Interiors

An Introduction

To Asa and to Kristine and to all our kids—at home, at school, and wherever they may find themselves in the world.

Interiors

An Introduction *fourth edition*

Karla J. Nielson
Brigham Young University

David A. Taylor
Brigham Young University

Boston   Burr Ridge, IL   Dubuque, IA   Madison, WI   New York   San Francisco   St. Louis
Bangkok   Bogotá   Caracas   Kuala Lumpur   Lisbon   London   Madrid   Mexico City
Milan   Montreal   New Delhi   Santiago   Seoul   Singapore   Sydney   Taipei   Toronto

Higher Education

Published by McGraw-Hill, an imprint of The McGraw-Hill Companies, Inc., 1221 Avenue of the Americas, New York, NY 10020. Copyright © 2007. All rights reserved. No part of this publication may be reproduced or distributed in any form or by any means, or stored in a database or retrieval system, without the prior written consent of The McGraw-Hill Companies, Inc., including, but not limited to, in any network or other electronic storage or transmission, or broadcast for distance learning.

This book is printed on acid-free paper.

1 2 3 4 5 6 7 8 9 0 DOW/DOW 0 9 8 7 6 5

ISBN-13: 978-0-07-296520-9
ISBN-10: 0-07-296520-7

Editor in Chief: *Emily Barrosse*
Publisher: *Lisa Moore*
Executive Marketing Manager: *Sharon Loeb*
Production Editor: *Chanda Feldman*
Manuscript Editor: *Jan Fehler*
Art Director: *Jeanne Schreiber*
Interior and Cover Designer: *Preston Thomas*
Art Editor: *Katherine McNab*
Photo Research Editor: *Alexandra Ambrose*
Photo Research Coordinator: *Judy K. Brody*
Production Supervisor: *Tandra Jorgensen*
Composition: *10/12 Palatino by Professional Graphics Inc.*
Printing: *70# Sterling Ultra Web Dull, R. R. Donnelley & Sons*

Cover: © Interiors: David Michael Miller Associates / photo: Bill Timmerman

Library of Congress Cataloging-in-Publication Data

Nielson, Karla J.
    Interiors : an introduction / Karla J. Nielson, David A. Taylor.—4th ed.
        p. cm.
    Includes index.
    ISBN 0-07-296520-7 (pbk. : acid-free paper)
        1. Interior decoration—Handbooks, manuals, etc. I. Taylor, David A. II. Title.

NK2115.N45 2005
729—dc22
                                                                            2005040882

The Internet addresses listed in the text were accurate at the time of publication. The inclusion of a Web site does not indicate an endorsement by the authors or McGraw-Hill, and McGraw-Hill does not guarantee the accuracy of the information presented at these sites.

www.mhhe.com

Contents

Preface   xv

Chapter 1 | The Process and Profession of Design

Interior Design: A Lifetime Pursuit   2

The Language of Design   3
Residential and Nonresidential Interior Design   3
Residential Interiors and Well-Being   4
The Need for Interior Design   4

The Process of Design   5

The Letter of Agreement   5
The Problem Statement   6
Research and Programming   6
Writing the Program   16
Design Development: Solving the Problem   16
Postoccupancy Evaluation   23
Nonresidential Considerations   23

The Interior Design Profession   24

The Design Profession: Past and Present   25
Designer Skills   25
Training and Professional Development   26
Interior Design Resources   27
Careers in Interior Design   31
The Future of Interior Design   36

Chapter 2 | Special Considerations in Design

Important Design Considerations   39

Environmental Considerations   39

Sustainability   39
Green Design   42
Other Environmental Issues   43

Considerations for Special Needs Users   46

Universal Design   46
The Americans with Disabilities Act of 1990   46
Accessible Design   47

Design for Special Populations   48

Design for Motion Impairments   48
Design for Hearing Impairment   51
Design for Visual Impairment   52
Design for the Elderly   53
Other Special Populations   53

Special Design Considerations as Fundamental Goals   55

Chapter 3 | Design Principles and Elements

The Principles of Design   58

Scale   58
Proportion   59
Balance   60
Rhythm   62
Emphasis   63
Harmony: Variety and Unity   64

The Elements of Design   66

Space   66
Shape or Form   67
Mass   68
Line   69
Texture   71
Pattern   71
Light   73
Color   74
Structural and Decorative Design   75

Design Discernment and Excellence   76

Cost Is Not the Issue   76
Training the Eye   77
Finding a Personal Style   79

Chapter 4 | Color

How We See Color   82

Subtractive Color   82
Visual Acuity and Deficiency   82
Metamerism   82

Color Theory   84

The Standard Color-Wheel Theory   84
The Munsell Theory   87
Other Color Theories   88

Color Harmony   88

Considerations in Color Harmonizing   88

Neutralized Colors   89
Neutrals   90
Other Color-Influencing Factors   92

Color Psychology   94

Afterimage Simultaneous Contrast   94
The Color Trend Market   94

Residential and Nonresidential Uses of Color   97

Color in Residential Interiors   97
Nonresidential Considerations   98

Chapter 5 | Lighting and Technology

Lighting in Interior Design   102

Natural Light   102

Combustion Lighting   103

Artificial Lighting   104

Categories of Lighting Effects   107
Lighting Effects in the Interior   110

Light and the Mind and Body   110

Seasonal Affective Disorder   111
Manipulating Mood with Interior Lighting   113
Glare   113

Power Terminology and Units of Measurement   114

Luminaires, or Lighting Fixtures   115

Architectural Lighting   115
Built-In Indirect Lighting   115
Lighting Economy   115

Lighting for the Future   115

Nonresidential Considerations   116

Types of Nonresidential Lighting   116
Lighting Economy in Nonresidential Interiors   119
Nonresidential Lighting for the Future   119

Technology   119

Information-Age Home Automation Systems   120
Information-Age Wiring and Installation   121
Wiring Plans   123
Residential Built-In Systems   124
Nonresidential Communication and Safety Systems   125

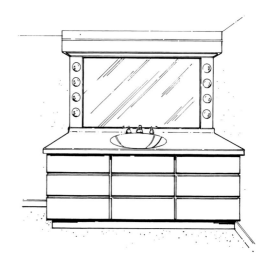

Chapter 6 | Space Planning Considerations

Prioritizing Needs and Wants   128

Function First   128
Interrelating Functions   129
Brainstorming   129
New Construction versus Remodeling   130
Economic Considerations   133
Other Factors That Affect Economy in Planning Home Space   134
Features and Benefits   136

Considerations for Specific Areas   136

The Entry or Foyer   136
Formal Living Spaces   139
Home Office Planning   139
The Library   143
Kitchen and Great Room Planning   143
The Laundry Room   151
Master Suite Planning   152
Family Bathrooms   154
Children's Spaces   157
Indoor-Outdoor Living   158
Media and Entertainment Rooms   158
Hobby and Special-Use Areas   159
Storage   159

Space Planning and the Principles and Elements of Design   160

Living with Less Space   161
Making Large Spaces Seem Smaller   162
Traffic Patterns   162
Rethinking the Box—Planning for Flexibility   163

Nonresidential Considerations   164

Function and Zoning   164
Traffic Patterns   168

Chapter 7 | Floor Plans and Building Systems

Floor Plans   172

Diagramming and Floor Plans   173

Measurements of Space: Cubic and Square Footage   173
Shaping the Space   175
Site, Orientation, and Climate   175

Floor Plans and Housing   175

Floor Plan Symbols   175
Floor Plan Types   175
Types of Housing   175
Buying an Existing Home   182
Obtaining the Floor Plan   182
Construction Documents: Working Drawings or Blueprints   186
Who Will Do the Work   187

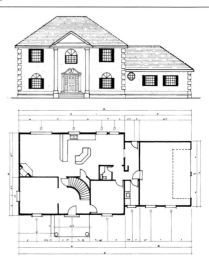

Constructing the Building 188

Structural Building Components and Systems   189
The Critical Path and the Punch List   195

Insulation and Energy Conservation   195

Active and Passive Solar Systems   195
Green Design   201

Nonresidential Considerations   201

Nonresidential Plumbing, HVAC, and Indoor Air Quality   204
Life Safety   208
Systems within the Plenum   208

Chapter 8 | Furniture Arrangement

Function   210

Combining Functions   210
Mechanical Functions   210
Circulation   210

Human Factors   212

Anthropometrics   212
Standard Clearances   212
Proxemics   212
Crowding   215
Territoriality   215

The Elements and Principles of Design   216

Balance, Scale, and Mass   216
Rhythm   217
Emphasis   217
Line and Harmony   218
Form and Space   219
Proportion   221

Basic Groupings   222

Nonresidential Considerations   225

Function   225
Nonresidential Furniture Types   225
Planning for Systems Furniture   226
Circulation   227

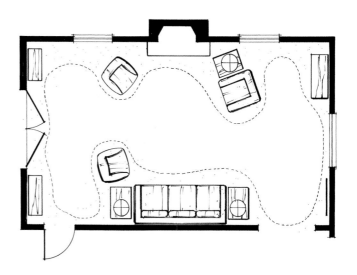

Chapter 9 | Furniture Selection

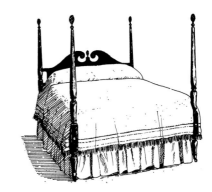

Wooden Furniture 230

Hardwood and Softwood 230
Other Forms of Wood 230
Case Goods 230
Wood Grains 231
Joining Methods 231
Wood Finishes 232

Metal Furniture 232

Types of Metal 232

Other Furniture Materials 234

Plastic 234
Leather 235
Wicker, Rattan, Cane, and Rush 235

Upholstered Furniture 236

Frames 236
Springs 236
Cushioning 236
Coverings 237

Furniture Harmony and Human Factors 237

Function 238
Anthropometrics and Ergonomics 238

Furniture Types 239

Systems Furniture 239
Ergonomic Superchairs 240
Custom Designs 240
Other Furniture Types 240

Nonresidential Considerations 240

Ergonomics 240
Durability 249

Chapter 10 | Architectural Detail

Walls 252

Wood Paneling 252
Moldings 253

Doors 254

Windows 257

Stairs 260

Fireplaces and Chimneypieces 264

Ceilings 266

Cabinetwork 268

Nonresidential Considerations 268

Chapter 11 | Wall, Ceiling, and Window Treatments

Wall and Ceiling Materials   272

    Selection Guidelines   272
    Hard or Rigid Wall Materials   273

Paint   282

    Painting Guidelines   283

Wall Coverings   286

    Wall-Covering Guidelines   286
    Fabric-Covered Walls   289

Ceiling Treatments   290

Window Treatments   290

    Window Treatment Considerations   290
    Soft Window Coverings   293
    Alternative Window Treatments   293

Nonresidential Considerations   304

    Durability   304
    Nonresidential Ceiling Treatments   305
    Nonresidential Window Treatments   305
    Less Pattern   306
    Safety Codes   306

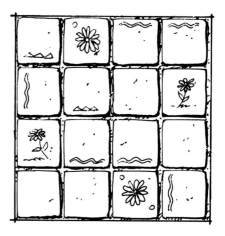

Chapter 12 | Floor Materials and Coverings

Floor Requirements and Specifications   308

    Calculations and Costs   308

Guidelines for Selecting Hard and Resilient Floor Materials   309

    Hard Floor Materials   309
    Resilient Floor Materials   314

Soft Floor Coverings   316

    Carpeting   316
    Rugs   321

Nonresidential Considerations   328

    Hard and Resilient Floorings   328
    Rugs and Carpeting   328

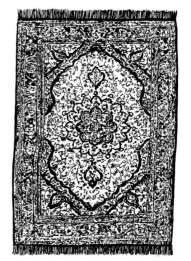

Chapter 13 | Fabric

Fibers   332

    Fabric Maintenance   336
    Fabric Construction   336
    Finishes   339
    Obtaining Fabric   340

Fabric—The Champion of Versatility   340

The Human Touch   341
Fabric Aesthetics   341
Fabric Weight and Applications   345

Nonresidential Considerations   345

Decorative Fabric Glossary   345

Chapter 14 | Art and Accessories

Fine Art   356

Sculpture   356
Painting   356
Mosaic   357
Drawing   357
Printmaking   357
Rubbings, Reproductions, and Graphic Art   358
Obtaining Fine Art   358
Preparing Art for Display   360

Decorative Art   360

Mirrors   360
Tableware and Cookware   360
Baskets   363
Clocks   363
Screens   363
Decorative Light Fixtures   364
Books   365
Textiles   365

Objects from Nature   366

Plants   366
Flowers and Greenery   367
Other Natural Objects   367

Other Accessories   367

The Use of Accessories   368

Collections   368
Overall Considerations   369
Emotionally Supportive Design   369

Nonresidential Considerations   370

Chapter 15 | Historic Design

Early Influences   374

Greece (Fifth Century B.C.)   374
Rome (200 B.C.–A.D. 400)   375
The Middle Ages (800–1500)   377
The Influence of Asia   382

The Renaissance (1420–1650)   383
The Baroque Period (1580–1750)   386

The English Influence in America   386

The Seventeenth-Century English Medieval Style (1608–95)   386
The Early Georgian Style (1695–1750)   389
The Late Georgian Style (1750–90)   390

American Styles   396

The Federal Style (1790–1830)   396
Jeffersonian Federal   397
The Vernacular Tradition (Seventeenth Century–Present)   397
The Greek Revival/American Empire Style (1820–60)   400
The Victorian Age in America (1837–1900)   405
Other Influences In America   410
The Beaux Arts Influence (1880–1945)   420

Modern Design (1857–Present)   420

The Skyscraper (1857–Present)   421
Art Nouveau/Jugendstil (1890–1900)   423
The Craftsman Style (1905–1929)   423
Frank Lloyd Wright's Organic Architecture (1908–Present)   425
Art Deco (1908–45)   428
The International Style (1932–Present)   429
Scandinavian and Mid-Century Design   431
Contemporary Trends   435

Putting Things in Perspective   437

Preservation   438

Glossary   441
Index   480

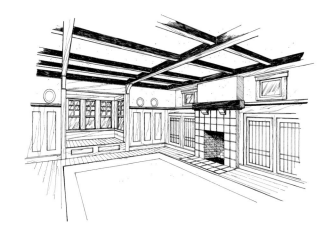

Preface

Interiors: An Introduction, Fourth Edition, is the starting point for a lifetime of design education, appreciation, and enjoyment. Interior design is an exciting discipline that makes life better through effective design solutions to spatial, functional, and aesthetic challenges. Whether your goal is a career in interior design, or simply a better understanding of how to enhance your own living space, the information and ideas found in *Interiors* will help you achieve it.

The objectives of *Interiors* are threefold:

1. to introduce a philosophy of and encourage an appreciation for fine design wherever it is found—in historical and modern examples, and in design that is continually evolving on the leading edge of technology;
2. to apply timeless design principles and elements to interiors;
3. and to make students aware of the wide variety of floor plans, materials, furnishings, and styles possible in interior design.

This book is the beginning of a study that can be expanded by searching the Internet, reading interior design magazines, and visiting museums, showcase homes, showrooms, and supply sources. Educated students are more astute consumers who are able to make selections with good design and practicality in mind.

Inside *Interiors*

Interiors: An Introduction, Fourth Edition, is an exciting look at the world of interior design. Today's interior design is thriving and continually changing, and this edition reflects those changes. The photos have been updated to illustrate contemporary trends and fresh interpretations of traditional styles. The line art, too, has been updated, and the design made more user-friendly.

Chapter 1: "The Process and Profession of Design," explores the way design problems are solved and the skills of the professionals who solve them. Information on the profession will guide those aspiring to careers in interior design and give all readers a better understanding of what interior designers do and how to work with them. In addition to being aesthetically pleasing, interiors need to be safe and functional. The complexities of balancing styles, functionality, and clients' preferences require that the study of interior design be thorough and detailed. The satisfaction and pride that come with well-designed interior solutions are well worth the time invested in learning how to create them.

Chapter 2 features a body of new information concerning energy-efficient appliances and high-tech appliances, along with updates to flooring (such as bamboo, which is highly sustainable) and fibers (such as polylactic acid, also completely sustainable). The chapter has been reorganized so that it covers sustainability first, followed by a case for modest living and then special populations. The vital importance of protecting our environment is much more than a passing whim—it is the key to thriving in the future and maintaining a high quality of life. The Americans with Disabilities Act, together with increased social concern for universal access in building design, have made it mandatory to consider special populations when designing any interior. By highlighting these topics early in the book, we encourage a philosophy of sensitivity to user needs and environmental considerations that carries through in every aspect of the study of interior design.

Chapter 5 describes the vital role technology has come to play in both the study and practice of interior design. Dramatic growth in the use of home computers and the demand for quicker telecommunications access make wiring systems a far more crucial topic today than in years past. As home automation systems become more widely available, they provide solutions to problems such as household scheduling and the need to conserve resources. This chapter presents information and ideas to help today's—and tomorrow's—designers utilize these technological solutions.

Chapter 6: "Space Planning Considerations," provides a detailed outline of the many crucial decisions that must be made before new construction or remodeling begins. Chapter 7: "Floor Plans and Building Systems," describes the successive phases of a construction or remodeling project, including a variety of examples of innovative and environmentally friendly professional plans and renderings.

As the home is the primary focus of most introductory courses in interior design, the concepts in *Interiors* apply first to the home and secondly to nonresidential interiors. In fact, most materials, principles, and considerations of good design are relevant in both environments. Information targeted especially at nonresidential design is presented throughout the book in sections entitled "Nonresidential Considerations." Through study and observation, the student of interior design learns from all environments—in residential settings as well as in the places where we work, shop, study, worship, and seek recreation or gain appreciation for design of the past.

Interiors concludes with an overview of historic style, beginning with ancient Greece and Rome and extending to Modern and Postmodern achievements. In this fourth edition, the overview includes additional and improved photos of architectural studies. Surveying 2,000 years of design history makes us realize that the world is at our feet. The style features of exotic places, historic times, and treasured culture are available to become a part of today's interiors, to enrich, to add significance, to connect the past with the present and the present with the future.

Because introductory interior design courses vary in their approach, *Interiors* is planned for flexibility: chapters can be used in the order preferred by the teacher, and selected chapters can be more heavily emphasized or left for another course of study. However this text is incorporated into a given course, we leave you our wish that it not be simply enjoyable reading, but the beginning of your lifetime of involvement in interiors.

Resources for Students and Instructors

Student Resources

Interiors is supported by a dynamic Online Learning Center website at www.mhhe.com/nielson4, where students can find a wide range of tools to help them in testing their knowledge. It includes chapter study tools, multiple-choice and essay quizzing, flash cards, crossword puzzles, and suggested websites.

Instructor Resources

The Online Learning Center for instructors at www.mhhe.com/nielson4 provides outlines for lecture preparation and detailed suggested class assignment. Instructors can also use PageOut, which allows them to create their own course websites simply and quickly.

The Instructor's Manual includes discussion outlines, suggested class assignments, and updated test banks for each chapter. It is available on the Instructor's section of the

Online Learning Center and on the Instructor's Resource CD-ROM. Adopters may obtain a password and/or CD-ROM from their local McGraw-Hill representative.

Acknowledgments

This book is the result of the efforts of many talented and supportive people. We would like to express our thanks to our spouses, Asa S. Nielson and Kristine B. Taylor, and to our children and extended families, our students at Brigham Young University, and our professional peers for their moral and thoughtful support.

We are grateful to those who provided illustrations: Jim Park for his masterful pen-and-ink work and the many photographers whose expertise is manifest. Also thanks to the individuals and corporations whose designs and products appear in this book, contributing to the state of the art in design excellence.

Reviewers Dr. Merlene Lyman Baird, Fort Hays State University; Dianne Batzkall, Harper College; Alinde Bittner, Saddleback College; Gigi Brown, Pima County Community College; Joyce Butts, Florida Community College at Jacksonville–Kent; Janet Crites, Fontbonne College; Sarajane Eisen, Lamar University; Dr. Barbara England, Freed-Hardeman University; Imelda Golik, CSU, Fresno; Bobanne Kalkofen, Johnson County Community College; Ryan Langemeirer, Minnesota State University–Mankato; Geoffrey Moore Langdon, Suffolk University; Dr. Robert Paul Meden, Marymount University; Dorothy Minarsch, College of the Canyons; Yvonne Moody, Chadron State College; Fred Oberkircher, Texas Christian University; and Suzanne Poslaiko, Scottsdale Community College contributed valuable feedback and suggestions for improvement.

Karla J. Nielson

David A. Taylor

Chapter 1 | The Process and Profession of Design

Interior Design: A Lifetime Pursuit 2

The Process of Design 5

The Interior Design Profession 24

© Norman McGrath

Interior Design: A Lifetime Pursuit

Interior design is an exciting career, and it is also a fascinating avocation, providing a lifetime of personal, aesthetic, and intellectual fulfillment. A single issue of a cutting-edge residential design magazine recently demonstrated that even those who do not practice interior design as a profession often create interiors worthy of recognition and publication. The magazine's colored pages featured the work of architects and designers, along with the designs of an illustrator, an account executive, an inventor, a hotel owner, a clothing fabricator, a law student, a housewares retailer, a writer, a contractor, and others. Anyone with a keen interest can become knowledgeable about design and can create interiors of charm and style.

Being involved in interior design is a rewarding pursuit that broadens intellectual horizons and deepens aesthetic sensitivity. Interior design is vital, vibrant, and dynamic; it is never static. As the world changes, life also changes and design keeps pace. An interior design will never really be "finished," because as life changes, so do we. Styles evolve, our outlook changes, the composition of our families and households alters, careers shift, and our designs adjust to life's ebb and flow. What an exciting thing it is to be fluent in the language of design, to know the historic roots of the design language, and to understand the new expressions of the language all around us. It is even more exciting to be able to speak the language of design by creating our own interiors. It is truly a rewarding lifelong avocation that is within the reach of all who are willing to invest the time and effort.

Figure 1.1 Interior design is a rewarding pursuit that leads to the creation of fine residential environments. © Peter Aaron/Esto

The Language of Design

The late design educator Sherrill Whiton compared studying interior design to learning a foreign language. If the vocabulary and the grammar of a language are mastered, we can adequately express ourselves. Interior design has a vocabulary of materials, styles, forms, details, light, colors, patterns, textures, lines, and mass. The grammar can be compared to design principles of balance, rhythm, emphasis, scale, proportion, unity, variety, and harmony. In the same way that we select words to form sentences according to rules of grammar, we use elements of design to create interiors according to established principles. Like master writers who manipulate the language in interesting new ways, talented designers often break with established rules and expectations to create new trends and tastes.

Residential and Nonresidential Interior Design

Although the focus of our interest in interior design is often personal, it certainly need not be limited to our personal home environment. Lifestyles today often dictate that we spend many of our waking hours in working situations, shopping, and dealing with various types of business services. We also spend time eating out, traveling, and staying in hotels. These nonresidential environments should be as well planned as the home environment. The focus of *Interiors: An Introduction* is general. The concepts discussed apply to both residential and nonresidential interiors. In cases where certain considerations do not apply equally to homes, separate sections with nonresidential considerations are included in the chapters.

Figure 1.2 Once you have studied interior design you will see nonresidential settings with new eyes and fresh perspectives.
© Tim Street-Porter/Beateworks.com

What we learn about interior design applies to the places where we shop, eat, stay, or receive public or professional services. After studying interior design, we will view all these places with new eyes. When they function well and are creatively developed, we will feel good about being there. Armed with a new awareness of design, we become amateur critics. Even though we may keep our critiques to ourselves, we find our appreciation and enjoyment increasing with each fresh exposure to design.

Residential Interiors and Well-Being

The great British prime minister Winston Churchill said, "We shape our environments; thereafter they shape us." This is certainly true of any place we spend time, but nowhere is it more true than in the home. The home is a refuge from the elements and the pressures of everyday life. It is the place where children are nurtured. Here they can be taught the value of work and cleanliness and the satisfaction that comes from a job well done. They can learn honesty, integrity, dependability, and service to others by taking appropriate responsibility for the home, its maintenance, and the quality of life it provides. The home is where we come for entertainment and relaxation. It is a place where we seek physical rest and sleep—no bed feels as good as the one at home. Here we can cook

in order to feed and fortify ourselves for the onslaught of daily living. Home should be a place of refreshment and support, and it should be important to us as a place where the finest values can be espoused and reinforced.

Interior design is the means to making homes pleasant and functional. In our fast-paced society, life is often filled with stress and sometimes unhappiness. Poorly planned interiors can add to this emotional burden and can be an unnecessary source of frustration. Well-planned and lovely homes are no guarantee of happiness, but a well-designed interior certainly helps smooth the rough edges of life. It is also important to note that there is no relationship between the size and luxury of a home and its ability to function. A modest cottage, if it meets the needs of those who call it home, can be a pleasant place to live. It is up to us to create the kind of interior that best meets our needs and our expectations of what will take place there.

A home filled with objects and materials of personal value will be unlike any other home elsewhere. It is pleasant to sit in the home of a musician or theater professional, for example, and sense his or her interests and experiences merely by looking around. When homes have the good fortune of growing and evolving with their occupants over a number of years, the charm will likely be even greater. This is the reason model homes often lack the emotional warmth of real home environments. Even though they may be designed and furnished with great sensitivity and filled with intriguing objects and ideas, they may still lack the sense of ownership and distinction that comes to a home that is lived in with love and care over a period of years.

The Need for Interior Design

The reasons for getting involved in an interior design project are varied:

• **New homes and buildings require complete designs.** New architecture should be completely planned—from the arrangement and allocation of space to the selection of new materials and furnishings. The extent of the purchase of new furnishings will often depend on whether one is starting fresh or moving from an existing building or home. Those starting fresh will have to select every item, whereas those who move from a more settled situation may be able to use existing furnishings.

Figure 1.3 Interesting pieces of personal value give this room great individuality and character. © Jessie Walker

Figure 1.4 Classic French doors and furnishings in a historical style give this interior a timeless quality. © *Jessie Walker*

- **Interiors need refurbishing.** With time, materials and furnishings become worn and are no longer suitable. The average life span for better-than-average soft goods (upholstery, draperies, and floor coverings), paint, and wall coverings is six to twelve years; when they wear out, they will need to be replaced.
- **The program changes.** As the composition of a household or business changes, the interior may need remodeling or refurnishing. For example, as children are born into a family, more bedroom space may be required. As the children grow and move on to college and out of the home, their rooms may be given to younger brothers and sisters, or they may become personal adult spaces, requiring some design alterations. In the same way, growth and expansion of a business or institution also require design changes. Environments that are updated in response to change function better.
- **Fashions change.** No matter how carefully interiors are designed, change is often welcome. As new materials and furnishings develop, there are expanded possibilities for change that will bring freshness to interiors. This is an area that requires careful balance. The interior furnishings industry thrives on changes in fashion, and new directions in design are exciting. Yet if durable furnishings are carefully chosen with an eye to classic styling, they will not date and will not need replacing. In a well-designed interior, updating with a new paint color, fabric, piece of furniture, or accessory may satisfy the craving for new fashion.

The Process of Design

Design is the process of solving problems. Good interior design solutions have the power to make people feel positive in their surroundings. Table 1.1 outlines the steps taken by designers to solve problems and answer questions posed by a design project.

The Letter of Agreement

As protection for both parties, most designers prepare a letter of agreement outlining the responsibilities of the designer and the financial obligation of the client to reimburse the designer for services rendered. The signed letter of agreement is a legal document; it avoids the waste of spending design time on researching, programming, and preparing conceptual designs in cases where the project never comes to fruition or the client selects a different designer. The letter also guarantees that the client will be supplied with whatever the designer agrees to provide for all or part of a project.

Table 1.1 | The Design Process

Letter of Agreement (Contract)
Problem Statement
Research and Programming

Identifies and seeks to understand:

- Users
- Lifestyle and function
- Relationships
- Space requirements
- Environmental factors
- Mechanical considerations
- Psychological and sociological considerations
- Economic factors
- Design preferences
- Codes and restrictions

Writing the Program

- Analysis of research data
- Organizing the data into a written program

Design Development

The program is implemented through:

- Concept development
- Working drawings and specifications
- Execution

Postoccupancy Evaluation

The Problem Statement

Initial identification of the problem might begin with some kind of **problem statement** indicating the basic nature of the project—as a primary residence, vacation house, office, clinic, retirement center, restaurant, hotel, or clothing store. Such a statement might also include the location of the project and even a specific address. The person or group commissioning the project could also be named in a design statement.

Research and Programming

A functional and successful design must solve problems. A clear understanding of the problems will lead to an effective design solution. The summary of goals, requirements, and restrictions associated with a design problem and its solution is known as the **program.** The process of **programming** is accomplished by gathering, compiling, analyzing, and verifying the information necessary to understand the problem and solve it. In nonresidential

Figure 1.5 Personal pieces reflect the owner's lifestyle and give this waterfront interior a nautical feeling. © *Jessie Walker*

design, the program is a formal written document; a program may be used formally or informally in residential design.

There are times when the program for a project will be provided by those commissioning the design, but it will probably still be necessary to collect additional data to complete the program. When designers are responsible for the program, they will conduct research, surveys, interviews, and studies and compile inventories as part of the programming process. The following are typical factors that might be considered in research and programming.

Users
The research process begins with identification of each of the **users**. The users, as the name implies, are those who will use the design directly or indirectly, from principal occupants to service people to guests and friends.

In a residential design, a **profile** may be developed for each of the principal residents who will live in the home. The profile could include such things as age, sex, background, culture, values, temperament, personality, personal habits, need for privacy, style preferences, responses to color, and an inventory of possessions and furnishings that need to be accommodated.

Profiles reveal household **demographics,** which is statistical information about numbers and kinds of residents. This would include traditional families with two parents, as well as nontraditional families such as those in combined households or single-parent households and special populations such as the elderly or handicapped. Household demographics can be determined through interviews of the principal users or by means of a questionnaire developed by the designer.

Lifestyle and Function
The profile helps the designer understand the **lifestyle** of the principal users. Lifestyle is a term frequently used in residential design to describe part of the program for a home. It represents the constantly changing way a person or group of people live and how they use their time. It includes such considerations as whether they like to read, write, or use a computer; whether they have special hobbies such as sewing, crafts, or woodworking; or to what extent they enjoy and participate in sports. The way people choose to entertain; how they prepare, serve, and eat meals; whether or not a grandparent lives with them; the way they use their leisure time; the type of musical instruments they play; the routine they use for dressing and their personal toilette; the amount and type of interaction they want with their children—all are examples of lifestyle considerations. As the composition of families or groups changes and as people grow older, interests, needs, and lifestyles also change. Consequently, flexibility in planning for potential modifications is very important in order to meet changes without major upheaval.

Since lifestyles are in a constant state of flux as household demographics change, it is important to be aware of the effect such changes will have. For example, many families with small children may find a playroom well suited to their needs. Tiny children can use the space for toys and for play. As children begin to bring friends into the home, the room will provide space for playing games with peers. As children become teenagers and young adults, the playroom can accommodate music and entertainment, and even parties and dancing. When the young adults leave home, the room may start the cycle all over again with space for grandchildren.

Another example of accommodating a changing lifestyle is the evolution of a bedroom from nursery into child's room and then into a teenager's or young adult's room. When the young adult leaves home, the room could be used for hobbies, study, television, a home office, a guest room, or a combination of uses.

The foresight to project changes in lifestyle is an important asset in the programming process.

Many kinds of design solutions have come to be accepted as standard. However, the lifestyle of the users will often dictate solutions to design problems that go beyond standard. Individual needs should be assessed in terms of the kinds of **functions** a user envisions for a space, as well as the kinds of furnishings and equipment required. For example, questions one might ask in planning a kitchen space are:

- How many of the users will be cooking at once?
- What kinds of equipment will be needed?
- Will there be minimal or gourmet cooking?
- What kind of supplies must be accommodated?
- How should supplies be stored?
- What kind of dining, if any, should be planned?

In a bedroom we might ask:

- Do the users like to read in bed?
- Will the bedroom be used for studying?
- Is an area for seating desirable?
- Will there be television or other forms of electronic entertainment?
- What are the storage needs?

In living areas we might want to know:

- Is the space used by company, family, or both?
- Will there be a piano or other musical instruments?
- Will television and entertainment be included here?
- Should books and reading be part of the planning?
- Will conversation be an important function?
- Will the space be used to display art?

Determinations should be made regarding every space and its use. For example, a bedroom could accommodate study or sewing space as well as sleeping. The family room could be used for dining, television, and stereo, as well as conversation and games. The dining room or guest room could double as a library or hobby room. This kind of flexibility is crucial because the cost of space is high, and infrequently used rooms need to be made more useful by planning for several functions. Every lifestyle will dictate different kinds of functions for each area; thorough inquiry will determine precisely what the functions are. With this exact data, planning can be effective and accurate, and lifestyle differences can be well accommodated.

Relationships

When the functions for each space have been assessed, the relationships of each function must be determined. Important lines of communication and the need for proximity must be identified. For example, it might be convenient to plan sewing and ironing near the laundry. The laundry may be close to the kitchen for daytime convenience, or it could be near the bedrooms and bathrooms where soiled clothes are removed. Bedrooms should be planned in relationship to bathrooms. Easy access from the nursery to the master bedroom may be ideal for some parents, but others might want children's rooms and activities isolated from their own. Kitchens and dining areas where food will be served should have logical and convenient relationships. A home office might most appropriately be located near the front door and close to a seating area such as a living room, for the convenience of those who visit the office.

Figure 1.6 Well-defined relationships allow integration of food preparation and other activities in this pleasant great room. *Dominic Mercadante, architect/photo © Brian Vanden Brink*

The consideration of relationships should even extend to the location of areas outside the building. For example, the convenient relationship of garbage containers to the kitchen or of kitchen to patio or garden is important. For bringing in groceries, the relationship of the garage or parking spaces to the kitchen or pantry is significant. Identifying these types of relationships facilitates efficient use of space and makes the design more effective because of its convenience. Well-planned relationships also smooth lines of communication, cut building costs, and make traffic patterns more efficient.

Space Requirements

When the designer puts pencil to paper, it is important to know exactly how to divide the space. Consequently, during the programming step, it is necessary to estimate the amount of space each function will demand. This requires some understanding of standard amounts of space allowed for traffic, as well as standard dimensions for furnishings. To program space requirements, the designer must establish inventories of furnishings, clothing, and special equipment belonging to the users. In most cases programming even includes taking actual measure-

ments of those items. Lifestyle profiles will also help in estimating space requirements. A sample checklist might include the following kinds of questions:

- How is entertaining handled, and how much space does that require?
- How many people might need to be seated for formal dining?
- What is the maximum number of guests that might stay at one time?
- What pieces of equipment will be used in the kitchen?
- How much food will be stored in the pantry?
- What kind of vacuums, mops, brooms, and other cleaning supplies are there?
- Are there collections of slides, videos, or DVDs that require space?
- Do card tables and folding chairs need to be stored?
- How many books, CDs, or tapes does the user have?
- How much sporting equipment needs storage?
- How many shirts, sweaters, etc., does the user own?
- How many pairs of shoes need to be stored?
- Are there seasonal decorations that require storage?

The old saying, "A place for everything, and everything in its place," neatly summarizes an important aspect

Figure 1.7 This delightful space was created expressly for the enjoyment of grandchildren who visit this home. *Interior design by MEA designs, M. Enid Arckless, ASID/Photos by Reed Kaestner*

of a well-designed space: Most interior environments need not be of any particular size to be well designed. If a space accommodates possessions and activities in a logical and orderly fashion, life will be more pleasant.

Consideration of space also extends beyond the functional measurement of actual space needs to the psychological realm of perception. Not only should there be adequate space for movement and circulation within a space, but the designer should also consider how the mind moves through a space. Inadequate space, or spaces without windows where the eye and mind cannot expand, is unpleasant for many and even claustrophobic for some. Psychological space perception is as important as actual space.

Environmental Factors

Our relationship with and responsibility toward the environment is a very important issue. As the developed nations in particular gobble resources, pollute, and destroy the environment at an alarming rate, the preservation of the environment has become not only an ethical issue but a political one as well.

Chapter 2 includes environmental considerations and lists some of the things that responsible designers can do to preserve the environment. An awareness of these issues can lead to action that will affect the quality of life for us and future generations.

Figure 1.8 The open arrangement of these spaces allows the eye and mind to expand. © *Melabee M. Miller*

Environmental considerations—such as climate, weather, and physical location—must be examined as part of the programming process. Some aesthetically pleasing designs are failures because they ignore important environmental questions. Environmental concerns cannot be subordinated to aesthetics; there must be a synthesis of the two.

Climate and Weather. Problems of climate and weather are generally straightforward. Climates with extremes of heat and/or cold will require ample insulation, as well as adequate heating and/or cooling systems. Climate and weather also influence the placement of a building to take advantage of favorable climate conditions—such as breezes or sunshine—or to avoid unpleasant ones. In fact, weather and climate should be keys to determining the

Figure 1.9 This room was designed to store a variety of possessions and accommodate several different activities.
© *Peter Aaron/Esto*

Figure 1.10 A mild climate allowed the designer to create a space that is completely open to the outdoors. *Photo*
© *Norman McGrath*

type of structure to be built. Building materials should be suitable to the climate so that they will not be subject to excessive deterioration.

Physical Location. Physical location involves factors such as site, view, prevailing winds, solar exposure, noise, and environmental hazards.

Site—The site of a building should influence its design. The building should be compatible with its neighbors, though the style need not be the same, merely harmonious. Where conservation and preservation of the environment are important, the design should be well suited to, and harmonious with, the natural surroundings. Plans should be developed to do the least possible damage to nature and to integrate the building with existing natural features.

In other cases, the design may be created to stand out in contrast to its environment; the environment may even be altered and reworked by the designer. Good and responsible judgment is paramount in such situations. Building and development are the natural results of growth and change and should be planned so that in years to come they will have improved with age.

View—Beautiful daytime or nighttime views are a valuable asset to an interior and should be featured in the design of the building. They should not be upstaged by excessively ornate window treatments. Where views are unpleasant or nonexistent, attention should be focused inward and treatments should be selected to deemphasize them.

Prevailing Winds—Prevailing winds can be a positive or negative feature of a location. They can provide pleasant breezes or disturbing winds. When breezes

Figure 1.11 The windows in this alcove take full advantage of the beautiful forest view. © Susan Gilmore/Esto

prevail, buildings should be oriented to use the wind for natural cooling. When winds are gusty or icy cold, the building and its landscaping should provide shelter and protection. **Berms** (small constructed hills) or trees planted in a **windbreak** can help minimize the effect of cold winter winds.

Solar Exposure—Like the wind, the sun can be both a positive and a negative factor. In the winter, the sun streaming through south windows may be warm and comforting, but without adequate protection from the sun, an interior may become difficult to cool, and ultraviolet rays and heat can damage furnishings as well as produce disturbing glare. Chapter 7, "Floor Plans and Building Systems," contains a thorough discussion of solar factors.

Noise—Some types of noise are enjoyable. The tumbling of a small creek or brook, the sound of waves breaking at the seashore, the crackle of a warm fire in the fireplace, or a breeze rustling through leaves can be comforting and pleasant. While most people enjoy an environment free from loud, annoying noise, it is amazing how humans can adapt to noise. Those who are accustomed to sleeping in rooms facing busy city streets may find it difficult to sleep in a completely quiet environment.

Noise from the outside and noise through interior walls can be controlled with extra insulation, adequate construction, and insulated glass. Noise within an environment can be controlled by the use of materials that **refract** (bend) and absorb sound waves. Textile applications (upholstery and floor, wall, and window coverings) refract and absorb sound waves and can largely eliminate echo noise, or **reverberation.**

Environmental Hazards—When planning, it is important to be aware of hazardous conditions, some serious enough to warrant selection of a new site. Fault lines, slide areas, eroding waterfronts, areas subject to flooding or forest fires, high-power lines, railroad lines, heavy industries, areas of extreme pollution, and even former pollution sites—all are examples of potential hazards. Streets with heavy traffic may be hazards for families with small children.

Mechanical Considerations

Mechanical considerations include heating, ventilation, air-conditioning (HVAC), plumbing, lighting, and telephone. A basic knowledge of the way these systems function will be helpful in understanding how they must integrate with the completed interior. Such understanding will also lead to a smoother and more productive working relationship with the skilled technicians who install these systems.

Psychological and Sociological Considerations

Psychological and sociological needs also must carefully be considered because the design of an interior has

tremendous power to make people feel good about their environments and can even affect the way they feel about each other. Most people recognize the effect that an interior environment can have (for both good and ill) on our well-being and even on some aspects of our character. Space, color, texture, pattern, scale, balance, furnishings, and all the other design elements and principles that constitute our interiors make us feel and act in certain ways. Knowledgeable use of these elements can lead to the creation of environments that make us feel emotional responses such as cool, warm, happy, romantic, nostalgic, awed, compassionate, hungry, restless, soothed, stimulated, or relaxed. That is why an interior designer must carefully consider the subtle manipulations that affect us so strongly.

Other sociological and psychological considerations include the need for privacy and interaction, cultural relationships, security and safety, and familiarity and stability.

Privacy and Interaction. Some people are rather private by nature, whereas others are more gregarious. Regardless of our basic social nature, we all have times when we need to be alone and times when we need to interact with others. Spaces such as living rooms, family rooms, game rooms, dining rooms, and even kitchens should be planned for interaction.

In many homes the kitchen is the heart. Even when homes are provided with areas for individual study, many times family members will end up studying around the kitchen table. When guests arrive for parties, they frequently gravitate to the kitchen. It is this tendency that has led to the popularity of **great rooms,** which are large kitchen/dining/family room spaces where most of the day-to-day living is centered.

It is equally important to plan spaces where members of the household can be alone. Libraries, studies, workrooms, or bedrooms are logical places for privacy. When children share a room, some means of division or separation should be planned so that a degree of privacy can be achieved when needed. A desire for solitude and introspection is a basic human need that must be planned for and respected.

Cultural Relationships. Distinctive aspects of local culture or family history can enhance the quality of an interior. For example, the Pueblo Indian design of New Mexico with its adobe construction has been adapted into a local style that is charming and well suited to its environment. It is also closely tied into the history and culture of the area and provides an emotional link with the prevailing culture. When an interior will be used by people with ties to a foreign culture, it can benefit from incorporating cultural elements, from structural features and choice of materials to displays of artwork or crafts. In this way the interior becomes an extension of personal history and experience.

Security and Safety. The physical safety of the occupants and possessions can affect the psychological well-being of a home. There are few things that compare with the feeling of terror and despair associated with a fire or other disaster. To help prevent accidents and fire, government agencies have established guidelines and rules (codes) for safety and fire prevention. Smoke detectors and fire extinguishers offer even greater security, both physical and emotional.

The need for protection is one of the most basic reasons for seeking the shelter of a home. Home security has become a multimillion-dollar industry providing alarm systems and other means of securing homes. Some of these security systems utilize complex equipment and sophisticated electronic surveillance, while others are as basic as well-engineered locking mechanisms. For many people, these kinds of measures provide a sense of calm and well-being that makes a home the center of security that it should be.

Familiarity and Stability. The design of an interior can include items that create stability and reassurance through their familiarity. For example, space might be designated for family photographs and other personal mementos. Art, accessories, and furnishings collected while traveling also have the same effect of tying us to our personal experiences. Such belongings are often reminders of events or people and are part of an emotional support system. The use or display of cherished collections, objects, or furnishings should be included as part of the planning process. Because of their familiarity and warm associations, our environments can support better mental and emotional health.

Economic Factors

Economic factors are one of the most important considerations because they have such an impact on the extent of the design. Without proper funding, a design can remain forever on paper. Economic considerations will govern

Figure 1.12 A dining area in a greenhouse is far from a standard design solution, but the result is charming, functional, and reflects user preference. © Norman McGrath

all aspects of the interior design—from the time allotted to research, develop, and execute the design to the quality of materials and furnishings.

Figure 1.13 Distinctive objects like these provide strong links to personal experience. © Jessie Walker

Figure 1.14 Pendleton blanket patterns and Native American accessories are tied to the local culture of this Western home. © Timothy Street-Porter

There are some considerations that will make designs more economical. For example, building materials that are plentiful or indigenous to an area will usually be cheaper. This means that brick is less costly near the factory because shipping costs are generally less. Where brick has to be transported many hundreds of miles, the cost will escalate. Wood is a natural choice in wooded areas and adds the economical quality of good insulation as well. Building and finish materials that require the least upkeep and give the greatest length of service or durability for the climate and location are also economical choices, a justification for selecting brick or siding instead of wood.

Exterior and interior building components that are standard sizes are less expensive than those special ordered or custom manufactured. Examples include doors, windows, and ceiling heights, and standard in-stock items such as appliances and plumbing fixtures.

The cost of replacement when materials wear out is also an important factor in planning for economy. It is sad when a home that has been mortgaged for fifteen, twenty, or even thirty years is outfitted with materials that need replacing in as few as five years. For example, a lower-grade vinyl flooring or carpet will likely wear out and cost more to replace than a better-quality, durable flooring would have cost in the beginning. Hardwood, tile, or even stone floors, which are initially expensive, will seldom wear out or need replacing. In the long run, cheap may cost more than expensive because poor-quality goods wear out before replacement is economically feasible and then those who use the design must live with shabby goods. The credo "Buy once and buy good quality" will serve well all choices for design materials and furnishings.

The cost of maintenance or upkeep of materials is another factor in planning for economy. If a finish or material requires constant dusting, cleaning, polishing, waxing, or other maintenance, it may not be the best choice. The cost is counted in two ways—the money for repair or hired cleaning help and the time and effort spent in maintaining it yourself.

Economy may also include planning ahead for future changes or additions. Plumbing and wiring can be installed for central vacuum systems, intercom units, or entertainment and sound systems that will be added later. Planning ahead saves costly remodeling, with its accompanying inconvenience and frustration. The list of projected changes and additions should include any item that is built-in and must be planned for in advance.

Design Preferences

As data are gathered, the client's or user's design preferences may be sought. They include preferences of theme, color, and even historic-period or contemporary styles (see Chapter 15). These preferences guide the designer through the concept-development phase of the design process. Personal preferences are particularly important in residential interiors where the client will be the principal user. In other cases, these kinds of choices may be left to the designer's discretion.

Codes

Codes and restrictions are laws established by federal, state, and local governments and their agencies for the health, safety, and welfare of the consumer. They are exacting and often complex, and they tie the designer to a considerable amount of liability. Codes provide requirements for mechanical systems that will function both safely and properly and for fire and occupational safety with certain types of materials, equipment, and structures.

Writing the Program

This list of considerations may seem lengthy, yet raising and answering as many questions as possible establishes a clear understanding or mastery of the problem. Such mastery becomes the basis for a good design solution. The only limiting factor in asking questions is time. At some point the information-gathering phase must end and the design must move forward.

Analysis

All the data uncovered in the programming process must be studied to establish design priorities; real "needs" should be separated from "wants." The prioritized data can then be organized into logical sequence for inclusion in the written document. If questions or discrepancies arise, they can be resolved through additional research.

Written Program

Putting the research information into written form is the last step in the critical programming phase of the design process. The resulting document is the key to a successful design solution. Table 1.2 is an example of a residential program and resulting floor plan.

Since the program is a constantly changing set of circumstances, the gathered data will reveal the program only at a given point in time. The program gives the direction the design solution must take, and in this way it is like a road map that helps the design stay on course. The length of the written program will vary according to the size of the project.

The finished design will be only as good as the quality of research and articulation of the data. A fine design is the result of spending adequate time to analyze and organize before beginning to create.

Design Development: Solving the Problem

The creative mind will be generating ideas for design solutions all the way through the research phase of the design process. However, only after the research data have been analyzed and clearly articulated in the written program can the development of the ideas, or **concepts,** be formulated with accuracy. The design comes into being through:

- Design concept development
- Working drawings and specifications
- Execution

Design Concept Development

Concept development usually begins with **brainstorming,** freely generating many ideas without stopping to judge their quality. The ideas can be verbal, sketched, or written. Some very good design solutions have been scrawled on table napkins and scraps of building lumber. The important part of brainstorming is the flow of ideas, as one idea often triggers another and the two may suggest a third or a combination idea. When the best ideas emerge, they are put on paper as the basis for the design solution.

The ideas take the form of quick drawings called **schematics,** which are used to help visualize space plans, traffic patterns, details, or even possible color schemes. These can be modified as the process continues until the parts begin to form the whole. As the design starts to come together, the brainstorming process continues as one scheme generates variations. These ideas must be examined, and at some point decisions must be made. Some ideas must be rejected, and those that survive can be accepted, altered, or expanded. This process continues until the pile of drawings reaches the ceiling or until time runs out. The ideation stage could go on indefinitely since solutions are limited only by imagination.

An important part of concept development is the selection of proposed materials, finishes, and furnishings. **Materials** consist of floor coverings, wall coverings, textiles for window coverings and upholstery, and materials

Table 1.2 | A Residential Program

Design for David and Kris Schneider Home

Design Concept Statement: This is the last home we will ever need, with master suite and all primary functions on one floor. The home should be well designed but need not have any extraordinary features that will drive up the cost of construction. The home should be adequate for entertaining friends and family who might come for an evening, a day, or for a stay of several days. The design should be traditional rather than contemporary, although open planning in the kitchen/family room area could impart a contemporary feeling.

User	Primary Users	David and Kristine Phillip: 21 Maren: 17 Katy: 13
	Secondary Users	• Extended family and friends who stay overnight • Married children and their families who stay overnight • Friends (groups up to 14) who come for dinner parties • Family groups (25–35) who come for holiday dinners
Function by room/area	Porches	• Covered porch on west and north for visiting in good weather • Private patio on east side—possibly covered—for outdoor dining, visiting, etc.
	Entry	• Wide enough to accommodate a console table • Privacy from family room/kitchen area • Wooden six-panel door with transom lights above • Coat closet for guests • Hardwood floors
	Parlor	• Small seating area • Hardwood floors
	Library	• Wall-to-wall, floor-to-ceiling bookcases • Could be same room as parlor
	Master Bedroom	• Queen-size bed • Walk-in closet • Limited seating • Carpet
	Master Bath	• Sink (1) with vanity, toilet, shower w/ recessed shelf and built-in seat • Storage for linen, medicine, cleaning supplies, TP, etc.
	Family Room	• Forced-air fireplace furnace with raised hearth • Built-in bookcases with space for TV/video, stereo system, and lots of books • Storage for DVDs and videotapes. • Relationship with back patio • Wall between TV/stereo and next room insulated for sound • Consider placement of Christmas tree • Carpet
	Dining	• Space for dining table to seat 14 • Table-height bar with seating on both dining and kitchen sides • Possible access to patio • Hardwood floor
	Kitchen	• Refrigerator, Viking gas cooktop, built-in oven, Viking range hood, dishwasher, and double sink with garbage disposal • Window above sink • Space for more than one cook: cooking will be important • Computer/phone center: desk • Cabinetry details will be worked out with manufacturer • Hardwood floor

(continued)

	Utility/ Workroom	• Large, with washer/dryer, ironing board, and sink • Counters for sewing, folding clothes, gift wrapping, and flower arranging • Cupboards and drawers for storing soap, bleach, sewing supplies and fabric, gift-wrapping supplies, crafts, and scrapbook materials and supplies • Filing cabinet • Place to hang ironing
	Utility Area Bath	• Full bath with tub for bathing grandchildren • Linen, TP, soap storage
	Utility, Kitchen, or elsewhere	• Large pantry for immediate-use food storage • Storage for brooms, mops, vacuum, and other cleaning equipment • Storage for household tools • Hanging space for coats, boots, etc. (could be cubbies) • A place to hang table cloths on hangers • Space for a chest-type freezer
	Garage	• Space for two cars • Near utility/kitchen area • Storage for garden tools, lawn mower, snowblower, and city-issued garbage dumpster
	Basement	• Three bedrooms • Recreation room • Bathroom with bathtub/shower • Mechanical room: HVAC, water heater, water softener • Unfinished area with shelves for storing food, camping equipment, Christmas decorations, and other types of "junk"
	General Considerations	• Storage in every bathroom for TP, soap, towels, and linens • Nine-foot ceilings throughout are desirable but not mandatory • Hardwood floors in entry, parlor, and passageways • Cement window wells • Vinyl windows may be acceptable if they can be recessed to provide adequate relief and shadow lines on exterior and interior • Larger-than-standard baseboards and moldings are desirable • Square (no rounded radius) corners on all wallboards • No texture on wallboard (smooth finish)
Relationships		• Family room and kitchen together—open • Utility and kitchen near each other • Garage and utility near each other
Environmental		• Fine view of mountains to the east • Climate with hot summers and cold, snowy winters • Neighbors on north quite close
Mechanical		• Full air-conditioning • Telephone and modem jacks in family/kitchen, bedrooms, and utility area • TV jacks in family room, basement rumpus room, and all bedrooms • Stereo system in family room with speakers in kitchen, utility, parlor, and library • Separate system to be added in recreation room later • Video system in family room, master bedroom, and recreation room
Psychological		The home should be a comfortable foil for daily living. The design should be solid but not overwhelming in terms of space or luxury. The home will serve as a backdrop for a personal, but unpretentious collection of art and accessories. The overriding feeling should be comfortable and welcoming.

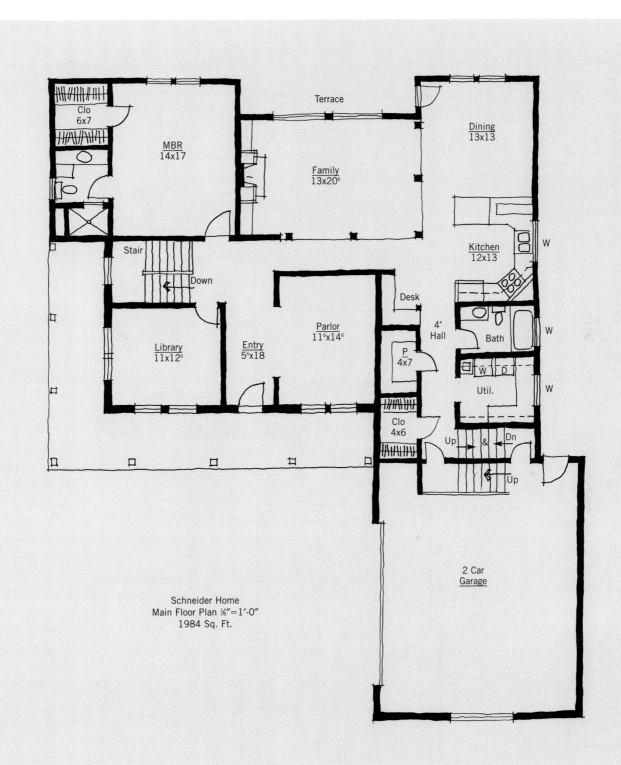

Clo
6x7

MBR
14x17

Terrace

Dining
13x13

Family
13x20^6

Kitchen
12x13

W

Stair

Down

Desk

Parlor
11^{6}x14^6

4'
Hall

Bath

W

Library
11x12^6

Entry
5^{6}x18

P
4x7

W D

W

Util.

Clo
4x6

Up & Dn

Up

2 Car
Garage

Schneider Home
Main Floor Plan ⅛"=1'-0"
1984 Sq. Ft.

(continued)

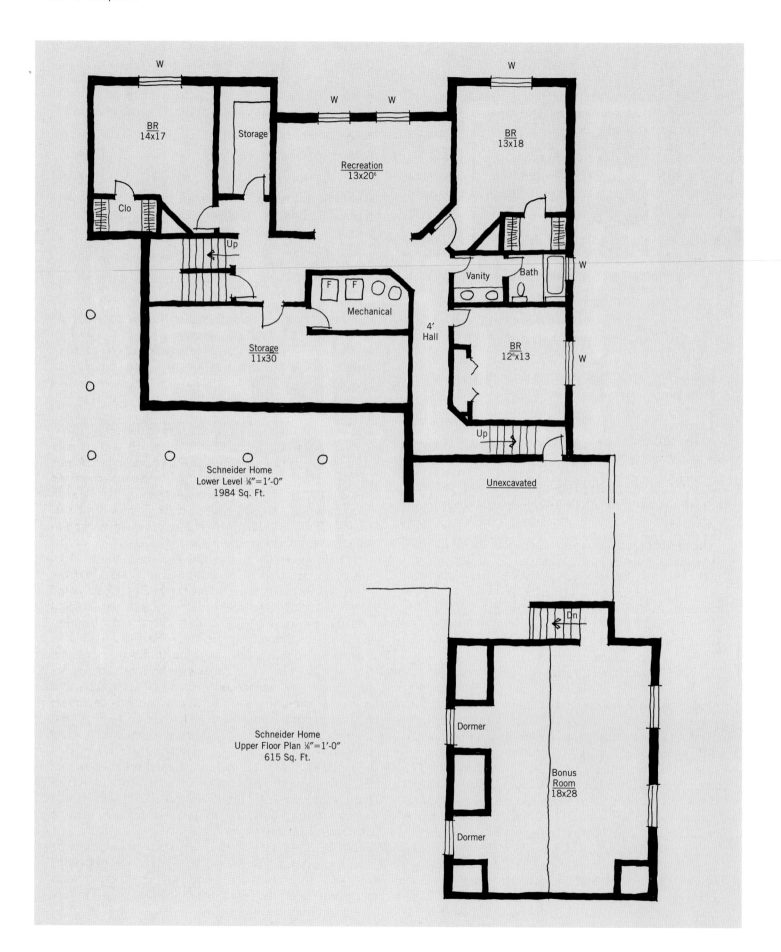

Schneider Home
Lower Level ⅛"=1'-0"
1984 Sq. Ft.

Schneider Home
Upper Floor Plan ⅛"=1'-0"
615 Sq. Ft.

for architectural trim and custom cabinetry. **Finishes** include paint and stain for walls, trim, cabinetry, and hard-surfaced floors. **Furnishings** are furniture and accessories such as rugs and lamps. Fixtures used for lighting and details as small as electrical switch plates could also be considered furnishings. These are chosen from a wide range of resources such as sample books, catalogs, showrooms, or Internet sites. Well-selected materials, finishes, and furnishings reinforce the design concept and make the project exciting because of their individuality and design harmony. Together with brainstorming notes and schematics, ideas for materials help the client/user understand what the completed design will look like.

When the best ideas are brought to a degree of completion, the design concept begins to emerge. A commitment is then made to the ideas, and they are refined to a level where they can be presented for analysis. The presentation of the proposed interior design is generally made with a series of boards (mat, foam-core, or illustration board) displaying the following:

- **Conceptual drawings** demonstrate the ideas or concepts for the design without the time-consuming precision of finished drawings. They include scaled drawings showing furniture placement.
- **Materials and finishes boards** are mounted with photos of furnishings and actual materials for the proposed design.
- **Renderings** are colored perspective drawings of the space that help to visualize how the finished design will appear.

On the basis of the presentation, the client may approve the concept. If it is not agreeable, the design must go back to the drawing board and the process begins again with additional client input. When the concept is approved, the design work may proceed.

Working Drawings and Specifications

The final design development includes working drawings; final selection of materials, finishes, and furnishings; and written specifications. When approved and signed, specifications and working drawings may become part of the agreement or legal contract between the client and the designer. The **working drawings** are the finished mechanical drawings or plans prepared for use by the contractors in making bids and completing the construction of the design. The working drawings are often prepared in blueprint form showing the details as they are to be executed. The complete set of working drawings (also called **construction drawings**) might include a title sheet, an index, perspective drawings, site plans, floor plans, electrical plans, reflected ceiling plans (showing lighting, ventilation, and other ceiling fixtures), sections (a view sliced through the building), elevations (straight-on views), detailed drawings of architectural el-

ements, fixtures, or cabinetwork, and schedules (listing types and finishes of architectural and design elements).

The furnishings and materials to be used in the design must be itemized and documented in lists called **specifications.** The specifications include:

- Identification of the item
- Its manufacturer
- Pricing per unit and extended total; labor costs
- Quantities and types of materials
- Standards of durability or fire resistance
- Types of finishes
- Special instructions for construction or installation
- Dimensions (sizes) and shipping weights
- Any other necessary data

If these are not carefully and completely spelled out, the item or construction may not turn out as intended because it was subject to interpretation. Bids may also be inaccurate and inconsistent. When the working drawings and specifications are complete and approved and the contract arrangements have been made, the design process moves into its final phase.

Execution

The **execution** is the implementation of the design. During the execution, demolition is done, the actual construction begins, and the materials and furnishings orders are finalized. Ordering can be time consuming, yet like each step in the design process, it must be done with great care and accuracy. When working to meet a deadline, nothing is more frustrating than receiving fewer materials or different furnishings than expected.

During this phase of the design process, the work of the contractors should be inspected to ensure that the plans are being carried out properly. This might entail working with builders who do the actual construction and with electricians and plumbers to make sure the electrical, lighting, and plumbing systems are installed as planned and specified. It usually includes meeting with the carpenters and cabinetmakers who construct and install custom woodwork to verify style, dimensions, and quality. It is necessary to check with window treatment fabricators and installers as well as wall-covering and flooring installers to ensure that the goods are correctly fabricated and installed. All of this supervision is a sort of a juggling act, but it is a crucial part of the process that will help guarantee success. This process is discussed further in Chapter 7, "Floor Plans and Building Systems," where scheduling, the critical path, and punch lists are explained and illustrated.

During installation, furnishings must be inspected for damage. Unfortunately, damage or flaws are somewhat common. In this case any necessary insurance claims with shipping firms and manufacturers must be processed without delay.

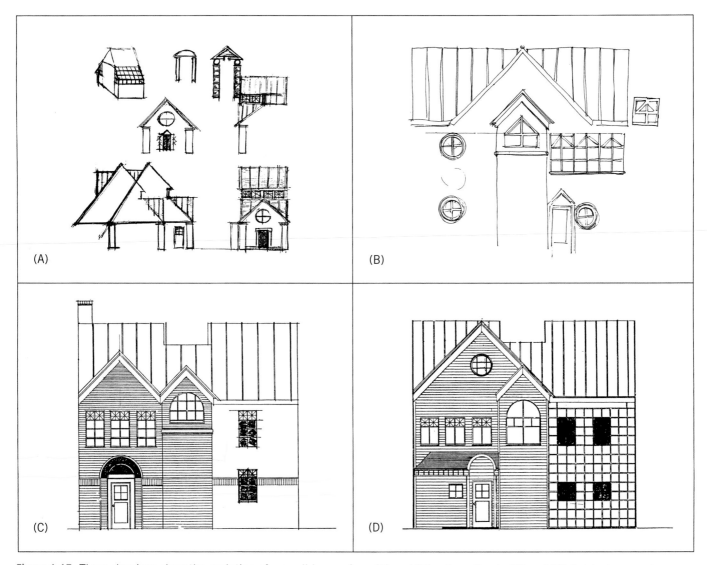

Figure 1.15 These drawings show the evolution of a small house, from (A) and (B) schematics to (C) and (D) finished concept.
Drawings by Carl Blake and Doug Beaudoin

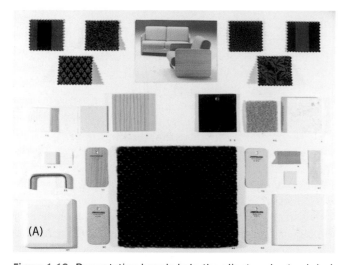

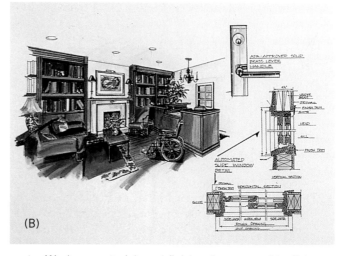

Figure 1.16 Presentation boards help the client understand design concepts. (A) shows materials and finishes for a nonresidential project. (B) is a rendering of a reception area in a small home office, together with details for a window. *(B) Rendering by Jonna Robison*

Although the execution phase inevitably has its moments of frustration, it can also be the most gratifying part of the design process. There is great satisfaction when the research and design development finally come together into a completed design. It is exciting to witness what was once a few scrawls on a scrap of paper emerging into something very real, innovative, beautiful, and functional.

Postoccupancy Evaluation

After a period of time in which users have lived with and tested the effectiveness of the design, the **postoccupancy evaluation (POE)** reveals how well the design functions. The evaluation can be accomplished by on-location interviews and open-ended questionnaires. It might seem that the information from such evaluations would be too late to be of any value. The value lies in future improvements and in the benefit of information that can be implemented in other projects. The evaluation is a tool that helps the designer perform better because of the added insight it provides.

Nonresidential Considerations

The design process for nonresidential interiors is largely the same as that for a residence with the exception of the following:

- Nonresidential design has a greater emphasis on the preparation of contracts and agreements between the client and the designer. This is the reason nonresidential design is often referred to as **contract design.** However, contracts for residential projects are not uncommon today.
- Preparation of bids is a more common procedure in nonresidential design. The designer develops a concept and prepares an estimate of how much the implementation of the concept will cost. This information is presented to the client, who can compare the concept and its cost with similar presentations by other designers.
- The specialties in nonresidential design are diverse, including health care, hospitality (hotels and restaurants), commercial (stores and businesses), and office planning. Specialization allows the designer to stay current on issues within his or her area of focus. However, any designer willing to invest the time in research might be able to develop a suitable design solution for any area of specialty.
- The profile for a nonresidential design may be more generic. Because customers, employees, and guests are transient, the design of a nonresidential space may be not for a specific person but rather for any person who performs a certain task or uses a certain space. Consequently, it is more important to identify most nonresi-

dential users in terms of numbers and functions, which are generic considerations. However, for others—such as a president, a chairman of the board, or the senior partner of a law firm—personal preferences will have to be assessed as they would for a residential user. Their offices might be furnished with more personal and costly items.
- Nonresidential designs are often larger in scope, size, and budget, so their planning may be more complex.

Figure 1.17 Hospitality design is a specialty that focuses on the creation of restaurants and hotels such as this. *© Jeff Greenberg/PhotoEdit*

For example, on large projects, such as hotels or hospitals that require several years for completion, it is usually necessary to substitute for items that may have been discontinued by the manufacturer in the interim. The designer will select substitutes that maintain the integrity of the original design.

• Codes and restrictions require that the designer be aware of the needs of the disabled. Today, all areas of a public building must be easily accessible to those with physical limitations. Codes are contained in documents available from state building boards; from health, safety, and welfare departments; and from agencies such as the American National Standards Institute, which have prepared specifications for making buildings accessible to the physically handicapped.

The International Conference of Building Officials has prepared a document called the Uniform Building Code (UBC). This is a set of guidelines for construction that is accepted nationwide.

The Interior Design Profession

As the preceding discussion of the design process shows, becoming an interior design professional requires more than enthusiasm and good taste. Successful interior designers possess technical and administrative skills as well as insights into problem solving, organization, and cooperation, and attention to detail. In the following section we examine the evolution of this relatively new specialty

Figure 1.18 The studio of Kelly Wearstler Interior Design in Los Angeles includes computer workstations, a space for greeting clients and vendors, and a table for conferences. © *Grey Crawford/Beateworks.com*

and the training, qualifying hurdles, and business aspects of the interior design profession as it exists today.

The Design Profession: Past and Present

Today's interior design profession may be said to have two ancestors: architecture and decorative arts. In past centuries, the role of an architect or builder often extended to determining and installing the features of a building's interior. Other aspects of the interior such as furnishings and carpets were fabricated by specialists such as cabinetmakers and weavers. Custom or "to-order" building and fabricating were the rule rather than the exception. Although the vast majority of people could not afford much choice in the character or quality of the buildings and furnishings they purchased, a few designers created tasteful interiors for the very wealthy. The works of **Robert Adam, William Morris,** and **Charles Rennie Mackintosh** in Great Britain and of **Samuel McIntire** in the United States endure today as admirable examples.

By the beginning of the twentieth century, many Americans had attained enough wealth and status to demand more elaborately planned interiors than what an architect or specialized craftsperson could provide. It was at this point that architecture and decorative arts merged to produce a new kind of professional: the interior designer, who would specify, coordinate, and oversee the plans, construction, and installation of interiors. Perhaps the greatest of these "society" designers was **Elsie deWolfe** (1865–1950).

The **Bauhaus** school of architecture and design, founded in Germany in 1919, trained designers to create interiors with a more functional, populist orientation. Unlike previous arbiters of style who had shunned mass-produced products, the Bauhaus actively promoted the use of machine-age materials, resulting in excellent designs such as the classic modern tubular steel chair. When the school was closed during the Nazi regime in 1933, many of its faculty—including **Ludwig Mies van der Rohe, Marcel Breuer, Walter Gropius,** and **Wassily Kandinsky**—emigrated to the United States. Their techniques and ideals, together with those of Scandinavian designers, have continued to define modernism in design from the 1950s to the present.

The post–World War II period in America witnessed a new level of affluence, commercial development, building, and population growth. Technology that had originated in the war effort was turned to manufacturing domestic products such as plastics, man-made fibers, and building systems. The general public was presented with an overwhelmingly wide variety of affordable goods. As a result, the demand for professionals to help navigate through the maze of materials and furnishings increased dramatically. Both residential and nonresidential users

appreciated the ability of knowledgeable interior design professionals to create an interior design plan and then guide their choices, administer their budgets, and oversee the execution of interiors that met their needs and wants.

Today's interior designers not only design creative and individual interiors but also act as specifiers, organizers, and buyers. Although the result of the design is still the completed interior, the profession has matured far beyond the era of artisans or society designers. The complexity of creating interiors increases as the diversity of styles, products, building systems, and user needs expands. Responding to the demand for excellence in design now involves a wide spectrum of professional tasks requiring extensive skill and training.

Designer Skills

The interior designer today must have skills, education, training, and experience to perform a great variety of tasks, which include the following:

- Developing the design, which includes generating and refining the design ideas leading to a design concept.
- Preparing the documents and letters of agreement pertaining to all contractual aspects of the interior and handling financial and business matters concerned with the design execution.
- Working with or specifying building systems, such as heating, plumbing, air-conditioning, and all aspects of lighting.
- Specifying materials, finishes, and furnishings, which requires a thorough knowledge of all types of floor, ceiling, and wall-covering materials and textile applications as well as a knowledge of period and contemporary architecture and furnishings and green design.

Figure 1.19 A designer verifies the accuracy of computer-generated drawings. © Alli Jagoda

- Preparing working drawings for cabinetry or interior details to be executed by a craftsperson or subcontractor.
- Overseeing the execution, installation, and completion of all contracted areas of the design project.
- Conducting the POE.

Among the specific skills and knowledge required for these tasks are:

- Technical skills including drafting or technical drawing, computer skills applicable to business management, as well as design and computational skills for measuring and costing
- Knowledge of construction methods, building systems, codes, architectural specifications, and safety requirements
- Ongoing awareness of innovations in materials, finishes, and furnishings
- Business skills such as employee management, budgeting, purchasing and lines of credit, marketing, and public relations
- Verbal communication skills, including the ability to present ideas, concepts, and contracts in written and verbal form
- Visual communication skills, including the ability to present ideas and concepts in sketches, renderings, and technical drawings

Training and Professional Development

Formal Design Education

There are many institutions offering accredited and fully developed interior design degree and certificate programs. They include departments and schools of architecture, fine arts, and home economics within universities, colleges, and design schools. Accreditation is granted by the **Foundation for Interior Design Education and Research (FIDER),** which provides a list of the schools and programs that meet its standards.

Education programs generally require from two to six years of study, with additional time needed to obtain graduate degrees. While it is possible to bypass formal education and learn the interior design profession through apprenticeship and on-the-job experience, this

Figure 1.20 Interior designers work closely with subcontractors, such as (A) painters and (B) electricians, to coordinate every element for an interior. *(A) © David A. Taylor, (B) © Judy K. Brody*

Figure 1.21 Designers oversee the work of fabricators who make draperies and other textile applications. *© Joey Moon*

process is ultimately more time consuming and difficult than a formal program of study. Most schools have internship options that allow students to receive academic credit while working in professional interior design firms; such options provide an advantageous opportunity to combine academic theories with practical applications. Table 1.3 lists topics of study in interior design programs.

NCIDQ Examination

The **National Council for Interior Design Qualification (NCIDQ)** serves to identify to the public those interior designers who have met the minimum standards for professional practice by passing the **NCIDQ examination.** The organization tries to maintain the most advanced procedures for examination and continually reviews the examination to include expanding techniques in design development and professional knowledge. A study guide to prepare a candidate for the exam is available on request from NCIDQ.

The NCIDQ exam is administered periodically at many locations around the country. It is now a requirement for full acceptance into several professional organizations. The exam covers the candidate's knowledge of interior design and poses a creative problem that the candidate must solve. A designer who has earned a baccalaureate degree and worked for a minimum of two years in the field should be eligible to take the exam. The NCIDQ exam sets a standard of excellence and competence so that professional interior designers may better serve the public.

Titlement and Licensing

In order to ensure professionalism, competency, and quality services, some states have passed title or licensing acts. This means that in order to use the title "interior designer," the professional must be licensed. Although requirements may vary from one state to another, generally, to obtain a license, the designer must pass the NCIDQ exam and have worked a minimum number of years in the profession.

In order to maintain that license, designers are required to earn a minimum number of continuing education units (CEUs) each year. As a general rule, one CEU is equal to ten "contact" or study hours. For example, a state that requires five CEUs per year would, in effect, require fifty hours of advanced CEU training. The CEU offers a way for designers to keep abreast of changes and developments in the interior design practice and profession.

Interior Design Resources

As the English writer Samuel Johnson said, knowledge is of two kinds: we know a subject ourselves, or we know where we can find information about it. Successful interior designers know where to go for information and how to access the resources that will best enable them to fulfill the needs of a given project.

Trade Resources

An immense number of **trade sources** exist to serve the interior design industry today. Trade sources are companies or vendors that sell goods and services to the trade (designers, architects, and specifiers) for purchase by their retail clients. These goods include every element of fixtures and furnishings needed in an interior. The goods and services are ordered through wholesale catalogs; through manufacturing and product representatives, or reps; or through regional showrooms, which may be closed (allowing only designers to enter and purchase) or open (allowing retail clients to accompany the designer). Craftspeople usually function independently of showrooms and sales representatives; quality craftspeople generally are in demand and have no need to market their services. Most major cities now have design **marketing centers** or **markets,** which are convenient clusters of trade-source showrooms that serve the designer. Many craftspeople are located near markets.

Computers and the Internet

A computer with Internet access is the most important tool available to interior designers today. It is used in every aspect of the interior design process, from programming to execution to billing for services rendered. Computer-generated animations even allow a client to

---

Table 1.3 | Topics of Study in Interior Design Education Programs

- Basic and creative arts such as two- and three-dimensional design, fine, and applied arts.
- Design theory, human factors, and spatial composition.
- Residential and nonresidential design.
- Design for special populations (handicapped, elderly, etc.), special problems (environmental, etc.), and special purposes (historic preservation, adaptive reuse).
- Design materials (textiles, lighting, furniture, color).
- Technical knowledge such as structure and construction, building systems, energy conservation, detailing, materials, laws, building codes, and ordinances.
- Communication skills, such as verbal, written, and visual presentation, drafting, and computer systems.
- Professional practice and organization and specification skills.
- History of art, architecture, interiors, furnishings, and materials.
- Research methodologies, survey, literature search, and observation.
- Computer application.

Figure 1.22 The Prairie Avenue Bookshop in Chicago offers interior design publications of the history, fashion trends, and technical advances in this complex and ever-changing field. *© Courtesy of the Prairie Avenue Bookshop Ltd., Chicago/photo: Christian Korab*

Figure 1.23 At design centers, marts, or showrooms, interior designers may assist customers in the selection of furnishings from a wealth of resources. *ThinkStock/SuperStock*

Figure 1.24 This swatch board provides samples for use in color comparison and selection for laminate surfaces. *© David A. Taylor*

Figure 1.25 Interior designers work with fabric samples, catalogs and computers to specify furnishings for both residential and nonresidential interiors. © David A. Taylor

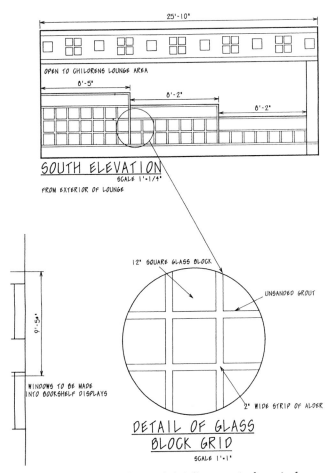

25'-10"

OPEN TO CHILDRENS LOUNGE AREA

6'-5"

6'-2"

6'-2"

SOUTH ELEVATION
SCALE 1"-1/4"

FROM EXTERIOR OF LOUNGE

9'-5"

WINDOWS TO BE MADE
INTO BOOKSHELF DISPLAYS

12" SQUARE GLASS BLOCK

UNSANDED GROUT

2" WIDE STRIP OF ALDER

DETAIL OF GLASS
BLOCK GRID
SCALE 1"-1"

Figure 1.26 This elevation and detail are part of a set of computer-generated design drawings for a children's library.

walk through a virtual version of the completed design. In some cases the computer and Internet access have made it possible for designers to work anywhere in the world without leaving the office; with laptop computers they can take their business with them when they travel. The computer has revolutionized the practice of interior design.

Designers use computers and the Internet for:

- **Computer-aided design (CAD)** to draw and render interior design concepts
- **Computer-aided design and drafting (CADD)** to draft, render, and animate design concepts as well as to create working drawings and details
- **Project management** to oversee calendars, critical paths, and deadlines so that the design is completed in a timely manner
- **Data management,** such as entering programming information in real time as the designer interviews the client
- **Managing accounts** that must be paid to suppliers and contractors and accounts receivable from clients to whom services have been rendered
- **Preparing specifications** of materials, finishes, and furnishings
- **Monitoring** procurement, delivery, and installation of materials, finishes, and furnishings
- **Networking with other designers** within an office or in other offices. Plans and drawings can be evaluated and changed on the screen in real time as the designers conference.
- **Networking with clients,** which can be done in a like manner
- **Videoconferencing,** which allows clients and designers or design teams to set up conferences over the Internet without the necessity of traveling
- **Product searches** on the Internet or via catalogs on CD-ROM
- **E-mail,** which allows almost instantaneous communication between designers or designers and clients. E-mail attachments allow for the immediate transfer of documents and drawings as well.

Professionals in Related Fields

The process of interior design is a team effort on the part of design professionals, craftspeople, and laypeople. In addition to having the interpersonal and business skills needed to work effectively with clients and users, interior designers must have the ability to participate in teams with professionals such as:

- **General contractors and builders,** who are licensed and legally responsible for the outcome of the structures they erect
- **Architects,** who are also licensed and legally responsible and are essential team members in projects for

Figure 1.27 The Pacific Design Center in Los Angeles, California, affectionately nicknamed "the Blue Whale," holds vast resources for interior designers. © *Allen Rubenstein/Corbis*

Figure 1.28 Quality craftspeople are important to successful interiors. (A) Upholsterers build and reupholster custom furniture. (B) Cabinetmakers construct built-in cabinetry for kitchen, bath, or office. *(A) © Joey Moon; (B) Bill Horsman/Stock, Boston*

upscale clientele. Many major architectural firms have interior design departments.

- **Subcontractors,** who specialize in handling specific aspects such as plumbing, HVAC, and electrical systems, drywall or plaster, masonry, siding, painting, and finishing carpentry
- **Cabinetmakers,** who create custom closets and cabinetry and other built-ins
- **Retailers and wholesalers** of products such as furniture, paint and wall coverings, lighting, window treatments, and floor coverings. Dealers who sell at retail to the public often provide discounts to interior designers.

- **Fabricators and craftspeople** such as upholsterers and other custom-furniture makers, restoration specialists, fine artists, stained-glass artisans, and stone carvers
- **Installers of materials** such as flooring and floor coverings, bath and kitchen fixtures, paneling, tile, wallpaper, and drapery rods and other window treatments. Installers may be involved in measuring and estimating when the design is in the planning stage.

Professional Organizations

Design organizations exist to research and make available to their members (through continuing education) new and improved design methods, information,

Figure 1.29 Bathroom design is an important specialty within residential interior design.
© Grey Crawford/Beateworks.com

Careers in Interior Design

An education in interior design provides professional opportunities in an almost endless variety of fields and specialties, and an important distinction is frequently made between residential and nonresidential design. Each of these two career categories has certain characteristics that tend to be consistent from one project to the next.

Residential Interior Design

Residential designers create interiors for homes, vacation homes, apartments and town houses, and other dwellings. They typically have close contact with users, often working directly for them, and strive to express their clients' personal tastes. In other cases they work with rental units, or new construction, in which the occupants are not present until the interiors are completed. Residential designers may specialize in particular rooms, such as kitchens or media rooms. They also may pursue careers in the retail sector, where they staff the interior design service departments that are incorporated into quality department stores, furniture stores, and home improvement stores.

Nonresidential Interior Design

Nonresidential design is far less personal than most residential work, and it entails a higher degree of attention to issues of project management and code compliance. While

sources, and materials. These organizations also lobby for licensing and title registration. Each organization has its own standards of excellence, various levels of association, and entrance requirements. See the *Interiors* website for further information.

some nonresidential firms do a variety of interiors, most specialize in a specific type, such as hospitals, hotels, or offices. Specialization allows nonresidential designers to gain the depth of experience and expertise that is often necessary to secure work assignments. It is not unusual

Figure 1.30 Interior design professionals assist residential and nonresidential customers in the selection and specification of textiles and furnishings from their extensive resources of product manufacturers and suppliers. *Bob Daemmrich/Stock, Boston*

for a nonresidential client to solicit competitive bids for interior design work, to examine candidates' business practices, and to require formal presentation of proposals before awarding a contract.

Specialized Design

As indicated above, interior designers—especially those working in nonresidential design—often become proficient and skilled in a particular specialty, such as hospitality (hotels, restaurants, resorts); commercial/retail (offices, stores); health care (hospitals, medical offices, hospices); and justice design (courthouses, jails, prisons). In addition to fostering in-depth knowledge, specialization allows designers to work in areas where their expertise can help prevent mistakes and consequent litigation. As interior designers are increasingly held legally responsible for the outcome of their projects, the importance of specialization as a risk management strat-

egy becomes greater. Table 1.4 describes many of the career specialties within the interior design field.

Table 1.4 | Design Specialties and Related Fields

- Acoustic design—planning the sound-reflecting and -absorbing qualities of an interior through the shape of the space and through specified finishes and materials. Theater design will incorporate acoustics.
- Adaptive reuse—the remodeling of old or historic structures to fit a purpose different from the original. A wharf warehouse, for example, could become a shopping plaza or mall; an old home could become a law, real estate, or insurance office; inner-city buildings could become luxury condominiums or co-ops. *Rehabilitation,* or *rehab,* is the process of bringing any older building up to current standards so that it can be inhabited.
- Amusement park design—carrying themes into every item of the park, from signs to trash cans and drinking fountains. It also deals with safety, traffic patterns, and efficiency.
- Aquarium design—for homes, offices, and aquatic parks and museums. This specialty could also include maintenance.
- Architectural space planning or floor plan design—drafting by hand or CADD.
- Art and accessory dealerships—selling fine art and/or unique accessories retail to the public or wholesale to interior designers.
- Color consultation—for marketing firms, industry, architectural, or interior design firms, business corporations, government.
- Buying—for large department and furniture stores. Buyers select floor merchandise or lines (merchandise offered by particular companies) carried by the company.
- Cabinet, closet, and storage design—custom design to suit individual needs or dealerships in retail modular storage furniture.
- Communication design—working with specialized needs in offices for computer terminal stations, telecommunication conference rooms, and other areas.
- Construction/project management—overseeing the construction and acting as liaison between client and contractor. This may include hiring the architect, engineers, subcontractors, craftspeople, and consultants.
- Drafting and/or CADD.
- Design for corporate parties, charity balls, design shows, or other large gatherings where there must be organization and orchestration of many details within a given length of time.
- Design for the handicapped, aged, or infirm—including design for medical facilities, rest homes, hospices, residences, or products.
- Energy conservation—acting as consultant to architectural firms or clients to increase energy efficiency (see also *solar design*).
- Entertainment center design—designing the storage units for television, videocassette recorders, stereo equipment, computers, media-center rooms, and home theater.
- Environmental safety—research into materials that will not burn or do not threaten the safety of the users or of the environment; consultation to manufacturers and architects.
- Environmental/green design—specifying materials and furnishings that are from renewable resources, minimally impact the environment, and contribute to a safe and healthy interior.

Figure 1.31 Facilities managers are responsible for the inventory and maintenance of systems furniture like this. *© Nick Merrick/ Hedrich Blessing, by courtesy of Herman Miller*

- Facilities management—a fast-growing field where corporations utilize a manager to plan and purchase furnishings and to coordinate and be responsible for all building repairs and maintenance. The facility may be one building or dozens of buildings in dozens of locations; the manager oversees other employees in the facilities department.
- Forensic consultation—studying a product's construction and appropriate use for manufacturing, for application, or for purposes of testifying in litigation proceedings.
- Furniture design—the design of new and innovative furnishing items such as case goods, upholstered furniture, and accessories.
- Furniture retail sales or rental business—residential and/or nonresidential.
- Graphic design and illustration, and signage graphics—such as creating a corporate image.
- Greenhouse and solarium design—designing spaces for healthy plants (including temperature and humidity control); also designing sun spaces for people to dine, socialize, or relax in a heated spa.
- Hard-surface floor-covering design—including both the actual design of the tiles or vinyl and the use/application of ceramic tiles, wood, brick, and stone on floors, walls, and ceilings (including mosaic and mural work).
- Hardware design—designing doorknobs, handles, and hinges.
- Health care design—designing hospitals, clinics, hospices, and doctors' offices.
- Health club/recreational facility design—buildings that house swimming pools, indoor ball courts, gyms for workout and aerobics. Safety as well as good design is important.
- Historic preservation and restoration of authentic interiors maintained as museums; also, restoring fine old buildings to their original state or an adaptation of it. Historic preservation is a growing concern in both residential and nonresidential inte-

Figure 1.32 Kitchen designers not only plan preparation areas, but also design service areas such as this desk and cabinet. *© Jessie Walker*

rior design and requires thorough knowledge of specialized goods and services.
- Hospitality design—interior design for hotels, convention centers, resorts, and restaurants. A large and important area in nonresidential design.
- Industrial facilities—manufacturing plants and accompanying offices and support areas.
- In-house corporate design—design, consult with experts, and coordinate components to keep the corporate image prestigious.
- Journalism—magazine and newspaper articles on design.

(continued)

Figure 1.33 Acoustic designers planned ceiling baffles to improve the acoustics of this refurbished concert hall.
© *Grey Crawford/Beateworks.com*

- Justice design—designing secured facilities such as prisons and courthouses.
- Kitchen design—planning the latest in cooking equipment and efficient food preparation and serving areas, plus accommodating a social environment. (A Certified Kitchen Designer uses CKD after his or her name.)
- Landscaping—design firms specializing in interior landscaping select, sell, rent, and maintain real and artificial plants.
- Law—handling litigation over interior design projects, working toward legislation, or serving as advisors concerning design laws, public safety, historic preservation, or a host of other design-related areas.
- Law office design—incorporating specialized needs, equipment, and personnel with an image.

- Library design—meeting needs of different kinds and locations (such as law libraries) and all the inherent equipment and space planning.
- Lighting design—a twofold career option: designing lighting plans and specialty lighting needs for interiors, and designing the lighting fixtures or luminaires.
- Management—in design firms, in industry, or in design-related business, or as facilities managers.
- Manufacturer's representatives (reps or sales reps)—liaisons between the trade and vendors. Call on design firms within a designated territory to whom they provide or sell product samples or catalogs. They order stock merchandise and provide the link between the manufacturer and retailer or designer in obtaining goods and services, providing swifter service, and troubleshoot-

ing. Reps also assist the designer in preparing specifications, selecting merchandise, preparing bids, and writing purchase orders.

- Marketing—consultants to wholesale and retail firms and to exporters/importers of design goods.
- Medical facilities—interior design for hospitals, clinics, and other medical care facilities.
- Model-home design—renting or selling furnishings to model homes. Similar to residential design but without having to deal with a user who will live there. Luxury models for condominiums, flats, or co-ops incorporate expensive and luxurious design.
- Museum design—planning spaces; meeting specialized needs for display design, background materials, specialized lighting, humidity control, and traffic flow. Curatorship—directors of museums or archives are yet another career option.
- Office design—a specialty in nonresidential design ranging from small offices to high-rise buildings. Professional offices, such as those for doctors and dentists, are another office specialty.
- Plumbing fixture design—designing sinks, lavatories, bathtubs and saunas, toilets and bidets, and faucets.
- Product design—new and innovative furnishing items such as furniture and accessories.
- Product evaluation—consulting with and recommending marketing strategies to companies that are introducing new designs and products.
- Publicity and public relations (PR)—establishing and/or marketing an image for corporations, company products, or other designers.
- Purchasing agent—an interior designer can act as purchaser for large companies, negotiating and overseeing correct ordering of furnishings.
- Real estate developer—interior designers often buy real estate, improve or remodel the building, and sell it at a profit. Building new nonresidential buildings and leasing them is another aspect. An interior designer–turned-developer can also arrange financing and sell homes or nonresidential buildings.
- Rendering—artists' conceptions of interior or exterior design.
- Restaurant design—a specialty in the interior design of restaurants, cafeterias, bars, and fast-food services.
- Retail design—from individual boutiques to large department stores and from single shops to entire shopping malls, creative designers are in demand.

- Retail selling—many interior designers own, manage, or work in retail stores. Specialty shops might include accessories, selected new or antique furniture, textiles, or fine art. Interior designers themselves are often expert sales people.
- Salon design—design of beauty and barber shops, tanning facilities, nail sculpturing, and other beauty services.
- Set design—set design is needed for television, theater, movies, and for taking photographs for furniture companies.
- Showroom designer—the interior design and space planning of permanent and seasonal showrooms of furniture, fabric, carpet, accessories. This can be done on a freelance basis or as a permanent employee of a manufacturing firm.
- Solar design—requiring knowledge of energy efficiency, sun control, and sunlight-resistant materials. Specialists in solar interior design are needed in both residential and nonresidential design.
- Textile design for fabrics, wallpaper, or carpeting—working in-house for large conversion companies, or freelancing and selling designs (or being paid royalties) for textile design. Custom design occasionally calls for one-of-a-kind textiles.
- Training specialists—in areas such as computers, retail sales and marketing, lighting, nonresidential specifications, or other design services.
- Transportation design—including specialties in aircraft interiors (passenger jets to corporate jets), marine design (interiors of luxury liners to private yachts), bus and train interior design, and even automobile design.
- Turnkey design—in which the designer sells the project and assumes complete responsibility to hire all consultants/subcontractors and finish the project with very little input from the client, who needs only to turn the key and walk in to a completed interior. Vacation homes are one application of this specialty.
- Universal or transgenerational design—planning and furnishing buildings that are easy to use without drawing attention to the user, regardless of age or physical abilities.
- Window treatment design—today so many style and mechanical options exist in window treatments that it takes expertise to know which treatments to specify. Fabric coordination with overall design and furnishings is also necessary.

Teaching Interior Design

To qualify for a full-time position in a university, college, or design school, a candidate is usually expected to have professional experience as well as a terminal degree: **master of arts (M.A.), master of science (M.S.), master of fine arts (M.F.A.),** or **doctor of philosophy (Ph.D.).** The degree may be in interior design or in a related field such as architecture, art history, business management, CAD, education, historic preservation, humanities, psychology, or housing. Hiring and advancement are based

on factors such as teaching effectiveness, creative work and research, and service to the institution and the community.

Teaching design in high schools or community colleges is another career option. High schools generally offer courses in interior design as a part of their home economics programs. Community colleges frequently offer interior design courses, and some offer vocational training or associate degrees that may emphasize design. A baccalaureate (bachelor's) degree may be the minimum requirement to teach in either of these situations, and high schools usually require a teaching certificate as well.

Teaching part-time is also a viable career option. Designers who are active in the profession or in a related field can add immeasurably to the strength of a design program by imparting the skills and experiences gleaned from real-life situations. Many academic design departments rely on practicing professionals who serve as part-time instructors.

Financial Considerations

As most clients usually view creating an interior as a major expense, they want to be sure the money they invest in a design project is being spent wisely. The designer will need not only good aesthetic sense and training, but also good budget sense. A thorough knowledge of sources and products is essential to allow the designer to suggest and obtain elements that the client can afford and that will meet the client's needs. By applying the elements and principles of design, the designer can avoid making aesthetic mistakes that would disappoint the client and require extra work to correct. The designer is also often charged with hiring and supervising subcontractors, installers, and craftspeople; the costs for these participants must also be monitored and accounted for.

Last but not least, designers themselves must be paid. The amount and structure of designer fees vary according to circumstance and are, of course, based on the type and extent of services the designer provides. For consulting with clients, a designer usually charges a flat fee or an hourly rate, freeing clients to shop on their own and purchase goods from whatever source they wish. For executing residential interiors, designers often receive payments based on retail sales or retail less a percentage. This arrangement may be combined with a design fee based on the time spent preparing estimates, drafting, rendering, shopping, and supervising installation, in which case the interior designer may be paid monthly or in increments as various phases of the design program are accomplished.

Letters of agreement outline the services to be rendered by the designer, whether purchasing is to be done by the designer on the client's behalf, and which arrangement (retail, retail less a percentage, or wholesale plus a percentage) is agreed upon. The letter will outline specific phases of the design job, the client's responsibility to third-party contractors and services, compensation arrangements, and collateral matters. Disclaimers (items and services for which the designer is not responsible) will limit the designer's liability and clarify the relationship between the designer and the client. A **retainer fee,** applicable to the design fees or the goods to be purchased, is customarily required to initiate work by the design firm.

Nonresidential interior design is often based on a flat fee, computing in advance the projected time necessary to complete the design. The flat fee may also be based on the square footage of the project. When fees are based on time, the salary of each person (principal, project manager, senior and junior designers, draftspersons, secretaries) who will be involved in a project is computed or projected, and the monthly salary of each person is multiplied by the number of months spent in each phase of the design job (programming, designing, construction, installation). That amount is multiplied by 3 to cover wages, overhead, profit, and anticipated overtime spent on the job. The square-foot method is used less often but is applicable for large spaces.

Purchasing arrangements for nonresidential furnishings are typically billed at wholesale plus 10 to 20 percent. The designer may not purchase for nonresidential jobs but may specify furnishings that are ordered by the purchasing department of the client's firm. Likewise, nonresidential clients are generally responsible to pay for third-party services such as those of architects, engineers, and general contractors. Billings for design goods and services are billed monthly or in prearranged installments that parallel each phase of the project.

The Future of Interior Design

It is clear that in the future there will be a greater need for designers to be knowledgeable about the complex and technical aspects of interior design. Increased litigation over design projects points to the increasing accountability of interior designers for the environments they create. Because of this, designers in the future will specialize further to gain expertise in one area of design.

As more states pass title registration acts and require licensing, qualified interior designers will enjoy increased recognition in the legal and business arenas. This trend should further protect the public against those who are not qualified to practice in the field.

Finally, computer technology promises to play a commanding role in the future of interior design. Increasingly capable databases and business management applications will assist in the coordination of research and documentation, analysis, organization, and processing of all the documentation handled by the interior designer. Financial programs will aid in preparing estimates, purchasing goods and services, and monitoring budgets. Graphic applications such as CAD will become more powerful; we might even expect that designers and clients will utilize **virtual reality** as a tool for visualizing and planning how an interior will look and feel. In addition to predictions we can make on the basis of what we presently know, we can be sure that computer technology will continue to burgeon and, as a result, that things we may not even be able to imagine will become possible as the interior design profession moves ahead in the twenty-first century.

Chapter 2 | Special Considerations in Design

Important Design
Considerations 39

Environmental
Considerations 39

Considerations for Special
Needs Users 46

Design for Special
Populations 48

Special Design Considerations
as Fundamental Goals 55

Figure 2.1 A former gymnasium has been adapted for reuse as a residence. *Reiter & Reiter Architects/photo © Brian Vanden Brink*

Important Design Considerations

Chapter 1 discussed the role of designers as problem solvers. Nowhere is this more crucial than in design that deals ethically with the environment and the special needs of users. Ethics are simply the moral obligation to do what is right. We have an ethical responsibility to care for the earth that is our home. We have similar ethical accountability to make life as free from design problems as possible for those whose needs differ from the norm. This chapter deals with design issues related to the environment and populations with special needs.

Environmental Considerations

Designers have an ethical responsibility to be aware of the impact their designs have on the environment and subsequently on users. That responsibility includes avoiding waste and pollution, as well as ensuring long life for design so that it will not be prematurely discarded. These are critical features of good design, and when design is good, both the environment and users benefit.

Sustainability

Sustainability means thinking about creating buildings and interior environments now, but also considering how they will be used 50, 100, or more years from now. It also includes strategies such as the use of environmentally friendly materials, recycling, and energy efficiency. Concepts of sustainability extend to include waste management, avoiding pollution, conserving resources, and utilizing materials and furnishings that are made from renewable resources with long life spans and requiring minimal upkeep. Sustainability is a healthy and educated mind-set about living and working to support rather than deplete natural resources. Ultimately, sustainability means creating long-lasting buildings and environments that tread lightly on the environment.

Use of Resources

There are two types of resources used by builders and developers: renewable and nonrenewable. **Renewable resources** include materials such as wood from trees that can be replanted in sustained-growth forests. **Nonrenewable resources** include minerals and metals in their raw form as well as fossil fuels. Fortunately, some forms of both renewable and nonrenewable resources, such as metals, plastics, and paper products, can be recycled. When buildings are demolished or interiors refurnished, the demolished or discarded materials and furnishings will have to be removed to a landfill unless they can be recycled.

Resource Efficiency and Sustainability

Because space for landfills is becoming increasingly hard to find, good ethics point to resource efficiency. "Reduce, reuse, recycle, and repair" are old but familiar ideas that constitute resource efficiency. Reduce simply means to use less. Reuse means to find new uses for things that have become obsolete. Recycle may be synonymous with reuse, but it also means saving used materials for reconstitution, so they can be used again as if they were new. Discarded paper, for example, can be reprocessed into new paper. Repair means doing what is necessary to return something that no longer functions, or has been damaged, to working condition, rather than discarding it. Resource efficiency has been imperative in times of hardship. Nineteenth-century pioneers and those who lived through the great depression of the twentieth century were experts at resource efficiency. In times of great abundance, resource efficiency becomes an ethical practice of those who value the environment.

Modest Living and Sustainability

Modest living is something few of us may consider when contemplating sustainability, but those who live modestly use their own and the earth's resources to meet needs rather than to fulfill wants. In doing so, they preserve the environment, simplify life, and amplify life's spiritual possibilities. Basic human needs include food, clothing, and shelter. In order to obtain these basic needs, some form of transportation—public or personal—is generally needed. Basic shelter includes places to prepare food, eat, sleep, sit, converse, and maintain hygiene. These needs include certain furnishings, fixtures, and appliances that are necessary to do household work. Beyond that, all things we possess are wants. It is startling to see how very few material goods and how little space many in the world live with, yet maintain lives of meaning and purpose.

Today, many luxuries seem to be necessities. Huge houses with soaring ceilings, enormous windows, and luxurious finishes and furnishings are considered by some to be very desirable because they are symbols of accomplishment or simply because of their luxury. Such houses, however, because of their size and luxury, consume more materials and are more costly to build and maintain than more modest dwellings. Environments that are larger than needed require more energy to light, heat, and cool and are more difficult and costly to maintain. When we build or purchase houses that are beyond our financial means, we incur debt that may lead to financial and emotional strain. Sustainability can be turned around to mean our ability to sustain ourselves, and when we overextend, we are incapable of sustaining ourselves.

Organization and maintenance are vital parts of modest living. Our lives can become so cluttered with possessions that we no longer know what we own. Thus, we buy unnecessarily to replace what we can no longer find. Modest living is also about being good stewards over that which we possess. Wise stewardship is not only caring for what we have, but having only what we really need. It means being aware of ways to contribute to the health of the earth while assuring personal or family well-being. If we buy wisely we need to buy only once. For example, a well-designed and well-built piece of furniture can be used for generations. Well-chosen carpets and other soft furnishings can be used for years—until they are worn out. They may require cleaning and maintenance, but if we organize and care for our possessions, they can be used for years, even indefinitely.

Figure 2.2 This pleasant interior is an example of modest living. Because of its moderate size, it required less materials and resources to build and furnish; uses less energy to light, heat, and cool; and is less difficult and costly to maintain than over-large, ostentatious homes. *Green Company, architects/photo © Brian Vanden Brink*

A writer for a respected American newspaper reports that there is a grassroots movement called Voluntary Simplicity, consisting of people who want to limit the size of their homes and number of their possessions in order to temper their pace of life. Many are attracted to the movement because of environmental concerns while others are drawn by spiritual benefits. The writer notes that people are starting to see that their possessions are a deterrent to peace of conscience, peace of mind, and happiness. They feel that the more they have, the more responsible they are for their possessions and the less breathing room they have. If they can create breathing room in their lives, they are more likely to find increased spiritual dimensions. Physical clutter is psychologically grating and emotionally taxing. Anyone who has "purged" a home in preparation for moving, knows the satisfaction and even happiness that come from discarding and simplifying.

By living modestly we consume less, reducing the impact we have on the environment while increasing peace of mind. Those who value leaving a light footprint on the earth should carefully consider modest living.

Design Longevity and Sustainability

In many areas, developers are turning farmland, greenbelts, and previously unused land into office and indus-

trial parks, neighborhoods, and shopping centers. Some find this kind of growth distressing, while others see it as a desirable sign of progress. Because development inevitably has an impact on the environment, it is an opportunity for design solutions that do the least possible harm to natural surroundings and leave a legacy of spaces and buildings that will become better with age.

The ultimate goals of most development are to build homes in which a growing population can live, to create places in which to obtain the goods we need, to establish centers of healing or learning, to facilitate the manufacture and transfer of new products and technologies, and to accommodate increased demands for transportation, as well as other worthy aims. Yet, because cost is often the most critical factor in development, communities are sometimes shortchanged by the poor quality of what is built. While vigilant communities establish design controls and restrictions that preserve and enhance the environment, those without design controls are vulnerable to the loss of open space in the name of profits.

Good design stands the test of time and adds quality to a community indefinitely. Historic sites or buildings often add value to an area. But poor design may never live to become historic; it will be razed to make way for

Figure 2.3 Because it is well-designed, this mid-century Scandinavian book case, purchased in Copenhagen in the 1950s, finds continued use as an entry piece in an Arizona condominium at the beginning of the new millennium. *© David A. Taylor*

new development. This consumes resources, and demolition creates waste and debris that go into landfills. If poor design escapes the wrecking ball, it may live on as blight. Ethical politicians, designers, and developers know that a development is more than a source of income. For good or ill, it will be a continuously visible part of the community environment until, quite naturally, with time it becomes a wonderful historic setting, blight, or is destroyed by the wrecking ball.

Design has great healing power for the environment because a good designer can turn blight into something wonderful. For example, derelict areas that have lain fallow for years have been given new functions and life with adroit design changes and the addition of green spaces. Older, but viable, buildings that no longer serve their original purposes have been given new life by thoughtful design changes. Good design can create and preserve communities that are pleasant and a genuine source of pride. Long-lasting design is a friend of the environment.

In order to be sustainable, materials, finishes, and furnishings used in interiors should also be chosen for good design and quality, which in turn produce longevity and decrease waste. Fashions come and go, and designers must be careful to weigh fashion against longevity. They should ensure that what they select and specify has lasting quality so that those design choices do not become tiresome and outdated before the materials, finishes, and furnishings themselves wear out. When they do wear out, materials, finishes, and furnishings should be recycled whenever possible.

Universal and Transgenerational Design and Sustainability

Two related concepts that increase sustainability are **universal design** (also discussed later in this chapter) and **transgenerational design.** The mission of the Center for Universal Design is to improve the quality and availability of housing for people with disabilities, including disabilities that result from aging. They define universal design as the design of products and environments to be usable by all people, to the greatest extent possible, without the need for adaptation or specialized design. Transgenerational design is the practice of making products and environments compatible with those physical and sensory impairments associated with human aging and which limit major activities of daily life. Principles of transgenerational design require designers to think not only about clients' present needs but also about what their needs will be throughout life. Transgenerational design does not focus on the occupant's age, but rather centers on an environment's usefulness to users of any age. Transgenerational and universal design are both about designing environments and household products that accommodate the widest market segments—for an environment to be truly universal or transgenerational, it has to feel comfortable to all users of all ages and abilities. If principles of universal and transgenerational design are applied, the life of an environment will be vastly extended because potential changes in need and ability will have been addressed at the start of the project.

Things to consider:

- Reduce, reuse, recycle, and repair possessions and furnishings.
- Learn to distinguish between wants and needs: build or buy only what you really need, leaving a lighter footprint on the earth.
- Encourage community governments to establish design-review commissions to monitor design quality and establish criteria for building and development.
- Encourage local governments to establish greenbelts and preserve green spaces as well as engage in city forestation or tree planting.
- Encourage preservation and adaptive reuse of existing buildings.

- Select well-designed and durable materials, finishes, and furnishings for longevity.
- Plan for the long haul, anticipating changing abilities and needs.

Green Design

Green specification describes selection of materials that produce a sustainable environment—the materials have come from a renewable source and removing them will not harm the earth's environment. Green products will also have been green-manufactured with no adverse effect on the environment, and can usually be recycled or reused. These kinds of products are free from harmful toxins, are made of renewable resources, and have not created environmentally harmful by-products in the manufacturing process.

Green products are items that are environmentally friendly because they do little or no harm to the environment or because they are made of postconsumer recycled materials. Wood used in such products comes from a certified forest management program. Most manufacturing requires the use of water, but responsible manufacturers that use large quantities of water, clean and reuse it rather than depleting fresh water sources.

Some problems of green specification are complex. For example, some regard the use of exotic woods—taken from endangered tropical forests—as unethical because it is felt that use of such woods depletes the forests. It is widely acknowledged that the tropical rain forests of the world are disappearing at an alarming rate and this may be affecting weather patterns and air quality throughout the world. Those responsible for the deforestation are often poor farmers who slash and burn the forest to plant their meager crops. The denuded soil is quickly depleted, and the slashing moves deeper into the forest. Some experts feel that if the emphasis could be changed from farming to the selective harvesting of exotic wood and the creation of sustained-growth forests, farmers would better be able to sustain life, slash-and-burn farming would become obsolete, and the forests would be preserved.

Things to consider:

- Specify green products whenever possible.
- Select and specify materials and finishes that will wear well.
- Reupholster furniture rather than discard it.
- Specify systems furniture (modular office landscape) from manufacturers that will refurbish their product when it is dated or worn.
- When possible, specify blanket wrapping rather than cardboard packing for shipping of new furniture and appliances.
- When appropriate, specify a patterned carpet that will hide soil and wear, extending its life.

Figure 2.4 Bamboo, a highly-renewable resource, was used to create this attractive and durable floor. *Bamtex courtesy of Wood Flooring International*

Figure 2.5 The Kohler Ingenium flushing system creates a low-volume flush that conserves water. When a larger volume is required, the lever can be held down a moment longer to augment the flush. *© Judy K. Brody*

- Recycle whenever possible, and encourage recycling in local communities by designing recycling centers in residential and nonresidential facilities.

Assistance for Designers

There are excellent resources for professionals who need assistance with green design and specification. One is the Leadership in Energy and Environmental Design (LEED™) Green Building Rating System developed by the U.S. Green Building Council (USGBC). LEED certifies buildings and systems based on credits obtained in the following categories: sustainable sites, water efficiency, energy and atmosphere, materials and resources, indoor environmental quality, and innovation and design process. LEED is a voluntary, consensus-based national standard for developing high-performance, sustainable buildings, created to define "green building" by establishing a common standard of measurement; to promote integrated, whole building design practices; to recognize environmental leadership in the building industry; to stimulate green competition; to raise consumer awareness of green building benefits; and to transform the building market. LEED provides a complete framework for assessing building performance and meeting sustainability goals. Based on well-founded scientific standards, LEED emphasizes state-of-the-art strategies for sustainable site development, water conservation, energy efficiency, materials selection, and indoor environmental quality. LEED recognizes achievements and promotes expertise in green building through comprehensive systems offering project certification, professional accreditation, training, and practical resources.

The Environmental Protection Agency (EPA) is another resource for designers. The EPA has established a certification system whereby manufactured items can earn the title "Environmentally Preferable Products" because they have a lesser or reduced negative effect on human health and the environment when compared to other products that serve the same purpose. To achieve this certification the product is evaluated according to the following criteria: product performance; total environmental impact of product manufacturing; use of "green energy" manufacturing; protection of safety, health, and environment; and end-of-life responsibility.

Other Environmental Issues

There are other important issues that affect our relationship with the environment. These should also be considered

Figure 2.6 This Arizona home is constructed of rammed earth and makes use of a ceiling fan and natural light to minimize energy consumption. *Palmer residence, Rick Joy Architect, Tucson/photo © Timothy Hursley/The Arkansas Office, Inc.*

Table 2.1 | Plants for Clean Air

Proven Pollution Fighters	Pollutant	Side Effects	Sources
English ivy, *dracena marginata*, Janet Craig, *warneckei*, chrysanthemum, gerbera daisy, peace lily.	Benzene	Skin and eye irritant; may be a contributing factor to chromosomal aberrations and leukemia in humans. Chronic exposure to even relatively low levels causes headaches, appetite loss, drowsiness, nervousness, psychological disturbances, anemia, bone marrow disease, carcinogenicity.	Inks, oils paints, plastics, rubber, dyes, detergents, gasoline, pharmaceuticals, tobacco smoke, synthetic fibers.
Azalea, philodendron, spider plant, golden pothos, bamboo palm, corn plant, chrysanthemum, mother-in-law's tongue.	Formaldehyde	Irritates mucous membranes of the eyes, nose, throat; can cause contact dermatitis, irritation of upper respiratory tract and eyes, headaches, and asthma and is suspected of causing a rare type of throat cancer.	Foam insulation, plywood, particle board, press-wood products, grocery bags, waxed papers, facial tissue, paper towels, wrinkle resisters, water repellants, fire retardants, adhesive binders in floor coverings, carpet backing, permanent-press clothing, cigarette smoke, natural gas, kerosene.
Gerbera daisy, chrysanthemum, peace lily, *warneckei*, *dracena marginata*	Trichloroethylene	Considered a potent liver carcinogen by the National Cancer Institute.	Primarily used in the metal-degreasing and dry-cleaning industries; also in printing inks, paints, lacquers, varnishes, adhesives.

From Plants for Clean Air Council.

along with sustainability and green design. Poor indoor air quality affects the health and productivity of users, and well-planned lighting and carefully specified windows can conserve energy.

Air Pollution in the Interior Environment

Some buildings are uninhabitable because of poor air quality that can cause users to become ill. This problem is sometimes referred to as "sick-building syndrome." Part of this syndrome is related to airborne toxins, poisons sometimes found in common building materials. Volatile organic compounds (VOCs) are found in artificial products such as plastics, resins, adhesives, solvents, cleaners, and some of the special finishes added to furnishings. VOCs produce toxic fumes and gases. The gases tend to dissipate with time in a process known as **off-gassing,** in which carpets, furniture, and other furnishings are allowed to air out before being used.

Other toxins are found in tobacco smoke (nitrogen oxides), exhaust from furnaces and automobiles (carbon monoxide), and human metabolism, which creates carbon dioxide. Radon gases are emitted by radioactive decay and may be present in groundwater, soil, and air. Radon has been linked to lung cancer. Special venting systems make radon-afflicted homes habitable. Asbestos is a common toxin found in buildings built prior to 1978. It is a neutral-colored fiber used in acoustical tile, ceiling and floor materials, insulation, and as a fireproofing material. When disturbed, asbestos separates into tiny particles that are easily inhaled into the lungs, affecting breathing and possibly causing cancer. Lead is a toxin that is particularly dangerous to infants. It is found in paint used in houses and buildings generally built prior to the 1950s. Ozone is produced by some kinds of office machinery such as old laser printers. Ozone can be explosive and may also damage lung tissue, even in low concentrations.

Bacteria and fungi are two main forms of microbial contamination in buildings. Fungus, consisting of mold and mildew, can cause respiratory problems as well as create unpleasant odors. Dampness and poor ventilation foster the growth of such toxins. Microbial contamination may be found in the heating, ventilation, and air-conditioning (HVAC) system because it may provide ideal conditions for growth.

Plants can mitigate many common toxins found in interiors. Plants have the ability to clean the air naturally and, when well cared for, they also provide a wonderful aesthetic quality of life in the interior space.

Things to consider:

- Allow at least twenty-four hours of good ventilation for off-gassing of new furnishings.
- When possible, specify particleboard and plywood products without formaldehyde.
- Make whatever design decisions are necessary to ensure adequate air circulation.
- Ensure that fresh-air intakes for HVAC systems are away from locations where automobile exhaust will be present.
- Work with local governments to prohibit smoking in public facilities.
- Ensure that building foundations are carefully sealed to prevent radon contamination.
- Use plants to clean the air naturally (see Table 2.1.)

Lighting and Energy Conservation

Lighting accounts for about one-fourth of all electricity used in the United States. Efficient electric lighting and increased use of natural light could save up to 90 percent of this electricity. Visible light from a **lamp** (bulb or tube) is measured in **watts.** An efficient light source provides as many lumens as possible for each watt expended. A standard incandescent light bulb (the most widely used form of residential lighting) is very inefficient, producing about 10 to 20 lumens per watt. By contrast, fluorescent lamps produce 30 to 110 lumens per watt.

Because of that great efficiency, one of the most significant developments in lighting technology is the **compact fluorescent lamp (CFL).** Because fluorescent light is shadowless and has typically been cool and unflattering, it may have a bad aesthetic reputation. CFLs, however, screw into standard sockets, making it possible to use them in recessed fixtures and with shades and baffles, giving their light a degree of direction. In addition, CFLs have a color quality that is very similar to incandescent, and they consume one-quarter of the energy of, and last up to thirteen times longer than, incandescent lamps. Standard fluorescent lamps (tubes) provide comparable efficiency, although some people find them aesthetically less pleasing. According to the Rocky Mountain Institute, every fluorescent lamp that replaces an incandescent prevents the emission of 1,000 to 2,000 pounds of carbon dioxide and 8 to 16 pounds of sulfur dioxide from power plants, thus helping to eliminate global warming and acid rain.

Halogen lamps, a bold first cousin to incandescent lamps, are about 10 percent more efficient than standard incandescent lamps. They produce a clearer, whiter light, have better color rendition than standard incandescent lamps, and last somewhat longer than regular incandescent lighting.

Natural light or daylight is healthy, economical, and aesthetically pleasing. Light from the sun is free, and because of improved window technology, natural light and heating and cooling need not conflict. Natural light can enter buildings through interior courtyards called atria (**atrium** is the singular form) and through **clerestory windows** set high up in a wall as well as through more standard kinds of windows. Light pipes and skylights can bring natural light to the interiors of buildings where no such light could normally reach.

Things to consider:

- Where possible, use fluorescent rather than incandescent lighting.
- Use incandescent lamps for spaces where occupancy time is limited.

Figure 2.7 Energy-saving compact fluorescent lamps are used to create ambient light in this restaurant. © Peter Mauss/Esto

Figure 2.8 Natural light is economical and pleasant in this health-care facility. *Payette Associates Architects/photo © Brian Vanden Brink*

- Use higher levels of light only where and when needed to accomplish specific tasks.
- Use dimmers and timers to save energy and extend the life of incandescent lamps.
- Use natural light from windows wherever possible before resorting to electric lighting.
- Also consider clerestories, skylights, light pipes, and atria to bring natural light into a building.

Windows and Energy Conservation

On average, 10 to 25 percent of internal winter heating is lost through windows, and similar amounts of heat gain occur through windows during warm seasons and in warm climates. Low-tech solutions include things as simple as caulking window frames to prevent air transfer or planting shade trees for natural cooling.

About half of all residential windows are single pane, with one sheet of glass. They keep rain and wind from entering a building but do little to stop heat and cold transfer. They typically have an R-value (ability to insulate) of 2.0, which is considered poor. Today's low-E glazing is double-pane, with two sheets of glass, and features special coatings, gas fill, good edge seals, insulated frames, and airtight construction that provide excellent insulation and prevent negative heat and cold transfer. They have an excellent R-value of 5.0 or more.

Things to consider:

- Where possible, specify high-performance windows for new construction or **retrofit.**
- Insulate and caulk window frames.
- Use low-tech solutions such as planting deciduous trees (those that lose their leaves seasonally) to block the sun's direct rays in the summer and let in the sun's rays in the winter.
- Design overhangs to block summer sun and admit winter sun as the sun's angle changes seasonally.
- Use screens or awnings for additional sun control.

Considerations for Special Needs Users

For years, the needs of users who found designed environments difficult or impossible to use were ignored. Today, however, because we have been made aware of special needs, and because the law requires that those needs be addressed, design for special populations is a standard component of design practice.

Universal Design

Universal design implies that well-planned designs will meet the needs of every user without drawing attention to persons with disabilities. For example, older buildings with many steps are not accessible to regular wheelchair users. Ramps can be installed to make the buildings accessible but the ramp is a special addition, and while it is functional, it draws attention to the wheelchair user, who must employ a different route of entry. New facilities designed on level grade, with automatic sliding doors where all can enter in the same manner, are examples of universal design—everyone is accommodated without drawing attention to distinctions of ability.

The Americans with Disabilities Act of 1990

In January 1992, the Americans with Disabilities Act of 1990 (the ADA) became law. This landmark civil rights legislation represents one of the most significant steps in eliminating widespread discrimination caused by the imposition of barriers restricting persons with disabilities. It is no longer satisfactory to provide separate facilities for people with disabilities; they must be integrated into facilities planned for the general public. The law recognizes that they *are* the general public and that they are entitled to the same treatment received by the public at large. Individuals who have difficulty or limitations with life activities such as walking, hearing, seeing, or using their hands are protected by the ADA. Designers have

Figure 2.9 Automatic doors are used in the same fashion by all users without calling attention to disability. © *Jim Whitmer*

to making life "normal" for those with limited ability. In Europe, where many buildings and much of the infrastructure are older, strategies for accessibility include the design of new wheelchairs capable of climbing stairs. Universal design is an ethical ideal that is seen more and more. In cases where universal design is impossible, however, accessibility is imperative.

We can never be sure if or when a disability will become a reality for a friend, an associate, a member of our family, or for us. Until that happens, we often ignore the kind of design that makes life better for persons with special needs. But with the passage of the ADA, many such considerations are law; they can no longer be ignored. The law has pushed us from a perspective of sympathy into a mode of action. In our homes the choice is still ours but in public, accessibility is the law.

Sympathy is one matter and empathy is another. If we all tried spending a day or two with a self-imposed disability, we would see how frustrating design can be, and we would quickly come to understand the need for the law. We can become aware of how special needs are being met in public spaces, but even more importantly, we can become advocates of good design for users with special needs.

responded to the challenge with the concept of universal design that goes beyond the accessibility required by the law.

The ADA allows that it is not necessary to tear down existing structures with steps; they need to be modified, not destroyed. It is doubtful that our world will ever be completely accessible without isolating, to some degree, those with disabilities. New planning and design will certainly be universal, but older facilities will always be a reminder of a time when little thought was given

Accessible Design

Accessibility is the law in nonresidential design; it is optional in design for single-family homes. Given the fact, however, that we may all encounter some form of impairment at some point in our lives, it is remarkable that home designs rarely are planned accordingly. The experiences of one woman, who spent many years caring for her wheelchair-bound mother, are not uncommon. Her

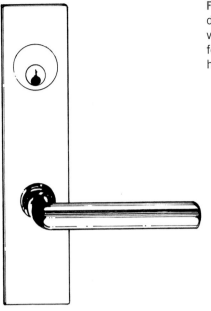

Figure 2.10 A lever door handle is a universal design solution for those with limited hand strength.

lump people into tidy groups, but it is important to note that impairments need not be measured by fixed standards and that each of us is prone to some type of limitation, whether temporary or chronic. For example, many of us wear glasses for impaired vision, some of us find ourselves with broken limbs, and those of us who have spent too much time listening to loud music will find that we have mild or significant hearing losses. The designation of "special populations" is helpful only because it makes us aware of needs.

Different kinds of physical impairments may require conflicting considerations. For example, curbs that are cut away for wheelchair-bound users do not signal blind users that they have reached the street. The wheelchair user prefers spaces that are open and larger than normal, while the blind user may be more comfortable in a smaller space where many things are within reach. The hearing-impaired user needs a space with little sound reverberation, while blind users need an acoustically "live" space to help find their way.

Design for Motion Impairments

People with impaired motion may be ambulant-disabled, meaning that difficulty in walking may require the use of crutches, a cane, or a walker. Chairbound-disabled people depend on a wheelchair for mobility. Those that are motion-impaired may also have some loss of ability to use their hands. Most of the design considerations for those with impaired motion center around physical barriers such as level changes introduced by curbs, multiple stories, steps, and paving or flooring materials of varying thicknesses. Doors, either by their narrow width or their weight, also form barriers. Standard bathroom and kitchen designs present a number of challenges for persons with impaired motion, particularly for those confined to wheelchairs.

This section presents lists of design recommendations for people with motion impairment that were prepared with the intention of heightening awareness. They are representative of the kinds of specifications found in the ADA but do not include all of its requirements.

Steps and Ramps

- Many ambulant-disabled users find stairs easier to negotiate than ramps (which are necessary for the chairbound). Consequently, a minimum slope for ramps is best, with a rise of 1 foot for every 12 feet of length (1:12).
- Steps should not have protruding nosing that will catch the toes of those with stiff legs, braces, or other leg problems.
- All ramps and steps should be well lit, with focus lighting directed at walking hazards. Whenever possible, they should be covered to remain dry and free from ice.

experience included dealing with the enormous difficulty created by barriers. Her mother's home was never planned to accommodate such limited mobility, and it was necessary to construct an inconvenient makeshift wooden ramp up the steep front steps. The kitchen and the bathroom designs made the situation even more difficult.

After the death of her mother, the woman planned and built her own home that was based on universal design principles. According to her **barrier-free design,** all of the entrances were level or accessed by gentle slopes, and the garage was level with the utility entrance. All doorways were wide enough to accommodate passage of a wheelchair, bathrooms were large enough to maneuver a wheelchair, and wall frames were reinforced to allow the later addition of grab bars. She commented that had it not been for the experience with her mother's disability, she would never have planned as she did. Visitors to the home are unaware of the subtle differences, and the costs in planning and building were negligible. The design is beautiful and functions perfectly for her, even though she may never need the features she has built in.

Few of us have the foresight to imagine that such planning will be of benefit to a family member or us at some point in our lives. Accessible design works well for everyone, whether impaired or not, and has the added benefit of making the design more sustainable.

Design for Special Populations

People with distinctive but similar design needs constitute special populations. Such populations include persons with limited motion, hearing, or vision, as well as the elderly who may have some form of impairment in one or more of these areas. Our tendency seems to be to

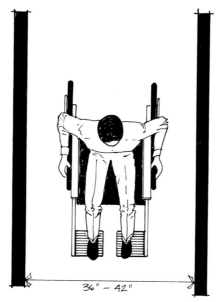

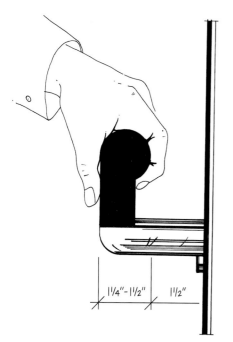

Figure 2.11 Handrail diagram.

Figure 2.13 Wheelchair clearance.

Figure 2.14 Wheelchair turning space.

Figure 2.12 A spacious and level approach, together with an automatic door, make this entrance barrier free. © *Aaron Haupt/Stock Boston*

- The top of a **handrail** should be 34 to 38 inches above the ramp or steps.
- Handrails should be oval or round, with 1-½-inch hand clearance between the rails and the wall. This will provide ease of grip but will prevent the hand or wrist from slipping between the handrail and the wall if the person loses balance.
- The handrail should have a gripping surface of 1 to 1-½ inches and should not be interrupted by newel posts or other elements.

Passage and Turning

- For a single wheelchair, 32 inches is minimum clearance at a point such as a door (36 inches is better), and 36 inches is minimum clearance in a continuous passage (42 to 48 inches is better). Minimum clearance for two chairs to pass each other is 60 inches.
- The space required by a wheelchair to make a 180-degree turn is a clear space of 60 inches.
- The clear floor space required for a wheelchair is 30 by 48 inches.
- The force needed to push a door open should not exceed 8 pounds of pressure.
- Lever-type door handles are easier to operate than round doorknobs, which are slippery and hard to operate with limited strength. Thumb-latch fixtures are equally hard to operate with limited strength or motion.
- A kickplate at the bottom of a door protects the door from the impact of a wheelchair's footrest.
- Floors should have a flat, nonskid surface. If carpet is used, then it should be securely attached, without a cushion or pad. Pile depth should not be more than ½-inch, since anything with a deeper pile makes passage difficult.

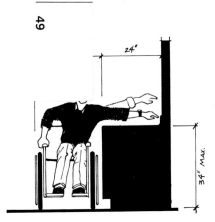

Figure 2.15 Counter dimensions.

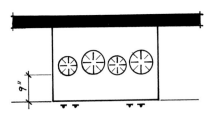

Figure 2.16 Cooktop arrangements.

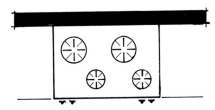

- Flooring materials should be flush, since a change in depth greater than ½-inch forms a barrier.

Kitchens

- All areas of the kitchen should be accessible to a frontal approach as well as a parallel approach by a wheelchair. This means an access space of no less than 30 by 48 inches, or a minimum distance of 48 inches between opposing elements. In a U-shaped kitchen, the distance should be increased to 60 inches.
- Varying countertop heights are recommended. A low counter near the sink for food preparation is helpful. Heights of 28, 32, and 36 inches are good, with a maximum depth of 24 inches so that items on the countertop can be easily reached.
- Upper cabinets should be adjustable to several heights. Eight inches above the counter is the minimum for very small users.
- Handles on upper cabinets should be mounted a maximum of 48 inches from the floor, with those on lower cabinets a minimum of 27 inches from the floor.
- Leaving space under the counter, especially at the sink, allows a wheelchair to approach. Hot-water pipes should be insulated so that the wheelchair user will not be burned.

- The sink controls should be mounted on the side or no more than 18 inches form the front of the counter for easy reach.
- A toe-kick space under cabinets should be 12 inches high and 8 inches deep to accommodate a wheelchair footrest.
- Pull-out trays allow better access than standard drawers and shelves.
- Wall-mounted ovens and microwaves allow wheelchair access.
- Cooktops should have staggered burners so that the users do not have to reach over a hot front burner to access a back burner.
- Cooktop controls should be front mounted for easy reach by a seated person.

Bathrooms

- Doors should be at least 36 inches wide (preferably 39 inches). Pocket doors keep the space clear and make access easier.
- No cabinet under the sink makes the vanity accessible.
- Toilets should be wall mounted 19 inches off the floor for easy approach by a wheelchair. The toilet is most easily accessed from the side or with a diagonal approach.
- Grab bars must be anchored in wood so that they will support at least 250 pounds. There should be a 24- to 36-inch horizontal grab bar located behind, and 3 inches above, the back of the toilet, as well as a 30-inch horizontal bar mounted 12 inches from the back wall beside the toilet.
- Some users will be able to negotiate a tub, and others will need to be able to wheel into a shower. Textured, non-slip grab bars mounted 32 to 38 inches above the floor make access easier. A seat in a shower is also helpful.
- Shower controls should be mounted no higher than 32 inches from the floor and should be a lever-type, single-mixing control. A handheld showerhead can be helpful to those with impaired motion.
- Faucets at the sink should also be lever controlled as well as side mounted. Water temperature should be set down to prevent scalding.
- Medicine cabinets should be mounted lower in a sidewall so that they can be easily accessed.
- Vanity mirrors should be installed low enough to be used by someone seated in a wheelchair. The mirror should be at least 16 by 20 inches and may need to be tilted for complete visibility.
- Non-slip flooring is imperative, as is good ventilation to prevent condensation that might cause slipping.

Bedrooms

- The height of the mattress should be equal to the height of the wheelchair. The nightstand should be the height of the bed.

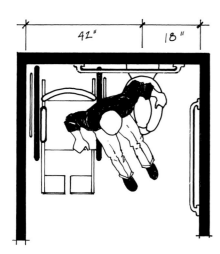

Figure 2.17 Diagonal approach.

Figure 2.18 Side approach.

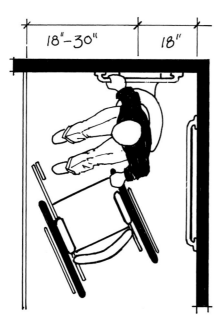

Figure 2.19 In a bathroom designed for an assisted living facility, grab bars aid bathing. © *Jim Whitmer*

- To accommodate a wheelchair, there must be a 60- by 60-inch clear space, usually between the bedroom door and the bed, or between the storage space and the bed. A minimum of 36 inches at the foot and far side of the bed will facilitate making the bed and cleaning.
- A footboard and headboard will often help in getting in and out, and a slatted headboard may be helpful in turning over or moving in bed.

Closets
- Bifold or sliding doors are best.
- Rods should be mounted 45 to 54 inches high for access from a wheelchair.
- Shelves higher than 50 inches are not accessible from a seated position.
- Slide-out shelves are more accessible.

Around the House
- Electrical outlets should be 27 to 28 inches above the floor. Switches should be 36 inches above the floor.
- At least one 60-inch-diameter turning space is required in each room of the house.
- Drawer pulls throughout the house should be D-shaped for better gripping.
- Windowsills set at a maximum of 36 inches make windows accessible to wheelchair users.
- Crank-operated casement windows are better for those with impaired motion.

Design for Hearing Impairment

Over 8 million people in the United States have extreme hearing loss. These people want to live normal and productive lives. Design can help make the quality of their lives better by alleviating some of the problems inherent in the interior environment. Many of the problems associated with hearing loss center around noise and sound reverberation, as well as adequate light for manual communication (signing and lip reading).

Things to consider:

- Carpet and fabric wall coverings reduce noise reverberation and improve the acoustics for the hearing impaired.
- Good lighting is imperative for adequate decoding of manual communication and lip reading.
- Good natural light helps visually and also creates the psychological feeling of openness and well-being.
- Furniture arranged in a semicircle or U-shape facilitates signing and lip reading by providing clear sight lines from speaker to listener.
- A round dining table is better than a rectangular table because it provides clear sight lines.

- Visual signals such as flashing lights can provide important visual cues. The lights are activated by the telephone, doorbell, alarm clock, fire alarm/smoke detector, or a crying baby. The lights can be placed in panels at strategic locations throughout the house.
- Special phone systems are available for the hearing impaired. These systems are called TDD, an acronym for telecommunication device for the deaf. The TDD includes a screen and keyboard and will require a specially planned space.
- Because of the addition of extra electronic devices, adequate outlets should be planned to avoid the unnecessary use of extension cords.

Design for Visual Impairment

People with impaired vision rely heavily on the senses of hearing and touch. Consequently, tactile indicators and acoustics are critical for day-to-day activities in familiar environments and for navigating in unfamiliar public spaces.

Things to consider:

- The blind may need tactile warning of danger. Door handles may be textured to indicate a dangerous area beyond the door, and landings and curbs can be textured to indicate steps or changes of grade.
- Outdoors, hanging or projecting objects (even plants and tree branches) that extend into the path of the blind person are dangerous because they cannot be detected with a cane.
- Handrails should extend 1 foot beyond the end of a stairway, even if this means extending the rail around a corner. Where there is more than one story, a handrail should extend continuously from floor to floor, rather than stopping at the landing.
- Signage is important. Small groups of letters and numbers can be easily read with the fingers, but larger groups of letters and long texts are difficult for the blind to read.
- Persons born blind learn Braille, while most persons blinded later in life do not. Signage should include both letters/numbers and Braille symbols.
- To be useful, tactile signals and signage should be uniform throughout a building.
- Audible signals for the blind are helpful at crosswalks, in elevators, and for emergency systems such as smoke detectors/fire alarms.
- Gas cooktops tend to be better for the blind because the gas makes a sound as it burns. In addition, electric elements retain heat after they are turned off, which can be dangerous. Controls should be mounted where the blind will not have to reach over the flame or coils to operate the cooktop. Elements, too, should be arranged to avoid reaching over one to get to the other.

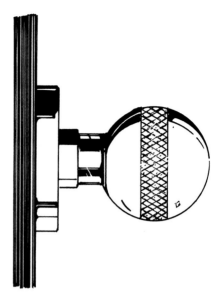

Figure 2.20 Textured door handle signals warning.

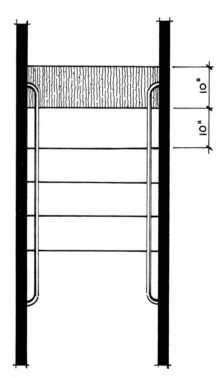

Figure 2.21 Texture under foot warns of possible danger.

- A lip on the counter may be helpful in preventing objects from being pushed off the edge.
- Furniture should have rounded corners and edges, and some padding of table edges may be advisable.
- A hook next to electrical outlets might be desirable to hang a plug where it can be found easily.
- Changes of grade in flooring materials are obstacles for the blind and should be avoided.

Figure 2.24 Keeping an electrical plug on a hook when not in use makes it easy to find when needed.

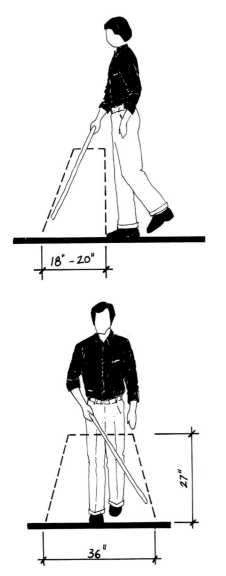

Figure 2.22 Unobstructed walking space is essential for those with visual impairment.

Figure 2.23 Raised numerals and braille help identify this classroom. © Joey Moon

Design for the Elderly

People are living longer today than ever before. As a result, the elderly population is growing rapidly and becoming an important political and social force. The concerns of the elderly include limited mobility, loss of hearing, and loss of visual acuity. Consequently, all of the considerations listed above apply to the elderly. There may also be loss of memory or other cognitive function that makes some tasks more difficult.

Things to consider:

• Visual contrast is important in judging space and distance. For example, a countertop should be light or dark in contrast with the floor. This helps with depth perception and makes the edges more obvious. The same is true for a tabletop, where depth perception is important.

• In some public spaces and facilities designed for the elderly, way finding is important. In a long hallway the location of doors can be indicated with a slight recess in the wall surrounding the doors. Distinctive pieces of furniture and art can be visual reminders of location. Color coding of areas or floors may also prove helpful.

• With age, there may be a tendency for the cornea of the eye to yellow. This causes a distortion of color perception and may make a color scheme appear drab and ugly to some. The designer can use a yellow lens to evaluate color schemes for the elderly, making selections that maintain their appeal.

• Decreased control over bodily functions may make it desirable to select textiles for upholstery that have been specially treated to resist moisture or laminated with a thin layer of plastic. The lamination process is almost undetectable.

Other Special Populations

The previous section focused on design for the elderly and persons with impaired motion, hearing, and vision.

But these represent just a fraction of those with special needs. Other special populations include children, homeless, abused, chemically dependent, religious groups, ethnic and cultural groups, convicted criminals, poor, rich, mentally ill, sick, terminally ill, and many others. Again, in some cases these are not fixed groups but rather situations through which the general population moves. Unlike the design needs of those with physical impairments, the design needs of these groups do not always lend themselves to universal design. For example, public toilets are not scaled to children because the population at large cannot use small-scaled facilities comfortably. The kind of security demanded by law for convicted criminals is inappropriate for other citizens. The considerations associated with these groups are important and worthy of the designer's attention, but they are not always applicable to the needs of users in general.

Figure 2.25 The yellow acetate lens allows the designer to see colors as older users might. © Bradley H. Slade

Figure 2.26 The reception area in a long-term care facility uses indirect lighting and elements from nature to create a relaxed and cheerful mood. *Lewis & Malm Architects/photo © Brian Vanden Brink*

Special Design Considerations as Fundamental Goals

The ideas and recommendations presented in this chapter can and should be applied to all the topics discussed throughout this book. Whether the subject is electrical systems and lighting, fabrics, historical styles, or any other topic, it is important to measure what we learn against the principles of sustainability and universal design. As we embrace sustainability and universal design, not only will the future be a better place, but also we will be better able to enjoy it.

Chapter 3 | Design Principles and Elements

The Principles of Design 58

The Elements of Design 66

Design Discernment and Excellence 76

Hutker Architects/photo © Brian Vanden Brink

The Principles of Design

The **principles of design**—**scale** and **proportion, balance, rhythm, emphasis,** and **harmony (variety** and **unity)**—are abstract concepts that have been important to great architecture, art, furnishings, textiles, and hard materials for centuries. These principles, listed in Table 3.1, form the **theory of design.** The theory of design implies that truly fine interior design incorporates appropriate scale and good proportion, as well as harmony of all the elements, achieved through sensitive balance of variety and unity. These design principles are the bylaws that are universally accepted as the philosophy or rules that should govern the use of the **elements of design,** listed in Table 3.2. Each element can be judged right or wrong in its use and placement through an evaluation of the *principles* of design.

For example, the use of color, an important and emotive element of design, can be judged or evaluated in this way according to each principle of design:

- **Scale.** Is the size or amount of the color appropriate for the decorative scheme, or is it used in too large or too small a quantity or an area?
- **Proportion.** Do colors complement each other, or is one ill-proportioned by too much or too little intensity or quantity?
- **Balance.** Is the color balanced with other colors in terms of size and intensity, and is the color distributed throughout the interior to create a balanced effect?
- **Rhythm.** Does the color carry the eye along with rhythmic smoothness, or is it too punctuated and abrupt in its use?

- **Emphasis.** Does the color create or support a focal point, or does it detract from the area of emphasis?
- **Harmony.** Does the use of color yield harmony through the adherence to a unified theme (unity) with enough subtle or dramatic difference to maintain interest in the scheme (variety)? Or does the interior lack harmony because the colors are too weak or competitive?

Each of the elements of design can be evaluated in this way.

Scale

Scale deals with actual and relative size and visual weight. Scale is generally categorized as small or light, medium, large or heavy, or grand (extra large). One of the goals of pleasing interior design is to select furnishings that are in scale with one another. This implies a similarity of objects in overall dimensions or in mass (density), in pattern, or in other forms of visual weight. When objects are out of scale with one another, they are not appropriate or harmonious selections.

Although the actual dimensions of two objects may be similar, one may be of a visually heavier scale than the other because of its weight or mass and the selection of material. For example, a glass table on legs will appear

---

Table 3.1 | Principles of Design

Design principles are the abstract concepts that constitute the theory, bylaws, or governing ideas that determine the success of a design. Each **element** in a design can be evaluated according to these principles.

Scale. Overall size, such as the largeness or smallness of a room, object, or pattern.

Proportion. Size relationship or ratio of parts to whole, such as the size of a chair in relation to the size of its arms.

Balance. Equilibrium achieved by arranging components symmetrically, asymmetrically, or radially.

Rhythm. Flow of elements, usually organized according to a scheme such as repetition or alternation, progression or gradation, transition, opposition or contrast, or radiation.

Emphasis. Enhancement that produces a point of interest or focal point in a design.

Harmony. Compatibility of elements to create a pleasing whole, achieved through unity and variety.

Figure 3.1 Large-scale chairs complement the large scale of the windows and room space in this home. *© Peter Aaron/Esto*

Table 3.2 | Elements of Design

Design elements are the concrete, quantifiable components of any design. They embody the principles of design and transform theory into reality.

Space. Open and closed areas; space may be positive (filled) or negative (open).

Shape. Two-dimensional outline, often seen as a geometric figure such as a rectangle or triangle.

Form. Three-dimensional shape, such as a cube, cone, or sphere.

Mass. Weight, density, or relative solidity of a form; mass may be actual or visual.

Line. Connection between two points; line may be vertical, horizontal, angular, or curved.

Texture. Smoothness or roughness of a surface; texture may be read visually or through touch.

Pattern. Arrangement of motifs in a repetitive or variegated order; a small pattern may be read visually as texture.

Light. Natural, artificial, or a combination of both; light affects the appearance of all other elements of design.

Color. Hues that vary from light to dark and from intense to dull and can be mixed with one another and combined in color schemes; color is the most personal and emotional of the elements of design.

Figure 3.2 Small-scale chair, balusters, and woodwork are charming and intimate. *© Courtesy Hunter Douglas Corp*

smaller-scaled than a solid wooden chest table. While the overall dimensions might be exactly the same, the glass-topped table allows us to see through the piece, which visually scales it down and makes it appear smaller than the wooden piece.

Pattern and ornament also visually determine scale. A pattern with large motifs may appear visually heavy or massive, while a pattern of the same overall dimensions filled with small motifs and empty areas will appear smaller-scaled overall. Likewise, color will affect our impression of scale. Bright, bold colors will appear larger than light, pastel ones.

The scale, or size, of the architecture will often determine the scale of furnishings; small-scale furnishings are used in small interiors and large-scale furnishings are used in large or lofty interiors. This rule can be broken to provide drama or excitement, such as a large-scale pattern in a small area (which also makes the space seem smaller). Conversely, small scale in a large interior might look tailored and may visually expand the space even further.

In choosing or judging scale, perhaps the most important consideration is human scale. Very large and very small scale often feel awkward to people. Although grand scale is impressive and dramatic in public architecture, and small scale is wonderful for children, for the majority of adults, scale is most appropriate when it complements and easily accommodates the average hu-

man form. Because we are most comfortable with these dimensions, the standard ceiling height in homes is 8 feet and chairs and sofas generally have a standard seating height and depth.

Floor plans are drawn to scale, with ¼, ⅛, or ¹⁄₁₆ inch usually equaling 1 foot.

Proportion

Proportion is closely related to scale and is usually expressed in terms of the size relationship of parts to one another and to the whole. Proportion also deals with shapes and forms and their dimensions. It is, for example, the relationship of a chair seat or back to its base or arms or that of the size and scale of the tabletop to its legs. When the relationship or ratio is pleasing, the furniture is well proportioned. The evaluation of proportion is based on ratios, or the comparison of sizes. For example, a table that is well proportioned has side dimensions (width and length) that relate well to each other, creating a nicely shaped rectangle—neither too wide nor too narrow for the function of the piece. A sofa table (placed behind the back of the sofa and the same height as the back) must be relatively narrow or it will be cumbersome and ill proportioned. Likewise, a family dining table that is wider than 3½ feet may be too wide for food to be comfortably passed across it.

Throughout the centuries that humans have worked toward pleasing proportions, many theories of what is good and acceptable have been espoused. One of the best known is that of the ancient Egyptians and, later, the classical Greeks. They stated that pleasing proportions were termed "golden." The **golden mean** is a line that visually divides an object, a wall, a tieback drapery treatment, or other furnishings into two unequal but harmonious parts; that line falls somewhere between one-half and one-third (vertically or horizontally). For example, a chair-rail or dado molding creates pleasing proportions above and below the molding when it is placed not in the middle of the wall or one-third of the way up the wall but somewhere in between. Tieback draperies or curtains are also divided into pleasing proportions somewhere between one-third to one-half of the way up from the bottom or down from the top of the treatment.

The **golden section** refers to proportions of parts to one another and to the whole. The progressions—3 to 5 to 8 to 13 to 21, and so on— are considered pleasing ratios or proportions as they relate to one another and roughly equate the theory of the golden mean. Further, these increments can be translated into sides of rectangles, called golden rectangles, that form the basis for a study of good proportions. For example, a table or art piece 3 feet by 5 feet is a pleasing proportion, as are multiples (or divisions) of those dimensions: 12 by 20 (4 times 3 and 4 times 5) or 15 by 25 (5 times 3 and 5 times 5). A room with golden-rectangle dimensions will theoretically be the easiest in which to arrange furnishings,

Figure 3.3 This chest is divided according to the golden section, just below the halfway mark.

and a golden-rectangle window should pose few aesthetic window-treatment problems. The golden mean, golden section, and golden rectangle are examples of how harmonious proportions can be calculated.

Many other philosophies of good proportion exist, but the bottom line is the "sense of rightness" that we feel or

Figure 3.4 Formal symmetrical balance (mirror image) is dignified and restrained. *Focal Point Architectural Products, Inc. Tarboro, NC, www.focalpointproducts.com*

recognize when good proportion is evident. Recognizing good proportion is an intuitive ability for some people; for others, it may take time and deliberate study to learn to recognize and to sense pleasing proportion. Much of what we learn about good proportion comes from studying historic architecture and furnishings and great works of art that have been recognized as good design with pleasing proportions.

Balance

Balance is **equilibrium,** or the arrangement of objects physically or visually to reach a state of stability and poise. Balance is important because of the human need for balance in our lives. It is necessary for physical confidence in our actions and movement, and it is a guidepost in achieving satisfaction and fulfillment in life itself. Thus we naturally seek balance in our interiors. This state of equilibrium is achieved in one of three ways: through **symmetrical** or **formal balance,** through **asymmetrical** or **informal balance,** or by **radial balance.**

Symmetrical Balance

Symmetrical balance is also known as **bisymmetrical, formal,** or **passive balance.** Symmetrical balance creates a mirror image by the placement of items that are exactly the same on both sides of a central point. This might be a

Figure 3.5 Studied symmetry is found in the matching bookcases, chairs, and accessories. The asymmetrical placement of the plants, art, and door relieves the exactness.

matching pair of mantel vases on each side of a painting or mirror. Or formal balance can be seen as matching nightstands or end tables with matching lamps placed on them. It could be a formal dining table where the chairs are placed exactly across from each other. Symmetrical balance suggests restraint, refinement, orderliness, and formality. Bisymmetrical balance is passive because it requires no judgment; we know exactly what to expect. Because formal balance is predictable, it adds a type of steadiness and durability to interior design. Much classical design—from the Greeks and Romans to the Renaissance, Baroque, and subsequent periods—was symmetrical. The symmetry created a sense of power and grandeur.

However, because of its unchanging nature, symmetrical balance can become stale and boring. In fact, it has been said that a really good symmetrical composition always contains elements of asymmetry. The symmetrical nature of historic designs was broken by asymmetric placement of figures in a frieze or by inclusion of dissimilar sculptural pieces in symmetrical niches. Rigid symmetry is less suitable to today's less formal and more relaxed lifestyle.

Asymmetrical Balance

Asymmetrical balance is also known as informal, "active," "optical," or **occult balance.** Asymmetrical balance can be accomplished in two ways:

1. Dissimilar objects can be placed at varying distances from the center point.
2. Objects of similar visual weight or form may be balanced at equal distance from an imaginary central dividing line.

Asymmetrical balance is often difficult to accomplish. It requires finding objects that are compatible yet varied enough to be interesting and then arranging the objects, judging the arrangement, and often rearranging them over and over until the sense of equilibrium is judged to "feel right." This effort justifies the nickname "active," because it requires active participation to accomplish. The

Figure 3.6 Asymmetrical or informal balance is seen in the design of this room.
© Peter Aaron/Esto

term *optical* is derived from the necessity of judging the composition with the eye, or the optic sense. Achieving asymmetrical balance demands patience and sensitivity and certainly comes easier to some people than to others. Yet the results are definitely worth the efforts because asymmetrical balance can be deeply pleasing and does not readily become tiresome.

Although "informal balance" is the most common of the alternative names of asymmetrical balance, it is also known as "occult" balance because it has no set rules of what is right and is, therefore, somewhat elusive or mysterious. The Western world has learned much of asymmetrical balance from the strong Japanese influence in architecture and design. Oriental philosophies are based on the intrinsic, harmonious, and asymmetrical arrangement seen in nature and then translated through careful study and application to interior design compositions.

Radial Balance

Radial balance is a state of equilibrium that is based on the circle. It is seen as chairs surrounding a round table or as concentric circles in a chandelier or lighting fixture. On a small scale, it is seen on the round dial of a clock; on a larger scale, as circular furniture arrangements of com-

fortable chairs for a group gathering. Radial balance can also be seen as spokes extending from a wheel, pedestal table, or chair base. A form of radial balance can be seen in the grain of a dining table where the veneer (top layer) is laid in quarter sections that meet in the center. Historic wooden pieces frequently incorporated radial balance with inlaid pieces of wood. Spiraling forms can also create a type of radial balance.

Rhythm

Rhythm is a concept familiar in music as the beat that continually carries along the melody. In interior design, rhythm carries the eye along a path at a pace determined by the elements that illustrate it. For example, rhythm might be found in the repetitive use of a color, pattern, texture, line, or furniture piece or style. Architectural detail such as stairs, window panes, and moldings illustrate rhythm. Rhythm is also a matter of expectation and anticipation and is a major part in the concept of emphasis or surprise. There are five types of rhythm:

1. Repetition and alternation
2. Progression or gradation
3. Transition
4. Opposition or contrast
5. Radiation

Repetition establishes rhythm through the repetitive use of an element of design, as previously suggested.

Figure 3.7 Repetitive rhythm is seen in the floor pattern, cabinetry detail, and even the rabbits on the soffit near the ceiling. *© Jessie Walker*

Figure 3.8 Rhythm by gradation is seen in the decreasing sizes of the nesting tables. *Photo by Gordon Lonsdale*

Repetition not only establishes a continuity and flow of rhythm but also provides unity, or sameness, which is a part of the principle of harmony. For example, a color repeated throughout an interior can establish rhythm if the eye can smoothly connect rather than jumping or leaping from colored object to colored object. Repetition is seen in rows of seats in a church or theater, in a set of books bound to match, or in the same style of lighting fixture used many times in a public space. In architectural detail, repetition may be seen in the same window in classic architecture such as the elegant Georgian home (see Chapter 15) or in moldings such as dentil trim.

Alternation is the sequence of two or more components by which the eye can follow a rhythmic pattern. It is seen in historic buildings with coffered ceilings, where a wafflelike pattern has both high and low areas. The egg-and-dart motif repeats two shapes, symbolizing birth and death, used in alternation.

Progression, or **gradation,** is seen in shapes progressing from large to small or small to large, such as the front steps leading to the **piano nobile** (raised entrance) in classic architecture or a set of nesting tables, where each smaller table fits beneath its next larger counterpart. A collection of different-size boxes or a candelabrum (descending branched candlestick) are accessory items that can create rhythm by progression, or gradation.

Progressive rhythm (rhythm by gradation) can also be seen in the value of color, where a color scheme contains shades that vary from very light values (perhaps on the ceiling) to medium values (on the wall) to dark values (on the floor) and where the values are further expanded in the furnishings. This light-to-medium-to-dark progressive sequence is also discussed in Chapter 4, "Color," as the concept of value distribution.

Transition is a rhythm that leads the eye without interruption from one point to another. Rhythm by transition can be established by a continuous line, usually an architectural element such as a crown or dado molding or an arched doorway. A stenciled or wallpaper border, a painted graphic, or a long carpet runner are methods of creating an uninterrupted visual, rhythmically flowing line.

Opposition, or **contrast,** is an abrupt change that forms interesting, repetitive rhythm and is seen in three ways. First, it can be seen as repetitive 90-degree angles—such as window frames or grids, as built-in units (such as cabinetry and luminous ceilings), and as the corners of angular furniture or framed artwork. Second, opposition or contrast can be seen in patterns: open and closed, busy and plain, light and dark combinations of fabric, area rugs, or other textiles or wall coverings. Third, forms can be placed to contrast in a pleasing rhythm. Angular shapes placed next to rounded shapes not only create rhythm by contrast or opposition but also give relief and a type of asymmetrical balance.

Figure 3.9 Rhythm by opposition is seen in the right angles of this window fenestration, chest, and screen.

Radiation, closely related to radial balance, is the final type of rhythm. Rhythm established by radiating concentric or spokelike lines or forms can be dramatic and impressive. It is sometimes employed as designs in large, custom floor coverings in places such as lobbies and ballrooms or in grand ceilings where architectural carving or cast plaster creates a radial effect. As such, it can give the room a circular, sweeping, rhythmic movement. On a smaller scale, radiation can be seen in place settings at a round or oval table or as furniture forms in a circular grouping.

Emphasis

Emphasis is the creation of a **focal point**—an area visually important enough to draw and hold attention. Examples of dramatic, demanding focal points include a beautiful fireplace, a view from a window (or even an art glass window), a wall of dramatic art, or an impressive piece or grouping of furniture. A rhythmic progression—a many-doored hallway, for example—can express the principle of emphasis by ending in a vista such as a fine piece of furniture or artwork.

Some interiors may have multiple focal points, each one with a different level of emphasis, progressing from the most to the least dominant in order to avoid conflict. Logically, smaller areas can handle fewer focal points than larger areas. An exception might be an art gallery, where each piece of art is given equal opportunity to be a point of interest and emphasis.

Where varying levels of emphasis are planned, the dominant focal point could migrate. For example, in the winter the fireplace is a logically comforting focal point that dominates interest. In warmer seasons, through rearrangement of the furnishings, the dominant focal point might become a large window with a view. Where no focal point exists, one can be created in the guise of bookcases, china cabinets, artwork (displayed individually or in group arrangements), tapestries, rugs, quilts or other art fabrics, and mirrors.

The elements of design can be manipulated to give greater emphasis to a focal point. Arranging furniture shapes to face the focal point, directing lines toward the focal point, grouping or massing objects to give visual weight to the focal point, or using more dramatic color at the area of the focal point are ways to increase emphasis.

Harmony: Variety and Unity

Harmony is the combination of design elements, architecture, and furnishings into a pleasing or orderly whole—a state of agreement or a feeling of rightness. Harmony is the result of a delicate balance of two subprinciples: unity and variety.

Unity suggests a oneness and uniformity—an identity that establishes a master plan. Unity is the goal that is be-ing sought and, hopefully, achieved when all the various elements and furnishings are brought together.

Unity can be achieved by carrying out a cohesive color scheme or by keeping the character and style of the furniture consistent. Unity dictates selecting background materials, fabrics, and accessories that all have a similar feeling. This means that the use of pattern or ornament, color and value, surface textures (smooth or rough), and even the grain of the wood (coarse or fine) is consistent in character with the master plan.

Variety is the absence of monotony or sameness, yet it is much more. Variety is a healthy, positive influence that brings about vitality, interest, and diversity. It can be seen through a selection of differing colors, textures, furniture and accessory styles, through the contrast of hard materials with soft materials, and through the combination of seemingly divergent old (historic) and new (modern) architecture and furnishings. Yet variety without some order or a master plan can become confusing and dissonant.

Figure 3.10 Rhythm by radiation is seen in concentric circles in the steps and as spokelike lines in the glass arch of the winter garden at the World Financial Center in New York City. © *Rafael Macia/Photo Researchers, Inc.*

Figure 3.11 The fireplace, which is the natural focal point of this room, is given greater emphasis by the parallel furniture grouping.
© Scott Frances/Esto

Figure 3.12 This room uses a variety of styles and materials, unified by their informal and rustic feeling. © *Jessie Walker Associates*

Every interior should have goals of identity and oneness, yet be varied enough to be interesting. This design statement, master plan, or set of goals should be set forth in written and graphic form, so that every furnishing item, whether purchased at once or over a period of years, will be selected to complement all other furnishings specified. It is wise and thoughtful planning that sets apart fine design from interiors that lack harmony.

The Elements of Design

The elements of design—**space, shape** or **form, mass, line, texture, pattern, light,** and **color**—are used by every designer in every discipline. These elements were not invented but discovered and skillfully incorporated and balanced by artisans and designers over the course of history. Because of the basic and crucial nature of the elements of design, they are discussed in nearly every fine-art textbook and wherever the education or evaluation of a designed work takes place.

Keep in mind that every element of design can be used effectively or ineffectively and that many compositions exist that are not perfect in their use of the elements. For example, an interior may have dramatic space, perfectly balanced light, well-proportioned form or mass, and appropriate line but may be filled with poorly selected pattern, texture, or color. Or perhaps the pattern, texture, and color are well chosen, yet some of the other elements are used ineffectively. As students of design, we seek to

Figure 3.13 Shape, form, line, and color are distinctive elements of design in this handsome bathroom vanity area. *Drysdale Associates Interior Design/photo © Brian Vanden Brink*

recognize and to perfect the skillful use of the elements of design in interiors.

Space

Space exists as a diffuse, endless entity until it is defined. The definition of space occurs with building construction, resulting in exterior and interior spacial allotments. Space-restricting devices within the building—walls, floors, ceilings, and furnishings—create a series of spaces with individual dimensions and qualities. These qualities can be discovered only as a person moves through spaces and perceives them one at a time: one space flowing into another or one abruptly ending and another beginning. When the space/time movement is complete, the perceptions are mentally assembled to give a true picture and judgment of the space.

The divisions and restrictions of space form the foundation of architectural planning. Interior designers often create unequal space allotments within buildings not only for aesthetic reasons but to answer human needs, as well. Treating spaces of different sizes addresses two basic human needs. First is the need to be protected, enclosed, and comforted. Small spaces give a sense of security from intruders and from the buffeting of the outside world. Small spaces establish territory; they give a sense of pride and of ownership, and they offer opportunity to personalize our own space. Conversely, small spaces can be restricting or confining and can spawn restlessness and frustration. Small spaces that are inadequate for functions that are performed there may visually be expanded through the use of light colors, wall-to-wall neutral floor coverings, small-scale furnishings, mirrors, and smoothly textured surfaces or textures with little pattern. Generous light from more than one source can also give the impression of more space than actually exists.

Large space fills a second basic human need as an outgrowth of the confinement of small space. This is the need to be free, to mentally soar into a space devoid of restrictions, to be stimulated by the immensity of space as compared to the insignificance of human scale. The lack of restriction, however, can create feelings of insecurity and inadequacy and a desire to return to the safe, secure quarters of small spaces. Large interior spaces can be difficult to handle; often there is a need to make the space seem smaller than it is. Effective ways of creating more intimacy in large spaces include using medium- to large-scale patterns and dark or vivid colors that visually advance, furniture that is heavy or solid looking, area rugs (particularly patterned or colored ones that visually break the floor space), large-scale artwork, and multiple furniture groupings (see also Chapter 8, "Furniture Arrangement").

Many well-planned interiors incorporate both small and large spaces. We see this in homes where a living area has a high ceiling, where a family room or great room has generous square footage, or where several rooms open onto a solarium, deck, or covered patio. In nonresidential interiors, such as business and professional centers, shopping malls, or hotels, the small, enclosed quarters are offices, boutiques, shops, or hotel rooms, and these are often grouped around a courtyard, atrium, ballroom, or multistoried open lobby area. To emerge from small spaces into large or tall spaces can be exhilarating and satisfying, yet the return to the small areas can bring about a needed sense of personal belonging, security, and safety.

Interior designers create interesting areas of **positive** and **negative space.** Positive space is space that is filled with color, texture, form, or mass. This could be walls, furnishings, art, area rugs, or even graphics or scenes painted on walls. Negative space is the empty space surrounding the positive space—the windows between walls, the floor around the area rug, the wall around and between works of art, the space between furniture pieces, or even the cubic footage. In a successful interior, the positive and negative spaces should be balanced in terms of both amount and placement. Some areas may be primarily positive space, others primarily negative, and still others equally distributed between the two. For example, the proportion of negative (empty wall) space between works of art hanging on walls may remain relatively even, or it may be unevenly distributed.

Shape or Form

While we sometimes think of shape as only a two-dimensional outline, form (which is an extension of shape) is the three-dimensional configuration of the objects within the interior. For example, furniture seen in silhouette has shape that can be perceived, and as we move around the furniture, the silhouette changes and we begin to comprehend the three-dimensional quality of the form.

Often an interior is successful because the forms that fill it are pleasing shapes and well proportioned one to another. There are several kinds of shapes: two-dimensional

Figure 3.14 The shape or form of new modern design is one of its most compelling features. Each of these pieces has a distinctive and pleasing form. *(A) Courtesy of Calger Lighting, Inc. (B and C) Photos courtesy Roset USA Corp., Smala designed by Pascal Mourgue; Yang designed by Francois Bauchet*

outline shapes or planes—such as rectangles, squares, triangles, circles, and other geometric shapes—or meandering, curved, or angular shapes that do not fit neatly into geometry. When these "2-D" planes are given a third dimension ("3-D"), they become forms such as cubes, cones, and spheres or forms that are sinuous or curving.

For example, a rectangular table can be an appreciated form and shape that is simple and pleasing, yet if the entire room were filled with similar shapes and forms, the room would become boring and repetitious. There needs to be a balance of form—a curved chair to soften the straight lines of the table form. The forms that are placed next to each other will have considerable effect on each other. Sometimes the juxtaposition of unlikely elements, such as the tandem placements of a vintage piece of furniture with a thoroughly modern piece, can create a delightful and charming surprise. On the other hand, certain forms destroy the integrity of each other and prove disastrous to both objects. This might be the placement of a delicate and lacy plant next to the abstract lines of a modern painting where the incongruity is jolting and disturbing. Perhaps a sculptural, abstract plant form, such as a cactus, would be better suited to the shapes in the painting.

The key to selecting forms is to balance them against the proportion and scale of the architecture for the desired psychological effect or feeling and to select each form to complement other nearby forms.

The sensitive and careful selection and arrangement of forms is crucial in an interior because forms have great power to persuade us to feel certain ways, such as alert and attentive or relaxed and secure. Shapes and forms appeal to the senses and can have amazing impact on the person who enters the room. For example, a person entering a room filled with cubes will probably perceive the interior as a no-nonsense one where, perhaps, business takes place. Curved forms are gracious, may make people feel more relaxed, and are commonly used in residential living rooms and bedrooms.

Being sensitive to sculptural forms can increase our appreciation for classical beauty and modern abstract expression. Historic furniture pieces (see Chapter 15) are sculptural forms that are so important that the character of an interior can become impressive with their added presence. Furniture pieces that have endured decades or centuries are revered and appreciated today as fine decorative art largely because of their timeless and appealing forms.

Mass

Mass is the solidity, matter, or density that is defined by shape or form. In furniture, mass is **actual density** when the material is filled in, such as a solid block of wood. Mass can also be **optical density** where the material may

not be solid. Heavier or more solid mass will make furniture pieces look larger than furniture with the same overall dimensions but with empty areas instead of solid areas. Examples of furniture with solid or heavy mass include sofas, chairs, and **ottomans** (oversized footstools) with skirts to the floor and/or with oversized cushions; end tables and nightstands supported with bracket feet or no feet or with doors or solid fronts; dining room tables with heavy solid legs or pedestals; and bookcases filled with books (as compared to bookcases with empty areas or areas of art or sculpture).

Heavy mass is desirable where the room is large and furnishings need to visually take up as much space as possible or where furniture needs to appear dignified or commanding.

Massing means grouping together components such as accessories, furniture, or blocks of architecture to create a unified "group mass." Massing will give a weighted, more solid, or imposing appearance. For example, several framed art pieces on a wall will create an important, heavier-looking arrangement than just one or two isolated small pieces. On the coffee table, a book, potted plant, and objects of art grouped into an interesting composition will draw more attention than would the book alone. Two sofas placed in an L shape or parallel to each other will look more impressive than a single sofa.

Furniture, accessories, and artwork can be massed together to balance other larger pieces or architectural components such as windows or fireplaces or to fit into the scale of a room. For example, a low chest with a table lamp could be massed together with a framed art piece to

Figure 3.15 Massing is a common element inside kitchen cabinetry. Here the collection of drinking glasses and pitchers are in a see-through massed grouping. *Hutker, architect/photo © Brian Vanden Brink*

become a visual unit. This unit could then balance a larger case piece such as a breakfront or secretary-type cabinet. Massing can be instrumental in giving richness and completeness to the other components that otherwise might look empty or unfinished when used alone. A framed artwork by itself on the wall may float awkwardly without something (a table, chair, or chest) to visually anchor it; this is the role of massing.

Architects use massing as a tool to create emphasis or to draw attention. For example, when an exterior is analyzed, it is often clear that the architect has manipulated window openings, wings, or shapes of the roof in such a way as to create areas of emphasis and balance via massing.

Line

Line is the connection of two or more points. The eye also perceives line when two planes meet and when shape is seen in silhouette as an outline. Lines may be **straight (horizontal** or **vertical), angular (diagonal** or **zigzag),** and **curved** (circular, **flowing,** or tightly curved). Lines are used by interior designers to create effects such as increased height, width, or the impression of movement. The psychology of line is important to creating ambience or a particular mood in interior design. The types of line are listed in Table 3.3, along with the psychological effect of each.

Figure 3.16 This kitchen features a balance of horizontal, vertical, and curved lines. © G. M. Wild Construction, builder/photo © Todd Caverly

Figure 3.17 Stair and window arrangements provide excellent studies in linear composition. *Left:* © Janis Schwartz/ Imagestate. *Right:* © Norman McGrath. *Below:* © Norman McGrath

Table 3.3 | Psychological Effects of Line

Straight Lines

Horizontal Lines: Weighty, Secure, Restful, Repose

Horizontal lines suggest a solid, harmonious relationship with the earth; earth's gravity has no further pull. Long horizontal lines can visually expand space, making rooms appear wider or longer. When found in a connecting architectural detail such as a molding, horizontal lines provide a smooth transition between rooms or areas. If they lead to a focal point, they help to emphasize it; when they stop at a window, the eye is guided to the exterior view. An interior with too many horizontal lines may become boring and lack interest.

Vertical Lines: Imposing, Lofty, Solid, Formal, Restrained

Vertical lines lift the eye upward. They have the ability to lift the mind and the spirit as

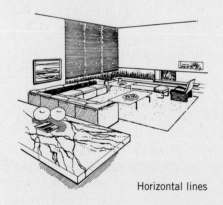
Horizontal lines

well. As such, vertical lines are a purposeful tool for architects and designers of churches and public buildings because they inspire awe and tend to diminish the significance of human scale. The use of vertical lines can make an interior seem higher, apparently increasing vertical space. Vertical lines are stable because they represent a perpendicular resistance to earth's gravity. They convey a feeling of strength and dignity and are quite appropriate in formal dining rooms, entryways, and formal living areas. This formality can bring a stiffness or commanding feeling to the interior. Too many vertical lines can cause a feeling of uneasiness, of too much confinement and predictability.

Angular Lines

Diagonal Lines: Action, Movement, Interest, Angular Stability

Diagonal lines are flexible because their exact direction may vary from shallow to steep

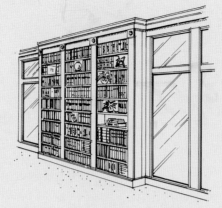
Vertical and diagonal lines

angles. Diagonal lines generally suggest movement, action, or dynamism, perhaps because diagonal lines are associated with going places: up or down a diagonal staircase or an escalator, the taking off or landing of an airplane. Interest is usually sustained longer with diagonal lines than with horizontal or vertical lines, possibly because the angles appear to defy gravity and the eye and mind are stimulated. Yet diagonal lines can also be secure, such as the reinforcing diagonals of an angled roof truss system. Too many diagonal lines, particularly on the wall, can be overstimulating and tiresome.

Zigzag Lines: Exciting, Lively, Rhythmic Movement

Zigzag lines are short diagonal lines that reverse upon themselves and form a regular or irregular pattern. A zigzag line can be one single line or several in a set. A set of regular zigzag lines is called a *chevron* or *herringbone pattern*, and irregular zigzag lines are called a *flamestitch pattern*. Angular zigzag lines can add energy and life to an interior. If too many zigzag lines are incorporated, however, the effect can be frenzied and agitating.

Curved Lines

Curved or Circular Lines: Soft, Humanizing, Repetitive Tempo, Gracefulness

Curved or circular lines provide relief and softness to straight and angular lines and balance the harshness of too many straight lines. Curved lines give a human quality to interiors; they can be easy on the eyes and pleasant to view. A series of curved lines, such as in an arcade (a procession of arches), gives a rhythmic cadence to the room, suggesting graceful movement. In architectural components, round or elliptic segments (sections of circles or ovals) such

as archways provide graceful dignity to interiors. Generously curved lines are viewed as feminine. An excess of curved lines may become too decorative and, consequently, visually disturbing.

Flowing Lines: Gentle Movement, Growth, Linear Development

Flowing lines are irregularly curved lines that move gently in a random or spiraling manner. Flowing lines may be seen in large, live interior trees, in spiral or curved staircases, or in the lines of fine Oriental rugs. Inspiration may be taken from the graceful curved lines of growing and changing plant forms. Because we are never certain where the line will end, flowing lines can provide a great deal of interest.

Tightly Curved or Busy Lines: Playful Activity, Zest, Lively Visual Stimulation

Tightly curved or busy lines are most often seen in textiles and in wall and floor coverings as complicated patterns that are lively, busy, or active. Tightly curved lines can add frivolity and fun to interiors and can make up a pattern that visually closes in space. Complicated tightly curved compositions, such as those in vivid floral fabric patterns or in area rugs, add life and may be visually stimulating and aesthetically satisfying. As such, busy lines may save interiors from becoming dull or boring, yet control over the quality of the design is imperative. Colors and contrast that are too bold or feature too much obvious pattern might prove displeasing and detract from the harmony of the interior.

Gently curved to flowing to tightly curved lines

Combining Lines

Lines are used in combination in every interior, yet often one line will be planned to dominate in order to accomplish a desired effect, such as the vertical lines that produce awe and lift the eye heavenward in a church. Furthermore, vertical and horizontal lines generally form the structural foundation for a building in the form of perpendicular floors, walls, and ceilings. Angular and curved lines are utilized for reinforcement, strength, interest, movement, and relief, as seen in triangular roof truss systems and angled ceilings or walls and in dignified archways and domed ceilings.

Texture

Texture is the surface characteristics and appearance inherent in every element and component of interior design. As the relative smoothness or roughness of a surface, texture is determined in two ways: by touching the physical texture and by visually reading the surface, which may appear quite different to the eye than it actually is to the touch. Some textures that read as rough are painted or printed tiny patterns that give the impression of a texture when it does not actually exist. An example is the painting of surfaces to look like rock, brick, or tile.

Smooth textures generally are associated with more formal, high-style interiors, while rough textures are often thought to be more casual. Textures generally need to be handled in a unified manner, with a compatible feeling to every other texture selected for the interior. However, some contrast in texture is vital for relief and for emphasis. If every texture reads as smooth and glassy, for example, the interior would seem cold and unwelcoming. If every texture is rough, the interior may become harsh and irritating. A balance or a variety of textures is necessary within the unified theme or ambience in order to achieve harmony.

Upkeep is also a consideration in selecting texture. Light-colored, rough textures will show very little dirt because the relief (high and low areas that produce highlight and shadow) will conceal soil. Smooth surfaces, such as flat walls, glass, or dark, polished wood, will reveal dust and fingerprints.

Pattern

Pattern is the arrangement of forms or designs to create an orderly whole. Pattern often consists of a number of motifs, or single-design units, arranged into a larger design composition. Pattern is seen in printed and woven textiles such as upholstery and drapery fabric, floor rugs, and carpeting. Pattern is also seen in wall coverings and in carved or inlaid furniture designs. Pattern that is too small to distinguish may read as texture.

Combining Patterns

Patterns are frequently combined in interior design. While some combinations are very successful, we often sense incompatibility in other combined pattern schemes. To achieve a feeling of rightness, four things need to be evaluated: (1) the placement of emphasis, (2) the character of the pattern, (3) the color scheme, and (4) the scale of the patterns to be combined:

- **The placement of emphasis.** Emphasis is giving importance to one pattern over another so that conflict is minimized. Emphasis is established by using a greater amount of one pattern or a larger scale of one pattern than another.

Figure 3.18 A variety of smooth and interesting textures make this living space a pleasing retreat. © *Jennifer Pacca, Award Interiors/photo © Melabee M. Miller*

Figure 3.19 The bold texture of the log walls is an important feature of this room. © *Jessie Walker Associates*

- **The character of the pattern.** When two or more patterns are used in the same interior, the characters or styles must be compatible. For example, a dignified Georgian damask or brocade fabric will not be compatible with a country Victorian printed cotton one. They will have an entirely different look or character.

- **The color scheme.** Generally, a closely related color scheme will foster harmony. If one pattern contains blues and yellows, for example, then other patterns should also contain exact, similar, or compatible hues, values, and intensities. If the colors are close but "off," then the patterns will not combine successfully.

- **The scale of the pattern.** Pattern scale or size can be similar if the style and the color are compatible. However, when the scale is the same, multiple patterns often seem to conflict. Varying the size or scale of the patterns by using, for example, a large pattern, a small pattern, a tiny pattern, a finely blended stripe, or a compatible geometric shape, along with appropriate textures, can be a good means of achieving success in combining pattern.

Figure 3.20 Patterns are combined in a quiltlike fashion in this cheerful space. © *Brad Simmons/Esto*

Figure 3.21 Natural light illuminates the lobby of International Business Machines (IBM) in Purchase, New York. © *Steve Rosenthal. Courtesy of Pei, Cobb, Freed & Partners, Architects*

Pattern Psychology

Consider line direction and the psychological effect when combining patterns. Angled and straight patterns are difficult to combine unless there are enough of each to have unity in the space. Curvilinear patterns combine more successfully with straight or angled patterns. In small spaces, too many pattern directions are confusing.

Light

Light in interior design has two sources: natural light and artificial light. Although natural light admitted in a large quantity through expanses of glass windows may need some means of screening to prevent glare (too much bright light) or heat buildup, natural light is a desirable and an appreciated element of design. The quality, quantity, and color of light affects the way we see our surroundings and, as such, needs direction, control, and perhaps supplemental sources of light.

When natural light cannot fully meet the needs of the interior design, artificial lighting can make up the difference. Artificial light generally comprises incandescent (the common lightbulb with a tungsten element that glows to produce heat) and fluorescent (luminous lamps) light. Both natural and artificial light are discussed in further detail in Chapter 5.

Light as an element of design affects all other elements. Light can make space appear large or small, friendly or cold. Areas well lit with clear, bright light will make spaces appear larger, whereas dim lights and shadows cast upon walls will seem to close in space.

Light can alter the apparent form or shape of furnishings. For example, lighting portions and leaving other areas in darkness can change the appearance of a form. Low-wattage light sources or backlighting (throwing light behind an object) can affect mass by making objects appear heavier than they really are.

Light affects the way we interpret texture when it highlights textural relief (surface irregularities), and light affects pattern by clarifying or by submerging details. For example, a rough texture can appear even rougher when a light is cast on it at a parallel angle. This "raking light" will emphasize the relief through highlight and shadow. A smooth texture will appear smoother with a directional band of light, such as a spotlight or a smooth wash of light. Likewise, clear light shining directly on a pattern will emphasize the pattern details, and low light casting shadows on a pattern will minimize the details.

Light can change the apparent identity of a color through the color and type of light that hits the surface. Further, different materials may reflect light and color in different ways, affecting the relationship of the colors to each other.

Color

Color, the last element of design, is the most emotional and personal of all the elements. Although everyone has individual preferences toward, and prejudices against, certain colors, humans generally respond similarly to color combinations within each culture. Here the psychology of color is based on the reaction of people in the United States and similar cultures in regard to color hue, value, and intensity.

Hues, or colors such as reds, oranges, and yellows are stimulating; blues, greens, and violets are calming. Hues as seen on the standard color wheel can be divided into equal groups where one half of the wheel consists of warm colors that are stimulating, friendly, cozy, and inviting, and the other half consists of calming cool colors that suggest restraint, dignity, and formality.

Color **values** are the relative lightness or darkness of the hues. For example, a high-value, light red is a pink; a low-value, dark red is a burgundy. Lighter colors seem to recede, making space appear larger and giving a more airy look to the interior, whereas darker values do the opposite—close in and give a cavelike coziness. Distribution of value is sought after in most fine interior design, where some values of light, medium, and dark hues are carefully placed to achieve the desired effect. When placed next to each other, light and dark values **(high contrast)** can be dramatic, whereas hues close in value **(low contrast)** create a subtly blended, calming environment.

Color **intensity** is the brightness versus the dullness of a hue. Pure colors can be lowered in intensity by adding a neighboring or a contrasting color or by adding white, black, gray, or any combination of these. Bright, bold, pure colors are exciting and happy. These need careful handling so as not to become overbearing through overuse or indiscriminate placement. Dull colors can be dark, medium, or light in value but are generally easy to live with because they are undemanding. Often a good balance is found in rooms that utilize the law of chromatic distribution: The larger areas are dulled and neutralized, and the smallest areas are brightest, with the intensity becoming brighter as the areas become smaller.

Color is examined in greater depth in Chapter 4.

Figure 3.22 This interior, devoid of decorative elements, has a strong feeling of structural design. © *Melabee M. Miller*

Figure 3.23 A structurally designed kitchen.

Structural and Decorative Design

Structural and decorative or ornamentive design are two basic divisions of design that are not generally considered with the principles and elements, yet they are important in evaluating the success of a design.

Structural Design

Structural design is seen in any element of interiors where the design is intrinsic to the structure and the form indicates the function of the piece. The concept of "form follows function" is a credo followed by architects and designers who have created modern classic works that are simple yet exactingly well thought out and executed. To say that form follows function means that the first priority in a design is its function, and the parameters of that purpose or function will dictate the shape or form of the design. For example, many modern chairs are designed primarily for the comfort and physical support of their users. The study of **ergonomics** or "ergofit" means that a chair (or even the entire range of furnishings and the building itself) is best suited for specific functions that will take place there. A chair designed to follow the dictum, "form follows function," will be stripped of embellishment and will fulfill only the needs of its function, with an eye to fine, sleek, and simplified design.

Structural design has no added decoration, and the design cannot be removed from the structure without destroying both the design (form) and the purpose (function) of the piece. In order for structural design to be considered fine or high-quality design, certain criteria must be met:

- **Structural design must be simple.** The form and materials will never be complicated or arbitrary. Ironically, however, simplicity is often much more difficult to design and execute than ornate design. Every curve, angle, and part of the design is absolutely necessary to the form and the function of the design.
- **Structural design is unadorned.** There will be no carving, decals, unnecessary color changes, or extras of any sort. The design is found in the form and the materials used—wood grain, for example, or stainless steel or plastic—all frankly exposed to reveal their real worth.
- **The function of the piece must be apparent.** For example, a well-designed structural clock will look exactly like a clock and not like anything else.
- **A structural piece must be well proportioned to be good design.** This is particularly true since there is no decoration to cover up the dimensions, the scale, and the relationship of parts.

Figure 3.24 Conventionalized details characterize the decorative design of this cozy bedroom. *Both © Brian Vanden Brink*

Figure 3.25 Decorative design seen as French Rococo furniture and ornament.

Much of today's minimalist midcentury furnishings are structural design.

Decorative Design

Decorative design is also called applied or ornamentive design and refers to the ornamentation, or embellishment, of the object or structure. Some subjects are in themselves decorative because of the way they are formed, whereas others may be structural pieces with decorative design added. Added decoration can be painted, inlaid, fired, engraved, or carved. There are four types or categories of decorative design:

1. **Naturalistic design** looks so real we could mistake it for a photo or the real plant, animal, or object from nature.
2. **Conventional design** uses designs from nature in a simplified, stylized, or adapted way. The design is "inspired" by nature but does not copy it accurately.
3. **Geometric design** is based on geometry: circles, diamonds, squares, and rectilinear shapes and patterns.
4. **Abstract design** is pattern or shape where the source or inspiration is not clear; it could be a combination, for example, of conventional and geometric designs.

When decorative architecture, interior architectural detail, or applied design on furnishings is well done, it will have the following characteristics:

- **There must be a sympathetic relationship between the style and method of decoration and the object,** such as precise etching or engraving of glass or carving or inlaying of wood.
- **The decoration must be suitable for the function and/or style of the piece.** If the object is a French Ro-

coco form, for example, then the decoration should not reflect unrelated Victorian motifs. Truly fine decorative design will complement the function. The decoration of a clock face, for example, should not obscure the ability to read the time but should enhance the clock's design richness.
- **The proportion of the decoration must be right for the size of the object.** This means two things: (1) The scale of the decoration should be right for the scale of the object (not too large or too small in proportion), and (2) the amount of decoration should be in accordance with the size of the object. A piece too heavily ornamented will likely be considered poor design.
- **The ornamentation should embrace the form and not interfere with its function.**

Design Discernment and Excellence

The principles and elements, together with an understanding of structural and decorative design, form a solid base from which we can judge any design. The **power of discernment** is defined as the ability to recognize and appreciate fine design wherever it is found. We study interior design to gain the ability to discern between levels of design excellence. Thereby we learn to appreciate and incorporate the best design possible into our lives and interiors. We often label design as to its quality or integrity; from most to least desirable, these labels include:

- **Excellent** or **fine design** is impeccable, great design. It is uplifting and visually rewarding, even thrilling to aesthetically sensitive people.
- **Good** or **fair design** is acceptable, though not perfect design. It is adequate for its purpose and is generally pleasing.
- **Average** or **mediocre design** is bland, uninspiring, unmotivating. Much mass-produced design is mediocre.
- **Poor design** is inadequate and disappointing. It is not aesthetically pleasing and usually doesn't function well either.
- **Bad design** or **kitsch** is repulsive or silly, unsupportive design. Some items that we label "kitsch," however, are used for humor in the same way cartoons give comic relief. Some kitsch items have sentimental value.

Cost Is Not the Issue

Keep in mind that these levels of design have little to do with cost. You can pay just as much or as little for bad design as for excellent design. The difference will be found in the inherent beauty and livability that make life more pleasant and rewarding. Fine design is the result of a commitment to fill life and our surroundings with the best design the world has to offer. Items and complete interiors of fine design endear themselves to us because of their timelessness, characterized by classic lines, pleasing forms, and superb use of textures and colors. This is true whether the design is structural or decorative.

Training the Eye

An eye for great design comes from consciously observing and comparing. Here are some places and ways to develop the power of discernment:

- **Visit public buildings** such as museums and art galleries, great public and church architecture, quality furniture stores and boutiques. These and other well-designed nonresidential places broaden our exposure to varying styles and can lead to discernment.

- **Walk through residential interiors** owned by family and friends; go to showcase homes and model homes. Visit historic homes open to the public or museum homes. These exposures help in judging what works aesthetically and what is poorly designed by comparing furnishings and considering how other people function and interact in the spaces.

- **Analyze the media,** which include design periodicals (interior design magazines), movie and video stage sets, CAD programs, and Internet sites. The media play an important role in shaping both short-lived fads

Figure 3.26 Analyzing the design of residential interiors will sharpen the eye. © *Jessie Walker Associates*

Figure 3.27 Showcase homes such as this provide opportunities to see what designers are doing today. © *Scott Frances/Esto*

and longer-lived trends. Much of what we see in the media is fair or good design, some is excellent, and some is poor to bad design. Don't be easily persuaded just because it's in a magazine or on the screen. Some "in-style" interiors have merit; others do not. It is just fine to let a fad pass by. Good design will stand the test of time. Don't be in a hurry to copy what you see. Take a little time to consider the merits of the design direction.

- **Observe nature.** It has been said that nature never makes an aesthetic mistake, and examples of nature's infallibility are all around us to study and learn from. The majesty we see in nature developed over a very long time. The result—a **patina** or mellow, warm, old beauty—is something that we can seek to create in our own interiors. As with nature, we need feel no rush to "complete" an interior. Our lives, like nature, evolve and never stay stagnant. Demographics change, careers change, possessions change. Let the process be part of the beauty, rather than thinking an interior should be "done." Great interiors, like nature, change and reflect the growth of those who live there.
- **Seek education** in the form of book and media learning, classroom instruction, and hands-on projects. Interior design is a complex field that involves many disciplines. A wide range of technical information and the creative capacity to solve problems often come from intense training, exposure, and seasoned experience. The study of historic styles yields a healthy perspective. Recognizing the designs that have withstood

Figure 3.28 This interior expresses affection for the rural past and willingness to break with convention. © *Jessie Walker Associates*

the test of time and are still considered beautiful cultivates appreciation and a love for fine design.

Finding a Personal Style

Just as no two people are the same, so no two interiors should be alike. Finding ideas that appeal to you can certainly serve as a source of inspiration, but copying others' styles will not help you develop a style of your own. Consider these suggestions:

- **Pare back** before piling on extras. Sorting through personal possessions and giving away things that are no longer useful or sentimental is a great starting point. Live with bare walls for a while—there is no shame in this. Then consider, ponder, observe, and live in the space before beginning to furnish.
- **Rearrange what you already have** before planning new purchases. Often the perceived need to own new things is folly. Good interior design rarely results from throwing out everything and starting from scratch with new furnishings. Rather, give new life by moving things around, rotating art and accessories, and moving furniture to different locations or different rooms.
- **Think "need," not "want."** Give serious thought to how you want to live and what you want to do in an interior. The space should first of all meet the functional needs of the occupants. Think "What do I need?" rather than "What do I want?" The ensuing solution will make the most sense. The design program discussed in Chapter 1 should spell this out well. Remember, the more data that are gathered, the better the design solution.
- **Cultivate creativity.** Look for the charms of your living or working space rather than its limitations. Build on what the best features seem to be, rather than lamenting what you don't have architecturally. Most importantly, look inside yourself—your lifestyle and needs—for the way you want to live. With so many furnishing choices and products available today, cre-

ativity has few bounds. Great ideas come to everyone who studies design. Do not be afraid or intimidated to implement a unique design plan. People with great style sometimes do things that are totally unexpected and out of the ordinary, perhaps ahead of their time. Although they may seem to abandon all trends in favor of their own preferences, their good choices are never made to shock, amaze, or impress anyone. True style and creativity involve tuning into and following what is naturally right. They have little to do with what is in fashion, although an awareness of fashion is always evident in interiors owned by people with good taste and creativity. Fashion passes; style remains. Style abhors cliché, cuteness, and conformity in favor of an uncompromising approach to first-class design quality and individuality. Truly great design is innovative yet demanding of the best.
- **Personalize** the space with things you love. Furnishings should reveal who you are, what you do, where you have been, what you have experienced, and who you love. And as you change, your home should respond to the person you become.
- **Cultivate good taste** by choosing wisely. When each item of furnishing is thoughtfully selected and considered an essential ingredient, there is promise of good taste and great style. It has been said that people with good taste know when to stop, just short of excess. Keep the plan simple; let every component be beautiful, and add to the mix only when the overall design will benefit. Look ahead to the future, and know that we never regret making good decisions, purchasing good quality, and insisting on design excellence.

Of all the objectives we may choose to incorporate in life, the dedication to creating welcoming, attractive, and individual personal interiors is one of the most worthwhile. An active knowledge of the principles and elements of design helps to ensure tasteful selections that will be cherished for years to come.

Chapter 4 | Color

© Mary McCulley/Imagestate

How We See Color 82

Color Theory 84

Color Harmony 88

Color Psychology 94

Residential and
Nonresidential Uses of
Color 97

How We See Color

Many factors influence the way we see color in interior design, but the color in our environments comes from only two sources: spectral colored light and pigment or dyestuffs. These combine with the physics of light and anatomy to allow us to perceive color, the most emotional element in interior design.

1. **Spectral light** is colored light inherent in nature. In a rainbow or white light shining through a prism we see the colored light bands known as the visible energy spectrum. These colored wave bands of energy, or **spectral colors,** appear in order from longest to shortest—red, orange, yellow, green, blue, and violet. Adjoining these on each side are invisible energy wave bands beginning with infrared (too long to see) and ending with ultraviolet (too short to see).

2. Colored **pigments** or **dyestuffs** come from two sources: natural compounds in the earth—minerals, plants, or animals—and chemically compounded colors that are artificial compositions. We apply them to our buildings and furnishings.

Subtractive Color

We see color through the **subtractive color theory.** When natural or artificial light hits a colored object, all of the spectral wave bands are absorbed or "subtracted" except the hues that are pigmented, painted, or dyed. These will reflect and travel back through space. When we look at that object, the reflected spectral and pigment-influenced colored wave bands of energy enter the eye, where they are received through the cells on the retina wall at the back of the eye. Known as cones and rods (for their shapes), these cells absorb hue and light and then send impulses to the visual center of the brain, where the colors are deciphered and identified. Colors placed very near one another are visually mixed by a process known as **subtractive color mixing** or **optical color mixing,** which allows us to see or interpret colors other than spectral colors.

Some of the impulses also travel to the master endocrine regulating glands, the pineal and the pituitary, where they become directed impulses that cause us to react to a color emotionally or psychologically. For example, when we see red, the heart rate and respiration rate rise and we feel excited or energized.

Visual Acuity and Deficiency

Most people see color in the same way, although some people can decipher or distinguish more of the over 10 million colors that the human eye can potentially see. These people have greater **visual acuity.** In contrast, a small percentage of people have various deficiencies in their cones and rods and decipher colors less accurately. What used to be called "color blindness" is now termed **color deficiency,** or the inability to distinguish value (light and dark) or pairs of complements one from another, the most common being red and green.

Metamerism

Metamerism or the **metameric effect** is the apparent change in color from one light to another. Judgment of the true color of an object is made under **full-spectrum light** or all the wavelengths of the visible energy band as

Figure 4.1 Metamerism is the apparent change of colors under different lighting. Here, the Ultralume, Designer 800 and Dulux series of lamps produce a high degree of visual clarity and definition, enhancing interiors, food and complexion colors while preserving daylight coloration. *Philips Lighting Company/photos © Melabee M. Miller*

Figure 4.2 Creative lighting and distinctive color are primary features of this middle school multipurpose room. *Stephen Blatt Architect/photo © Brian Vanden Brink*

seen on a clear, cloudless day. However, because most artificial light sources lean toward warm or cool, the **spectral energy distribution** varies, so it is wise to try out color in the setting where it will be used. From the showroom floor to the home or nonresidential setting, colors can appear decidedly different:

- When the light is warm (contains more yellow and less blue spectral colors), more warm hues are reflected and the object appears more yellow-based.
- When the light is cool (contains more blue spectrum and less yellow spectrum), colors appear more bluish.

Spectral Energy Distribution Factors

- **Orientation,** or the direction of natural light, means a slant to the spectrum that affects the way colors appear:
  - East light is clear and bright.

- North light is clear and cool.
- South light is constant and warm.
- West light is hazy and hot.
- **Season and climate** affect color. Winter has fewer warm wavelengths, and summer has more; hazy or cloudy conditions screen out warm wavelengths.
- **Artificial lighting** is in some forms nearly full spectrum; these bulbs or lamps are relatively costly.
- **Incandescent lighting** contains more warm wavelengths than cool.
- Economy **fluorescent lighting** contains more cool spectral colors than warm.
- **Warm fluorescent lighting** is closer to full-spectral energy distribution light.
- **Combustion lighting** (candlelight and firelight) contains more warm wavelengths, although the flickering quality is generally darker, making colors appear darker.

Color Theory

Artists, scientists, and observers of nature have theorized about color, studying how it is made; what it is made of; how nature uses color; how people use color; how colors affect one another; and how colors affect people both emotionally and physiologically. They observed what lightness, darkness, and intensity do to color; how colors may be combined, blended, broken up, or otherwise manipulated to achieve specific results; and what colors make pleasing harmonies or schemes. Of the many who theorized about color, a few have made significant observations that still guide our understanding and use of color in interiors. **M. E. Chevreul** (1786–1889), a French chemist and head of dyestuffs at the Gobelin Tapestry Works near Paris, published a book in 1825 that has been translated into English and is still in use today: *The Principles of Harmony and Contrast of Colors*. This book is considered one of the best ever written on color; in it are found the roots of all our present theories.

The Standard Color-Wheel Theory

The **Standard Color-Wheel theory,** or system, is also known as the **Palette theory,** the **Prang theory,** and the **David Brewster Color theory.** This theory is based on a conventional color circle or wheel where three **primary hues**—red, yellow, and blue—are placed equidistant. **Secondary hues** are placed between these primaries and are a result of mixing any two of them: red plus yellow yields orange; yellow plus blue yields green; blue plus red yields violet. Hence, the secondary colors are orange, green, and violet and are placed in their proper places between the primaries. By mixing a primary and a secondary color on the color wheel, an **intermediate** or **tertiary hue** emerges—for example, yellow plus orange yields yellow-orange. These colors are yellow-orange, yellow-green, blue-green, blue-violet, red-violet, and red-orange. (Note that the primary color is written first.)

These twelve primary, secondary, and intermediate colors, placed in a circle, constitute the conventional color wheel. However, variously mixing the colors on the wheel—along with black and white—yields an unlimited number of colors (hence the name "Palette theory"). This method can be used to mix paint in literally any hue, value, and intensity, to match or blend with any wall covering or fabric, or to achieve any artistic result. We have only to observe the number of choices of paint-chip colors on the market to see that this is so.

When a color wheel is divided between red-violet and violet and across to green and yellow-green, the colors related to red and yellow are considered **warm colors**—red-violet, red, red-orange, orange, yellow-orange, yellow, and yellow-green. The colors related to blue are considered **cool colors**—green, blue-green, blue, blue-

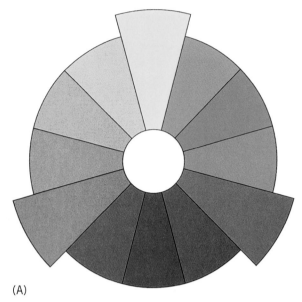

(A)

Figure 4.3 (A) The standard color wheel. (B) Color wheel theory/color schemes.

violet, and violet. The warmth or coolness of a color is also relative to the amount of white or black added. For example, very light yellow may be rendered cool because it recedes away from the viewer and gives feelings of light and space. The visual temperature is also dependent on the strength or intensity of the color and by the placement of colors next to each other. The psychology of these warm and cool hues will be considered later in this chapter.

Chevreul discovered through his studies that color combinations could be divided into "analogous and contrasting harmonies."

Monochromatic color schemes are based on one color. In interiors, successful monochromatic schemes often utilize light, medium, and dark values, varieties of the color in intensity and dullness, and the addition of other hues such as a complement to neutralize or to vary the hue slightly. Ample amounts of white or off-white, or small amounts of black or the complement hue, can be added to a monochromatic interior to balance the color distribution or relieve a potentially overwhelming use of color.

Analogous harmonies or schemes are colors adjacent to each other on the color wheel. Generally, three to six colors are used in analogous harmonies, with one color predominating, another secondary in importance, and a third (up to the sixth) used as accents. Here, a key to success often lies in the variety of the lightness, darkness, intensity or clarity, dullness, and exactness of the hue and in the uneven use of the different colors. For example, in a scheme of orange, yellow-orange, yellow, and yellow-green, perhaps a softened or neutralized yellow would dominate, with yellow-orange used in smaller proportions and more

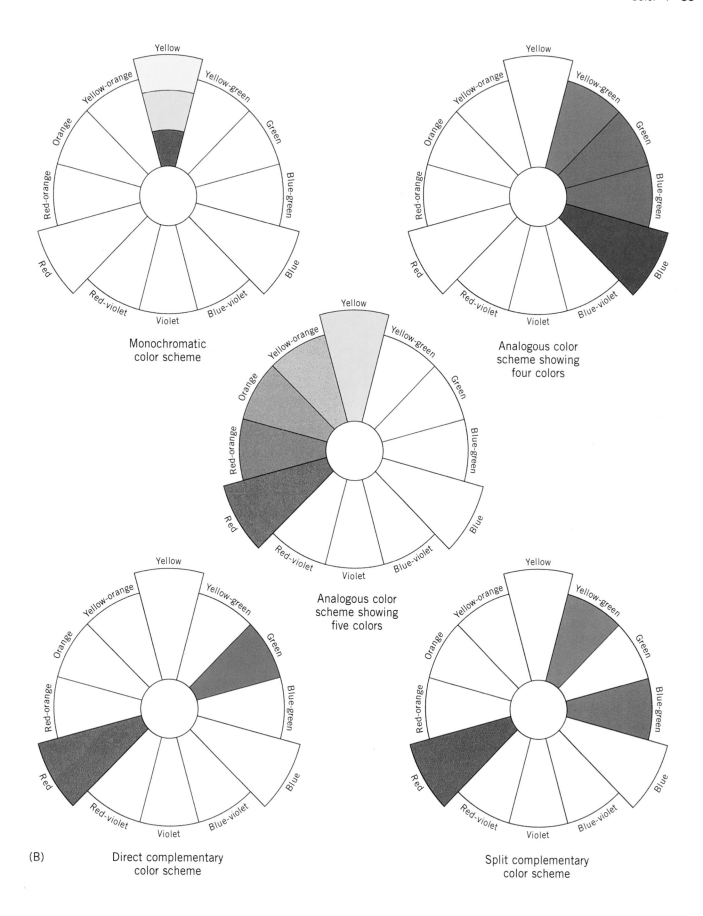

Monochromatic
color scheme

Analogous color
scheme showing
four colors

Analogous color
scheme showing
five colors

(B)   Direct complementary
color scheme

Split complementary
color scheme

neutralized tones and the orange and yellow-green as accent colors.

Complementary colors are those opposite each other on the color wheel:

- **Direct complement** colors are pairs exactly opposite—red and green; yellow and violet; blue and orange. Or they may be intermediate colors such as blue-green and red-orange, for example, that when lightened and/or dulled are a lovely combination.
- **Split complements** contain a base hue and the two colors on each side of its direct complement—yellow, red-violet, and blue-violet, for example.
- **Triadic complements** are three colors that are equidistant on the color wheel. Examples include the primary colors, (red, yellow, and blue) or the secondary colors (green, orange, and violet) or a set of intermediate hues (yellow-green, blue-violet, and red-orange).
- **Double complements** are two pairs of direct complements that are adjacent or next to each other, such as yellow and violet and yellow-orange and blue-violet.
- **Tetrad complements** are four colors that are equidistant on the color wheel, such as yellow-orange, green, blue-violet, and red.

Figure 4.4 A green monochromatic color scheme with Oriental toile fabric and exotic Asian theme is carried out with painted white trim and wicker, faux bamboo and other natural furnishings and accessories. *George Snead Interior Design/photo © Todd Caverly*

Figure 4.5 The combination of oranges, yellows, and greens makes an analogous scheme. *© Mark Darley/Esto*

Figure 4.6 Complementary red and green form a lively contemporary color scheme *© Scott Frances/Esto*

- **Alternate complements** are triad schemes with a direct complement of one of the hues.

Chevreul noted that colors that are far apart on the wheel enhance the intensity of one another. In other words, the greater the difference, the more apparent or obvious the difference. He deemed complementary combinations more beautiful than analogous ones. Both analogous and complementary harmonies are generally more aesthetically pleasing when the colors are used in unequal proportions with one color clearly dominating.

The Munsell Theory

The **Munsell theory** is a major color theory in general use for interior design today. **Albert H. Munsell** (1858–1918), an American colorist, published his studies in several

books. One study published in 1905 and still in use today is his *Color Notation*. His basic theory is widely used today in industry, manufacturing, interior design, and other fields such as science and medicine. Munsell "packets" are available today from Munsell Color for color study and implementation of exact color needs.

The Munsell theory is a precise, formula-based system for notating specific colors. Munsell formulated a color wheel and then expanded it to a three-dimensional globe with leaves or pages of color variations. The system is based on three attributes that determine the exact color identity:

1. **Hue**—the color name; for example the hue red. The Munsell system is based on five hues: red, yellow, green, blue, and purple (not violet). The colors between these are red-yellow, yellow-green, blue-green,

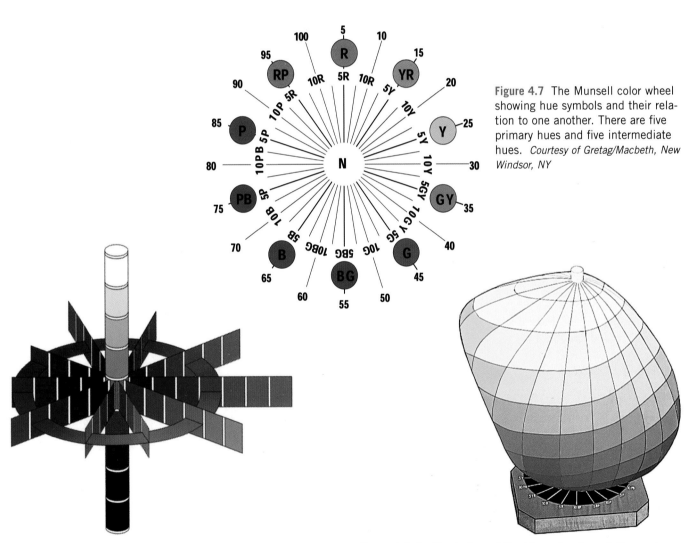

Figure 4.7 The Munsell color wheel showing hue symbols and their relation to one another. There are five primary hues and five intermediate hues. *Courtesy of Gretag/Macbeth, New Windsor, NY*

Figure 4.8 A center cutaway revealing the core of neutrals at the 5/ value level shows how hues extend from neutral to the greatest chroma, or brightness. *Courtesy of Gretag/Macbeth, New Windsor, NY.*

Figure 4.9 An illustration of the Munsell color notation system in three-dimensional form. *Courtesy of Gretag/Macbeth, New Windsor, NY.*

blue-purple, and red-purple. Hue families are given a letter and a numerical notation, 2.5, 5, 7.5, and 10, where 5 is the pure hue. Pure red (R), for example, without any of its neighbors to the left (purple hues) or to the right (yellow hues) is assigned a 5, or 5R. If the red page or palette has some yellow in it, the hue page is assigned 7.5R. This is essentially red-orange. If the red hue is slightly red-purple, the page is 2.5R. Yellow without any yellow-red or green added is 5Y; 5B is blue without any green or purple influence; and so on.

2. **Value**—the lightness or darkness of the hue. Value is geared to a central column of value. White, at the top, is designated as 10; black, at the bottom, is designated as 0; in between is a step series of grays going from dark gray, or 1 (next to black at the bottom), to light gray, or 9 (next to white at the top). Every color has what is termed a normal value (see Table 4.1). This means that every hue has a certain value level as it occurs naturally or in its most natural-appearing state. Yellow is naturally very light and has the lightest **natural saturation point.** Violet is the darkest.

3. **Chroma** or **intensity**—the amount of pure chroma in a given hue; the relative brightness versus the dullness. At the normal value level more intense colors or bright hues exist. For example, more light yellows exist than dark yellows, because yellow is light at normal value. More darker purples exist than light purples because purple is dark at normal value. Chroma is also designated with a number that follows the value number and a slash. The numbers range from 1 to 16; the lower numbers are neutralized or dulled. A color is dulled or lessened in intensity by adding its color-wheel complement. The higher numbers indicate less of that complementary color, so the color becomes clearer and purer, and sometimes brighter, as the numbers increase.

A sample of the Munsell notation for a pure, light, clear yellow would be 5Y 8/12; a clear, naturally occurring red would be 5R 4/14. A dull, medium-value purple would be 5P 5/2. A less pure red, one with some purple added and found in a light value and dull intensity, would be 2.5R 7/4. The advantage to this system is that it states clearly the attributes of a color. The precision of the system is also a boon to color use where exactness is paramount.

Other Color Theories

Other outstanding colorists who have strongly influenced interior design include **Wilhelm Ostwald, Johannes Itten,** and **Josef Albers.**

The **Ostwald theory** is plotted as triangular pages with hues varied not by chroma but by the amount of black and white. The formula bases pure hue or color (C)

Table 4.1	Normal Values	
Yellow	Light value	8
Green	Medium-light value	6
Blue	Medium value	5
Red	Medium-dark value	4
Purple	Dark value	3

at one angle, white (W) at the second angle, and black (B) at the third. Harmonious colors are those that have the same content or amount of hue, white, and black—$(C + W + B = 1)$. Harmonies can be established in parallels, where colors with the same whiteness work nicely with colors of the same content of black. Harmonies of verticals and of step values (called shadow series) are also harmonious. Complex ring-star and elliptic-path harmonies were also plotted by Ostwald. Wilhelm Ostwald (1853–1932) was a physicist who won the Nobel Prize in 1909 for chemistry. He turned his research to color and produced the book *Die Farbenfibel,* translated into English as *The Color Primer.*

Johannes Itten (1888–1967), a teacher at the Bauhaus in Germany, did comprehensive work in color theory. He later taught at Yale University and published two important works: *The Art of Color* and *The Elements of Color.*

Josef Albers (1888–1976), who also taught at the Bauhaus and at Yale University, has become famous for his studies in simultaneous and successive contrast. He experimented with the optics of color. As author of the text *Interaction of Color,* he is considered one of the most influential teachers of this century.

Color Harmony

Color harmony exists wherever colors are combined in a manner pleasing to the eye and to the senses. Color harmonizing comes naturally to some and only after struggle and effort for others. It has been said that there is no such thing as an ugly color, only colors that are used incorrectly. Colors change identity and character literally as they are blended with other hues and visually when placed next to other hues.

Considerations in Color Harmonizing

Hue Identity

Examine a color closely to determine its character. For example, blue is considered one of the most difficult colors to work with because it is so easily swayed by other hues or by white or black. A few of the common blue identities include:

- Navy—blue with black added
- Teal—blue with green added
- Baby blue—a cool, light blue
- Country blue—a neutralized midtone blue
- American blue—a pure, deep blue
- Royal blue—a darker, slightly violet blue

Undertones

The colors that are added to a base hue are called **undertones.** The blue examples listed above illustrate undertones that change the identity of blue. Undertones can render any color cool, even if it is warm. Undertones can render a color more warm or cool. Warm colors—yellow, orange, and red—become cooler when blues, greens, and violets are mixed into them, and vice versa. Colors that are neutralized or grayed will harmonize as a group, browned colors will harmonize with each other, and pure colors or their tints and/or shades will harmonize.

Color Samples

Small samples make selecting colors difficult. A tiny paint chip rarely has the color effect of an entire painted wall. It may appear darker, lighter, or more intense, and the undertones will become more obvious. Working with large samples in situ (where the installation will take place) is not always possible. However, a quart of paint applied to the wall or to a large piece of board or sheetrock can help in evaluation of the true color and effects. A large piece of carpet sample can often be obtained from the warehouse, and a yard or two of fabric or a roll of wall covering can confirm the rightness of the choice and save anguish as well as money.

Shibusa

The Japanese concept of **Shibusa** is a theory of harmonizing color so that combined hues are appealing for a long period of time. Based on the ratios and proportions seen in nature, Shibusa dictates that colors used together be pleasing optical interrelationships. They are subtly harmonious so that nothing offends the eye. Colors are close in value and intensity with just a bit of sharp accent and enough variety to avoid boredom. A Shibui (the adjective) color scheme also incorporates subtle patterns and uneven textures to ensure that the hues remain interesting while being soothing and long-lived. Shibusa is an appropriate choice for interiors where a sense of peace, patience, or detail appreciation is the program goal.

Bold or High-Contrast Colors

Bold or high-contrast colors are pure, bright, or intense colors of any hue. They are often seen in retail design, where lively contrast stimulates shoppers to impulse buy through a sense of euphoria. They are also used in places that people visit briefly—fast-food restaurants or gas stations, where the colors encourage people to hurry through their purchases.

Neutralized Colors

Neutralized colors have been mixed to become less pure, or dulled in intensity. They fall into four categories:

- **Shades** are achieved by mixing black with a hue, or black and then white. They are darker versions, also achieved by adding gray or brown.
- **Tints** are hues made less pure by adding white. Very pale tints are clear and cool, as white paint or pigment

Figure 4.10 Neutralized yellow is emphasized by crisp white trim. *© Jessie Walker Associates*

Figure 4.11 Neutralized yellows form a warm yet livable color scheme well-suited for conversation and reading. *© Mark Darley/Esto*

contains blue. Midtone tints are clean and can be brighter.

- **Tones** are neutralized with a complement or contrasting color(s). Tones have undertones that can be identified with careful examination.
- **Pastels** are lightened tones, or tints of tones made by adding white. They are dull or "dirty" and livable as wall colors. They are rich but nonassertive.

The Law of Chromatic Distribution

A technique for using chroma successfully is found in the **law of chromatic distribution.** It states: "The more neutralized colors of the scheme are found in the largest areas, and the smaller the area, the brighter or more intense the chroma becomes." This means that backgrounds—floors, walls, ceilings, and large window treatments—should use neutralized colors: shades, tones, and pastels. The smaller the area, the brighter the colors should become, with very small areas receiving the intense, bold accents. It is large/dull to small/bright in chromatic progression.

Neutrals

Neutrals are the families of whites and off-whites, grays, and blacks and off-blacks. Browns and beiges are also often considered neutrals, even though they are actually neutralized colored hues.

Whites and Off-Whites

Whites and off-whites give interiors increased visual space. Whitened backgrounds look light, spacious, and farther away. Furnishings that are hues seem cleaner and crisper surrounded with whites. This approach is effective in retail merchandising, where the product to be sold and the clothing of the customers are considered part of the color scheme.

Off-whites are produced by adding other neutrals (gray, black, brown) to white or by mixing color and neutrals into white. These undertones produce off-whites that may be warm or cool, clean or dirty, more neutralized or more colored. Thousands of different off-whites are used in today's interiors. They are seen in paints, wall coverings, textiles, floor coverings, and accessories. It is usually wise to avoid using off-whites that are not similar in undertone. For example, a clear yellowish off-white and a dirty neutralized pinkish off-white will be disturbing; one will appear as the wrong color. Off-whites with similar warmth, clarity, and color undertones will blend harmoniously.

Grays

Grays are achieved by mixing various amounts of black and white, which makes true **achromatic** (no-color) grays. Gray is often an ideal background color against which to show other colors. Grays are easily colored with other hues to produce a wide variety of pinkish grays, yellowish grays, greenish grays, brownish grays, and so on. Colored grays need to be carefully matched or blended to be harmonious, and, like off-white, gray may be rendered cool or warm, depending on the undertones. Warm grays can be welcoming and comforting; cool grays tend to be cold and uninviting.

Black and Off-Blacks

Blacks and off-blacks give deep, dark value to the set-off neutrals. Black sharpens and adds richness to other colors placed next to it. Black used generously may create a dramatic and theatrical setting, although it might produce feelings of depression in some people. Accents of black give richness to interiors. Off-blacks may be very dark grays or tinted blacks where the hue is barely discernible and can effectively tie into color schemes.

Browns

Browns and beiges are often favored because of the warm qualities that they bring to an interior. Browns are achieved by mixing several colors on the color wheel or by neutralizing orange. Often browns are introduced into an interior through stained woods, which do not need to match as long as they

Figure 4.12 The Law of Chromatic Distribution as seen in predominantly neutralized color with small areas of bright chroma. © Peter Aaron/Esto

Figure 4.13 Two examples of interiors furnished in neutrals. (A) Browns and beiges fill this sophisticated Mid-century revival living space with a new, updated color scheme *© Grey Crawford/Beateworks.com* (B) A palette of grays, beige and browns with black accents form a clean, contemporary interior. *Courtesy of Del Mar Window Coverings*

(A)

(B)

harmonize. Used in large amounts, browns can produce either a cavelike coziness or a feeling of oppression. Browns are often at their peak when good value distribution is employed, utilizing many steps of lightness from beige to very dark brown.

Designing rooms in neutrals is not a new idea, nor will it readily be a dated one. Many beautiful interiors are created using achromatic whites, grays, and blacks, along with the brown/beige group. These environments make fine backgrounds for colorful artwork and accessories. One major advantage of selecting neutrals for interiors is the flexibility to change color schemes without being locked into a set color. Interiors employing neutrals in every room also allow furnishings to be moved from one room to another.

Other Color-Influencing Factors

In addition to light, discussed at the beginning of this chapter, other factors that influence our perception of color include texture and material, color placement, and value distribution contrast.

Texture and Material

Texture and materials catch and absorb or reflect light. Smooth surfaces reflect light, which makes colors appear lighter and more intense. Grained wood and textures absorb or refract (break up) the light, causing colors to appear darker. Thus, an exact match in colored samples will not appear as precise when in-

Figure 4.14 Light, both natural and artificial, affects the perception and appearance of color. © Brian Vanden Brink

stalled. The attempt to match paint, drapery, carpet, upholstery, and laminates may cause frustration and dissonance in the finished interior. It is wiser to blend color by selecting various values or harmonious undertones and allow inherent differences to enhance the entire color scheme.

Wood furniture sets, groups, or suites have been produced in single-colored stains for many years. This has sometimes led people to believe that all wood furniture and backgrounds should match. Today successful interiors often feature different woods in varying stains and values.

Color Placement

Color placement of hues in **juxtaposition,** or close together, will cause colors to affect one another. A color

placed near green, for example, may take on a greenish cast or bring out a greenish undertone. A color selected alone and then installed in combination with other hues may take on undertones that give a different character to that color. The result may be pleasing or disharmonious. Coordinating samples under similar lighting conditions or on the site before installation may avoid unpleasant surprises when the colors become permanent in the interior.

Value Distribution and Contrast

As defined under the Munsell theory, **value** is the relative lightness or darkness of a hue or neutral, or the amount of white and black added. **Value distribution** is the utilization or placement of value for a desired result.

High values are light hues (tints and pastels) or light achromatics (about 7 to 10 on the Munsell chart). High values visually expand space; they are a useful tool when walls, floors, or ceilings need to seem farther away. High values make juxtaposed colors seem crisper and cleaner and can unify interiors when used as backgrounds.

High-key interiors have predominantly high values. The effect of many tints is an airy, somewhat carefree feeling. Pastels produce a soothing and calming interior. High-key interiors may seem romantic or ethereal and less connected to the earth, an effect that can relieve stress but also may cause feelings of insecurity.

Midtones are colors at their normal value or natural saturation point and with achromatic values from about 4 to 6 according to Munsell. They are also midvalue neutralized tones. Midtones give a sense of normality and calm. They evoke less reaction and are

Figure 4.15 High-key schemes have a predominance of light values.
© Peter Aaron/Esto

safe, stable, and easy to live with; yet without relief of light and dark values, midtones can become boring and uninteresting. The addition of accents of high/low values and bits of bright chroma and shine creates a Shibui effect—a pleasantly long-lived scheme.

Dark or **low values** are shades and darker tones from about 1 to 3 according to Munsell. Dark or low values seem to advance and close in space; they are useful when walls, floors, or ceilings need to seem closer for warmth or visual effect.

Low-key interiors focus on dark or low values. They can produce a stable, anchored, ponderous, or historic effect; an intellectual or research/reading mode; or even a cavelike coziness or comfort or theatrical setting.

High contrast means that light and dark values are used to give a sharp or bold contrast, precision, drama, or excitement and a clean contemporary scheme. High-contrast values also look professional and no-nonsense.

Value distribution based on nature is the placing of values in the general pattern seen in nature:

- Darker colors are underfoot, creating a sense of security and harmony with gravity.
- Midtones are in the middle—on walls and around windows, on upholstery, and on linens—giving stability and normality.
- Lighter values are above—in the window and near/on the ceiling—for a sense of expanse and visual or mental freedom.

Figure 4.16 In a low-key scheme, dark values predominate.
© Aronson/Stock Boston

Figure 4.17 An example of soft tones. © Design by Sheyla Huff-Hrenya, Hollywoodhomeware.com/ photo © Marc Anthony Photography

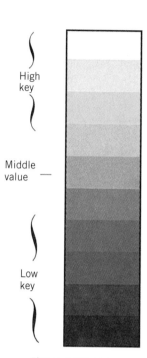

High key

Middle value —

Low key

Figure 4.18 Value scale indicating high key (light values), middle values, and low key (low values).

Color Psychology

The psychology of color is a valuable tool that the interior designer can use to fulfill the needs of the users. In homes as well as public buildings, a knowledge of how people typically view and understand colors can help the designer create effective and efficient interiors. Color psychology is both physiological and cultural. Some common associations or color symbolisms in Western societies are listed in Table 4.2.

Color-group moods can also be determined through research. Philip Thiel, in his book *Visual Awareness and Design,* reports his finding that groups of colors produce specific emotional responses:

- Light-value and bright color groups produce feelings of spontaneity and happiness.
- Light and dull or neutralized colors produce feelings of calm and relaxation.
- Dark and dull or neutralized colors are serious and profound.
- Dark values and bright chroma (jewel tones) suggest richness and strength.

The psychology of color can be seen in the effects produced by warm and cool colors. **Warm colors** visually and psychologically warm the temperature of an interior.

They are inviting, homey, optimistic, encouraging, and stimulating to the appetite, and they facilitate the blending of objects, patterns, and textures. Warm colors also tend to reduce space and create more intimate interiors. Keep in mind that these are generalities. Depending on the value and the intensity of the chroma, colors can be very warm (high chroma, which intensifies these attributes), warm, or only slightly warm (middle to low chroma, which deemphasizes the qualities listed).

Cool colors generally calm and relax the mind and body, giving the impression of lack of pressure and plenty of time to wait or to accomplish tasks. Cool colors often suggest more formality and precision of detail, pattern, and color. They visually expand space, and thus are effective tools in small, cramped quarters. Cool colors subdue the appetite and emotions. Very cool colors are intense, cool colors are middle chroma, and slightly cool colors are low in chroma (neutralized).

Afterimage Simultaneous Contrast

When the eye focuses on an intense color for as few as thirty seconds and then focuses on a neutral area, the complementary color appears in the same pattern as a ghostly **afterimage. Simultaneous contrast** is most evident in pairs of intense, high-chroma complementary colors of

Table 4.2 | Common Color Associations

Red

Pure, intense: Danger, passion, love, excitement, stimulus, conspicuousness.
Dark, neutralized: Wealth, power, sometimes evil.
Pure chroma pink: Cheerfulness, youth, festivity.
Light or pastel pink: Femininity, innocence, relaxation, delicacy.

Orange

Pure, intense: Friendliness, warmth, celebration, clarity.
Dark, neutralized: Wealth, success, fame, rich depth.
Light or pastel: Stimulation (to the appetites), security, relaxed euphoria (sense of well-being).

Yellow

Pure, bright: Cheerful optimism, sunshine, springtime, renewal, intensity, demanding, revealing, warmth (too much is hot), intellect, stimulation.
Dark, neutralized golden yellow: Wealth, affluence, status, distinction, high esteem. Too much is brash, garish, or ostentatious.
Middle to light value: Intelligence, wisdom, compassion, freshness, cheerfulness, optimism, goodness, clarity, cleanliness.

Green

Pure, bright: Nature, calmness, friendliness, integrity, practicality, frankness.

Dark, neutralized: Solidity, wealth, anchored tenacity, security.
Blue-green: Sea and sky, cleanliness, nostalgia, calmness.
Yellow-green: Youthfulness, freshness, happiness.

Blue

Pure, intense: Loyalty, honesty, integrity, royalty, stimulation, restlessness. These also apply to deep or neutralized blues.
Deep, neutralized: Sincerity, conservatism, safety, peacefulness, kindness, compassion. These also apply to pure or intense blues.
Light or pastel: Tentativeness, cleanliness, calm, expanded time and space, lack of security.

Purple or Violet

Pure, intense: Optimism, imagination, royalty, dignity, poise, renewal, commitment, drama.
Dark, neutralized: Depth, richness, security, sternness, soberness, sobriety, dullness.
Light or pastel: Freshness, springtime, flowers, imaginativeness, femininity, kindness, sensitivity.

---

equal value placed in juxtaposition: A vibrating or moire afterimage appears where they border. This can cause eye-focusing problems, irritation, and headaches.

Afterimages and vibrating simultaneous contrast can create a disturbing visual and, hence, emotional state of being. Afterimages can be reduced by varying the intensity of colors placed together, by separating them in distance, or by carefully handling strong graphics and patterns. A stark white background is more likely to create an afterimage than a neutralized color or a gray. A strong chroma of a hue will bring the complement into the visual area, which will be seen in the neutrals. Varying the value of colors will also reduce visual discomfort.

The Color Trend Market

Today color trends or palettes are established by color forecasting organizations, who provide annual color palettes or color forecasts.

Figure 4.19 Reds and golds create a rich, warm color scheme. *Elizabeth Gillin Interiors/ photo © Melabee M. Miller*

Figure 4.20 Deep blues are cool and sophisticated in this historically styled interior. *Brad Simmons/Esto*

Figure 4.21 Pink gives this formal room a soft, feminine feel. *Photo from Laura Ashley's archive of past product lines*

There are a number of explanations for the yearly change:

1. The public responds to new colors introduced by the mass media. When interior fashion changes and a new look is introduced, people are generally quite receptive in order to stay in style or to stay on the forefront of fashion change.
2. Our fast-paced society leads us to not only accept change but expect and even be impatient for it.
3. High technology—instant access to pools of computer or media-based information—has made us a change-oriented society.
4. Economic growth paves the way for expansion of the interior design profession. Consequently, further research into organizational and individual behavior based on color response is also possible.

Color organizations (see Table 4.3) research color direction and forecast color trends with remarkable accuracy. Their forecasts aid manufacturers who are anxious to keep products selling well in the marketplace, where appealing and popular color is of primary importance in item selection. Color trends are established by professional groups. Three of the best known and most influential are the Color Marketing Group (CMG), the Color Association of the United States (CAUS), and the International Colour Authority (ICA). As these groups trace the advance and recession of color popularity, they select new hues while also freshening hues currently on the market. In addition, they look at and decide which hues the public is most likely to accept. These decisions are based on the following:

- An awareness of color trend evolutions and past and present trends
- An awareness of the constant demand by consumers for change in color preference
- The input from national and international companies that produce the colors and from association members who market these colors
- An understanding of human response or psychological reaction to specific hues, and an intuition for color based on this understanding
- National or international events that affect color trends, as they have in the past
- Creative designers and artists, whose well-known works influence decisions, or high-profile people whose style is watched and imitated
- The influence of high technology and computer-screen colors

Color consultants provide specific consulting services for groups or manufacturers. On the basis of interior design training and trend knowledge, color consultants can:

- Select colors for a wide variety of products
- Provide schemes for entire interiors
- Specify colors for architectural projects

Residential and Nonresidential Uses of Color

Color in Residential Interiors

In the home we are free to select colors that are the most personally appealing. When color schemes are neutralized, children and extended-family members can express themselves more with art and accessories. As neutrals

---

Table 4.3 | Color Organizations

- **Color Marketing Group** (CMG), 4001 North Ninth Street, Suite 102, Arlington, VA 22203, is a nonprofit organization whose membership is involved in the process of color selection or specification. The association selects colors for marketing services and products. Members pay an association fee and attend meetings—regional and semiannual national meetings. At the spring meeting, colors are chosen, and at the fall meeting, they are presented to the members. Members are sent resourceful newsletters and have access to workshops and educational seminars.
- **Color Association of the United States** (CAUS), 24 East 48th Street, New York, NY 10016, issues color charts for home and contract furnishings each September and apparel swatches each March and September, intended to be eighteen to twenty months ahead of the actual selling season. Members receive the charts and monthly color newsletters and may attend New York–based seminars. Colors each year are selected by a rotating panel of eight to ten members recognized for their color expertise and professionalism.
- Members of the **International Colour Authority** (ICA), c/o Benjamin Dent & Company, 33 Bedford Place, London WC1B 5JX, England, meet in the spring and fall in London, where forecasts emerge from international members' panels on both home furnishings and apparel. Members receive a continuous printout of ICA data that indicates colors to be promoted worldwide. Monthly reports from subscribers are tabulated and divided into specific areas. The information is then sent back to the subscribers and is followed up with a written report that evaluates and documents trend development and forecasted color use.
- **Munsell Color,** 2441 N. Calvert Street, Baltimore, MD 21218, is a resource for designers and educators. Munsell Color can provide many tools and educational materials for use in defining, identifying, and recording or matching colors through the Munsell color notation system.

and neutralized color schemes convey a sense of rest and repose, a home in which they are used can become a calming, peaceful sanctuary. Similarly, bright color and deep chroma can be powerfully effective for immersing the occupants in a planned psychological response.

Color is a good way to change a home's look, mood, or formality without spending a lot of money. Although re-upholstering furniture, replacing carpeting, and selecting custom window coverings often are costly, many other colored items are usually not. Paint, for example, is relatively inexpensive considering the square footage it covers. Bed, bath, and kitchen linens can change the look entirely when backgrounds are neutral, and art and accessories may be changed with the seasons or moods. Smaller colored areas that are bright and cheerful might be preferred by younger children. Tailored for their needs, the same areas may provide a source of identity and individuality for teens and young adults, may be soothing and relaxing for working adults, and may be comforting and reminiscent for senior citizens.

Color in homes can be tailor-made to individual needs beyond age. People who are housebound or prone to depression can be cheered with warm, encouraging colors. People with poor eyesight may benefit from light, clear color and value. Those who need reassuring environments in which to work at home can select colors that are calming or stable. Various task or hobby areas within the home can also be outfitted for individuality. Living areas where people congregate or are entertained should be neutralized enough to be generally appealing to everyone.

Colors not only have to "live" well; they also must physically wear well. One cliché states that the best carpeting choice is the "nicest dirty color you can find." Dull or neutralized colors can conceal dirt, require less cleaning, and conceal wear better. This increases the life of the product, whether it be carpet, hard flooring, wall or window treatments, furniture, or other fabric items. Patterned and textured products also wear well, provided there is long-term appeal. Ask yourself, "Will I still want this pattern-texture-color combination in ten years?" If you sincerely think you will, it is probably a good color choice.

Nonresidential Considerations

Color in public and in work spaces is a complex topic. For example, color in medical facilities will often be handled differently than in hospitality interiors, office interiors, retail businesses, or production or assembly-line facilities. The differences lie in the specialized needs of the users of these various environments. Designers must be knowledgeable about and sensitive to these needs, which govern emotional responses, since they can affect behavior, attitude, productivity, or patronization.

Medical facilities include hospitals, doctors' offices, outpatient facilities, and geriatric facilities. Here the philosophy of color has changed significantly in the past several years. Medical facilities used to be white or pale tints, cool-looking, and full of hard surfaces, an echo of the sterile environment. Today, we know from research that soft or neutralized colors in a variety of values, from dark to light, can promote healing. Also, colored background elements are no longer always hard. Medical facilities often incorporate carpet, warm wood textures, and fireproof fabric or wall coverings on the partitions and walls. This offers a more human, caring atmosphere to persons in sometimes frightening and bewildering circumstances.

Hospitality facilities include hotels and motels, resorts and spas, and restaurants. Their interiors are areas where color and design are dictated by the culture and the climate. Lavish colors and patterns may dominate reception areas and rooms and suites. In restaurants, red- and orange-related hues are found to be the most

Figure 4.22 Gray and off-white neutrals (A) and neutralized soft green (B) are easy to live with and create a calm, restful mood in these residential interiors. *(A) Peter Aaron/Esto (B) Susan Gilmore/Esto*

(A)

stimulating to the appetite, and colors that complement the food color enhance the visual appeal and flavor of the food. Where climates are very warm, cooler colors are often used, and in colder climates, warmer colors are often more welcoming.

Office interiors have become sophisticated in terms of equipment and furniture systems and the use of computers to simplify procedures, storage, and retrieval systems ("the paperless office"). Color trends are reflected in contemporary office design, with neutralized hues and complex neutrals considered most professional.

The objective of design for **retail businesses** is to entice customers to purchase goods and services. Stimulating, warm, cheerful, and advancing colors are often utilized in large stores and shopping malls, where the bright colors help customers locate departments and services. To an extent, glitter and neon-bright colors have been incorporated into retail businesses that appeal to youth. The use of subtle, deep-value tones and neutralized pastels, accented with pure chroma, with polished wood and metal gives retail businesses an exclusive or rich appearance. This method does not necessarily limit the clientele to those with money. Rather, it is aimed toward making customers feel that they deserve quality merchandise and can afford it. White, neutrals, and neutralized hues form a background for colorful merchandise and provide flexibility.

Production plants have requirements of psychological comfort, productivity, and safety. Light pastel colors that reflect light are generally more pleasing than stark whites, intense colors, or dark values. Cheerful colors influence workers to be cheerful.

Productivity can be increased by eliminating eye fatigue caused by afterimages, intense chroma, stark whites, very dark values, or shiny or glossy surfaces at the workstation. Matte or dull surfaces in colors that

(B)

provide a pleasing contrast to the material or object being worked on will add texture contrast necessary for both comfort and productivity. Primary colors used to identify controls or parts of machinery will increase efficiency. Warm colors in cool environments and cool colors in warm environments will help workers feel more comfortable.

Safety can be enhanced by using bold or intense colors on dangerous parts of machinery or in areas of potential hazard. The use of color to reduce eye fatigue will help workers be more alert and help prevent accidents.

Figure 4.23 Pure, jewel-like color contributes to the impressive mood in this restaurant setting. © Peter Aaron/Esto

Chapter 5 | Lighting and Technology

Lighting in Interior
Design 102

Natural Light 102

Artificial Lighting 104

Light and the Mind and
Body 110

Power Terminology and Units
of Measurement 114

Luminaires, or Lighting
Fixtures 115

Lighting for the Future 115

Nonresidential
Considerations 116

Technology 119

Scogin Elam & Bray Architects/photo © Brian Vanden Brink

Lighting in Interior Design

Light—both natural and artificial—is such an important element of interior design that we devote most of this chapter to examining its aesthetic, practical, and technical aspects. It is through light that we see color, and by light we discern all the elements and components of an interior. In the following sections we discuss the ways lighting is handled, what effects it has on an interior, the types of lighting and lamps (bulbs), and lighting's effects on our minds. We also examine technical terms and information to help us make wise, informed lighting choices.

In lighting an interior, we should strive toward these goals:

- To make lighting effective and practical for the activities and purposes of the interior
- To make the interior more aesthetically pleasing
- To make the interior psychologically useful
- To select lighting wisely and use it economically in terms of both product and power

Natural Light

Natural light, or light from the sun, has a **full spectrum** of colors. Natural light makes colors appear rich and vibrant and is a healthful, cheerful light necessary for living. A balance of natural light evenly distributed from two or more directions is desirable since it helps reduce shadows in the interior and consequent visual and physical fatigue.

Yet even natural light can lean toward one color, depending on factors such as the time of day, season, weather conditions, orientation, climate, and location. The color of light is different at morning, noon, and evening and, within any one of those times, will vary according to the season and weather conditions. The morning sun in the summer is brighter and warmer than the morning winter sun, and it is more brilliant and yellow on clear days than on overcast days.

Orientation refers to the direction of the light. For example, southern-exposure light will be warmer and northern light will be cooler. Orientation also takes into account reflected surfaces. If a northern exposure faces a large orange building, then certainly orange will be reflected into the north-facing interior, rendering the light warmer than it would otherwise be. Light reflecting a deep blue sea or an azure sky will bring bluish light into the interior.

Natural light is not completely predictable. When there is no cloud cover or screening at the window, natural light can become too bright and intense, resulting in **glare,** excessive **luminance** in the visual field that can cause irritation and fatigue. Natural glare is a problem that requires interior shading or screening window treatments. (Artificial glare will be discussed later on.) There

Figure 5.1 A variety of artificial lighting strategies from candles to sconces, table lamps and art accent luminaries provide effective mood lighting to this living space. © Scott Frances/Esto

Figure 5.2 Welcome sunlight floods the Spa Café at the Cliff Lodge, Snowbird, Utah. © *Ricke-Hults/ Photo Researchers, Inc.*

are also times when overcast conditions or the size and orientation of the window cause natural light to be inadequate. Too little natural light for activities such as reading, writing, or other detailed tasks can cause eyestrain and fatigue. When natural light is too dim for the occupants to function well, it must be combined with an artificial light source to become fully effective. Most people turn on lights during the day when cloud cover, fog, or smog reduces the luminance of natural light.

Combustion Lighting

Firelight, candlelight, and lanterns are another natural source of lighting called **combustion lighting.** Light from fires and candles flickers, as do lanterns when they are moved about. This inconsistency can be charming and create coziness.

Figure 5.3 Candlelight is a warm and intriguing form of combustion lighting. *Photo by David A. Taylor*

Figure 5.4 Artistic and effective lighting is a key element in this successful carry-out restaurant, Rice to Riches. *Focus Lighting, NY/photo copyright J.R. Krauza*

The warmth from a combustion source can also be an asset. A fireplace draws people near it for warmth and comfort as much as for the light. Gas logs flicker—imitative of a real fire but without the work and mess. **Luminaires** (lighting fixtures) may incorporate flame-shaped bulbs that flicker to copy the light of real candles.

Artificial Lighting

Artificial lighting can create moods, add sparkle and emphasis, and be directed and manipulated to meet the goals of the interior. Although artificial lighting is often considered a stable source of light, it is interesting to note that over the life of the lamp, the lumen output (level of brightness) is reduced. There is also a color shift when dimming the lamp and a gradual color change over the life of the lamp.

Although many kinds of artificial lighting sources exist today, the most commonly used are incandescent (common filament lightbulbs), **fluorescent** (tubes for general, luminous lighting), **HID (high-intensity discharge) lighting,** and **cold-cathode lighting.** HID lighting and cold-cathode lighting are discussed under "Nonresidential Considerations" at the end of this chapter.

Incandescent Lighting
Incandescent light is produced by heating a highly resistant **tungsten filament** with an electric current until it glows. Incandescent light contains a continuous, warm, mellow color spectrum. Incandescent lighting produces heat and is costly. Lamps (or bulbs) wear out quickly and are discarded (or recycled into other materials, such as ceramic tiles). Long-life bulbs cost more, but they last longer.

Incandescent lighting is used in ceiling and portable fixtures such as table lamps. This lighting is flattering and best for warm mood lighting.

Colored incandescent lighting can be achieved by using colored glass on the lamps or by placing a colored screen over the light. The most familiar are colored Christmas bulbs.

Figure 5.5 Small blue halogen fixtures cast crisp and sparkling pools of light. © *Grey Crawford/Beateworks.com*

Table 5.1 | Types of Incandescent Lamps

Types of incandescent lamps (bulbs) vary according to shape and purpose. Commonly used lamps, available in a wide range of wattage, are listed in this chart. The numerical system that indicates the size of the lamp uses numbers such as R-20, R-30, R-40 and indicates the diameter of the lamp in inches divided by one-eighth of an inch. For example, R-20 is a lamp 21/2 inches wide.

Lamp Shapes

A lamp: Arbitrary-shaped bulb; the most common lamp shape.

B lamp: Candleabra lamp—a smooth torpedo-shaped (oval or ovoid) bulb.

C lamp: Cone-shaped bulb.

F lamp: Common cone-shaped reflector—brighter and shaped to spread the beam wider.

G lamp: Globe-shaped (spherical or round) bulb.

T lamp: Tubular lamp, also a designation for tungsten halogen lamps.

PS lamp: Pear-shaped lamp—a rounded, longer shape.

R lamp: Flame-shaped bulb.

Other Reflective Lamps

ER lamp: Elliptic-shaped reflector lamps focus the light beam to 2 inches in front of the lamp, thereby saving energy with increased light in one spot.

PAR lamp: Parabolic aluminized reflector lamps have heavy, protective glass that makes them suitable for both interior and exterior (outdoor) use. Silvering is used to establish the beam spread and the reflective quality of the lamp and to determine whether the beam will spread out into a **floodlight** or will be used for a spotlight. Silvering also creates **glare-free** lamps. The lamp face (the nonsilvered portion) also affects the beam spread.

HID lamp: Mercury vapor and high-pressure sodium are two of the most common high-intensity discharge lamps. Commonly used outdoors.

PL lamp: Compact twin fluorescent lamp bulb.

Tungsten Halogen Lighting

Another type of incandescent light is the **tungsten halogen lamp.** The filament of the small lamp is surrounded with halogen gas. As the tungsten burns off, the halogen reacts with the tungsten, creating a bright light. This type of light enables one to direct light to a certain area and to intensify the light by placing the bulb inside a reflective (PAR) lamp. Tungsten halogen lights cost more than common incandescent lighting but will usually last longer and produce more lumens per watt.

Tungsten halogen bulbs are available as standard lamps that look similar to the arbitrary bulbs and screw into any incandescent socket. Tungsten halogens are also used as flood, spotlight, or low-voltage lighting. In lamps of standard wattage, halogens last three times longer, burn 10 percent brighter, and are closer to the natural sunlight spectrum.

Low-Voltage Lighting

Low-voltage lighting uses a type of lamp that controls the beam spread usually to about 9 degrees. The lamp typically has a built-in reflector with a tungsten halogen bulb that produces superior accent lighting or spotlighting. It also incorporates transformers to reduce voltage to

Figure 5.6 This fitness center is lit with ambient fluorescent fixtures. © *David Sundberg/Esto*

Fluorescent Lighting

Fluorescent light is produced by an arc between two electrodes inside a glass tube filled with very low pressure mercury vapor. The arc or discharge produces ultraviolet (invisible) radiation in wavelengths that excite or activate the white powder (phosphorus crystals) lining the lamp. The phosphorus **fluoresces** (glows), converting the ultraviolet energy into visible light energy.

Fluorescent light is a relatively shadowless, even light, making it ideal for general lighting of environments where tasks are performed but where task lighting would be impractical or undesirable. In homes, fluorescent lighting is most commonly used in luminous ceiling panels, recessed into a dropped ceiling and covered with textured, translucent panels. Fluorescent lights are also commonly used in under-the-cabinet lighting over counters, in bathroom lighting, and over work surfaces in hobby rooms or offices. This type of even, clear light provides an environment where work can take place for hours without lighting-caused fatigue.

Fluorescent lamps are available in straight, circular, or U- or V-shaped tubes and as **compact fluorescents** in

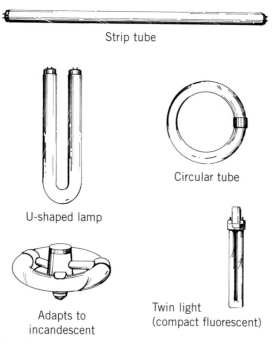

Strip tube

U-shaped lamp

Circular tube

Adapts to incandescent

Twin light (compact fluorescent)

Figure 5.7 Shapes of fluorescent lamps.

the source. Indoor low-voltage lighting is often used inside recessed or track fixtures.

These lights are particularly useful in retail stores to highlight specific merchandise such as jewelry, which sparkles under a low-voltage halogen beam. Low-voltage halogen is the lamp of choice where artwork is displayed.

Figure 5.8 Compact fluorescent lamps. *Courtesy of General Electric Company*

many shapes. Although they initially cost more than incandescent bulbs, they require far less energy to run and last far longer than incandescent lamps. The exact difference in cost, energy saved, and longevity varies according to the type of fluorescent lamp and the type of incandescent lamp it is compared with. Fluorescent tubes become less effective as they age because they lose lumens and may hum or flicker prior to burning out. **Rapid-start fluorescent lamps** have eliminated the problem of blinking when the lights are switched on.

Fluorescent lighting is available in both warm and cool color spectrums. Cool, economical fluorescent lamps are cold and unflattering although the lumens per watt are high and the light is cost efficient. **Cool white deluxe** and **warm white deluxe** lamps have a balanced spectrum and are more flattering, but they are more costly. Fluorescent lamps are available in a wide range of styles and types; each dealer will have a chart with all the kinds of fluorescent lamps listed. When shopping for fluorescent lamps, it is wise to consult with the lighting personnel for help in selecting lamps that will be most appropriate.

Compact Fluorescent Lamps Compact fluorescent lamps (CFL) are initially more expensive, yet they consume as little as one-fifth of the power and last up to sixteen times longer than incandescent lamps. CFL lamps also offer the same color options and degrees of "warmth" as linear fluorescent lamps. Some can even be dimmed. The choices are not just in the lamps but also in the ballasts that connect the lamp to the fixture and can convert an incandescent fixture into a fluorescent one. Ballasts can be classified as standard electromagnetic, energy-efficient electromagnetic, or electronic, with novel options such as radio-interference suppression or power-factor correction.

Dimmable Fluorescent Lighting Fluorescent lighting has been slow to be adopted into residential interior design partially because until recently there was no safe and economical way to use fluorescents with a dimmer switch.

Now, however, these components are more reliable, economical, and readily available.

A **dimmable fluorescent system** consists of an electronic dimming ballast, control wiring, power wiring, a wall-box dimmer switch, and dimmable fluorescent fixtures. (Caution: Using a nondimmable fluorescent lamp in a dimmer circuit is a fire hazard.) Although dimmable components cost more than nondimmable ones, the savings will be seen in lower electric bills and longer life, depending on the frequency of the switching. Lamps can even be set as a nightlight without affecting the life of the lamp. Fluorescent lighting maintains its whiteness when dimmed, whereas dimming incandescent lighting results in a slight color change.

Note that compact fluorescent (CFL) lamps emit electronic frequency wavelengths, which may interfere with signals received by television and radio. CFL should be placed at least 8 feet away from these devices.

Colored Fluorescent Lighting Colored fluorescent light is **cold-cathode lighting,** commonly called **neon lamps.** These use different gases or vapors to produce colors. Traditionally used to light exterior signs in business districts, today creative uses of neon lighting have brought this type of light to residential interiors. Lighting as art frequently incorporates neon lighting in homes with surprising and intriguing effects.

Categories of Lighting Effects

In order to accomplish the goals of lighting, categories are useful in directing the design. In homes, they include **general, ambient, task, accent and mood lighting,** and **lighting as art.** These are discussed here, and other categories are found under "Nonresidential Considerations" later in the chapter.

General and Ambient Lighting
General lighting is usually planned into the blueprints of the home (see "Wiring Plans" later in the chapter).

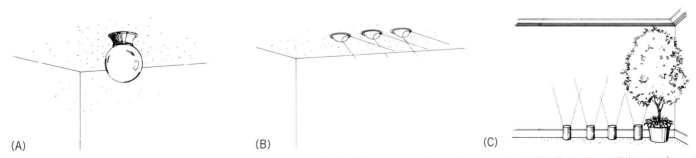

(A) (B) (C)

Figure 5.9 General and ambient lighting. (A) The ceiling luminaire lights an area from above eye level. (B) Eyeball spotlights wash the wall from ceiling level. (C) Uplighters wash this wall with light, illuminating the ceiling and the area nearby. Light-colored walls will reflect and increase footlamberts.

General lighting provides a uniform, even, broad plane of light. It may be accomplished with **direct lighting** such as ceiling fixtures that shine downward. Direct general lighting often takes the form of fluorescent or other utilitarian incandescent ceiling fixtures. These fixtures, particularly the fluorescent type, may provide good general lighting for kitchens, offices, workrooms, and classrooms, where tasks are performed throughout the space. However, one of the drawbacks is that such lighting is bland or monotonous and unsuitable for areas such as living rooms and bedrooms where aesthetics are an important part of the lighting plan.

Ambient lighting comes from an indirect source that throws background light against a surface such as a wall or ceiling, reflecting the light back into the room. Recessed **eyeball spotlights** in the ceiling around the perimeter of a room "wash" the walls with light, and **up-lighters** cast light onto the ceiling, where it is reflected back into the room, creating a soft general illumination. Ambient lighting creates a pleasant quality of illumination but may not be adequate for specific tasks. Thus ambient lighting is often combined with other types of task or accent lighting.

Task Lighting

Task lighting directs the right amount of light where it is needed to perform tasks requiring hand-eye coordination. Examples of such tasks include reading, typing or word processing, writing, drawing, assembling parts, working with tools, cooking, dining, sewing, and personal grooming. Task lighting should not be high-contrast areas of light and dark. If the pool of light abruptly ends and darkness begins, unnecessary eyestrain and fatigue will result. It is wise to combine task lighting with general, ambient, or natural lighting whenever possible. In the kitchen, for example, the **luminous ceiling** (general lighting) may be accompanied by task lighting such as recessed downlighters, soffit, or under-cupboard lighting.

Task lighting may also be seen as strip lights placed around a mirror or above a work area. **Track lighting** and **spotlights** are also used to focus light onto a task area.

Task lighting can also be accomplished with **portable luminaires,** which can be moved from one area to another. These include **floor** and **table lamps,** plug-in wall sconces, and under-the-counter strips.

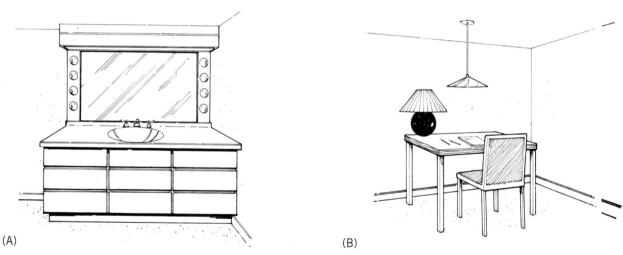

(A) (B)

Figure 5.10 Task lighting for specific purposes: (A) personal grooming; (B) reading, writing, or studying.

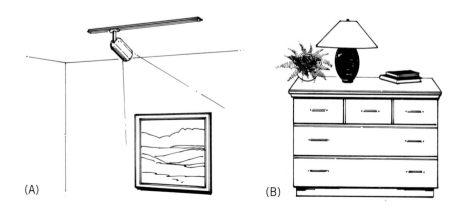

(A) (B)

Figure 5.11 Accent or mood lighting. (A) Track spotlight accentuates artwork. (B) Low lighting from a small luminaire (table lamp) creates a mellow mood.

Accent and Mood Lighting

Accent lighting is sometimes referred to as **artistic lighting.** Accent lighting may focus on a piece of art or an accessory item, emphasizing the object. Accent lighting creates interest and drama through small spots of light or by casting light in small areas against a dark background. This **high contrast** of dark and light areas gives interest through the patterns of light and dark, such as those created by art spotlights or a play of **brilliants**—a myriad of pinpoints of light, the tiny lights on a tree, for example.

Mood lighting creates a sense of inviting coziness, such as the contrast of soft, low, or glittering light against a dark background. Examples include dimmed recessed lights and table and floor lamps. Lighting from a fireplace is also mood lighting. It emotionally draws people near for visual interest and for comfort and warmth. The heart of the home has long been its hearth, where meals were prepared and served for centuries. Today a seating area around a flickering fireplace is still inviting. It can become even more effective and beautiful with the addition of spotlights or directed low-voltage lighting.

General and ambient, task, and accent lighting are frequently combined, since each type of lighting fulfills different purposes. They may overlap to fit the time of day or night or activities taking place. For example, on an overcast day general lighting can be a backup for natural lighting. General lighting is mandatory where no windows exist and for nighttime occupation. Task lighting supplements general lighting for specific work projects during the day or night. Accent lighting is used primarily at night and in windowless interiors during the day. When lighting is used concurrently, there needs to be usage control for the sake of conserving bulb life and energy.

Lighting as Art

In lighting as art, the light fixture and method of lighting become art itself. Besides traditional **decorative luminaire** lamps, here are ways that lighting can become artistic:

Figure 5.12 Accent lighting is used to highlight a work of art. *© Peter Aaron/Esto*

Figure 5.13 The connecting concourse of the United Airlines terminal at O'Hare Airport in Chicago, with its dazzling light show, is an engaging art lighting experience. *© Timothy Hursley*

- The fixture or luminaire itself may be the emphasized point of vision, as in a neon sign or artistic lighting fixture. Innovative artists combine light with other materials and textures for intriguing artistic effects.
- Colored light and patterns of light and dark from one or many sources can turn lighting into art.
- Lighted, etched **acrylic sheets** allow light to shine through the etched areas, giving unlimited design possibilities to art, floors, walls, and other areas.
- **Light pipes** made of acrylic can conduct a variety of lights in artistic ways: by sunlight and by a selection of lamps that produce intense light up to 1,000 watts. Subtle and/or changing color can be inserted into the pipe. When the pipe is formed into shapes such as prisms, the effect can be multiplied, giving the interior designer phenomenal freedom in creating color impressions.
- **Laser** lights, commonly used in light shows, can be made stationary or changeable and can project images of art, furniture, and people or even the illusion of more interior space.
- **Holograms** produce amazing three-dimensional images in midair.

Lighting Effects in the Interior

Lighting effects can change the apparent shape, color, and texture of the interior. These effects include the following:

- An **ambient bank** or **plane of light** is a large, well-lit area. It may encompass the entire interior, or it can designate smaller areas within a large space.
- An even **wash** is a soft plane of light from spotlights or track lights aimed at a wall or ceiling.
- A light shining at a steep angle or very close to the object or to a surface **grazes** it with luminescence—an effective way of emphasizing texture.
- A **pool of light** is a circle of light thrown by a downlighter or spotlight. Spotlighting from more than one direction can **balance light** and emphasize detail by eliminating shadows.
- **Perimeter lighting,** around the outside of a room or an area, visually expands the space.
- **Point** or **pinpoint lighting** spotlights a tiny area. Pinpoint lighting can emphasize or create shiny, glittery accents if it strikes a reflective surface.
- **Line** or **outline lighting** emphasizes a shape or lights an area, such as a dressing table and mirror, with a line of incandescent lamps or with fluorescent or neon tubes.
- **Silhouette lighting** is accomplished by shining a light directly on an object so that the shadow behind it echoes its shape.
- Lights that shine upward behind objects such as plants and art will "model" the object's shape, thereby creating patterns on the wall or ceiling.
- Lights shining directly downward will cause shadows beneath and around the object. Downward light on people casts unflattering shadows.

Light and the Mind and Body

It is important not to overlook the dramatic effects that lighting can have on the mind and body. Most of us have experienced mood variations in response to natural light: On sunny days we're likely to have a lighthearted, cheerful outlook, while dark, dreary days put us in a negative, sluggish mood. Similarly, artificial lighting that is too

Figure 5.14 Recessed spotlights are used to create perimeter lighting in this study. © Tim Street-Porter/Beateworks.com

Figure 5.16 Sunlight pours deeply into this bedroom. Bringing natural light into the interior may help to prevent feelings of depression.
Peter Breeze, architect/photo © Brian Vanden Brink

Figure 5.15 Recessed downlighters illuminate carefully planned areas in this restaurant. In the daytime, the spacious skylight brings in natural light to supplement the light from outdoors.
© Douglas Hill/Beateworks.com

bright or dim may annoy us or make us feel exhausted or even ill. A well-designed lighting plan not only will avoid these extremes but also will make use of high levels of illumination to enhance people's energy and motivation and will provide low, subtle lighting to encourage relaxation and mellow feelings.

Seasonal Affective Disorder

A form of depression called **seasonal affective disorder (SAD),** first identified by psychiatrists around 1980, is a dramatic example of how light can affect the mind and body. SAD symptoms include lethargy, irritability, and an increased desire to sleep and eat carbohydrates. Because symptoms typically occur as winter approaches and disappear when spring arrives, experts believe SAD is caused by a disruption of the circadian entrainment rhythms, the process by which we "set" our biological clocks.

It is not surprising, then, that psychiatrists recommend activities in daylight, such as morning walks, as a way to alleviate winter depression. They have also developed a system of bright-light therapy as a treatment for SAD. In this therapy, the patient uses a specially designed light-box or light helmet for a prescribed period, usually 30 to 60 minutes a day. Therapeutic light devices are sold under several brand names, including Northern Light, Photo Therapeutics, True Sun, and Vita-Light. These devices resemble natural full-spectrum sunlight in both their brightness and their color balance. Patients need to find the timing and distance of exposure that works best for them and be aware that bright-light therapy does not help everyone.

Because improper use can cause problems such as headaches, eyestrain, and other damage to the eyes, SAD therapy lights should *never* be used to self-medicate a case of winter "blahs," much less for general lighting. However, in designing interior lighting, we can take

Figure 5.17 Low levels of ambient light and an exciting cold-cathode light sculpture set the mood of this nonresidential interior.
© Grey Crawford/Beateworks.com

advantage of what we know about SAD to create an environment that helps people feel their best year-round. One way to admit natural light is to plan or remodel homes to include large expanses of glass such as picture windows, bay windows, and skylights. The solarium or greenhouse, discussed in Chapter 7, is another means of bringing light into our homes. A very simple and affordable method is to use lamps (lightbulbs) balanced to resemble the full spectrum of sunlight. We tend to feel more rested, energetic, and optimistic when natural light is a part of our daily regime.

Manipulating Mood with Interior Lighting

Factors that determine the physical and emotional effects of lighting include:

- Size and source of the lighting
- Direction of the lighting
- Color spectrum of the lighting
- Color and texture of the furnishings being lit

For example, a plane or bank of light minimizes form and bulk, reducing the importance of objects and even people. It can fill a person with a sense of space and freedom and can be restful and reassuring. This type of general lighting is effective in open areas of public buildings, offices, hotels, and retail businesses. In homes it is often used in kitchens, bathrooms, workrooms, or hobby rooms, where moderately bright light produces a general feeling of well-being.

Large areas of bright light stimulate a temporary psychological and physical surge of energy, which may cause undue fatigue after periods of prolonged exposure. The mind will become bored or dulled after a barrage of continuous bright lights. If the light becomes too brilliant, it can cause malaise, or a feeling of illness. This is one reason why phototherapy lights for treating SAD should not be installed as general lighting.

Moderate to low levels of indirect lighting, accomplished with dimmer switches on ambient lighting, are sometimes called **mood lighting,** meaning that the area is inviting, cozy, and intimate. This type of lighting is used in restaurants where the clientele come not only for good food but for a relaxed, private, and unhurried conversation. Mood lighting is favored in homes in formal living or dining rooms, master bedrooms, family rooms, media or theater rooms, and upscale kitchens and great rooms and as an alternative in computer rooms and home offices, where low lighting diminishes eyestrain. It

helps establish the perimeter of the room and produces a sense of security. Mood lighting can be accomplished with backlighting (placing lights behind furnishings) and **flickering light** emitted from candles, fireplaces, or electric flame lamps. Flickering light is usually warm in color, casting a healthy glow.

Colored light also has profound effect on the mind and body. Warm white light and soft, warm colored light generally are welcoming and uplifting. However, intensely colored light, such as bright red, orange, and yellow, produces considerable eyestrain. This may lead to an eventual feeling of physical exhaustion as the mind struggles to avoid coping with the intensity.

Cool white light and cool-colored lights (blue, cool green, and violet) produce calm, restful environments but can eventually become unfriendly, cold, or depressing.

Glare

Glare is excessive light that causes irritation or fatigue. These unpleasant effects result from heat buildup as well as too much brightness and can be caused by natural or artificial light. Dark areas surrounding lighted areas cause eyestrain, fatigue, and even depression as peripheral vision constantly has to deal with the dark-bright contrast.

Natural daylighting often requires shading window treatments to reduce glare. Glare from artificial light can be controlled by lowering the wattage, using a **cool-beam**

Figure 5.18 Lighting behind undulating fabric wall art gives drama and evocative mood to the MoriMoto Restaurant in Philadelphia. © *Focus Lighting, NY/ photo copyright J.R. Krauza*

Table 5.2 | Types of Glare

Direct glare is bright light or insufficiently shielded light sources in the field of view. Placement of lighting sources is very important; light in the center of a room can produce direct glare, as can some accent lighting. Direct glare is a problem in offices where the desk faces the window. This may be corrected by turning the desk so that the light is coming from the side rather than the front. (Note that light from behind a seated person will cause shadows on the work surface and will be equally unacceptable.)

Reflecting glare is excessive light that bounces off a shiny surface such as a glass tabletop. Fatigue is augmented when reflecting glare is present.

Veiling glare prevents us from seeing a task clearly. It is caused by light reflecting off a surface, creating a reflection. We see the reflected images of the light source rather than the task at hand. Veiling glare can make seeing extremely difficult and cause eyestrain; it is due to incorrect placement of the lighting source or an inadequate baffle (screening device) of the light fixture.

Table 5.3 | Measuring Electricity and Light

Electricity and light are quantified according to the SI (Système Internationale, or International System of Units). Note the relationships among the various units.

Electricity

Ampere or **amperage.** The unit of electric current, equal to the current produced by 1 volt across a resistance of 1 ohm. A typical residence has a 15-amp circuit fed into it from the main utility line.

Kilowatt-hour. The work done by 1,000 watts in one hour. Electric utility companies measure consumption and bill customers in kilowatt-hours.

Volt or **voltage.** The unit for electric potential, defining the force or pressure of electricity in the power line. Standard household current in the United States is 110 volts, and major appliances require dedicated 220-volt hookups.

Watt or **wattage.** The unit of electric power equal to that produced by 1 ampere across a potential of 1 volt. Standard luminaires in the United States typically accommodate bulbs that consume 60 to 150 watts.

Light

Candela, candle, or **candlepower.** The unit of luminous intensity.

Footcandle or **footlambert.** The amount of light thrown by one candle on a square foot of surface, equal to 1 lumen per square foot. Conventional office lighting may be from 50 to 150 footlambert (fl).

Lumen. The unit of luminous flux, measured against the luminous intensity of one candle. A typical 60-watt lightbulb has a light output of 840 lumens.

Lux. The unit of illumination, equal to 1 lumen per square meter. The illumination of bright sunlight outdoors is 10,000 lux, of a very well-lit office is 500 to 1,000 lux, and of conventional home lighting is 300 to 500 lux.

lamp, or adjusting the direction of the lighting source. Another means of diverting or diffusing glare is through **baffles.** Baffles come in many forms:

- A length of wood placed in front of lights directs the light upward or downward.
- Louvers or grooves on or inside a luminaire or fixture act as baffles.
- A metal or wooden grid diffuses the light and produces more even distribution.
- The lens or glass covering can be textured or coated to diffuse glare.
- Reflectors inside the bulb itself can further control the light and glare.

The most common types of glare are listed in Table 5.2. These are **direct glare, reflecting glare,** and **veiling glare.**

Power Terminology and Units of Measurement

To understand how incandescent and fluorescent lighting is measured, it is necessary to understand basic power terminology and units of measurement.

Incandescent and fluorescent lighting is measured in **footcandles, footlamberts,** and **lumens** (see Table 5.3). These terms allow lighting engineers and designers to create and evaluate lamps for specific purposes. They are a part of the general body of interior design knowledge.

Incandescent lamps, or lightbulbs, typically vary in wattage—15, 25, 60, 75, 100, 120, 150, and 175. In a lumi-

naire that contains two or more lamps, there is often a limitation on the wattage so that the fixture will not be overheated and at risk of catching fire. The most common halogen wattages are 50 and 65. The wattage of fluorescent lamps is 18, 20, 32, 40, 60, or 80; they deliver greater brightness per watt than incandescent lighting, making fluorescent lamps more energy efficient.

Ordinary incandescent lamps (bulbs) last from 750 to 2,500 hours, and **long-life bulbs** (which cost more initially and deliver less light for the electricity used) last from 2,500 to 3,500 hours. Low-voltage lamps use less wattage or electric power and deliver greater control and a wider range of beam spread.

Note that it is not the size of the lamp or the level of wattage that makes an impact in lighting. Lighting becomes most interesting when the size of the beam is controlled to create pools of light or emphasize certain areas or focal points in the interior. This is the advantage of incandescent lighting over fluorescent lighting.

Luminaires, or Lighting Fixtures

Luminaires, or **lighting fixtures,** fall into two broad categories: **architectural or structural lighting** and **nonarchitectural lighting,** or **portable luminaires.** Architectural or structural luminaires are permanently installed and planned for in the lighting or wiring plan. They include ceiling and wall fixtures that are installed to permanent wiring.

Many architectural luminaires are simple and inconspicuous. They emphasize what they light, not the luminaire. Other luminaires are quite decorative and/or dramatic and can make up an important part of the design scheme.

Portable luminaires (nonarchitectural lighting) are those that plug in; they (1) hang on the wall or from a ceiling hook or (2) are placed on a table or on the floor. Decorative luminaires are discussed in Chapter 14, "Art and Accessories."

Many styles, colors or finishes, and types of glass in luminaires are on the market today. The appeal of decorative luminaires is found in styles for every interior design. Be aware that good, poor, and mediocre design and quality exist; thus the power of discrimination discussed in Chapter 3 becomes paramount when selecting luminaires.

Architectural Lighting

The categories of architectural lighting include **luminous panels, built-in indirect lighting, recessed** and **adjustable fixtures,** and **surface-mounted** and **suspended fixtures.**

Luminous Panels

Luminous panels are strips or lines of lights, usually fluorescent, over which glass or plastic translucent panels are placed. The translucent panel glows, producing a soft white or colored light, according to the texture and color of the glass or plastic. It can also cause glare in some situations. Luminous ceiling panels, quite common in kitchens, are referred to as **luminous ceilings.**

Built-In Indirect Lighting

Refer to Table 5.4.

Fixed and Adjustable Luminaires

This category (see Table 5.5) includes various luminaires that are "fixed" or set into the ceiling, called **recessed**

luminaires, and those that are adjustable. **Adjustable luminaires** can be recessed or surface mounted.

Surface-Mounted and Suspended Luminaires These luminaires are clearly visible, perhaps even obvious to the eye. Translucent covers are called **diffusers** and serve to soften the light. Clear or tinted glass covers may require a decorative lamp.

Suspended fixtures such as **chandeliers** or **dropped-pendant luminaires** may be dropped only a few inches from the ceiling (over a dining or conference table) or may be suspended several feet (in an open area such as a hotel atrium or an entrance). Sizes vary dramatically from about 6 inches to several feet in diameter. The size and placement are dependent upon the scale of the interior, the use, the scale of the luminaire, and the ceiling height, as well as the scale and placement of the furniture. In a dining area, the chandelier should be approximately 30 inches above the table. Suspended lamps, often used in reading corners, should drop to about 40 inches from the floor or 20 inches above the seat level.

Lighting Economy

The upward surge of electricity rates, predicted to continue, is the major factor in economizing with light. Lighting consumes less electricity than heat-producing appliances such as dryers, water heaters, dishwashers, ovens, and ranges. However, lighting does consume more power than smaller appliances. Ways that lighting can be more effectively and economically used are listed in Table 5.6.

Lighting for the Future

The direction and future for residential lighting is multi-faceted. The buzzwords will be convenience, energy efficiency, and specialized and flexible lighting effects. Consider these trends:

- Increased energy efficiency via electronic sensors that can turn selected lights on and off according to the level of natural light, and sensing devices that operate lighting in response to radiated heat caused by human presence and movement
- Devices such as timers that switch lights on and off to discourage burglary when the home is unoccupied
- Control systems, including wall-mounted, programmable units for total home or area control
- Handheld devices that operate on infrared frequencies to send instructions to wall receivers
- Greater flexibility in lighting effects, such as more combination of types of lighting and greater use of dimmer switches to accommodate different tasks, as

Table 5.4 | Indirect Lighting

Indirect lighting is placing a light behind a built-in or portable feature. Types of indirect lighting placed behind deflectors include the following.

Cornice Lighting

A light behind a board mounted into the ceiling washes light down onto the wall.

Valance Lighting

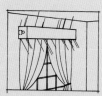

A light used over the top of windows washes both the ceiling and the window treatment.

Bracket Lighting
(Up and Down)

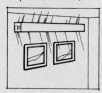

Valance lighting mounted lower on the wall washes the upper (and perhaps lower) wall with light.

Bracket Lighting
(Up Only)

A light placed just below the ceiling has the board or deflector beneath it.

Soffit Lighting
(In a Kitchen)

A light built into the soffit shines downward from the top of the cabinet overhead.

Soffit Lighting
(In a Bath)

Soffit lighting provides even illumination for personal grooming.

Base or Toe-Mold Lighting

A strip of light is placed against the floor where a deflector directs the light upward or perhaps downward, giving the effect of theatrical usher lights.

Toe-Kick or Riser Lighting

Lighting is placed under the toe-kick area of cabinets or stairs. This can also take the form of usher lights.

well as corresponding flexibility in levels of mood lighting within the same area
- Increased use of artistic lighting in residential design, including more cold-cathode lighting and motivational lighting (see "Nonresidential Considerations")
- Increased use of the services of **lighting designers,** who create maximum effectiveness for lighting, both practical and aesthetic

The *Interiors* website lists lighting organizations and sources of information for the latest developments in lighting.

Nonresidential Considerations

Many of the topics discussed in this chapter are applicable to nonresidential situations as well. Here we also discuss other considerations that apply specifically to nonresidential interiors.

Types of Nonresidential Lighting

Natural Daylighting

In nonresidential settings such as offices, natural daylight is often desired by employees—sometimes even considered a luxury. However, problems exist with **natural daylighting** (as discussed under "Glare," earlier in this chapter). Temperature control is another major consideration linked to daylighting. Excessive heat and cold can be the result of poor insulation or large expanses of glass. Natural daylight almost always needs to be supplemented with artificial light; the lighting systems need careful control to maintain a healthy balance of light.

HID Lighting

HID, or high-intensity discharge, lighting is used for bright interior and exterior lighting. HID lamps establish an arc between two very close electrodes set in opposite ends of small, sealed, translucent or transparent glass

Table 5.5 | Fixed and Adjustable Lighting

Recessed Downlights

Canisters set into the ceiling cast pools of light downward.

Surface-Mounted Downlights

Ceiling-mounted canisters that hang down are used in place of recessed downlights where there is insufficient ceiling clearance, or they are added later in a remodeling situation.

Eyeball Lighting

Fixtures that project an adjustable lamp from the ceiling and throw pools of light onto the wall are eyeball spotlights. A series of these can form wall washers.

Strip Lighting

Strip or theatrical lighting is often used for personal grooming areas.

Adjustable Track Lighting

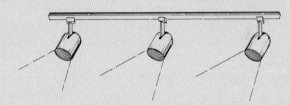

Flexible ceiling-mounted fixtures hold spotlights or floodlights mounted anywhere and at any position on a fixed track. (Track luminaires come in various sizes, shapes, colors, and finishes. They are ideal for accent lighting and wall-wash lighting.)

Table 5.6 | Suggestions for Lighting Economy

- Turn out lights when not in use.
- Put light only where it is needed, keeping in mind that high contrast (a pool of light surrounded by dark) can cause fatigue and even distress.
- Use dimmer switches to lower wattage.
- Use photoelectric cells or timers to turn outdoor lights on and off automatically.
- Open window treatments to allow daylight in.
- Use light-colored surfaces to reflect and thereby increase light, and avoid textures that absorb light.
- Use only some of the lights in an interior (use one, rather than two, table lamps).
- Illuminate local tasks with portable luminaires with fewer lamps or lower wattage rather than general overhead lighting.
- Use one higher-wattage bulb rather than multiple lower-wattage bulbs. For example, one 100-watt bulb uses less energy than two 60-watt bulbs.
- Install extra light switches so that at each doorway the light can be turned off without inconvenience.
- Use low-voltage or lower-wattage lamps.

- Use new materials (such as acrylic) that conduct and reflect light but use a fraction of the electricity required for traditional incandescent lighting.
- Use energy-saving fluorescent lighting in place of incandescent lighting where aesthetically practical. Fluorescent lighting uses only one-fifth to one-third as much electricity as incandescent lighting with comparable lumen ratings. Warm white deluxe fluorescent lamps can replace incandescent lighting in the home.
- Replace incandescent lamps with CF lamps screwed in their place, using only about 18 watts in place of a 75-watt incandescent lamp. These fluorescent lamps, when properly installed and ventilated, last as long as ten average incandescent lamps. There is no humming of the ballast or interference with radio or television reception.
- Line new or retrofitted older light fixtures with reflective material, which dramatically reduces the number of lamps required and the amount of electricity used to produce the same number of lumens.
- Use motion sensors to turn lights on when the room is occupied and off when unoccupied.

tubes. The electric arc generates heat and pressure high enough to vaporize the atoms of various metallic elements inside the lamp, causing the atoms to emit large amounts of visible-range electromagnetic energy.

HID lamps are used to "uplight" exteriors of large buildings and are being used more often in interiors of nonresidential buildings. They produce a greater quantity of light using less energy than an incandescent lamp. The problems being overcome in HID lighting are the noise or hum of the arc or ballast and the length of time to restart the lamp after a power failure.

Cold-Cathode Lighting

Cold-cathode lighting, or **neon lighting,** uses different gases or vapors to produce colors. Neon lighting has been an important part of exterior lighting for advertising and storefronts, but it is being increasingly used in interiors such as restaurants and retail businesses to emphasize a color scheme and add drama and excitement. Lighting designers often create unique neon lighting for nonresidential interiors.

Motivational Lighting

The behavior of people can be altered or directed with **motivational** or **illusion lighting.** This means that people will be motivated to sit, walk, or face a particular direction because of the impressions given them by special lighting (particularly the manipulation of bright versus dark areas) and finishes. Motivational lighting can create environments where the quality, intensity, and angle of light cause the illusory appearance or disappearance of objects, walls, ceilings, and even entire rooms. Lighting designers are often utilized by interior designers to accomplish special effects in an interior. The manipulation of areas of intense brightness or darkness can affect both the mind and body, making us believe that something exists that really is not there (a wall, for example) or that something is not as close as it actually is. In addition to making us behave in a predicted manner, this can make spaces fit the needs of the people in the environment.

Figure 5.19 (A) Table lamps and wall sconces are an appropriate traditional approach to lighting. (B) The combination of lighting types—including a skylight for natural light—is typical of future directions in lighting. *(A) Jessie Walker Associates; (B) Grey Crawford/Beateworks.com*

Safety Lighting

Safety lighting is required in public spaces where there are egress signs, such as exit signs. Other safety lighting mandated by building codes includes aisle or egress lighting and lighting for stairs and landings. (New developments in egress lighting are discussed in "Nonresidential Lighting for the Future.")

Lighting Economy in Nonresidential Interiors

In nonresidential interiors, lighting is a major monthly expense, and because of the tremendous amount of electricity used, nonresidential buildings are limited by law to the amount of electricity consumed per square foot. These limitations are roughly one-tenth of what they were before the energy crunch of the 1970s. The cost and the consumption limits of lighting do, therefore, constitute a legitimate reason for controlling lighting use while maintaining effectiveness.

In addition to the suggestions presented in Table 5.6, there are other ways to control energy consumption and costs in nonresidential lighting. One is the addition of central programmable monitoring systems that will automatically turn lights off and on in various parts of a building when required. Another is the increased usage of sensing devices (see "Nonresidential Lighting for the Future") that monitor light usage, turning it on and off according to time, daylight levels, or whether people are moving in the room.

Fluorescent luminaires in the ceiling can be retrofitted with reflective materials that deliver the same lumens with half the number of lamps. For example, a luminaire that ordinarily contains four 60-watt fluorescent lamps will produce the same light with only two 60-watt lamps after retrofitting. In this way, energy consumption can be cut in half, greatly reducing the cost of electricity.

Electric costs can also be reduced by retrofitting incandescent luminaires with adaptable compact fluorescent (CF) lighting that delivers the same lumens or brightness with far fewer watts. These lamp bulbs connect to ballasts fitted into adapters that screw into incandescent fixtures, cutting costs immediately by up to 80 percent and producing a longer life span. For example, PL-type fluorescent lamps that use 7 or 9 watts can replace 150-watt incandescent lighting. The PL-type lamp is a small, low-wattage fluorescent twin tube with a prong base that fits into the adapter containing a ballast.

New laws are being passed in many states that limit the amount of electricity a building can consume. This, in turn, limits the number, placement, and usage of lights in nonresidential interiors. Some feel that this will limit the creativity of lighting designers. However, we are already seeing advances in economical lighting. Look for new products and innovative ways lighting can be functional, beautiful—even dazzling—and still use less electricity.

Nonresidential Lighting for the Future

- Motivational and illusion lighting will play key roles in nonresidential design in the future in public spaces such as banks, offices, medical facilities, museums, theaters, and all types of staged events. The laser show is a standard attraction in night clubs and planetariums and is now making its way into homes as well.
- **LEDs (light-emitting diodes)** are solid-state lamps without filaments whose life expectancy projections range from 700,000 to over 5 million hours (80 to 570 years). LEDs have application in emergency exits or in situations where lights burn out or are shaken loose due to vibration (such as in airports, in railway stations, in industrial plants, and over doorways). Egress exit signs can also be made of etched acrylic plates that eliminate the necessity of breakable glass. LED nightlights are now used in homes, as well.
- Other developments will continue to become important, such as sensing devices and central computerized monitoring systems.
- Reduced office glare can be accomplished by improved light dispersion at the work surface where the user can control the levels of illumination. Tilting fixtures are available to adjust the direction of light and control glare at workstations.
- Lower maintenance through retrofitted longer-life lamp bulbs and fluorescent lamps is another trend.
- Fluorescent luminaire fixtures are now available that screw into existing fixtures, as previously discussed.
- Remote-control devices are available that send instructions for reprogramming back to a central unit or that control lights from a remote location. Dimming controls can likewise be computer-controlled.
- New products such as oak-wrapped or molding-encased strips for fluorescent ceiling boxes and unbreakable diffuser lenses for luminous ceilings continue to augment aesthetics. New designs are continually emerging in the lighting-as-art field and as decorative luminaire fixtures. Lighting design is a viable field for a design professional because of the continual demand for new products and designs in the marketplace.

Technology

Technology is now so much a part of our lives at home and in public that the issue is not whether or not to incorporate the latest technological devices but which ones to select or replace and how to accommodate them in the home and workplace. Whereas wiring for electrical, phone, and coaxial cable is still the means whereby much of the technology is run in the home and workplace, the direction for the future will be more digitized appliances and technological devices that can be operated via remote control, from a cellular telephone or other hand-held device. The same portable computers and electronics can be

(A)

(B)

Figure 5.20 (A) Beyond™ *iCEBOX* FlipScreen/*Courtesy Salton Inc.* (B) Beyond™ waterproof wireless keyboard/*Courtesy Salton Inc.*

operated from home, from the office, from the car, and from any remote location where a power source can recharge the battery when needed.

Whereas technological communications are a given in the workplace, a major trend in new-home construction and upgrading existing homes is to make technology more livable. Developments such as wall-mounted larger flat-screen televisions allow technology to be smoother and less imposing. Fitting computers, televisions, DVD players, and stereo equipment into the home without overpowering it continues to be an important task in interior design. Creative solutions continue to evolve, such as creating a nook for a child's computer station off the family room or kitchen to satisfy a parent's desire for monitoring homework progress and Internet access. Home offices also are becoming more functional and include more shelving and custom cabinetry, with the wiring in place for power, phone, and cable.

According to the National Association of Home Builders (NAHB), one survey found that nearly three-fourths of American adults know about home automation systems and a majority are interested in owning products that use technology to manage a wide range of

tasks. For further information on technology issues from the NAHB, lighting and technology associations, and product manufacturers, go to the *Interiors* website.

Information-Age Home Automation Systems

There are many connection options of home automation systems, including the programmable control of lighting, appliances, computer networks, television and tape or digital players, digital satellite connections, and television monitoring of exterior door and window security and baby's room. Home automation systems can augment energy savings by electronically turning off appliances and lighting and adjusting thermostats when no one is at home and at night. The system can even shop for the best electrical rates and can connect to other companies, returning unused electricity generated from the building's own solar collectors. The system can also turn off specified appliances during times when rates are highest. A single control center with a television screen is where the monitoring and programming takes place. In addition, the control center can accept telephone messages, via cellular phone command, for example, so that appliances, heating and cooling systems, and even the hot tub can be programmed to turn on just before the homeowner arrives.

Another growth area of technology is the increased demand for multimedia in the home. Computers require electrical outlets and phone jacks, and cable television demands that the cable be prewired to areas where televisions will be placed. With the explosion of digital and wireless electronic equipment, virtually any room in the home can be a mini-office or part of the entertainment scene.

Home automation systems are available from a number of manufacturers whose Web addresses are listed at the *Interiors* website, Chapter 5, under "Home Automation Systems."

Information-Age Wiring and Installation

For both home automation and multimedia, specialized **structured wiring** is necessary. Rather than conventional wiring, Category 5 unshielded twisted-pair cable is faster and less prone to interference for telephone and computer networking than standard telephone wire. This allows for very high-speed Internet connections and advanced energy management via energy consumption control and energy charges. RG-6 quad-shielded coaxial cable can deliver clear signals from digital satellite or high-definition television transmitters. Manufacturer-certified installers and some electricians are qualified to install Category 5 and RG-6 cable structured wiring for home automation systems. Some proprietary or well-known brand-name home automation systems can be installed only by a manufacturer-certified installer.

Cost estimates for information-age wiring and installation are lower when the wiring is installed during construction ($600 to $2,000) than when it is part of retrofitting an existing home ($1,000 to $3,000). Most complete home automation systems on the market run about $3,500 and up. Wireless digital connections are also an option on the horizon, and they will cost approximately $100 to $150 per connected device.

Home Automation for Existing Houses

Although the ideal time for upgrading wiring is in the building process, discussed above, there are several options for retrofitting home automation in existing structures. These include the power-line carrier (PLC) system, infrared (IR), radio frequency (RF), and digital subscriber lines (DSLs)—telephone line networking.

Of the **power-line carrier (PLC) systems,** the most well-known uses X-10, a proprietary communications product that transmits coded communications signals over the existing AC wires that power the house. Many companies make X-10–compliant products. This means that nearly any appliance that uses AC power can be turned on or off remotely by using external plug-in modules or modules that fit inside the electrical box. Interface cards that fit into the computer will work with control software for PLC systems. Even higher data rates than X-10 are available in products that use a technique called

Figure 5.21 Beyond™ Home Hub2/*Courtesy Salton Inc.*

Figure 5.22 Older, existing homes can be retrofitted for today's technology. © *Grey Crawford/Beateworks.com*

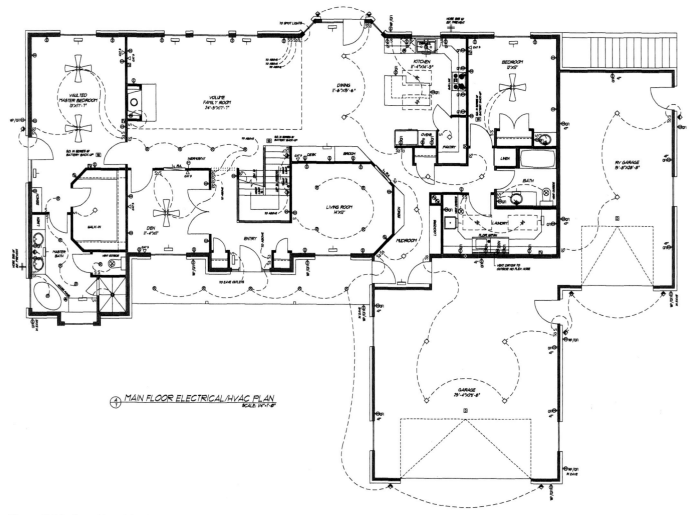

Figure 5.23 A residential wiring plan.

a *spread spectrum.* These conform to the consumer electronics bus [CEBus] standard of the Electronics Industries Association. Two companies that manufacture them are Intellon and Echelon.

Infrared (IR) is a wireless method for short-distance operation of entertainment equipment or connecting computer to printer via a remote-control device. However, the signals cannot go through walls or around corners.

Radio frequency (RF) transmission, familiar to us as cordless telephones, will become a standard that allows users a range of wireless computers, phones, and other devices to network with each other in multiple locations.

Digital subscriber lines (DSLs) give new life to copper telephone wires by providing increased speed of Internet access and allowing Internet and telephone use on the same telephone line at the same time.

Of these choices, RF-based networking ranks just ahead of phone-line networking as a first choice in the "no-new-wires" data networking solutions. Power-line

networking is also a viable solution in multiple personal computer (PC) households.

Electrical Raceways

An alternative installation technique that has been used for years in commercial buildings and is now available for residential applications is **electrical raceways.** These encased PVC baseboard wiring covers come in white and wood laminate to blend into decor. They can be mounted on any kind of surface and consist of a two-compartment design that separates electrical from low-voltage phone, data, and coaxial cables. An advantage of electrical raceways is that device plates can be installed anywhere along the raceway for power receptacles, phone jacks, and cable outlets. Installation consists of mounting the base, running the wires, and snapping on the cover. Raceways can be installed in new construction and in retrofits and have the further advantage of being accessible for future changes without the need to tear into walls. The disadvantage is that some homeowners may find the

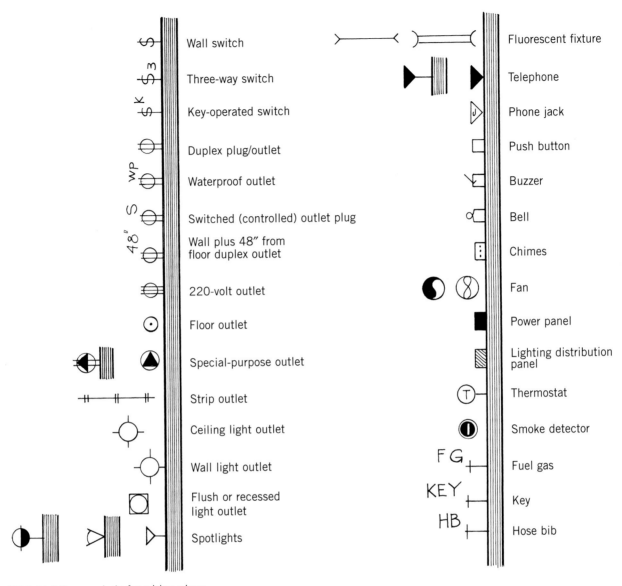

Figure 5.24 Lighting symbols for wiring plans.

raceways visually unacceptable. The retail cost is approximately $8 per linear foot. For more information, see the addresses at the *Interiors* website.

Wiring Plans

The planning of lighting systems requires training, experience, and thinking through what lighting must accomplish in an interior. Interior designers are often actively involved in this process. A **wiring** or **lighting plan** is a part of the working drawings. The wiring plan indicates where outlets, switches, and wall and ceiling light fixtures will be located.

Switches and Outlets

Light switches can be placed in one, two, or even three locations. Switches should easily be accessible at the door-

way on the open side so that lights can be turned on at the doorway. Careful thought should be given to the type and placement of switches, according to the needs of the users. If, for example, the user is an aged or infirm person, then a "rocker switch" may be easier to operate than a standard flip switch.

Dimmer switches increase or decrease the level of illumination or brightness. Dimmers make it possible to create levels of interest and different moods in the interior. **Automatic sensor dimmers** are used to turn on interior lights automatically to supplement natural daylight to a proportionate, preprogrammed level.

Switched outlets are plugs that are activated by switches. This allows for lamps, lighting as art, or decorative lights (such as holiday decorations) to be turned on at the switch—the light is plugged in and turned on at the source but controlled at the switch. Switched outlets contribute convenience and safety to the interior and its occupants. If, for example, a portable table luminaire is the only or desired source of light in the room, it can be turned on at the door. This will eliminate the necessity of first turning on general lighting to reach the portable light and then returning to turn off the general lighting. It also reduces the danger of walking across a dark room. In addition, the inconvenience of fumbling over holiday packages, decorations, or the tree to reach Christmas lights—or walking outside to turn on exterior lights—can be removed through switched outlets.

According to state and local building codes, outlets must be located from 6 to 12 feet along the wall for portable luminaires (floor, table, and wall lamps). The frequent placement of outlets minimizes the need for extension cords and precludes plugging too many lights or appliances into one outlet. Therefore, the building code helps ensure safety against tripping and falling and against fire from overloading a circuit and outlet. Stretching cords tight can also increase danger of damage, loose connections, and possibly tenuous circumstances where the luminaire is placed too close to the edge of a surface and could easily fall off, break, and perhaps even burst into flames.

Convenience is another major reason for including frequent outlets: It is easy to place the luminaire, appliance, or piece of equipment where it is needed. Vertical placement is an important part of planning outlets and switches for the sake of convenience. For example, a table-height outlet may be desirable for units such as entertainment components or computers. Appliances for kitchens, workrooms, or hobby areas need outlets above counter height.

Outlets should have a **grounding receiver** (three-prong plug outlet) as standard in all areas for high-electric-use lights, appliances, and components. **Multiple-outlet strips**—casings with spaced outlets that are prewired or portable—are useful in home workbenches, home offices, and kitchens.

The exact placement of switches and outlets can be determined when the building has been framed. It is common for the client and/or interior designer to meet the electrician at the site and mark the exact location of fixtures, outlets, and switches. There may be a need to adjust placement because of the heat ducts. Before mechanical systems are installed, it is wise to plan where the luminaires, outlets, and switches will be needed.

Nonresidential Wiring

The planning of lighting systems in nonresidential complexes and high-rise buildings entails technical studies of lighting needs, electrical code requirements, and restrictions.

Nonresidential lighting plans constitute a **network of lighting fixtures** that are controlled from a central loca-

tion or are automated. The lighting designer need not visit the site to determine exact location, since nonresidential lighting placement is firmly established by the architectural plans. However, special needs and considerations can be met.

Prewired office systems that contain outlets for business equipment and lighting are connected to architectural wiring in the wall, ceiling, or floor. Where additional electric plugs are required, multiple outlet strips are commonly installed after the building is completed.

Residential Built-In Systems

- **Fire alert systems** are single or interconnected networks of **smoke detectors** and heat-sensing devices that alert the occupants of a potential fire hazard. They may emit a shrill whistle or a long or interrupted buzz or beep that will indicate danger. They may be wired or battery operated.
- **Security systems** guard against unlawful entry. They are sensing devices that take many forms. When activated, they may turn on lights, set off alarms, or automatically notify security guards. Security systems can become quite elaborate, even to the point of being connected with the local police dispatcher. Security systems vary dramatically in price and options.

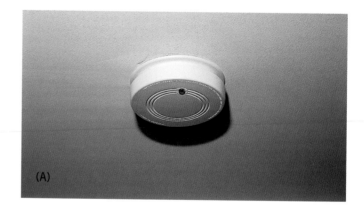

(A)

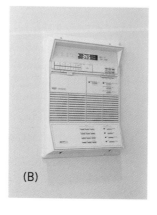

(B)

Figure 5.25 Typical residential electronic devices include (A) a smoke detector and (B) an intercom. *(A) photo © Judy Brody; (B) photo © Sarah Hanson*

- **Communication systems** in the home are an effective means of communicating from one area to another without raising the voice. The **intercom**-system wiring should be installed when the home is being built, although radiolike units can be purchased and installed at a later date. The intercom can also pipe music to various rooms, and it enables parents to listen to children in other parts of the house.

Nonresidential Communication and Safety Systems

- **Intercom systems** allow occupants to talk through wall-mounted or desk units with persons in other areas of the building. In nonresidential installations, the intercom can become rather sophisticated, including loudspeakers and two-way response without pushing buttons. Telephones also can form intercom systems. The intercom may also carry taped or radio music.
- **Computer networks** link personal computers together or connect computer terminals (a keyboard and monitor, or screen) with a mainframe computer (large computer processing unit). This allows workers to call up information and interface (compare or put together) information for projects and business dealings. Computer systems that network outside the immediate building are often linked by telephone systems.
- **Telephone systems** connect workstations, sometimes with a central operator, and allow calls to be transferred, put on hold, and computer dialed, among other options. In some offices telephones can also access information from a computer.
- **Fire alert systems** are mandatory in all nonresidential design. In large complexes, the sensing devices are connected to a central monitor. Sprinkling systems are also required to help fight fires.
- **Security systems** are routinely installed in nonresidential interiors, particularly retail and high-security areas.

Chapter 6 | Space Planning Considerations

Prioritizing Needs and
Wants 128

Considerations for Specific
Areas 136

Space Planning and the
Principles and Elements
of Design 160

Nonresidential
Considerations 164

Christine Oliver, architect/photo © Brian Vanden Brink

Prioritizing Needs and Wants

In the space planning process, many things need to be considered before the floor plans are drawn and construction (or demolition and reconstruction) begins. It is far better to make changes on paper than to rip out and reconstruct a space that should have been better planned in the first place. As part of the design process discussed in Chapter 1, research and programming take place by asking questions. This chapter will address and further explore those questions and present considerations and suggestions for making wise and carefully thought out decisions.

Basic human needs include food, shelter, and clothing. All homes provide shelter, a place to prepare and eat food, and space to store and change clothing. Other human needs are to feel safe and accepted through relationships of trust and to rest and restore physical and emotional health. There are also individual needs: to be productive and creative, to successfully accomplish tasks, and, as a result, to feel worthwhile. Residential interiors that meet these needs offer comfortable spaces for interacting socially with others, quiet places in which to rest and be alone in order to rejuvenate, and functional areas for work or performance of tasks. In nonresidential settings, the needs vary according to the function of the space, but they often parallel those listed here. **Wants** comprise a large category of luxuries. It is human nature to want to improve one's surroundings and to upgrade to nicer, more convenient and beautiful spaces and furnishings. The justification is perceived to be an enhanced quality of life. Yet every want or indulgence should be weighed against the need it will fulfill and then be compared to the cost it will require—in time, effort and money—and the long-term usefulness of that item. The result is common sense, meaning the planning of space that meets both needs and wants in a reasonable way.

Function First

Functional analysis is perhaps the most important of the space planning criteria. Function means the intended use of the space; it can be graphically illustrated as zones, as seen in Figure 6.1. In nonresidential interiors, the zones vary dramatically according to the intended use—from health care to retail, from hospitality to office planning. (Suggestions for nonresidential areas are found at the end of this chapter.) However, in the home, there are typically four zones. These zones may be planned in one area each in a floor plan, as seen in the simplicity of Figure 6.1, or they may be planned in separate areas as needs dictate.

- **Work zones** include the kitchen, the laundry, and other task areas such as sewing, tool or repair, and craft or hobby areas, as well as an area or office for tak-

ing care of household organization, bill paying, and family scheduling. If a business is conducted at home, the work zone might include a professionally equipped home office or, in the case of a "cottage industry," a place for the manufacture and storage of products, perhaps with a separate entrance, if zoning laws permit. The need for employment work space may dictate two or more work zones, as separate areas are often required in order to maintain professionalism.

- **Social zones** include entryways; formal living and dining spaces; and informal family rooms and dining spaces, great rooms, multipurpose or recreation areas,

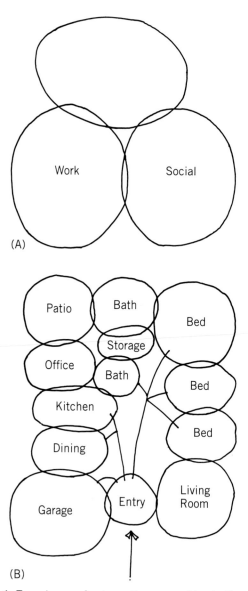

Figure 6.1 Two phases of schematics or graphics in the evolution of the floor plan. (A) The general zones—private, work, and social. (B) Divisions within these zones for specific rooms and their relationship to one another.

media or home theater rooms; as well as solariums or outdoor living spaces. Hallways may be part of the social zones.

- **Private zones** are those allotted for private living: the bedrooms, bathrooms, and private sitting or retreat areas.
- **Zone within zone** may be a feasible solution for specific tasks. For example, a work zone involving a computer may be placed in a social zone (living, dining, or family room) because space is available there; this arrangement is convenient and doesn't take the user away from the center of family activity. Or a work zone may be placed within a private zone. A computer station, for instance, could occupy a corner of a bedroom or a private retreat area.

Interrelating Functions

At this point, a list or "bubble" of the major zones and where they might be duplicated could be explored. The next task is to determine how many rooms and what specific functions these zones will contain and how they will interrelate (Figure 6.2a and 6.2b). Typical is the placement of the formal living zone next to the formal dining area, the kitchen next to the service (laundry, garage, or outside-entry) areas, and the bedrooms next to the bathrooms. Include in the list what areas or functions the user wishes to interrelate. There is great latitude for customization in new construction. For example, some clients may request a home office in a private, quiet area of the home, while others may want it near the front door or in or near the kitchen. Some prefer the family room open to the kitchen and informal dining (a combination known as the great room), while others want the informal social zone separated from the kitchen. When functions interrelate, or flow smoothly from one zone to another, and when the design program is well executed, the result is quality interior design.

Brainstorming

Once the basic zones are established, brainstorming exactly what should occupy those zones is next. Brainstorming is a useful tool for putting down on paper a list of everything that is needed or wanted in each zone. Specifics are listed, from the size of the bathtub to the number of places for shoes and sweaters, how many people will occupy the entry or the outdoor living space, and where each family member will go for solitude. In nonresidential brainstorming sessions, the zoning ideas will center around work productivity, ease of communication, and which functions interrelate. These are also considerations in home planning.

One important rule of a brainstorming session, no matter how many prospective users participate, is that

Figure 6.2 Work zones in a single kitchen. (A) Food preparation and informal dining. (B) Cookbook storage and meal planning. *Both © Mark Darley/Esto*

every idea be recorded for further consideration and no one be allowed to say anything negative about anyone else's idea, no matter how absurd it may appear. Rather, the rule is to write down every idea, look for the needs and wants that it may fulfill, and allow it to spawn even more creativity. After brainstorming, which can take place in one or several sessions or can be a posted list to which ideas can be added, let some time pass for the ideas to be considered by each work team or family member. Then begin the process of culling out or discarding the ideas that, after careful thought, are not desirable and building on the ones that are feasible and justifiable.

New Construction versus Remodeling

Deciding wisely whether to build a new home or remodel an existing one requires careful thought. Construction and remodeling both demand a commitment of time, money, and effort. Consider the following advantages and disadvantages of each option.

New Construction

Building a home from the ground up requires architect- or engineered-approved blueprints drawn in accordance with local zoning laws and any restrictive covenants for the area or development, a building permit approved by the municipality, someone to oversee the construction, and building inspectors to ensure that the work is sound and safe and meets the local laws known as building codes.

The advantages of new construction are these:

- The location and orientation of the home on the site can be custom selected.
- There is satisfaction in designing and building a unique, personal space that has never before been occupied.
- The plan can be completely customized as to number, placement, and shape of rooms, site orientation, exterior style, and window and door openings.
- New construction can incorporate the newest developments in building materials, technology, wiring, heating and cooling and communication systems, plumbing and other fixtures, and finish materials.

Figure 6.3 Interrelated functions of social zone and reading/retreat private zone are seen in this library–family room. *John Martin Architect/photo © Brian Vanden Brink*

- New materials require less upkeep because of their newness. Wisely chosen, they can be relatively maintenance free and aesthetically pleasing for many years to come.
- The space is unoccupied during construction. There is no need to live with or work in the mess.
  The disadvantages of new construction include:
- Costs for new construction are almost always higher than the costs of buying existing structures. Both material and labor costs have risen sharply in the past decade.
- The time frame typically extends longer in reality than in the estimate. This can cause frustration and problems with moving or current occupancy.
- Travel to and from the site is time consuming.

Figure 6.4 This newly constructed master bedroom contains luxury features, including a king-size bed, upholstered seating, fireplace, television, study area, and built-in storage. *Fentel Housing Corporation/photo © Melabee M. Miller*

- The need to oversee the construction, even with a general contractor, is real. The owner should be a part of the process to determine if the interim results are satisfactory.

Remodeling

Remodeling is a process that has a wide scope. A remodel can be as small as adding a closet or building in a water fountain or as large as doubling the size of the building or home through a major addition. Some remodeling requires building permits, contracts with those who will perform all or parts of the work, and major time and expense. Other remodeling projects can be accomplished in a short time by the owner or subcontractors.

Remodeling often entails demolition and reconstruction, again, as a large or small project. Remodeling assumes that parts of the building or home are satisfactory but others need rework to make them more functional.

Figure 6.5 New construction allows for flexibility in planning and customizing. *© Chip Henderson Photography*

However, sometimes a building or home will be completely gutted, interior walls realigned, and new electrical, plumbing, and HVAC systems installed.

The advantages of remodeling are:

- Relocation can be avoided. This is a major reason why most people remodel. Business location or residential neighborhood, friends, schools, and proximity to shopping and services may be so advantageous that there is no desire to uproot and move.
- Changes in an existing plan can take place one at a time, over a long period of time, with much less pressure to accomplish than new construction. There is time to live with the idea, plan it out carefully, execute it in a way that suits the owner or occupant, and control the size or scale of the project.
- Remodels can be accomplished in stages or in parts of the structure and by various individuals or teams. A general contractor or remodeler may do the work, or the owner may hire professionals, such as a framer, plumber, electrician, drywall installer, or painter, or may elect a do-it-yourself approach.
- The cost may be less than that of new construction, depending on the extent of the remodel, who does the work, and how it is accomplished.
- The area to be remodeled may not dramatically affect living or working in the space.
- The great features of a building or home can be kept while upgrading. This often produces a very satisfying result. There is no need to give up what works or what you love about the space; just improve it to work out the little things that may be causing current frustration or not meeting a need.
- Older homes, with their vintage charms and historical character, often need upgrading of the structure or of electrical, plumbing, or HVAC systems. They may also have too many small rooms for today's lifestyles, or the owner may desire to remove previous remodeling to restore the home or building to a prior or original floor plan. Historic buildings and homes are often adapted to new uses; an old warehouse can become new offices, an old home can become a boutique, or a barn can become a home through the process of remodeling.

The disadvantages of remodeling are as follows:

- Living with the mess is an emotional and physical strain. It may cause people to be irritable and put strain on relationships. Moving out during a remodel is often advisable, depending on the extent and location of the remodel. This also requires effort, is expensive and time consuming, and is difficult for everyone involved.
- The presence of subcontractors in the work or living space impinges on privacy and disrupts routines.
- Removing walls sometimes yields a surprise. It's not uncommon, especially in older buildings, to discover unexpected conditions, such as a hidden fireplace or chimney flue, rotted floorboards or ceiling joists, or a complete change in building methods. These will require more time and money to correct and at times may completely alter the master plan; what you thought you could do may not be possible after all.
- Whether or not there are unhappy surprises, making decisions and discussing the project as it progresses is necessary, takes time, and can be stressful.

In both the new construction and remodeling processes, a few rules apply:

- Each is a difficult process; it is physically, mentally, and emotionally exhausting to build or remodel. Many decisions must be made, and disagreement is common. Cooperation and negotiating will help save sanity and preserve relationships.
- Not everything runs smoothly. Problems arise in delivery, materials, interpretation, and workmanship. These frustrations can cause bad feelings and real frustration. Murphy's law applies: If anything can go wrong, it will.
- Most projects take longer than anticipated—especially if the project is a DIY (do it yourself), which typically takes two to three times what was originally estimated.
- Costs often go up as decisions are made to upgrade to a better product or expand the plan in some way. Ideally this should not happen if thorough research has been done in advance and commitments to specific products have been made. However, there are many variables, particularly in remodeling. When the demolition portion of the remodel begins, the structure or new perspective of the space will often change the master plan a little and may require extra structural support, upgraded wiring, or repair of other defects. Sometimes you don't know exactly what you're working with until the walls come down.

Figure 6.6 Older homes may offer charm but require upgrading of systems as well as refurbishing. © *Phyllis Picardi/Stock Boston*

- People doing the work may not always use the techniques you would choose. Also, if they have other projects going on at the same time and therefore must divide their time, they may not come to your job consistently. Waiting for subcontractors is a common frustration.
- The necessity of having building inspectors often costs additional time, effort, and money. They typically find more things to be fixed with each inspection and will not issue an occupancy permit until all their demands are satisfied.

Economic Considerations

Economy is an important consideration in planning space. In most cases, new construction will have a financial limit (a maximum amount that can be spent) imposed by the client or by the lending institution. Therefore, the architect, designer, and builder, as well as the client or homeowner, need to make careful and wise decisions concerning the amount of space. This is because the actual square footage is proportional to the cost of the building or home. Total price is estimated on a cost per square foot. The cost per square foot will vary according to the location, the building materials used, the amount of skilled labor involved, and the number of luxury items incorporated.

A total building cost of $100 per square foot (excluding the building lot or property costs) can be calculated as follows:

1. An 800-square-foot building would cost approximately $80,000.
2. A 1,200-square-foot building would be about $120,000.
3. A 2,000-square-foot building would cost $200,000.

Therefore, smaller total square footage means lower building costs when building one-story or main-level-only homes.

However, second-story and basement living space is less costly to construct than main-floor living space. This is because the roof and foundation can serve all levels and because plumbing and electrical systems can be centralized and fireplaces stacked. Further, room inside an attic (termed a half story) can be quite economical since the attic space would often be there anyway. With the addition of dormer windows or skylights and per-haps a steeper pitch in the roof, the attic space can become not only livable but charming because of its angles and nooks. In the case of basements, there may be need for a crawl space or, where there is a deep frost line that would require sinking a deeper foundation, this space can be extended to become living space. Basements are a modest addition to the initial building cost in most cases. The attic or basement space may be framed with the home but finished at a later date, offering added living space as the need arises. Therefore, the initial cost of the home would not reflect the potential of that addition of living space in a high cost per square foot. In this way, a home with half-story and basement space can be more affordable in the long run than a home of the same square footage on one level only.

Figure 6.7 In both new construction and remodeled older homes, the end result may yield traditional character. © *John M. Hall*

Figure 6.8 An unused attic in an existing home can be turned into useful space like this guest suite. *Alan Freysinger Architect/Christina Oliver Interior Design/photo © Brian Vanden Brink*

Financing

While a fortunate few home owners can afford to spend limitless amounts of money on their projects, most building and remodeling are governed by what the clients can afford. Financing the project often entails taking out a loan. The amount of money a person or family can borrow is based on credit history plus guidelines and ratios for debt management.

A general rule is that a home purchase price should not exceed two and one-half times the annual income. Housing costs (mortgage payment, property taxes, insurance, utilities, repairs, maintenance, and any cooperative or condominium fees) should not exceed 28% of the gross monthly income. This **housing-to-income ratio** is expressed:

$$\frac{\text{Housing costs}}{\text{Gross Income}} = 28\% \text{ or Less}$$

A second guideline expressed as a ratio is **debt-to-income,** where debt including housing costs plus other long-term debts (more than 10 months to repay) should not exceed 36% of the gross monthly income:

$$\frac{\text{Housing costs} + \text{Debts}}{\text{Gross Income}} = 36\% \text{ or Less}$$

Other Factors That Affect Economy in Planning Home Space

- Interest rates also affect the cost of the payments and, hence, whether or not the home or building can be afforded. Table 6.1 lists examples for monthly payments of fixed-interest loans of $100,000, $140,000, and $180,000 at 6, 8, and 10 percent over both fifteen and thirty years. These amounts represent only the principal and interest, however; they do not take into

Table 6.1 | Comparison of Monthly Mortgate Payment

Principal and Interest Only—Fixed Rates

Fifteen-Year Loan

Loan Amount	6% Interest	8% Interest	10% Interest
$100,000	$843	$955	$1,074
$140,000	$1,181	$1,337	$1,504
$180,000	$1,518	$1,720	$1,934

Thirty-Year Loan

Loan Amount	6% Interest	8% Interest	10% Interest
$100,000	$599	$733	$877
$140,000	$839	$1,027	$1,228
$180,000	$1,079	$1,320	$1,579

Totals: When the Loan Is Paid in Full, the Following Amounts Will Have Been Paid:

Fifteen-Year Loan

$100,000 at 6% ($843 × 180 payments) = $151,740
$100,000 at 8% ($955 × 180 payments) = $171,900
$100,000 at 10% ($1,074 × 180 payments) = $193,320

$140,000 at 6% ($1,181 × 180 payments) = $212,580
$140,000 at 8% ($1,337 × 180 payments) = $240,660
$140,000 at 10% ($1,504 × 180 payments) = $270,720

$180,000 at 6% ($1,518 × 180 payments) = $273,240
$180,000 at 8% ($1,720 × 180 payments) = $309,600
$180,000 at 10% ($1,934 × 180 payments) = $348,120

Thirty-Year Loan

$100,000 at 6% ($599 × 360 payments) = $215,640
$100,000 at 8% ($733 × 360 payments) = $263,880
$100,000 at 10% ($877 × 360 payments) = $315,720

$140,000 at 6% ($839 × 360 payments) = $302,040
$140,000 at 8% ($1,027 × 360 payments) = $369,720
$140,000 at 10% ($1,228 × 360 payments) = $442,080

$180,000 at 6% ($1,079 × 360 payments) = $388,440
$180,000 at 8% ($1,320 × 360 payments) = $475,200
$180,000 at 10% ($1,579 × 360 payments) = $568,440

NOTES:

- As shown above, for a fifteen-year loan, the cost of the loan when paid in full is between one-and-one-half and two times the loan amount. For a thirty-year loan, it is from two to three times the loan amount.
- Lenders apply the payments in such a way that most of the interest is paid at the beginning of the loan. By increasing the amount of principal paid each month, the borrower can shorten the term of the loan. For example, an additional $50.00 a month applied to the principal on a thirty-year loan can reduce the years of payment to around fourteen to eighteen years. Making a half-monthly payment every two weeks—a convenient schedule for borrowers who receive a paycheck twice a month—is another way to reduce the overall loan term.
- This chart calculates principle and interest only. Property taxes and home owners or hazard insurance will increase payment amounts, to be held in escrow by the lending institution or paid directly by the home owner.
- Mortgage payments typically include money to be set aside, or escrowed, for home owners insurance and property taxes. Some borrowers are also required to carry private mortgage insurance (PMI). The calculations in this table do not include these amounts, nor do they include loan origination costs such as points or commitment fees.
- The hypothetical mortgages in this table are fixed-rate loans. Payment calculations for adjustable-rate or balloon mortgages would be significantly different from the calculations shown here.

account escrow amounts required for taxes and insurance, which can easily add up to another $200 or $300 a month.

- Environmentally sound building and furnishing materials, such as ICF forms (see Chapter 7), will stay functional for many years, thus avoiding replacement and high energy consumption. Likewise, modest square footage and standard-sized ceilings cost less to build, finish, heat, and cool. This is considered long-term economy.
- The cubic footage affects the cost. Areas with very high ceilings will be more costly to construct because of the additional building materials required.
- Simple building shapes contribute to economy. A home with many jogs, angles, gables (roof points), and dormers (windows in the roof) will make the cost per square foot rise, increasing the cost of the interior space. The closer the home is to a simple box, the more economical it will be to build.
- Long-range space planning can be a boon to saving money. When a space is to be finished or remodeled at a later date, structural planning or framing can accommodate the future changes. For example, if a room will one day adjoin another via French doors, the framework for that doorway can be put in place as the home is built, thus avoiding major remodeling. The exterior style and shape should always be taken into consideration when planning additions so that the home will look as though the addition belonged there all along, not as if it were an awkward

Table 6.2 | Residential Space Planning for the Human Scale

Room/Function	Moderate	Large Size
Entry	35 sq. ft.	over 35 sq. ft.
Hall	3 ft. wide	4 ft. wide
Living room	13×15 (195 sq. ft.)	18×30 (540 sq. ft.)
Kitchen	8×12 (96 sq. ft.)	12×16 (192 sq. ft.)
Great room	12×20 (240 sq. ft.)	20×30 (600 sq. ft.)
Family room	13×18 (234 sq. ft.)	15×25 (375 sq. ft.)
Dining room/area	10×13 (130 sq. ft.)	13×16 (208 sq. ft.)
Bathroom	5×10 (50 sq. ft.)	10×15 (150 sq. ft.)
Bedroom	10×12 (120 sq. ft.)	15×20 (300 sq. ft.)
Two-car garage	22×22 (484 sq. ft.)	25×40 (1,000 sq. ft.)

afterthought. Careful space planning will reduce the frustrations and increase the rewards of an eventual remodel.

- Economy can be increased by planning to avoid unusable wasted space or poor traffic patterns.
- The proper scale and proportion of rooms in relation to the interior space should be considered. This means judging the intended function of the area and planning square and cubic footage to meet the demands for that space. (Table 6.2 lists several types of rooms/functions and typical dimensions and/or square footage for moderate rooms versus large rooms.)
- Economy is evident when the size of rooms allows the user to function without crowding or frustration. A space that is too small can necessitate costly expansion by remodeling.
- It can be economical to double up purposes in an area, called a **multiuse area,** and to make space appear larger than it is.

Features and Benefits

The motivator for building or remodeling is rooted in function; users have functional needs and wants that are not being fulfilled by the features of their existing home. Knowing that the process is going to be difficult, lengthy, and costly, people are willing to endure these inconveniences because they envision a home with design solutions that will provide a better environment for rest, recreation, work, or other activities.

One of the first things an individual or family should do when considering building or remodeling is to make a **wish list** (see Table 6.3), an extensive list of the features the users want and the reasons why they want them. It is important to take a hard, realistic look at the "why" dur-

ing this brainstorming stage. As the best designs are based on wants justified by needs, the "why" will determine how seriously a given feature is needed. An attractive or fashionable feature that will be only rarely used by anyone in the household is probably not a good investment. In fact, there may be a variety of design features that will convey the same benefit, so after giving careful consideration to function, the user may end up choosing an entirely different feature from the one originally named. The more benefits a feature can provide, the more likely it is to be a viable option.

Considerations for Specific Areas

Several areas need in-depth thinking through before the floor plans are drawn. These include the entry, formal living spaces, the home office, the kitchen/great room, the master suite, indoor-outdoor living spaces, children's rooms, bathrooms, work and hobby areas, and other special-use areas. Consider the guidelines below.

The Entry or Foyer

An entryway allows for traffic to flow to all areas of the house without having to cross a main or formal living space.

- There should be ample room to accommodate the number of people who would occupy the space at any given time. If entertaining is customary, an entry or foyer larger than 35 square feet (approximately 5 feet × 7 feet) should be considered.
- Two-story open entryways, or atria, are dramatic and impressive. They allow for grand chandeliers and

Table 6.3 | The Wish List: Features and Benefits

Here are a few features that are popular in today's homes, along with some of their benefits. While it would be unusual to find all these features in one home or on an individual user's wish list, think of this table as the springboard for an actual wish list. (Other wish-list ideas are found in the section "Considerations for Specific Areas.")

Features	Benefits
Water	
Indoor or outdoor fountain or wall of cascading water; pond	To calm and refresh emotionally
	To humidify in dry climates
	To provide a focal point for conversation or solitary seating areas
Spa, large jetted tub and/or swimming pool	Therapeutic effects; social experience; exercise and recreation
Built-in saltwater fish tank	To support a hobby and love for water and living organisms
Heating Alternatives	
Indoor or outdoor fireplace or cooking station	To establish a cozy hearth-and-home feeling
	To provide an aesthetic focal point
	A place for people to gather
	The heat will be needed and is a good source of heat
	As an alternative place for food preparation
Solar heating	To conserve nonrenewable energy resources
	To physically and mentally benefit from the healthful effects of sunlight indoors
Warmed bathroom floors, heated towel bars	To give greater physical and emotional comfort
	To augment heat in an area that may tend to be cold during personal grooming
Technology	
Home automation:	Ensure security for valuable possessions
Video-accessible security system	Mental and emotional peace of mind
	Full participation in the information age
Upgraded wiring for Internet access	Research/business communication
Intercom wiring and surround-sound speakers	Communication with others without raising the voice
throughout the home or building	Music everywhere
Livable technology (incorporating the latest	To focus on comfort and coziness first with convenient access to technology
technology in a livable human atmosphere)	
Living with Nature: Feeding the Spirit	
Natural materials (wood, tile, stone, including tumbled marble, granite countertops, stainless steel plumbing fixtures and appliances)	Classic, timeless look that allows design flexibility for years to come Low maintenance and inherent beauty
Outdoor living spaces (including fireplace; large porch, lanai, or patio with a variety of flooring, with roof or pergola beams or open)	To extend the living space to the out-of-doors To give an alternative place for eating, conversation, work, and recreation
Large windows*	To maximize view, enhance light, bring the outdoors visually inside
Spaces that feed the spirit:	To counterpoint the stresses of modern life
Zen gardens, Chinese Feng Shui design features (wind chimes, plants, mirrors, furniture placement), water garden, tabletop fountain, candles or low lighting, aromatherapy or home fragrance	To enhance a feeling of well-being To create peace in the interior, thereby enhancing communication, relationships, and personal emotional stability

*These dictate costly window treatments and may let in too much heat and light and too much cold and dark.
Source: Adapted from trend reports from the National Association of Home Builders (NAHB). Go to the *Interiors* website for the NAHB and other website addresses.

(continued)

Table 6.3 | The Wish List: Features and Benefits (continued)

Soothing music via surround sound	To utilize technology to calm and balance
Exercise or personal spa room (with fitness equipment, television, and massage table)	A safe, convenient exercise/health area To work out and be informed; to relax and heal

Function and Storage

Increased storage (deeper and more drawers versus cabinets, huge closets, storage dormers)	Ergonomically easier to use Open organization for seasonal storage
Refrigerated or warming kitchen drawers, wine storage, wet bar	Storage at point of use
Stepped custom cabinetry, various finishes	Architectural interest in taller rooms
Moldings (everywhere from kitchen to home office)	Attention to detail and the finishing touches
Upscale kitchen (integrated and computer-connected appliances, open to dining, conversation, outdoor living areas)	Kitchens are now total centers of entertainment and living
Lots of drawers and custom kitchen island	Storage and space for gatherings of people

Personalized Design

Minimalist design, nostalgic design	Select a style, then plan with design in mind

Figure 6.9 Water features such as this pool provide emotional, aesthetic, and physical benefits. *Payette Associates Architects/photo © Brian Vanden Brink*

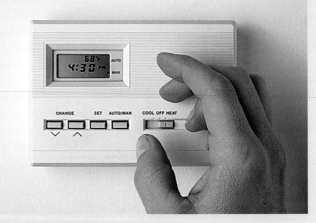

Figure 6.10 Controls for programming a home automation system. *© Index Stock Imagery, Inc.*

Figure 6.11 A cozy fireplace creates a warm and inviting focal point. © Jessie Walker Associates

Figure 6.12 Upscale appliances such as the commercial range are an important feature of this kitchen. *Peter Rose Architect/photo © Brian Vanden Brink*

sweeping staircases. However, they typically have windows above the doorway that are ill-proportioned and allow a clear view into the upper story, radically diminishing privacy.

Formal Living Spaces

Living rooms, dining rooms, and showcase dens or libraries seen from the entry or foyer are considered formal living spaces.

- Formal living spaces are typically separated from the kitchen and other work spaces. This allows them to stay more tidy, and precious furnishings placed in them can be protected.
- Formal spaces are ideal for reclusiveness and study, music listening or rehearsal, formal gatherings and dinners. They provide a restrained, subdued atmosphere and encourage seemly behavior.
- Formal living spaces may be occupied so infrequently that they are economically difficult to justify.

Home Office Planning

Planning Home Office Functions

Office space in the home has become a necessity for a great many individuals and families as telecommuting, home-based businesses, and computer management of personal finances continue to rise in popularity. As with other space planning, it is best to consider function before making other decisions about the home office. Here are some of the possible functions the office may fulfill:

- "Home base," where a worker who has a conventional office can accomplish work during nonoffice hours or sit while resolving "on-call" emergencies
- Work area for an employee who telecommutes full- or part-time
- Accommodation for a home-based business, which may or may not call for additional employees or customers to spend periods of time in the house
- Household financial center, where personal bills are paid and tax returns prepared

Figure 6.13 The inherent beauty of wood is a striking feature of this impressively scaled space. © *Tim Street-Porter/Beateworks.com*

- Internet-access and study area for adults and/or children

On the basis of the functions the office needs to fulfill, consider the issues below. Some users may decide that their home needs more than one office space to meet all their needs.

- Will more than one user utilize the office space at the same time or different times?
- Does quiet and privacy play a role in the work to be done? If so, then having a separate room that is not near the noise or activity center is wise planning. Where work is ongoing or creates a necessary mess, it is wise to plan for a room with a door that can close and even lock.
- Plan for shelves, filing cabinets, and closets or furniture that can hold items that need to be stored. These might include boxes of computer paper, extra office supplies, noncurrent files, and reports or client or school information that should be saved.
- Allot space for a work table for projects that need storing or will be worked on over an extended time period.
- Make a list of the electronic equipment desired or necessary for the computer. Such peripherals might include a printer, scanner, photocopier, fax machine, and phone with caller ID or answering machine. Also list the items that are routinely used in the office, including everything from the tape dispenser to the stapler, pen holder, and paper clips. "A place for everything, and everything in its place" is a key to a well-organized office, higher work efficiency, and less stress.
- Many computer-holding furniture pieces are designed to close up so that when the work is done, the computer area can be closed to view.
- If the office will double as another room, plan space to accommodate furniture for that other room.

Where to Locate the Home Office

Once the functional issues of the home office—or offices—are examined and the equipment needed to support the functions is identified, then space within the home can be chosen. In addition to using a laptop or notebook anywhere, here are some location possibilities:

- On the main floor, just off the entry. This is a good location if the office will never be untidy and if clients are expected to come to the front door.
- At a separate entrance, if the office accommodates many clients or delivery personnel or an employee or two.

Figure 6.14 Traditional details support the formal mood of this space. *Focal Point Architectural Products, Inc. Tarboro, NC, www.focalpointproducts.com*

Figure 6.15 This home office is located within a family room. *© Grey Crawford/ Beateworks.com*

- Near the kitchen in a location that is easily seen and accessible. Monitoring the use of the Internet has become a priority for many parents in order to protect their family members from exposure to influences conflicting with family standards. This area might be a den, family or great room, or even a hallway within sight of major traffic patterns. It is best kept away from the actual food preparation/cooking area but easily seen from there. Some families need more than one computer, and when monitoring is a priority, space planning for carrels or long electrically wired tables takes special thought.

- At a desk within the kitchen. This is convenient for the daily routine, but the desk should be kept outside the major work triangle(s) of the kitchen. The advantage is that cooking, family interaction, and supervising of others' activities can take place simultaneously. The disadvantage is that it is difficult or impossible to concentrate where there is noise.

- In a bedroom with a door that can close. This may be on the main floor, upstairs, or even in a basement. The advantage is quiet seclusion for long periods of writing or study. It is also good to be able to shut a door when the day's work is over. If the office is in sight, the work seems to beckon at all hours. Peace of mind in being able to leave and forget a home office is very important. Disadvantages to this location include the isolation from what's going on in the home and the risk of other users accessing undesirable Internet sites.

- In a living room, family room, or dining room. Any of these rooms can house a home office, particularly when the computer-housing furniture is handsome and has doors that can close over the equipment and work in progress.

- A corner of a bedroom. This is an acceptable location when the use will not disturb other occupants and when the work does not get in the way of the user's ability to relax and leave the work. The advantage is being able to work in privacy, in any dress mode, and at any hour of the day. These features can also constitute disadvantages.

- Multiple locations. It is not uncommon for adults who use their office for employment or professional projects to be unwilling to allow other users into their space and at their equipment. One solution to this

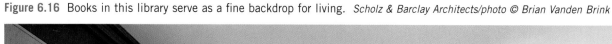

Figure 6.16 Books in this library serve as a fine backdrop for living. *Scholz & Barclay Architects/photo © Brian Vanden Brink*

dilemma is to plan for a child's computer station near the adult home office.

The Library

The library has been incorporated into many new homes in recent years. Even in this information age, with all the advantages of learning online, nothing can take the place of holding a book in hand or reading a book to a child. Bookcases can be beautiful, and a room with books can set the stage for a lifetime of literacy and learning, thereby enhancing the quality of life.

- Location: A library can be a separate room with doors that close (consider pocket or French doors) or can be incorporated into the family room section of the great room or be a part of the home office or the master suite. A formal living room can double as a library, and so can a formal den just off the entryway. Formal dining tables are often underutilized, so dining rooms can make good libraries with the addition of an armchair or other comfortable seating beyond the dining table.
- Bookcases can be ceiling to floor, located in segments around the room or in an open loft above a family or living area. Lower bookcases can be for children's books, memory books or scrapbooks, and educational learning toys. Upper bookcases can hold the treasured and valuable books that are for mature readers. Planning for custom cabinetry, shelves, and cupboards at this wish-list stage is a good idea so that the space will be adequate.
- Good lighting is a must. Plan to wire for lighting that washes or spotlights the bookcases and gives good illumination to reading and study areas. Windows in a library give the eyes a chance to rest and to ponder what's being read and are a must for a computer station, where eyestrain should be relieved every few minutes by looking off into the distance for at least a few seconds.
- Plan adequate space for comfortable seating. For solitary reading, consider support furnishings such as a footstool, table and lamp, and blanket or throw; for group reading sessions, plan to have one or more love seats or sofas with a coffee table and end tables for laying down books.
- Consider a table or desk where the user can sit down and spread books out for research or homework.
- A fireplace is often desirable in a library to give warmth and emotional comfort.

Kitchen and Great Room Planning

The kitchen has long been the hub of the home, but in recent decades it has taken on a multifaceted role. No longer a room where all cabinetry has to match or the single working triangle is the norm, today's kitchen is the room where a majority of living and interacting takes place, and it is designed with space and equipment for a variety of activities. A **great room** is an area that comprises three formerly separate spaces: kitchen, dining, and family room. The following suggestions may be just a beginning; many good books on kitchen planning are available. Certified Kitchen Designers (CKDs) or Certified Kitchen and Bath Designers (CKBDs) can create optimum kitchen and great room spaces. See the *Interiors* website for pertinent website addresses. When working with building construction professionals who specialize in kitchens and remodeling, check out their references and visit remodeled kitchens they completed, and be sure that contracts are signed that spell out everyone's responsibilities.

Kitchens and great rooms may include these features:

- Areas for preparation of snacks and quick meals, larger family meals, formal meals, and meals for event crowds
- A quick-eating bar or island or some other informal dining area, with access to formal dining
- Space for events or parties where participating in cooking and interaction of the guests is part of the fun
- Space for home office duties: taking care of family finances, doing Internet shopping or research, running a business, or having children do homework at a computer station
- Casual, comfortable seating for conversation, music and video/television, and entertaining
- Direct access to mudroom, laundry room, and outside service areas

Features and Trends for Kitchens and Great Rooms
- With the advent of multiple users, kitchens may feature duplicate workstations, appliances, and fixtures, such as two ovens, two microwaves (one near the eating area, one in the cooking area), two refrigerators, two sinks, and two dishwashers. These may or may not be located next to each other; more likely they are not, except for the double ovens.
- Multiple islands, one for food preparation and one for serving;
- Drawers that contain warming ovens, and refrigerator drawers;
- Cabinets that are architecturally beautiful, with various heights (stepped cabinetry), moldings, and pieces that look like furniture rather than cabinets. Thematic styles, such as Traditional, Modern, Arts and Crafts, Shaker, Country French, and American Country, provide the basis for wall, window, and floor coverings as well as furniture and accessories.
- Walk-in pantry and cabinetry with special features such as rolling shelves and pull-out panels, bins, and work surfaces;

Figure 6.17 (A) This well-planned kitchen features bar, kitchen table and dining table seating and a great-room sitting area in the back behind the Windsor bar stools. In a modest space, many people can enjoy dining and conversation. *Green Company, architects/photo © Brian Vanden Brink*

- Universal design elements, such as surfaces that are safe to walk on, good lighting to decrease accidents, electricity located away from plumbing and water, lock-out options on ranges and ovens, water temperature–regulating devices, and safe cooktops;
- Appliance features are now so numerous that research and comparison is a must. Many models offer a chip that allows operation to be monitored on the home computer or hand-held digital assistant. See the Web addresses for appliance companies on the *Interiors* website.
- Special placement may be designed for cabinetry and appliances to accommodate the needs of the wheelchair bound or ambulatory impaired. Likewise, think safety and empowerment through good planning for children and adolescents, who will use the kitchen when home alone.
- More than one working triangle and various working zones to meet the needs of multiple users;
- The return of the Butler's Pantry. A separate room or open as an appendage to the kitchen, it contains cabinetry to hold larger serving dishes and extra tableware, and it often houses an extra sink, dishwasher, and refrigerator.

Zones and the Working Triangle

Kitchen planning includes working arrangements in zones or work areas. The three zones that are considered the basic working triangle include:

- The refrigerator zone

Figure 6.17 (B) A home office station with ergonomic chair and natural light from a window is convenient to this handsome kitchen. *© Andrea Rugg/Beateworks.com*

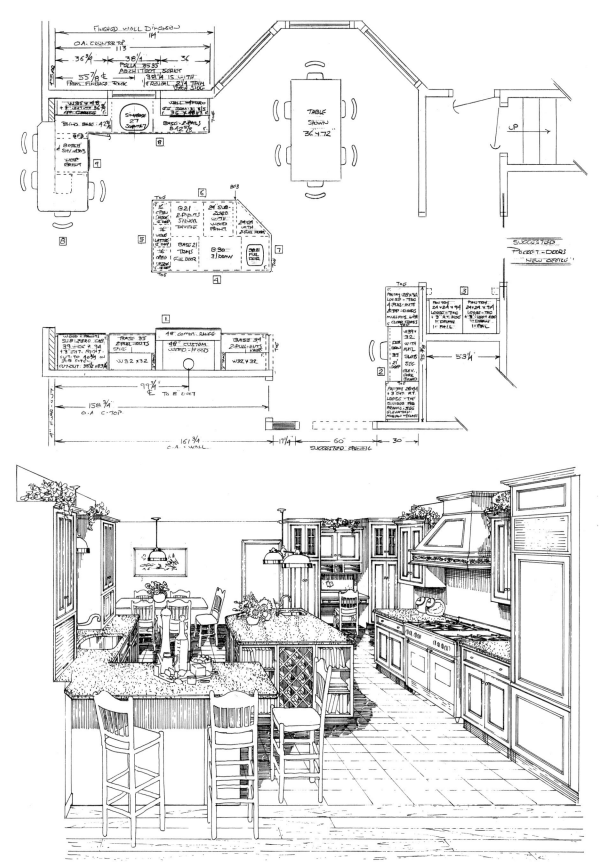

Figure 6.18 Upscale kitchen with custom design elements. *Kitchen designs by Laido Designs, Franklin Lakes, NJ. Floor plan by Michael B. Laido, CKD. Rendering by Patricia Carmen.*

- The cooking zone (range and ovens)
- The sink/cleanup zone

Total walking distance among these three areas should not be fewer than 12 feet (too crowded—produces frustration) and not more than 26 feet (too spread out—leads to exhaustion). Where multiple cooks work together, two basic work triangles may be planned. Other zones that

add convenience and are considered essential to modern kitchens include any or all of the following:

- Additional food storage zones
- Various specialized food preparation zones
- A second cooking zone and/or a quick-cooking zone
- A second cleanup/sink zone
- Tableware storage zone(s)

Table 6.4 | Cabinetry Considerations for Kitchen Zone Planning

Food Storage Cabinetry

Food storage can be divided into three main categories:
1. Perishables: These items require refrigeration or freezing.
2. Regularly used dry food supplies: Foods used on a daily basis such as flour (flour bin drawers with metal liners are available), baking powders, spices and supplies, boxed cereal, various pastas, rice, and legumes. These should be located in the kitchen near the zone where they will be used in food preparation or cooking. Generally, the flour and heavy supplies go in the lower cabinets and smaller supplies above. A spice rack or specially designed cabinet is desirable to keep spices organized and handy. A cabinet or cupboard specifically for boxed cereal or for items such as sugar, cornmeal, popcorn, rice, beans, and other legumes may be preferred. The shelf heights should be adjustable and the interiors must be easily cleaned.
3. Staples and canned goods: Occasionally used. These might be located in a pantry or larder—a wall of cabinets or a walk-in closet. By keeping extra supplies in the pantry, the cook can save kitchen space and cut down on trips to the store. The pantry may also be located between the kitchen and dining room as a place from which to serve food to the formal dining room. An extension of the concept of the pantry is the food storage room that is located in a cool area (such as a basement), and that stores staples, cases of food (such as canned goods), flour, cooking supplies, legumes, other items with a long shelf life (which replenish the pantry supply), and bulky cooking pots and pans. Underground storage space may also be designed to include a root cellar and/or wine cellar.

Food Preparation Countertop/Cabinet-Top Areas

Determine the kind of food preparation that will take place and plan countertop areas accordingly. In kitchens where much food preparation takes place, a minimum of two long counters (over 3 feet) are required. An island or a peninsula often provides wide countertops. Where bread is frequently mixed, a large area near flour bins and cooking supplies is imperative. If vegetables are often chopped, cutting boards that are built into the countertop or that pull out near the sink will be appreciated. Some kitchens are planned with two or more cutting boards of various sizes—larger ones for mixing, smaller ones for cutting. As another example, if candymaking is a specialty, a separate area with supplies nearby and a counter of marble is ideal. The type of food preparation, then, should be the topic of careful consideration in planning the size and location of countertop or cabinet-top space. There may be a small sink for food preparation and a large sink for cleanup, often placed in an island or peninsula.

Cooking containers such as pots and pans need to be close to the range or cooktop. Cupboards with sliding drawers eliminate awkward hunting situations. Vertical panels hold cooking sheets, dripper pans, muffin tins, and other flat dishes upright and should be located near the oven where they are used. Cooking utensils can be located in drawers near the stove, placed in a crock, or hung on the wall. Items used every day should be most convenient.

An appliance garage consists of cabinet doors on the countertop with space behind to hide portable appliances; sliding shelves in lower cabinets can also hold appliances, and electric plugs can be installed inside these special cupboards. Cabinets can be designed with solid or glass doors (or without any doors at all) and to hold any special item.

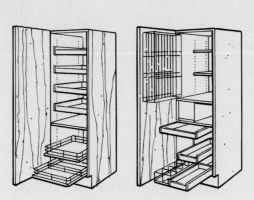 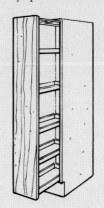 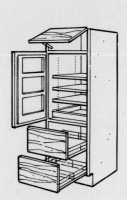

Table 6.4 | Cabinetry Considerations for Kitchen Zone Planning (continued)

Cleanup Cabinetry

Cabinets for cleaning supplies need to be planned near the sink. Typically, the cabinet beneath the sink contains everyday cleaning supplies and often a trash can. A separate, taller cupboard keeps the smell away from the sink and allows for a larger trash can (trash compactors are discussed in Table 6.5). A broom closet should be planned to make brooms, mops, and vacuum cleaners conveniently accessible.

Towels and washcloths should be handy to the sink. A rack for dish towels that slides into the lower cabinets helps to control clutter and to keep towels dry and more sanitary. A drawer or two should be allotted for clean kitchen linen. Drawers should be added for extra paper towels or cleaning cloths or rags, paper or plastic garbage bags, and extra disposable items such as rubber gloves or scouring pads.

Tableware Storage Cabinetry

Cabinetry for tableware includes cupboards for plates, dishes, and stemware (cups, glasses). Lower cabinets next to the dishwasher might hold dishes for everyday use (children can then easily set the table), and upper cabinets could contain special, breakable tableware. Drawers should be planned for silverware, placemats, cloth or paper napkins, and folded tablecloths; a closet can be used for hanging tablecloths (pressed and ready for special occasions). A set of shelves for centerpieces and vases is valuable.

Dining Cabinetry

Islands and peninsula eating bars augment or even replace the conventional table in many of today's kitchens. The bar may accom-modate two or more stools or chairs, depending on the number of people in the household. The bar is planned and built as a part of the cabinets; it may contain drawers, cupboards, or appliances on one or two sides. It may double as a desk or contain a space for a computer. It may have no cabinets and function as a cabinet-top eating surface with only bar-stool space beneath it. The bar, island, or peninsula may also be lowered so that shorter bar stools or standard chairs can be used, rather than tall bar stools.

Service/Storage Cabinetry

Planning cabinets for table service or serving dishes also requires thought because some dishes, platters, and utensils are used on a regular basis and others may be used only occasionally, such as on holidays or at more formal meals. Therefore, the serving pieces most often used should be accessible, and the items seldom used can go in less accessible places, such as above the oven or the refrigerator. Keep in mind that lightweight items should go overhead, and heavier items should be placed in lower cabinets to allow for ease and safety in removal. Glass or plastic dishes/lids, used for storing perishable items in the refrigerator or freezing unit, should be fairly close to the refrigerator and near a countertop or cabinet top. Consider drawers just for lids, perhaps one for plastic and one for glass, plus a drawer or two for plastic wrap and bags, aluminum foil, and waxed paper.

It has often been said that there is never too much storage space. Although people do tend to fill up whatever kitchen storage is available, it is far better to plan generous storage space than to produce clutter and frustration by allowing too little.

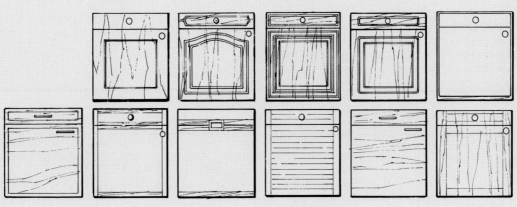

- Serving and service storage zone
- Cleaning supplies storage zone

These zones should be planned for the convenience and consideration of the family members who cook and should be laid out logically according to individual needs. However, certain checkpoints, presented in Tables 6.4 and 6.5, are fairly consistent.

Part of the kitchen planning process is deciding which types of appliances to purchase; making selections among the many makes, styles, and options of those appliances; and making sure the cabinetry dimensions will accommodate them with precision. Table 6.5 lists the major types or categories of appliances and surveys options and considerations in their selection and placement.

Figure 6.19 A contemporary kitchen designed for serious cooking. © Jessie Walker Associates

(A)

(B)

Figure 6.20 (A) The Energy Guide label from the Federal Trade Commission (FTC) is to appear on all appliances so the consumer may compare energy usage and associated costs. (B) The Energy Star label, sponsored by the Environmental Protection Agency (EPA) is affixed to specific products to indicate that the item exceeds energy efficient and conservation guidelines.

Figure 6.21 HomePad refrigerator with computer screen. *Courtesy of SAMSUNG*

Table 6.5 | Appliance Planning Considerations

Appliances, devices powered by gas or electricity, fall into two categories. These are large or major appliances such as refrigerators, ovens, ranges, and washer/dryers, and small appliances such as toasters and specialized food-preparation or cooking devices. Models, options, and price ranges have expanded considerably, making it worth the time to research new appliance selection, perhaps beginning with an Internet search of consumer reports. Integration with other appliances or home systems, convenience features and energy-saving options, and appearance are some items to be considered. Generally, appliances will last as long as the warranty. Whereas in the past appliances were designed to last for twenty to thirty years, today six to eight years seems to be the average life span. As technology moves forward at an accelerated pace, features in current models are outdated quickly and replaced with newer, faster conveniences.

Price Point vs. Energy Costs

Appliances are costly investments, and research both instore and online will be worth the effort. Sales on appliances are typically in January and June when current models are discounted to make room for newer models. Price points can vary greatly, with more expensive appliances having more features. Yet the purchase price is only part of the true costs. The cost of running the appliance should also be considered.

Energy Guide labels are now required on new refrigerators, freezers, clothes washers and dryers, dishwashers, and water heaters. Furnaces and room air conditioners have a rating rather than a label. The Energy Guide lists energy use compared to other similar appliances, with an estimate of how much it will cost to run that appliance.

The **Energy Star** label, sponsored by the U.S. Department of Energy (DOE) and the U.S. Environmental Protection Agency (EPA), is on thirty categories of products including appliances, electronics, lighting, office equipment, HVAC, and even homes. The Energy Star label indicates the product is at least 10 percent more efficient than comparable products, using less energy or water, promoting cleaner air, and using materials wisely. Clothes washers with the Energy Star label are 50 percent more efficient; dishwashers are 25 percent more efficient.

Refrigerator and Freezers

Refrigerators are available with a variety of features and price points. Adjustable shelves, special compartments (for meat, vegetables, and dairy products), frost-free and energy-saving features, and stainless steel or painted doors or with insert paneling in fashionable colors are a few of the features available today. Many refrigerators contain a freezer unit, which can be located at the top, bottom, or side. Side-by-side refrigerators are also available in wider sizes for better width storage inside. Side-by-side units often feature cold-water and ice dispensers, eliminating the need to continually open and close the door (energy-saving). Refrigerated or freezer drawers may be a part of the unit or be "integrated" into cabinetry, placed at the point of most convenient use.

As the twenty-first century leads to greater digital convergence, the refrigerator may be equipped with a computer with available options including electronic bulletin boards, Internet access and e-mail, recipe databanks, a shopping list cross-referenced with a menu planner to work with available ingredients, and a barcode scanner that alerts as to expiration dates of scanned products placed inside.

A second refrigerator or large freezer may be placed in a garage, basement, or butler's pantry. Freezers come with side-hinged doors or as a chest where the lid lifts. Chest freezers keep the cold air inside rather than rushing out, but make it more difficult to organize and access food. The area in front of the refrigerator or freezer should allow for a minimum of 3 feet to open and close the door and access the food without crowding. There should be a countertop nearby for loading and unloading food.

Ovens/Ranges/Cooktops

Ovens and ranges or cooktops can be located together or separately. Conventional or convection ovens may be placed below the range or above it. If below, the unit may have a smaller conventional or microwave oven above as well. A cooktop contains cooking elements only and is placed in the countertop or cabinet top wherever it is desired—along the wall or in an island, for example. The microwave oven is usually placed in one of three locations: on the counter, suspended under the upper cabinets, or built into the wall. Microwaves are least attractive placed on a counter; suspended types are smaller microwave units, and built-in units are often combined with a conventional oven. Multipurpose ovens are also available for both microwave and conventional or convection cooking. Self-cleaning or continuous-cleaning options are also worth considering in new ovens. A smaller convection oven can be placed by itself in a wall away from the microwave, which may be in a quick-cooking center. Ample counter space on each side of a range is sound kitchen planning, and counter space on at least one side of an oven to place food before and after cooking while opening the door is also very important to avoid spills and burns. Experts agree that electric ovens and gas cooktops are ideal. Upscale cooktops have up to eight burners and grill options. Warming drawers keep food warm till serving, and may be placed in the dining room or other rooms.

Dishwashers

Most dishwashers are built-in units that slide under the countertop or cabinet top. Portable dishwashers are rolled to the sink and attached to the faucet and drain. For faster cleaning of smaller loads of dishes, select a drawer dishwasher or optional in-sink dishwasher. Drawer diswashers provide you the opportunity to run half-full cycles, and new optional in-sink dishwashers, in addition to eliminating bending, can provide either an extra deep sink or more counter space. Other options include top-rack-only wash, hidden controls and heating elements, and a food disposer to eliminate food particles. Energy- and water-saving features qualify some models as Energy Star approved. Various colors and finishes

(continued)

Table 6.5 | **Appliance Planning Considerations** (continued)

are available. A special frame can hold wood or laminate to match the kitchen cabinets. The dishwasher should be located just to the left or right of the sink and next to the storage area for tableware. Select a quiet-operation dishwasher.

Garbage Disposals

The garbage disposal is a standard appliance in one side of the sink, in the center of a three-compartment sink, or in a second food preparation sink.

Trash Compactors

Trash compactors are appliances that compress garbage and thereby eliminate frequent trips to an outside garbage can. Trash compactors are located next to the sink or virtually any place in the kitchen. For those who do not desire a trash compactor, the same space can contain a garbage container that slides or swings out.

Sinks

Many styles of sinks are available today in a variety of contemporary colors. Porcelain and stainless steel are the two most popular materials for sinks. Double sinks are common, and sinks with a third, central compartment for a garbage disposal are available. Sinks may have different-sized compartments and different depths.

Smaller sinks for rinsing vegetables or alternate cleanup areas are a nice addition.

Portable Appliances

There are two major categories of portable appliances: appliances for food preparation and food-cooking appliances. The number of choices increases every year. When planning a kitchen, it is wise to make a list of the appliances to be used and to prioritize their location—the most frequently used will need to be most accessible, perhaps even on the countertop or cabinet top. For convenient use and elimination of clutter, plan for appliance cubbyholes or compartments on the counter. It is important to remember that portable appliances will be used only if they are convenient and accessible. If it is necessary to move bulky items out of the way and reach to the back of low or high cabinets for an appliance, it will seldom be used.

- **Portable appliances for food preparation:** Blender, food processor, cabinet-top mixer, hand mixer, food mill, chopper/grinder, can opener, electric knife, knife sharpener, food slicer, pasta maker, dough roller, drink mixer, coffee grinder, juicer, ice cream maker, weight scale, food dehydrator.
- **Portable food-cooking appliances:** Microwave oven (may also be built-in), toaster, toaster oven, coffeemaker, rice cooker, Crock-Pot, electric skillet/grill, waffle iron, popcorn popper, electric wok, warming tray, hot plate/portable range, yogurt maker, deep fryer.

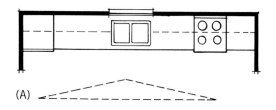

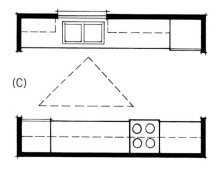

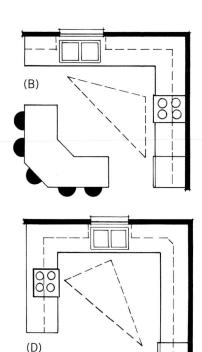

Figure 6.22 Working triangles. (A) The single-wall kitchen with refrigerator at left, stove/oven at right. (B) L-shaped kitchen with an eating bar and stove and refrigerator right of sink. (C) The galley or tunnel kitchen uses space economically but can conflict with traffic patterns. (D) The U-shaped kitchen eliminates traffic problems and provides ample counter space.

Table 6.6 | Standard Sizes of Fixtures and Cabinet Work*

Item	Width/Length	Height	Depth	Special
Kitchen counter	as needed	36″	20–35″	28″ high (wheelchair bound)
Refrigerator	28–36″	5–6′	2′6″	34–36″ high
Dishwasher	24″	34″	24″	
Range	30–36″	36″	24″	
Oven	24–30″	24–30″	26″	two units make "double-oven" size
Washer	30″	36″	30″	
Dryer	30″	36″	30″	
Stacked washer/dryer	30″	72″	30″	
Bathroom counter	as needed	30–34″	20″	28″ high (chairbound-disabled)
Toilet	15″ (seat)	28–30″ (tank)	26″	
Regular bathtub	5′	16″	2′8″	
Oversize bathtub	6–7′8″	to 24″	3–4′	
Spa (sauna/steam room)	6′	8′	8′	8′ wide316′ long
Interior door	2′6″–3′	6′8″	1³⁄₈″	
Exterior door	3′	6′8″	1³⁄₈″ (Wider as needed)	
Ceiling	—	8′ (Higher as desired)	8′ (Higher as desired)	

*Sizes and shapes vary by manufacture, and a wide variety of nonstandard-size fixtures can be purchased through specialty suppliers.

The Laundry Room

Because the laundry room features permanent cabinetry and stationary appliances, foresight and flexibility in planning are required. Sizes for washers and dryers are listed in Table 6.6. Cabinets should contain shelves high enough for laundry detergents, whiteners, softeners, and other frequently used products and items. Counter space for folding clothes and a closet or rod for hanging permanent press clothing are important. The laundry room most often contains an ironing board—perhaps the built-in variety, which is excellent for saving space and keeping iron and board accessible and orderly. Drawers or cabinets can hold clothes to be ironed or mended as well as mending supplies. Sewing rooms are favorite combinations with laundry facilities because the ironing board is necessary for laundry and sewing and because mending often takes place before or after laundering. Sewing cabinetry can contain work surfaces that fold or slide behind doors, keeping the clutter out of sight when no sewing is taking place. The laundry room may also double with a mudroom and may contain closets or "lockers" for coats, winter gear, or sports equipment according to the season. The laundry/utility room may hold a food freezer, and the cabinetry may be organized for tools such as screwdrivers and pliers. If the laundry room is located near the kitchen, it could double as a storage room for bulky cooking appliances.

There are at least five options of laundry location in space planning a home:

- Most typical is to locate the laundry near the kitchen. Some smaller homes and apartments have the washer and dryer in the kitchen itself, although ideally, the laundry needs to be in a place where clothes sorting can take place and where the door can be closed on the mess if necessary. Placing it near the kitchen is convenient since much of the daily household work revolves around the kitchen and only a few steps are needed to tend to the laundry in progress.

In two-story homes where the laundry is on the main floor, careful planning can locate the laundry beneath at least one bathroom and over a clothes drop, which could empty into a cabinet above the washer and dryer. It is also possible to install two or three clothes drops so that sorting takes place as clothes are being dropped: one for whites, one for dark colors and jeans, and one for bright or light colors. This concept

Figure 6.23 Good planning makes processing laundry more efficient. *Elliott & Elliott Architects/photo © Brian Vanden Brink*

Figure 6.24 A stacking washer and dryer conserve space. *© Brian Vanden Brink*

can be extended with the idea of drawers or baskets belonging to each family member. As clothes are folded, they are put into the drawer and that individual is responsible for taking the clothes and putting them away.

- A second location is in a basement. This location will keep the noise and clutter off the main floor but will necessitate climbing stairs with loads of dirty and clean laundry.
- The third location is in the bedroom wing, next to the family bathroom. This location is popular in larger two-story homes and eliminates carrying laundry up and down stairs.
- A fourth location is in a hallway, but this may not be good planning since the clothes have to be sorted in the hall and a mess is created in the traffic pattern.
- In smaller homes and apartments, the bathroom may house the laundry. Theoretically this may be a good location since soiled clothing is often taken off there at bath time. Some conflict could easily arise between functions and users, although in households of one or two users this is not an issue. Lack of adequate space for laundry activities may also be a disadvantage.

Master Suite Planning

The master suite is one area in which money can be invested with an assurance of a return if the home is resold. A bit of upscale luxury in the master suite is a major trend, perhaps because two-career couples feel they need a private place to unwind after a long day. The master bedroom is often a master suite, consisting of various areas and adjoining rooms that become a mini-apartment supporting a variety of activities. Consider these options:

- Incorporate space for seating or conversation. A single chair and ottoman or chaise lounge is a good alternative to sitting on the bed for reading or conversing. Consider a conversation area with sofas or love seats and comfortable chairs. Support them with end tables, lamps, magazine racks, or case piece furniture such as a bookshelf.
- Wire and plan space for an entertainment unit. An armoire or television cabinet flanked by bookcases makes the master suite a place for private home theater. Surround-sound speakers wired into the ceiling for movies and stereo music are a luxury easily accomplished in new construction and remodeling.

- A small home office desk or hutch can be placed in the master suite. Placing a full-scale home office in a room adjoining or close by the master bedroom makes working at odd hours much less dreaded.
- An area just off the bedroom can accommodate exercise equipment, spa facilities, or a massage therapy room.
- The master suite can accommodate a library that focuses on bookshelves, comfortable seating, and perhaps a fireplace or a window with a great view. In this room, the computer station may be played down, perhaps placed behind doors in a built-in or furniture unit.
- Consider dual closets, or double walk-in closets, and built-in closet organizer shelves. Also consider a sky-light or translucent glass windows in the closet areas or a window for fresh air.
- Vaulted, domed, or high ceilings, fine millwork (moldings), and creatively planned spaces are other sought-after luxuries in master suites.

Master bathrooms are an important part of the master suite. Consider:

- Luxury spa or whirlpool bathtub.
- Separate roomy shower with dual heads at different heights, or water walls of multiple small jet spray heads. Luxury showers are often deep walk-in room-like areas. Ammenties include surround sound speakers for music, radio or television, and television screens.
- Warming towel bars.

Figure 6.25 This master bedroom utilizes vertical open attic space to give more cubic footage to a modest square foot area. © *Peter Aaron/Esto*

- Above counter lavatory bowls (sinks) and extensive use of stone or tile.
- Where the bath area is large and open, the toilet is often inside a small room or "closet" with good lighting and ventilation fans.
- Closet or dressing areas adjoining the master bathroom.
- Vaulted ceilings and creative shapes can make this area seem larger than it is.
- Consider double vanities, custom-built for the height of each person. Vanities may be in separate areas, with large mirrors and custom storage for each user's needs.
- A sit-down vanity area with drawers and cupboards, electrical outlets, and a sink close by.
- Ample drawers and cupboards for bathroom linens, supplies, and personal care items.
- Windows with a view. If near the bathtub, plan for remote-controlled window shades—down when entering and exiting the tub, up when submerged in the bubbles. Art or stained-glass windows are also popular.
- A wet or dry sauna or massage area.
- Technology: Telephone, television, and surround sound for music and radio are incorporated in today's master bath. Waterproof electronics are widely available.

(A)

Family Bathrooms

Family bathrooms are often a point of contention, with one person locking the door and staying for lengths of time, often just grooming, while others grow impatient. Some ideas to help alleviate the tension are listed here:

- Compartmentalize the bathroom with a pocket, folding, or swinging door between the vanity and bath/toilet area.
- Place the toilet in a closet.
- Separate the vanities; lengthen the vanity; consider double sinks.
- Place a vanity with sink in each bedroom.
- Place a small bathroom between each two bedrooms with an access door on each side. This works especially well when the bathroom contains the toilet and bathtub or shower and the vanities are in a hallway or bedroom.
- Put the bathtub and shower in separate areas.
- Small bathroom spaces can appear larger by the use of increased ceiling height, plumbing fixtures without bulky cabinetry, and well-placed mirrors.
- Upscale or luxury homes usually feature a full-scale private bathroom with each bedroom. This plan makes ideal guest suites and is a boon to family harmony when the children marry and come home for a visit with their own children or when an aged parent comes to stay in the home.

(B)

Figure 6.26 (A), (B), and (C) This upscale master bathroom is a luxurious extension of the master suite. *All © Melabee M. Miller*

(C)

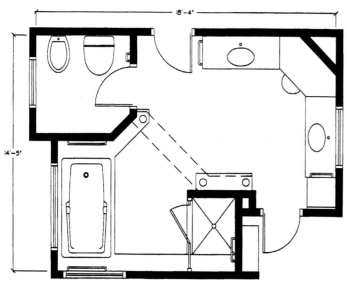

Figure 6.26 (D) This bathroom floor plan shows separate vanity areas, closet room for toilet, and area for bathtub and shower. This creates an upscale, luxury bathroom with compartments.

Figure 6.27 (A) A seating vanity area is a feature of this contemporary bathroom. (B) Two sinks make this family bathroom more functional. *(A) and (B) © Jessie Walker*

- Be sure to plan doorways so that plumbing fixtures are not in plain view.
- Many styles of bathtubs, showers, vanities, and sinks are available. Website addresses for plumbing fixture companies are listed on the *Interiors* website.

Children's Spaces

Whereas demographic research indicates that fewer children live in each home today than did so a generation ago, the emphasis on making a child's world wonderful has never known such enthusiasm. Here is a list of considerations for children's spaces:

- Small bedrooms that adjoin a playroom allow for a separation of sleep and play areas.
- Larger bedrooms that are carefully planned with action or move-about space make a child's world private.
- Planning a desk with good lighting and perhaps built-in with shelves encourages children to study. Most parents will want each child to have computer access. Not all, however, will choose to connect children's computers to the Internet, as there are concerns about online content that conflicts with family values and about the effect of extensive Internet use on children's development of social skills and family relationships.
- Luxuries such as a telephone and television are also personal considerations, influenced by concerns about unmonitored telephone use and television viewing. The amount of family interaction desired versus the autonomy and indulgence a child is afforded should be an open matter of discussion, with research to back the decision.
- Surround-sound speakers for the inevitable stereo system are an option that must be planned in advance.
- As alternatives to a plethora of electronic devices, consider these ideas for bedrooms or playrooms: built-in fantasy play areas with climbing devices and a slide; a performing stage; a wall of full-length mirrors for dancing; a toy car racetrack or a table for model trains and jigsaw puzzles; built-in shelves for books, with comfortable and inviting seating such as chairs, love seats, or cushioned and pillowed window seats.

Figure 6.28 A children's space stimulates the imagination. © *Tim Street-Porter/Beateworks.com*

Figure 6.29 Distinctive architectural features add beauty to this outdoor living space. © *Tim Street-Porter/Beateworks.com*

Children's play areas can also contain organized closets with compartmentalized shelves and drawers for educational toys and experimental science kits.

Indoor-Outdoor Living

Whether a minuscule deck, a broad porch, or an expansive lawn, in many climates and seasons the outdoors offers an ideal place to converse and connect with family and friends. Fresh air and sunshine promote good health. Watching the children or pets play while visiting is a pleasant pastime. A well-designed yard can be an extension of the living spaces. Consider these advantages of connecting the indoor environment to the outdoors:

- The visual expanse of an outdoor living space seen through windows and doors makes the interior seem larger.
- A pleasant view, even of a small patio or backyard, can make indoor living psychologically more enjoyable.
- An indoor-outdoor traffic flow and outdoor seating can at least double the space for entertaining and gracious family living.
- Outdoor living spaces may incorporate many amenities: durable well-designed furniture; beautiful architectural features such as columns, roofed porches, and well-chosen flooring materials; even area rugs, art, and accessories. A whirlpool spa or swimming pool, perhaps with a retractable roof; a fireplace or upscale cooking grill; or even a small kitchenette containing a refrigerator and microwave oven behind lockable cabinet doors can be a part of the outdoor living experience.
- Wiring on the outside of the home allows for working on a computer laptop or notebook. A DSL or telephone jack makes connecting to the Internet possible while sipping lemonade on the porch.

Media and Entertainment Rooms

The **home theater** or **media room** can employ the following space planning concepts:

- A big-screen television with ample storage space for videos or DVDs and audio CDs

Figure 6.30 This media room features comfortable individual seating. © Norman McGrath

Figure 6.31 A billiard table expands the use of this family room. *Design by Custom Electronics/photo © Brian Vanden Brink*

- A slanted or stepped (terraced) floor to afford everyone viewing the "big screen" an unimpeded view
- Surround sound wired in during construction
- Dimmable lights; usher lights low on the walls
- A kitchenette or snack bar (check building codes ahead of time to determine what is allowed)

Entertainment rooms beyond the media or home theater room might include:

- Active game tables: Ping-Pong, foosball, billiards
- A dance floor
- Arcade machines
- Soda machines or a soda fountain or snack bar with bar stools
- Indoor racket ball or tennis court
- Swimming pool and/or hot tub (consider retractable roofing)

Hobby and Special-Use Areas

Other rooms to consider in the wish list include rooms where hobbies or special activities take place:

- Art studio for painting or printmaking, graphics, ceramics, stained glass, or other artisan skills or crafts
- Darkroom and processing area for photography
- Music practice and study room; sound or recording studio (sound-insulated)

- Workshop for building or working with machinery or devices or making a product for sale

Storage

Storage is a precious commodity; it fills up so quickly and is difficult to empty because possessions are hard to part with. A cardinal rule is that storage should be located at the point of first or most frequent use. It has also been suggested that in order to determine real storage needs, one should list things owned and their corresponding sizes and then list where these items should be stored and what size that storage area should be. Storage zones are desirable in specific locations:

- The kitchen should include storage for dry goods (such as a wall or walk-in pantry) and ample storage for pots and pans, small appliances, serving bowls, informal and formal plates and dishes and glasses (stemware), silverware and utensils, linens, soaps and cleansers, and cleaning appliances (brooms, mops, or vacuums), all located within convenient reach.

Figure 6.32 This spacious artist's loft uses a multilevel plan to establish zones and make the space more usable. *Reiter & Reiter Architects/photo © Brian Vanden Brink*

Figure 6.33 Carefully planned storage is also an important visual feature of this kitchen. *Robert Currie Interior Design/photo © Brian Vanden Brink*

- The laundry facility should have storage for extra soap, bleach, softener, and other cleaning preparations.
- The front hall closet is for family and/or guest coats. Depending on the weather and the lifestyle, there may be a place for wet outerwear such as raincoats, umbrellas, or boots. It may not always be possible, however, to accommodate all the guests' coats, scarves, and gloves when a sizable group is being entertained. In this case, the outerwear might be placed in a den or on a bed.
- Closets, lockers, a walk-in closet, or a wall of hooks near the back entrance, garage entrance, or mudroom are for winter gear (coats, boots, school bags) and individual sports gear, again depending on lifestyle. In the summer, such an area could double for summer sports gear: tennis, baseball, and soccer equipment and even swimming towels and gear.
- A closet for the vacuum cleaner should be placed where it is needed. In two-story houses, a vacuum might be located in a closet on each floor.
- Linen closets are usually located in a hall near bedrooms to hold extra sheets, pillowcases, pillows, and blankets.
- Bathroom storage needs include paper goods, personal hygiene sundries, and extra towels, as well as cleaning supplies.
- Bedrooms are often shortchanged in storage. Sizable, compartmentalized closets will be appreciated.
- Any area where a hobby is performed requires individualized storage.
- Home offices need closets, shelves, and/or units that can hold reference books, files, paper, and other supplies. The personal computer demands certain storage items such as printer paper and disks.
- The family room or entertainment room will need storage for items such as cassettes, records, compact discs, and videotapes.
- The library, often combined with a home office or another room, will need plenty of shelves and perhaps some storage with locking doors for valuable books or papers.
- The tool shed is a place to store lawn and garden tools and equipment, and tools for use in other maintenance projects.
- Where no tool shed or yard storage shed exists, the garage is often used for lawn and garden equipment,

Figure 6.34 This modest and handsome great room features cabinetry shelves for the storage of an impressive book collection for cozy reading near a contemporary fireplace. *Rick Burt, architect/photo © Brian Vanden Brink*

tools, bicycles, and a myriad of items too bulky for home storage. With careful planning, the garage that is also a storage area can be organized to avoid a cluttered appearance.

Space Planning and the Principles and Elements of Design

Effective space planning incorporates careful consideration of the principles and elements of design (discussed in Chapter 3) in order to create interiors that are pleasing and effective. And since people are the most important ingredient of the space, the proportion and scale in particular should always be judged according to that of the human body. With this in mind, the space can be planned to fit the purpose. A very large or grand scale—seen in places such as cathedrals, hotel lobbies, or open atrium areas of office buildings—is awesome compared to the human scale. But in these places, that overwhelming feeling serves a purpose—to give a different perspective or alternative to viewing space. The perspective may create a feeling of reverence, awe, contemplation, or simply relief from closed, small-scale quarters. However, the overall size or scale of the space best relates to the human frame in most interiors. Table 6.2, on page 136, indicates typical sizes for living areas in homes that have proved their effectiveness in relating to the human scale.

Other design principles and elements are readily applied in the space planning process. Scale, proportion, balance, rhythm, emphasis, and harmony (the principles of design) are sought in order to make space functional and pleasing for many years to come. These aspects of function and pleasantness in space planning are accomplished through the manipulation of the elements of design—the delineation of space with shape or form through mass, line, pattern, texture, light, and color.

Living with Less Space

Smaller seems to be the direction of the future. This is not necessarily bad, since large spaces demand upkeep and extra furnishings and can pose not only cleaning burdens but security problems as well.

Skillful and creative planning makes the best use of the space available. This can be done in advance in the blueprint stage. Multiuse space is generally open space as large as two or three rooms. The omission of walls is a cost-saving factor, and one large room rather than cubicles of smaller ones can give the entire interior a more spacious and luxurious feeling. A large space allows for greater flexibility in meeting current needs and in arranging furniture as the function changes over time.

Figure 6.35 Mirrors visually expand the space of this bathroom. © *Jessie Walker Associates*

In a home where the cost disallows space for every desired purpose, some rooms can serve two or more functions. For example, a little-used but desired formal dining room can double as a library; the home office or den could act as a guest room. The most dramatic multiuse area, however, is the **great room,** a term taken from medieval England when the **great hall** was the place where dining, entertaining, conversation, and sleeping all took place. Today's great room frequently includes a kitchen; a snack bar or island for both food preparation and eating; a seating conversation area, often grouped around a fireplace, window, or other focal point; an entertainment system of television/video/stereo equipment; perhaps a sit-down eating area (in lieu of the formal dining room); and a desk for study, scheduling, and handling personal finances, which may contain space for a personal computer and filing system.

Use of this area evolved not only from rising building costs but also from today's lifestyle. People today are busy, often employed in or outside the home, and time is a precious commodity. Conversely, the presence of many rooms, or a duplication of formal/informal spaces, requires that time be spent cleaning and maintaining those

spaces. Today's lifestyle is less formal than that in the past. Whereas a formal dinner party may have been the standard through the mid-twentieth century, today even the boss is entertained comfortably in the great room (and may even enjoy pitching in and helping with the cooking). Further, hired help today is used in a different sense. The home owner may have someone come in to clean but will rarely employ servants to prepare meals, serve, and clean up as was commonly the case among well-to-do families in past eras. Convenience foods and equipment, such as microwave ovens and dishwashers, have simplified lifestyles and reduced much of the burden of food preparation and entertaining.

Stretching Space

Because of smaller spaces in today's homes, it is often desirable to make spaces seem larger than they actually are. A **space-saving device** is a method of making space appear larger. Some of these devices are:

- The use of **open plans** with few structural walls. Many homes have been remodeled to remove walls. However, a general contractor should be consulted first to determine if walls can safely be removed without posing a threat to the structural soundness of the building. In no case should load-bearing walls be removed.

- Vertical space, accomplished with vaulted (high, angled) ceilings, 1½- or 2-story ceilings, or skylights.
- Half walls that allow visual and audible communication to the upper area of an adjoining room.
- Extensive use of glass windows, doors, and walls. In the past, glass building materials admitted too much heat and cold. Now, however, we are able to control solar gain and heat loss through new glass types, high-performance window film, shading devices, and energy-conserving window treatments.

Once the building is complete, decorative space-saving devices can also seem to expand space. These devices include the following:

- Light colors seem to recede, as do dull colors.
- Smooth textures expand space more than do rough textures.
- Properly used mirrors can expand space if, for example, the mirror reflects a view out a window and not a decoratively furnished or busy, patterned area.
- Floor-to-ceiling draperies make walls look taller, as do top treatments and strong vertical lines in the window treatments.
- Long vertical or horizontal moldings carry the eye and expand visual space, giving the impression of greater height or width, respectively.

Figure 6.36 Colors of deep value make a space feel smaller.
© Grey Crawford/Beateworks.com

- Plain, wall-to-wall floor coverings will give the impression of greater floor area, particularly in contrast to patterned or layered floor coverings.
- Furnishings that are small scale, are lighter in color, use small or no patterns, have legs rather than upholstered skirts or solid wood to the floor, and utilize glass or other see-through materials will also help expand small spaces. A common design error is to place large, patterned upholstered pieces and large-scale wooden furniture in small spaces.

Making Large Spaces Seem Smaller

Too much space can be as big a dilemma as too little space. Feelings of unfriendliness and insecurity are common in areas that are larger than human scale in height and/or horizontal space. Noises are often amplified, or they may echo or reverberate, particularly when there are large areas of hard surfaces. Communication can be difficult because of this. Another pitfall is a lack of privacy and the inability to physically or emotionally claim an area as one's own.

Space-reducing devices are largely the converse of space-saving devices. The following suggestions call for groupings and techniques to make the space become more human in scale and more friendly:

- Furniture can be arranged into several conversation or function groupings.
- Area rugs, such as colored and patterned Oriental or designer rugs, can define groupings.
- Darker colors on walls, floors, and ceilings make space seem smaller, as do patterns or heavy rough textures.
- Space will appear to decrease with large-scale furniture such as upholstery with skirts, or the overstuffed variety; wood furniture that is heavy (literally); furniture that is solid right to the floor; and tall and wide pieces.

Traffic Patterns

Traffic patterns are also referred to as circulation or traffic flow. A traffic pattern is the repeatedly used walking path from room to room or area to area. Traffic patterns are necessary and unavoidable and require careful evaluation as an important part of space planning. Traffic patterns may be drawn in lines and arrows on the diagram or floor plan, indicating where people will be walking or where objects will be moved regularly through the space. These traffic patterns should be left free and kept as direct as possible. In a home, major traffic patterns typically lead from:

- Front door to a central circulation system that leads to all areas of the house
- Garage to kitchen for carrying groceries

Figure 6.37 Two phases of schematics or graphics in the evolution of the floor plan. (A) The size and shape of the rooms and the traffic patterns. (B) The floor plan where doorways, windows, and walls are clearly defined.

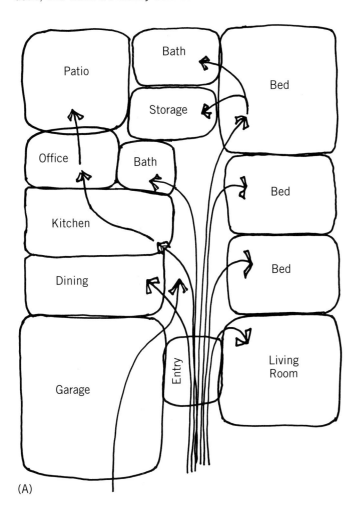

(A)

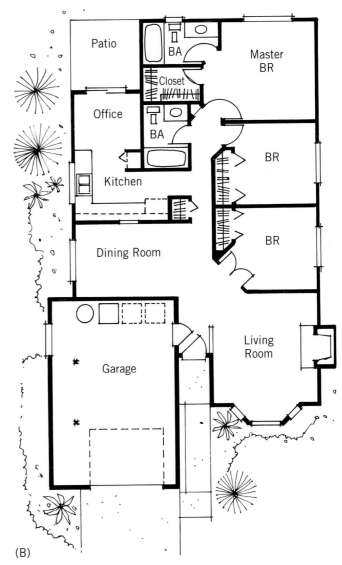

(B)

- Garage to hall closet, service area, or mudroom
- Kitchen to formal, informal, and private living areas
- Kitchen to dining room
- Kitchen to service areas and entry areas
- Laundry areas to bedrooms
- Bedrooms to bathrooms
- Back door to kitchen, mudroom, or service area

Some pitfalls to avoid in arranging traffic patterns:

- Rooms that act as hallways, where a room must be crossed to reach another room
- Door locations that force circulation through conversation furniture groupings
- Areas too small for furniture and circulation
- Areas where bathroom fixtures, beds, or other private spaces are open to view
- Traffic flow through work areas that tend to be untidy, such as the kitchen sink or laundry area

Traffic patterns must be planned for adequate width. Hallways and stairs in homes have typically been 3 feet to 3 feet 6 inches wide. However, a 4-foot-wide corridor and stairs will more comfortably allow two-way traffic, not to mention users with special needs.

Another traffic planning feature is the location of doors and the direction the doors swing. Generally, doors should be placed toward the corner of a room to avoid cutting up the wall space, and the door should swing inward against the adjoining wall. Where **swinging doors** will be a problem, **pocket doors** or sliding doors that will not impede traffic may be a good choice.

Rethinking the Box— Planning for Flexibility

The saying "Nothing is as permanent as change" is good to remember when summarizing space planning

Figure 6.38 Families who want to monitor computer use will plan for it in centers of activity. *© 2002 Bruce Ayres/Stone*

considerations. What is reality today may be just a memory tomorrow. For example, a college student leaving home for school or leaving home permanently, to return only for short visits, creates a demographic shift as well as an empty bedroom that can be reallocated for another spatial need. It may become a home office, a guest room, a hobby room. With a little remodeling, it may be absorbed to create a long-desired master suite sitting area.

Planning for flexibility is the wisest sort of planning. Consider some of these potential changes in the needs of a family:

- A couple with no children can use space in any way they want and can adapt any extra bedrooms for their own personal needs.
- As children become a part of the family, spatial needs vary dramatically. Not only is the bedroom the child's world, but the entire home becomes his or her playground unless limits are placed on where and how the child can interact with his or her surroundings.
- With a growing family, play space, study space, friend-interaction space, and even getting-away-from-the-children space become priorities.
- When students are a part of the family mix, there is increased need for computer and printer access. Many families desire to monitor use of the Internet and will opt to have computers the children use within sight of the daily task routine. This requires good advance space planning to meet the needs of the student as well as the adult.
- As the children grow up and leave home and then return for visits or to live with their own children, a need exists for both integrated and separated family living spaces. Many families will plan for an "apartment" where grown family members can be autonomous.

This may include a kitchenette or small kitchen and eating area, a second laundry room, and another living space as well as bathroom and bedroom.

- As an increasing number of children, children-in-law, grandchildren, and all their friends come to visit, the family home may need to accommodate crowds. Advance planning will provide space where they can sit, visit, and eat.
- Another important consideration is the plight of aged parents, who, typically between the ages of 70 and 90, can no longer live independently and need to be taken into the family home. Advance planning for a "mother-in-law apartment" can benefit all family members if and when the need arises. With the increased good health of the elderly making nursing home care unnecessary for many, this becomes a very real possibility. If the apartment is on ground level and other family members can move to another level, the inevitable stress can be reduced. Planning for a secondary master suite on another level or in another location in the house will accommodate this demand. That secondary suite would make a nice guest room when not occupied by a live-in family member.

Take note: Check local codes first to find out exact parameters of apartments within the home. For example, a second kitchen may not be allowed if the stove is full-size. A separate entrance may not be allowed—or it may be required. To minimize difficulties with the building inspector, research the laws before making plans and beginning a project.

Nonresidential Considerations

The discipline of space planning for nonresidential spaces is far more complex than that for residential spaces. Each area—medical facilities, hospitality, business and office space, retail space, and production plants—has highly complex and specialized considerations, often based on local or state building codes. As such, an evaluation of all nonresidential space is beyond the scope of this book. However, since most of us have at least visited many or all of these spaces, it is possible to evaluate what we see as it pertains to space planning.

To this end, the following information is an extension of the space planning principles discussed in this chapter; most of the information that applies to homes can, in some form or another, also apply to many nonresidential interiors.

Function and Zoning

In each type of nonresidential building, the zoning will be specific to its functions. Below are some things to look for.

A Design for 21st Century Living

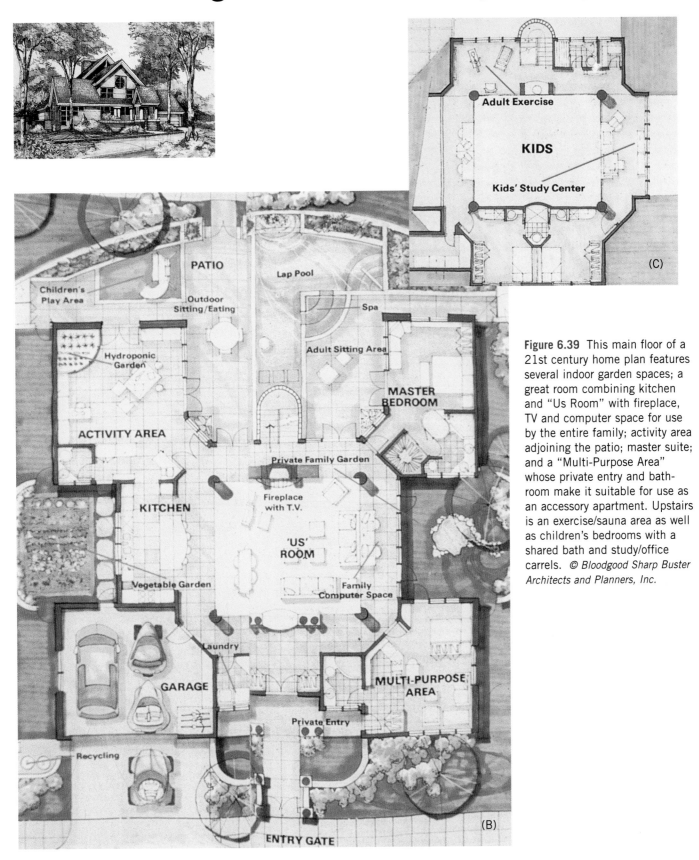

Figure 6.39 This main floor of a 21st century home plan features several indoor garden spaces; a great room combining kitchen and "Us Room" with fireplace, TV and computer space for use by the entire family; activity area adjoining the patio; master suite; and a "Multi-Purpose Area" whose private entry and bathroom make it suitable for use as an accessory apartment. Upstairs is an exercise/sauna area as well as children's bedrooms with a shared bath and study/office carrels. © *Bloodgood Sharp Buster Architects and Planners, Inc.*

Figure 6.40 A gym/spa facility includes a snack bar featuring healthy foods. © David Sundberg/Esto

Figure 6.41 The reception area of a library where traffic is directed by means of color, signage, and space planning. *Perry Dean Rogers & Partners Architects/photo © Brian Vanden Brink*

Restaurants

- Reception/payment, waiting area including some seating, coat rack or check
- Open seating at tables and booths, sometimes a bar zone (less formal dining), possibly al fresco dining area
- Take-out area (casual or fast-food eateries)
- Self-serve buffet area (less formal dining)
- Rest room zone
- Food preparation and storage zone, delivery and receiving area

Hospitality

- Hotels and motels are planned with one or more open-seating areas in the reception area, some within view of the check-in counter.
- In multistory hotels, elevator banks constitute a zone, generally located near stairs or escalators.
- Luggage bellhop stations and luggage storage/holding rooms.
- A lounge is often a part of the large lobby area, where people wait for friends or relax before going out to a restaurant for dinner and even where business is conducted.
- Informal dining, often referred to as a coffee shop, and one or more formal restaurants may be located on the main level; the nicest restaurants are often on the penthouse level or top floor with a commanding view of the city.
- Meeting rooms for business gatherings, conferences, and trade show seminars.
- Ballrooms and banquet rooms that can be divided into smaller rooms.
- Business centers with copying, faxing, and mailing services.
- Support areas with small shops; some luxury hotels have mini-shopping malls as a part of the hotel or adjoin larger indoor, sometimes multistory shopping or business centers.

Shopping Malls and Retail Stores

- In shopping malls, both general large entrances with clear signage and entrances to the anchor stores and larger retail shops.
- Open (one- or two-story) central mall spaces with benches and perhaps fountains and other nonretail images for resting the eye and body and meeting other shoppers.
- Open food court, where order and pickup counters can be seen from all seating/dining areas. Notice that the shape, architectural detail, and furnishings of this open space are often interesting—the atmosphere needs to be emotionally nourishing, even fun.
- Department store zones should be clearly marked with graphics or signage so that shoppers can find their way in, find what they need, and find their way out.
- Smaller shops or boutiques generally have a more open layout, where the entire store may be visible from the mall or street entrance. Notice, however, how fixtures and signage separate the merchandise into zones.
- Merchandise checkout or payment stations should also be obvious, as should important support stations where functions such as repair, customer support, or gift wrap are located.

Medical or Healing Centers

- Reception and patient waiting zone, checkout area
- File storage and retrieval, support-staff stations, insurance processing and billing desk area
- Patient exam rooms for doctors or non-Western healers
- In-office lab space; general weigh-in area, rest rooms
- Doctors' personal office space
- Surgery area
- Support/supply areas
  In healing centers there may also be:
- A sauna and/or spa treatment area
- Massage, exercise, and other therapy areas including exercise equipment
- Group instruction rooms or areas, in both seated classroom and open space for yoga/exercise

Hospitals

- In addition to the above, hospitals have more surgery space and areas for specialties such as obstetrics, laboratories, x-ray and nuclear medicine, various forms of therapy and counseling.
- Patient rooms and support facilities
- Nurses' stations
- Administrative areas including an extensive business office
- A kitchen, cafeteria, pharmacy, and chapel are figured into most hospital plans.

Public Transportation

- Train stations, bus stations, and airports need specific areas to function: check-in at counters and curbside, spaces to manage crowds and long lines, and security checkpoint areas.
- Elevator, escalator, and stairs
- Public rest rooms
- Administrative and customer services; baggage-hold offices
- Baggage-processing areas connecting or convenient to planes, buses, or trains
- Shops and casual dining
- Signage and connecting walkways and trams

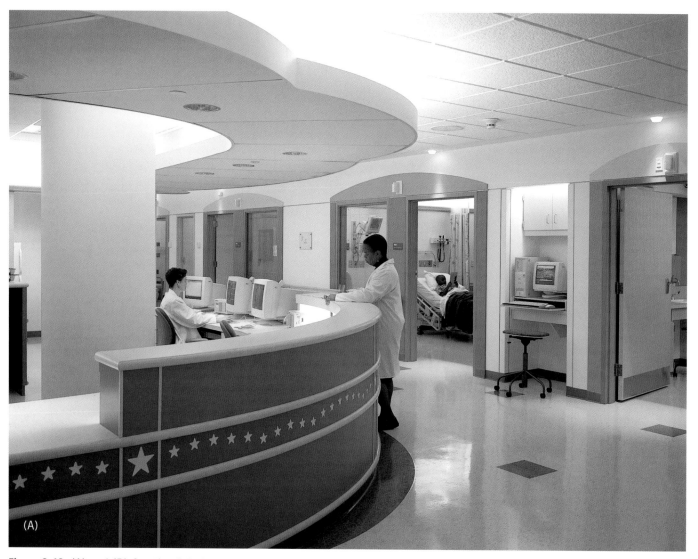

(A)

Figure 6.42 (A) and (B) Creative light-hearted design in the pediatric wing of a hospital helps children and parents as well as professionals to feel more optimistic. *S.B.R.A. Architects/photos © Brian Vanden Brink*

Office Buildings
- Multistory office buildings have a lobby area with a directory of businesses per floor.
- Elevator banks and stairwells; rest rooms
- Lobby areas on each floor and entrances for each business that typically include a reception area, waiting area, support facilities and administration, offices, and conference rooms

Other Public Facilities
With the above areas in mind, think about space planning in every public place you visit: look for spatial allotments in grocery stores, churches, gym or spa facilities, and schools. By observing and evaluating the use of the space, we can determine if the space planning was wise and well thought out or if more research in the design process should have been conducted before floor plans were finalized.

Traffic Patterns
The greater the volume of people or objects, the wider the traffic pattern or **corridors** will need to be. This is evident in public architecture such as hospitals and shopping centers, where the traffic is heavy and corridors are wide. Local building codes must be met for corridor widths in nonresidential buildings.

Two separate sets of doors are often employed in nonresidential settings as air-lock entries, or vestibules, to keep out excess cold air, rain, and snow. This arrangement can also be a security enhancement. The vestibule area should be sizable so that foot traffic will not pile up and there is room for shelter.

Traffic patterns in settings such as department or specialty stores can be quite complex, and architects use visible markers or guideposts to aid the users. People entering nonresidential spaces need to know three things

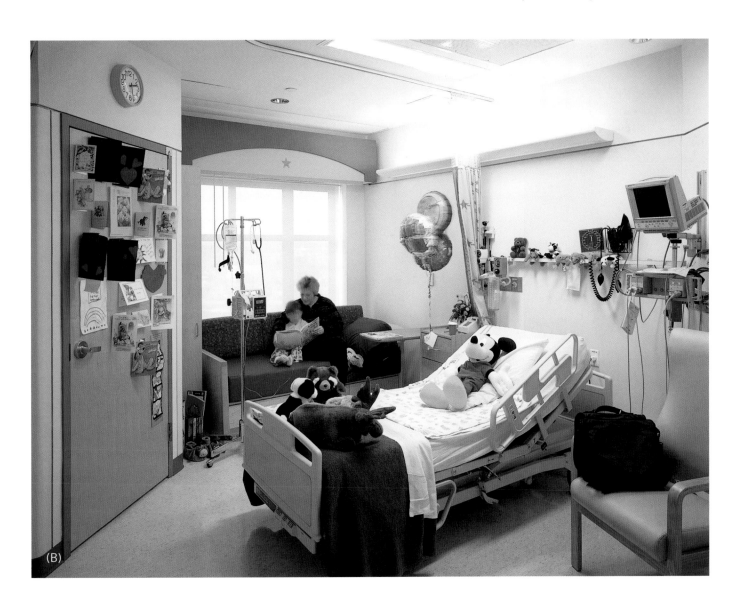

(B)

Figure 6.43 Signage is a critical element in airport space planning. © *Steve Vidler/ SuperStock*

in order for traffic to flow smoothly: (1) how to get in, (2) how to find their way around, and (3) how to get out.

Some spaces do this quite effectively. For example, in a well-planned grocery store or supermarket, the buyer is able to find grocery carts near the entrance, locate items by checking the bright wall signs and the smaller hanging signs over spacious aisles, and then find the checkout counter with easy egress to the doors and the street or parking lot.

Traffic patterns also need to be planned in open, multi-use areas such as the open-plan office. Where several functions take place in one area, the furnishings or planning systems can be the delineators of space. A free-standing wall partition, desk, computer terminal desk, filing system, or shelf can be moved to accommodate changing needs, providing flexibility. Fewer structural walls allow for easier traffic flow, and the removal of visual obstructions makes spaces seem larger.

Chapter 7 | Floor Plans and Building Systems

Floor Plans 172

Diagramming and Floor Plans 173

Floor Plans and Housing 175

Constructing the Building 188

Insulation and Energy Conservation 195

Nonresidential Considerations 201

Winton Scott, architect/photo © Brian Vanden Brink

Floor Plans

Floor plans are part of the working drawings or documents required to build a new space or remodel an existing one. A custom floor plan may evolve slowly by hand, beginning with a bubble and then overlay through steps of refinement, or drafting may be accomplished with computer software tools. Stock plans can be edited or modified or can be left as is, with the home built from readily available plans.

This chapter explores the types of floor plans and housing, explains floor plan symbols, and presents a brief overview of the most commonly used **structural building system** or construction methods. Alternative building system methods are sometimes used in homes, although they are chiefly seen in nonresidential buildings, as discussed at the end of this chapter. Since the finishing and furnishing of an interior are an integral part of the entire process, persons involved in interior design benefit from an understanding of the entire process.

The chapter also presents an overview of **interior environmental control systems**—plumbing, heating, and air-conditioning. Electrical systems and home automation are discussed in Chapter 5, "Lighting and Technology." The **interior finish components** are listed, as are **project-managing tools,** including **technology tools** used by architects, general contractors, design professionals, and laypersons who act as their own general contractors or do the work themselves.

A building system based on the use of **solar energy** utilizes heat and energy from the sun to warm flooring, cubic living space, or water. Insulation is part of the building process, but it can be incorporated after the

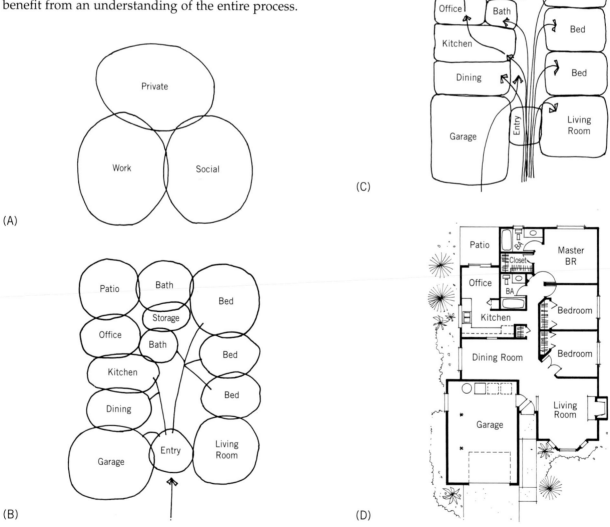

(A)

(B)

(C)

(D)

Figure 7.1 Two phases of schematics or graphics in the evolution of the floor plan. (A) The general zones—private, work, and social. (B) Divisions within these zones for specific rooms and their relationship to one another. (C) The size and shape of the rooms and the traffic patterns. (D) The floor plan where doorways, windows, and walls are clearly defined.

completion of any building. Building components that conserve natural resources and use recycled products or products that are environmentally safe are termed **green design,** discussed in Chapter 2. Green design should be a part of the thought process and be incorporated at every opportunity in every building, remodeling, or refurnishing project.

For further information on any of the topics in this chapter, go to the *Interiors* website, which lists Web addresses for the National Association of Home Builders (NAHB) and other organizations and businesses that supply a wealth of information on the latest developments in building processes.

Diagramming and Floor Plans

Diagramming is the process of placing a two- or three-dimensional representation of the proposed space on paper. The **graphics** evolve by refining the schematics (drawings and allocation of space) to finally become a finished **floor plan.** The evolution of diagramming takes place as follows:

- **Bubble planning**—the placement of zones on paper according to function.
- Size and shape determination—the allocation of square footage and cubic footage and the shape of rooms and areas.
- **Refinement**—this step could take up to several **overlays,** the laying of tracing paper over the previous graphic to tighten and refine the sketch, or it could be accomplished through CADD software tools.
- **Perspective sketches** and **renderings**—three-dimensional pencil, pen-and-ink, or full-color representations of the proposed space or how a portion of the interior will appear upon completion.
- **Floor plans**—the finished product that indicates specific and exact placement of walls and systems within the home. Floor plans are drawn to scale (usually ¼ inch equals 1 foot) and consist of symbols that make the plan understandable to the general contractor and subcontractors. Other components of the construction documents are discussed later in this chapter.

Measurements of Space: Cubic and Square Footage

Cubic footage is three-dimensional space or the space we walk through. It is determined by multiplying a room's width by its length and then by its height. Rooms with a typical 8-foot ceiling will contain fewer cubic feet than rooms with higher ceilings. Greater cubic footage suggests the possibility of vaulted ceilings and interesting vertical shapes, with the accompanying illusion of greater square footage or floor space.

Square footage is two-dimensional space (floor area), which equals the length of the room or building multiplied by its width. Square footage may be the determining

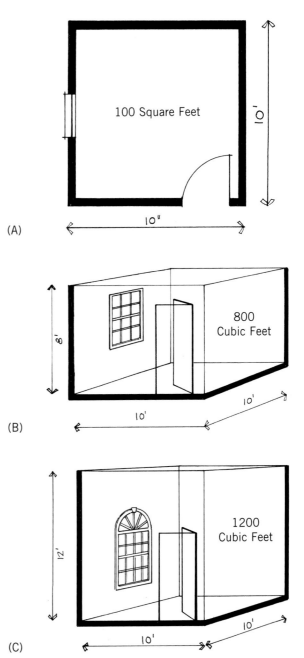

Figure 7.2 Calculation of square footage and cubic footage. (A) Square footage is derived by multiplying the width of a room by its length. The 10 feet by 10 feet yields 100 square feet. (B) Cubic footage is the width multiplied by the length and then by the height of the room. The 100 square feet multiplied by 8-foot walls yields 800 cubic feet. (C) The same room with a 12-foot ceiling contains more cubic footage and will cost more in both material and labor, even though the square footage remains the same.

factor of the building size based on an estimated **cost per square foot.** Square footage may also be limited by the size of the building lot. In neighborhoods of new homes, there may also be a minimum acceptable square footage requirement, part of the restrictive covenants established by the developer or residents to ensure a consistent level of quality and price range in the neighborhood's homes.

Figure 7.3 Curved walls and vaulted skylights make this an exciting architectural space. *© Peter Aaron/Esto*

A breakdown for square footage may be based on a percentage for each general area. In homes, a general rule of thumb is to allot 80 percent of the space for living space, 10 percent for halls, and 10 percent for storage.

Another factor in determining square footage may be the number of people who will occupy the space. Psychological studies have repeatedly demonstrated that **overcrowding** can lead to adverse emotional consequences as well as physical limitations and discomfort. However, the number of square feet allotted per person varies according to society. Whereas in Hong Kong 60 feet per person is considered adequate, in the United States 400 to 500 square feet per person is generally considered the minimum for comfortable living standards, although fewer square feet may be alloted for children and modest living.

Shaping the Space

The shape of the interior space has horizontal and vertical components. Although a rectangular room is the easiest to build and simplest to decorate, it can also be the most boring architecturally. Angled or curved walls, vaulted or curved ceilings, half walls or transparent walls, or even cutout sections between rooms can add interest and visually expand the actual dimensions of the room. Altering room shapes has been a boon to new smaller homes and to the remodeling of older ones, as the alternatives give the impression of greater space and provide architectural interest where none may otherwise have existed.

The shape of interior spaces can also affect the exterior shape and dimensions of the home; this, too, must be taken into careful consideration when designing custom housing. From the interior living standpoint, it is ideal to first determine the spatial arrangements and shapes within the floor plan, then let the exterior shape be determined by the sizes and shapes of the interior spaces. However, the desired style or proportions of the exterior will often limit or restrict the interior shapes or sizes. Realistically, some compromise is often necessary. A room may need to be altered in dimension or size to make the exterior more pleasing, or the placement of doors and windows in the rooms may be dictated by their fenestration, or arrangement, from the exterior.

Site, Orientation, and Climate

The shape of the space may also be dictated by the limitations or special considerations of the building site. Look carefully at the direction of the prevailing breezes in both summer and winter, the slope of the lot, any natural vegetation, the location and types of nearby buildings, and property values of surrounding architecture. Also consider the orientation, or direction the site faces, so that solar aspects and fenestration can be incorporated. The orientation is also important in relation to the climate. A sunbelt home will have different planning than a New England home, for example, because the former must provide control of heat from the sun and the latter must control excessive winter cold. The needs and criteria of the climate, then, are important aspects of planning a home.

Floor Plans and Housing

Floor Plan Symbols

Floor plan symbols are illustrated in Figure 7.4a through 7.4d. These include symbols for windows, doors, plumbing fixtures, appliances, walls, stairs, and mechanical equipment. (Electrical symbols are found in Chapter 5, "Lighting and Technology.") Keep in mind these are examples only; the number and types of symbols vary.

A study of these symbols will increase the ability to "read" or understand the floor plans that follow.

Floor Plan Types

There are three types of floor plans:

- A **closed floor plan** is one in which most or all of the rooms are units that are opened to others only by a door, and when the door is shut, the room is completely enclosed. This gives privacy and control over sound, yet often it creates a chopped-up floor plan without flexibility.
- An **open floor plan** has several areas that are open to one another without walls or with only partial walls or dividers. The cost to build may be less, and the space seems much larger than with a closed plan. There is flexibility in the use of the space. The disadvantages lie in the lack of privacy that may result and the transmission of more sound than is desirable. These floor plans may open vertically (high ceilings), horizontally (few walls), or both.
- **Combination** (open and closed) **plans** have both open and closed areas or areas that can be opened to permit a flexible use of the space. This can be accomplished with double doors (such as a pair of pocket sliding doors, French doors, or accordion doors) and with some areas with high ceilings that open to areas such as lofts or balconies or other living space.

Types of Housing

Housing can be divided into two broad categories: the **single family residence (SFR),** which is an independent house with a yard, and **attached dwellings,** those that share walls, with or without a yard.

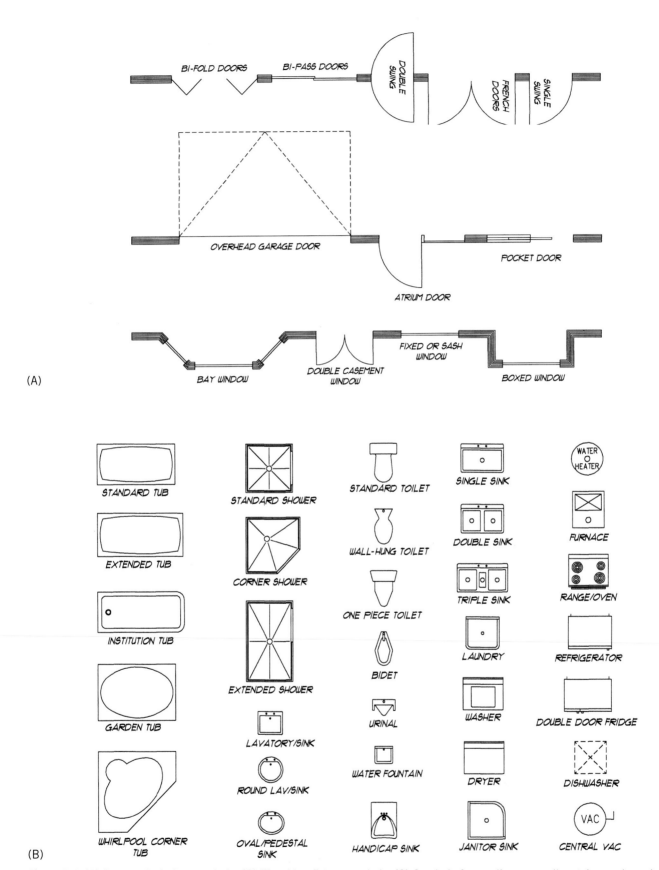

Figure 7.4 (A) Door and window symbols. (B) Plumbing fixture symbols. (C) Symbols for appliances, walls, stairs, and mechanical support equipment. (D) Representations of finish building materials as indicated on the elevations—part of the blueprint plans. *(A & B) CAD by Gary Stewart*

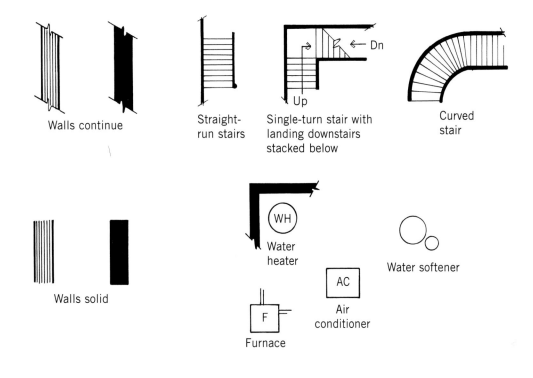

Walls continue

Straight-run stairs

Single-turn stair with landing downstairs stacked below

Curved stair

Walls solid

Water heater

Furnace

Air conditioner

Water softener

(C)

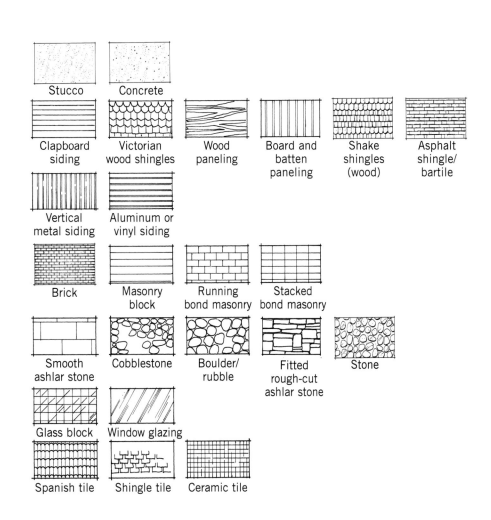

Stucco

Concrete

Clapboard siding

Victorian wood shingles

Wood paneling

Board and batten paneling

Shake shingles (wood)

Asphalt shingle/ bartile

Vertical metal siding

Aluminum or vinyl siding

Brick

Masonry block

Running bond masonry

Stacked bond masonry

Smooth ashlar stone

Cobblestone

Boulder/ rubble

Fitted rough-cut ashlar stone

Stone

Glass block

Window glazing

Spanish tile

Shingle tile

Ceramic tile

(D)

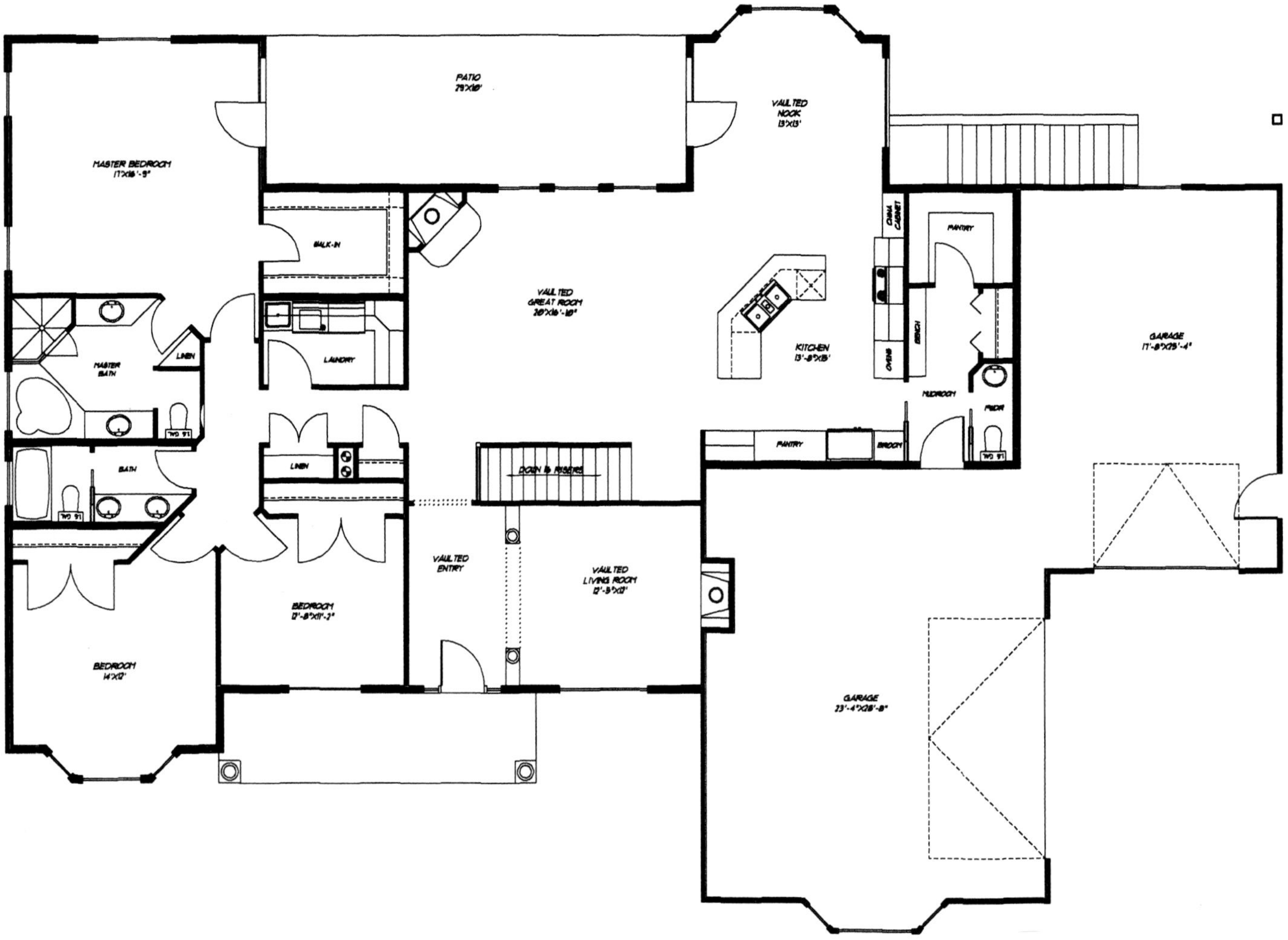

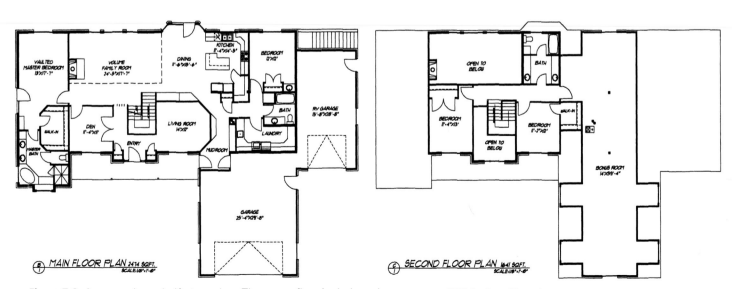

Figure 7.5 A rambler or ranch-style plan with optional basement. *CAD by Gary Stewart*

Figure 7.6 A one-and-one-half-story plan. The upper floor includes a bonus room. *CAD by Gary Stewart*

The Single Family Residence

The single family residence, or a home with a yard, has the greatest potential for individuality. Although some are rental units, the majority of homes are owner-occupied. Ownership means that the plan can be originated or remodeled to fit the needs of the owners. Here are the types of plans:

- A **rambler** or **ranch.** A one-story home, with living room, dining room, kitchen, bedrooms, and bathroom all on one level. A basement, if any, typically contains a family room, utility area (laundry, half-bath, mudroom), additional bedrooms, bathroom, and/or storage. When built with a slope in the backyard, the downstairs area may be a walk-out basement, which allows for full-size windows and patio doors. In this case, a deck and perhaps steps down to the backyard will service the main floor. A rambler or ranch can be a prefabricated house moved onto the site and placed on a waiting foundation or over a basement; such homes are also built in developments ranging from modest to upscale and may even be spacious with luxury features.
- **One-and-one-half story.** A plan with bedrooms upstairs inside the attic, usually with dormer windows. The main floor contains the living and dining rooms, kitchen, bath or half-bath, and perhaps a den or family room and/or master bedroom.
- **Two-story.** A plan similar to a one-and-one-half story, except that the roof line begins above the second floor, allowing full-height ceilings. There is usually a full- or partial-height attic above the second floor.
- **Split level.** A house with three or more levels. Typical plans put the living room, dining room, kitchen, and perhaps a half-bath on the main floor. Up one-half flight is the bedroom wing, and down one-half flight from the entry is the family room and utility space. Another level below the main floor may house storage or extra bedrooms.
- **Split entry** or **raised ranch.** A rambler with a raised basement, where half the basement is above ground level. The entry is on a landing, and stairs go up to the main floor or down to the basement. Being halfway above ground level, the basement is better-lit with larger windows, making the lower level a more livable space.
- **Patio home.** A plan suitable for a narrow lot. It may be one, one-and-one-half, or two stories. Such homes are economical because of the modest number of square feet and smaller lot size. One-story patio homes are especially well suited to the retirement-age owner who does not want to or cannot climb stairs. Patio homes are also a good choice for first or starter homes.
- **Mobile home.** A prefabricated home that is a part of a mobile home park. Single-wide mobile homes are 12- to 15-feet wide; double-wide mobile homes are 20- to 30-feet wide and are fabricated as two units and moved to the site. Originally called trailers, and meant to be mobile, most of these are now permanent.

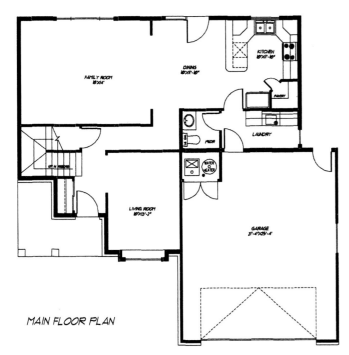

MAIN FLOOR PLAN

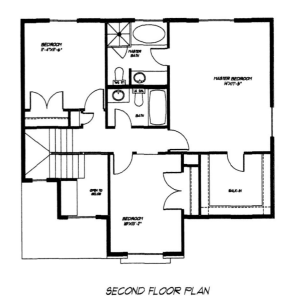

SECOND FLOOR PLAN

MAIN FLOOR 962 SQ.FT.
2ND FLOOR 991 SQ.FT.

Figure 7.7 A two-story plan showing a great room along the rear of the home. Bedrooms and private areas are zoned upstairs. *CAD by Gary Stewart*

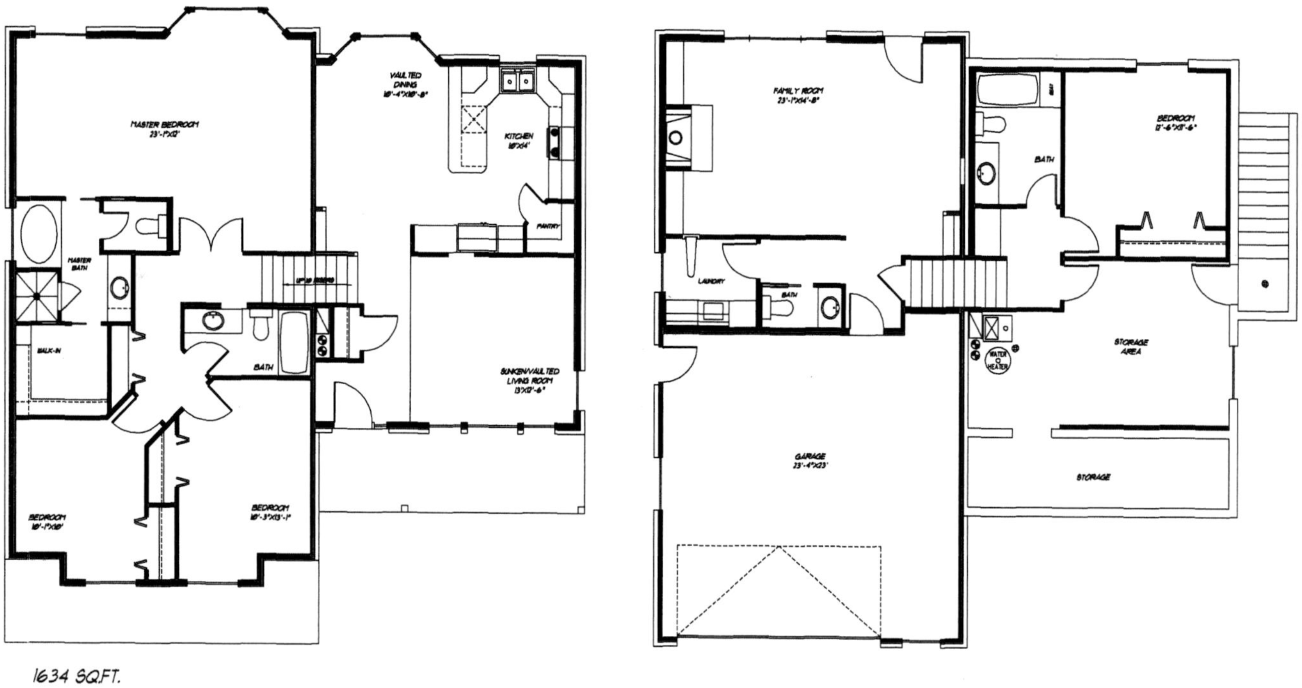

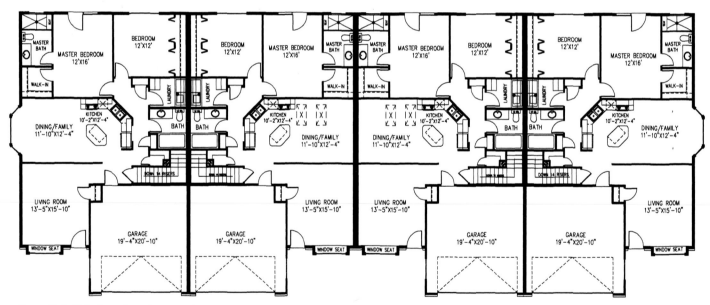

1634 SQ.FT.

Figure 7.8 A split-level home showing three steps down to the family room and 10 steps up to the bedroom wing above the garage. Storage and one more bedroom are beneath the kitchen and living room. *CAD by Gary Stewart*

Figure 7.9 This fourplex plan may be apartments (to rent) or condominiums (to own). *CAD by Gary Stewart*

Attached Dwellings

Attached dwellings have many advantages: better use of land so that more people can live in locations convenient to urban centers, schools, or business; less cost; and more freedom from the yardwork and upkeep that a larger home and yard require. Their major categories are as follows:

- **Apartment buildings** are multistory buildings where multiple units are housed on each floor, accessed by stairs and in high-rise complexes also by elevators. **Apartments** typically have one living area, one kitchen/dining area, one or two bathrooms, and one to four bedrooms.

- **Multiplex units** are small apartment buildings. A two-family or-unit building is a **duplex,** which may be one level with a basement apartment or may be side-by-side apartments. A three-unit building is a **triplex,** a

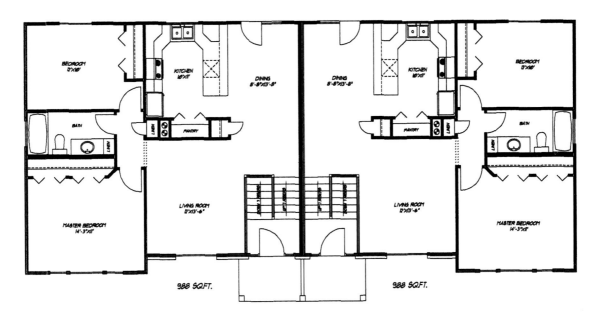

MAIN FLOOR PLAN (UNIT 1)   MAIN FLOOR PLAN (UNIT 2)

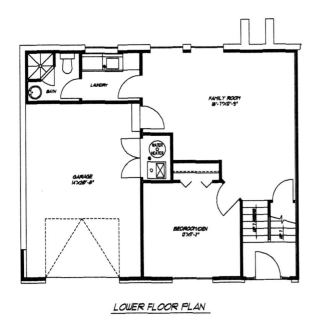

LOWER FLOOR PLAN

FRONT ELEVATION (UNITS 1 & 2)

Figure 7.10 A twin home or semi-detached house plan. *CAD by Gary Stewart*

four-unit building is a **fourplex** or **quadplex,** and so on. Each unit may have a separate or shared entrance.

- **Accessory apartments** are located in a detached dwelling in a portion of the home, such as in the basement, in the back of the house, over the garage, or in an upstairs location. Many locales have zoning restrictions on accessory apartments; they will often require, for example, at least three off-street parking spaces.

- **Twin homes** or **semidetached houses** are two homes built on a lot with a shared wall between them. They may be one, one-and-one-half, or two stories high. These homes may also be called duplexes.

- **Luxury apartments or flats** are usually larger and have more upscale or luxury features. The bottom or ground floor and nearby buildings typically have all the support services required for convenient living: parking spaces, a post office, grocery and apparel stores, a drugstore, dry cleaners, and so on. The living space is called a suite, a flat, a condominium, or an apartment.

- **Town houses, brownstones,** and **row houses** are attached city houses built as a series or development. They are narrow, usually only one or two rooms wide, and two, three, or four stories high.

- **Flats** are a group of rooms on one level of a building, such as an apartment or luxury high-rise suite. When larger brownstones are subdivided, each unit is often called a flat.

- *Pied-à-terre* is a French term for a flat or house for occasional use (literally, "foot on the ground"), typically kept as a second home in a city distant from the primary dwelling.

Note: These terms may vary regionally.

Buying an Existing Home

Most people will not build a custom home but will purchase or rent an existing one. Although the list of things

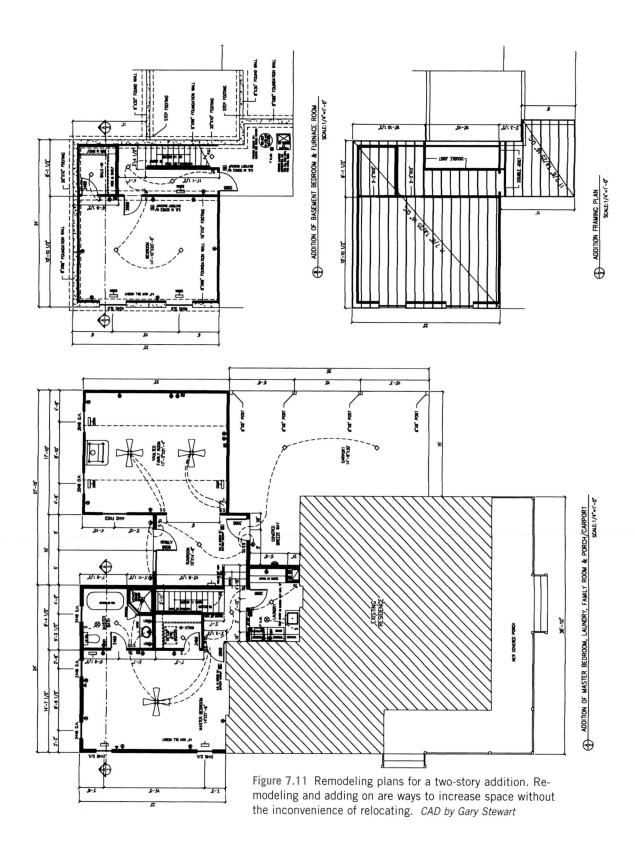

Figure 7.11 Remodeling plans for a two-story addition. Remodeling and adding on are ways to increase space without the inconvenience of relocating. *CAD by Gary Stewart*

to know when selecting a home is extensive and more information is available through the Web addresses listed on the *Interiors* website, here are a few of the important considerations:

- **Location, location, and location** are said to be the three most important criteria in buying a home. It is wise to buy the most modest home in a nice neighborhood (increased value) but unwise to own the nicest home in any neighborhood (decreased value). Location has to do with neighborhood, proximity to support services, ease of access, and even things like view and property values.
- **Buy a home that meets your present and future needs.** If you expect to increase or decrease your family size, operate a home business, or add luxury features, choose a plan that will allow modifications without major remodeling.
- **Consider upkeep.** You'll never regret buying a home with materials and systems that are relatively maintenance free.
- **Look for warranties** on the environmental control systems (heating, air-conditioning, plumbing, electrical).
- **Check for structural soundness** in construction—framing, roofing, walls and windows, doors, flooring.
- **Be aware of defects** or potential problems; negotiate with the seller as to who will repair existing problems. Older homes require more upkeep; be sure your budget will allow for this. A building inspector will verify if the home is soundly built and safe for occupancy. In addition, prospective buyers can hire private home inspection services to evaluate the building and its systems and fixtures. The findings of the inspection help buyers decide if the home is worth the asking price. Some defects are serious, others are just cosmetic, and still others are perceived defects because the plan or features do not suit the lifestyle of the new occupants. Go in with your eyes wide open about what will be required to make the home truly yours.
- **Utilize online real estate services**—both listings and virtual tours. A photo bubble allows viewers to look upward to the ceiling and down at the floor and to pan right and left. As rooms are strung together, the Internet tour re-creates a walking tour. Also available are views outside to see the neighborhood and the backyard.

Obtaining the Floor Plan

Before construction or remodeling can begin, the owners and contractors must obtain a floor plan specific to the project. This can be done in one of several ways.

- **Custom floor plans** are unique, or one-of-a-kind, plans that meet the needs of the client, the uses, and the site. There are three ways to get custom floor plans:

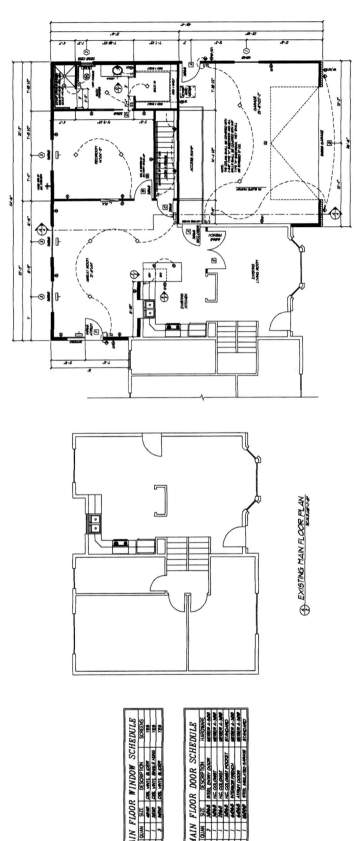

Figure 7.12 This split-level home has been remodeled to meet the needs of an ambulant disabled user. *CAD by Gary Stewart*

Table 7.1 | Types of Home Occupancy

Three principal forms of home occupancy are private, condominium, and rental. Each type has advantages and disadvantages for certain groups of people and for those in different stages of life.

Private Ownership

Like the single detached house, private ownership—owning one's own home—is a part of the American dream that is becoming less obtainable as the cost of housing and financing increases (see Table 6.1). Private ownership brings with it a great deal of responsibility for upkeep, maintenance, security, and care of the house and grounds. For some, this responsibility is an unwanted burden that is eliminated by other forms of ownership.

Condominium

The word *condominium* comes from Latin and literally means "ownership with." Condominiums are complexes of any type of dwelling, from high rise to town house, that are owned privately but maintained and governed by groups of owners. These groups form home owners' associations that use the owner's monthly fees to provide for general maintenance, security, snow removal, and care of the landscape. The home owners' associations also establish the rules and restrictions for the condominiums. Some condominiums feature amenities such as club houses, health and fitness centers, swimming pools, tennis courts, stables, and parks—also maintained through the monthly fees. Condominiums can be geared to people with similar interests or ages such as singles, young families, and "empty-nesters" (couples whose children have left home). Condominiums are ideal for those who want to own property without all of the worries of private ownership.

Rental

Those who are unable to afford condominiums or private ownership will usually rent housing from a landlord who owns and maintains the rental properties such as **apartments.** Others choose to rent because renting generally carries no responsibility for maintenance or upkeep, and in some cases all or part of the cost of utilities (electricity, gas, water, sewer, and garbage) is included in the rent. Any type of housing, from detached houses to high-rise apartments to duplexes, can be rented, although costs and quality of rental units vary greatly.

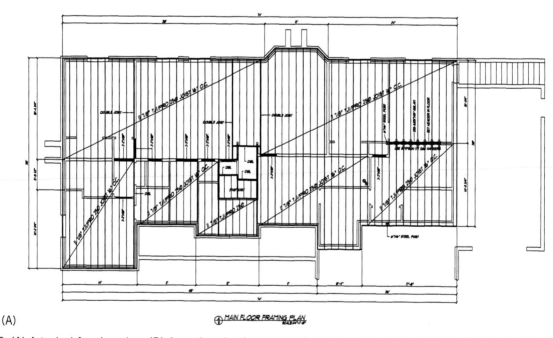

(A)

⊕ MAIN FLOOR FRAMING PLAN

Figure 7.13 (A) A typical framing plan. (B) A section showing a crosswise slice through the building. (C) Cabinet details. (D) Construction details. *CAD by Gary Stewart*

through an architect, through a home designer, or by means of computer software.

- **Architects.** The more custom the plan, the more likely that an architect will be hired to design and perhaps oversee the building project. Architects are schooled in structural soundness and the skill of taking a prospective home owner's wish list and creating the home that fulfills his or her needs and wants. Architects may also hire computer draftsmen to produce the actual floor plans.

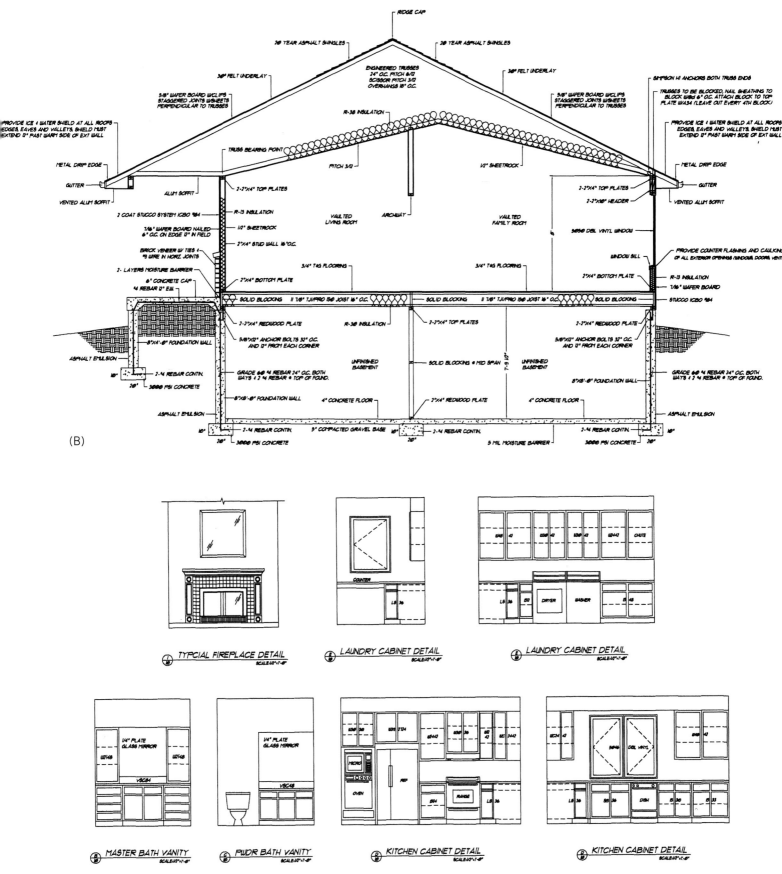

(B)

(C)

- **Home designers.** Many people have their plans drafted by a computer-trained home designer without the use of an architect. This provides a level of expertise and experience at a cost less than that of an architect. Home designers will have their plans approved by structural engineers.

- **Computer software.** Laypeople can create their own floor plans with any of several computer software packages, some of which are capable of producing contractor-ready plans. Some software allows the user to edit, or modify, existing stock plans. Most have the tools to create floor plans, including the selection or design of all interior components—fireplaces, window and wall configurations, stairs, kitchen and appliances, decks. Some have a database of appliances and plumbing fixtures to select and drop in, allowing users to experiment with the workability of the plan. Some have landscaping tools, and most have interior furnishings tools such as furniture, lighting, accessory, and surface texture databases that aid in the planning of everything from aesthetics to traffic patterns or circulation. Most packages include a 3-D tour, allowing the user to see what any given space will look like, with or without furniture and accessories.

- **Stock plans** are plans designed by architects and home designers that are available for purchase. They are found in floor plan magazines, on computer software, and on Internet websites. Both software and floor plan websites contain thousands of plans that can be purchased or printed on blueprint-size printers. Some people will customize or modify plans slightly with the help of a home designer. Modest changes—say, the location of a door—can be made by communicating with the home builder.

Computer-aided drafting (or design) (CAD) is the way nearly all custom and stock floor plans are accomplished. Most professionals are schooled in hand-drafting techniques, and hand drawn bubble sketches are often utilized at the brainstorming stages of a custom project. CAD plans, however, are accurate and allow for

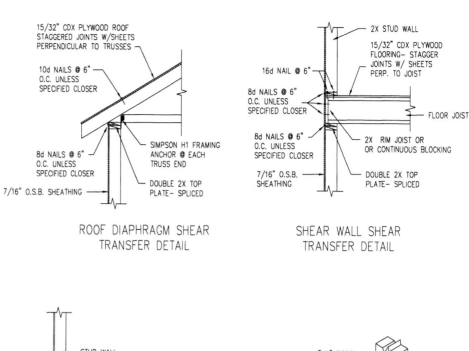

ROOF DIAPHRAGM SHEAR
TRANSFER DETAIL

SHEAR WALL SHEAR
TRANSFER DETAIL

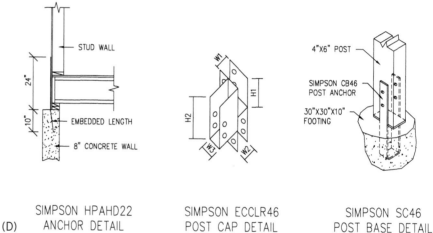

(D) SIMPSON HPAHD22
ANCHOR DETAIL

SIMPSON ECCLR46
POST CAP DETAIL

SIMPSON SC46
POST BASE DETAIL

changes to be made without an eraser. In fact, as the designer and client experiment with various options, each option can be saved in a computer file. This provides freedom and flexibility during the design process.

Construction Documents: Working Drawings or Blueprints

The working drawings, sometimes called **blueprints,** are the sets of plans that specify designs, materials, and dimensions to guide each subcontractor who works on the home or building. Working drawings include the following:

- **Floor plans** are drawn to scale (¼ inch or ⅛ inch equals 1 foot) and show the layout of the rooms and their relationship to one another. They are used for estimating cost, for scheduling, and for actual construction of the building.

- **Exterior elevations** are the exterior views of each side of the building in flat drawings (no perspective) showing the finish building materials, the location and style of doors, windows, architectural detail, roof, chimney, and other details. Exterior elevations help us judge the building style aesthetics, or curb appeal.

- **Schedules** indicate how various parts of the building are to be finished. Materials and finishes for components such as doors, floors, walls, and ceilings are listed.
- **Site plans** show the situation of the building on the land, legal boundaries, slope, key reference points, and possibly information on soils and vegetation. Site plans also indicate details on water, sewer, and electrical system grids (hookups).
- **Foundation drawings** indicate necessary details on footings, fireplace footings, anchor bolts, breaks in walls, and drains. They are used to estimate labor and materials and to direct foundation work.
- **Framing plans** give projections of the building from the lowest level and up to the roof. It shows sections, key connections, and the layout of the floors and roof, with necessary information on columns, beams, and joists. Details are enlarged.
- **Cross sections** are vertical drawings of a slice through the interior of the building, showing the relationship and scale of the foundation, walls, beams, rooms, stairs, and other architectural elements.
- **Utility plans** show a building's mechanical systems: heating, ventilation, air-conditioning, plumbing (usually presented separately), electrical, and lighting plans and cable wiring. These plans will include layout for other systems such as fire protection, security, and communications (intercom).
- **Interior elevations** show types of cabinets and millwork (molding, railings) and other special interior features. They are used to obtain bids and construct the items.
- **Details** are enlargements of construction components where clarification or additional information is needed (for example, custom window arrangement to be framed).
- **Specifications** are written documents that describe structural or finish materials or custom work—what is needed, where it is to be located, what quality and craftsmanship level is desired, how it is to be assembled, and any other special considerations needed for correct construction.
- The **subcontract** is the agreement for specialized work performed by a person or company and specified for a building's construction or finish work. The **subcontractor** will take information from the blueprints, determine how much labor and materials are required for their specialty (framing, plumbing, sheetroof, roofing, electrical, for example), and produce a bid or solid estimate of the job. The general contractor will usually get three or more bids and select the lowest bid, the

subcontractor with the reputation for the best quality work, or the subcontractor with a reasonable bid and proven quality. The **interior design package** or parts of it, such as carpeting, window treatments, wall coverings, or furnishings, may also be bid in this manner.

Who Will Do the Work

With blueprints in hand, a commitment must be made as to the actual construction of the new home or building remodel. This should not be a quick decision but should be carefully researched and thought out. Home owners should check references for all professionals they consider working with. There are three ways to accomplish a building project:

1. **An architect** can oversee a building project and will be responsible to hire the general contractor and insist that every detail be perfect. The architect then becomes the only person the home owner deals with, and this arrangement may save a lot of frustration. Architects will typically charge a fee based on a percent of the finished building costs.

2. **A home builder, general contractor, or remodeler** holds a state-issued general contractor's license and hires subcontractors to build each phase of the building, sometimes personally participating in parts or all of the building process. The general contractor will oversee every stage and work directly with subcontractors, the client, and the building inspectors. Check out credentials and talk to people for whom the builder has completed work. Look at the craftsmanship in finished projects, and ask hard questions about the builder's reliability, ease of communication, and customer satisfaction. A contract will be signed, and money given to the builder in draws from the lending institution or from your checking account. Never pay the balance until all the details are satisfied, within reason.

3. **Hiring subcontractors yourself** is an economical option if you have some experience and a basic knowledge of the building and remodeling process. Keep in mind that subcontractors (masons, carpenters, installers, painters, etc.) may be more accustomed to working for a general contractor, for whom they work regularly; this may make your project less important in terms of quality or reliability. It takes a certain amount of grit to be your own general contractor. It requires time, effort, and diligence. Be sure to read up on the topic both before and during the process.

4. **Do it yourself** is ideal for people with the skills, the tools, the time, the vision, and the support of family members. Without these, the level of frustration can run high, and keep in mind that fixing a botched job often takes more money than the cost of hiring professionals in the first place. DIY jobs are ideal for smaller remodeling jobs; a person building an entire home

alone or with help will need many months away from his or her regular employment, or else the job will drag on for an inordinate amount of time.

Constructing the Building

When construction begins, the architect or general contractor will set up a method for making everything happen at the right time. A critical path (see Table 7.2 on page 196) indicates the time frame, in consecutive and overlapping order, of every step in the building and finishing process. **Scheduling** means setting up and reconfirming dates for the selected subcontractors to arrive on the site and perform their work. If one subcontractor fails to meet the deadline for completion, it could disrupt the entire schedule. The next subcontractor on the critical path may not be available at a slightly later date because of other commitments. It is therefore the responsibility of the general contractor, architect, or project manager to coordinate the schedule by frequently contacting the subcontractors and reconfirming the schedule. This responsibility may affect the work of the interior designer at the finish and/or decoration and furnishing stage. However, the smooth flow of the construction critical path is crucial to the success of the finish critical path, and in many cases, they are not separated. Large interior design firms that specialize in nonresidential work routinely work out complex and extensive critical paths that track the flow of jobs to be performed.

The interior designer must understand the aspects of construction in order to communicate effectively with subcontractors, architects, engineers, and other professionals. A mutual respect and understanding between designers and these professionals will allow the designer to better discuss structural plans, architectural details, finish materials, and furnishing instructions. As a result, these aspects will be more successfully completed.

The designer has the responsibility of notifying the builder of special materials or finishes that could interfere with the critical path. For example, if the designer and client change the floor-covering selection from carpeting to a wood floor, the building must be left empty for a week or longer to accommodate the floor installers and finishers. This could cause serious problems with the critical path if the designer does not notify the builder in advance. It is the responsibility of the architect or designer and the builder to see that all aspects of the design are properly and correctly executed.

The jobs performed by subcontractors are explained in the sections below. They are broken into two categories: the structural building components and systems and the interior finish components.

High-technology devices are revolutionizing the way work is done at the construction site. Rather than requir-

ing rolls of cumbersome blueprints, the entire set, no matter how large the project, can now be installed on a handheld "personal digital assistant." Each project manager can then scroll to the section of the work at hand, zoom in on the details, and, if a larger view is necessary, plug the handheld device in to a notebook or laptop at the site. In addition, all the information concerning specifications, bids, critical paths, and punch lists can be kept on personal digital assistants, as can information for the materials and furnishings for a building's interior.

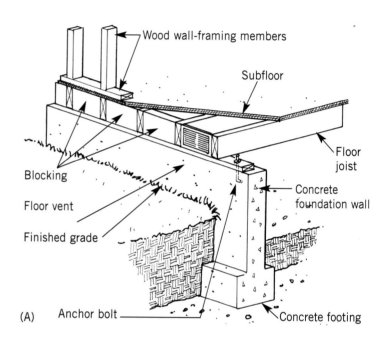

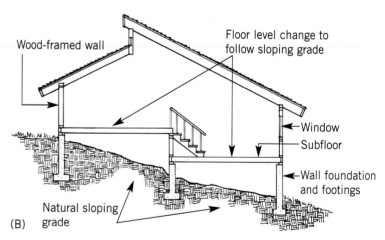

Figure 7.14 (A) A close-up, cutaway view of a foundation wall, floor joist system, and subfloor with placement of wood wall-framing members. This illustration shows only a crawl space under the main floor—no basement. (B) A cross section showing a floor change to accommodate the natural slope of the site grade.

Structural Building Components and Systems

Many kinds of **structural systems** are in use today. A few are quite common; some are unusual and rarely seen. Building methods vary according to the environment, available materials, and local building codes. The system described here is **wood** or **steel frame** or **truss system** construction, used primarily in homes and smaller nonresidential buildings. Nonresidential structural systems are illustrated and identified at the end of this chapter.

The Foundation

After the lot has been surveyed and laid out with chalk lines, and after the hole for new construction has been excavated (dug), cement contractors set up wooden and metal frames, pour, and finish foundation footings. **Footings** are the strips of concrete set into the ground several inches to several feet below the excavated basement or crawl space area. Footings anchor the foundation walls and serve as a base for the weight of the building.

Foundations are the concrete block or poured concrete walls of the basement or sublevel. After the concrete

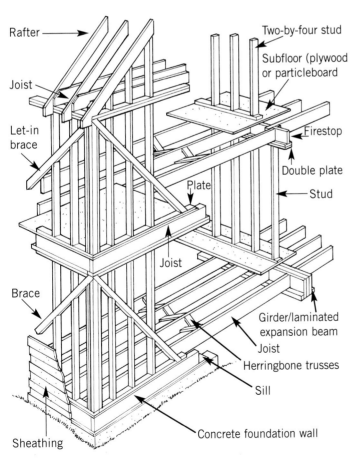

Rafter

Joist

Let-in brace

Brace

Sheathing

Two-by-four stud

Subfloor (plywood or particleboard)

Firestop

Double plate

Plate

Stud

Joist

Girder/laminated expansion beam

Joist

Herringbone trusses

Sill

Concrete foundation wall

Figure 7.15 The wood-framing system.

forms are stripped or removed, the walls must cure for a period of time. **Cement** is a dry mixture of lime, silica, alumina, and other minerals used to bring nonadhesive materials together into a strong, cohesive unit. **Concrete** is the building material made by mixing cement and a mineral aggregate (gravel) with sufficient water to cause the cement to set into a hard mass. Before it sets, concrete is relatively easy to work and may be poured into forms to become a durable material used where strength and stability are requirements and where moisture may permeate interiors (moisture will rot a wooden structure but may not damage concrete). **Reinforced concrete** has **rebar** (strong, bendable steel bars) or wire mesh set into the wet mixture before it is dried, which gives structural strength and helps prevent cracking. **Flatwork** refers to cement for basement floors, garage floors, driveways, and walkways; it may be reinforced and poured over sand, gravel, wire mesh, or rebar to minimize shifting and settling that produce cracks.

Masonry (concrete) block is another type of foundation frequently used in frame construction. **Waterproofing** the foundation is done by spraying or rolling a sealant—such as a tar mixture and perhaps a sheet of heavy black plastic or tar paper—onto the foundation walls before the dirt is backfilled around it. The sealant prevents water seepage into the foundation. The foundation walls may also be insulated with styrofoam board before the backfill. **Window wells** are corrugated rounded steel or cement units that keep dirt away from a basement window. They may be open at the ground level or can be covered over with ironwork, plastic bubbles, or glass block.

Backfilling and **compacting** mean that some of the excavated dirt is filled into the area outside the completed footings. Compacting, coupled with wetting the excavated area, hastens the settling process so that the dirt will be prepared for the subgrade or foundation floors.

Plumbing (see also pages 192–193) takes place at three stages.

1. Before the foundation floor is poured, the underground plumbing brings water and sewer pipe into the sublevel and heating (natural gas lines where applicable).
2. The rough plumbing (water systems, tubs and showers, and a central vacuum) is installed and connected when the building is framed.
3. The finish plumbing is the installation of fixtures, such as sinks and toilets.

Framing

Framing, the next step, is the wood or steel skeleton. This is a crucial step in the construction process, because the wooden or steel frame that is set onto the foundation (called frame or truss construction) supports the entire building. Wood or steel **joists** (beams) are secured with **trusses** (triangular braces) and form the base for the **subfloors** (plywood or other material) and the walls. Walls are built of 2-by-4 studs (8-foot lengths of lumber approximately 1¾ by 3¾ inches) or with steel studs. Load-bearing walls carry the weight of the structure and the roof. Lightweight foam blocks can also be used to frame walls. These are also strong enough to support a roof system. The roof truss system, which may be triangular or flat, is made of rafters and joists. These systems are usually prefabricated to specification and called **roof trusses.** (Other wall components, such as various kinds of blocks, may be used instead of wood or steel framing.)

Once the walls are framed, the interior spaces are firmly established, and although it is possible to move walls after the building is framed, it is costly in terms of time, labor, and inconvenience. Framing is finished with the addition of plywood, Celotex, paperboard, styrofoam, or other exterior panel materials. These add stability to the frame, add some insulation, and provide closure.

A new material made of recycled content with significant potential to positively impact the environment is **Insulating Concrete Forms (ICF).** These are blocks or panels made of special plastic foams that are filled with reinforced concrete. They are easily shaped into basements, walls, landscaping curves, or any shape imaginable, with convenient scrap usability. In the framing process, the blocks are most frequently used as exterior walls and are easily cut for electrical, plumbing, and window placement. They are also strong enough to hold concrete and serve as the backer for interior and exterior finishes. ICF forms are simple to install; walls go up quickly.

A 2,000-square-foot home, built with ECO Block ICF, will save about 47 trees with a net extra cost per square foot about $0.25 to $3.25 more than a traditional wood frame house. The plastic foams used to create ICF vary in price and properties with main differences determined by use. ICF homes rank high in safety and comfort ratings. They provide more security against fire, insect problems, and wind and water damage, and reduce noise pollution. ICF buildings are also air-tight, dramatically reducing residential heating and cooling costs when compared to a typical new home by cutting energy consumption by 30 to 50 percent.

Interior Environmental Control Systems

Interior systems are now installed, which include the **rough plumbing, rough electrical,** and **rough heating.** Rough plumbing is the installation of pipes that will connect water to the taps; drains from sinks, tubs, showers, and toilets; and vents for pressure balance, allowing the pipes to drain. Tubs are set at this time so the wall material can be set around them. Rough heating includes forced-air ducts and vents run from the clothes dryer hookup. Rough electrical is the wiring from the breaker box to each area of the interior where electricity will be needed for light fixtures, light switches, and electric outlets. Wiring is also installed now for intercoms, telephones, computer, fax, built-in stereo, and media equipment. A master computer panel is a luxury feature, installed at convenient locations, that can control all electric lights and major appliances. (See "Information Age Home Automation Systems," in Chapter 5.)

Insulation is added at this time, in the form of batts, rigid panels, or blown (loose) insulation. A **superinsulated** structure has a deeper skeleton framework (up to 14 inches) filled with insulation and layered with a thick **vapor barrier** plastic. Very **tight** superinsulation will require **air-exchange units** to bring necessary fresh air into the interior. Several materials can be used to deaden sound such as **sound board,** which absorbs noise and is used with Sheetrock or plasterboard.

Windows are set in place, and the **exterior veneer** and finish materials such as brickwork, siding, and stucco are added. The roof is finished with **tar paper, shingles,**

Figure 7.16 Scheduling facilitates smooth progress from (A) construction to (B) finished home. *Photos by Karla J. Nielson*

Figure 7.17 Window set into brick-veneered home. © Alli Jagoda

(A)   (B)

Figure 7.18 Sheetrock installation. (A) Screwing the Sheetrock in place. (B) Taping and mudding to cover seams. *Both* © Joey Moon

(**shake shingles** are made of wood; **asbestos,** or fireproof, **shingles** are common) or other roofing materials such as **bartile** or metal shingles or panels.

Exterior finishing includes installing any garage doors, finishing the **soffit** (area under the eaves), the **fascia** (the front of the eaves), and **rain gutters** (channel rainfall as it drains off the roof), plastering the foundation, and any exterior painting of trim.

Interior Finish Components

The interior finish materials and components include wall, ceiling, and floor finish materials, woodwork and cabinetry, countertops, optional wall coverings, and optional window coverings. The most common wall and ceiling material is **Sheetrock,** made of pulverized gypsum rock (also called **drywall, gypsum board, plasterboard,** or **wallboard**) (see Chapter 11). The Sheetrock is installed by nailing, screwing, or gluing horizontal or vertical panels to the wall studs and ceiling joists. To move walls after the Sheetrock has been hung constitutes major remodeling and is very costly. Wallboard panels measure 10-by-4 or 8-by-4 feet and are cut to fit the space. Seams are covered with **perfa-tape** (3-inch-wide stiff paper tape), attached and smoothed with plaster called mud. A smooth finish is more costly than **texturizing,** which is spraying or hand-troweling textures of plaster and then lightly sanding the wall or ceiling to a desired smoothness. Light texturizing is called orange peel, and heavy texturizing is sometimes termed brocade texture.

Other finish wall materials include wallpaper, ceramic or quarry tile, wood, stone, cork, and fabric. Other ceiling materials include acoustical tile (suspended ceilings), wood, fabric, and wall coverings.

The **finish package**—built-in shelves and closet systems, baseboard/door/window trim, and railings—is installed next, then painted along with the walls and ceilings. Any woodwork to be painted is also installed at this point. Doors are removed from the prehung frames, painted or stained separately, then hinged. If wood trim is to be stained, it may be installed after the general painting is done.

Railings are then installed and finished. Cabinets, countertops, and any other built-in units (prefinished) are installed as are **windowsills** of wood, marble, or tile, and tub and shower **surrounds**

(B)

Figure 7.19 Rough plumbing is installed after the home is framed. *Photo by Karla J. Nielson*

Figure 7.20 Smoothly finished sheetrock and extensive molding give this interior architectural character. *Robert Currie Interior Design/photo © Brian Vanden Brink*

(cultured marble, onyx, or tile). Finish flooring is set in bathrooms and laundry areas so that the **finish plumbing** (sinks, toilets) can be installed. Finish electric work (lighting fixtures) is done before, after, or concurrently with finish flooring and plumbing.

The wallpaper is installed next. Following that, the carpet or other floors that need some protection (such as wood) are installed, and hardware (door handles and strike plates) is set in place. Appliances are installed, and window treatments may now also be installed. The last step is the delivery and arrangement of furniture and accessories.

Plumbing Systems

Plumbing is a term that indicates pipe installed within a building for carrying a volume of air or water. Plumbing typically means the water intake system, water-conditioning and/or water-heating system (including components of passive or active solar systems discussed later in this chapter), and water disposal systems—drains and sewer lines. The plumbing carried within the framework or threaded through the masonry block is termed rough plumbing. Copper pipe is generally used for water intake, and cast-iron (more costly but quieter) or plastic (PVC—polyvinyl chloride) pipe is used for sewer or waste-water disposal. Finish plumbing includes hookups to appliances (dishwashers and clothes washers) and installation of **fixtures** (sinks, toilets, urinals). Shower units and bathtubs/whirlpools are installed during the framing before the sheetrock is hung.

Plumbing is also used to facilitate **central vacuum systems** and may also be used for fresh air intake for wood-burning stoves and for furnace (heating) and central air-conditioning (cooling) units.

In nonresidential design, space will usually be allotted for a **plumbing chase** (the thick plumbing wall area) that provides access for maintenance.

While details of plumbing systems are beyond the scope of this text, here are a few considerations for both new construction and remodeling:

- Plumbing is installed within ceilings, floors, and walls, and its location is generally permanent. Although some modification is possible, the process of relocating plumbing is difficult, messy, and expensive.
- Central plumbing—stacked or back-to-back bathrooms/kitchen/laundry—is

more economical and prevents waste of materials and energy.

- A slope or grade of about ⅛ inch per 10 feet is recommended for indoor waste plumbing so that gravity will aid draining, although in many cases this is not mandatory. Waste lines need to be direct (no curves or elbows) to main plumbing stacks (drains) or exit lines in order to drain properly. Vents that connect to the roof are also necessary for correct draw and drain.
- Water that has a shorter distance to travel from the water heater to the point of use will stay hotter than water that travels a greater distance.
- Two water heaters are useful in large homes; multiple water heaters are used routinely in nonresidential interiors. A second water heater may be necessary for a hot tub or spa, or example.
- Conservation should be a consideration. Controls on the water heater allow for the adjustment of temperatures. Natural gas may be less costly for water heating than electricity or heating oil, although costs vary according to geographical region and from time to time.
- Running pipes through the floor to a designated water heater is an excellent, even form of radiant floor heating, especially under tile.

Heating, Ventilation, and Air-Conditioning

Central heating or **space heating** of the interior is generally handled through a **furnace** and connecting hot water pipes or **duct work** or **ducts** (run through the walls, floors, and ceiling joists).

With **forced-air heating,** the furnace heats an element that in turn heats air that passes by it and is blown out. **Cold air return** vents draw air back to the furnace where it is reheated for recirculation. Warm air typically enters a room at the floor or ceiling level through **registers.** Many types and price ranges of furnaces exist, fueled by electricity, natural gas, coal, or oil. A **high-efficiency furnace** uses less fuel to heat the interior and therefore costs less to run, although these units have a higher initial purchase price. Furnaces may also be fitted with humidify-

ing devices **(humidifiers)** that add moisture to the heated air. (Any method of heating will draw moisture out of the air, which is harmful to health, plants, and furnishings.)

Radiant heat is produced by using a furnace to heat water in a boiler. The hot water passes through pipes to a **radiator** that warms the room. This type of system is not used commonly today, but it may be found in older homes.

Most heating systems are controlled with a **thermostat,** which can be set to maintain a specified temperature. Thermostats for small systems are often programmable to accommodate needs according to the time of day or the use of the building. Large **HVAC** (heating, ventilation, and air-conditioning) systems will be monitored and controlled by computer.

Interior furnishings must never obstruct heat registers or cold air returns. Where draperies hang to the floor, clear plastic deflectors can be placed over a vent or register that channel or direct the hot air into the room.

Room or area heating can also be handled by electric or gas-fueled **baseboard units,** radiant ceiling panels, radiators, **portable space heaters,** or **wood-** or **coal-burning stoves** and fireplaces or fireplace inserts. These units also must not be obstructed with furnishings that may combust or catch on fire. Local building codes will require a **clearance,** or distance (usually about 3 feet), that restricts placement of combustible materials, including walls and structural components, near the heat source. An exception is for insulated **zero-clearance fireplace units,** which can be placed in combustible walls. (Space and room

Figure 7.22 A traditional wood-burning stove supplements heating and complements the style of this home. *Centerbrook Architects/photo © Brian Vanden Brink*

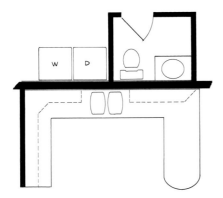

Figure 7.21 Back-to-back plumbing.

heating are also discussed later in this chapter under "Active and Passive Solar Systems.")

Ventilation and air-conditioning are interrelated terms. **Ventilation** refers to natural breezes or air currents from open windows and doors. The designer must be aware that window treatments and furniture placement should allow for, and not obstruct, desired natural ventilation. Ventilation may sufficiently cool the interior for most of the year, supplemented by air-conditioning only in the hottest seasons. However, hot, arid, or humid regions rely heavily on air-conditioning for livable comfort for much of the year.

Air-conditioning can be handled similarly to heating in small-scale settings: by a central system or by cooling one room at a time. A **central air-conditioning system** may be handled through the forced-air furnace unit or by a separate unit located outside or inside the building. In very humid climates, the air-conditioning unit may have a **dehumidifier,** a unit that removes excess humidity (moisture) from the air. In dry climates, an **evaporative cooling system,** or **swamp cooler,** may be less costly to run and may cool more efficiently. The evaporative or swamp cooler works by forcing air through moistened pads or filters. It is installed in a wall, window, or ceiling and connected with central duct work. With this system, windows or doors are kept ajar in the rooms where the cooled air is to be drawn.

Heating and/or cooling can also be accomplished or augmented by a **heat pump,** which uses a geothermal connection to exchange cold and hot above-ground temperatures for the moderate temperatures that prevail several feet beneath the earth's surface.

The designer should be aware of the heating and cooling system and duct work in the case of remodeling or structural changes in the interior design. Walls or ceilings that carry duct work cannot easily be removed or altered. Contractors and HVAC specialists are valuable resources for the designer in this regard and should be consulted before structural changes are made.

Acoustics

Also integral to the planning of space is the need to control noise through the shape of the interior space and the materials selected for walls, windows, ceilings, and flooring. In most nonresidential interiors where many people walk or meet, noise control is imperative. Here are some tools through which acoustics are controlled:

- Rough materials as opposed to smooth materials. Even hard surfaces, if they are substantially textured with high/low relief or are rough-hewn, will refract sound.
- Shape and volume of space can be planned to break up noise level.
- Materials that are part of the interior package: carpeting, wall materials, window treatments, and furnishings will have a great deal to do with the quality and

Figure 7.23 (A) Ductwork carries cooled or heated air through the building. (B) A central air-conditioning unit cools air by refrigerating it. A dehumidifier can be added to the unit. (C) An evaporative or "swamp" cooler cools air by forcing it through water-soaked pads. *Photos by Karla J. Nielson*

control of acoustics. Carpeting and textile applications absorb sound.

- In large concert halls, churches, or public areas where sound needs to be evenly distributed and enhanced, acoustic specialists plan for the exact length, width, and height of the space, the specific shapes of the floors, walls, and ceilings, and materials that will perfectly balance absorption and reflection of sound waves. This is done through mathematical equations and formulas.

The Critical Path and the Punch List

The **critical path** graphically illustrates the overlapping order of everything that must be accomplished in a job. The exact items will vary according to the nature of the job—whether it is new construction or remodeling. The **punch list** is a series of items that must be accomplished as the project progresses. The sample includes spaces for noting the start and finish dates.

Table 7.2 is a sample construction/finish critical path, and Table 7.3 is a sample punch list. Both represent the types of things that are done in new construction, remodeling, and interior design, though neither is intended to address every detail of the construction/design process.

This sample critical path represents a typical time frame for a small home, which can be completed within two months. Larger homes with more features typically take from four to six months or longer to complete. Remodeling projects can take from two weeks to two years, depending on factors such as extent of demolition and reconstruction, funds available, and size of the work force. Small nonresidential buildings will take from three to eight months to build and furnish, and large nonresidential buildings require a time frame of four months to three years.

Not taken into account in this sample critical path is the preliminary design process. Chapter 1, "The Process and Profession of Design," outlines the method involved in gathering data and developing the design before the actual building begins. This sample critical path also does not include lead time, which is the time required to file for and obtain a building permit, to take the plans to the city and receive approval, to survey and establish the relationship of the building to the lot, and to prepare the property before the excavation begins. Lead time is also required to prequalify the client for the loan and to begin the loan processing—which can take longer to finalize than it takes to construct and finish the building.

The critical path and punch list are typically expanded to fit the job requirements. The punch list may consist of several sublists and may include specific items requested by a client as the job progresses. A punch list is also used to note unresolved problems observed during inspection tours of a project. These problems must be resolved by the contractor and subcontractors before the project is finished.

Insulation and Energy Conservation

Insulation refers to standard materials used in building construction: rigid panels or sheets of insulation, batting (rolls of fluffy fiberglass insulation), and blown-in attic and wall insulation, often made of recycled paper or chopped manufactured fiberglass. Heavy plastic sheeting can aid insulation by forming a vapor barrier that will not allow heat or cold to penetrate by convection or air movement.

Additional window glazing can increase insulative values. Two or even three panes of glass, called double or triple glazing, will significantly reduce heat loss or gain. Triple glazing can be found in the form of storm windows. A tinted "summer storm window" cuts down unwanted solar gain, as does solar window film. **Weatherstripping** around doors and windows also helps stop drafts or air infiltration. **Draft dodgers** are any material (heavy rug, fabric tube filled with sand) pushed tightly against a door to prevent cold air infiltration. Storm doors and **vestibules** (air-lock entries) are other means of keeping out cold air.

The comfort of conventional and solar buildings often depends on the control of excessive heat loss or heat gain. In the winter when the heat loss occurs during overcast days and cold nights, the windows or collectors will need either **movable insulation,** such as fiberglass insulation panels on the interior or exterior, or **insulative window treatments,** such as layered fabric shades, insulating shutters, or lined and interlined draperies.

In the summer, excessive heat gain will need control through exterior or interior **shading devices.** Exterior shading devices include awnings; rolling, hinged, or angled shutters; solar screens or sunscreens; architectural projections or roof extensions; vine-covered trellises; or deciduous trees. Interior shading window treatments include metallized pleated shades, horizontal and vertical blinds, opaque roller shades, shutters, and soft window treatments such as curtains, draperies, and shades.

Active and Passive Solar Systems

Many buildings incorporate active or passive solar heating. The designer needs to understand the terms and concepts of solar energy so that the interior design may complement and augment the system.

Active Solar Systems
An **active solar system** is made of mechanical parts that convert **incident solar radiation (insolation)** to thermal

Table 7.2 | Critical Path

Activity		Week 1					Week 2					Week 3					Week 4					Week 5					Week 6					Week 7					Week 8					Week 9					Week 10					Week 11					Week 12					Week 13					Week 14					Week 15					Week 16					Week 17				
	Construction Days	1	2	3	4	5	6	7	8	9	10	11	12	13	14	15	16	17	18	19	20	21	22	23	24	25	26	27	28	29	30	31	32	33	34	35	36	37	38	39	40	41	42	43	44	45	46	47	48	49	50	51	52	53	54	55	56	57	58	59	60	61	62	63	64	65	66	67	68	69	70	71	72	73	74	75	76	77	78	79	80	81	82	83	84	85
	Calendar Days	1	2	3	4	5	8	9	10	11	12	15	16	17	18	19	22	23	24	25	26	29	30	31	32	33	36	37	38	39	40	43	44	45	46	47	50	51	52	53	54	57	58	59	60	61	64	65	66	67	68	71	72	73	74	75	78	79	80	81	82	85	86	87	88	89	92	93	94	95	96	99	100	101	102	103	106	107	108	109	110	113	114	115	116	117

Activities:
- Stake Out and Excavation
- Dig and Pour Footings
- Pour Foundation
- Utility Hook-Up
- Strip and Cure Foundation
- Subgrade Rough Plumbing
- Grade and Pour Basement Floor
- Backfill
- Framing and Building Erection
- Window Glazing
- Rough Plumbing
- Rough Heating
- Rough Electrical
- Roof Shingles
- Masonry/Siding, Soffit, Facia, Gutter
- Form and Pour Exterior Concrete
- Insulation
- Cleanup
- Dry Wall (Sheetrock)
- Ceramic Tile (a. Surround); (b. Countertops)
- Install Finish Package (Woodwork)
- Interior/Exterior Painting
- Install Cabinets/Countertops/Hardware
- Finish Electrical
- Install Vinyl/Tile Flooring
- Install Wallcoverings
- Finish Plumbing
- Finish Cleanup
- Grade Site
- Landscaping
- Paint Touch-Up
- Finish Punch List
- Install Carpet
- Finish Heating-Registers
- Clean Windows
- Install Window Treatments
- Furniture/Accessories
- Finalize Billing

energy to warm air space, heat water, and even run air-conditioning units. The system consists of six basic components that may be altered as needed. These components are:

1. **Collectors** capture or collect the sun's warmth by means of panels mounted to face the sun at approximately 90-degree angles. They may be focusing (like a magnifying glass) or nonfocusing (like a greenhouse—

heating a material, which in turn heats a gas or liquid medium).

2. This thermal energy is moved by **transport,** usually via a fluid or air, from the collectors. This may require pumps, valves, and pipes for liquid transport or blowers, dampers, and ducts for hot air.

3. The transport component moves the heat to **storage,** a reservoir that stores the thermal energy. It may be simple or complex, made of water, rocks, aluminum

---

Table 7.3 | Punch List

	Start Date	Finish Date		Start Date	Finish Date
Architectural plans			Windows set in place/glazed		
Turn in plans to city			Bricking/masonry exterior		
Order temporary power			Order cabinets/built-ins		
Lay out lot			Order flooring		
Order footing material			Ceiling insulation		
Order steel for footing/walls			Order finish package		
Dig hole (excavate)			Hang sheetrock		
Order concrete for footing			Cleanup after this phase		
Deliver footing material			Order tub & shower surrounds		
Set footing			Taping & texture walls/ceiling		
Call to confirm foundation crew			Confirm painter		
Pour footing			Brick interior (fireplaces)		
Strip & stack footing material			Finish work (woodwork)		
Order underground plumbing			Cleanup after this phase		
Order underground heating hook-up			Confirm cabinets/countertops		
Caulk footing			Interior painting		
Order waterproofing of walls			Confirm tile installer		
Call for inspection of walls			Confirm flooring installers		
Order window wells			Setting of cabinets		
Waterproofing of foundation			Confirm finish plumbing		
Call for inspection plumb. & heat.			Confirm heating		
Backfill house & floor			Confirm electrical		
Grading & compaction of floors			Setting of countertops		
Run water and sewer laterals			Setting of marble and tile		
Order framing material			Order garage doors		
Pour concrete floor and garage			Ceramic tile in entry		
Deliver framing material			Confirm carpet and vinyl		
Framing of house			Finish electrical		
Cleanup after this phase			Set vinyl in bathrooms		
Confirm windows/doors			Finish plumbing		
Confirm plumbing			Finish heating		
Confirm heating			Install garage doors		
Confirm electrical			Install wall coverings		
Order brick/masonry			Finish setting vinyl/carpet		
Rough heating			Install hardware		
Rough electrical			Appliances		
Run dryer/bathroom vents			Install window treatments		
Install fireplace			Finish soffit, fascia, rain gutters		
Inspection of plumbing, heating, electrical			Cleanup after this phase		
			Call for final move-in inspection		
Cleanup after this phase			Set furnishings in place		

Note: The critical path and punch list are typically expanded to fit the job requirements. The punch list may consist of several sublists, and it may include specific items requested by a client as the job progresses.

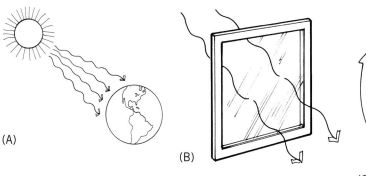
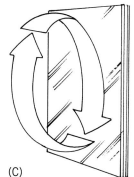

(A) (B) (C)

Figure 7.24 Passive solar systems: (A) radiation, (B) conduction, and (C) convection

oxide, or other materials. The storage ensures warmth at night and on cloudy days when no thermal energy is being collected.

4. **Distribution** carries the heat through pipes and ducts to the space to be heated. It usually requires larger ducts and radiating surfaces than conventional furnace systems.

5. **Auxiliary heating** is usually a central or localized system. Hooked into the solar distribution unit, the furnace is capable of taking over heating needs if the active solar system cannot produce enough heat on successive sunless days.

6. **Control,** perhaps in the form of a thermostat, is an automatic or a manual system to control heat and energy flow.

Passive Solar Systems

Passive designs share common aspects with active systems. Both collect, store, and distribute thermal solar energy for space heating and water heating. The difference is that passive designs are dependent on natural heat and cold movement. Heat is naturally transferred in three ways:

1. Radiation is the spreading of heat through space, as in the radiating heat from the Sun to the Earth. Heated elements that send forth warmth (fireplaces and space room heaters) are called radiant heat sources. The heat waves from the Sun, called solar energy or solar gain, are long, strong electromagnetic waves. These waves are strong enough to pass through glass windows, where they refract against floors, walls, ceilings, furnishings, and people. As solar waves bounce off surfaces, some of that energy is absorbed, and the remainder becomes shorter, weaker wavelengths that cannot repenetrate the glass windows. Thus, heat is trapped and builds up inside glass-enclosed spaces, a phenomenon known as the **greenhouse effect.**

2. Conduction is the transference of heat through matter. Certain materials such as glass and metal are excellent conductors, allowing heat and cold to pass easily through their molecules (which is why they are most

often used as cooking utensils). Glass- and metal-framed windows conduct heat and cold into the interior; metal also makes an excellent component of solar collectors used in active solar systems and passive water heaters.

3. Convection or air movement is based on **natural thermal flow** (the path of rising warm air and the subsequent falling of cool air). The greenhouse effect warms interior air, making convection work to our advantage through these natural thermal air flows.

When the passive system is augmented by mechanical devices such as pumps, fans or blowers, and duct work—or even connected to an existing furnace system—it becomes a **hybrid solar energy system.**

New buildings may integrate passive solar design principles or hybrid systems into the design of the building. Existing buildings that are remodeled, or have additions, to include an active, passive, or hybrid solar system are **retrofitted.** It is important to note that most solar systems are custom designed for the architecture and space; effectiveness will therefore vary.

Direct Gain. The simplest form of passive solar heating is **direct solar gain,** which is sunshine coming through south-facing windows. The heat is generally absorbed by a thermal mass (dense material slow to heat and cool) such as floors or walls of concrete; ceramic or quarry tiles over cement or rocks; bricks or stone; or barrels or pools of water or sand. Direct gain may allow too much heat, light, and direct sunshine to enter the interior (causing fading and damage to furnishings), and too much heat loss may occur at night. For this reason, direct gain windows may require light-filtering or shading devices and movable insulation to guard against excessive heat loss.

Indirect and Isolated Gain. Indirect and isolated passive solar gain means gathering the heat or energy separate from the occupied areas. Listed and illustrated here are some of the most commonly used passive solar systems:

- **Trombe walls** are thermal storage walls named after the French scientist who developed them. A Trombe

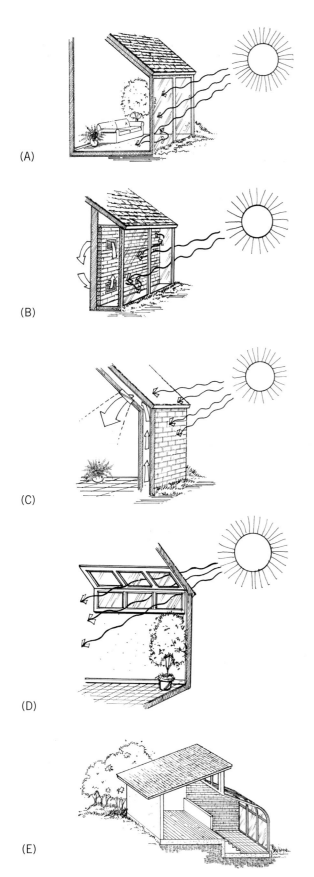

wall system uses large areas of south-facing glass as collectors. Within a few inches of the glass, a dark-colored masonry of brick, concrete, or stone slowly conducts the collected heat to radiate warmth to the interior at night. The Trombe walls have vents at the top and bottom to utilize a natural convection loop—hot air becomes lighter and rises so that vents high in the wall bring warm air into the interior; low vents allow cooler, heavier air to return to the heat trap to be warmed.

- **Thermosiphoning** traps air in spaces in the walls and roof. The air is heated and rises to a point where it can be drawn off with fans through ducts. Fiberglass panels used in the ceilings can also admit translucent light. A thermosiphonic system is less effective than thermal mass Trombe walls but also is less costly.

- **Roof monitors** are window arrangements set high in the wall or ceiling such as clerestory windows, skylights, or cupolas (glassed-in extensions, also called sun-scoops, in the roof). Monitors admit light and solar winter heat, and they ventilate out summer heat. In the winter the lighter hot air must be circulated to the floor level and the monitors should be protected against heat loss at night.

- **Solar greenhouses** or solariums are the most popular of all indirect passive solar system options, probably because they are the easiest to retrofit and because a greenhouse sun space is a delightful, healthful, and versatile extension of interior space. They are even popular in restaurants and nonresidential settings, and in homes they can serve as living/dining space, as a hot tub or swimming pool area, or as a gardening greenhouse. A solarium works best with a thermal mass (rock or sand) surrounded by rigid insulation. Insulated glass facing within 14 degrees of due south works best to collect sunshine. The thermal mass stores the heat in direct-gain fashion to be released through convection and reradiation in cold weather and at night. The solarium/greenhouse can be designed to close off from the interior at night and during cold, cloudy spells in order to control excessive heat gain and heat loss in the main body of the house.

Greenhouses can produce 10 to 50 percent of the heat for the interior, depending on the size and insulation of the building, the climate, the size and orientation of the greenhouse, and factors such as protection from prevailing winds, landscaping, movable insulation, interior air flow (an unobstructed convection loop through the house and back to the greenhouse is essential), and the design and quality of the greenhouse itself. Diagonal glass, used in many greenhouses, is the most difficult to protect against heat loss at night and excessive heat gain in the summer, making it less efficient than vertical glass.

Figure 7.25 (A) Direct solar gain, (B) Trombe wall, (C) thermosiphoning, (D) roof monitor, (E) solar greenhouse.

Figure 7.26 This Arizona home receives abundant natural light through a long, narrow north-facing skylight and expanses of south-facing glass. Direct solar gain from the south is permitted in winter and obstructed in summer by a deep, precisely angled roof overhang. A high-efficiency heat pump fulfills all heating and cooling functions. *Eddie Jones Architect, Phoenix. Photo © Timothy Hursley/The Arkansas Office, Inc.*

Figure 7.27 An example of an integrated solarium, this room is sometimes referred to as a sun room, Florida room, or Arizona room. Greenhouse rooms are popular in all areas of the United States, and are often pleasant places that can be closed off during uncomfortably hot or inclement weather. They may also be artificially heated and cooled to be pleasant year-round. *© Jessie Walker*

When air is trapped in or around a home, it forms a natural insulative barrier that conserves energy. The **envelope** concept, originated by architect Lee Porter Butler, has an integral solarium on the building's south side, and vents carry the heated air through channels over the ceiling in the attic, down a double north wall, and through channels under the lower floor. The continuous air convection loop utilizes passive solar gain with or without a thermal mass.

A **berm** is an earth mass placed on the north side of a building. Southern window exposure brings in winter heat; shading devices such as trees cool in the summer.

Green Design

Green design is not only a major trend in building and interior design; it is also a responsibility we have to future generations. Every decision made during the building and systems selection process should be checked against whether or not the following criteria are met:

- The efficiency and long-term durability of the product. A material or mechanical system component that fails to perform will likely end up in the landfill. Quality counts, even if the initial cost is a little higher. Efficiency in utilizing natural resources is of utmost importance.
- Materials and furnishings should come from sustainable resources, not from resources that are too difficult or take too much time to replant or regrow or that cannot be replenished.
- How efficiently the interior will function, and whether the lifestyle and/or working conditions within the building support green design. The monitoring or conservation of water, electricity (light and appliances), natural gas, or heating fuel is one example. Another is the ease of recycling products such as paper, cardboard, plastics, cans, and glass. Yet another efficiency factor is the ease of controlling heat and cold and light and dark through window coverings.
- Green design does make a difference. Through attitude and commitment, each act of conservation, recycling, or reuse (longevity) can add to our ability to ensure a safe, quality life for future generations.

Nonresidential Considerations

Structural building systems (seen in Table 7.4) for nonresidential interiors often utilize complex planning that must meet code restrictions and specifications and thus are beyond the scope of this introductory text. However, the beginning interior design student can recognize the following structural building systems that are commonly seen in both historic and new building construction.

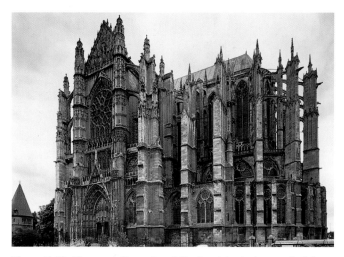

Figure 7.28 The evolution of architectural techniques. Gothic structural block construction with flying buttresses. *Peter Willi/Bridgeman Art Library*

Figure 7.29 The curtain wall construction of the Empire State Building is visible in this photo, taken before completion. *Bridgman Art Library*

Table 7.4 | Additional Structural Systems

In nonresidential buildings, metal, concrete, and masonry are the most common building materials. The most often used structural systems are illustrated here.

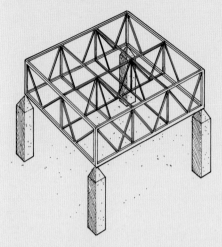

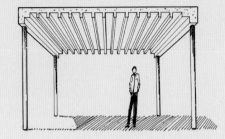

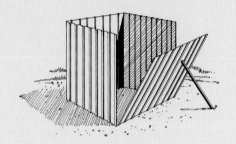

Metal or space frame is a three-dimensional truss/beam and column system assembly that creates a steel skeleton and is also called curtain wall construction. The exterior finish material can be glass or brick veneer or siding, for example.

Slab system is reinforced concrete ribbed or waffle design that transfers the lateral loads to supporting end beams; slabs can span short distances and are widely used.

Frame system is made of a rigid steel skeleton sheathed with prefabricated rolled steel or precast concrete.

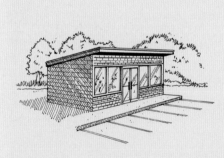

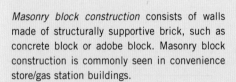

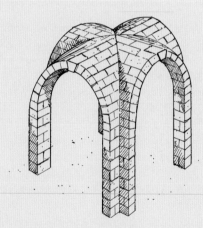

Masonry block construction consists of walls made of structurally supportive brick, such as concrete block or adobe block. Masonry block construction is commonly seen in convenience store/gas station buildings.

Arch systems are stone blocks cut and fitted to form a curved shape, anchored firmly in vertical supports and with a keystone to stabilize the compression and friction needed to bind the arch together. The arch system has been in existence since ancient Romans built viaducts.

Vaulted systems form an elongated arch such as seen in Medieval cathedrals. The vaulted system is used in ecclesiastical and public architecture where lofty spaces are desirable.

Additional Structural Systems (continued)

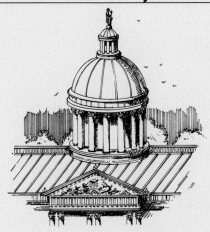

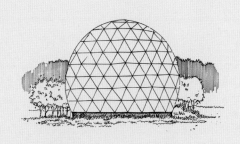

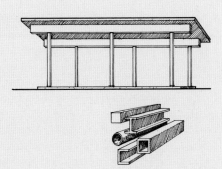

Dome systems are an arch rotated about a circular plan, with a compression ring rather than a keystone that stabilizes the dome. The dome system is most often seen in rotundas of government buildings and in some churches. The dome is a soaring space inside the building and is essentially an arch system rotated around an axis.

Geodesic domes are constructed of triangular steel skeleton components filled with opaque or transparent materials. The geodesic dome was developed in the twentieth century by American architect Buckminster Fuller. Based on the strongest and most stable building shape, the triangle, this interlocking system creates lightweight and economical spaces for a variety of purposes and even for transportable buildings and shelters.

Beam systems are often seen in gas station canopies and are straight, solid structural elements of reinforced concrete, solid or laminated wood, or rolled steel section based on compressive and tensile stress. The load is laterally transmitted along the axis to the vertical support beams.

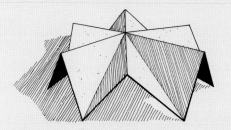

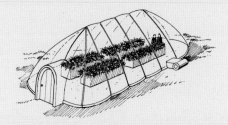

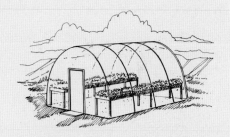

Folded plate systems are of thin, reinforced concrete in a strong, rigid geometric form.

Pneumatic systems are air-inflated or air-supported lightweight, flexible membranes.

Tensile systems are fabric structures stretched over vertical posts or frames like a tent.

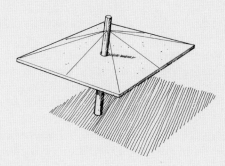

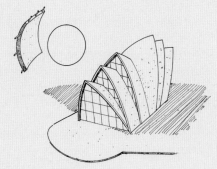

Cable systems are based on a vertical column and horizontal slab connected with flexible steel cables.

Thin shell membranes are self-supporting concrete or lightweight foam membranes over a steel-reinforcing mesh (like an eggshell) with free-form curvatures as seen in the cutaway illustration.

In historic buildings mass density was the measure of strength, where, for example the weight of the building rested on the thickness of the walls and foundation. Tall structures, such as medieval churches, were supported with flying buttresses built upon massive walls and foundations so that the upper walls and ceilings would not collapse. Fitting these blocks together through skillful engineering and utilizing friction versus the earth's gravitational pull made possible the great cathedrals with their soaring rib-vault ceilings and also the domes of great public and church architecture.

In the mid-1800s, as iron and steel were mass produced and utilized for steel skeletons, much larger and taller built spaces were possible. Skyscrapers and steel-framed houses were referred to as space frames or "curtain wall construction," meaning that the "skin" of the house between the steel members could be all glass. Steel also made possible the many forms in use from the early 1900s through the present as reinforced concrete, where reinforced concrete slabs allowed for flexibility in shape.

In the mid- to late twentieth century, new building materials were developed, and more continue to be developed today. Plastic and other artificial fibers, extruded materials, and foams used for framing, building blocks, or skins have made possible structures with shapes that are the antithesis of medieval architecture. Buildings that appear to float, bend, or lean challenge our perceptions about what architecture really is, and give us new horizons for both creativity and function.

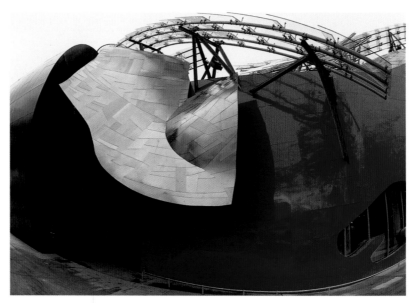

Figure 7.30 Using advanced technology, this nonresidential building by Frank Gehry appears to float and flow, challenging our assumptions about architecture. © Grey Crawford/Beateworks.com

Nonresidential Plumbing, HVAC, and Indoor Air Quality

Plumbing systems for nonresidential interiors will be gauged by the local building codes. Major plumbing is typically located within a central location in a section of the wall called the plumbing chase, which connects directly to the rough plumbing beneath the building. Size or capacity of plumbing systems as well as restrictions for intake and waste are governed by code.

In many large buildings such as hotels and office buildings, windows are fixed or nonoperable, thus creating a mechanically sealed environment that eliminates natural ventilation. This ensures that the HVAC system can efficiently deliver a mix of warm and cool air to achieve a constant temperature. The rate of air exchange—the infusion of clean, fresh air into an environment to replace stale air—is also dictated by code. The number of people and frequency of occupancy compared to the size of the space yields the quantity of cubic feet exchanged per minute or per hour. Additionally, individual rooms sometimes have heating or air-exchange units, typically located beneath the windows, so that the air temperature can be regulated or fresh air can be taken into the space.

The desire for enhanced **indoor air quality,** air that is free of toxins, smoke, mold, and dust, as discussed in Chapter 2, has led many people to incorporate portable air purifiers in homes and nonresidential spaces. In large buildings, such as huge office complexes, clean indoor air is often a serious problem. If the air-intake units are drawing poor-quality air from the outside, the indoor quality will suffer. In the miles of nonresidential HVAC ductwork in a single building, it is not uncommon to find construction debris, buildup of dust, mold, dead insects, and even rodent dung and remains, which contribute to poor indoor air quality. A combination of low air-volume exchange (sometimes sacrificed to save energy costs) and poor air quality creates the **sick building syndrome.** Studies have linked such poor air quality to a wide spectrum of physical maladies and illnesses that are difficult to diagnose and cure. Optimum air quality can enhance the productivity of the workforce, who will think more clearly, feel more energized, and experience less illness. Ductwork in both homes and nonresidential buildings should be vacuumed and sanitized as a part of routine maintenance.

In addition to the discussion in Chapter 2 about air quality, consider that when remodeling older buildings, special care must be taken to protect the remodelers or occupants against the toxins that may be released, including asbestos microfibers and lead paint.

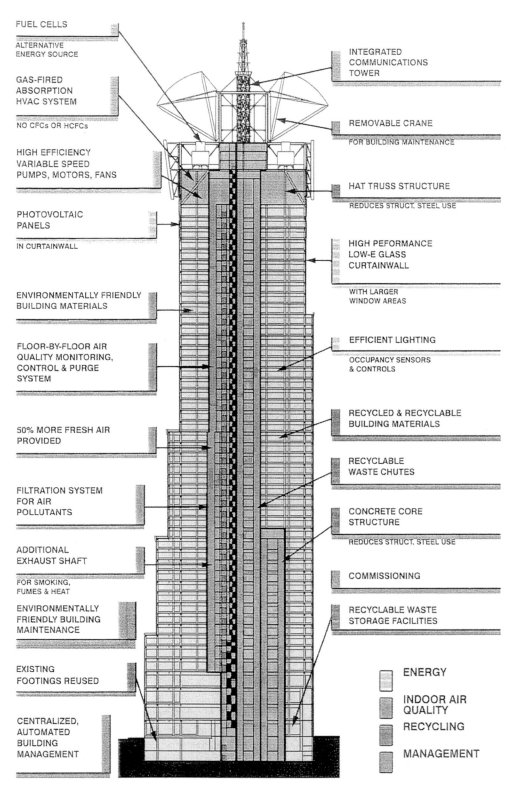

FUEL CELLS
ALTERNATIVE
ENERGY SOURCE

GAS-FIRED
ABSORPTION
HVAC SYSTEM
NO CFCs OR HCFCs

HIGH EFFICIENCY
VARIABLE SPEED
PUMPS, MOTORS, FANS

PHOTOVOLTAIC
PANELS
IN CURTAINWALL

ENVIRONMENTALLY FRIENDLY
BUILDING MATERIALS

FLOOR-BY-FLOOR AIR
QUALITY MONITORING,
CONTROL & PURGE
SYSTEM

50% MORE FRESH AIR
PROVIDED

FILTRATION SYSTEM
FOR AIR
POLLUTANTS

ADDITIONAL
EXHAUST SHAFT
FOR SMOKING,
FUMES & HEAT

ENVIRONMENTALLY
FRIENDLY BUILDING
MAINTENANCE

EXISTING
FOOTINGS REUSED

CENTRALIZED,
AUTOMATED
BUILDING
MANAGEMENT

INTEGRATED
COMMUNICATIONS
TOWER

REMOVABLE CRANE
FOR BUILDING MAINTENANCE

HAT TRUSS STRUCTURE
REDUCES STRUCT. STEEL USE

HIGH PEFORMANCE
LOW-E GLASS
CURTAINWALL
WITH LARGER
WINDOW AREAS

EFFICIENT LIGHTING
OCCUPANCY SENSORS
& CONTROLS

RECYCLED & RECYCLABLE
BUILDING MATERIALS

RECYCLABLE
WASTE CHUTES

CONCRETE CORE
STRUCTURE
REDUCES STRUCT. STEEL USE

COMMISSIONING

RECYCLABLE WASTE
STORAGE FACILITIES

ENERGY

INDOOR AIR
QUALITY

RECYCLING

MANAGEMENT

FOX & FOWLE ARCHITECTS
ARCHITECTURE FOR THE ENVIRONMENT

Figure 7.31 The green design features of an award-winning New York skyscraper, known as the most environmentally friendly office building in Manhattan. *Four Times Square—Developed and owned by The Durst Organization, Inc. Fox and Fowle Architects*

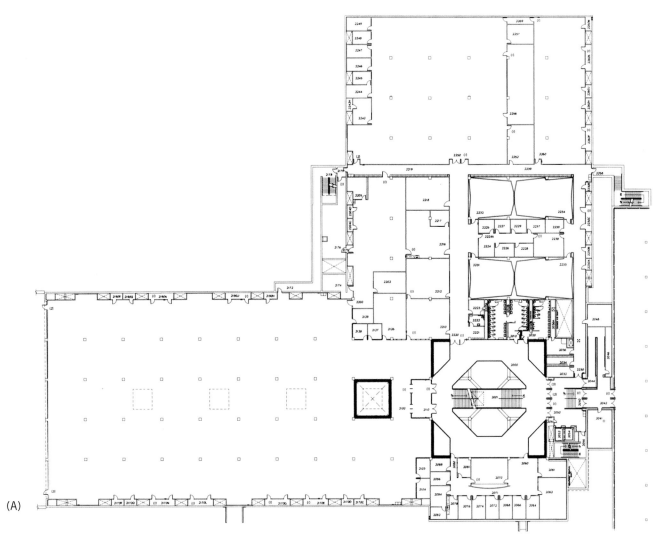

(A)

(B)

Figure 7.32 The library underground addition at Brigham Young University. (A) Floor plan; (B) Exterior view; (C) Entry with a view of the underground addition; (D) Students studying near lightwell; (E) Study area and stacks near north window; (F) Students using laptops with "wired furniture." *All courtesy of Brigham Young University*

(C)

(D)

(E)

(F)

Life Safety

Nonresidential buildings must include life safety systems. The most imminent life safety danger is fire, which can be potentially averted if the following system devices are in effect:

- Smoke detectors and fire alarm systems
- Sprinkler systems to put out fires
- Automatic closing doors in case of fire
- Egress/exit lighting via light-emitting diodes that require no electricity
- Easy-to-follow directions posted in an obvious location for escape plan and stair/exit locations in case of fire
- Portable fire extinguishers in obvious locations
- Back-up lighting and power systems for any part of a building that is without natural daylighting and for nighttime emergencies

Systems within the Plenum

Life safety and interior comfort-control systems are generally located in the area known as the **plenum,** a space between the roof/ceiling and the suspended ceiling, which is a metal grid that holds acoustical tile. The plenum contains wiring for smoke detectors and/or fire-extinguishing sprinklers, lighting, possibly telephone and intercom (these may also be run in the floor), and HVAC ductwork and registers. The advantage of the acoustical tiles set into the grid is easy access to the plenum when maintenance is required.

Figure 7.33 (A) Systems in the plenum include heating, air-condition, and ventilation (HVAC), lighting, fire alarms, sprinkling systems, and high-technology connection. (B) Egress lighting connected through the plenum. *(A) © Karla J. Nielson; (B) © Sarah Hanson*

Chapter 8 | Furniture Arrangement

Function 210

Human Factors 212

The Elements and Principles of Design 216

Basic Groupings 222

Nonresidential Considerations 225

© William Waldron

The placement of furniture and fixtures in an interior is an extension of space planning and is directly linked to aesthetics and function. Arrangement of furniture according to aesthetic principles adds to the visual appeal of a space and may make its use more satisfying. But furnishings placed without regard for function and user needs will fall short of intended goals, and the aesthetic appeal of the design will vanish as users begin to move furniture around to make the space meet their needs. A good arrangement of furniture will be both functional and pleasing to the senses.

Function

Function is the use an environment will have and the activities that will take place there; it dictates the selection and the arrangement of furniture. For example, a living-room space could be used to accommodate conversation, a library, musical instruments, a stereo, a television, video equipment, slides or movies, games, reading, napping, formal or informal dining, writing letters, paying bills, growing plants, displaying art, or any combination of these or other functions. The arrangement of furniture should be planned to accommodate appropriate activities in the amount of space available. If the primary use of the space is conversation, then it is logical that the comfortable seating pieces should be placed in groupings that facilitate communication and maximize interaction between users. If the main function of the room is television viewing, the sofas and chairs should be arranged to face the screen. Reading will require the placement of lamps near seating pieces to avoid the eyestrain caused by inadequate lighting.

The consideration of function extends to every area of the home. A bedroom will naturally be used for sleeping, but it might also serve for dressing, conversation, a studio, an office, a library, an art gallery, a sewing room, or computer or stereo use. Each requires appropriate arrangement of furniture. For example, if reading in bed is important, then a table must be placed close enough to the bedside to reach books. A lamp may be placed on the table, or some other form of lighting should be provided. Another very simple function that often takes place in a bedroom is putting on shoes and stockings. Something as obvious as a small chair or ottoman, appropriately placed in or near the dressing area, can make this simple task much more pleasant. Such considerations, though they may seem insignificant, can make life run much more smoothly.

Combining Functions

Often, functions will have a strong relationship to each other. For example, the conversation area previously mentioned might also accommodate informal **buffet-style dining,** and the way those two activities interface should be considered. Tables should be arranged close enough to seating for easy placement of drinks or plates, and a serving table should be conveniently located near the seating area. Tables used with seating pieces should be approximately the same height as the arm of the seating piece so that food or drink can be reached easily.

The combination of functions is an absolute necessity in small homes or apartments. Such spaces must often include both a dining table and comfortable seating in the same room. Some creative planning not only will solve the problem but will create a solution with a great deal of functional and aesthetic appeal. One such solution might include moving the sofa to the center of the room. A drop-leaf table could then be placed behind the sofa to provide dining space for one or two people. With the table pulled away from the sofa or with one leaf extended, even more diners could be accommodated. When not being used for dining, the drop-leaf table could double as a sofa table.

Mechanical Functions

It is also important that furniture be arranged so as not to interfere with the mechanical functions of an interior. Heating vents and **cold-air returns** should not be covered by furniture. Blocking them causes the heating, ventilation, and air-conditioning systems to function much less efficiently. Doors should be able to swing and open freely without interference from furniture pieces, and furniture placement should not hinder the opening and closing of windows.

Furniture designed to hold lamps or telephones should be placed near electric outlets and phone jacks for convenience and safety and to prevent tripping over cords. Unless they are custom designed and carefully planned from the beginning, most residences do not offer the kind of flexibility that allows an electric outlet in the middle of the floor. Consequently, furniture groupings will have to be "anchored" to a wall where there are electric and phone connections. Careful planning before construction or during remodeling might include floor plugs for greater flexibility in arranging furniture.

Circulation

Furniture arrangement needs to accommodate free movement or **circulation** from one space to another. Furniture should be placed to enhance that movement by allowing **traffic** to flow or by restricting and redirecting the traffic when necessary. This kind of control provides the best utilization of space because it eliminates unnecessary traffic patterns. The specific amounts of space necessary for free circulation are addressed in the next section.

Figure 8.1 This bedroom space is arranged to accommodate not only sleeping, but also conversation, reading, and relaxation. *Tom Catalano Architect/photo © Brian Vanden Brink*

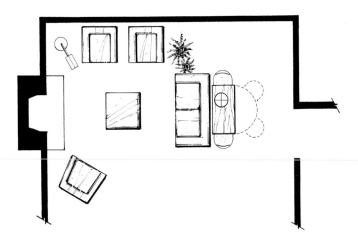

Figure 8.2 An arrangement showing combined function.

As discussed in Chapter 6, interiors have natural **traffic patterns.** These patterns can easily be seen by drawing lines on a floor plan to represent where we would most logically walk to get from one space to another—the **natural traffic pattern.** The complexity and lack of organization in the completed pattern usually shows quite clearly the need to control traffic.

We can control the flow of traffic by placing furniture at key locations so that it forces traffic to flow away from areas that should be used for seating and conversation or other functions where traffic might be disruptive. These locations can be determined by preparing a corrected plan indicating where the traffic should flow. Laying the corrected plan over the natural traffic plan will show where furniture should be placed to control the flow. For example, some homes have no entries—the front door opens directly into the living area. In this kind of plan, a sofa or other large piece of furniture could be used to divide the seating area from the door area and establish a visual entry that directs traffic behind the seating area instead of through it. Such placement avoids cutting the room in half with an unnecessary traffic pattern. Thus, a well-placed piece of furniture can be a simple deterrent to misdirected traffic.

Human Factors

Anthropometrics

Anthropometrics, the dimensions of the human form, are an important consideration in arranging furniture because human dimensions must be the standard of measure for interior design.

One must also consider people whose needs for circulation are different from the norm. For example, the needs of those who use wheelchairs, canes, crutches, or walkers must be addressed if they are to be able to move freely in an interior (see Chapter 2).

Standard Clearances

Users without physical impairments require variable amounts of space or **clearance** to circulate comfortably within an environment.

- Major traffic paths should be 3 feet or wider.
- Minimal clearance for traffic is 1 foot 6 inches.
- Seating pieces used with coffee tables need slightly over 1 foot of clearance between the table and the front of the seat.
- For a user to be able to extend his or her legs in front of a seating piece, about 3 feet of space is required, depending on leg length and the degree of extension.
- Desks and pianos require a minimum of 3 feet of clearance for chairs, benches, and users.
- Comfortable dining requires slightly more than 2 feet of space per user along the perimeter of the table.
- In order to accommodate a seated diner and space behind for passage and serving, 3 feet of space should be planned.
- Getting in and out of a dining chair requires about 1 foot 6 inches of space.
- Three feet is considered good clearance between a bed and dresser.
- Space between two beds should be from 2 feet 6 inches to 3 feet.
- Minimal clearance to facilitate bed making is 1 foot 6 inches between the bed and the wall.
- In a bathroom, clearance of 2 feet 6 inches to 3 feet 6 inches in front of the toilet provides adequate space for most functions.

Proxemics

Proxemics, a term coined by anthropologist Edward T. Hall, describes the way people use space and the way that use is related to culture. Proxemic patterns vary in different cultures; the distances suggested here apply to North Americans. Hall's study identifies four distances:

1. The space from 1 foot 6 inches to actual physical contact is considered intimate distance and is reserved for displays of affection, comfort, protection, or physical aggression.

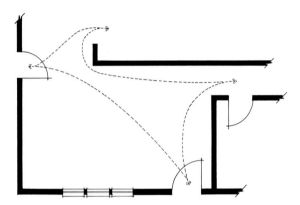

Figure 8.3 The natural traffic pattern of this room consumes nearly half of the available space.

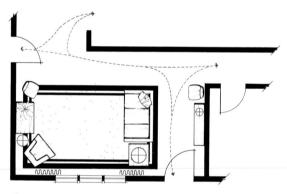

Figure 8.4 The arrangement of furniture corrects the problem and makes the flow of traffic more efficient.

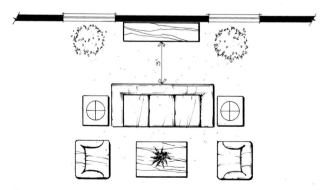

Figure 8.5 This arrangement allows three feet of clearance for major traffic.

Figure 8.6 Three feet of clearance for extending the legs.

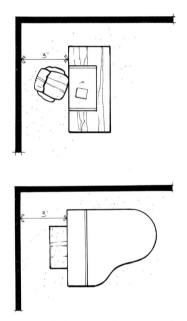

Figure 8.7 Three feet of clearance for a piano bench and a desk chair.

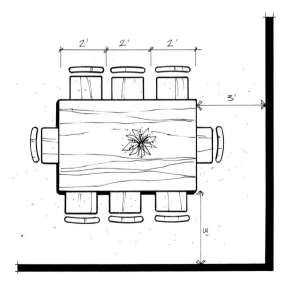

Figure 8.8 Three feet of clearance for dining chairs.

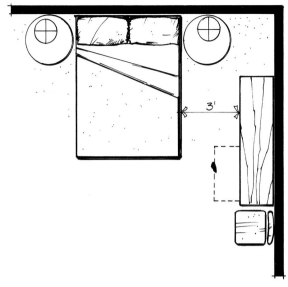

Figure 8.9 Three feet of clearance between bed and dresser.

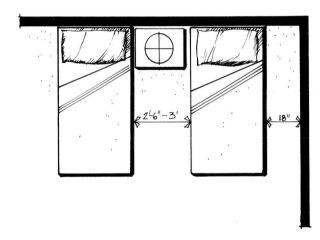

Figure 8.10 Three feet of clearance between beds.

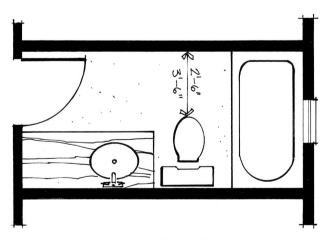

Figure 8.11 Standard clearance in a bathroom.

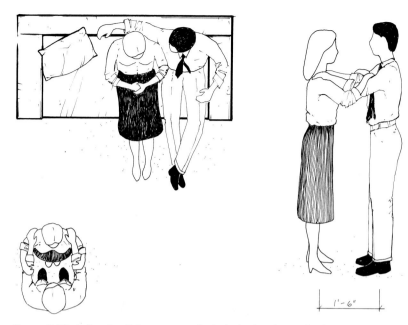

Figure 8.12 Intimate distance—one foot six inches to contact.

Figure 8.13 Personal distance—one foot six inches to four feet.

2. Personal distance is equal to the invisible "bubble" of space with which we separate ourselves from others. Everyone has a different perception of this space, and many are made uncomfortable by those with smaller bubbles who stand too close and violate **personal space.** Personal distance usually extends from 1 foot 6 inches to 4 feet. In many cultures, particularly those of southern Europe, the Middle East, and Latin America, the personal-space bubble is much smaller;

people are customarily seen appropriately touching and even embracing without any threat or discomfort.

The way people normally use furniture is also affected by their perception of personal space; for example, few people choose to sit in the center of a sofa. Most people sit at one end, and most often they prop one arm on the armrest. In this way, a sofa that can comfortably hold three people is most often occupied by only two people, since no one wants to sit in the middle. A third person sitting on an 8-foot sofa between two people leaves only about 1 foot between each person. This comes very close to intimate distance, leaving people who are just friends—or, worse yet, acquaintances or strangers—in the uncomfortable position of being too close. Furthermore, the middle person has no "anchor" in the form of an armrest to cling to for mental protection when that personal space is invaded.

When forced into close contact, we become uncomfortable because we perceive our personal-space bubble as a necessary privacy. Those who use crowded public transportation or elevators have methods of coping with the unnatural intimacy of such situations. Most will become immobile and avoid eye contact. Body contact is avoided, and when touching does occur, the tendency is to recoil quickly. Eyes are kept focused away from others; to help avoid eye contact, some may keep their eyes fixed on a book or other object.

When strangers enter an empty seating space, they tend to take seats at opposite ends, gradually filling the space but leaving a seat between themselves and others. When the only spaces left are next to a stranger, some people will choose to stand or will hesitate before taking a seat. Many would consider a person aggressive who sits next to them when there are still areas of open seating available. Under difficult circumstances, such as when airports are filled with grounded travelers, many of these notions of personal space are repressed. In such conditions, strangers may be viewed as colleagues in discomfort and the crowding perceived as more tolerable.

3. From 4 to 12 feet is considered social distance. At the far end of that scale interaction tends to be more formal, and at the close end interaction is characterized by greater involvement and less formality.
4. More than 12 feet is considered public distance. In public distance there is little personal interaction.

These distances can be helpful in planning interiors. For example, furniture groupings for conversation should be planned within the 4- to 12-foot bounds of social distance. Optimal distance for conversation is 8 feet—it seems to feel neither too close nor too distant.

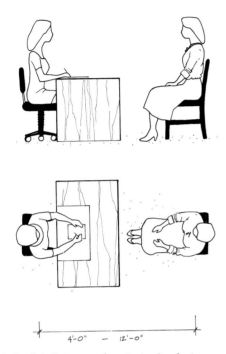

Figure 8.14 Social distance—four to twelve feet.

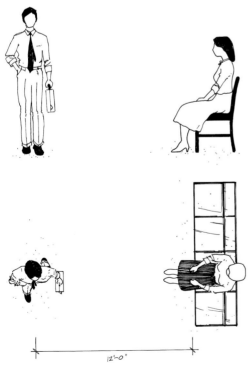

Figure 8.15 Public distance—more than twelve feet.

Crowding

The effects of **crowding** on animals are well known. In crowded conditions, animals begin to suffer stress, abnormal social behavior, illness, and in some cases death. Studies of crowding in humans have shown confusing results. Hall cites a study by Frenchman Paul Chombart de Lauwe, who discovered that when the subjects of his study had less than 8 to 10 square meters of space per person in their residences, their social and physical pathology doubled. He also discovered that when the space grew beyond 14 square meters per person, the problems also increased, though not as dramatically.

Crowding is not strictly a function of dimensions. It also seems to be closely related to culture, personality, and the desire for involvement with other people. Those who enjoy involvement and interaction with others tolerate and, in some cases, even enjoy crowding. They find a crowded, lively environment exciting. Shops, cafés, restaurants, clubs, shopping areas, and markets are areas where one might expect to see planned crowding. The crowded environment should also provide islands of tranquility for those who enjoy less involvement or for those who need to retreat periodically. This type of person may find the effects of crowding (sounds, smells, and touch) overstimulating.

In home environments, some people enjoy being surrounded by lots of furniture, books, and art objects. Others need more visual or actual space in which to mentally expand. Designers must be sensitive to these differences in personality and preferences when planning furniture arrangements because the amount of furniture and its placement will affect the way users feel about their homes.

Territoriality

Territoriality is an aspect of proxemics that deals with the need to have a space of our own. This need manifests itself in many ways. For example, you may have noticed

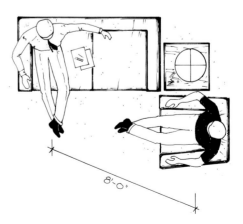

Figure 8.16 Eight feet is optimal for conversation.

that many people select a classroom seat at the beginning of a school term and sit in the same seat each time the class meets. When someone else sits in that place, they are annoyed and feel displaced. The same kind of behavior occurs in families where adults and children have determined their places at the table or in the car. Variations from the normal seating pattern may lead to conflict. Those who share bedrooms may find that certain parts of the room or even a certain side of a bed "belongs" to one person. When it is time to clean or straighten the space, things not belonging to one person may end up in a pile somewhere in the area that is perceived as the other person's territory. These behaviors are expressions of the need to claim space.

It is important to understand this need so that, when placing furniture, we can not only allocate adequate

space for each person but also design shared areas with space and amenities that give users the opportunity to personalize and establish territoriality.

The Elements and Principles of Design

Several of the elements and principles of design are directly applicable to the arrangement of furniture. Understanding how these important tools apply to furniture placement leads to attractive and pleasant furniture arrangements.

Balance, Scale, and Mass

Furniture should be arranged to provide a feeling of balance within the interior. Mass or **visual weight** (how heavy the piece appears to be) is a primary consideration in arranging furniture to create balance. Furniture is particularly effective in achieving equal distribution of mass because it is available in so many different sizes, shapes, materials, and colors, which are all factors that influence mass. For example, darker pieces appear heavier than lighter pieces, bold and large-scale patterns have more mass than subdued or smaller-scaled patterns, heavier textures are more massive than smooth textures, and pieces the eye can penetrate are less massive than solid pieces. For this reason a glass table appears to be lighter scaled and less massive than a solid wood table, and a piece that sits up on legs has a lighter appearance than a piece that is solid or upholstered clear to the floor. Following are some guidelines for considering balance and scale in the arrangement of furniture:

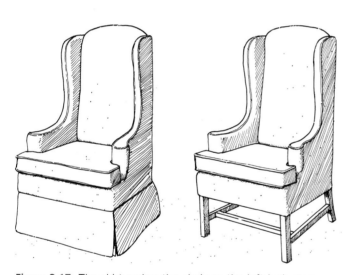

Figure 8.17 The skirt makes the chair on the left look more massive.

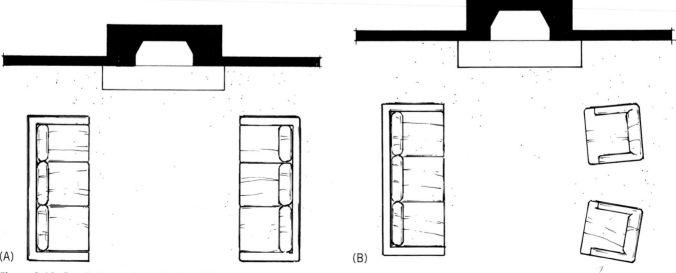

(A)   (B)

Figure 8.18 Parallel groupings showing (A) symmetrical and (B) asymmetrical arrangements.

- The visual weight or mass of the pieces is more important than actual dimensions or scale in creating a well-balanced arrangement.
- Furniture can be balanced with other pieces of furniture. For example, two chairs of the same visual scale placed across from each other will be visually balanced.
- Furniture can also be used to balance **architectural elements** in an interior. For example, a sofa or love seat could be used opposite a fireplace to create balance.
- Massing furniture together may create heavier mass in order to achieve balance. For example, a large-scale wing chair does not balance with a small side chair. However, if the side chair is arranged with a table and lamp, the three pieces massed together may balance the heavier wing chair.
- Groupings may be arranged to create symmetrical or asymmetrical balance. For example, a pair of matching sofas facing each other in front of a fireplace creates a symmetrical grouping. If one of the sofas were replaced with a pair of chairs, the grouping would be asymmetrical but balanced nonetheless. One form of balance is not better than the other—each type has its own appeal. In a symmetrical grouping when small details such as lamps, tables, or even small **occasional chairs** are varied, the feeling will still be one of symmetry, but the grouping will have the intriguing quality of asymmetry. (An occasional chair is a small-scaled piece that sits away from the main seating area and can be drawn up on occasion when it is needed for additional seating.)
- Lighting should also be considered in planning the balance of a furniture arrangement. At night the balance of a room can be drastically altered by lighting. Artificial light will create areas of emphasis that should be balanced along with the furniture. If the lighting is well placed and the levels of light are appropriate, the balance will be maintained.
- The final judgment as to whether balance has been achieved will have to be personal, visual, and intuitive—no device exists for such measurement other than the eye.

Rhythm

The placement of furniture is an exercise in rhythm. One particularly important aspect of rhythm to consider when creating furniture arrangements is rhythm through alternation. Here are some considerations for the use of rhythm by alternation:

- An interior will be more interesting when upholstered and wooden pieces or hard and soft textures are alternated. A number of upholstered pieces without contrasting textures of wood or other hard materials to break the flow may feel monotonous.
- The alternation of textures creates contrast, an element that makes any design more pleasing.
- Alternation of rectilinear and curvilinear forms will also make the interior more appealing. The addition of rounded forms in an otherwise rectilinear design softens the impact of the straight lines and lessens any harshness such lines may have implied.
- The same subtle appeal is created when high and low forms are alternated. Particularly when seen in **elevation** (a flat, straight-on view), an arrangement of furniture is more interesting when high and low pieces are mixed in such a way that wall space is broken into interesting shapes and proportions.
- Alternation of high and low pieces away from the walls, in the open space of an environment, helps relieve monotony and can provide interest.

Emphasis

Emphasis deals with the creation of a focal point. A focal point is the object or area where the eye is drawn first. Furniture arrangement is an important factor in creating an area of focus within an interior. The planning of **primary and secondary focal points** gives the environment a sense of purpose and subtly involves and stimulates the senses as the eye moves from one area of emphasis to another. Fireplaces, windows, and other architectural

Figure 8.19 This U-shaped grouping creates a focal point where no natural focal point exists. © *Jessie Walker*

Figure 8.20 Very large spaces like this can accommodate more than one primary focal area. *Courtesy of Noel Jeffrey, Inc.*

features are natural focal points that draw the eye. Following are some guidelines for creating emphasis:

- In rooms with natural focal points, furniture can be placed to emphasize and take advantage of them. A grouping around a window or fireplace will emphasize the fine natural features of the room.
- In rooms that lack natural focal points, furniture can be placed to create groupings that take their place. For example, a case piece such as a chest or secretary could be placed against a wall with a pair of sofas placed facing each other at right angles to the case piece. The seating area would then be focused on the case piece.
- Most rooms will have just one primary focal area and other secondary or minor focal areas. In a standard-size living room, the area around the fireplace could be the primary focal area, and the secondary focal points could be (1) a desk with a chair and a lamp, (2) a console table with a painting or mirror and a lamp, or (3) a comfortable chair with a table and lamp for reading

tucked into a corner. A chest with an occasional chair could also be a secondary focal point.
- Very large spaces may require more than one primary focal area. For example, very large living rooms may need more than one main seating area to adequately fill the space.
- The table will be the primary focal point in a dining room, and a serving piece with a painting or mirror and side chairs could be a secondary focal point.
- The bed will generally be the primary focal point in a bedroom, and a small area with comfortable seating, tables, and lighting could be the secondary focal point.

Line and Harmony

Whenever a piece of furniture is placed in an environment, a line is created where the piece meets the floor or where its silhouette is seen against the background. In **plan drawing** (a view drawn from above), the furniture

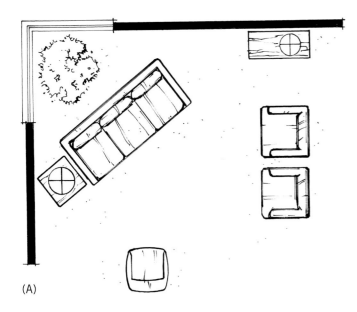

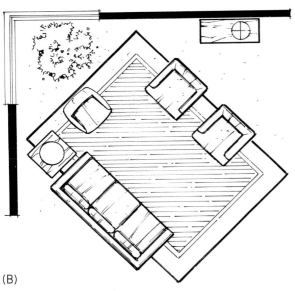

(A)

(B)

Figure 8.21 (A) Incorrect and (B) correct placement of furniture using angles that contrast with the natural lines of the room.

arrangement is also a study in line. Line is a powerful tool and should be used judiciously to create harmonious furniture arrangements. Some points to consider about the harmony of line when planning furniture arrangements include the following:

- If a line is introduced into a space, it should relate harmoniously to the other existing lines. For example, a sofa or other large piece placed diagonally across the corner of a room feels awkward unless other elements repeat and enhance the diagonal line of the piece.
- Placing large pieces at an angle often disregards the basic lines of the architecture. However, if other elements are arranged in concert with the diagonal line, the result may be very harmonious and interesting. For example, if an area rug turned on an angle is used as the format for an arrangement in a room of sufficient scale, the grouping will feel right. If the other pieces or the architectural elements in a room follow the same diagonal format and repeat and accentuate the diagonal lines, the arrangement will be pleasing.
- Chairs in a grouping placed at a slight angle tend to make the arrangement feel less formal and rigid because they soften the solid feeling of a rectilinear composition.

Form and Space

The forms in a furniture arrangement are the individual pieces of furniture. The space is the empty area between the furniture pieces. The design of space is as important as the furniture forms themselves. Furniture arrangement is a two- and three-dimensional study in space

Figure 8.22 The angular placement of this furniture is in harmony with the lines of the fireplace. *Studio Tagland Architecture, P.C./photo © Melabee M. Miller*

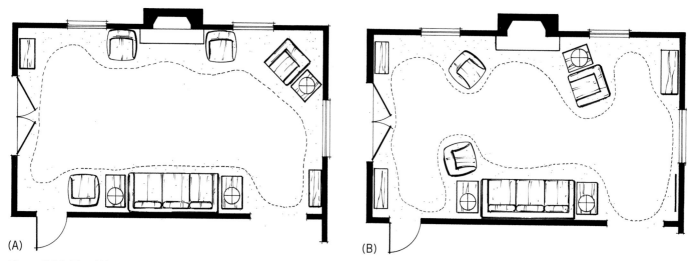

Figure 8.23 The (A) negative space in a grouping is made more interesting (B) by pulling pieces away from the wall.

and form and should be planned with sensitivity to **negative space.** Seen in plan, the arrangement should make interesting use of space. Seen in elevation, the furniture placement should break the wall space into interesting forms and create well-proportioned negative spaces. Art and accessories hung on the wall must be treated as part of the composition. Consider the following when arranging furniture and hanging accessories:

- Negative space needs to be interesting; avoid arrangements with the furniture "holding hands" in dancehall fashion around the perimeter of the room. This type of arrangement is often safe but without the interest it could have if some of the furniture were drawn into the room instead of being placed flat against the wall.
- Large pieces of furniture pushed tightly into corners are not as pleasing as pieces placed leaving some negative space. This is true in both plan and elevation—the piece needs breathing room to separate it from the corner or some negative space to separate it from a doorway or window.
- A desk that is placed perpendicular to a wall or actually moved out into the room may be more interesting than one that is pushed flat facing the wall. Turned perpendicularly, it extends into the negative space and changes the shape of the space, making it more interesting.

Vertical Space

In considering form and space, it is important to recognize the way that the interior will be experienced in elevation. Together with the architectural openings (windows and doors), the furniture and **accessories** (art pieces, hangings, collections) form a vertical pattern or **wall composition.** Thus the planning of where to place furniture and accessories in relation to walls is an integral part of applying the elements of form and space to design:

- In many instances the accessories can be used to complete the composition and finish the balancing process. There are no rules governing the hanging of pictures and other accessories, only the consideration of form, negative space, and balance.
- When hanging more than one piece in a grouping, it is important to lay the pieces out on a table or on the floor just as they will be hung. By doing this, one can evaluate the composition and see how the pieces relate to each other and how the proportion of the negative spaces between the pieces relates to the pieces themselves.
- Accessories must be considered in relationship to the furniture with which they share a wall. Art pieces should not be hung so high above the furniture that the relationship between the pieces is lost.
- The scale of the accessory should relate well to the scale of the furniture with which it will be placed. If the scale of a piece is too small, several smaller pieces could be massed to create a grouping of appropriate scale and mass for the furniture. For example, a mirror or painting can be massed together with a chest or table to balance a higher case piece on the opposite side of a fireplace.
- On walls without furniture or architectural openings, the accessory pieces could be massed in groupings or hung gallery fashion. Hanging pictures gallery fashion requires that the pieces be placed in a row at eye level with appropriate spacing between each piece. If the pieces are all close to the same size, an imaginary line could be traced along the wall to mark the top or bottom edge of the pictures. If this seems too rigid, then an imaginary line could be used instead to mark the center of each picture.
- The height of hangings should relate to other pieces in the room as well as to the composition of all the other walls.

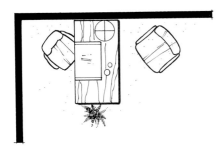

Figure 8.24 A desk placed at a right angle to the wall makes a functional and an interesting composition.

(A)

(A)

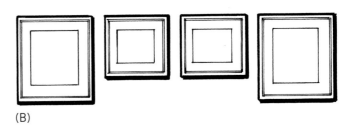

(B)

Figure 8.26 Two ways of hanging art pieces: (A) in a grouping and (B) gallery style.

(B)

Figure 8.25 In (A) the paintings are hung too high. In (B) the paintings relate better to the furniture.

Proportion

Every space has its own shape and proportions. Some spaces are long and narrow, some are square, and others are well-proportioned rectangles. In a large-scale interior, the proportions will be less apparent and consequently of less concern when arranging furniture. In most environments, however, the proportions of a room should be carefully considered when placing furniture. Furniture arrangements can be planned to make best use of awkward spaces, and in some cases the proportions of a space can visually be altered by a good furniture arrangement. The following considerations may be helpful:

- Rectangular rooms, if not too narrow, are the most flexible and easy to arrange.
- A square room is more difficult but could be arranged with a rectangular grouping as a primary focal point on one side, with open space along the opposite side for secondary focal points. An area rug could be used to help define the primary focal point.

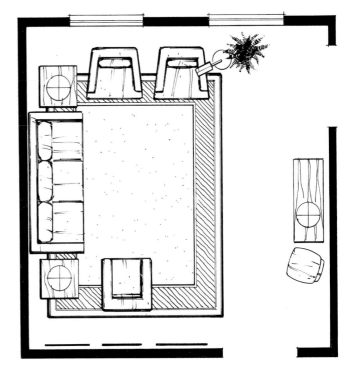

Figure 8.27 A possible solution for furniture arrangement in a square room.

- If the square room is large enough, an area rug could also be used to create a central focal point with a square or rectangular grouping placed in the center of the room. This would require careful planning of floor plugs or the use of recessed or other ceiling lighting.
- Long, narrow spaces can be challenging. The best way to handle this type of space is by dividing it into

areas of function or use. For example, in long, narrow family rooms or game rooms, part of the space could be devoted to conversation and music/video. The next section of the room could be planned for a game, pool, or Ping-Pong table or for eating space. The back of a sofa could serve as a divider between the spaces and help alter the **visual proportion** of the room.

- A narrow living room could also be divided according to use into seating area, music area, dining area, or even into more than one area for conversation and seating.

- Long, narrow rooms do not need extra-long sofas to match the proportion of the space. The long sofa only tends to exaggerate the uncomfortable proportions. It is wiser to divide the space into smaller modules with furniture groupings.

- In nonresidential interiors, narrow spaces can be intriguing. For example, a narrow space with a row of tables can make a restaurant more interesting because the function fits the space.

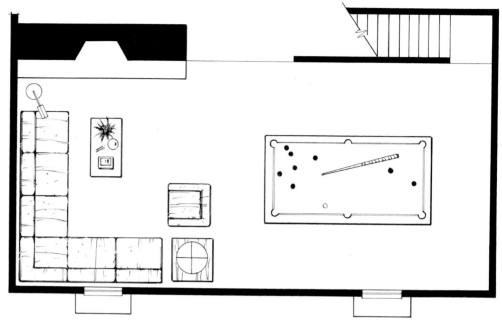

Figure 8.28 The proportions of a long narrow room are improved by dividing the space visually according to function.

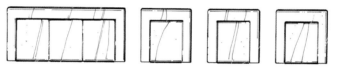

Figure 8.29 A straight-line grouping.

Basic Groupings

Most seating arrangements fit into seven basic configurations. The seven groupings can be composed of any combination of benches, ottomans, chairs, sofas, lounges, or love seats, and each grouping will be appropriate for different functions:

1. **Straight-line groupings** are formed by arranging furniture in continuous lines. Because this configuration is the most efficient for seating the largest number of people in a space, it is a popular choice for nonresidential interiors. It is used in theaters, airplanes, waiting rooms, classrooms, churches, and arenas, as well as in homes when they have been arranged for club

Figure 8.30 An inviting straight-line grouping at the Grand Hotel on Mackinac Island, Michigan. © Lowell Georgia/Photo Researchers, Inc.

meetings or other large gatherings. This type of grouping makes interaction difficult since it requires leaning forward, weaving back and forth, or craning your neck to talk with anyone except the person next to you. Its principal advantage is its ability to handle crowds.

2. **L-shaped groupings,** formed with two seating pieces placed at right angles to each other, are more conducive to interaction. The L could be an intimate arrangement of two chairs and a small table tucked into a corner or a pair of sofas capable of seating several people. It could be formed by something as simple as a chair placed at a right angle to the end of a love seat or sofa. The L-shaped grouping allows people to converse easily because the angle of conversation is comfortable. They do not face each other directly but sit at a slight angle, elbow to elbow.

3. **U-shaped groupings** are an extension of the L shape. They can be formed by adding a chair, sofa, love seat, or any seating piece to the L. This configuration also enables interaction and further expands the space for seating.

4. **Box-shaped groupings** are formed by adding seating pieces to partially close the opening of the U-shaped grouping. This is the best configuration for interaction among the largest possible group of users. Conversation pits, which are built-in seating areas designed as an integral part of the environment, are often box-shaped. If built around a fire pit, the interaction is often diminished by the fire hood, which interferes with visual contact. But if the line of sight is carefully maintained, the interaction can be excellent. In more standard furniture groupings, the opening of the U will usually be closed with a chair or pair of chairs allowing sufficient room for users to enter and exit the grouping with ease.

5. **Circular groupings** are much like box-shaped groupings except that, as the name implies, they are arranged in circular shapes. Some modular furniture pieces are designed in a circular or curving fashion.

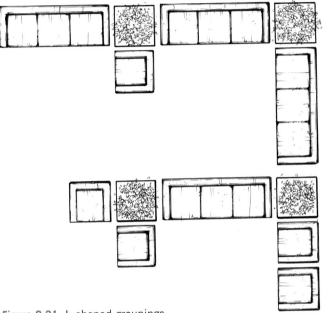

Figure 8.31 L-shaped groupings.

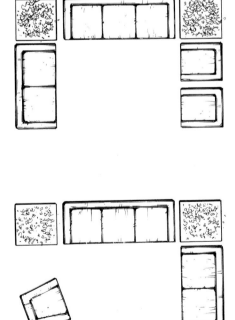

Figure 8.32 U-shaped groupings.

Figure 8.33 Placed around a table, these chairs create a flexible circular grouping. *John Silverio Architect/photo © Brian Vanden Brink*

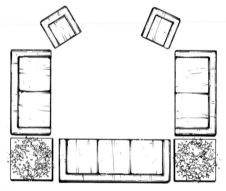

Figure 8.34 Box-shaped grouping.

These groupings, like the box-shaped groupings, are excellent for interaction because eye contact can be maintained with nearly everyone in the group. However, their unusual shape makes them unsuited to many situations.

6. **Parallel groupings** are an excellent arrangement for emphasizing a natural focal point or creating one where none exists. Two seating pieces are placed so that they face each other at right angles to a window, fireplace, or other natural focal point. The seating pieces frame the focal point, and the users face each other for good interaction. Where no natural focal point exists, the grouping can focus on a case piece or some other object of interest.

7. **Solo groupings** may sound like a paradox—the ideas may not seem compatible. However, it is important to remember that single pieces placed away from main groupings of furniture generally need some form of accompaniment. For example, a reading chair at least needs a lamp and would be even better with a table to hold a book and a refreshment. The chair becomes more functional and feels more purposeful with the table and lamp. Consider also that when a single chair is placed in a particularly beautiful spot to complete a

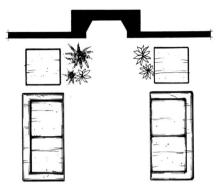

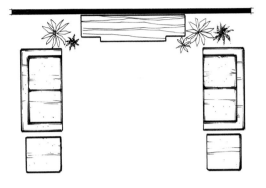

Figure 8.36
Solo grouping.

Figure 8.35 Parallel groupings.

Figure 8.37 The chair and ottoman are made more comfortable and usable with the addition of a table and lamp in this solo grouping. © *Peter Aaron/Esto*

furniture is often treated as sculpture whose principal purpose is aesthetic. The lighting in these spaces will often be architectural and preclude the need for tables and lamps. The appeal of such designs is in their clarity and lack of embellishment; extra pieces of furniture would only detract. However, most rooms are designed with a wider range of purpose in mind and are made better by grouping pieces that extend the function of the furniture. Even a wall of books can be made more functional by placing an ottoman or occasional chair next to the bookcase for browsing.

Nonresidential Considerations

Function

Many nonresidential designs will include areas of seating, dining, or sleeping that are treated in the same way they would be in a residence. However, in other cases of nonresidential design, the list of functions will not always relate to a specific person but rather to a generic need or function. For example, in an office with a receptionist, those who enter should have their attention drawn directly to the reception desk. The reception area must then be placed so that it is the first thing seen as a person enters. The designer will not ask the receptionist if a center-stage position is agreeable because in this situation the function supersedes the personal preferences of a specific user.

point of emphasis, it may never be occupied. Where the design may call for a chair as part of a vista—placed under a window or at the end of a hallway—people may feel "on stage" if they use it.

Seating pieces in some sleek, modern rooms may have no need for accompaniment. In such environments, the

Nonresidential Furniture Types

Nonresidential design often includes placement of fixtures that are quite unlike any furniture used in residential design. For example, in health care facilities, such as doctors' offices, clinics, and hospitals, there will be furniture specially designed for examination and procedures. The design must reflect understanding of each procedure and the relationship between different procedures so that the fixtures and equipment can be placed for efficiency and convenience. This kind of specialized need is one of the main reasons designers develop and practice in specialty areas such as health care design, restaurant design, hotel design, and office planning. Such specialization allows a design group to stay current with the latest technology and developments in each area and with the ways to best implement these developments in a design.

Planning for Systems Furniture

Many businesses and institutions are designed with large, open work spaces for many users. To make efficient use of such spaces, designers often specify **systems furniture** (discussed in Chapter 9, "Furniture Selection"). This consists of prefabricated modules that can be arranged in a number of different ways to create spaces and workstations for an endless number of different needs and functions. Systems furniture provides a great deal of flexibility, but determining space and function needs for each area is an enormous undertaking. This task is made much simpler by the use of computer software provided by the systems furniture manufacturer for collecting and analyzing data on needs and functions. These programs generate specifications for the types of modules that best meet the users' needs. The systems furniture is also laid out by the software as the designer plans the space. Those representing the manufacturer and selling the systems furniture are also available to help the designer specify the right components and plan their optimal arrangement.

Figure 8.38 Systems furniture provides versatility and has great design interest as well. *Courtesy of Herman Miller*

Circulation

Because many of the basic problems of circulation and traffic control are the same for residential and nonresidential design, principles or solutions observed in one setting can be applied in the other. For example, many nonresidential environments are designed with open plans, where one enters directly into open areas. Spaces with open plans have a particular need for traffic control. In retail stores and restaurants, furniture and fixtures are often used to define areas for traffic. In restaurants, the placement of tables will create aisles for circulation; the patterns can be altered by rearranging the tables. In retail stores, fixtures such as clothing racks or display tables are used to create lanes for traffic. Changes in material will sometimes suggest traffic patterns to a user. For example, in a store or restaurant, the main traffic lanes might be paved in slate or tile, and the seating or sales area covered with hardwood or carpet. The change in material indicates where major traffic should flow.

By plotting natural patterns of circulation and then determining where traffic should flow, open spaces with carefully placed furniture or fixtures can be designed to function as well as they would if they had actual walls or dividers to control traffic.

Chapter 9 | Furniture Selection

Wooden Furniture 230

Metal Furniture 232

Other Furniture
Materials 234

Upholstered Furniture 236

Furniture Harmony and
Human Factors 237

Furniture Types 239

Nonresidential
Considerations 240

Jeffrey S. Quéripel, Quéripel Interiors/© Melabee M. Miller

Furniture selection is a prime means of expressing individuality in interiors. Furniture has become an art form that can move us with its beauty, and whether or not we are conscious of it, the furniture we choose says much about our values and design sense. Because furniture often represents a sizable investment it is particularly important that it be well chosen for its quality of design, construction, function, and comfort, as well as for its lasting good looks.

In order to make the best possible selection when specifying furniture, it is important to understand relative quality and its relationship to price. Only when the quality of design, materials, and construction are in line with the price can furniture be considered a good value. Consequently, a knowledge of materials and construction is important to making wise selections.

Wooden Furniture

Because wood is an excellent material for furniture construction, it has been utilized by craftspeople for thousands of years. It is a renewable resource that can be regenerated by reforestation or by planting seedlings to replace trees that have been cut down for lumber. Wood is strong yet relatively easy to cut, carve, join, finish, and refinish. Wooden pieces are easily cared for, and if well constructed and carefully maintained, they may become better looking with age and last almost indefinitely. Beautifully finished wood appeals to our senses because of the unity and infinite variety of its grain patterns and the warmth of its colors. Wood was once part of a living organism, and even after the tree has been felled and the wood cured, worked, and finished, it still has that appealing quality of life.

Hardwood and Softwood

Woods are categorized as **hardwood** or **softwood.** Hardwoods such as oak, pecan, walnut, birch, maple, and cherry come from broad-leaf deciduous trees that lose their leaves in the winter. These tend to have tighter **grains** than softwoods and consequently are stronger and harder and can be carved and worked in more detail. Exotic hardwoods, such as ebony, mahogany, and rosewood, come from broad-leaf evergreen trees grown in tropical rain forests. Because many of these forests are being destroyed by excessive logging, it is important when specifying tropical hardwoods to obtain them from a reputable source, preferably one that harvests the lumber from sustainable groves. Softwoods such as pine, cedar, cypress, spruce, fir, and redwood come from conifer or cone-bearing trees. These trees do not drop their needles, and they grow more rapidly than hardwoods. Softwood has generally been less expensive than hardwood, making it well suited as a building material. Because it is less costly and can easily be worked without expensive, sophisticated machinery, it has been widely used by provincial craftspeople for furniture construction. Softwood has a more open grain than hardwood and, in the proper setting, adds simple warmth and character to an environment.

Other Forms of Wood

Wood in several other forms is also used for construction of furniture:

- **Plywood** is used as a substitute for solid woods and is made by **lamination**— laminating (gluing) thin sheets **(plies)** of wood or other materials, sandwich fashion, in successive layers to make a panel. When each ply is rotated a quarter turn so that the grain of each layer runs perpendicular (at a 90-degree angle) to the layer below it, a material of great strength is created. If the grain of each layer runs in the same direction, the plywood can be bent and shaped with heat, pressure, and chemicals to create beautiful furniture designs.
- **Particleboard,** or **chipboard,** is made by compressing flakes of wood with resin under heat and pressure to form a solid panel. Particleboard will not warp and can be used as a base for veneers of wood or plastic laminates and can be vinyl-wrapped for use in drawers.
- **Hardboard** is also produced by gluing fine wood fibers under heat and pressure. MDF, or medium-density fiberboard, is a widely used type of hardboard. MDF contains a substance called urea formaldehyde that irritates the eyes and lungs, and may be released when the material is cut or sanded. Another type of hardboard (often known by the brand name Masonite) is used for drawer construction, dust panels between drawers, and backing on mirrors and case goods. Hardboard is also used as paneling with simulated wood-grain veneers, textures, or drilled with holes for attaching hooks and brackets.

Case Goods

Furniture pieces made without upholstery such as desks, dressers, cabinets, and chests are called **case goods** by the furniture industry. Some case goods are made of solid wood, but many pieces are made using other combinations of materials:

- **All-wood** construction means that the visible parts of the piece are made of wood.
- **Combination** indicates that more than one type of wood is used on the exposed parts of the piece.
- **Genuine** denotes the use of veneers of a particular wood over hardwood plywood on all the exposed parts of a piece.

- **Solid** refers to the use of solid pieces of a certain wood in the construction of all the external (visible) parts.
- **Veneer** is a thin slice of beautifully grained wood bonded to plywood or particleboard. Veneers have been used since earliest times to create pieces of great appeal and strength. Because beautiful pieces of wood are used in thin slices, handsome effects with matched grains and inlaid patterns (called **marquetry**) can be achieved with veneers. One frequently used type, **burl veneer,** comes from the scarlike growths where trees have been diseased or repeatedly pruned. This results in an irregular growth pattern that becomes a beautiful and complex grain in the finished piece of furniture.

Wood Grains

By using several cutting methods, different grain patterns can be revealed in most woods:

- **Plain slicing** means that the half log **(flitch)** is cut parallel to a line through the center of the log, producing a vaulted or cathedral-like grain.
- **Quarter slicing** indicates that the quarter log (also called a *flitch*) is cut so that the blade meets the grain at right angles to the growth rings, resulting in a generally straight, striped grain.
- **Rotary slicing** shaves a continuous, thin layer of wood from a log mounted to a lathe. It is as if the log were being unwound like a roll of paper. The grain produced by this method is broad, open, and bold.

Joining Methods

A well-made piece of wooden furniture is assembled by fastening pieces of lumber together in junctions or closures called **joints.** There are several ways of joining and reinforcing furniture. The most common of these are listed below:

- **Corner blocks** are triangular pieces of wood that are glued and screwed into place at an angle. These blocks are considered not true joints but rather reinforcements. Corner blocks are used in points requiring extra strength, such as points where legs join tabletops, frames for case pieces, or frames for chair and sofa seats.
- **Dowels** are a third piece of wood used to join the other two parts of the frame together. The rounded dowel is

glued into holes that have been drilled into the other pieces. The quality of this type of joint relies on the strength of the dowel.

- **Dovetail** joints are used to secure drawer fronts and sides. This joint takes its name from a series of dovetail or fan-shaped notches carved into one piece and projections on the other that are carved to fit the notches.
- **Miter** joints are two pieces of wood that meet at a 45-degree angle. Mitered corners must be reinforced with screws, dowels, nails, or metal splines in order to be strong and functional.
- **Mortise and tenon** is an ancient method of joinery that imparts great strength. It is formed by two pieces of wood that have been carved to interlock. Into one of the pieces a square hole (mortise) is carved, and the second piece is carved with a projection (tenon) that fits into the hole. Mortise-and-tenon joints make secure connections for furniture frames.

Wood Finishes

Finishes are applied to wood for its protection and to enhance grain characteristics that cannot readily be seen in unfinished pieces. The first step in the finishing process is the preparation of the surface by smoothing and sanding to remove any unevenness and imperfections. The wood may then be filled with a liquid or paste **wood filler** to level the pores inherent in the natural grain. After further sanding, color may be applied to the wood.

Color is generally added in the form of **stains** mixed with water, oils, or other agents; the natural color of the wood grain can be lightened by **bleaching.** Paint can also be used to color a finish. When paint is applied to a surface and then wiped away, leaving a "scum" of paint, the finish is called **antique finish.** When no color is added to or extracted from the wood, the finish is referred to as **natural.**

The next step in the finishing process is the application of a transparent film to protect the piece from moisture and stains. One of the oldest finishing films is **shellac,** made by dissolving a secretion of the lac bug in denatured alcohol. Shellac produces a beautiful finish that, unfortunately, is not resistant to moisture, alcohol, or heat. A much stronger finish can be obtained with **varnish.** Varnish, a preparation of resinous substances dissolved in oil or alcohol, can be used on almost every surface and is very durable as well as moisture- and alcohol-resistant. **Polyurethane** is a synthetic resin used to give today's varnish its remarkably durable properties. **Lacquer** is a resin that has been dissolved in ethyl alcohol. With the addition of pigments to the lacquer, beautiful colored finishes are possible. Interestingly, lacquer is also used as a finish remover. Consequently, a sealer must

be applied between stains or other finishes and the lacquer in order to keep the lacquer from softening the previous finish.

Finishes are frequently polished with mild abrasives to soften or refine the finish film. Waxes and oils are used to polish and protect finished wood surfaces; the manufacturer's instructions for specific care of wood should be followed so that finishes will not be damaged.

Some furniture is **distressed** to make it appear used and worn like an **antique.** The surface of the wood is intentionally dented, scratched, and flecked with dark paint as part of the finishing process. As with any phase of the furniture manufacturing process, this can be done very well or in a poor manner. It is the care that is taken at each step, together with the quality of the materials used, that determines the value of a piece of wooden furniture.

When case goods are being purchased directly from a showroom, or even when a selection is being made from a catalog (and a comparable piece is available in the showroom), simple quality checks can be made:

- Doors and drawers should fit tightly without sticking.
- Drawers should slide easily on **glides** or ball bearings.
- Drawer interiors should be smooth and free from splinters that might snag clothing.
- Pieces should be checked for quality of joinery and presence of corner blocks.
- **Back panels** and **dust panels** should be placed between drawers.
- Sanding and finishing of unexposed surfaces should be examined for smoothness.
- **Hardware** can be examined for quality and style.
- The exterior finish can be checked for clarity and possible defects.

Metal Furniture

Like wood, metal is an important material for furniture construction and has been used as such for thousands of years. Metal has great durability and strength and can be worked in many different ways. It can be cast into solid forms, rolled into thin sheets that can be manipulated into an infinite variety of pieces and components, and **extruded** (forced through an opening) into tubes and other shapes that can also be bent and formed into beautiful furniture pieces.

Types of Metal

Though furniture could be made from most metals, only a few are commonly used:

- **Aluminum** is used for some outdoor furniture because it is lightweight and does not rust. It is also used for window frames and can be enameled, left its natural silver color, or **anodized** a dark bronze color. (Aluminum is anodized with an electrolytic process, whereby it is subjected to a chemical solution together with an electrical charge.)

- **Brass** is a gold-colored metal made from an *alloy* (combination) of zinc and copper. It is used either in solid form or as a plating for furniture and accessories.
- **Chromium,** or **chrome,** is used as a plating on steel furniture. It is known for its brilliant silver shine. Chromium is also used as a plating on lighting fixtures and plumbing accessories.
- **Iron** is a strong black metal that can easily be wrought (worked) to create indoor and outdoor furniture, railings, grates, grills, and accessories. It will rust, so it must be protected with paint.
- **Steel** is an alloy of iron and carbon. The combination has greater hardness and strength than iron but still can easily be worked. Steel is used extensively for nonresidential furniture and fittings, office systems and furniture, and residential pieces. Steel furniture is usually chrome-plated or painted.
- **Stainless steel** is an alloy of steel with chromium. The addition of chromium makes the steel rustproof. Stainless steel is used for furniture hardware and trim, as well as for a variety of fittings in nonresidential applications.
- Other metals such as silver, gold, pewter, bronze, copper, tin, and lead are used principally for accessories or for specific functions within the building structure.

Most metals need to be finished, for if the unfinished metal is left exposed to the natural elements in an environment, it will tarnish or rust. This quality is sometimes exploited by the designer to create a desired effect. Copper weathers to a beautiful blue-green color often referred to as a verdigris finish; a 588 **steel** weathers to a self-protecting coat of rich reddish brown rust. Metals can be polished to a high gloss and maintained with a coat of lacquer

or with continued polishing, and if a less lustrous finish is desired, the metal can be **brushed.** Metal pieces can also be painted or plastic coated in every conceivable color.

The quality of metal pieces will depend on the care and craftsmanship used in their construction. Like a fine automobile, the components of a piece of metal furniture should fit together tightly and the finish should be smooth and free from imperfections. Metal furniture can be found in many ranges of price and quality, and

Figure 9.2 Metal furniture is often used in outdoor settings such as this patio. © *Jessie Walker Associates*

Figure 9.3 Leather adds softness to this exciting hard-edged interior. *© Peter Aaron/Esto*

because of its durability and aesthetic flexibility, it can be used in almost every environment.

Other Furniture Materials

Over the years, creative designers have used every material imaginable—from animal horns to **papier-mâché**—to create furniture. Today a range of natural and synthetic materials other than wood and metal are available to those who design and manufacture furniture. The most common of these are plastic, leather, wicker, rattan, cane, and rush.

Plastic

Plastic is a type of nonmetallic compound, produced synthetically, that can be molded and hardened for a wide

range of design uses. It is a complex product that is in a constant state of development and redevelopment. Consequently, it may be difficult for the interior designer to stay abreast of new technology in this field. Fortunately, of the thousands of plastics that have been created, only a few are used for furniture and interior design. Families of plastics such as **vinyls, acrylics, polyurethanes,** and **melamines** (laminates) are the most common. Each of these families belongs to a larger group of either **thermoplastics** or **thermoset plastics:**

- Thermoplastics change their form by heating and can be damaged by too much heat. Acrylics and vinyls are thermoplastics.
- Thermoset plastics use a combination of compounds that are set by heat, so they are not easily damaged by it. Melamines are thermoset, and polyurethanes are both thermoset and thermoplastic.

Plastics today can be foamed, molded, **vacuformed,** sprayed, **calendered** (rolled), or blown in just about any weight or consistency, from spongy to rigid, to create a surprising variety of forms. This great flexibility makes plastics an ideal material for creative expression as well as function. Plastics have been maligned because they are often used to imitate natural materials or intricately designed details traditionally executed by hand. Yet when plastics are used in the context of their own potential, novel pieces of great aesthetic value are possible.

Because technology changes so rapidly, it is important for the designer to understand the specifications for a particular plastic before selecting it. Some plastics may be highly flammable, and some may give off poisonous or explosive gases if they burn. Since the designer may be liable for the health and safety of the user, understanding the performance of the material under every condition is most important. Care of plastics should be according to the manufacturer's directions.

Figure 9.4 Wicker furniture adds the right quality of informality to this sunroom. © *Jessie Walker Associates*

Leather

Leather is most frequently used as a covering material for chairs and other upholstered furniture, where its ability to "breathe" makes it an exceptionally comfortable and luxurious choice. It is also found as an inlay or embellishment to case goods, notably leather-topped desks and writing tables. Leather can be tanned to varying degrees of softness and durability, embossed or tooled with decorative patterns, and dyed in colors ranging from subtle to vivid.

- **Full-grain** leather retains the natural texture and imperfections of the animal hide.
- **Top grain** is the outer, most durable layer of the hide. This is the leather most suitable for furniture use.
- **Suede** and **nubuck** are leathers that have been buffed to produce a soft, velvety nap. Nubuck, which is made from top-grain leather buffed on the upper side, offers superior durability.

Full-aniline leather is processed with a natural, transparent dye that allows the grain to show through. Other color processes include **semianiline** or **protected aniline,** in which aniline-dyed leather is treated with additional substances to increase color saturation and resistance to stains, and **pigmenting,** in which chemical dyes are used to give the leather a deeply saturated color.

Wicker, Rattan, Cane, and Rush

Wicker, rattan, cane, and rush are all natural materials used to make furniture or certain furniture components. These materials tend to be rather informal, although cane is used to make formal pieces as well. Following are some considerations of these materials:

- **Wicker** is not a specific material, but rather the term is used to identify any piece that is fashioned from small twigs or flexible strips of wood. Common wicker pieces include chairs, tables, and baskets.
- **Rattan** is made from the unbranched stem of an Indian palm and is used to manufacture wicker furniture. Rattan poles are flexible, can be bent into beautiful forms, can be stained, lacquered, or painted, and, unlike

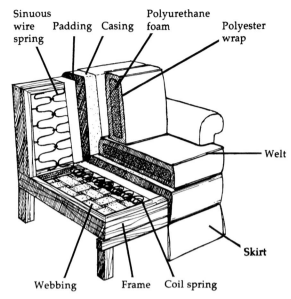

Sinuous wire spring   Padding   Casing   Polyurethane foam   Polyester wrap

Welt

Skirt

Webbing   Frame   Coil spring

Figure 9.5 The upholstery process showing the frame, webbing, coil springs hand-tied eight ways, and sinuous wire springs (in the back).

bamboo (which is brittle and hollow), can be nailed or screwed.

- **Cane** is made from grasses, palm stems, or plants such as rattan or bamboo. Thin strips of these materials are woven to form a mesh that is usually fitted into the seat or back of chair frames. The mesh allows air to pass through and is strong yet has the ability to flex and give, providing a degree of comfort. Cane has been used throughout history to create beautiful pieces of furniture; today manufacturers continue to use it on pieces of classic design.
- **Rush** is a type of long grass that is twisted to form a thin cord. Rush is a strong and long-lasting material with great appeal and has been used for centuries to weave floor mats as well as chair seats. Today, rush is sometimes duplicated with strong paper cords. The paper version is nearly identical to real rush and is particularly well suited to dry climates, where rush can dry out and split.

Upholstered Furniture

The quality of fabric-covered furniture is more difficult to assess than case goods because upholstered pieces are "blind" items; one cannot see what is inside. This means that one must rely on written specifications of a particular product as well as the information that a sales representative might furnish about the product. Because quality is important to the durability of a design, designers often choose manufacturers and products with which they are most familiar and whose quality they know and

trust. Understanding the construction and composition of fine upholstered goods leads to the selection of pieces of quality and value.

Frames

Frames for upholstered furniture are made from the same materials as case goods: wood, metal, or plastic. Wooden frames are made of hardwood, since softwoods generally lack the necessary strength and may split when joined. Wooden frames should be securely joined with double dowels and glue, and the corners should be braced with blocks or metal plates and securely glued and screwed into place.

Springs

Springs are generally of two types:

1. **Coil springs** are attached to a tightly woven webbing of rubber and metal, linen, jute, or synthetic. The webbing is stretched across and attached to the bottom of the frame and serves as the base for the springs, which are then tied together at the top in at least eight places per spring.
2. **Sinuous wire (no-sag) springs** are fashioned from a single wire that is bent in a continuously curved zigzag and attached to the frame. This type of spring is used in chair backs or in upholstered pieces with particularly thin profiles because it requires less vertical space than traditional coil springs.

Cushioning

A layer of burlap or other material protects and supports the padding and keeps it from working into the springs. The **padding** is a soft layer of **batting** made from a fibrous material such as cotton or polyester that covers the

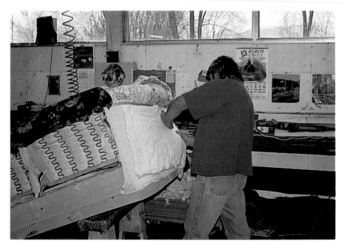

Figure 9.6 An upholsterer adds padding to a sofa. © *Joey Moon*

springs and frame and gives shape and form to the up-holstered piece. A **casing** of muslin holds the padding in place and keeps the final cover from abrading the padding.

Some seating pieces are designed with **loose cushions** for reasons of aesthetics and comfort. Such cushions or pillows can be filled with foam-covered springs, down and feathers, foam, polyester fiberfill, or a combination of these materials. **Reversible cushions** can help extend the life of an upholstered piece because the cushions can be turned.

Down is considered luxurious and is distinguished by its rumpled look. Because down and feathers are not re-silient, such cushions require frequent plumping. Down cushions are increasingly rare due to high cost.

The most common cushioning material is polyurethane foam with a wrapping of polyester batting. Polyurethane foam comes in a variety of densities and is resilient, non-allergenic, and impervious to moisture. The polyester fiberfill gives added softness and comfort to the cushion and has the quality of resilience missing in down fill.

Lower-quality furniture typically has solid foam or **laminated (sandwiched) foam,** where the thinner outer layers are less dense and resilient than the thicker middle layer, giving some of the feeling of more costly polyester-wrapped foam.

Coverings

Coverings have a major impact on the aesthetics of up-holstered furniture. Identical pieces covered in dissimilar covers will have very different finished appearances. Be-cause the cover is such a visible part of the piece, it will often be a major factor in the selection process.

Covers are available in a wide range of materials and qualities; manufacturers use the cover quality as a means to set prices for upholstered goods. A piece may be cov-ered in material the client has obtained through a de-signer or elsewhere. These goods are referred to as "C.O.M." (customer's own material) and are shipped to the manufacturer for upholstery on the selected piece. The manufacturer also maintains a supply of fabrics in several grades of quality that can be specified and or-dered from catalogs and sample books. Each sample is assigned a grade corresponding to its quality; different prices are listed for each grade of material. An uphol-stered piece may be covered with **slipcovers** that can be changed seasonally. The quality of the covering is de-pendent upon the material and finesse used in tailoring the piece.

It is often necessary to order goods from catalogs with-out actually inspecting the pieces; one must rely on man-ufacturers that have an established reputation for quality and service.

In some cases, however, where pieces are available in showrooms, quality can be observed firsthand:

- Evaluate the comfort of the piece by sitting in it.
- Check for careful matching of patterns or **naps** (direc-tion of pile).
- Look for smooth seams and straight **welts** (covered cords) without puckering.
- Verify that cushions fit properly.
- Be aware of loose or hanging threads that might indi-cate poor craftsmanship.
- Ensure that buttons are tight on **tufted** pieces.
- Examine quilted fabric to see that the quilting has been carefully executed.

When delivered, upholstered furniture should be allowed to off-gas for 24 hours before the interior is occupied.

Furniture Harmony and Human Factors

Harmonious and aesthetically pleasing combinations of furniture are the result of a selection process that may be partially intuitive but is also based on an understanding of styles, themes, and pieces that have classic quality. By studying and knowing styles from history, and by keep-ing abreast of innovative developments in the market-place, we can make sound judgments about the kinds of furniture that will best suit our aesthetic needs.

Because many people find selecting furniture a be-wildering task, manufacturers have always made matched sets or "suites" of furniture. For example, they produce bedroom sets with dressers, nightstands, chests of drawers, headboards, armoires, and mirrors with matching details, woods, and styling. This is an easy so-lution for those who lack the confidence to choose, but as we know from studying the principles of design, har-mony is made up of unity and variety. Matched sets are unified, but they often lack variety. The most interesting rooms have a personal mix of pieces that results in a harmonious setting with a pleasing balance of unity and variety.

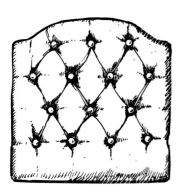

Figure 9.7 This buttoned upholstery is an example of tufting.

Figure 9.8 Furniture in this space was selected in response to its function: conversation, reading, and television/entertainment. © *Keith Swan/Esto*

Function

The first consideration in selecting individual pieces of furniture and built-in fittings and fixtures for an environment is the users and the tasks they will perform in the environment.

Each environment has a certain function or group of functions for which it is designed. It is important to be familiar with all of these functions so that furniture and fittings can be designed or selected to enhance the desired function. For example, soft, deep, low seating pieces for casual television viewing and music listening are very different from the kinds of seating one might choose for work at a sewing machine or computer. Such pieces should provide proper height and back support and should be based on actual human dimensions.

Anthropometrics and Ergonomics

Anthropometrics are human physical dimensions, including height, weight, and volume. **Ergonomics,** or biotechnology, is the study of human relationships to the furniture and products that fill our environments. These terms may seem formidable, but their application to furniture design is simple: The human form, its dimensions, and its need for movement are the bases for functional and comfortable furniture design.

The ideas of comfort and function are often linked to culture. For example, people in parts of Asia and South America learn from childhood to sit on their haunches in squatting fashion. Given the choice of a stool or a grassy spot by the roadside, these people might opt for the grass. Those from other areas of the world could certainly argue the relative comforts of sleeping in hammocks, on a Japanese futon mattress atop tatami mats, or on more conventional mattresses filled with coil springs. The ancient Egyptians developed sleeping arrangements with a headrest that today appears anything but comfortable.

Regardless of cultural influences, the best measure of function and comfort is the human form. Ideally furniture and fittings should be scaled to the average human form—but unfortunately, there is no such thing as an average person. Hertzberg, Daniels, and Churchill measured 132 different features of 4,000 air force flyers and found that there were no men who fell in the average range on ten key measurements. Nonetheless, most design is keyed to an average set of dimensions. These average measurements will not be optimum for everyone but will likely cause less inconvenience than would be the case if furniture, fittings, and fixtures were designed for the very short or the very tall. Personal environments can be custom designed to the dimensions of extreme individual

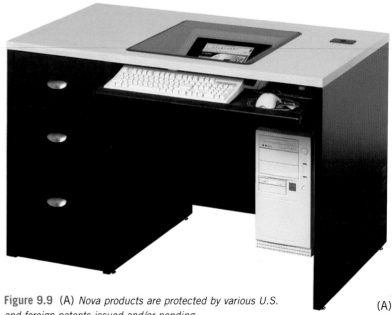

Figure 9.9 (A) *Nova products are protected by various U.S. and foreign patents issued and/or pending.*

(A)

sizes, and where possible, this should be an important goal of the design.

With all the research and developments in furniture design, it is remarkable how little the overall form and dimensions of furniture have changed over the millennia. Today's ergonomic superchairs differ very little in general dimensions from the chairs used in ancient Egypt.

Furniture Types

There is an infinite variety of furniture types that has been used through the ages in response to specific needs. Most of these types have changed very little over the years, responding primarily to changes in taste and style. Recently, developments have introduced new types of furniture such as the systems used extensively in nonresidential design. Even these, however, were need-based designs.

Systems Furniture

To meet the challenge of flexibility created by complex and changing needs, particularly in nonresidential design, product designers developed systems furniture, manufactured in modules that can be assembled and reassembled in different configurations. The spaces created may be open, private, semiprivate, or a combination. The mod-

Figure 9.9 (A and B) The ergonomic placement of the computer screen helps eliminate fatigue because the head is maintained at a natural angle for reading.

(B)

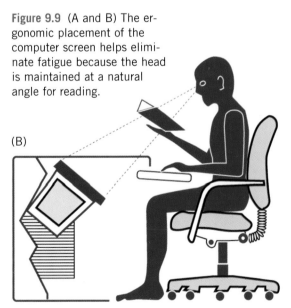

Read your computer like a book.™

Figure 9.9 (B) *Nova products are protected by various U.S. and foreign patents issued and/or pending.*

Figure 9.10 (A) Systems furniture provides personal workstations in an open workspace. *Ethospace photo courtesy Herman Miller*

(B)

Figure 9.10 (B) Different components in each module allow individual users flexibility to accomplish specific tasks. *Ethospace photo courtesy Herman Miller*

ules might consist of full- or partial-height panels or divider units to which coat racks, filing cabinets, bookcases, storage bins, writing surfaces, computer stations, work surfaces, drawing surfaces, and drawer units can be attached. The systems can also be integrated with freestanding furniture components. These systems contain all the wiring for task lighting, ambient lighting, telephones, computer links, and electric power. The systems designed for laboratories even provide flexible plumbing connections.

The wide acceptance of systems furniture is the result of its tremendous flexibility. The inflexibility and permanence of wall construction is eliminated by the use of modular dividers and components that define space in much the same way as conventional constructed walls.

Figure 9.11 An ergonomic chair provides sustained comfort.
Alan Freysinger Architect/Christina Oliver Interior Design/photo Brian Vanden Brink

These modules also allow, with very little effort or disturbance, users to reclaim unused space or space whose designated function has changed. Because of their wide use, manufacturers find it worthwhile to invest in the aesthetic design of modular components; the result is exciting lines of systems furniture with great appeal as well as utility.

Ergonomic Superchairs

In today's society many people spend the greater part of their day in work situations where they must be seated. In order to be functional, seating must offer sustained comfort. Consequently, research has led to the design of highly flexible seating pieces. These self-adjusting chairs are designed to sustain and support the human form and to accommodate the body, which is constantly shifting and changing. These chairs absorb the shock of sitting down and support the body in an upright position until the user decides to lean back. When reclining, the chair shifts to transfer body weight from the buttocks to the back, legs, and thighs. The feet remain on the floor as the user tips back, and the back of the chair flexes to provide

constant support for the lumbar area. The result is sustained comfort, reduced physical strain, and less muscle fatigue in the lower back. This kind of comfort is a boon to productivity and satisfaction.

Custom Designs

Design projects often include needs and functions that require specialized fittings and furniture that may not be available from manufacturers. Such pieces can be custom designed and built to exact specifications. For example, a restaurant design may include a long padded bench (banquette) against a wall, intended for seating with a series of tables. Such pieces must be custom designed and built for a particular set of dimensions—they cannot be ordered from a catalog. Custom designs help establish a distinctive look for an interior because they are one of a kind, created for a unique set of requirements.

Other Furniture Types

The vocabulary of furniture selection includes the names of a wide variety of types. These are not styles, but simply different kinds of pieces with varying functions that are often available in a wide range of styles. Table 9.1 illustrates many types of furniture.

Nonresidential Considerations

Ergonomics

Unlike residential work, in which the designer often knows the users and can cater to individual body sizes and types, nonresidential design entails the ergonomic challenge of selecting furniture for a continually changing group of users whom the designer has never seen. In many interiors, a profile of the typical, or target, user can be created from demographic information supplied by the client. For example, target users in a fine restaurant will be different from those in a sporting goods store or a pediatrician's office. While individual patrons and employees will change, their statistical similarities in age, height and weight, physical condition, and special needs will remain fairly constant. The designer's goal is to select furnishings of the right height, shape, and feel to satisfy the user that the particular interior is intended to serve.

In some interiors, the ergonomics of furniture selection are governed by the interests of the client rather than those of the users. You may have noticed that the seating in fast-food restaurants, airports, and shopping malls is somewhat uncomfortable. This is not an accident; the managers of these locales intend to discourage loitering. Visually, too, the furniture in a nonresidential interior may be less "comfortable" than that in a residential one, where the same users will live with it day after day.

Table 9.1 | **Furniture Identification**

Side Chair

No Arms

Hitchcock, nineteenth century

Side Chair

No Arms

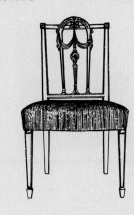

Sheraton, eighteenth century

Side Chair

No Arms

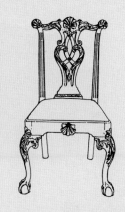

Chippendale, eighteenth century

Open Armchair

With Arms

Queen Anne, eighteenth century

Open Armchair

Belter Designer

Rococo Revival, nineteenth century

Open Armchair

Hoffman Designer

Prague chair, twentieth century

Fauteuil

French Open Arm

Règence, eighteenth century

Fauteuil

French Open Arm

Rococo, eighteenth century

Fauteuil

French Open Arm

Neoclassic, eighteenth century

Furniture Identification (continued)

Bergère

French Closed Arm

Rococo, eighteenth century

Bergère

French Closed Arm

Neoclassic, eighteenth century

Windsor Chair

Bow Back

American, eighteenth/nineteenth centuries

Windsor Chair

Comb Back

American, eighteenth/nineteenth centuries

Windsor Chair

Pierced Splat

English, eighteenth/nineteenth centuries

Lawson Lounge Chair

Rolled Arm

Contemporary

Armless Chair

Slipper Chair

Contemporary

Ottoman

Upholstered Footstool

Contemporary

Settee

Deacon's Bench

American, eighteenth/nineteenth centuries

Furniture Identification (continued)

Settee

Double Pierced Splat

Chippendale, eighteenth century

Settee

Bentwood

Thonet, late nineteenth century

Sofa

Camel Back

Chippendale, eighteenth century

Sofa

Bow Back

Hepplewhite, eighteenth century

Sofa

Tuxedo

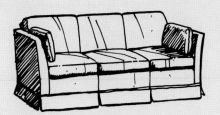

Contemporary

Sofa

Lawson with Rolled Arms

Contemporary

Sofa

Chesterfield with Tufted Back and Rolled Arms

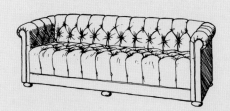

Contemporary

Chaise Longue

Reclining Sofa

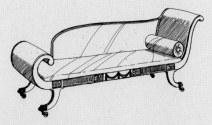

American Empire, nineteenth century

Chaise Longue

Pony Chaise

Le Corbusier, twentieth century

Furniture Identification (continued)

Chaise Longue

Also Called Chaise Lounge

Contemporary

Wing Chair

Upholstered Wings

Queen Anne, eighteenth century

Wing Chair

Upholstered Wings

Chippendale, eighteenth century

Tub Chair

Rounded Back

Contemporary

Club Chair

Oversized Upholstered

Contemporary, Victorian reproduction

Ladder-Back

Sausage-Shaped Turnings/Rush Seat

American, eighteenth/nineteenth centuries

Ladder-Back

Chaise á Capucine

Country French

Ladder-Back

Pierced Slats

Chippendale, eighteenth century

Ladder-Back

Rocker

Shaker, nineteenth century

Furniture Identification (continued)

Ladder-Back

Hill Chair

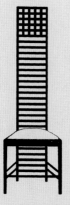

Mackintosh, twentieth century

Rolltop Desk

Tambour Top Rolls Shut

American, early twentieth century

Secretary

Drop-Front Desk with Bookcase

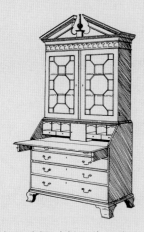

Chippendale, eighteenth century

Table Desk

French Bureau Plat

Neoclassical, eighteenth century

Rolltop Desk

French Bureau á Cylindre

Rococo, eighteenth century

Chest on Chest

Stacked Double Chest

Chippendale, eighteenth century

Knee-Hole Desk

Space for Knees

Chippendale, eighteenth century

Tall Case Clock

Also Called Grandfather Clock

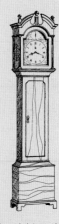

Chippendale, eighteenth century

Chest of Drawers

French Commode

Rococo, eighteenth century

Furniture Identification (continued)

Chest of Drawers

Block Front

Chippendale, eighteenth century

Highboy

Chest on Raised Legs

Queen Anne, eighteenth century

Highboy

Also Called Tall Boy

Chippendale, eighteenth century

Breakfront

Front Breaks or Comes Forward

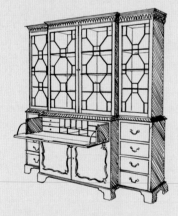

Chippendale, eighteenth century

Armoire

Closet: Also Called Wardrobe

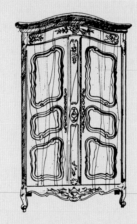

Country French

Hutch

Open Cupboard

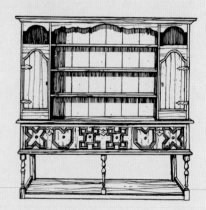

American vernacular

Buffet

Serving Piece: Also Called Sideboard

Hepplewhite, eighteenth century

Nesting Tables

Stack Underneath One Another

Hepplewhite, eighteenth century

Tilt-Top Table

Top Tilts, Also Called Tip-Top

Chippendale, eighteenth century

Furniture Identification (continued)

Pedestal Table

Also Called Tripod

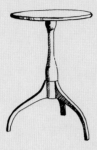

Shaker candlestand

Gateleg Table

Legs Swing Out on Drop Leaf

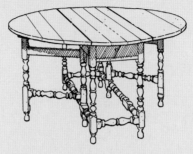

English/American vernacular

Butterfly Table

Small Drop Leaf

Vernacular, seventeenth/eighteenth centuries

Pembroke Table

Tea Table-Sized Drop Leaf

Hepplewhite/Sheraton, eighteenth century

Tea Table

Small Tall Table

Queen Anne, eighteenth century

Flap-Top Table

Top Opens for Games

Duncan Phyfe, nineteenth century

Console Table

Goes Against the Wall

American Empire, nineteenth century

Console Table

French

Rococo, eighteenth century

Butler's Tray Table

Used as a Coffee Table

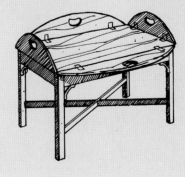

Chippendale, eighteenth century

Furniture Identification (continued)

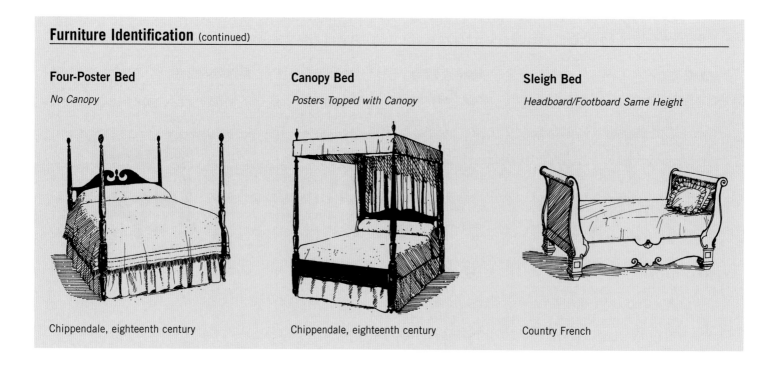

Four-Poster Bed	**Canopy Bed**	**Sleigh Bed**
No Canopy	*Posters Topped with Canopy*	*Headboard/Footboard Same Height*
Chippendale, eighteenth century	Chippendale, eighteenth century	Country French

Figure 9.12 Novel furniture is an important part of the overall feeling of this restaurant. *© Peter Mauss/Esto*

Hotel lobbies, restaurants, and retail stores may utilize elaborately decorative, even outrageous furniture to evoke a memorable impression during the short time the target user is present.

Durability

While it may be obvious that furniture selected for non-residential use needs to be durable, it is worth considering specific characteristics that can help furniture meet the test of hard wear over time:

- Patterns, lightly textured surfaces, and medium-dark colors camouflage dirt and scratches better than solids, smooth surfaces, and light colors.
- Materials and finishes should be suitable for thorough cleaning with detergents or other solvents.
- Drawer pulls, cabinet handles, and other operational parts should be chosen with the first-time user in mind. If the method of operation is not evident at first glance, some users will inevitably misuse the piece and damage it.
- Quality materials and construction methods are worth the investment. Many manufacturers describe their merchandise as suitable for both home and institutional settings, but the designer should evaluate it according to the planned use before accepting this generalization.
- Cabinets in nonresidential interiors are often custom made. Even on a modest per-unit budget, custom-designed furniture may be an option if the project calls for enough units to create an economy of scale.
- The designer should read any warranties in advance to make sure that they cover nonresidential use.

Chapter 10 | Architectural Detail

Walls 252

Doors 254

Windows 257

Stairs 260

Fireplaces and
Chimneypieces 264

Ceilings 266

Cabinetwork 268

Nonresidential
Considerations 268

© Paul Warchol

Architectural details are permanent features such as stairs, doors, windows, panels, moldings, trim, chimneypieces, fireplaces, and cabinetwork. During a given historic era, certain details were popular and commonly used. The details became typical of the period, and today they are an important key to identifying rooms of a particular era. Now, as in times past, designers and builders choose details to provide an element of finish in an interior, as well as to make the design more interesting and appealing.

Walls

In common dwellings from many periods, the wall treatment was generally the same as the building materials. For example, Medieval interiors often included a timber framework and stucco infill as a wall treatment. They might also have stone walls left plain, stuccoed with rough plaster, or simply whitewashed. Panels of wood that were joined (fitted together) and carved like furniture were used in the great churches of the Middle Ages. This type of paneling was also used in castles and manor houses as a barrier from the dampness of stone walls and as a form of decoration. This paneling, which usually reached above the level of the doors, was called a **wainscot.** The wood was framed in small vertical panels that were carved with a motif resembling a stylized piece of folded linen called **linenfold.** Wainscoting in this style was also popular in some interiors from the nineteenth and twentieth centuries. These more recent wainscots were frequently finished at the top with a **plate rail** (a narrow shelf used to display plates).

The Renaissance brought a return to classicism, and the designs of Rome became the basis for most wall detailing. The Roman temple was built with columns resting on a raised podium. The columns supported a complete entablature, including an architrave, frieze, and cornice. During the Renaissance the exterior details of the Roman temple were translated into interior wall details, executed in materials such as wood, plaster, and marble. The podium became the **dado** (the lower portion of a wall set apart by moldings). The columns were applied decoratively as flat **pilasters** with appropriate bases and capitals (also treated in a flat manner), and the entablature was interpreted as a series of moldings where the wall meets the ceiling. The spaces between the pilasters were filled with molded panels that varied in size and style. During certain periods the pilasters disappeared, leaving just the simple panels. These basic classical details have been reinterpreted many times in every culture touched by the Renaissance.

Certainly, one of the most popular treatments through the years has been panels of wood. However, the influence of the International style (with its lack of historical ornament) and the rising cost of fine historic detailing have made historic paneling less common. In some historically styled homes and in certain nonresidential settings requiring a traditional feeling, paneled walls are still used.

Figure 10.1 Linenfold panel.

Wood Paneling

The three most common panel types are traditional, board and batten, and tongue and groove (types of wood, finishes, and joints are discussed in Chapter 9, "Furniture Selection"):

- Traditional **paneling** is made with panels that may be flat, **beveled** (perimeter of panel is cut at an angle to meet the frame), or raised (panel projects beyond the frame). The panels are framed with **stiles** (vertical part of the frame) and **rails** (horizontal part of the frame). The frames are joined with mortise-and-tenon or dowel joints. The frame is grooved where the panel and the frame are joined, and a small space is left to allow for expansion and contraction of the panel.

Figure 10.2 Dado and pilaster.

Dado

- **Beadboard** is a type of nineteenth- and early-twentieth-century paneling that became very popular again at the end of the last century and the beginning of the new millennium because it is so well suited to informal vernacular/country-style design. It is made with narrow vertical strips separated by a rounded vertical bead. The fiberboard paneling comes prefinished or primed, ready for painting. Beadboard is often used as a wainscot or dado.

- **Board and batten** is paneling made from wide vertical boards. The gap between the boards is covered with a 1-inch by 2-inch strip of wood called a batten. This type of paneling was used in America during the seventeenth century to cover the fireplace wall, creating what was referred to as a **palisade wall.** Reverse board and batten produces the opposite effect of boards with a wide reveal or groove between.

- **Tongue-and-groove** paneling consists of boards **coped** (cut to fit an adjoining piece) with a projecting tongue on one edge that matches and fits into the recessed groove on the opposite edge. The two edges of the board are generally beveled producing a V-shaped groove where the boards meet. The groove hides any irregularities in the thickness of the boards. Inexpensive plywood or pressboard paneling sheets are produced to imitate the look of genuine tongue-and-groove paneling.

Moldings

Moldings are trims used to create decorative effects. At the same time, they may cover the unfinished ragged edges of the wall left in the construction process. Moldings are frequently made of wood that can be worked easily—most often pine and oak. Mitering the corners (cutting and fitting together the trim at a 45-degree angle) allows for a pleasing fit where pieces are joined. Moldings may be stained or painted. When they are painted the same color as the walls, they tend to have less visual importance. When they are painted to contrast with

Figure 10.3 Traditional wooden paneling adds depth and character to this interior. *Elizabeth Gillin Interiors, Designer/photo © Melabee M. Miller*

Figure 10.4 Beadboard wainscot with plate rail.

Figure 10.5 Board and batten paneling.

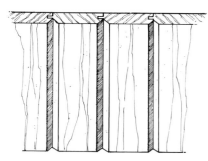

Figure 10.6 Tongue-and-groove paneling.

Doors

The selection of a door is important for practical reasons. Major considerations are security against breakage and unlawful entry, upkeep with regard to climate and the amount of wear and tear it will receive, and protection against fire (burn time). Beyond these crucial safety and maintenance factors come the considerations of initial cost and upkeep cost. Upkeep considerations include painting, refinishing, and ability to withstand breaking or shattering. The initial cost should be balanced with the upkeep costs. When these considerations are met, aesthetics will be the determining factor in style selection.

The front doorway sets the tone of the building. The scale of a large door can inspire awe and indicate the importance of the structure. The captivating doors of London, painted bright "London bus" red, cornflower blue, butter yellow, shiny black, or Georgian green, trimmed with brass hardware, are a striking counterpoint to the white stucco or somber brick of the town houses. They

the walls, they become a more dynamic feature of the room. Following is a list of trim types:

- **Base** describes the molding used to finish the wall where it meets the floor. Any workable material, including rubber or plastic, can be used to make a base.
- **Baseboard** designates bases of wood. The base hides any slight irregularities in the level of the floor and keeps the wall from being scuffed by vacuums or other equipment. This trim is sometimes called a mopboard because it protects the wall during cleaning.
- **Chair rail** is a molding placed at the usual height of a chair back to protect the wall from damage. If the section below the rail is paneled, dado fashion, the trim is called a **dado cap.** The portion below the rail is sometimes called a wainscot, although *wainscot* is a term better used to describe a door-height section of paneling. The height of the chair rail may vary from approximately 30 to 36 inches.
- **Crown** or **bed moldings** are placed where the wall meets the ceiling to add a finishing touch to traditionally styled rooms. They are generally simple; the more complex and ornate ceiling molding is called cornice molding.
- **Cornice moldings** often include decorative ornamentation such as the acanthus leaf, egg and dart, modillions, or dentils.
- **Cove molding** is a rounded piece placed where the wall meets the ceiling. It makes a clean smooth transition from the ceiling to the wall.

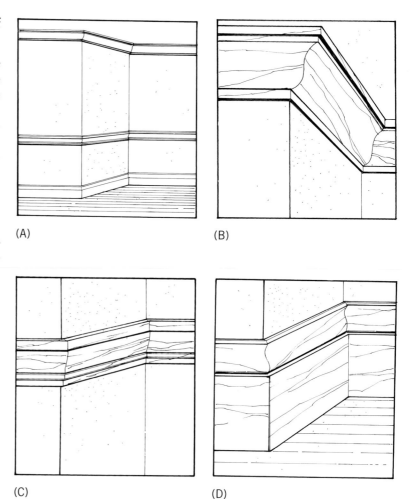

(A)

(B)

(C)

(D)

Figure 10.7 (A) Example of crown, chair rail, and base molding. Details of (B) crown molding, (C) chair rail, and (D) base.

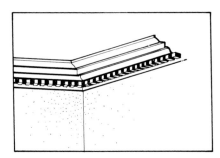

Figure 10.8 Cornice molding.

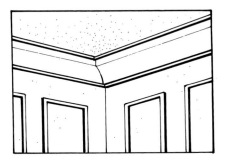

Figure 10.9 Cove molding.

Figure 10.10 Paneled door.   Figure 10.11 Flush door.

also provide the touch of individuality that a door demands. The doors on the interior of a house serve more common functions but are no less worthy of attention. Interior doors are framed with moldings to conceal the ragged space between the door frame and the wall. Doors may be made of wood or from metal, glass, or plastic. They are available in many decorative styles. Doors fall into two basic categories, paneled doors and flush doors:

- Traditional **paneled doors** of wood are made in the same manner as traditional wooden wall panels. This type of door consists of wooden stiles and rails that secure the molded panels.
- **Flush doors,** as the name indicates, are flat with no raised or sunken panels. They are made of wood using two principal methods. The first utilizes a **solid core** of wood, also called **lumber core.** In this type of construction, a thin cross banding (veneer with a horizontal grain) is laminated (glued) to a core of wood blocks that has been framed with rails and stiles. The door is finished with a vertical-grained face veneer. The second type is **hollow core,** which is made with a stile-and-rail frame filled with a lightweight honeycomb of cardboard and covered with as many as three veneers of thin wood. These doors are not as strong as the lumber-core type.
- Metal doors, once used only for areas with serious security problems, today have become quite acceptable in most settings. They are now made of steel and filled with a core of high-density polystyrene or polyurethane plastic foam, which makes them well insulated. Compared to wooden doors, metal doors are less subject to dimension changes resulting from temperature

and humidity shifts. They can be formed in traditional paneled styles or fitted with panes of glass, and when painted, they are almost indistinguishable from wooden doors when seen from a distance.

- High-strength tempered glass doors in metal frames (or unframed) are functional, particularly in nonresidential settings, because they permit visibility in areas of high traffic and allow passersby to see into areas where products or services are available.
- Glass doors with metal or wooden frames make inviting entrances to patios or balconies or attractive dividers between rooms. When the glass is leaded (smaller pieces held together with lead strips), **beveled** (edges cut at an angle), or stained (colored leaded glass), it creates beautiful effects with light and can be an important decorative feature of the interior. Sliding glass doors have become less popular because they are heavy and difficult to operate. They often develop problems with their glides (sliding tracks) and are also difficult to secure.
- Molded plastic doors in many designs, including the traditional paneled type, are available today. They

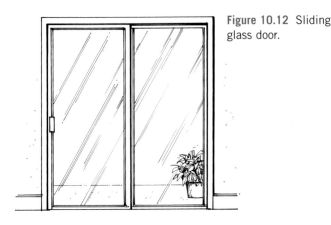

Figure 10.12 Sliding glass door.

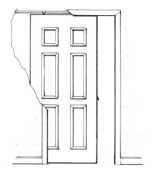

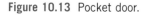

Figure 10.13 Pocket door.

Figure 10.14 Bifold doors.

Figure 10.15 Accordion doors.

Figure 10.16 Louvered doors.

may be embossed with a faint wood grain or perfectly smooth. When painted, they have the appearance of a wooden door, especially from a distance.

Several other types of doors are seen in today's interiors. Among the most important are those described below:

- **Pocket doors** glide on a metal track from which they are suspended. When they are opened, they slide into a recessed pocket in the framing of the wall. They come as a preframed package that is installed during the framing phase of the construction process. They are particularly advantageous in areas where a door that swings open would be in the way.
- **Bifold doors** are hinged with two sections. One section is anchored on the side, both top and bottom, so that the doors pivot and glide freely. They are kept in place by a small wheel fixed to the top of the unanchored section that guides the door along a metal track fixed to the top frame of the door. They stack against the **doorjamb** and project slightly into the room when open. They are also used in double configurations with four sections that stack on both sides of wider doors.
- **Accordion doors** are made with narrow panels of wood, metal, or plastic. They fold accordion-style on a track from which they are suspended, and they stack neatly in a small space.
- **Louvered doors** are wooden-framed with angled louvers or slats like shutters. Louvered doors allow circulation of air yet still provide visual privacy. They are commonly installed on closets or other spaces where air circulation is advisable. Louvered panels are used on pocket doors, bifold doors, and standard doors.

- **French doors** are double doors similar to paneled doors, but the wooden frames are filled with glass rather than wooden panels. One door is often kept

Figure 10.17 Beautiful French doors with a round fanlight together with pilasters create a striking frame for this garden view. *Textiles by and photo courtesy of Brunschwig & Fils/Peter Vitale, photographer*

Figure 10.18 French doors.

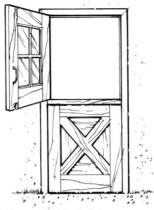

Figure 10.19 Dutch door.

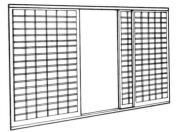

Figure 10.20 Shoji screens.

latched in place and the other is used for passage. New French-type doors with one permanently stationary door are called atrium or patio doors and frequently replace sliding glass doors.

- **Dutch doors** break horizontally in two sections so that each can open or shut separately or the two can be latched together into a single door. They may have windows in the top section. Dutch doors were originally designed to admit fresh air through the opening above and to keep out animals by closing the section below. In nonresidential settings, Dutch doors are used for service areas to keep out unauthorized traffic yet still allow communication or act as a service counter.
- **Shoji screens** are Japanese sliding panels made with wooden frames filled with oriental paper (or frosted glass or Plexiglas). A grid is placed on one or both sides to divide the screen into panes that resemble traditional windows. The grids can be simple rectangles or quite complex and ingenious in their design. They were used like sliding walls as dividers in the traditional Japanese house and are used today in some Western interiors for the same purpose or for a purely decorative effect.

Windows

Through windows we look out at the world and the world looks in at us. The placement of windows not only is important to the wall composition of the interior but largely determines the fenestration (architectural arrangement of windows)—a crucial part of the style and character of the exterior. Some major considerations in the selection and placement of windows follow:

- **Security.** Windows are the easiest point of unlawful entry; the greater the quantity and the more accessible and poorly lit the windows are on the exterior, the greater that risk.

- **Orientation and solar gain.** Where solar gain is desirable, windows should be most plentiful on the south of the building and least plentiful on the north. Limiting their number, strategically placing them, and protecting against bright sun on the east and the west orientations are imperative. Light is clearest and most steady from the north, most warm and constant on the south, clearest and brightest on the east, and most colored and hottest on the west.
- **Quantity of light desired.** Great quantities of light can be healthful to mind and body, yet when accompanied by heat and glare, light can be emotionally and physically unhealthy. Too much light and heat can also be damaging to interior furnishings.
- **The view.** Windows should be planned to frame any pleasant view. The view can serve to visually expand space and bring the exterior into the interior as an extension of the design.
- **Privacy.** The location, the height of the wall, and the number of windows can largely determine the amount of privacy afforded the occupant. Windows high in the wall give greater privacy, as do smaller windows.

There are few architectural details that can compare in elegance to beautifully designed windows. The exquisite Federal-style fanlight with its delicate **tracery** and the boldly handsome Palladian window (Figure 10.22) are treasured features of many older buildings. They represent the finest historic architectural development. Like doors, windows are trimmed in appropriately styled moldings to complete their finished appearance.

Windows have evolved from crude openings draped with animal skins to Medieval leaded panes to large Late Renaissance windows to the glass houses of the twentieth century. Not surprisingly, glass has been an important part of that evolution. Setting the glass in place is called **glazing** and can be done with one or more sheets of glass:

Figure 10.21 Double and single glazing.

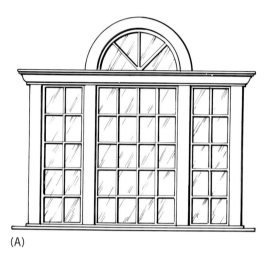

(A)

(B)

Figure 10.22 (A) Palladian window. (B) Federal-style elliptic fanlight.

Figure 10.23 Round porthole window.

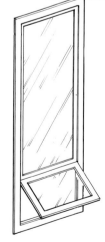

Figure 10.24 Awning window.

- A single layer of glass is called **single glazing.**
- **Double glazing,** or **thermal pane,** is two sheets of glass sandwiched in a frame to deter heat and/or cold transfer.
- Energy efficiency can be further enhanced with the addition of a third sheet of glass to produce **triple glazing.** This is often used for winter **storm windows.**

Windows that can be opened mechanically or by hand are termed **operable.** The obvious benefit to operable windows is their ability to admit fresh air. Certain types of operable windows also offer the advantage of being easy to clean because both inside and outside glass surfaces can be reached from the inside. **Fixed,** stationary, or inoperable windows are used where ventilation is undesirable because the HVAC system is sealed, where the window is out of reach, or where a view is to be framed without being interrupted by a divider bar.

Windows are made in a wide range of types. Each type is appropriate to a historic style or to a functional purpose. Following are common window types:

- Arched and round windows have been appreciated for centuries. The **Palladian window,** previously mentioned, is an arched window with two lower sidelights framed with classical columns, pilasters, and moldings. The **fanlight** is also an elliptic arch form of the Neoclassic era. Round **porthole** windows were especially popular during the Victorian era and may be seen in some vintage houses. Hexagonal windows are six-sided variations of the rounded window.
- **Awning windows** are hinged on the top to swing outward at an angle like an awning. They may be stacked or grouped in horizontal bands along a high wall, clerestory fashion, for privacy. They may also be used as the bottom component in a sashlike window or some other window arrangement. They have the advantage of being able to remain open in a rainstorm.
- **Bay** and **bow windows** are projecting windows. The bay is **canted** (angular) or projects straight out, and the bow has a curved projection. Bay and bow windows provide attractive interest to the exterior of a building. They add extra space to the interior, as well as admit light. They may, however, be costly to drape because they require custom drapery rods.
- **Casement windows** are side-hinged, swinging windows. They are an important historical style popular in many countries. Casement windows may be used as operable sections beside large, fixed picture windows. They have great appeal because they provide maximum ventilation, and if they swing out, they keep the interior free for draperies or other window treatments.
- The clerestory was the highest window in the Gothic church, and today **clerestory windows** are still those that are set high in the wall. These windows may be for light only or for light and ventilation. They may be

of almost any style; it is their location at the top of the wall that makes them clerestory. They provide light while ensuring privacy.

- **Cathedral windows** are angled, A-frame windows that follow the pitch of a vaulted ceiling. They embody a strong architectural quality that makes them particularly well suited to contemporary interiors. They work best in settings with pleasant views where no window coverings are necessary.

- The **greenhouse window** is a projecting glass box used to catch the sun's rays. Some may be just large enough to fill a kitchen window, and others may be room size. Like botanical greenhouses, they are ideal for plants; the room-size version can also be a favored spot for dining and relaxing. They can also be designed as sunrooms with hot tubs, spas, or comfortable areas for conversation and relaxation.

- The **jalousie window** is made with a set of louvered slats that tilt open and closed. The principal benefit of this window is the ability to provide ventilation while restricting entrance of rain. The name is French for "jealousy"; a wooden blind, slatted like the jalousie window, may have allowed jealous lovers to see in without being seen.

- The **sash window** is made with two window panels designed to slide up and down in a vertical channel of the window frame. The panels may be larger, single sheets of glass or may be divided into several smaller panes. The smaller-paned windows were designated historically by the number of "lights" (panes) in each panel; for example, twelve over twelve indicates twelve panes in the top frame and twelve in the bottom, and six over six indicates six above and six below. A **single-hung sash** window has an operable lower window that can be raised and lowered. In the **double-hung sash** window, both sashes are operable, allowing good air circulation. Cooler air enters through the lower opening, and warm air rises out through the top. The traditional sash window, divided into smaller panes, is a classic. Those that are well proportioned and well built add a clear note of distinction to traditionally styled buildings. Because they are so popular, manufacturers have been experimenting with new methods of fabrication. Some have designed wooden grids that fit over a single pane, giving the appearance of individual panes. The grid can easily be removed and then snapped back into the frame, making it easier to wash the windows. Others have placed metal grids between two panes of glass to create the impression of panes. The traditional framing method, with individually framed panes, is called a **true-divider** system.

- A **sidelight** is a narrow window next to a door. A pair of sidelights is used to flank a door. A **transom** is a window above a door. Arched transom windows are called

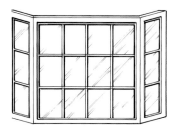

Figure 10.25 Bay window.

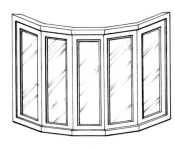

Figure 10.26 Bow window.

Figure 10.27 French casement window.

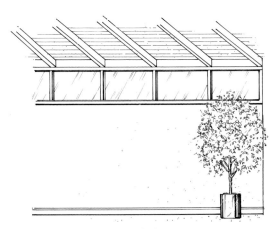

Figure 10.28 Clerestory window.

Figure 10.29 Cathedral window.

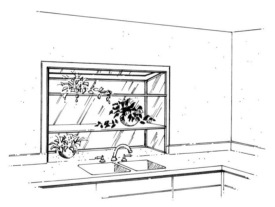

Figure 10.30 Greenhouse window.

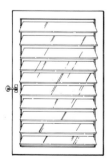

Figure 10.31 Jalousie window.

Figure 10.32 Sash window (nine over nine).

Figure 10.33 Sidelights and transom.

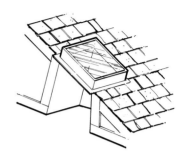

Figure 10.34 Skylight.

fanlights. In older buildings, operable transoms were often used between rooms to improve air circulation.

- **Skylights** are custom-installed or prefabricated units mounted in the roof and ceiling to bring natural light into interiors that have no direct access to windows and would otherwise be dark. Light pipes require only small roof openings, as they use mirror-like inserts to magnify the light they admit. Skylights are made of glass, plastic, or Plexiglas.
- **Attic windows** are operable pivoting windows placed in an angled roof in lieu of dormers. They are less expensive than framing a dormer and admit more light. They are utilized in new construction and remodeling projects where unused attic space is being transformed into living or working space.
- **Sliding windows** are technically the same as sash windows but are designed to slide horizontally. A sliding window may be a single operable panel of a larger window. Sliding windows may be framed in wood or vinyl-clad wood as well as aluminum.

Stairs

During the Middle Ages, stairs were tucked into tiny turrets (towers) or hidden between walls. In the Renaissance the stairway became more imposing, and by the eighteenth century it was often a dramatic focal point of the house. These same choices govern the design of stairs today. They may be functional and unobtrusive or a very dramatic part of the design. Stairs often have some romantic associations, such as sliding down banisters or hiding on stairways decked with pine boughs to sneak an early peek on Christmas morning. They may conjure up mental pictures of a grand entry on the night of a first date or of children watching and listening from an upstairs landing as guests arrive for a party. Stairways can be a beautiful and exciting part of an interior. Because the components from which they are assembled may be unfamiliar, they are listed, defined, and illustrated as follows:

Figure 10.35 Large-scale sash windows are a striking feature of this retrofitted loft space. © *Jessie Walker Associates*

Figure 10.36 Attic window.

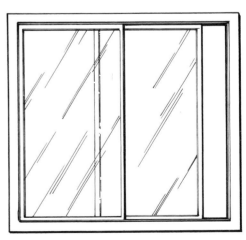

Figure 10.37 Sliding window.

- The **stringer** is the diagonal, notched structural piece that supports and gives form to the stair. On the completed stair, the structural stringers are not visible because they are usually covered by the treads and risers. On the finished stair, the diagonal molding on the wall next to the steps is also called a stringer.
- **Treads** are the flat, horizontal pieces on which the feet step when going up or down a stair.
- **Nosing** is the rounded edge of the tread. The nosing makes the stair less sharp and dangerous. It also prevents carpet on the stair from wearing against a sharp edge.
- The **riser** is the vertical member between the treads. It is the riser that acts as a toe kick on the staircase. In certain designs the riser is omitted, creating an **open-riser stair.** Some people feel nervous and insecure on open-riser stairs because the stairs may not appear solid.
- The **starting step** is the first step of the stair. It is often **bullnosed** (with a rounded curve) on the open end to support a newel post.
- **Landings** are the intermediate platforms on a stair (often where it turns) or the area at the bottom and top of the stair. These are important because they allow the stair to turn and because they make the stair safer. People who have difficulty climbing stairs are able to rest on the landing. The landing also provides exciting design possibilities—it makes a perfect place for a beautiful window.
- The **handrail** or banister is the piece that follows the pitch of the stair and is held by the hand. **Easements** are the short bends that allow for a change of direction in the handrail. A **volute** is the spiral or scroll end of the handrail that rests on the newel post. Handrails may be the traditional carved type, or they can be formed with metal pipes, tubes, flat pieces of wood or metal, or any device that is compatible with the design of the stair.
- The **baluster** is the vertical member that supports the handrail. In traditional stairways the balusters are usually turned wood. However, they can also be bent metal, square wooden pieces, or panels of glass.
- The **newel post** is a larger baluster that supports or receives the handrail at points of the stair, such as the starting step, the landing, and the top of the stair. The design of the newel post can be elaborate or simple. The balusters, handrail, and newel posts together make a **balustrade,** or railing.
- The **stairwell** is the open space in which the stair is set. Its shape and size will vary with the design of the stair.

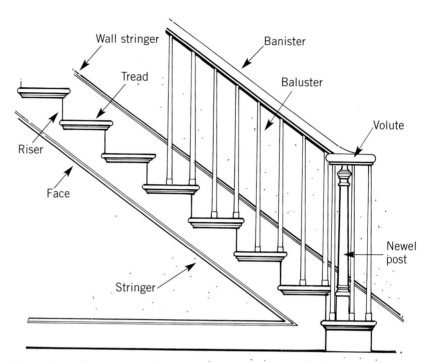

Figure 10.38 Stairway components.

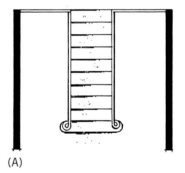

(A)

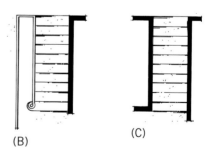

(B) (C)

Figure 10.39 Stair forms. (A) Open stair (no walls). (B) Semi-housed stair (wall on one side). (C) Closed stair (enclosed by walls).

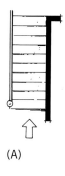
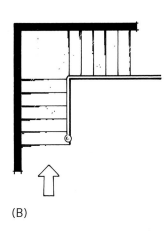

(A)

(B)

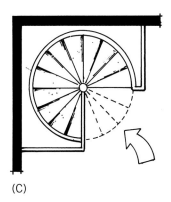
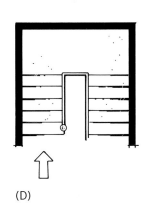

(C)

(D)

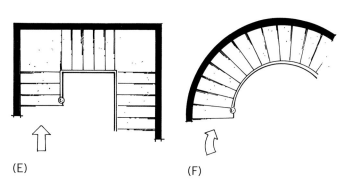

(E)

(F)

Figure 10.40 Stair forms. (A) Straight-run stair. (B) One-turn stair (with landing). (C) Spiral staircase. (D) U-stair (with one landing). (E) Double-turn stair (with two landings). (F) Semi-housed curved stair.

Stairs may take several different forms. The most common forms are listed here:

- A stair whose sides are not attached to any wall is termed an **open stair.**
- A **semihoused stair** is connected to the wall on one side and open on the other.
- A stairway with walls on both sides is called a **closed** or **housed stair.**
- A straight stairway without any turns is said to have a **straight run.**
- A stairway that turns 90 degrees at a landing is a **one-turn stair.**
- A **double-turn stair** makes two 90-degree turns at two separate landings.
- A **U-stair** turns 180 degrees at a single landing.
- A **spiral staircase** twists around a central axis like a corkscrew. This type of stair takes the least amount of space but is often difficult to negotiate and makes moving furniture difficult.
- A **curved staircase** may be open or semihoused and forms a graceful curve.

Figure 10.41 This graceful curve of this traditional staircase is an important feature of this home. © *Jessie Walker*

Fireplaces and Chimneypieces

The fireplace is another detail often associated with pleasant memories. The leap and flicker of constantly changing flames and the crackle of the burning wood create a mood of warmth and evoke memories of a chilly winter evening by a fire with family or friends.

For thousands of years, fire was the only source of heat in buildings. During the Middle Ages, when someone discovered that a hole in the wall with a hood could siphon the smoke from a fire, the design significance of the fireplace was instantly elevated. Before that, the fire had been built in a pit in the floor and the smoke escaped through cracks or vents in the roof. The hood provided new possibilities for design. Because it was a source of warmth, the fireplace was the logical focal point in the room, and designers lavished it with attention. Through the years, the basic technology of the fireplace has changed very little. It is the design of the decorative **chimneypiece** that has changed the most. Each new period saw changes in the style of the chimneypiece that gave the fireplace the proper character for its surroundings. The projecting shelf of a chimneypiece is called a **mantel.**

A fire requires fuel, heat, and oxygen. As it burns, the fire consumes oxygen, and this creates a draft as more air is drawn in to feed the fire that warms the air. The fireplace works on the principle that warm air rises, drawing the smoke off as it ascends and radiating some heat into the room. The rising air creates a suction that also pulls air from the room. As the intensity of the fire dies, it begins to suck precious warm air from the room. To keep the warm air in the house from escaping, it is necessary to close the front of the fireplace with glass or metal doors.

The fireplace is made of several components:

- The **hearth** is the noncombustible slab that forms the base for the fire and projects into the room to prevent embers or sparks from charring the floor.

Figure 10.42 The fireplace is the focal point of this comfortable room. *Green Company, architect/photo © Brian Vanden Brink*

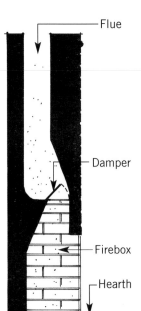

Figure 10.43 Fireplace components.

- The **firebox** contains the fire and is built of masonry or metal on top of the hearth.
- The **surround** is the noncombustible piece that frames the opening of the firebox. It is frequently made of tile, marble, or other stone.
- The **flue** is the chimney pipe that is separated from the firebox by a movable **damper** that controls the flow of air and escape of smoke.
- **Zero-clearance fireplace units** are self-contained units with triple-insulated walls that allow placement in walls without firebrick or masonry.

Fireplaces can be built in any form—imagination and function are the only real restrictions. However, the most common types are flush-face, projecting, hooded, corner, raised, freestanding, and stoves:

- The **breast** (face) of the **flush-face fireplace** is even, or flush, with the plane of the surrounding wall. Because

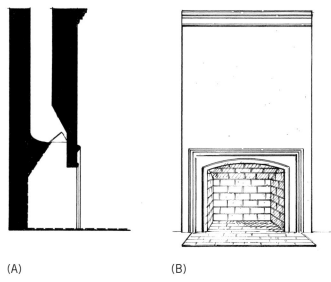

(A)   (B)

Figure 10.44 Flush-face fireplace. (A) Side cutaway section view. (B) Front view elevation.

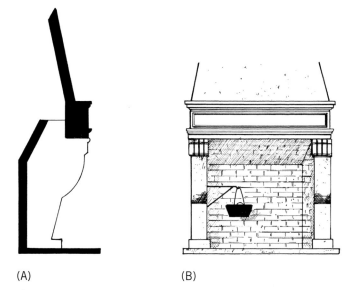

(A)   (B)

Figure 10.46 Hooded fireplace. (A) Side cutaway section view. (B) Front view elevation.

the flush-face tends to be less decorative, it is well suited to contemporary interiors where it often consists of a surround and a simple molding. Several historically styled fireplaces are also flush-faced with or without a mantel.

• The breast of a **projecting fireplace** projects into the room, forming a mantel. This type is adaptable to clean contemporary versions as well as more decorative historical types.

• A **hooded fireplace** incorporates a projecting hood that may be formed in nearly any shape, from rounded to an-

gled to boxlike. This was the first type of fireplace to be built during the late Middle Ages and early Renaissance.

• The **corner fireplace** is located in the corner of a room; it may have a hood or may be built like a standard fireplace. Because they cut off the corner of a room, corner fireplaces often have inherent problems of balance and line and may present challenges in furniture placement.

• Many fireplaces are designed with a **raised hearth** built just in front of the firebox or extending the entire length of the wall. With a raised hearth, the firebox is elevated so that it can be seen more easily through the

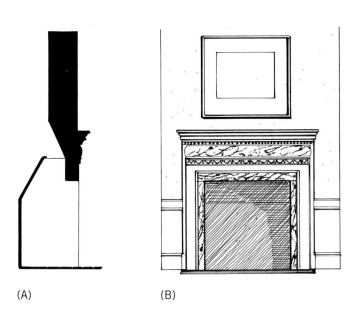

(A)   (B)

Figure 10.45 Projecting fireplace. (A) Side cutaway section view. (B) Front view elevation.

Figure 10.47 Corner fireplace in a Southwest adobe home.

furniture grouping that often surrounds a fireplace. The raised hearth requires less stooping and has the added advantage of making the fireplace easier to fuel and clean. This type of hearth also provides a nice place to sit next to the fire.

- A **freestanding fireplace** is a metal unit or other fireplace that is placed in the room away from the wall, with the flue or chimney pipe exposed. The fireplace unit may be placed on a raised platform or may rest at floor level.
- Until the advent of central heating, the pot-bellied stove was a standard fixture in homes, churches, schools, and stores. Today, in areas with cold winters, **stoves** are still used in some homes. Stoves are generally freestanding units placed in front of a noncombustible wall with clearance between the wall and the stove. Fireplaces can also be fitted with enclosed stove units called **fireplace**

inserts for more efficient use of fuel and little loss of warmed house air. Some stoves and fireplace inserts are designed with forced-air systems that can heat most of a medium-sized house. These draw air from outside; the air is warmed by the stove and then forced by a fan into the house, creating positive pressure. When a vent or window at the opposite end of the house is opened slightly, the warm air will be drawn to that part of the house. A fresh-air intake pipe to the stove will eliminate drafts caused by combustion.

Ceilings

Ceilings are literally the crowning glory of a room. For example, the great hammer-beam ceilings of Early Renais-

Figure 10.48 A vaulted ceiling adds height and grace to this contemporary interior. © *John Linden/Esto*

sance England—with their Tudor arch-shaped trusses supported on magnificently carved brackets—are awe-inspiring. And the delicate-patterned plaster ceilings, designed by Robert Adam in eighteenth-century England, are still beautiful examples of the importance a ceiling design can have in a room. Today, there is a vast selection of ceiling materials and types from which to choose. Ceilings may be decorative or structural and may even serve the important function of covering, yet providing access to, mechanical systems located in the ceiling. Ceilings can provide dramatic changes in plane or space. A low, cozy fireplace nook can suddenly open to the main body of the room that soars to the rafters. Angled ceilings are interesting because of the variety of line and form they create. Ceilings can be formed in many ways. The most common types of ceilings are plain flat, vaulted, domed, coffered, coved, baffled, and suspended:

- The simplest type of ceiling is flat plaster or sheetrock. This plain treatment is ideal when the intent of the design is to emphasize other areas of the room. The flat ceiling may be embellished with textured plaster, raised patterns, moldings, or medallions, which may be painted to harmonize or contrast with the ceiling. These embellishments are called **anaglypta,** which is the Greek

Figure 10.49 A structural beamed ceiling adds visual strength and interest to this space. *Mark Hutker & Associates Architects/photo © Brian Vanden Brink*

word for "raised ornament." Today, anaglypta patterns are frequently made of hardened plastic foam.

- A **vault** is a ceiling constructed on the principle of an arch. Therefore, a vaulted ceiling may be round (a barrel vault) or pointed like the Gothic church ceiling. In today's interiors, the tall, open, cathedral ceiling belongs to this group. Rooms with barrel-vaulted ceilings often have rounded ends with half-domed ceilings called **niches.**
- **Cathedral ceilings** are pointed with two slopes. Those with one slope are **shed** ceilings. These can be exciting because of the way they open up the space, making a relatively small room feel much larger than it actually is. Cathedral and shed ceilings can also add grandeur

to large spaces such as hotel lobbies, office atriums, and churches.

- **Domes** are bowl-shaped, rounded ceilings. When the dome covers a drum-shaped (round) room, the space is called a **rotunda.** Domes may be quite flat and dish shaped or deep and high. Because its form is the shape of the heavens, the dome draws the eye upward and creates a feeling of expanse. In public spaces such as capitol buildings, domes create spaces of great dignity and grandeur. In a residence, a shallow recessed dome in an entry or dining room expands the visual space.
- **Beamed ceilings** frankly expose the rafters or trusses as a decorative feature of a room. They can be very simple and rough or richly carved or painted. Beams

Figure 10.50
Anaglypta.

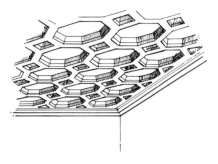

Figure 10.51 Traditional coffered ceiling.

Mass-produced cabinetwork is installed wherever standard sizes will fit the space and where a tight budget demands economy. Prefabricated units may be purchased at home improvement stores and builder supply houses.

Custom pieces are planned by the designer and executed by the cabinetmaker or finish carpenter; for example, custom cabinetwork is seen in living/dining rooms, kitchens, bathrooms, laundry rooms, and sewing areas of luxury homes. One area of the home where custom cabinetwork is particularly impressive is the home office, study, den, or library. Custom details make such interiors more individual, distinctive, and functional.

Nonresidential Considerations

Many of the details used in residential design are the same as those in nonresidential design. However, the following details are more common to nonresidential design:

can impart a provincial or rustic feeling to an environment. The buildings of the Southwest incorporate large pine beams called **vigas** as structural support for the smaller cross beams, called **latillas,** which form the ceiling. Logs add a rugged feeling to cabins and ski lodges in any geographic setting. Squared, finely finished hardwood beams trimmed with molding are favored in rich traditional interiors such as law offices, libraries, and luxury housing. Since buildings are generally no longer made of timbers, these will usually be false beams used just for effect. Metal trusses are left exposed in some of today's designs because, like their wooden counterparts from earlier times, they have interest and strength as design forms.

- **Coffers** are boxes constructed in the recesses between beams and cross beams.
- **Coved ceilings** are formed with a curved radius or straight angle where the wall meets the ceiling. This is accomplished by actually structuring the ceiling in that fashion or by the application of cove moldings. The absence of a sharp right angle has a softening effect on the room.

Cabinetwork

Cabinetwork, or **cabinetry,** is finished interior woodwork such as shelves and cabinets. Those who custom-build freestanding and built-in units are called **finish carpenters.** Cabinetwork is manufactured in two basic ways. Cabinets can be mass produced on an assembly line in standard sizes or crafted to custom specifications in large or small woodworking shops by skilled finish carpenters. These units are brought to the site as components and installed, fitted, and trimmed with molding.

Figure 10.52 Fine custom cabinets provide attractive storage in this kitchen. *G.M. Wild Construction, builder/photo © Todd Caverly*

- Today, coffered ceilings are formed when concrete is poured over inverted "pans" or forms in such a way that when the concrete has set and the pans have been removed from below, a wafflelike pattern of coffers is produced.
- A **baffled ceiling** is hung with wooden or metal slats or fabric banners. These are installed in parallel or grid patterns that act as a screen for the lighting system and also serve as an acoustic treatment. The fabric banners provide an excellent opportunity to add color and texture. The wooden and metal slats also create patterns that add an interesting quality to the environment.
- **Suspended ceilings** are metal grid systems hung from the superstructure of the building with wires. The **plenum,** or space between the grid and the building structure above, contains ducts for the HVAC (heating,

ventilation, and air-conditioning) system, as well as plumbing and electrical systems (see Chapter 7, "Floor Plans and Building Systems"). The grids are filled with acoustic panels that can be removed and replaced, allowing easy access to the equipment above the ceiling. Lighting systems, sound systems, sprinkler systems, smoke detectors, and vents for the HVAC system are often integrated with the suspended ceiling.

- Custom cabinetwork is extremely common in nonresidential design. For example, the reception desk in a hotel must be designed to fit the physical and aesthetic requirements of the project. The same is true of a nurses' station in a hospital or the cashier/host station in a restaurant. All of these kinds of pieces are custom designed and built.

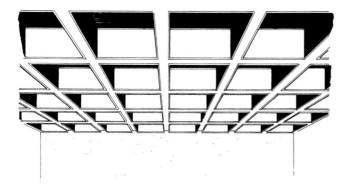

Figure 10.53 Contemporary coffered ceiling.

Figure 10.54 Baffled ceiling.

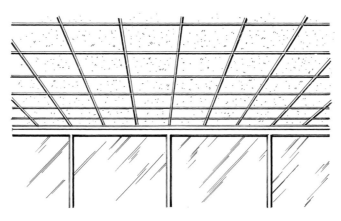

Figure 10.55 Suspended ceiling.

Chapter 11 | Wall, Ceiling, and Window Treatments

Wall and Ceiling
Materials 272

Paint 282

Wall Coverings 286

Ceiling Treatments 290

Window Treatments 290

Nonresidential
Considerations 304

Christina Oliver Interior Design/photo © Brian Vanden Brink

Wall and Ceiling Materials

Materials for walls and ceilings come from a variety of sources, both natural and fabricated. Some materials used on walls and ceilings can also be used on floors; others are appropriate only for walls or ceilings. Wall and ceiling materials are hard or rigid, flexible or soft, and their weight varies from heavy to light. Table 11.1 provides an overview of the selection of materials typically used.

Selection Guidelines

- Generally, hard materials echo and reflect or amplify sound; flexible and soft materials absorb sound.
- Permanently installed materials initially cost more but may be the least costly in the long run, as they require little finishing, upkeep, or replacement. These include stone, wood, tile, and brick. The time frame of occupancy must also be a factor in selecting permanent materials. A long occupation can justify the costs, whereas frequent moves will not.
- Interiors need to be flexible for change. Shifts in the lifestyles of occupants will benefit from flexible materials that can be replaced, such as paint, wall coverings, or fabric.
- Pattern on the walls will lock in a style or color scheme and can be restrictive.
- Upkeep is a major consideration where there is limited time or budget for cleaning or where traffic or youngsters would tend to soil, mark, or damage the wall surfaces.
- Authenticity and style are factors in selecting wall materials. The reproduction of a period room or the general look or feeling or level of formality will largely

Table 11.1 | Wall and Ceiling Materials—an Overview

Brick. Heavy, hard, costly material, expensive to install. Lasts indefinitely and is structurally handsome. No upkeep.

Concrete. Heavy, hard **building blocks** or **cast slabs.** Can be painted or left natural gray or colored before casting. Cold to the eye and touch. Moderate cost of material; can be costly to install. No upkeep unless painted.

Cork. Very lightweight, flexible, sound absorbent; costly material but moderate installation. Handsome and subtle appearance. Easy upkeep.

Fabric. Flexible, sound absorbent, three-dimensional; can carry out a fabric scheme by coordinating with other furnishing fabrics. Several methods and styles of applications. Can be changed at will. Cost of fabric varies from low to high; installation is moderate. Easy upkeep.

Glass. Architectural glass (windows), **glass block, stained glass** used as transparent or translucent building materials. Can be very structural and moderately to very decorative. Costs vary from moderate to expensive. Upkeep varies according to use and environment. **Glass tile** requires little upkeep, but cost is high as an imported item. Fiberglass is used in tub surrounds. Upkeep requires nonabrasive cleaners. **Mirrors** enhance space visually.

Metal. Aluminum, brass, bronze, copper, stainless steel, and **tin** are costly to purchase and install. Effects are rich whether structural or decorative. Permanent material. Upkeep depends on finishes and location or use; most require little or no upkeep.

Paint. The least expensive of the wall treatments, but must be applied over a prepared, rigid surface such as Sheetrock or wood. Color range and effects are unlimited, and paint can be reapplied at will. Paint can imitate many materials, such as marble and wood. Professional painting services are costly. Upkeep depends on the use, environment, and type of paint used.

Plaster. Versatile, from very smooth to very rough **(stucco).** Can be cast into decorative anaglypta moldings and ornaments to document a particular period. Cost is moderate; upkeep depends on the type of paint or finish the plaster is given.

Stone. Fieldstone, flagstone, granite, limestone, marble, and **travertine** are all heavy, costly materials that are also expensive to install. Structural or decorative effects, but all with natural beauty and little or no upkeep. Lasts indefinitely.

Cultured stone (imitation onyx and marble) is used for tub and shower surrounds and countertops or cabinet tops. Lightweight; moderate cost; requires nonabrasive cleansers.

Tile. Acoustical tile absorbs sound. Set into a ceiling grid framework; lightweight; decorative or structural; moderate cost, no upkeep—tiles that become stained are replaced or painted.

Ceramic, quarry, Mexican, and **mosaic tile** installations are heavy and costly in terms of material and labor to install. Permanent material, they require little or no upkeep. Tile is also popular in kitchens and bath or hot tub areas as a countertop or cabinet-top material.

Wallboard. Sheetrock, wood paneling, particleboard—all come in sheet form to cover large areas. **Sheetrock (plasterboard, drywall)** is the most common wall and ceiling material and requires painting or wall coverings. Moderate material and installation cost. Upkeep depends on finish methods and materials.

Wall coverings. A variety of paper, vinyl, or cloth products that come in rolls or bolts. Subtle and structural to very decorative patterned effects. Moderate cost of goods, moderate installation costs. Upkeep depends on final layer (fabric, paper, vinyl) and placement and use. In most cases, upkeep is minimal.

Wood and **wood moldings, planks, paneling.** Wood is costly to purchase but modest to install. Wood has lasting beauty. It can be stained, sealed, or painted. Little or no upkeep.

dictate the actual surface and visual texture as well as the pattern.

- The size of the space can be a determining factor. Heavy textures, large patterns, and dark or intense colors close in spaces, making them appear smaller, whereas smooth or subtle textures, small patterns, and light or dull colors visually expand spaces.
- The function of the interior should determine wall material durability. Heavily used areas need impervious materials; little-used areas can accommodate more fragile treatments. High levels of humidity, smoke, fumes, or airborne oils or dirt may dictate nonabsorbent materials.

Hard or Rigid Wall Materials

Most hard or rigid materials are permanent installations with common characteristics:

- Are costly to purchase and to install
- Require little or no upkeep, depending on the finish or character of the surface
- Have inherently handsome natural texture or pattern
- Have withstood the test of time and are considered classic wall and ceiling treatments

Tables 11.2 through 11.6 describe various types of wall and ceiling materials and provide details of applications, maintenance, special considerations, and cost structure.

Figure 11.1 Slate is cut into rectangles that are installed like tiles in this refurbished bathroom. *I.O.I., Inc. Interior Design/photo* © *Brian Vanden Brink*

Table 11.2 | Stone

Stone

Description. Natural stone includes flagstone, granite, limestone, marble, and terrazzo, all described in this table. In addition, other general types fit the definition of stone:

Ashlar refers to a stone that is cut into rectangular shapes so that it can be fitted together into a geometric pattern with grout.

Cobblestone (or river cobbles) are large, rounded, somewhat smooth rocks used to face walls and fireplaces in rustic settings.

Fieldstone is a rugged type of large rocks that may or may not be rounded and smooth. When laid, fieldstone has a random pattern.

Sandstone is a soft, reddish stone that is a type of fieldstone and may be cut into ashlar shape.

Rubble means rough uncut stone or stone that is not uniform.

Artificial stone is made to imitate rubble or ashlar.

Granite

Description. A very hard crystalline rock with small amounts of feldspar, quartz, and other minerals in crystal or grain form. The size of the crystals varies from very fine to fairly coarse. The colors vary from light to dark values and variations of gray, pink, green, brown, and black and may be combinations such as greenish or pinkish gray. May be highly polished or rough cut.

Applications. Walls, countertops, fireplace surrounds. Used in both residential and nonresidential settings.

Maintenance. Low upkeep; wipe with a damp cloth.

Special considerations. Exact color match will need to be carefully coordinated between the designer and the quarry or supplier.

Cost structure. High.

Limestone

Description. A calcite (calcium carbonate) stone with a light-grayish neutralized color. Has little to no pattern and subtle texture, with a typically matte or dull finish. Formed from the calcium carbonate that crystallizes out of a freshwater or saltwater solution and settles via evaporation, leaving a limestone "mud"; also formed from shells and bones of sea animals, which are broken up by waves into mud.

Application. An excellent building stone, as it can be easily carved or cut in any direction without splitting. Because of this, limestone and sandstone are often called **freestone.** An unpolished, largely ungrained wall material in the form of slabs and tiles. Also used for fireplace surrounds and shaped mantelpieces.

Maintenance. Dust or wipe with clear lukewarm water or mild, nonoily detergent if stone is sealed.

Cost structure. High.

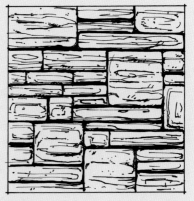

Ashlar

River cobbles

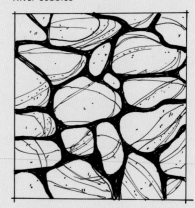

Fieldstone, sandstone, or rubble

Granite

Stone (continued)

Marble

Description. A metamorphic limestone, granular or crystalline, white or colored, often with streaks. The hardest and typically the most expensive of the stones. May be cut into thin sheets or slabs. Can be polished to a high sheen. Cold to the touch.

    Terrazzo is a composite flooring of broken chips of marble set into cement and polished to a sheen. This is a practical use of marble, since up to 50 percent waste occurs from breakage at the quarry.

Applications. Walls, fireplace surrounds, tiles for special or custom installations. Exclusive look for both residential and nonresidential installations.

Maintenance. Clean with warm water and infrequently with soap and water.

Special considerations. The most formal of the stones; rich-looking finish material.

Cost structure. Very high.

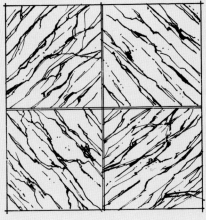

Marble

Travertine

Description. A light-colored limestone rock formed near mineral springs. Trapped gas in the stone causes holes and interesting textures that can be filled according to the intended use.

Applications. Walls, fireplace surrounds and hearths, bathrooms. Used frequently in nonresidential settings and as accents and for custom installations in residential interiors.

Maintenance. Wash when necessary with clear lukewarm water. Wash no more often than every six months with soap and water and rinse thoroughly. On vertical surfaces it needs little if any cleaning.

Special considerations. Travertine is slightly less formal than marble and widely used.

Cost structure. High.

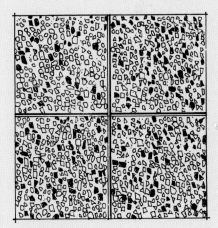

Marble terrazzo

Figure 11.2 Rough slate walls contrast with smooth marble slabs and mirrors in this modern master bathroom. © *Tim Street-Porter/Beateworks.com*

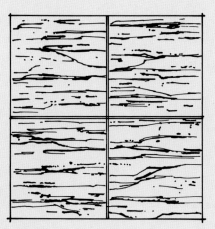

Travertine

Table 11.3 | Brick, Concrete, Tile

Brick

Description. Clay, shale, and water mixed and shaped into solid or hollow rectangular blocks, etc., then baked or fired to harden. Brick is colored according to the clay used (red is most typical) or the dyes added before firing. Brick used for constructing walls is typically 7 to 8 inches long by 3 to 4 inches wide and 2 to 3 inches thick.

Applications. Interior and exterior walls and fireplace surrounds, vaulted or arched ceilings, residential and nonresidential.

Maintenance. Low upkeep—dust or use a mild soap and water solution. Often no upkeep is required.

Special considerations. Can be treated with a sealant such as polyurethane that will prevent the brick from absorbing oil-based spills.

Cost structure. Moderate to high.

Brick

Concrete Block and Slab

Description. Large porous bricks made of concrete with air pockets that make the material lightweight enough to handle but also somewhat fragile during handling. Poured slabs of concrete form walls and can be relatively smooth or very rusticated or brutalistic.

Applications. Walls, some nonresidential ceilings.

Maintenance. Little or no maintenance. Concrete block surfaces are usually painted and then treated as any porous painted surface. Concrete slabs are rarely painted but are used as a frank and structural building material.

Special considerations. May be used for an exterior building material; then it must be sealed against water permeation.

Cost structure. Low to moderate, although installation or labor to install is high.

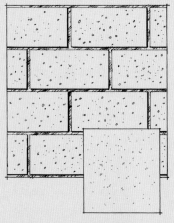

Concrete block / Concrete slab

Ceramic Tile

Description. Fine, white clays formed into tile shape (bisque), glazed, and fired at very high temperatures. Finishes vary from shiny and smooth to painted/decal-patterned to rough. **Mosaic tiles** are very small tiles used to create permanent patterns and pictures on walls. Today mosaic tile comes in preset sheets, a face mount or back mount, ready to be set with grout.

Applications. Walls, counters, backsplash areas, ceilings. Used extensively in nonresidential settings because of its durability. Often used in entries, bathrooms, kitchens, and solariums or in any room in warm climates.

Maintenance. Low upkeep. Dust or wipe with clear water, vinegar water, or soap and water for heavy dirt. Grout may soil and discolor. Silicone treatments will make grout less susceptible to soil. Newer developments in grout are more resistant to stains.

Special considerations. Durable surface that maintains good looks indefinitely. Ceramic tile can break, is cold, and is very hard.

Cost structure. Low to high—costs vary considerably in ceramic tiles. Imported tiles from France and Italy can be expensive. Labor to install is also high. However, because it is permanent, the life-cycle cost is low.

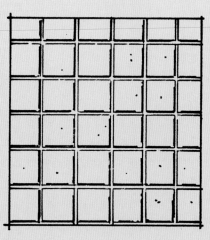

Ceramic tile

Brick, Concrete, Tile (continued)

Figure 11.3 Ceramic tile walls and granite countertops are a practical and attractive choice for kitchens. *Alan Freysinger Architect/Christina Oliver Interior Design/photo © Brian Vanden Brink*

Quarry Tile

Description. Made of fine clay and graded shale, with color distributed through the body of the tile. Most is a **terra-cotta** rust/red, the color of the natural clay. May be glazed but usually left natural. Typical square or hexagonal shapes are most popular.

Applications. Walls, counters, backsplashes, ceilings, residential and nonresidential applications, similar to ceramic tile.

Maintenance. Same as for ceramic tile.

Special considerations. Natural terra-cotta color gives quarry tile a timeless appeal.

Cost structure. Tile cost is low to moderate, although installation is costly.

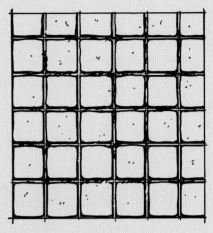

Quarry tile

Mexican Tile

Description. Hand-shaped clay taken from the ground and left to set before firing, reflecting imperfections of hand labor that add to its charm.

Applications. Large squares are not often used on walls; smaller, glazed tiles are used for decorative effects on walls, countertops, backsplashes, stair risers, and doorway surround trim.

Maintenance. Glazed tiles clean the same as ceramic or quarry tiles.

Special considerations. Mexican tile is durable, but if not sealed it is susceptible to oily stains. The softest of all the tiles, it can be chipped or broken more easily than quarry or ceramic tile.

Cost structure. Tiles are low to moderate cost; installation is costly.

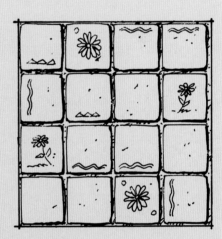

Mexican tile

Acoustical Tile

Description. Acoustical ceiling tiles or panels are made from mineral fiberboard or from fabric or plastic-clad fiber, fiberglass, and even metal.

Applications. Ceilings in primarily nonresidential settings; occasionally for walls.

Maintenance. Maintenance is low. Ceiling installations may show soil around air distribution openings. Follow manufacturer's directions for cleaning. Tiles that become stained are usually replaced or painted.

Special considerations. Acoustical tiles may not be tiles at all but strips of insulative materials. Square, rectangular, and strip materials are usually mounted on a track or grid system, making it relatively easy to install, replace, or access the plenum area above, which houses lighting, HVAC, and other systems.

Cost structure. Moderate.

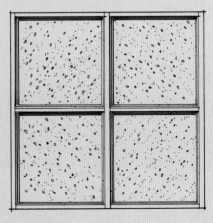

Acoustical tile

Table 11.4 | Glass, Mirror, Metal

Architectural Glazing

Description. Transparent or translucent brittle material of molten sand, potash, lime, and perhaps metal oxides for color or for reflecting and screening properties.

Applications. Window glazing, curtain wall construction (glass walls over a steel skeleton frame), both residential and nonresidential; interior office walls and dividers; and one-way-visibility windows and dividers.

Maintenance. Transparent glass will show dirt easily and needs occasional maintenance with a glass-cleaning solution. Professional window washers are usually employed for nonresidential installations.

Special considerations. Glass for angled (skylight, greenhouse) installations must be tempered for strength (known as tempered or safety glass). Low-E (low-emission) glass screens out the harmful ultraviolet rays.

Cost structure. Moderate to moderately high.

Architectural glass (glazing)

Glass Block

Description. Transparent or translucent glass pressed and formed as two halves and fused together. The semihollow blocks offer light diffusion and transmission and good insulation. Designs may be imprinted on one or both sides.

Applications. Residential and nonresidential applications where light diffusion is needed with some privacy. May also be used in wall and ceiling installations with artificial light behind the blocks. Glass blocks are not for use in load-bearing situations.

Maintenance. Little upkeep. If the blocks become dirty or greasy, soap and water will clean them. Polishing is not necessary.

Special considerations. Variations of glass block include a fibrous glass insert that controls glare, brightness, and excessive heat gain. Solid glass blocks are available for wall installations for greater protection against breakage and forced entry.

Cost structure. Moderately high.

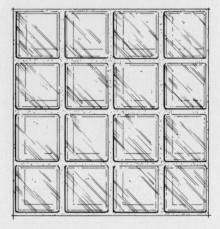

Glass block

Fiberglass

Description. Glass fibers spun or pressed into a lightweight, insulative mass; translucent or opaque.

Applications. Wall panels and dividers, bathtub and shower surrounds and units. Fibrous fiberglass "wool" is an insulative material used in wall and ceiling structures. Fiberglass panels are also used for corrugated ceiling panels and patio covers. Both residential and nonresidential applications.

Maintenance. Fiberglass panels and pressed forms are easily scratched and need to be cleaned with a nonabrasive cleanser.

Special considerations. Used where little hard use is anticipated, since it loses its shiny finish with abrasion or hard-water deposits.

Cost structure. Moderate.

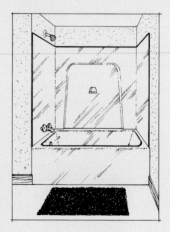

Fiberglass

Glass, Mirror, Metal (continued)

Mirror

Description. Flawless float glass backed with a coating of silver or silver alloy. May be bronzed, grayed, antiqued (smokey), veined with gold color, or etched with a design.

Applications. Walls and ceilings, residential and nonresidential.

Maintenance. Clean with glass cleaner; polish with soft cloths or paper products.

Special considerations. Mirrors will visually expand the space and may be set in place as flat, flawless panels or shaped into patterns such as tile. Mirrors may be used on folding screens or sliding closet doors.

Cost structure. Moderately high.

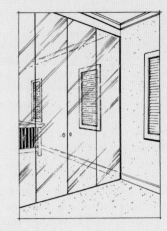

Mirror

Metal—Aluminum, Brass, Bronze, Copper, Stainless Steel, Tin

Description. An extremely durable material that can be used in several forms. Sheets of aluminum, brass, bronze, copper, and stainless steel may be cut and fitted in place; strips of metal may be installed on clips. Metal panels are available, solid or perforated. Tin panels, with stamped patterns, document Victorian designs.

Applications. Walls, ceilings, and custom installations such as wrapped columns. Custom residences and nonresidential installations.

Maintenance. Little upkeep. If surfaces should become spotted from handling, use a metal polish preparation. Painted metals can be washed with soap and water. Follow manufacturer's instructions for cleaning. Most metals are treated to be impervious to oil, dirt, and corrosion.

Special considerations. Metals are available in shiny or brushed surfaces. Some metal ceiling systems are designed to be installed over existing ceilings in renovation or remodeling work, making it possible to maintain existing heat and air-conditioning ducts and wiring. Finishes (see Chapter 9) include anodized satin, polished, and brushed.

Cost structure. Moderately high to high.

Metal

Table 11.5 | Wallboard, Plaster

Wallboard

Description. A general category of drywall goods including **Sheetrock** or **drywall** (gypsum board—made of crushed and processed gypsum rock). Available in sheets 4 feet by 8 feet or 4 feet by 12 feet and hung with nails or screws to wooden or metal studs. Seams are sealed with perfatape (paper) and covered with plaster mud, smoothed out to be inconspicuous. The wallboard may be left smooth or be textured. Smooth wallboard is best for wallpaper installations.

Applications. The most common of the wall finish materials for both residential and nonresidential settings. It is a basic material that may be finished as described or overlayed with wall coverings or fabric.

Maintenance. Upkeep will depend on the texture and finish given the wallboard. Paints vary in their ability to withstand repeated cleanings, as do wall coverings and fabric.

Special considerations. Economical wall-covering material. It is also fragile. It will dent and scratch and can be punctured when doorknobs or other hard objects are thrust against it.

Cost structure. Moderate.

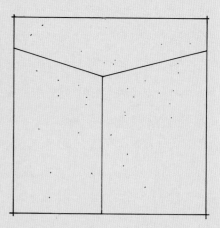

Wallboard—Sheetrock or gypsum board

Plaster

Description. A paste mixture of lime, sand, and water that hardens as it dries. May be applied as a finish material to be smooth, textured, or rough. **Stucco** may be a smooth or rough consistency, depending on the fineness of the sand used. Plaster may also be cast into decorative ornaments or cornices, generally called **anaglypta** or **anaglyphs,** that can imitate handcarved wood and be nailed or glued in place and painted.

Applications. Walls, exterior and interior, ceilings; anaglypta ornament, moldings. Authentic smooth plaster walls are coated over **lath** (thin strips of wood nailed to the wall studs horizontally, about three-eighths of an inch apart) or over wire mesh. Today, plaster is more often applied over plasterboard or Sheetrock (see wallboard) or concrete block.

Plaster is applied as "mud" to seal the **perfatape** to conceal wallboard seams or applied as rough-textured stucco. It is also sprayed on or hand-applied in a **texturizing** process and then sanded into the desired texture. A light application of blown plaster is usually called orange peel. Plain plaster applications are more common in nonresidential settings.

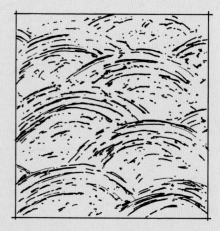

Plaster or stucco

Maintenance. Upkeep of plaster depends on the use or abuse, as it can chip, crack, and peel. It scratches and mars easily, and smooth plaster is difficult to touch up with paint. Washability depends on the type of paint used.

Special considerations. Smooth plaster applied over Sheetrock is more costly than sprayed or textured walls. New lath-and-plaster walls are nearly nonexistent because of the labor involved.

Cost structure. Moderate.

Figure 11.4 Rough wall textures can be enhanced or created visually by special painting techniques. © Tim Street-Porter/Beateworks.com

Table 11.6 | Wood, Cork

Wood: Millwork Traditional Paneling

Description. Stock and custom-milled wood applied to walls and as cabinetry in the form of flat and raised panels, shelving, and moldings. The wood may be hardwood or softwood, plywood or solid wood.

Applications. Walls in residential and now, to a substantial extent, in nonresidential work.

Maintenance. Depends on the finish it is given. Oiled or waxed wood may need protection against moisture and will show fingerprints. Millwork is usually sealed with lacquer, acrylic, or urethane, which then is easy to clean with a mild detergent solution.

Special considerations. Installation is considered to be part of the architectural detail and hence a permanent part of the building that is rarely removed unless remodeling takes place. It gives visual richness to the interior, particularly when stained rather than painted.

Cost structure. Moderate to high, depending on whether the millwork is paint grade (less costly) or stained wood (very costly).

Traditional paneling

Wood Paneling

Description. Solid wood paneling comes in thin 4- by 8-foot sheets of hardwoods. More typical, however, is high-quality veneer plywood with a thin layer of hardwood (veneer) laminated to the surface. **Hardboard** (Masonite) is made of wood fibers compressed under heat or pressure. These may have a veneer or a photo reproduction of wood applied to the surface and grooved to represent a plank wall material. They may also be formed with a surface texture to imitate carved wood panels. **Tongue-and-groove strips** (milled to interlock) are also used for walls as a paneling. **Board-and-batten** walls are long strips of wood with narrow strips or lath nailed or screwed over the seams. **Beadboard** has grooves to imitate board and batten.

Applications. Walls and ceilings. The quality of the wood will determine the type of residential or nonresidential application.

Maintenance. This depends on the surface of the product. Paneling may be oiled, waxed, urethaned, or treated with acrylic or other products, or it may have a plastic finish, which varies from a very thin coat to a durable, permanent finish capable of withstanding the wear of any contract installation. Wall-cleaning products are available for wood only, or follow the manufacturer's instructions. Durable finishes may be washed with soap and water.

Special considerations. Wood paneling ranges from a do-it-yourself-project look to a very exquisite and costly appearance.

Cost structure. Moderately low to moderately high. Solid wood will be most costly.

Board and batten or Beadboard

Cork

Description. The thick outer layer of the cork oak tree, a broad-leaf evergreen that grows in the Mediterranean region. It is light in color, elastic, and insulative. It is resilient and may be treated with a vinyl coating, making it more durable. It is sound absorbent.

Applications. Residential and nonresidential settings where a quiet, resilient surface is required.

Maintenance. Dust or wipe with a damp cloth.

Special considerations. Due to its insulative properties, cork should not be used where solar gain is desired. It will absorb bumps well but can be broken off and is very difficult or impossible to repair. In very thin sheets it may be laminated to paper for wall coverings.

Cost structure. Moderate to high.

Cork

Figure 11.5 Painted "trompe l'oeil" scenes transform the walls of this California laundry room into an ocean view. *Courtesy of Amy Weiss Design*

Paint

Paint is used on walls and ceilings more than any other finish material. The reasons are diverse and all valid:

- Paint is a versatile, inexpensive wall finish and is relatively easy to apply.
- Paint offers color and texture variety and ensures protection to the surface.
- Painted walls can reinforce interior architecture through neutral, noncompetitive colors.
- Paint has contrast and graphic ability, providing visual excitement or drama.
- Paint can add richness and subtlety through low-contrast, deep, or soft colors.

- Bright-colored paint can accent or draw attention to surfaces and details.
- Dark-colored paint reflects little light, thus making the surface seem to advance, and light-colored paints can visually expand spaces.
- The chromatic and textural variety of paint allows it to imitate other materials—wood, marble or other polished stones, tortoiseshell, or fabric, for example.
- **Trompe l'oeil,** painted three-dimensional scenes that fool the eye, adds architectural interest and sometimes humor as scenes of architecture, accessories, or even people that are not really there.
- Skilled professional painters can produce texture and pattern, contrast and camouflage; they can create imitations of nearly any type of material. Professional

painting is not inexpensive, although the cost for painting faux (false or imitation) marble, for example, is far less than surfacing with real marble.

Painting Guidelines

Because paint varies in versatility and ease of application, careful planning and preparation are imperative to achieve truly beautiful results. Some guidelines and cautions for using paint include the following:

- Surfaces must be properly prepared. Old paint that is cracked, bubbled, flaked, or peeling must be removed or sanded. Remove wallpaper. Cracks, holes, and damaged areas must be patched and sanded smooth. A clean, dust-free surface will help ensure a flawless finish.
- Before selecting paint colors or textures, evaluate the room itself. Look at the dimensions, the moldings, the architectural assets and defects. Evaluate the number of windows, the direction they face, and the amount of light admitted.
- Don't try to judge color from a small paint chip. Instead, try painting a small wall, portions of the wall, or a paper that can be taped to the wall. Judge the color during different times of the day and under different types of light.
- Consider **glazing** (transparent paints) for unique light-revealing effects and texturizing techniques. Experiment with different color combinations.
- Consider orientation and climate when selecting the hue for painted walls. For example, a lively yellow may be warm and comforting in a cool room with a north exposure or in a cooler climate, whereas that same color would visually and psychologically bake the inhabitants of an interior with a broad southern exposure or in a hot climate.

Figure 11.6 Contrasting paint color on trim, or "picking out" emphasizes the architectural detail in this interior. *© Brian Vanden Brink*

- Evaluate what contrast in the paint will do to the room. High-value contrast (very light hues against very dark hues) will accentuate and draw attention to that contrast. This can be dramatically effective where the contrast is in large planes and busy if the contrast is, say, around every door and window. On the other hand, light values next to medium ones or medium values near dark values can provide depth and richness.
- Consider the psychological effect of the color. The way people feel about color should be respected. Warm colors are lively and welcoming; cool colors are calm, providing a restful, restrained environment.

Table 11.7 | Types of Paints

By understanding the characteristics of each type of paint, you can make the best selection. It is also wise to describe the project to painting contractors or retail paint store specialists who can recommend a suitable product.

Acrylic paint is a synthetic resin water-based paint. It is odorless, quick-drying, durable, and easy to use. It cleans up with soap and water and is moderately priced.

Alkyds and **alkyd enamels** are durable resins, oil-modified, that dry faster and harder than oil paints. Alkyd enamels produce a glossy surface. Alkyds are moderately priced, are easy to work with, and have very good coverage and color range. Cleanup is with solvents or paint thinners.

Artist's paints—oil or acrylic—come in small bottles or tubes and can be thinned with mineral spirits or water and used as glazing for transparent color-overlay painting techniques.

Enamel paints are oil-based or sometimes water-based. They usually come in gloss or semigloss (may have flattening agents added for a matte finish). These paints are used most often for their hard, glossy, smooth finish.

Epoxy paints come already mixed or have hardeners mixed in at the site. Epoxies can be used to paint metal and water-holding surfaces such as bathtubs and swimming pools.

Fillers and **sealers** are used prior to staining or painting. Fillers are putty or stick-putty materials that fill in holes or cracks. Sealers are liquid preparations that make a smoother surface.

Finishes refer to the relative shine (see Table 11.8). Finishes also consist of a separate group of liquid sealants used on cabinetry and furniture, including shellac, lacquer, polyurethanes, and acrylics.

Flame-retardant paints retard the spread of flames or the toxic fumes and smoke given off by burning paints. Most specifications for new or remodeled nonresidential buildings require that paint meet a Class A flame spread, the lowest possible.

Latex paint is the least costly of the paints. Latex paints vary in their quality and durability. They are easy to apply and dry quickly, reducing recoating time. They have an excellent color range and are fairly durable but must be protected from freezing temperatures. They are not as scrubbable as alkyds but do have the ability to breathe, allowing moisture to escape. Cleanup is with soap and water.

Oil-based paints were for a number of years considered the best paint to buy. They were thought to be the most durable, were the most expensive, had the strongest odor, and took the longest to dry. Cleanup of oil-based paints is with paint thinner or solvent. These paints have largely been replaced with alkyds, and they may eventually be off the market due to environmental concerns.

Primers are liquid sealers applied to some surfaces before the paint. They fill in small pores and help the paint become more durable.

Solvents are liquids that dissolve resins, gums, or oils and are used to thin or clean up oils, alkyds, and oil-based enamels.

Stains are thin liquids used to color woods by penetrating the porous surface. Stains come in water base, oil base, varnish, and wax.

Table 11.8 | Paint Finishes

Flat or **matte paint** reflects very little sheen. It is appropriate for walls and ceilings to give a soft, velvetlike texture. Flat paints are the least washable of the lusters. Flat paints are available in enamel, often called **eggshell enamel,** which gives a matte finish and is more washable.

Satin or **eggshell paint** has a small amount of light-reflecting quality, so it hides fingerprints better and is more washable.

Semigloss paint has some sheen to hide marks, is more washable than flat or satin, and contrasts nicely with either flat or gloss paints.

High-gloss, or **gloss enamel, paint** is the shiniest of the paint lusters and the most durable and scrubbable. Its reflecting qualities, however, will show every flaw on a surface that has not been properly prepared for painting.

Texturizing paint comes in various textures. While the majority of the paints used are smooth, some thicker paints are available that can be applied to give the effect of stucco or of suede. These texturizing paints will also absorb more sound.

Table 11.9 | Paint-Texturizing Techniques

Visual texturizing can be achieved in many ways; just about any effect the design calls for can be accomplished by a skilled painter.

Smooth textures are achieved by using one of the four common methods of applying paint listed below. These techniques may produce an even surface appropriate in many period settings and modern interiors where woodwork and architectural detail are not important. They also make appropriate backgrounds for the broken and textured paint techniques presented in this chart.

1. **Brush painting** is used for corners; small, hard-to-reach areas; and detail work such as window grids and moldings.
2. **Roller painting** is very useful for large areas such as walls and ceilings. Small rollers are handy for narrow areas. A different sleeve should be used for each color. Rollers do spatter somewhat, and the roller should never be too full of paint.
3. **Pad painting** is useful for smaller areas and will not spatter. Pads cover evenly and are easy to work with.
4. **Spray painting** takes on two forms. Airless spraying uses fluid pressure and undiluted paint—it gives a better coverage but uses more paint. Air-compression spray guns use diluted paint and give less-complete coverage. Spraying is common in new buildings, both residential and nonresidential. It is fast and economical. It should be followed with a roller to even out the paint.

Antiquing means to make a surface look old, to soften and blur slightly in imitation of the mellow patina that naturally accompanies the aging process. Techniques frequently used in antiquing include color washing, glazing, spattering, and dragging.

Color washing is a technique of applying a coat of thinned, sometimes translucent, paint over a white or colored background. It is versatile, attractive, and easy to use, giving effects from rugged texture (over rough walls) to shimmering translucence (over smooth walls).

Dragging and **combing** are techniques that produce fine lines and may be used in wood graining. Dragging or coasting a dry brush over a wet glaze reveals a base color and can imitate fine fabric yarns. Combing uses any hard comblike tool. Dragging and combing can be done in straight lines, curving lines, or fan shapes. Cross-hatching by combing can produce a fabric burlaplike texture; by dragging with a brush, a variety of interesting crosshatch textures are possible.

Glazing is a technique in which transparent colors are overlayed in sequence, thereby producing various gradations of color.

Marbling is the technique of imitating polished marble stone. If it is done by artisans with a high degree of skill and artistic sense, the marbled surface cannot be distinguished from the real stone. Marbling can also simply be a mottled whirling, moving flow painted onto the surface.

Outlining means painting contrasting colors or white values on architectural molding.

Picking out means highlighting features on molding, such as dentil trim or carved bas-relief.

Porphyry is a granitelike texture achieved by crisscross brushing, then stippling, spattering, and finally **cissing** (dropping mineral spirits on the splatters to dilute and make shadows of the spatters).

Ragging and **rag rolling** are the basis for marbling where the wet paint or glaze is partially removed by dabbing with a rag or rolling the paint off with a rolled rag.

Shading is the technique of blending color values from light to dark across a wall or ceiling.

Spattering is achieved by filling a brush and flipping the paint onto the base color to produce uneven spots or spatters. Lighter or darker colors can be used, with lighter or darker base colors. Spattering can vary from tiny irregular dots to large globs of paint, and the spacing can be very close or sparsely spattered on an open ground.

Smooshing is a slightly marbled effect achieved by applying a plastic dropcloth to a wall of wet paint, rubbing or "smooshing" the hands over the plastic, and then peeling off the plastic.

Sponging (or paint applied with sponges) produces a broken, splotchy effect. Larger sponge pores will produce a more coarse-looking texture and a larger splotch than finer sponges. Sponging can yield rich-looking walls and ceilings, somewhat akin to granite when more than two colors of very carefully coordinated paint of two or more shades of one hue are used. Oil-based paints will look more crisp; latex paint will look softer.

Stippling is similar to sponging but uses a stippling brush to dab on a colored glaze or paint, revealing some of the base color. The result is finer than that from sponging.

Wood graining is done by brushing on a glaze and drawing wood grains and lines with an artist's brush. Techniques vary according to the type of wood being imitated. When well done, wood graining can be very beautiful.

Figure 11.7 Paint texturing techniques: (A) crackle finish, (B) sponging, (C) ragging or rag rolling, (D) combing, and (E) color washing. (F) Red painted crackle technique beneath a chair rail exposes the acidic green beneath it, which is also painted above the rail. *Courtesy of the Sherwin-Williams Company*

Wall Coverings

Wall coverings—including wallpaper, vinyl and textile wall coverings, and fabric—provide tremendous variety in pattern, color, texture, sound absorption, and flexibility. Walls and ceilings benefit from the many wall coverings that add visual and architectural interest. The reasons for utilizing wall coverings include the following:

- Colors, patterns, and textures of wall coverings are unlimited.
- Wall coverings can imitate natural materials such as stone, wood, brick, or tile at a fraction of the cost of those materials.
- Costs vary, but they can be modest. Installation can be done professionally or by the layperson.
- Three-dimensional fabric wall coverings absorb sound and give a sense of quiet or peace to the interior.

- Wall coverings can cover badly cracked walls or old paint; they can even camouflage architectural flaws or defects.
- Fabric installed on the wall can coordinate with fabric used in other areas of the interior. Many wall-covering companies offer companion fabrics to match wallpapers.
- Wall coverings can provide "instant decor"—they can add charm, beauty, and character to interiors.
- Fabric wall coverings can be installed flat, pleated, shirred, draped, or folded, allowing creativity in the way the pattern, color, or texture is utilized.

Wall-Covering Guidelines

Wall coverings are so extensively used as "instant decorating" that some guidelines and cautions are in order:

Select wall coverings that are compatible with the style of furnishings and with the architecture of the building.

Figure 11.8 A coral plaid wall covering placed above a traditional dado ties together the niche paint and Neoclassic dining chairs fabric. © *Scott Frances/Esto*

Formal Baroque or Renaissance designs in a modern building are not only out of character; they may insult the integrity of both the wall covering and the architecture.

Choose pattern with great discrimination. Consider how long a pattern will stay stylish and aesthetically appealing. A general rule is that the more dramatic or flamboyant the pattern, the more quickly it will become tiresome.

Limit the number of patterns in an interior and coordinate them to provide harmony from one area to another. Patterns that differ in style or color will be discordant, and if two or more clashing wall coverings are visible from any one vantage point, the effect can be disastrous.

Obvious patterns on the ceiling will visually lower the ceiling and can be psychologically disturbing.

Patterns that clash with fabrics in the interior are poor choices. Keep in mind how often the furnishings may be changed or replaced.

Many textured and colorful wall coverings are lovely and sophisticated, and their subtle qualities establish pleasing transitions from one room or area to another. However, very intense colors, or cheap imitations (such as plastic grass cloth), may not be considered good design.

Installation is a key factor in how nice a wall covering looks. The work of professional wall-covering installers will look far superior to a careless do-it-yourself job.

Wall covering terms useful in selecting and ordering are found in Tables 11.10 and 11.12. Table 11.11 lists methods of fabric installation as wall-covering material.

Figure 11.9 A William Morris wall covering is installed between oak stiles and rails in this Craftsman Bungalow interior. © *Jessie Walker*

Table 11.10 | Wall-Covering Terms

Single rolls contain 30 to 36 square feet, being about 28 feet long by 27 inches wide. When calculating wall-covering quantity, figure that single roll will cover 25 to 30 square feet, which allows for waste. European papers have 28 feet per single roll. Wallpapers are priced as single rolls and may be purchased by the single roll (abbreviated S/R).

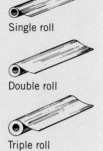

Single roll

Double roll is the equivalent of, and is priced as, two single rolls rolled into one—it usually contains about 72 square feet. It saves waste and is therefore more economical.

Double roll

Triple roll is priced as and equals three single rolls in one length, about 108 square feet. The most economical use of the paper.

Triple roll

Dye lot is a single run of colors or a single production. The dye-lot shades may vary. If it becomes necessary to reorder, always specify the dye-lot number (included on a piece of paper with the roll) or send in a swatch of the paper. It is not always possible to obtain the same dye lot at a later date, so do not skimp when ordering.

Border is a narrow or wide band of wallpaper used to trim and accent. Borders are usually packaged in single "spools" of 15 feet (5 yards).

Pattern repeat comes in two directions. A vertical pattern repeat is the complete motif or pattern from the top of one length to the top of the next. A large pattern repeat is more wasteful, since a complete pattern repeat must begin at the top of each length. A horizontal pattern repeat means that the pattern can be matched straight across or drop-matched by lowering the next length of paper.

Peelable wall covering means the top layer of the wallpaper will peel off, leaving a substrate (lining) material that can be papered over again.

Prepasted wall covering means the paper has a dry coating of paste and will need only to be moistened to be applied.

Pretrimmed wall covering means ready to hang. Hand-printed wallpapers have a selvage (border) with separate printed information, including blocks of color used in the paper. This must be trimmed off before the paper is hung. Pretrimmed papers have the selvage cut off.

Semitrimmed has only one side of the selvage trimmed, so the selvage left on is under an overlap or is trimmed off at the site.

Scrubbable denotes a wall covering that can withstand repeated wet cleaning. Most vinyl wall coverings are scrubbable.

Sizing is a thin liquid painted onto the wall surface that reduces the amount of paste absorbed by the wallpaper. It also gives the surface "tooth," or enough abrasiveness to stick well, and it seals the surface so that alkali cannot penetrate into the wallpaper.

Strippable is a term applied to papers that can be stripped off the wall completely without scraping or steaming.

Washable means the paper can be cleaned gently with a little soap and water.

Table 11.11 | Methods of Installing Wall Farbic

Covered-frame method uses a lath frame (1-inch by 2-inch wooden strips) laid on the back of the fabric. The fabric is pulled tightly over the frame and stapled. The result is a blind wooden frame with top and sides covered with fabric. This can be mounted or hung on protruding nails as panels and may not cover the entire wall. Smaller fabric-framed panels may be accessory items.

Direct pasteup uses fabrics that come prepared for installation as a wall covering with a paper or foam backing, or the installer may apply a spray backing or iron on a stiffening fabric backing. Sometimes the preparation or paste causes the fabric grain to slip, making it difficult to match patterns horizontally. A skilled professional is an asset in direct fabric pasteup.

    A less permanent method is to sponge liquid laundry starch onto the wall or dip the fabric in it. The fabric will stick to the wall until it is remoistened and pulled off.

Hook-and-loop fasteners may be used to install fabric in cases where the fabric needs to be taken down frequently for cleaning. The best-known brand of hook-and-loop fasteners is Velcro. One half of the tape is sewn or glued to the fabric and the companion part is applied to the wall.

Lath method uses wood lath strips nailed to the wall perimeter. The fabric is stapled, glued, or fastened to the strips with hook-and-loop tape. This saves the effort of preparing badly damaged walls or stiffening the fabric for direct pasteup.

Panel-track method can use several brands of metal or plastic tracks that are on the market for the professional, usually nonresidential installation of fabric on the wall. These include office systems furniture which provides a flexible wall where fabrics can be changed when necessary.

Stapling with a staple gun is a fast, easy method of applying fabric to the wall. The staples may be covered with trim such as welt or gimp or braid or with wood or plastic molding.

Strapping-tape method is a very inexpensive and easy method. Simply roll lengths of strapping tape into circles and flatten against the wall; then press the fabric in place. High humidity or certain paint surfaces may make this method unsatisfactory, however.

Upholstered walls mean that there is a layer of batting applied first to the wall in the form of polyester or cotton batting or foam. The fabric is then stapled over the padding, and a trim is placed on top. This gives extra sound-absorption and insulation values.

Table 11.12 | Types of Wall Coverings

Coordinating or **companion fabrics** are now available with many wall coverings. This is a convenient, although not inexpensive, way to coordinate fabric installations with wall coverings.

Cork wall coverings use cork, a natural resilient bark, cut into very thin layers with a paper backing.

Embossed wall coverings are calendered to produce a three-dimensional, raised pattern. **Anaglypta wall coverings** are embossed to resemble sculptured plaster, hammered copper, or hand-tooled leather and may be paintable.

Fabric or **textile wall coverings** are fabrics laminated to a paper backing and sold in rolls or bolts. The most common fabric wall coverings are linen, jute, and wool. They give a rich natural-textured look and are very appropriate for both residential and nonresidential interiors.

Fabric-backed wall coverings are used for heavy-face papers or vinyl to give strength to the installation. Most nonresidential wall coverings and heavy vinyl residential wall coverings are fabric backed.

Flocked wallpapers use **flocking,** which is a process of gluing tiny fibers in a pattern to the surface of the paper. It is a decorative effect, in imitation of cut velvet.

Foil/mylar wall coverings have a shiny, highly reflective quality.

Grass cloth is made of dried grasses that are left natural or dyed a color and woven into a textile with fine cotton threads (a more refined product) or other grasses (coarser looking). They have a paper backing.

Leather is a luxurious and quieting wall covering. Leather squares or **leather tiles,** the tanned hide of cattle and swine, are dyed brown or other colors and possibly embossed with patterns.

Murals are printed scenic wallpapers that come in panels. They have traditionally been scenes of romantic or faraway places, sometimes ruins of ancient civilizations.

Paper wall coverings are the most common wall coverings. They may be coated with vinyl (explained below). They are easy to hang and come in a wide variety of patterns and colors.

Vinyl wall coverings come in several types, from light to heavy weight. They are:

> **Vinyl-protected wall coverings** in which a thin layer of vinyl is applied over wallpaper to make it more washable and durable.
>
> **Vinyl latex,** paper impregnated with vinyl and applied to a fabric or paper backing.
>
> **Coated fabric,** coated or laminated fabric wall covering.

Vinyl wall coverings are the heaviest of the wall coverings, the most scrubbable and strippable, and possibly even reusable. Vinyl wall coverings are more difficult to hang because of their weight. They may imitate wood, leather, tile, marble, or any other hard material.

Figure 11.10 A sporty, masculine wall covering enhances the mood of this recreation room. *Arnold Palmer Lifestyles collection, Eisenhart® brand by and photo courtesy of Eisenhart Wallcoverings Co.*

Fabric-Covered Walls

Fabric installed or upholstered onto a wall or ceiling has many advantages. It is the most **flexible wall covering,** as it can be applied flat, gathered (shirred), pleated, or folded. Fabrics can change their character with the different methods of installation. A patterned fabric laid flat looks quite different from one that is shirred, pleated, or folded. Installations can be quite temporary, permanent, or semipermanent. Fabrics:

- Are highly insulative against both noise and temperature extremes
- Offer visual comfort as well as physical softness
- Offer the ability to use the same material on other installations, such as upholstered furniture, bedspreads, and accessory items

Fabrics used on the wall may be subject to soiling and may discolor or stain when spot cleaned, making upkeep difficult. Fabrics should not be used in heavy traffic areas

Figure 11.11 Fabric on the wall, here wrapped as blocks or upholstered, absorbs noise and increases comfort. *Courtesy of DuPont "Teflon" soil and stain repellent*

where people, particularly children, tend to touch the wall frequently.

Ceiling Treatments

While most of the materials discussed for wall treatments may also be applied to ceilings, the most typical ceiling materials are those that are lighter in weight, such as acoustical tile, wallboard, plaster, wood, and cork. Most guidelines for the use of paint and wall coverings on walls will also hold true for ceiling treatments.

The ceiling treatment can have a powerful, yet subtle, influence on the overall feeling of space in the interior. For ceilings that need to be visually lowered, use patterns, dark or bright colors, or texture. To visually raise the height, use smooth surfaces and light, pale, or dull colors. Horizontal beams or bands will visually lower a ceiling, whereas angled ceilings with beams that carry the eye upward—an effect often seen in church interiors—will increase the visual height. Fabric is sometimes draped on a ceiling in sunburst or tentlike fashion to create a cozy atmosphere.

In interiors where sound needs to be absorbed, fabric is a good choice. It can be upholstered onto the ceiling as well as draped, and it is also available in fabric panels and acoustical panels. Acoustical tile, of course, is also a good sound absorber, as is textured acoustical plaster. In addition, texturing is frequently desirable as a way of covering up blemishes before the ceiling is painted.

Chapter 10, "Architectural Detail," discusses and illustrates different architectural ceilings.

Window Treatments

Because of consumer demands for beauty, privacy, energy conservation, comfort, and cost efficiency, today's window treatments offer a variety of options that continually expands with advancing technology.

Window treatments are generally divided into two categories—soft and alternative. **Soft window treatments** include draperies, curtains, fabric shades, and top treatments; alternative coverings include a wide array of art glass, horizontal and vertical slat blinds, screens, shades, and shutters. These treatments are presented in Tables 11.13 through 11.19. Recent trends have favored layered treatments—two or more fabric treatments, or a practical and durable alternative treatment (a blind, shutter, screen, or shade) layered with a soft fabric treatment of curtain, drapery, or top treatment.

Window-Treatment Considerations

Many factors go into making a wise choice for a window covering. These include aesthetic coordination, privacy, energy consciousness, light control, and also operational control.

Aesthetic Coordination
Aesthetic coordination is the careful selection of window treatments to not only look beautiful but to blend with and support the interior and exterior design and architecture.

Aesthetic coordination also requires sensitivity to good proportion. It helps to judge proportion by sketching the window treatment to scale. Window treatments that are top heavy, too wide, overdone—or, on the other hand, too skimpy—can throw off the proportions of the entire room. This is because the window itself is an important architectural feature that will inevitably draw attention because of the light and view. If the window treatment is aesthetically disturbing, the interior will

vide total privacy either. Only opaque treatments that can be closed fully provide complete nighttime privacy. These include opaque draperies and shades, solid vane vertical louvers, opaque cellular pleated shades, and routless (no holes) horizontal blinds.

Energy Consciousness

Energy consciousness is important for two reasons:

1. The cost of heating or cooling a room is reduced through energy-efficient treatments.
2. The comfort of the room is enhanced by controlling excess heat gain and heat loss.

Heat gain or **solar heat gain** can be a problem not only in hot climates and in the summer but anytime heat from the sun becomes uncomfortable and begins to fade or damage interior furnishings. Treatments that control heat gain are referred to as **shading devices.** The ideal shading device is actually on the exterior, preventing the sun from hitting the glass of the window.

Once the sun hits the glass, temperatures between the window and the interior window

Figure 11.12 Smoothly finished sheetrock painted deep green makes a pleasing background for these self-valanced draperies placed over two-inch blinds, which adjust for light control and privacy. *George Snead Interior Design/photo © Todd Caverly*

seem incomplete and lacking in harmony, no matter how handsome other furnishings are.

Privacy

Privacy protects valuable belongings against burglary. Privacy also gives a psychological sense of well-being and makes a space more usable after dark.

During the day, adequate privacy can be obtained with translucent treatments, which also offer the advantage of allowing daylight into the interior. Sheer and semisheer curtains, pleated fabric shades, louvered blinds or shutters, and pierced screens all give good daytime privacy.

Translucent treatments do not give nighttime privacy. Alternative treatments that have holes or slats that do not close completely do not pro-

Figure 11.13 (A) Silhouette shades control glare and soften this mountain home. *Hunter Douglas Window Fashions, 1-800-937-STYLE www.hunterdouglas.com*

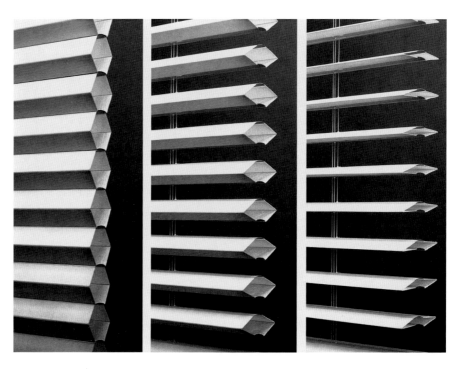

Figure 11.13 (B) The Trio® Convertible shade is a newly engineered alternative to cellular shades. 1⅛-inch individual, hexagonally shaped horizontal vanes open by compressing and close by expanding, even when the shade is partially raised, providing new light control options. The shade offers an R-value of 3.94 and prevents 75 percent heat loss. *Hunter Douglas Window Fashions, 1-800-937-STYLE www.hunterdouglas.com*

treatment can climb to as high as 300 degrees Fahrenheit, heating the room and causing damage to furnishings. The most effective interior shading devices are those that can reflect a high percentage of sunlight back through the glass. Window film and metallized pleated shades and light-colored treatments do this best. Room-darkening treatments also effectively control heat and brightness.

Heat loss is a problem in moderate to cold climates in the winter. When heated interior air rises and travels toward the window, it comes in contact with cold glass, cooling the heated air, which then drops to the floor and circulates at ankle level, where we may feel a draft. Preventing the warm air from striking the glass is the best preventative for heat loss. Insulated fabric shades sealed on the sides and at the bottom and insulated shutters are the best treatments. Other good choices are opaque roller shades and heavy lined/interlined draperies that reach to the floor, are securely attached to the walls, and have sealed top treatments. The heavier and more solid the treatment, the better it insulates.

Light Control

Control of light is a major consideration in selecting window treatments. Light-controlling needs should be noted in the design program. If the room needs to be completely darkened, certain opaque treatments will fill that requirement. Light is often desirable, although glare (intense directional light) causes irritation and fatigue. Many treatments do a good job of controlling glare: draperies, curtains, shades (of light to medium weight), all types of vertical and horizontal **blinds,** pleated and translucent shades, **louvered** shutters, screens, and bamboo shades.

Within an interior, the need for light and glare control may vary according to the **orientation,** or direction, the windows face. Whereas north-facing windows may need little light control, the bright east light, constant south light, or hot, piercing west light may require shading devices during particular times of the day when the sunlight comes directly through windows facing those directions.

Figure 11.13 (C) This manufactured waterfall Roman shade is energy efficient and easily rolls into the head rail. *Torino Marble fabric in color Candlewax. Courtesy of Comfortex Window Fashions*

convenience of automation or remote control. There are also mechanisms that can sense, by light or temperature change, when to close treatments, thus enhancing energy efficiency.

Soft Window Coverings

Fabric at the window gives softness to an inherently hard and poorly insulative material. Fabric provides sound and temperature insulation, visual comfort, and interest through color, texture, and perhaps pattern. In addition, light-filtering fabrics can give daytime privacy (and be layered with opaque fabrics or hard materials for nighttime privacy) and can effectively reduce or eliminate glare. Fabrics can be installed on **traverse rods** to be drawn off the window. Fabrics also can be made into many decorative shapes, giving architectural support, authenticity, or decorative effects. There seems to be no limit to the styles and combinations of fabrics used at the window, making the window perhaps the most creative of

Figure 11.15 Elegant striped draperies are tied back in the Neoclassic high position, the "golden mean" between ½ and ⅓ from the top of the draperies. *Jeffrey S. Quéripel, Quéripel Interiors/photo © Melabee M. Miller*

Figure 11.14 These Heritance® hardwood shutters offer the beauty and durability of wood and a state-of-the-art finish and fine dovetail panel construction that ensures the shutters will not separate over time and create light gaps. *Hunter Douglas Window Fashions, 1-800-937-STYLE www.hunterdouglas.com*

Operational Control

The selection of a window treatment should also be based on whether or not it needs to be operable, and this will largely be dictated by the needs previously discussed. Stationary treatments—tied-back draperies, ruffled curtains, top treatments, stationary screens—cannot be closed for privacy, nor can they be removed for desirable solar gain or maximum light penetration. Ventilation may be inhibited by a treatment that is difficult to operate or that will not adequately stack out of the window area.

For many treatments on cord- or pulley-operated hardware, motorized units can operate the opening and closing of the treatment. Many situations can benefit from motorized units—from hard-to-reach controls (such as solarium shades) to control by a disabled person to the

all background material installations. See Table 11.18 for calculations.

Draperies

Draperies are pleated fabric panels hung on a rod. Draperies may be opaque, casement (semi-opaque), or translucent. There are many types of pleats, the most common being the French or pinch pleat. See Table 11.13.

Curtains

Curtains are often shirred, or gathered, onto a rod, making them stationary or hand operable. **Shirred curtains** may be formal or informal. Curtains can also have a variety of headings depending on the use. Table 11.14 lists some types of curtains.

Fabric Window Shades

Fabric shades are panels of fabric that operate top to bottom. In Great Britain they are called blinds. See Table 11.15.

Top Treatments

Top treatments are used for a number of reasons: to hide rods or pleats, to cover the area from the top of the window to the ceiling, to give a soft and finished look to the room. Top treatments may be shaped according to architectural detailing or may be inspired by furnishings. They are often an effective medium to unite a room and carry the eye gracefully along the top of the walls. Types of top treatments are discussed in Table 11.16.

Drapery Hardware

Much of the versatility possible in soft window coverings is due to the many kinds of hardware that have been developed during this century, some of which are presented in Table 11.17. Many variations of each type are available through interior designers and window-treatment specialists.

Alternative Window Treatments

Alternative materials are generally very durable and require little maintenance. They can be clean and contemporary or very traditional, crossing boundaries in many cases. They serve as versatile backgrounds and are often simple statements that will coordinate with many styles of furnishings. Some are moderately priced and offer both privacy and light control. Alternative treatments are presented in Table 11.19.

Table 11.13 | Types of Draperies

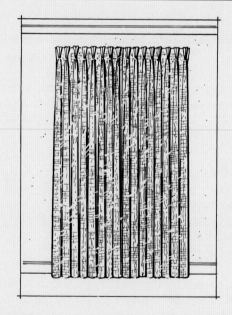

Draw draperies are installed on a traverse (cord-operated) rod and may be pulled or drawn open and closed. **Privacy draperies** are installed under a transparent fabric or separated tiebacks to provide nighttime privacy or insulation. **Sheer draperies** include transparent and translucent fabrics, often placed next to the glass and historically called glass curtains.

Casement draperies are draw draperies made of a woven or knit fabric with novelty yarns and a strong textural look. They are popular in non-residential settings, such as offices, and in casual settings at home. They screen light and cut down on glare but do not provide nighttime privacy.

Types of Draperies (continued)

Parisian pleat or **inverted pleat draperies** are installed on rings that slide along a designer rod.

Tieback draperies are ideally slender stationary panels that meet in the center on narrow windows or are separated on wider windows. They are tied back with fabric bands (ties) or metal holdbacks.

Table 11.14 | Types of Curtains

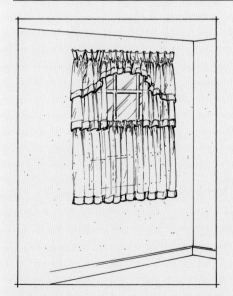

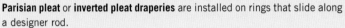

Cottage curtains are short lengths, shirred, and hung in informal style within or on the window frame. They may be **tiered** or layered. **Café curtains** cover the bottom half of the window.

Priscilla curtains are cottage curtains that fill the window with a sheer, semisheer, or muslin fabric. Priscillas have a ruffle sewn on the front leading and bottom edges and on the tiebacks and have a ruffled valance. They meet in the middle or crisscross with one panel in front of the other.

(continued)

Types of Curtains (continued)

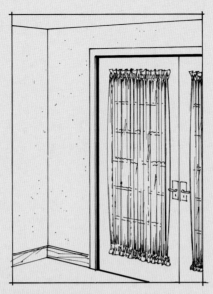

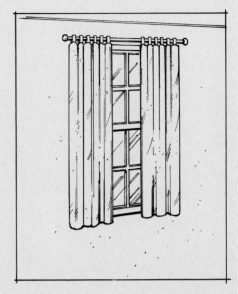

Long or **formal** curtains are shirred (gathered) onto the rod and are nonoperational.

Sash curtains are sheer or semisheer fabrics shirred at the top and bottom and installed most often on casement windows and French doors so as to swing with the sash or door.

Tab curtains are flat panels with straps of fabric sewn to the top and looped over dowel rods—a simple, classic treatment.

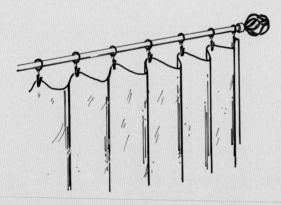

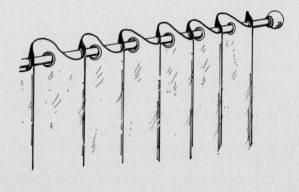

The **standard ring top panel** is installed with rings that slide along the rod and attach to the curtain with metal clips or thread loops.

The **grommet panel** uses metal grommets, installed in the curtain fabric, to slide along the rod.

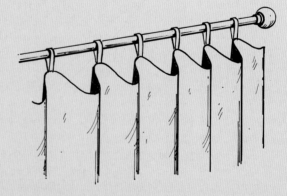

The **flounce top panel** is constructed with a flap of fabric that gives a visual effect similar to a valance. It is attached to the rod with ties.

The **camisole panel** uses narrow fabric straps to attach the curtain to the rod.

Table 11.15 | Fabric Window Shades

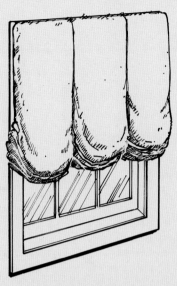

Waterfall Roman

London shades are constructed with inverted pleats that are nearly flat at the top and fall softly to form one or more swags. The fabric stacks in neat pleats when the shade is raised.

Balloon (pouf or **cloud) shades** are softly gathered to be billowy at the bottom, forming poufs or balloons. The top may be constructed in several ways including shirring, flat-box pleats, and French pleats.

Flat Roman

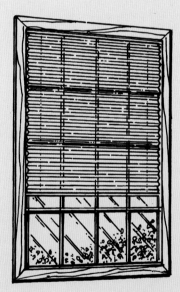

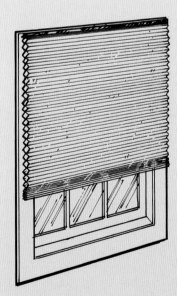

Relaxed Roman

Pleated shades are factory-made products of stiffened fabric, plan or printed, that fold up in narrow according pleats. They may be translucent or opaque.

Cellular (honeycomb) shades are energy-conscious, constructed in layers that fold in opposite directions to leave an insulating channel of air inside. They may have a single, double, or triple cell construction.

Roman shades are sewn in horizontal folds that stack when the shade is raised.

Table 11.16 | Types of Top Treatments

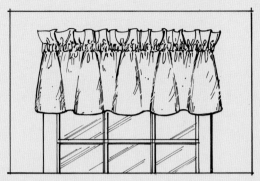

Shirred valances are gathered at the top. They may have plain, shaped or scalloped hems or may be gathered onto a bottom rod.

Flat inverted box pleat valances may be stiffened with an interlining. Many other styles of pleats can also be used to construct valances.

Cornice

Cornices are straight or shaped wooden or resin top treatments. When covered with padding and fabric, they are called **upholstered cornices.** When cornices extend down the sides to the floor or partway, they are called lambrequins or cantonnieres. When upholstered, these are energy efficient because they inhibit the exchange of cool and warm air at the window.

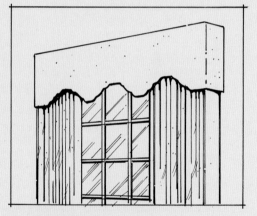

Upholstered Cornice

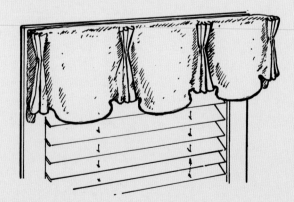

Shaped valances are made of fabric with a stiffened interlining. Their shape might carry out a theme, document a historic period, or echo forms found in other features of the room. Shown here is a shaped pleated valance.

Swags or **festoons**—half-round fabric treatments in overlapping arrangements—are the top treatment perhaps most used throughout history. Many widths, depths, and variations are possible. Cascades, falling from above or beneath the valance, are often added to frame swags or festoons.

Types of Top Treatments (continued)

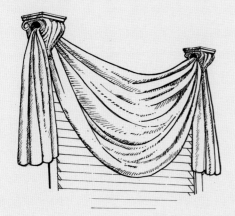

Swagged scarf valances are made of simple lengths of fabric, looped through swag holders which come in a wide range of shapes, sizes, and styles.

Swag holder

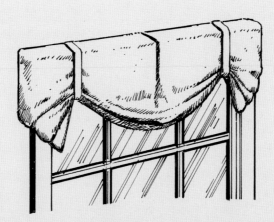

Balloon tab valances or **London valances** are constructed of fabric that falls in a soft swag shape and is attached with tabs or straps.

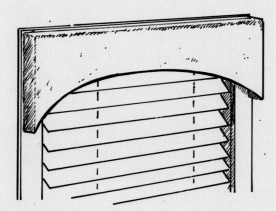

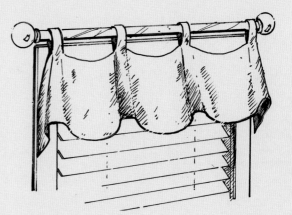

Arched flat valances may be constructed like cornices or shaped valances.

Tabbed relaxed swagged valances fall in soft folds, and are attached with fabric loops or tabs which slide along a designer rod.

Table 11.17 | Types of Drapery Hardware

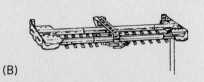

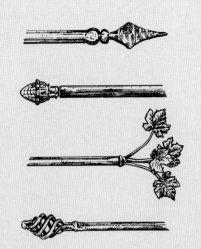

Conventional traverse rods are cord-operated rods with carriers to hold the drapery hooks. Conventional traverse rods come in single-hung (for one pair of draperies), in double-hung (for two sets of draperies), and with a plain curtain rod underneath or a curtain or valance rod on top. They also come in one-way draw for stacking draperies to one side.

Curtain rods come in oval shapes. Some curtain rods are made with spring tension, so no brackets are necessary on an inside frame mount. Curtain rods also come in (B) round shapes or (C) with attached finials and may have rings to hold drapery hooks or clips to clip onto pleats or panels.

Wrought iron rods are available with finials styled to give a rustic or traditional look. There are dozens of styles available, and wrought iron can be custom designed.

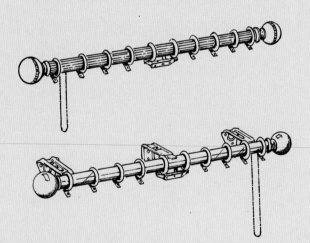
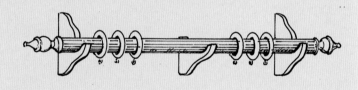

Decorator rods have special carriers that look like rings but operate as traverse (cord-operated) rods. They come in wood colors, white, antique, brass, chrome, black, and specialty finishes.

Wood rods come plain and fluted, and they may be stained or painted or covered with fabric or wallpaper. Curtains may be shirred onto wood rods, the fabric may be draped over in loose swag fashion, or the wood ring carriers may hold drapery hooks, which must be hand operated.

Types of Drapery Hardware (continued)

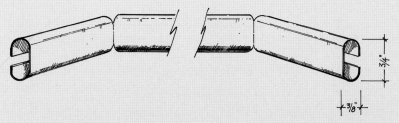

Bay and bow rods are available in nearly as many varieties as listed for conventional traverse and curtain rods. **Motorized rods** are for hard-to-reach draperies or large installations or simply for the convenience of pushing a button rather than drawing a cord or wand. Motorized systems are common in nonresidential settings.

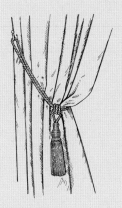

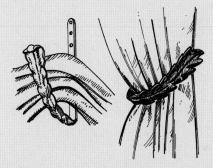

Swag holders or **metal tieback holders** come in patterns such as decorative rosettes and as concealed (clear plastic placed under the drapery) holders.

Tieback holder of braided rope and tassel.

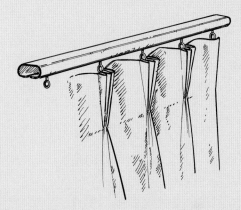

Architectural rodding comes in several varieties, and each company has patented names for its products. Nonresidential or architectural rods have sturdy ball-bearing carriers, and many of the styles are operated with a wand rather than a cord, which eliminates many problems of cord-operated rods in places such as hotels, offices, and institutions. While components can be specified for any type of custom installation, nonresidential rods are usually for flat panels or for less full draperies with few pleats.

Table 11.18 | Calculating Yardage for Window Treatments

For Curtains and Draperies

1. Determine rod width (end of rod to end of rod).
2. Add on for overlaps (for traverse draperies that meet in the center) and returns (around the corner to the wall), if applicable. A measure of 12 inches is standard for a single-hung layer, 16 inches for a double-hung layer, and 4 inches for an underlayer.
3. Divide by 20 inches to determine the number of widths or cuts (a typical 45- to 48-inch fabric will pleat or gather down to about 20 inches including side hems).
4. Determine the desired finished length (add 6 inches for puddling if desired); then add for hems, headings, and any ruffles to determine the cut length. Hems are usually 4 inches doubled, or 8 inches. For pleated headings add 8 inches. Ruffled headings will need 6 to 12 inches added depending on the depth of the ruffle and the width of the rod. (Figure the finished length plus the rod pocket, the ruffle, and another 2 inches for the self-lining and hem, which is turned under.)
5. Multiply the cut length by the number of widths or cuts to find the total inches; then divide by 36 inches to yield the number of yards. Always round up. For pattern repeats, figure the number of complete pattern repeats needed for each cut; then multiply that number by the inches in one pattern; repeat for the total inches needed per cut. There will be waste in pattern-repeat fabrics because the pattern must start at the same point at the top of each cut. Yardage will be an average of 20 percent greater.
6. Costs for sewing, installation (charged by the width or foot), and the rods are additional.

For Balloon Shades

1. Determine finished width; then divide by 20 inches for the number of cuts or widths.
2. Add 6 to 8 inches for hems and headings; then add 20 inches for the pouf at the bottom.
3. Ruffle yardage is figured in widthwise or lengthwise strips. Total inches of ruffle needed will be multiplied by 2 or 3 (for desired fullness), and the depth of the ruffle doubled plus 1 inch for self-lining. These dimensions are calculated or sketched out in scale into the width of the goods either widthwise or lengthwise.
4. Cost to sew is figured per square foot (ruffles are extra, charged per linear foot), and fabrication costs are greater if the shade is operable.
5. Installation board and cost to install are priced per linear foot. Board may be included in cost of shade fabrication.

For Flat, Shaped, and Pleated Valances

1. Determine whether the width should run vertically in cuts or horizontally (railroaded) with no seams. Railroaded fabric may appear a different color than the curtain or shade beneath it because of the way the light hits the weave.
2. Determine the cuts or widths (if selected) as previously determined for curtains, eliminating the overlap but figuring in returns. Multiply the cuts by doubling the finished length for self-lining, plus 2 to 4 inches for seams, or multiply by the finished length plus 2 to 4 inches if lining fabric is used. Divide by 36 inches for yardage; then round up. Order the same quantity of lining fabric if the fabric is not to be self-lined.
3. Railroaded valances and curtains/draperies turn the width to run the lengthwise direction of the goods. Multiply the finished width by 2½ (or fullness desired) and divide by 36 inches for yardage. For valances, figure strips this way—finished length—face only or self-lined measurement divided into the width of the goods.

For Swags and Cascades

1. Determine the number of swags or festoons by sketching them in the configuration desired and determining the overlap and width of each swag. Measure for desired depth.
2. A self-lined swag up to 20 inches wide and 12 inches deep will need 1 to 1½ yards each; a self-lined swag up to 40 inches wide and 24 inches deep will need 3 yards each.
3. Cascades and jabots need yardage equal to double their finished length. Costs to sew are determined by the workroom. Sewing on ruffles or trimmings will cost extra (trimming yardage is 2½ times the top of the swag); installation is per swag or cascade or per linear foot of installation board.

Table 11.19 | Types of Alternative Window Treatments

Stained and **art glass** gives pattern, color, and interest to the glass. Patterns and privacy levels vary. Costly.

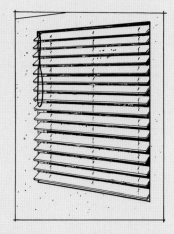

Two-inch metal or **wood blinds** are handsome and provide light control and privacy. Moderate cost.

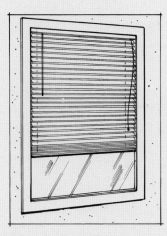

Miniblinds control light and glare, give relative privacy, and are sleek. Inexpensive.

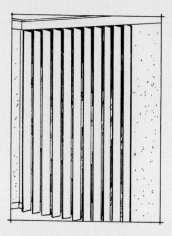

Vertical louvers are durable, can provide good light control, can offer privacy (when heavy or opaque), and can conserve energy. Moderate cost.

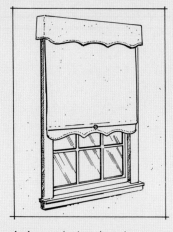

Roller shades can be translucent or opaque, with the latter being energy efficient. Low to moderate cost.

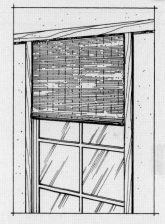

Bamboo shades give a natural look as they screen glare and diffuse light. They offer no nighttime privacy. Modest cost.

Shoji screens provide light diffusion and the serenity of old Japan. They operate by sliding on tracks. Costly.

One-inch movable louver shutters shown here as double-hung, give light control, privacy, and the warmth of woods. Costly.

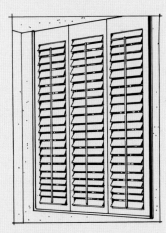

Plantation shutters have wide blades and have a permanent look to them. Costly.

Figure 11.16 For centuries marble has been a preferred finish material in large public spaces, such as seen here in the Utah State Capitol building. Columns, walls, and floors are stone, a material that provides a sense of permanence and stability and one that will last through generations of heavy traffic. *Photo by John Wang*

Nonresidential Considerations

Materials for nonresidential walls, ceilings, and windows often differ from those used in the home. The differences are threefold. Nonresidential materials generally must be:

1. More durable—they should be able to withstand harder abuse from greater traffic and in less controlled situations.
2. Less patterned and more textured in appearance. Non-residential materials are plain compared to the variety of decorative materials used in homes.
3. Flame-retardant, fire-resistant or fireproof, and static- and microorganism-resistant—in order to meet state and local building codes for public safety.

Durability

Because of the durability requirement, permanent hard materials are often used in nonresidential settings. It is not uncommon to see stone, tile, or brick used not only on the exterior but on the interior. This allows people to touch, bump, soil, or abrade the surface without worry that it will be damaged. Wall-covering materials are specially made to be durable for nonresidential applications. For example, vinyl and fabric wall coverings can withstand a great deal of physical abuse, and many **nonresidential wall coverings** have been tested and rated, so the architect or designer can match the durability rating to the traffic classification required by code or building specification:

- Class I. Decorative wall coverings.
- Class II. Decorative and serviceable wall coverings. Serviceability includes colorfastness (low) and washability.
- Class III. Decorative wall coverings that have good serviceability. Serviceability includes colorfastness (low to moderate), washability, scrubbability, and resistance to abrasion, breaking, crocking, and staining.
- Class IV. Wall coverings that are decorative with full serviceability, including colorfastness (low to moderate),

washability, scrubbability, and resistance to abrasion, breaking, crocking, staining, and tearing.

- Class V. Medium-commercial-serviceability wall coverings that include colorfastness (very good), washability, scrubbability, and resistance to abrasion, breaking, crocking, staining, tearing, heat aging, cracking, and shrinkage.
- Class VI. Full-commercial-serviceability wall coverings that are the same as Class V coverings but have greater resistance to tearing.

Nonresidential wall coverings are classified as either nonmildew resistant or mildew resistant. They may also need to meet fire code restrictions, and this makes the product selection somewhat different from that for residential wall coverings. The range of selections tends to be more textured and subtle, without the many changing designer patterns found in residential wall coverings.

Nonresidential wall coverings often are 52 to 54 inches wide and contain 30 square yards, dimensions that are more convenient and economical for large installations. However, this much weight is unwieldy and requires expert installation.

Nonresidential Ceiling Treatments

There are many materials and types of treatments used in nonresidential interiors that are worth mentioning. These include acoustical ceilings in tile or larger panel sections, mounted in suspended grid systems and dropped to accommodate heating, ventilation, and air-conditioning systems, lighting systems, communication systems, and fire-extinguishing systems within the plenum area. The ceiling must allow access to these systems in case of system or component breakdown. Ceilings may consist largely of indirect lighting; they may contain soffits for lighting or for accommodating the previously mentioned systems. The ceiling may be of glass, such as a solarium ceiling, in which case it must be safety glass.

Nonresidential Window Treatments

Window treatments for nonresidential interiors must be able to withstand operation from many different people who are unfamiliar with them. Therefore, mechanisms are usually engineered to be as trouble free as possible. Drapery rods without pull cords are often specified. Draperies are often slid open and closed one panel at a time with a wand attached to the leading carrier. This not only prevents breakdowns that would occur in a cord-and-pulley system but discourages the handling (and soiling/damaging) of the fabric to find the cords.

Window-treatment materials must be able to reduce glare for office use, a particularly important facet for those working at computer terminals (glare on the screen

Figure 11.17 Wood blinds control light and glare and are easy to operate. Swags and side draperies of a rich, complex fabric frame and soften the hard lines. *Courtesy of Hunter Douglas*

must be minimized or eliminated). Daytime privacy in working/nonresidential situations is also of prime importance. Therefore, alternative window treatments are used frequently. Of these, the most popular are mini-blinds, vertical louvers, roller shades (opaque and film), and cellular shades. Casement draperies—generally an open-constructed cloth—are standard in offices and situations where glare control and sound control are required.

Window treatments may also be required to provide any or all of the following six energy conservation functions:

1. Allow winter solar heat gain
2. Allow daylighting all year
3. Reflect summer solar heat gain
4. "Seal" the window from the room air when mechanical heating and air-conditioning are operating
5. Insulate against heat and cold extremes
6. Allow for natural ventilation during temperate weather

Nighttime privacy is a need in some installations, requiring a hard treatment that can close fully or a fabric that is lined, opaque, or a combination of hard and soft materials—such as a casement fabric over a blind or shade. Printed fabrics are sometimes used in hospitality and medical facilities. Hotels, for example, will often have coordinated or matching draperies and bedspreads; hospitals and clinics may have patterned draperies in patient rooms and sometimes as cubicle curtains. These are finished with soil- and stain-resistant treatments. Patterns are good choices where the fabric will be handled, since patterns will not readily show soil and will hide wear better than plain fabrics (unless, of course, the patterns fade from sunlight, which makes them look worn-out prematurely).

Less Pattern

Most of the materials used in nonresidential installations, however, do not include much pattern. Rather, texture is seen for nearly every surface installation. Hard materials (stone, brick, tile, concrete) often have natural patterns that read as texture and cannot be removed. Where plaster is used, it is often textured as well. Flexible wall coverings are frequently given textures that imitate natural materials such as grass cloth, leather, suede, or marble. Fabric wall coverings can be amazingly durable as well as handsome. Natural linen and wool coverings are fine-quality examples of beauty combined with durability. Artificial fibers can also make tough, good-looking wall-covering fabrics and are often used in wall partitions or dividers in open office planning where they serve to absorb sound. Acoustical ceiling tiles, likewise, have texture and very subtle pattern, as do other ceiling panel materials—metal or fabric, for example. Textures show less soil and wear and will last longer under use and abuse than will plain fabrics. Whereas patterned fabrics and wall coverings soon become dated and the color schemes last only a few years, textured fabrics do not go out of style as quickly. This is important in nonresidential settings where the design scheme may not be changed for many years.

Safety Codes

Safety codes are laws that ensure the safety of the occupants in public spaces. Codes routinely govern fire safety, static resistance, and protection against microorganism and bacteria growth. The architect or designer must find materials that meet building codes or written building specifications. These materials have been tested and rated for their resistance to fire, static, and microorganisms. Most materials will have been tested in most of these areas, and the information will be written on the samples (part of product specifications) or available from the manufacturer. The documentation of these ratings is of prime importance in designer liability. Fire safety is obviously the most crucial of these standards. The material should also have been tested for smoke density and for the emission of toxic or poisonous gases while burning or smoldering. Flammability terms are presented under "Nonresidential Considerations" in Chapter 13, "Fabric."

Chapter 12 | Floor Materials and Coverings

Flooring Requirements and Specifications 308

Guidelines for Selecting Hard and Resilient Floor Materials 309

Soft Floor Coverings 316

Nonresidential Considerations 328

Dominic Mercadante Architect/photo © Brian Vanden Brink

Floor Requirements and Specifications

Floor coverings are a major element in an interior and deserve careful consideration as they are often permanent or long lived. The criteria that determine the choice include:

- The durability required. High-traffic areas must have floors of high durability.
- Cost of materials, installation, and maintenance in terms of time, effort, and expenses.
- Aesthetic considerations, such as establishing a particular architectural style.
- The necessity of acoustic noise control.
- Applicable insulative and solar absorption or reflection needs.
- Fire or building codes that must be met.

Calculations and Costs

Floor materials are calculated and priced per square foot or square yard:

- Hard materials such as stone, wood, wood combined with another material, and some tiles are calculated per square foot and are costly, although they are also very durable.

Figure 12.1 Slab stone is a low-upkeep, cool material well suited to the hot and sun-filled Southwestern United States. © Timothy Hursley

Figure 12.2 In this men's store, the vividly colorful tie display counterpoints a classic black and white tile flooring. *Courtesy of Zakaspace*

- **Sheet vinyl** and carpeting are calculated per square yard and cost less than most hard materials, though they are less durable.

To find the square footage, multiply the room's width by its length (in feet). Divide this figure by 9 to find the square yardage (9 square feet in 1 square yard). Because roll goods (vinyl and carpet) must be installed all in the same direction with no quarter turns, roll goods are "plotted" on a floor plan to determine exact widths and cuts (vinyl is usually 6 feet wide; carpet, 12 feet wide). Each cut (width) is multiplied by its length and then divided to determine the yardage to be ordered.

Installation costs for **stone** and **tile** are high and figured per square foot according to the charges of the installer ($6.00 or more per square foot—pr/sq/ft). Wood installation is also costly and is charged by the square foot ($4.00 or more pr/sq/ft). Wood may need professional finishing (acrylic or polyurethane), and brick may need a sealant. Carpet costs are figured per square yard and generally include pad or underlay and installation (using the tackless strip method or the direct glue-down method) at $8.00 and up.

Flooring materials are divided into three categories—hard (nonresilient), resilient, and soft. **Nonresilient flooring materials** include brick, concrete, stone, tile, and wood. **Resilient** flooring materials are asphalt tile, cork, fabric, leather, linoleum, rubber, and vinyl. Soft floor coverings include wall-to-wall carpeting and a wide selection of area rugs.

Guidelines for Selecting Hard and Resilient Floor Materials

Hard and resilient floor materials form a substantial part of the character of an interior. The integrity of flooring is so important that it is impossible to create successful interiors if the flooring appears to be cheap, a poor imitation, or of poor design or quality. Flooring is not only a background but also a material that will provide years of satisfaction in terms of beauty, durability, and upkeep.

With that in mind, it is wise to select flooring according to the following criteria:

- **Beauty** means good design merit and integrity. Flooring should be appealing even if there were no other furnishings in the interior.
- **Harmony** as a background for a variety of furnishing styles over time. Look for neutralized colors, subtle textures, and lack of a definite pattern.
- **Graceful aging** in the form of a **patina,** or mellowing of the finish through continued use. Permanent flooring is often in place for ten or twenty years, and many historic interiors that have stood the test of time feature hard materials that have lasted and continued to be beautiful for a century or more.
- **Subfloor preparation** supports and enhances the finishing material. Thin resilient floors such as vinyl require a smooth subfloor, or irregularities will show through the finish flooring. Heavy materials such as stone, tile, or brick require a sturdy subfloor, which will raise the floor level.
- **Life-cycle costing** is the total cost divided by the number of years of expected use. Surprisingly, more costly products often have a lower life-cycle cost because they don't require replacing.

- **Upkeep** means maintenance frequency and ease of cleaning. Hard flooring materials generally require less care than resilient ones. Surfaces with grooves or indentations tend to trap dirt. Natural materials are superior at camouflaging tracked-in soil.
- **Durability** is the ability to withstand traffic. Particularly in high-traffic areas, avoid flooring materials that are vulnerable to wear.
- **Safety.** Smooth hard resilient floorings without added texture are slippery, especially when wet. To avoid accidents due to visual confusion, flooring should avoid glare, three-dimensional patterns, or abrupt pattern changes that would create a depth illusion. Strollers, wheelchairs, and walkers operate best on flooring with a medium texture; avoid extremes of rugged textures (including deep carpet pile) or highly polished smooth hard materials.

Hard Floor Materials

Hard floor materials, such as brick, concrete, stone, and tile, have several advantages. Generally these materials are:

- Strong and durable.
- Nonabsorbent and relatively impervious to soiling and staining.
- Easy to maintain and clean.
- Timeless—"classics" with aesthetic appeal that lasts indefinitely.
- Versatile—adaptable for use in formal or informal, structural or decorative, textured or patterned interiors.
- Able to serve as structure as well as finish materials.

Disadvantages of hard materials include the following:

- High initial cost—although the life-cycle cost is often comparatively low.
- Subfloor preparation.
- Rigidity—a hazard for objects (and people) that may fall on the hard surface.

Table 12.1 | Stone Flooring

Exposed Aggregate

Description. Aggregate (smooth rocks or small pebbles) set or rolled into wet concrete. Part of the concrete is hosed off before it dries in order to expose the aggregate. Also called **pebble tile** or **pebble concrete.**

Applications. Interior and exterior paving. Residential and nonresidential.

Maintenance. When sealed with a polyurethane or another finish, exposed aggregate has very low upkeep. Brush vacuum.

Cost structure. Moderate to high.

Exposed Aggregate

(continued)

Stone Flooring (continued)

Flagstone

Description. Flagging describes exterior or interior paving: bluestone, quartzite, sandstone, and slate. Shape can be regular or irregular and surface will be fairly uniform.
Applications. Residential and nonresidential.
Maintenance. Little upkeep: Sweep, vacuum, or damp mop if necessary.
Cost structure. High.

Flagstone

Granite

Description. A very hard crystalline rock with small amounts of feldspar, quartz, and other minerals in crystal or grain form. Crystals vary from very fine to fairly coarse. The colors vary from light to dark values and variations of gray, pink, green, brown, and black. May be rough-hewn or smooth and polished.
Applications. Floors and countertops; used in high-end residential and nonresidential settings.
Maintenance. Low upkeep: Wipe, sweep, vacuum, or damp mop if necessary. Use very mild detergent and remove soap residue. Polish with cloths.
Cost structure. High.

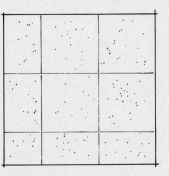

Granite

Limestone

Description. A calcite (calcium carbonate) stone with a light-grayish neutralized color. It has little to no grain, with a typically matte or dull finish.
Applications. Residential and nonresidential flooring in high-traffic areas. Fireplace surrounds and mantelpieces.
Maintenance. Sweep, vacuum, or damp mop with clear lukewarm water.
Cost structure. High.

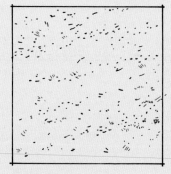

Limestone

Marble and Terrazzo

Description. A metamorphic stone, granular or crystalline, white or colored, often with streaks. The hardest and typically the most expensive of the stones. May be cut into thin sheets or slabs. Can be polished to a high sheen. Cold to the touch. **Terrazzo** is a composite flooring of broken chips of marble set into cement and polished to a sheen. May be tiles or poured as a solid floor. This is a practical use of marble, since up to 50 percent waste occurs from breakage at the quarry.
Applications. Floors, fireplace hearths. High-end residential and nonresidential installations.
Maintenance. Clean with warm water and infrequently with soap and water, taking care to rinse well; soap residue will render the floor slippery.
Cost structure. High.

Marble parquet

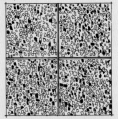

Terrazzo

Stone Flooring (continued)

Slate

Description. A metamorphic, finely grained rock that cleaves or splits naturally into layers. Slabs are ½- to **1**-inch thick. The surface may be (1) fairly rough (if it is a natural cleft or split); (2) rubbed with sand to achieve an even plane; or (3) honed, producing a smooth finish with a patina or mellow glow. Colors vary from grays to greenish or reddish grays to blacks and browns.

Applications. Residential and nonresidential settings.

Maintenance. Low upkeep: Sweep, vacuum, clean with mild soap and water. Do not wax.

Cost structure. Moderate to high.

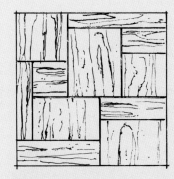

Slate

Travertine

Description. A light-colored limestone rock formed near mineral springs. Trapped gas in the stone causes holes and interesting textures. When used as flooring, the holes are filled with cement or epoxy.

Applications. Residential and nonresidential. Floors, stair treads, fireplace hearths.

Maintenance. Vacuum, wash when necessary with clear lukewarm water. Wash no more often than every six months with soap and water and rinse thoroughly to prevent a slippery surface.

Cost structure. High.

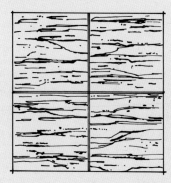

Travertine

Table 12.2 | **Tile, Brick, and Concrete Flooring**

Ceramic Tile

Description. Fine, white clays formed and glazed before the first or second firing. Shiny or smooth to patterned to rough and matte (dull). **Mosaic** tiles are small tiles set into a pattern; may be preset sheets, a face mount or back mount, ready to be set with grout.

Applications. Nonresidential and residential. Entryways, bathrooms/rest rooms, kitchens, solariums, high-traffic areas, countertops.

Maintenance. Low upkeep: Sweep, vacuum, wipe, damp mop, or soap and water for heavy dirt. Grout may soil and discolor. Silicone treatments will make grout less susceptible to soil.

Cost structure. Low to high—with moderate to high installation.

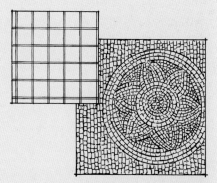

Ceramic Tile   Mosaic Tile

Mexican Tile

Description. Hand-shaped clay taken from the ground and left to set before firing. Imperfections of hand labor add to the tiles' charm. Thick, fragile, rustic. Tiles may be decorated and glazed.

Applications. Large squares are used in residential and nonresidential settings.

Maintenance. Porous surface should be treated with linseed oil or paste wax. Sweep, dust mop, wax, and buff. Rewax or reoil when tile shows signs of wear.

Cost structure. Low to moderate, plus installation.

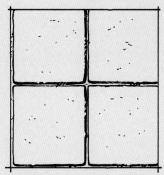

Mexican Tile   *(continued)*

Tile, Brick, and Concrete Flooring (continued)

Quarry Tile

Description. Fine-colored clay and graded shale. Most is a terra-cotta rust/red, the color of the natural clay. It may be glazed but usually is left natural. Square or hexagonal shapes are most popular.

Applications. Residential and nonresidential flooring and countertops.

Maintenance. Same as for ceramic tile.

Cost structure. Low to moderate, plus installation.

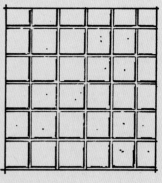

Quarry Tile

Brick

Description. Clay, shale, and water mixed, colored, and shaped into solid or hollow rectanglar blocks and then fired to harden. Solid bricks for flooring are ¾ to 2 inches thick and are referred to as pavers.

Applications. Interior and exterior floors and patio paving, residential and nonresidential.

Maintenance. Low upkeep: Sweep, dust, vacuum, damp mop, or buff.

Cost structure. Moderate to high.

Brick

Concrete

Description. Portland cement, sand, gravel or rock aggregate, and water mixed and poured into forms or slabs, texturized. Hardens as it sets. Naturally gray but may be colored.

Applications. Subfloors and floors may be cast or stamped into shapes. Nonresidential flooring. May be both structural element and finish material.

Sealed, textured concrete is used for custom countertops.

Maintenance. Raw concrete absorbs stains and generates dust; painted or sealed concrete is impervious to stains as long as the paint or finish remains intact. Sweep, damp mop, or hose off where possible.

Sealed countertops: Use mild detergent; wipe as customary.

Cost structure. Moderate.

Concrete

Table 12.3 | Wood and Laminate Flooring

Wood Planks and Parquet

Description. Oak, maple, cherry, teak, or pine strips range from 1½ to 2¼ inches wide and 2 to 7 feet in length. **Random-plank** widths range from 3 to 8 inches, typically installed in three varying sizes. Strips and random plank are tongue and groove to fit snugly together. **Parquet** is strips or squares set into shapes.

Applications. Residential and nonresidential flooring. Solid wood may come prefinished or may be impregnated with stain and acrylic for a durable nonresidential surface.

Maintenance. Depends on the finish: Oiled or waxed wood will need protection against moisture, require dust mopping frequently, and need rewaxing. Two finishes used frequently today are polyurethane and acrylic. These require only sweeping, dust mopping, or vacuuming and occasionally damp mopping with a water-vinegar solution. Hard (liquid) wax can be used on top.

Cost structure. Moderate to high.

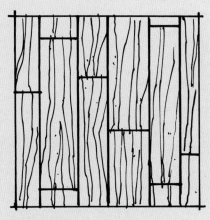

Random plank

Basketweave parquet

Basketweave/octagonal parquet

Herringbone parquet

Bamboo Flooring

Description. Bamboo flooring is a rapidly renewable resource made from hollow round shoots of the bamboo Asian grass plant that matures in three years, regenerates without need for replanting, and requires minimal fertilization or pesticides. Although it is not wood, bamboo flooring is categorized with hardwood flooring. Bamboo is attractive because it is very hard, strong, and dimensionally stable. Bamboo floors provide a very rich visual texture, with thin strips of varying color interrupted by the bamboo nodes. It installs similar to standard hardwood flooring.

Applications. Residential and nonresidential flooring where green products are desirable.

Maintenance. Comparable to wood flooring.

Cost structure. Slightly more expensive than flooring from domestic hardwoods.

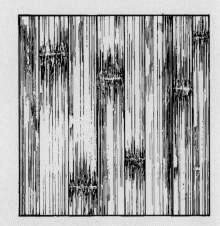

Bamboo

Wood and Laminate Flooring (continued)

Laminate

Description. Wood particleboard with a hard, durable composite vinyl layer laminated (glued under heat and pressure) to bond to the wood core.

Applications. Imitation-wood floor planks and parquet; countertops. Flooring for residential or lower traffic areas of nonresidential interiors.

Maintenance. Dust mop, sweep, or damp mop. Countertops: Wipe with cloths or nonabrasive scrubbers and cleaning preparations as needed.

Cost structure. Moderate.

Figure 12.3 Wood flooring provides a visual connection between living spaces. *Stephen Blatt Architects/photo © Brian Vanden Brink*

- Chilliness—hard materials tend to be cold to the touch unless heated artificially or by sunshine.
- Acoustic "liveness"—being nonporous, hard materials reflect sound and amplify noise. This effect is often mitigated by using hard materials as a background for softer, sound-absorbing area rugs.

Resilient Floor Materials

Resilient materials have flexibility or give. These include cork, fabric, leather, rubber, and most vinyls. Like hard materials, resilient floor materials have common sets of advantages and disadvantages.

The advantages of resilient flooring are:

- Initial cost is generally lower than that for hard materials.
- Resilient floor materials are warmer to the touch.
- By absorbing more sound, they produce quieter, more comforting interiors.
- They are easier on the body for standing and thereby produce less fatigue.

- Items dropped are less likely to break, and less damage is done to the floor itself because of its ability to give (resilience).
- There is a wide variety of designs or patterns, colors, and even visual textures (particularly in the vinyl flooring types).
- The maintenance is moderate, depending on the finish and the durability of the finish.

Disadvantages of resilient flooring include the following:

- They may require more maintenance and cleaning if the surface has no protection or as a no-wax surface treatment wears off.
- Resilient floors can be damaged, dented, or torn by dropping sharp objects such as kitchen knives or by dragging furniture or appliances across the surface.
- Resilient floorings are less durable than hard floor materials, making them a costly choice in the long run due to the necessity of replacement.
- If poorly installed, seams will open and will become worn.

Table 12.4 | Resilient Floor Materials

Cork

Description. The outer layer of cork of the cork oak tree, a broadleaf evergreen that grows in the Mediterranean region. Light in color, elastic, insulative, and sound absorbent. Usually treated with a vinyl coating or impregnation, removing some of its resilience but making it a more durable product.

Applications. Residential and nonresidential settings where a quiet surface is required for low or limited traffic.

Maintenance. Vinyl-cork floors may be damp mopped or buffed. They tend to show dust and footprints easily.

Cost structure. Moderate to high.

Leather

Description. Squares or tiles of leather, the tanned hide of cattle and swine. Dyed brown or other colors. Embossed with patterns historically. Leather may be cut into strips and made into shag-type area rugs.

Applications. High-end residential in small, low-traffic areas. Quiet flooring.

Maintenance. Damp mop with very mild detergent; no saddle soap.

Cost structure. Very high.

Linoleum

Description. A mixture of oxidized linseed oil, ground cork and wood, color pigments, and gums, poured onto a backing of canvas, burlap, or jute. **Linoleum** is a highly durable, ecologically friendly substance. Unlike vinyl, it does not release PVCs into the air. It can last fifty years and more and still be an excellent flooring. In fact, it continues to become more durable after installation due to the oxidation of the linseed oil. This smooth and washable flooring is primarily produced in Europe.

Application. Residential and some nonresidential.

Maintenance. Damp mop, sweep, vacuum. Polish/wax products are optional.

Cost structure. Moderate

Rubber

Description. Tiles made of butadiene styrene rubber and synthetic materials come in two forms: a flat surface with a marbleized pattern and with raised discs or squares—a solid colored three-dimensional surface. The latter was designed to knock dirt off shoes and to provide water drainage off the surface.

Applications. Primarily nonresidential flooring.

Maintenance. Sweep or vacuum. May be washed with detergent and water. Rinsed and mopped with a water and 5 percent liquid bleach solution. Buff for shine return. New floors require more buffing.

Cost structure. Moderately high.

Vinyl

Description. Vinyl is a shortened name for polyvinyl chloride (or PVC), a plastic solution that hardens to a solid film. Many materials may be coated with vinyl, such as cork and fabric.

Vinyl Composition

Description. A blended composition of vinyl, resin, plasticizer, and coloring agents formed into sheets under pressure and heat. Sheets or tiles. Vinyl is also called resilient sheet flooring.

Applications. Both residential and nonresidential settings, primarily health care, as it is an even, solid surface that can be kept clean.

Maintenance. Sweep, vacuum, damp mop; detergent. May be waxed.

Cost structure. Moderate to moderately high.

(continued)

Figure 12.4 Resilient sheet flooring provides graphic design and relative warmth and quiet in the Portland, Maine, Children's Museum. *Stephen Blatt Architects/photo © Brian Vanden Brink*

Resilient Floor Materials (continued)

Sheet Vinyl

Description. Vinyl resilient sheet flooring comes in 6-, 9-, and 12-foot widths. There are two kinds of sheet vinyl. One is a solid or **inlaid vinyl,** built up with successive layers of vinyl granules that are usually plain or patterned with a suggestion of texture. The other type, called **rotogravure or roto,** is a printed pattern. The surface is coated with vinyl or vinyl/urethane (a thinner layer), called the wear layer. Both types of vinyl may or may not have a cushioned backing.

Applications. Flooring, both residential and nonresidential. Nonresidential vinyls are thicker or have a thicker wear layer.

Maintenance. Most sheet vinyl is given a no-wax surface to help maintain a shiny surface. However, heavy traffic, furniture movement, and detergents may remove the shine. Damp mopping with a water and vinegar solution will help keep the shine. Vinyl floors may be waxed.

Cost structure. Moderate to moderately high.

Vinyl Tile

Description. Solid vinyl is composed of PVC, plasticizers, pigments or coloring agents, mineral fillers, and stabilizers. Available in solid colors, plus patterns such as marble, travertine, slate, brick, and stone. Some vinyl tiles may have a wood veneer sealed between layers.

Applications. Flooring, both residential and nonresidential.

Maintenance. Sweep, vacuum, damp mop (as for sheet vinyl) without detergents, which can dull the finish.

Cost structure. Moderately low.

Vinyl resilient sheet flooring

Soft Floor Coverings

Carpeting

Carpet, particularly wall-to-wall installed carpet, has become a standard item in interior design. The use and placement of **broadloom carpet** (12-feet wide on average) is restricted only by the aesthetic and maintenance requirements of the room. Carpets are made in many fibers and in a wide selection of colors, textures, and prices. The quality of the carpet and how well it will wear can be difficult to determine when examining the store sample. The small size of most carpet samples also makes it hard to visualize the effect of an entire area covered in that carpet. The following guidelines may be helpful:

- **Understand the fibers** used in carpeting (Table 12.5) and the advantages and disadvantages of each.
- **Learn carpet constructions** and the selection of textures available.
- **Look for guarantees** against flaws (holes, streaks, color variations) or after-installation problems (such as fading, premature crushing, or pile loss).
- **Purchase locally** from carpet dealers known for business integrity, quality installation, and service.
- **Compare quality.** Poor-quality, inexpensive carpets can appear similar to moderately priced carpets yet have inferior-quality yarns, less latex glue to hold the primary and secondary backing together (see "Tufted Broadloom Carpets"), and other compromises not immediately apparent. These carpets will wear out faster and need replacing much sooner, thereby costing more than a good-quality carpet.
- **Ask for recommendations** from sales personnel for carpets that will stand up to wear and traffic. See if there is a written guarantee of quality and durability.
- **Determine quality** with hand tests. Bend back the face of a tufted carpet to reveal the primary backing. This is called making the carpet "grin." If a lot of primary backing is exposed, the tufts are not close together and the carpet will likely mat or crush under traffic. When close together or dense, the carpet will have better resilience. Also try untwisting the pile to see if it may become fuzzy, and pull the pile to determine if the face will lose fibers.
- **Take the carpet sample to the site** where it will be installed. Evaluate color during different times of the day and at night with artificial light, and walk on it to determine whether it will show footprints or crush easily. Drop thread or other debris on the surface and evaluate whether it will readily show soil.
- **Select color wisely.** For a heavy-traffic area, select a color medium in value (not too light or not too dark) and

Figure 12.5 Results from a wear test in a Hong Kong subway station, where a half-million commuters walked across it. (A) Anything Goes! ® Carpet retained resilience and surface appearance. (B) An ordinary pile with similar density and thickness, subjected to the same half-million commuters, lost its tuft twist and remained frayed and matted even after cleaning. *Photos courtesy of Shaw Industries*

Carpet Fibers

Most carpets are constructed of a single fiber, such as nylon. However, there are an increasing number of carpets made of blended fibers, such as 65 percent wool and 35 percent acrylic, or 80 percent nylon and 20 percent wool or polyester. These and other blends are popular for three reasons:

1. A blend has the positive qualities of each fiber; it is durable and may be pleasing to the touch.
2. A more costly fiber can be extended with the combination of less expensive fibers.
3. Cross-dyeing effects can be obtained by coloring the yarn with a single dyestuff—the two different fibers take the dye differently, creating a two-tone effect.

Table 12.5 lists carpet fibers and their sources, advantages and disadvantages, maintenance requirements, and cost structures. There are many quality levels of each of these fibers, both natural and synthetic. Higher-quality fibers make the carpet perform better and last longer, but they cost more per square yard.

Woven Broadloom Carpet

Broadloom carpets are woven or tufted by machine and are typically 12 feet wide.

- A **Wilton carpet** is woven on the **Jacquard** loom. It allows complex patterns to be constructed, and each color is carried as a separate **weft** or bank of yarns beneath the face of the design, making Wilton carpets

low in intensity (fairly dull). This will hide the shadows and soiling caused by foot traffic. Patterned carpet will increase the life span of a carpet under heavy use because pattern can effectively hide both soil and wear.

- **Compare the carpet's life span to its aesthetics.** A vivid or demanding color may prove tiresome sooner than would a more neutralized carpet. Neutrals and neutralized colors are flexible for redecorating, which may take place several times during the life span of a carpet.
- **Select a quality padding or underlay,** and check to see that the padding delivered to the site is the one you selected.
- **The quality of installation** may determine how the carpet looks, lays, and performs. Insist on the most highly skilled carpet installers that can be hired in your vicinity.
- **Upgrade carpeting** to a better quality than the standard allotment for carpet in new construction. Lower-quality carpeting costs more in the long run because it will wear out quickly and require replacement and labor to remove and install.

Figure 12.6 Wilton carpet, as seen here, is a quality soft flooring custom-designed and woven to meet high-end interior design specifications. *Old World Weavers, fabric division of Stark Carpet, room design by Scott Salvator Inc.*

Table 12.5 | Carpet Fibers Comparison

Wool

Source. Wool is the fiber taken from domesticated sheep. It varies from very fine to very coarse, as well as varying in length. Shorter staple lengths are used in lesser-quality and longer staple lengths in higher-quality wool carpets. Wool may be dyed any color or left in natural white, cream, brown, or gray, as are **berber carpets.**

Advantages. Long a standard of comparison as a durable carpet fiber, wool is resilient due to its overlapping scale, giving it long life and resistance to crushing. It takes dyes beautifully and is woven and tufted into carpets of high quality. It is used in pile for Oriental, folk, and designer rugs.

Disadvantages. Wool carpets must be treated for moth resistance. When wet, wool emits a distinctive animal smell. Some people are allergic to wool. It is susceptible to **fuzzing** (fibers working loose) and **pilling** (fibers working into small balls or pills). Wool is the most costly of the carpet fibers.

Maintenance. Wool should be vacuumed regularly and spots cleaned immediately. Wool takes a long time to dry but may be wet cleaned. Professional dry-cleaning methods are recommended. Avoid scrubbing brushes that could untwist the pile or encourage pilling.

Cost structure. High.

Nylon

Source. A manufactured synthetic based on the raw materials phenol, hydrogen, oxygen, and nitrogen. Nylon is heated into a solution and then extruded into long threads that may be texturized and cut into staple (short fibers) to meet requirements of the many textures found in nylon carpet.

Advantages. Nylon is the most widely used carpet fiber, accounting for over 90 percent of all carpeting sold alone or combined with other fibers. A flexible fiber used for level-loop carpets and cut piles, both tufted and woven, and used often for **accent** or **scatter rugs.** Nylon is strong, durable, resilient, and abrasion resistant, has good color retention, hides dirt, and has excellent bulk. There is a minimum of fuzzing and pilling; it is nonallergenic and mildew and insect resistant. It also has good flame resistance.

Disadvantages. First- and second-generation (chemical composition) nylons are prone to static electricity and have a harsh sheen and unpleasant touch. However, these weaknesses have been overcome. Fifth-generation nylons are guaranteed against stains and soiling. However, there are many quality levels of nylon, and some of these problems may still exist.

Maintenance. Nylon cleans exceptionally well. It should be vacuumed regularly and spot cleaned as needed. Both steam or wet and dry or chemical cleaning are effective. Accent or scatter rugs may be machine washed and dried.

Cost structure. Moderate.

Olefin/Polypropylene

Source. Olefin and **polypropylene** carpets are made of ethylene or propane gas constituted into a synthetic long-chain polymer. Polypropylenes are modified olefins.

Advantages. Olefin is lightweight, inexpensive, durable, and strong. It resists fuzzing, pilling, and abrasion. Used for indoor and outdoor carpeting, nonresidential carpeting, and carpet tiles. Also used for artificial turf.

Disadvantages. Olefin is less soft to the touch. Must be treated for resistance to sunlight fading and deterioration. Tends to crush, pill, and stain. Less durable than nylon.

Maintenance. Vacuum regularly. Cleans well; is unaffected by moisture and most chemicals and acids.

Cost structure. Low to moderate.

Polyester

Source. Polyester is a synthetic long-chain polymer derived from a reaction between dicarboxylic acid and dihydric alcohol.

Advantages. Polyester takes and holds dyes well. Next to acrylic, it most closely resembles wool because of its dyeability and softness. Polyester is mildew and moth resistant, nonallergenic, and nonabsorbent. It is a durable fiber that resists fuzzing and pilling. Polyester is soft and cool to the touch.

Disadvantages. Polyester crushes easily and must be **heat-set** to maintain yarn twist. Heat-set polyesters are good selections for residential areas with light traffic. Polyester lacks warmth and tends to hold oil-borne stains.

Cost structure. Moderate to moderately high, depending on the quality of the fiber.

Acrylic

Source. Acrylic is a synthetic fiber composed mainly of acrylonitrile and can be texturized and cut into staple fibers and spun into a bulky yarn.

Advantages. Acrylic is the fiber that is most similar to wool. It looks like wool, so it is often combined with wool to lower the cost. It is soft and warm to the touch. Acrylic is often used to imitate wool berber carpet.

Disadvantages. Acrylic has low resilience, mats easily, and fuzzes and pills. It has a relatively short life span compared to wool or nylon, but its life span increases dramatically when blended with either of these two fibers. Acrylic is vulnerable to oil-borne stains, which are difficult to remove.

Maintenance. Acrylic responds well to wet cleaning, but care must be taken to avoid brushing and untwisting the fibers, as they will mat down and pill more easily when they have been loosened. Vacuum regularly and remove spots immediately.

Cost structure. Moderate.

heavy and substantial. Wiltons are nearly always of quality wool and are very costly. They are seen most often in exclusive areas of nonresidential interior design.

- **Axminster carpets** are also Jacquard woven but without the extra **warps.** Only the colors needed are inserted, making complex patterns possible without great expense. Axminster carpets are of wool or nylon and are seen in many kinds of nonresidential settings such as restaurants, theaters, retail businesses, and hotels. Axminster carpets are readily adaptable to custom design, and in cases where they are still cost prohibitive, carpeting can be printed to imitate the design.
- **Velvet weave carpets** are also woven but without any design. They may be solid or woven of variegated yarn, usually of wool or a wool and nylon blend.

Tufted Broadloom Carpets

Tufted carpets make up the majority of carpets today. They are constructed on a loom that employs multiple needles threaded with the yarn. The carpet yarn is punched into the primary backing in a zigzag pattern, which holds the yarn in place in case of a loose tuft that is pulled. The tufts are held securely with a **latex** coating (rubber-based glue) that also holds on a secondary backing of polypropylene.

Some tufted carpets have no secondary backing, and custom hand-tufted area rugs have a layer of latex to which is affixed a loosely woven scrim textile that adds some stability to the construction. **Rubber-backed tufted carpets** are tufted into a thick rubber-cushioned backing and directly glued to the surface. **Fuse-bonded carpets** (such as artificial turf) are tufted into a heavy layer of latex and are also directly glued down without padding. There are many levels of quality in the construction of tufted carpets.

Other Carpet Constructions

- **Knitted carpets** are constructed of knitted yarns held together with a latex backing. They account for very few carpets on the market.
- **Needlepunch carpets** are masses of fibers (rather than yarns) that are held together by an interlocking fiber-punching machine. They are inexpensive and durable and come in yardage and square tiles with or without a latex backing. They may be installed over a pad or glued down directly.

Carpet Textures

Carpet texture means the pile surface. Yarns are cut or looped, fine or bulky, one level or multilevel:

- **Cut-pile** surfaces are sheared to one height or multilevel. This term encompasses all textures that are not loop textures.

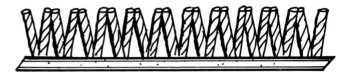

(A)

- **Plush** carpets are cut pile, densely tufted (close together) and with a short pile. Residential plush carpeting is typically one solid color; it tends to show traffic and vacuum marks, which emphasize the plush quality that imitates the density of Oriental rugs. Nonresidential plush carpeting can also be two-tone or subtle patterns, which hide wear.

(B)

- **Frieze** (fri-zay') yarns are tightly twisted, for greater resilience. Many residential frieze carpets are slightly two-toned and referred to as "trackless" since they hide dirt and footprints. Frieze is physically and visually a durable carpet texture.

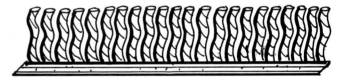

(C)

- **Sculptured** multilevel textures consist of various levels of cut pile or of loops (also called multiloop or embossed loop). They may also be tufted of variegated yarn (colors vary), producing a type of random pattern. Deep sculpturing of cut pile, seen in some residential carpeting, can weaken the resilience, whereas tightly tufted carpet with understated sculpturing (nonresidential) can be very strong and resilient.

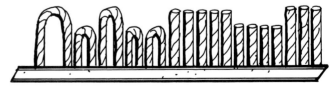

(D)

Figure 12.7 Carpet textures. (A) cut pile; (B) plush; (C) frieze; (D) sculptured.

- **Deep-pile** or **shag** carpets have returned to the residential market. Quality deep-pile carpets are tufted tightly and are both durable and luxurious. They are an "upgrade" carpet, costing more than a typical cut-pile carpet.

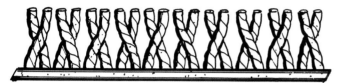

(E)

- **Level loop,** also called **round-wire construction,** is the most common short-pile nonresidential carpeting. Yarns are looped over wires for uniformity and then the wires are removed. Level-loop textures are strong, durable, and resilient but not soft to the touch.

(F)

- **Random** or **level-tip** is a nonresidential short pile of cut and loop texture in which the cut pile is the same height as the loops, creating a more plush texture with the strength of level-loop textures.

(G)

- **Nonresidential carpet textures** are often used in residential interiors where durability, strength, and longevity are more important than luxury and softness. Applications often include hallways, stairs, home offices, family rooms, and perhaps children's rooms.

Installation Methods and Padding

Carpet can be installed according to two basic methods.

Direct glue-down uses no separate cushion and is suitable for any type of carpet. Reasons for direct glue-down include:

- Averting potentially dangerous ripples, which are a hazard in high-traffic and especially nonresidential installations
- Saving the expense of the pad, tackless strip, and labor to install two layers
- Doing installations where no softness is required

Pad and tackless strip uses a pad attached to a thin board with tacks that protrude toward the wall. The pad is stapled, nailed, or glued down. Using equipment that stretches the carpet, the installer hooks the carpet over the tacks and then pounds the tacks into the carpet. The padding for this method is available in several types, listed here in order of popularity:

- **Urethane foam** is made from synthetic polymers in varying thicknesses. It may be formed to be extra dense.
- **Chopped urethane,** or **rebond,** is bonded into sheets with additives such as paper, vinyl, fabric-backed foam, or wood chips. This factor makes bonded foam subject to various quality levels.
- **Foam rubber pads** are firm, flat sheets made from natural or synthetic rubbers. They are suitable for medium traffic.
- **Sponge rubber pads** combine natural and synthetic rubber and fillers to form a flat or a waffle sponge, suitable for light to medium traffic. With age and wear, rubber will disintegrate.
- **Felt padding** was originally animal hair. Though **animal-hair felt padding** is now rare, a **combination felt padding** made of some animal hair and some synthetic fibers is more common, while **fiber felt padding** is all synthetic. Felt is firmer than other padding materials, making it an excellent substrate for Oriental rugs, whose backing can be damaged by too much resilience.

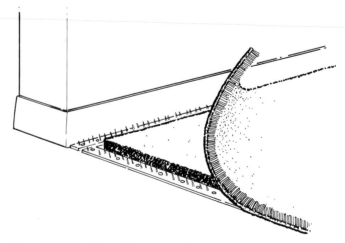

Figure 12.8 Tackless strips are nailed next to the wall, then padding or underlay is stapled down (if subfloor is wood), and carpet backing is hooked into angled staples to anchor it securely to the floor.

Figure 12.7 (continued) Carpet textures. (E) shag; (F) level loop or round-wire construction; (G) random or level-tip.

Carpet Maintenance and Cleaning

The appearance and life span of a carpet often depend on the way it is maintained. Although heavy traffic will wear carpet out faster, keeping the carpet clean is a key to good looks and to increasing its life span. Soil allowed to stay on the surface of a carpet is not only unsightly; the longer it is left, the more difficult it is to remove. When dirt, grit, or sand settles to the bottom of the pile, it can abrade the yarns at the base, wear them off, and eventually destroy the carpet.

In heavy-traffic areas such as hallways and rooms that contain traffic lanes, carpeting should be vacuumed every day. Areas of little traffic, such as bedrooms, usually require vacuuming only once a week. A light vacuuming is three times back and forth, and a thorough vacuuming is seven times back and forth. Repetitive vacuuming loosens and pulls the dirt from the base to the surface and then sucks it up into the machine.

Spots should be removed as quickly as possible and never allowed to remain on the carpet long enough to become set. Mild detergent and clear water are useful for many stains, and oil- or tar-based stains can be removed with a commercially prepared dry-cleaning solution. Carpet stores will often recommend products or sell kits for cleaning spots.

Carpets should be cleaned when they become so soiled that vacuuming or spot-cleaning the carpet no longer keeps the surface looking good.

- Steam extraction forces very hot detergent solution into the carpet and then extracts it immediately with a suction or wet vacuum.

- Carpet cleaning can also be done by spraying a solution onto the carpet and following with suction extraction. This may be called dry cleaning as there is less moisture in the carpet.

Rugs

Rugs add softness and warmth, provide positive acoustical properties, and give character and richness to interiors. A fine rug can be the basis for interior design furnishings and may even be the focal point in a room. **Area rugs** define an area, such as a conversation area or placement under a dining table, and may include many of the types of rugs discussed below.

Authentic Oriental Rugs

Oriental rugs are knotted or tied by hand by native craftspeople from Iran, Turkey, Romania, the Caucasus, Afghanistan, Pakistan, India, Tibet, and China. The finest Oriental rugs originated in what was called Persia (today primarily Iran) at the height of the rug-weaving era in the fifteenth century. An Oriental rug is typically composed of a cotton warp, pile knots of wool or sometimes silk, and a cotton weft inserted after every two rows of knots. The design and colors are drawn on graph paper and called a cartoon. Patterns are symmetrical, often mirroring the design on all four corners. The finer the warp and knots and the greater the number of knots per square inch, the more intricate the patterns. Fine rugs have 400 knots or more per square inch and can take months to weave in a rug-weaving center and years if the weaver is working alone.

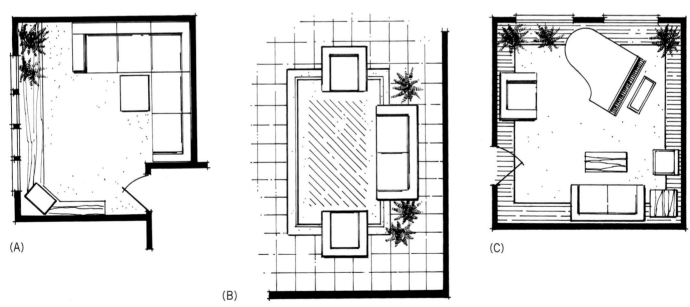

(A) (B) (C)

Figure 12.9 Floor coverings help define space. (A) Wall-to-wall carpeting unifies an entire room. (B) An area rug defines a portion of the room, such as a conversation grouping. (C) A room-sized rug nearly covers the room; the exposed floor forms a border adjoining the walls.

Figure 12.10 An authentic Persian oriental rug placed over a wood floor of wide, random planks. © *Susan Gilmore/Esto*

Oriental rug weaving is an art and skill of the highest order, and this is reflected in prices of the finer rugs:

- **Antique Oriental rugs** are older than seventy-five years and are the most costly if they are in good to excellent condition.
- **Semiantique rugs** are those from twenty-five to seventy-five years.
- **New rugs** are less than twenty-five years old.

Oriental rugs will often increase in value over the years despite some wear. This is true even of new rugs if they are authentic and woven in the area where they originate, called the traditional rug-weaving area. Nontraditional rug-weaving areas, such as India, have made traditional designs readily available.

It takes an expert to evaluate and appraise a rug. It is best to shop for an Oriental rug at a reputable dealership that specializes in them.

Oriental rugs are divided into Persian, Caucasian, Tibetan, and Chinese rugs.

Persian rugs have intricate curving patterns, are often floral, and have high knot counts. Persian rugs from Iran are considered the finest rugs, although there is a great variety in quality. Persian rugs are also produced in India and surrounding countries. The best-known types are the Hamadan, Hereke, Herez, Isfahan, Kashan, Kerman (Kirman), Nain, Qum, Sarouk (Saruk), Senneh, Sereband, Shiraz, Shirvan, and Tabriz.

Figure 12.11 An abstract Turkish Oriental rug warms and anchors the conversation grouping in this clean, contemporary interior. *Elliott Elliott Norelius Architecture/photo* © *Brian Vanden Brink*

Figure 12.12 Types of Oriental and area rugs.

Complex Persian Oriental rug. Fine rugs have over 400 hand-tied knots per square inch; more knots yield curved lines.

Persian prayer rugs are unique in that they contain a Moorish arch imitative of those found in mosques. These rugs are often very finely woven with complex designs and may have a wool or silk pile. They are used as wall hangings as well as accent rugs. Historically, these rugs were carried by Islamic peoples, who would point the arch toward the holy city of Mecca to prostrate and pray at designated times.

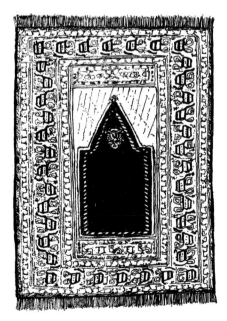

Persian prayer rug

Caucasian or **Turkish rugs** are generally those from the Caucasus region in the former Soviet republic, and Turkish rugs originated in Turkey, though many are produced in Afghanistan, Pakistan, and India. These rugs are generally coarser, of brighter primary colors, and with simpler and geometric designs. Best known are the Afghan, Belouch, Bokhara, Kazak, Kurd, Qashqa'i (Kashkai), Tekke (Tekke Turkoman), and Yomut (Yamout).

Caucasian or Turkish rug

Tibetan rugs are a type of deeper-pile Caucasian rugs. Made in Tibet and Nepal in styles dictated by Western tastes, these rugs are woven of very coarse yarns and in abstract, almost undefined patterns in earthy or faded colors and with streaked effects. They are primitive and

Tibetan rug

coarse and have been well received in contemporary interiors as a counterpoint to the world of high technology.

Chinese rugs are woven with a deeper pile of coarse wool (fewer knots per square inch). By law, all modern Chinese rugs have the same number of knots per square inch. Designs may be traditional—with open background, central medallion, and a large-scale border, typically in cream, Ming blue, gold, and/or red. They may also copy designs from Persia and France, or they may be contemporary patterns. All will be sculptured or beveled on both sides of the design, giving a deeper, richer look and emphasizing the design.

Indian dhurrie rug

Chinese rug

Rugs from India and surrounding countries have made Oriental rugs more readily available. Since labor costs are low and skill is high, rugs of all types are produced there. By law, all wool is native, and quality varies. Chinese rug depth and sculpturing is applied to French patterns and termed **Indo-Aubusson rugs.** Flat folk rugs are also produced in great quantity in India.

Folk Rugs

Folk rugs can be defined as any rug woven by an ethnic group or reflecting the native heritage of a country. Folk rugs are flat weave or pile weave, generally of wool.

The **dhurrie** (dhurry, durry) and **kilim rugs** have been produced for centuries in India and Romania, respectively. Indian dhurries were traditionally of cotton, so few authentic antiques exist; Romanian kilims were of wool. In both rugs, folk designs are woven with no pile. They are reversible, and they vary from dark and vivid to pale colors. Designs are often geometric but may be

Romanian kilim

based on floral patterns or have only textures and no patterns. Today the designs and colors are largely dictated by Western tastes, where the market has been strong.

Navajo rugs are made in the southwestern United States—Arizona and New Mexico, primarily. These flat tapestry rugs reflect Native American (Indian) tribe motifs and colors—geometric, angular, simple patterns in gray, cream, white, black, brown, rust, and red. Navajo rugs can be valuable as investments, although they are imitated by Mexican laborers who produce knockoffs,

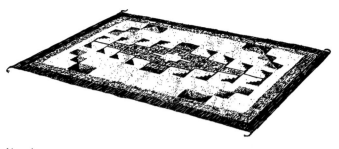

Navajo rug

Rag rug

Braided rug

Scandinavian rya rug

which are not valuable. The types of Navajo rugs include the Chinle, Crystal, Ganado-Klagetoh (Ganado Red), Shiprock-Lukachukai (Yei and Yeibechi), the Storm Pattern, Teec Nos Pos, Two Gray Hills, and Wide Ruins. Of these, the finest weave and most valuable are the Two Gray Hills rugs.

The **rya** and **rollikan rugs** are the best known of the Scandinavian rugs. The rya is a hand-knotted deep pile rug in abstract designs and contemporary colors. The rollikan is a flat tapestry rug that reflects the simplified, modern tastes influenced by the folk arts and flowers of Scandinavia.

Rag, braided, and **hooked rugs** are the New England colonists' contribution to folk rugs. These rugs were made of clothing that was no longer usable (rags) and turned into utilitarian floor coverings. Rag rugs are plain-weave, flat rugs, originally woven on a floor or hand loom. Braided rugs are made of strips of fabric, braided and sewn into an oval or circle. Both rag and braided rugs are produced by hand and machine today. Hooked rugs are made by inserting strips of fabric into a heavy scrim or burlap backing cloth; they form simple patterns, usually floral.

European Handmade Rugs

The best known of the European rugs are the French Savonnerie and Aubusson, the Portuguese needlepoint, and the Spanish rugs.

Savonnerie rugs have been produced at the Savonnerie factory in France for over 300 years. These rugs are a hand-knotted pile, traditionally with deep, rich, vivid colors and large-scale patterns. The Savonnerie rugs produced there today may be of very contemporary patterns as well as the historical French motifs of the Baroque (Louis XIV) and Empire periods.

Aubusson rugs are named after the factory where they were first produced. These French rugs are flat tapestry weaves, historically of Oriental rug–inspired motifs in faded or muted colors. These rugs were particularly favored during the reign of Louis XVI, when light-scaled Neoclassic designs were in vogue. Today Aubusson rugs may have floral or abstract/modern patterns.

Needlepoint rugs are mainly produced in Portugal and China. Although some needlepoints are machine made, authentic needlepoints are still hand-embroidered wool on a heavy scrim. The characteristic round stitches are usually formed into lovely floral patterns. These rugs are popular because of their European flavor.

French Savonnerie rug

French Aubusson rug

Portuguese needlepoint rug

Designer Rugs

Designer rugs are made to custom specifications by several companies in America. The rugs are most often hand or machine tufted of quality wool onto a canvaslike fabric and then coated with a latex to hold the stitches in place. There may be a heavy fabric sewn onto the back as a secondary backing. The value of designer rugs lies in the freedom and creativity possible. The rug may be a simplified, enlarged version of a selected textile. It may have large- or small-scale patterns and a variety of pile heights and yarn textures. The size and shape are also custom. In nonresidential applications, designer rugs may center around a corporate logo or carry out a specific theme. Designer rugs can be used as focal points or as wall tapestries. They may be pictorial, reflecting regional histories, architecture, geology, or industry. Manufacturers work with interior designers to create the exact colors, textures, and designs. Designer rugs are less costly than Oriental rugs.

Machine-Made Rugs

Rugs that are mass produced on machine looms can imitate many kinds of rug designs—Oriental rugs, folk rugs, French rugs, needlepoint rugs, and designer rugs. They are easily recognized in home improvement and furnishings stores by their economical prices, standardized patterns, and fiber content—wool, nylon, or olefin. Machine-made rugs that imitate orientals are called **domestic oriental rugs,** and when these are made of high-quality wool with an extended warranty they are often used in custom interior design.

Natural Fiber Rugs

Natural fiber rugs include animal skins, berber rugs, cotton rugs, floccati rugs, sisal/maize mats, tatami mats, and wool rugs.

Animal skins include zebra; black, brown, and polar bear skins; and any other animal skins laid on the floor or hung on the wall. The use of animal skins has been curtailed in recent years due to conservation efforts.

Berber rugs, originally woven by the Berber tribal natives of North Africa, are made of wool that is not dyed

Figure 12.13 An antique Aubusson tapestry hangs as textile art above the fireplace complemented by a room-sized Neoclassic-patterned French Savonnerie rug. *Photo © Rafael Macia/Photo Researchers, Inc.*

but left in its natural color state—cream, brown, and black. The wool hues are mixed to frankly expose the natural flecks of the various colors. Berber rugs come in off-white, beige, darker brown, and charcoal. Berbers today are most often nylon or wool machine-tufted broadlooms for nonresidential and residential application. A berber area rug may be a portion of a broadloom with bound edges, cut or shaped to cover an area.

Floccati, or **flokati,** rugs originate in Greece. They are tufts of sheared goat hair worked into a knit or woven fabric. They have a deep, luxurious pile. Floccati rugs are used in both informal and formal settings and have been favored area rugs in contemporary settings for many years. They are available in off-white and brown and are surprisingly inexpensive.

Sisal and **maize** mats are also available in squares or tiles, so the installations can cover small or large areas. They are not known for their comfort; sisal is particularly prickly to the touch. But these natural fibers form interesting and handsome floor textures.

Tatami mats are traditional floor coverings for Japanese homes and are seen in contemporary Western residences as well. They are woven of dried sea grasses and edged with black fabric and are set together in geometric patterns. The

Figure 12.14 This entryway designer rug features powerful geometric shapes. *Christina Oliver Interior Design/photo © Brian Vanden Brink*

Figure 12.15 Intriguing one-point perspective is accentuated with the grid lines of the ceramic tile floor in this New York subway station. Ceramic tile can withstand years of hard non-residential abuse and still look good. *Italian Trade Commission, Ceramic Tile Department*

thickness of tatami mats varies from about 1 to 4 inches. They offer good insulation as well as a precise appearance.

Natural wool rugs are often woven or tufted into neutral, subtly patterned area rugs. Surface textures vary from cut pile to beveled designs to level-loop construction.

Cotton rugs are woven by hand or machine and left neutral or yarn dyed to form simple patterns and textures. Cotton rugs may be machine washable and dryable if they are small rugs, and in larger installations they absorb dirt but clean up nicely.

Nonresidential Considerations

In addition to the guidelines in this chapter for selection of residential flooring, nonresidential flooring has further criteria and considerations.

Hard and Resilient Floorings

Hard flooring is frequently specified by interior designers for nonresidential settings. Factors that dictate this decision include the flooring budget and the traffic level or classification. A Class A or I traffic rating indicates extremely heavy traffic flow. Many residential floorings such as medium-grade vinyl or tufted carpeting would wear out quickly under heavy traffic. Thus, nonresidential floorings are more durable. They include solid vinyl, rubber, and particularly tile, brick, and stone. Although initially very costly, tile, brick, and stone will outwear any other flooring because they last indefinitely under even very heavy traffic. Because of their weight, the subfloor must have extra strength and support.

Another advantage of hard materials is that they will generally not show dirt or traffic-pattern shadows and will be easy to clean and maintain. Tile, brick, and stone will not be damaged unless a very hard blow is struck; then the material will need to be replaced. Rubber and solid vinyl have other advantages. In addition to their resilience and resistance to damage, they are easier on the feet and are quieter than nonresilient flooring.

Rugs and Carpeting

Carpeting selected for nonresidential installations varies somewhat from that used in residential settings, where color, price, and durability are the criteria. Nonresidential carpets must meet some or all of the following requirements:

- Cost of all nonresidential carpets must meet budget limitations.

Figure 12.16 Patterned carpet is a key element in this hotel lobby design. Patterned carpet can have a life span double that of a plain carpet; it hides both soil and wear. *Photo by Andy Battenfield and Kelly Haas*

- Flammability resistance forms a stringent requirement in many public buildings. Testing for flammability is often conducted, and ratings are available to the client through the designer.
- Construction is an important criterion. In order for a nonresidential carpet to be durable, minimum requirements must be filled for **pile density,** which means the number of **tufts** or **stitches per square inch,** together with the distance between rows and the pile height. The more dense the tufting or the weave, the stronger the carpet is likely to be. The strength of the **tuft bind,** or how tenaciously the face yarn is held onto the primary and secondary backings, is also a construction criterion. A thin layer of latex, for example, may not prevent the yarn from unraveling when pulled.
- Weight of the face yarn will be one measure of carpet durability. Heavier **face weight** will indicate the amount of yarn per square measure. **Finished pile weight** includes the backings as well.

- Abrasion resistance includes the type and quality of fibers and the type, thickness, and twist tightness of the yarn, as well as the density.
- Resilience means the carpet must have the ability to withstand light, medium, heavy, or extra-heavy traffic without undue crushing or matting.
- Appearance means the carpet will hide and release soil and will resist staining and fading, fuzzing and pilling.
- Maintenance is an important factor. Carpets must not show dirt easily. Many nonresidential carpets are patterned because they show about 50 percent less wear and soiling than an unpatterned carpet.
- Static resistance is important where delicate machinery such as computer terminals may be affected or where highly flammable materials are present.
- Sanitation is a requirement for carpet cleaning and maintenance in clinical and institutional facilities.

Chapter 13 | Fabric

Fibers 332

Fabric—The Champion of
Versatility 340

Nonresidential
Considerations 345

Decorative Fabric
Glossary 345

Drysdale Associates Interior Design/photo © Brian Vanden Brink

Fibers

The study of fabric begins by examining the substance from which fabrics are made: fiber. Because fibers vary in strength, dimensional stability, and a host of other criteria, a knowledge of fibers is essential to both interior design professionals and consumers. When selecting fibers, one should take close look at the level of expectation for the given installation, as no one fiber can do everything and meet every need. To increase their usefulness, fibers may be blended, either in the viscose-solution stage (man-made fibers) or the raw-fiber stage (natural fibers). In addition, threads may be spun together to make intimate blends, or two or more fibers can be used in fabrics—one as a base and the other(s) as pile or as one direction of yarns (the warp or the weft). The reasons for blending fibers are threefold:

1. To extend a costly fiber with one that is less expensive
2. To strengthen a weaker fiber with a stronger fiber
3. To give different characteristics such as bulk, texture, and different color reactions to one dye

Fibers are two general types: natural and man made. **Natural fibers** come from two sources: cellulose and protein. **Cellulosic fibers** are derived from plants—from the fruit, such as cotton, or from plant leaves, stems, or stalks, called **bast fibers,** such as **linen** (from flax), **jute,** ramie (China grass or linen), sisal, coir (coconut), piña (pineapple), maize (corn), and Oriental grasses.

Protein fibers come from animals (wool of sheep, hair of goats, camels, horses, rabbits, and other animals) and insects (silk from the silkworm caterpillar). **Sericulture** is the tedious process of producing silk under cultivation. **Leather** is the tanned hide of cattle and swine.

Man-made fibers are **cellulosic** and **noncellulosic** or **synthetic.** Rayon and acetate come from cellulose—cotton linters or wood chips—to which various chemicals are added. Noncellulosic or synthetic fibers—**nylon, acrylic, polyester, saran, olefin, vinyl,** and many others not frequently used in interior design—begin with organic compounds such as petroleum, natural gas, coal, air, and water. (See Table 13.1.) These **generic** fibers are produced for specific end uses. **Trademarks** or **trade names** identify generic fibers by manufacturer.

An independent fiber category is natural/mineral fibers that must be processed in ways similar to man-made fibers. These include asbestos, rubber, and metal.

All man-made fibers are formed in much the same way. The compound is made into liquid or viscose form, then forced through holes in a shower-head-like orifice called a **spinnerette.** The size and shape of the openings can build in certain fiber characteristics. Variety in the yarns comes through **texturizing** the **filaments,** through types of yarn formations, and through the tension and direction of the yarn twists. In addition, generic fibers may

Table 13.1 | Man-Made Fiber Production

The man-made cellulosic fibers rayon and acetate come from cotton linters, wood chips, and chemicals blended into a liquid or viscose solution.

Petroleum, natural gas, coal, and chemicals are the ingredients for the noncellulosic or synthetic fibers nylon, acrylic, modacrylic, polyester, vinyl, and others.

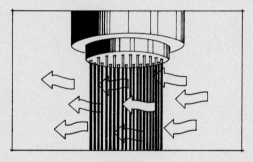

The spinnerette extrudes liquid that solidifies into filaments that are twisted into man-made fiber yarns.

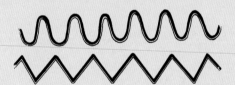

Filaments can be crimped or given texture before spinning into thread or yarn.

be combined in the viscose stage, making blended fibers that can be engineered to meet specific needs.

Table 13.2 lists the most commonly used interior design fibers and their sources, natural types or man-made trademarks, positive and negative characteristics, and uses in residential and nonresidential settings, as well as the care and cleaning of each fiber, its relative cost structure, and its flammability rating.

Table 13.2 | Fiber Comparison

Natural Cellulosic Fibers

Cotton boll   The Cotton Council and Cotton Incorporated logo.

Cotton

Source. Fruit of the cotton plant, a member of the mallow family. Needs extended sunlight and a long growing season.

Types. Short, long, extra long, carded, combed, mercerized. Egyptian and Sea Island are the finest cotton fibers.

Positive characteristics. Versatile, dyes and prints well; good **hand,** dimensionally stable; absorbent fiber.

Negative characteristics. Wrinkles, fades, shrinks unless mercerized and preshrunk. Mildews if kept moist. Eventually rots from sunlight exposure. Low abrasion resistance.

Residential uses. Draperies, walls, upholstery and padding, slipcovers, bed and bath linens, trimmings, accessories, rugs.

Nonresidential uses. With a flame-resistant finish, used for draperies, upholstery, and accessory items.

Care and cleaning. Washable or dry-cleanable. Washing removes more finishes; dry cleaning recommended. May require ironing. Remove spots with mild detergent.

Cost structure. Depending on grade, varies from low to moderately high.

Flammability. Burns readily; flammable. Must be chemically treated for flame resistance.

Flax   International Linen Promotion Commission logo

Linen

Source. Fibers within the stalks of the flax plant; a bast fiber. Grows in moist, moderate climates such as Great Britain and the low European countries.

Types. Tow linen (short **staple**), demiline, line linen (long staple). Ramie or China grass is a bast fiber with some similarities to linen.

Positive characteristics. Crisp, strong fiber. Appealing natural texture in tow linens. Dyes well, maintains good appearance. Absorbent. Line linens are smooth, lustrous. Durable.

Negative characteristics. Brittle, stiff, inflexible; sun fades; short fibers have low abrasion resistance. Stains are difficult to remove. Permanently creases.

Residential uses. Upholstery, slipcovers, draperies, semisheer casements, wall coverings, fine table linens (line linen), kitchen linens.

Nonresidential uses. Wall coverings. When treated for flame resistance, casement draperies, upholstery blends.

Care and cleaning. Dry-clean. Table and kitchen linens may be washed in hot water and machine dried. Ironing is required for table linens.

Cost structure. Depending on fiber length and finishes, medium to moderately high.

Flammability. Flammable, burns readily. Must be treated for flame retardance in nonresidential settings. Paper-backed, adhered linen wall coverings are inherently flame resistant, receiving a class A rating.

Jute

Source. Fibers within the stalks of the jute plant; a bast fiber.

Types. Burlap, gunnysack cloth.

Positive characteristics. Dyes bright colors, inexpensive, strong when dry.

Negative characteristics. Will rot if kept damp, fades, is brittle.

Residential uses. Crafts, wall covering. Drapery blends.

Nonresidential uses. None.

Care and cleaning. Hand wash, dry thoroughly. Dry cleaning recommended.

Cost structure. Low.

Flammability. Burns readily; flammable.

Natural Protein Fibers

Wool comes from sheep   The "Wool Mark" logo

Wool

Source. Wool of sheep; hair of goats and camels.

Types. Virgin—100 percent new wool; worsted—longer staple; woolen—short-, medium-staple fibers. Mohair—Angora goat hair.

Positive characteristics. Great resilience, dyes well, durable, flame resistant. Appealing hand. Dimensionally stable. High absorbency.

Negative characteristics. Some wools are scratchy, and some people are allergic to wool. Susceptible to moths. No resistance to alkalis. Low tensile strength.

Residential uses. Upholstery; draperies; casements; wall coverings; broadloom carpets; designer, folk, Oriental, and other area rugs.

Nonresidential uses. Upholstery, carpeting, rugs (designer, folk, Oriental), wall upholstery accessory items, draperies.

Care and cleaning. Dry-clean or clean by professional wet method.

Cost structure. Moderate to very high.

Flammability. Flame resistant; slow to ignite, self-extinguishes when flame is removed.

(continued)

Fiber Comparison (continued)

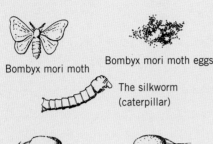

Bombyx mori moth

Bombyx mori moth eggs

The silkworm (caterpillar)

Moth escapes to lay more eggs

Cocoon filaments twisted to form silk threads

Leather is the tanned hide of swine and cattle

Silk

Source. Filament of domesticated or wild silkworm cocoons.

Types. Cultivated, reeled—Bombyx mori produced via sericulture. Wild (raw)—off-white tussah silk with slubs from A. myllita and A. perny moth species.

Positive characteristics. Lustrous, smooth to slubby, dry hand, excellent **drapability.** Strong when dry. Dimensionally stable. Resists organic acids. Not harmed by wetting.

Negative characteristics. Subject to sunlight deterioration as well as soil and moisture decomposition. Low resistance to alkalis. May be eaten by carpet beetles.

Residential uses. Draperies (must be lined), trimmings, upholstery, wall hangings and coverings, fine Oriental rugs. Accessories—pillows, scrolls, embroidered art fabric.

Nonresidential uses. Draperies (lined), fine trimmings, luxury upholstery.

Care and cleaning. Dry cleaning recommended. Some silks are washable.

Cost structure. Moderately high to very high.

Flammability. Burns slowly. Self-extinguishes when flame is removed.

Leather

Source. Hides or skins of cattle or swine.

Types. Full, top grain, split leather. Sueded, buffed, embossed, glazed. Aniline, pigment dyed.

Positive characteristics. Extremely durable. Wears well and long. Resists fading, tearing, stretching, cracking.

Negative characteristics. Quality varies according to hide, tanning, and company branding. Susceptible to marks, holes, and tears.

Residential uses. Upholstery, desktops, book bindings. Rarely for floor tiles, wall coverings, and area rugs.

Nonresidential uses. Upholstery, desktops, book bindings. Executive situations—floor coverings and wall coverings.

Care and cleaning. Mild soap and water; no saddle soap.

Cost structure. High.

Flammability. Flame resistant/fire retardant. Emits no toxic fumes.

Man-Made Cellulosic Fibers

The Man-Made Fibers Industry logo

Rayon

Source. Regenerated cellulosic from wood chips and cotton linters.

Trade names. Avril, Coloray, Colorspun, Enkrome, Jet-spun, Zantrel, Bemberg, Cordura, XL, Fibro, Beau-Grip.

Positive characteristics. Imitates silk in luster, drapability. Good solvent, insect resistance.

Negative characteristics. Low abrasion resistance, susceptible to sun, low moisture resistance; will mildew.

Residential uses. Draperies (should be lined), trimmings, bedspreads, upholstery, slipcovers, scatter rugs.

Nonresidential uses. As blends, some draperies and upholstery fabrics.

Care and cleaning. Dry-clean.

Cost structure. Low to medium.

Flammability. Flammable—ignites readily; melts before burning.

Acetate

Source. Reconstituted cellulosic, wood chips, cotton linters, and acetic acid.

Trade names. Airloft, Celanese, Chromspun, Estrom, Acele, Celaperm, Lanese, Loftura.

Positive characteristics. A silklike sheen and hand. Stable fiber, low absorbency; good solvent resistance.

Negative characteristics. Low resistance to abrasion, acids. Susceptible to sunlight deterioration. Mildew; will discolor. Weakens with age.

Residential uses. Bedspreads, draperies (should be lined), curtains, fiberfill, mattress ticking, lining, slipcovers, upholstery.

Nonresidential uses. As blends, some draperies.

Care and cleaning. Dry-clean. Some acetates are washable.

Cost structure. Low to medium.

Flammability. Flammable—ignites readily; melts before burning.

Man-Made Noncellulosic/ Synthetic Fibers

Nylon

Source. Amide linkages attached to two aramid rings.

Trade names. Anso, Antron, Cadon, Caprolan, Cumuloft, Nomex, Perlon, Quiana, Cantrese, Courtaulds, Cordura, Ultron, X-Static, Zefran, Zeflon.

Positive characteristics. Strong, stable, durable, resilient, versatile. Sheer to thick. Not affected by water, moisture, insects, microorganisms, aging. Resists alkalis, acids, solvents.

Negative characteristics. Conducts static electricity; sheen, harsh hand; low sunlight resistance.

Residential uses. Bedspreads, carpets, mattress pads, scatter rugs, slipcovers, upholstery, wall coverings.

Nonresidential uses. Carpets, curtains, upholstery, wall coverings.

Care and cleaning. Dry-clean or wet-clean.

Cost structure. Low to medium.

Flammability. Some flame resistance; melts before burning; self-extinguishes when flame is removed.

Fiber Comparison (continued)

Acrylic

Source. Over 85 percent acrylonitrile units, synthetic long-chain polymer.

Trade names. Acrilan, Bi-loft, Creslan, Dolan, Dralon, Fina, Leacril, Orlon, Zefran.

Positive characteristics. Excellent resilience. Soft wool-like texture, hand, and appearance; dyes well. Resists alkalis, acids, solvents, mildew, insects, and aging.

Negative characteristics. Oleophilic—holds oil-borne stains; variable strength and stability; may fuzz and pull.

Residential uses. Carpets, upholstery blends, curtains, draperies.

Nonresidential uses. Carpets, wall coverings.

Care and cleaning. Dry cleaning recommended.

Cost structure. Low to medium.

Flammability. Flammable; melts, then burns slowly.

Modacrylic

Source. From 35 to 85 percent acrylonitrile units, long-chain polymer.

Trade names. Acrilan, Dynel, Kanekalon, Elura, Sef, Verel.

Positive characteristics. Soft, buoyant, good hand, drapability, texture. Resists water, aging, insects, alkalis, acids.

Negative characteristics. Restricted application, low abrasion resistance; heat sensitive; moderate strength.

Residential uses. Casement draperies, fake-fur blends, upholstery.

Nonresidential uses. Casement curtains, draperies, walls.

Care and cleaning. Dry cleaning recommended.

Cost structure. Medium.

Flammability. Flame resistant; burns only with flame source; self-extinguishes when flame is removed.

Polylactic Acid Fiber (PLA)

Source. A manufactured fiber in which the fiber-forming substance is composed of at least 85 percent by weight of lactic acid ester units derived from naturally occurring sugars, such as those in corn or sugar beets. PLA relies on basic fermentation and distillation followed by polymerization. The Federal Trade Commission (FTC) granted PLA a new generic category designation in 2002.

Trade names. Nature Works(TM) Ingeo. In Japan: Ecodear, Lactron, Terramac, Plastarch.

Positive characteristics. Sustainable and renewable resource. Lightweight, low absorption, high wicking, breathable. Similar to cotton in appearance, natural fiber hand, good drapability. High ultraviolet (UV) resistance, color absorption. May blend with cotton or polyester.

Negative characteristics. Low moisture absorption, moderate strength.

Residential uses. Upholstery, carpeting, draperies.

Nonresidential uses. Upholstery, carpeting, draperies.

Care and cleaning. Dry clean or machine wash, according to product and manufacturer's recommendations.

Cost structure. Moderate.

Flammability. Low flammability and smoke generation.

Polyester

Source. Synthetic polymer ester of substituted aromatic carboxylic acid.

Trade names. Alvin, Blue C, Caprolan, Dacron, Encron, Fortrel, Hollofil, Kodel, Lanese, Quintess, Shantura, Spectran, Strialine, Tergal, Terylene, Textura, Trevira, Twistloc, Vycron, Zefran.

Positive characteristics. Resists sunlight fading and deterioration, mildew, insects; dimensionally stable; good strength. Soft hand, dyes well, resembles wool appearance. Water, heat, aging have no effect.

Negative characteristics. Susceptible to abrasion, low resilience, oleophilic (holds oil-borne stains), pills.

Residential uses. Sheer curtains, draperies, wall fabric, upholstery, slipcovers, carpets, awnings, fiberfill battings.

Nonresidential uses. Curtains and draperies, wall fabric, upholstery.

Care and cleaning. Wash or dry-clean.

Cost structure. Low to medium.

Flammability. Flammable; will burn with flame source; self-extinguishes when flame is removed. Easily flame-retardant treated.

Olefin

Source. Long-chain polymer of ethylene, propylene, or other olefin units.

Trade names. Durel, Herculon, Marvess, Polybloom, Polypropylene, Vectra, Patlon, Fibralon.

Positive characteristics. Durable, economical, good resilience. Oily stains easily removed with water and detergent. Resists acids, alkalis.

Negative characteristics. Low melting point, susceptible to sunlight and heat deterioration, oily, rough texture.

Residential uses. Awnings, carpets—face and backing, upholstery, floor mats.

Nonresidential uses. Indoor-outdoor carpeting, upholstery, carpet backing, artificial turf.

Care and cleaning. Dry-clean or wet-clean.

Cost structure. Low to medium.

Flammability. Flammable; burns slowly. Melts and burns when flame is removed.

Vinyon/Vinyl

Source. Vinyl chloride, long-grain polymer.

Trade names. Naugahyde, Valcren, Vinyon, PVC, Phovyl, Eibranyl, HH, Leayl, Teylron, Thermoyyl, Cordelan.

Positive characteristics. Imitates leather; many colors and textures.

Negative characteristics. Splits; holes difficult to repair.

Residential uses. Artificial leather upholstery, wall coverings.

Nonresidential uses. Artificial leather upholstery, wall coverings.

Care and cleaning. Mild soap and water; solvents for ink removal.

Cost structure. Low to medium.

Flammability. Melts, self-extinguishes.

Lyocell

Source. Lyocell is a manufactured fiber, but it is not synthetic. It is made from wood pulp harvested from tree farms. In 1996, lyocell became the first new generic fiber group in thirty years to be approved by the Federal Trade Commission.

Trade names. Tencel® lyocell, Lenzing lyocell.

Fiber Comparison (continued)

Positive characteristics. Breathable, absorbent, and generally comfortable; moderate resiliency. Strong and durable. Lustrous, may have soft drape, particularly in microfibers. Short staple–length fibers give a cotton-like look. Long filament fibers are silk-like.

Negative characteristics. May be unresilient and may wrinkle, may shrink. May be susceptible to mildew and damage by silverfish.

Residential uses. Bath towels, sheets, pillowcases, window treatments.

Nonresidential uses. None yet.

Care and cleaning. Interior design lyocell fabrics perform best when dry-cleaned. Bed and bath linens may be hand or machine washed and tumble-dried at moderate temperatures. Avoid oxygen or chlorine bleaches which may affect either dyes or resin finishes applied to the fabrics. Avoid excessive rubbing during stain removal. It can take high ironing temperatures, will scorch, not melt.

Cost structure. Moderate.

Flammability. Flammable unless treated.

Note: Other fibers—such as saran, spandex, fiberglass, latex, and metallic—have limited use in interiors and are therefore not included in this chart.

Table 13.3 | Fabric Maintenance Guidelines

- Regularly vacuum upholstery and window treatments to prevent soil from becoming embedded and prevent dust from combining with humidity and air impurities to become sticky grime.
- Remove spots promptly with a dry-cleaning solution, very mild detergent (1 teaspoon detergent per quart lukewarm water), or a weak water and vinegar solution, depending on the fiber and finish. Always blot the excess, lifting it out rather than rubbing it in.
- Vacuuming and spotting can decrease major cleanings. This is desirable for a number of reasons:
  1. Repeated cleaning can weaken fibers.
  2. Cleaning solutions can remove finishes and fade colors.
  3. Repeated cleaning can take body out of fabric, causing it to hang limply or lose shape.
  4. Cleaning involves cost, time, and effort.
- When selecting professional cleaners, inquire as to method and guarantee. Seek personal recommendation for quality work.

Fabric Maintenance

In addition to the points in Table 13.2, there are some general guidelines in Table 13.3 that, when followed, maintain the appearance and long life of fabric.

Fabric Construction

Fibers are made into fabric in a variety of ways; textiles may be woven or **nonwoven, knitted** or **needle constructed, layered** or **compounded,** and **extruded.**

The majority of fabrics are still woven on looms, which vary from simple, hand-operated instruments to sophisticated, computer-controlled elaborate machinery.

Figure 13.2 Twill weaves seen here as Scottish Lomond Clan Tartan and a subtle plaid with herringbone weave lay atop a Jacquard weave in a coordinated palette of persimmon, copper, yellow and green. *Courtesy of Highland Court®*

Figure 13.1 Plain weave fabric—Oxford plaid. © *D. E. Lanners/ Courtesy SoFro Fabrics/House of Fabrics*

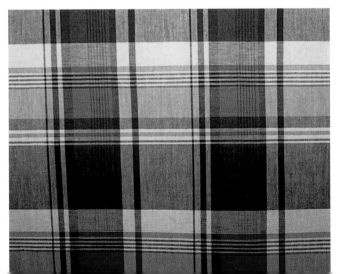

Figure 13.3 These 100 percent solution-dyed acrylic Sunbrella® fiber trims are guaranteed not to fade or stain and are both water and mildew resistant, making them good choices for pool, patio, or sunroom. The striped fabric is a satin weave. *Courtesy of Duralee® Fabrics*

Figure 13.4 This Scottish lace tablecloth is named "A tribute to Charles Rennie MacIntosh" and features his famous MacIntosh rose design. *Scottish Lace and Gifts by Mary Keil/photo © David A. Leviton*

Figure 13.5 These woven Jacquard textiles show a variety of styles from traditional to contemporary designs. *Courtesy of Stroheim and Romann*

Figure 13.6 A lively mix of fabrics featuring a bright floral, two plaids, a check, and stripe patterns are coordinated in happy colors and informal theme. *Courtesy of Stroheim and Romann*

Table 13.4 | Fabric Construction

Woven

The Plain Weave

A host of fabrics are plain weaves, including chintz, broadcloth, ninon, batiste, and tweed, for example.

Plain weave. The plain weave is formed by interlacing yarns one over, one under (1/1) in regular sequence. Variety is introduced through different-sized yarns or by varying the plain weave.

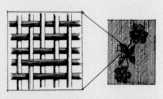
Plain weave

Plain basket weave. Basket weaves are equal, two over two or three over three.

Plain basket weave

Plain oxford weave. The oxford weave variation floats two fine warp threads over and under one heavier weft thread.

Plain oxford weave

Plain leno weave. Another variation is the leno weave in which the warp threads form an hourglass twist.

The dobby attachment weaves in small geometric one-color figures.

Plain leno weave

Twill weave. The warp-face twill weave is made of an interlacing pattern that floats one warp thread over two or three weft threads and then under one, called a weft tiedown. This order produces a diagonal **wale**. Steep wales result when two low-pitch wales float over three.

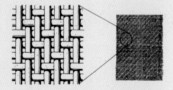
The twill weave, identified by the diagonal wale, is often used for sturdy fabric

Novelty twills are formed by reversing or altering the order of interlacing, such as the herringbone (a zigzag chevron pattern) and the houndstooth (a four-pointed star, or a square with a tooth projecting from each side). Twills can be incorporated into complex Jacquard-woven patterns, as well. Duck and serge, as well as houndstooth and chevron, are twill fabrics.

Satin weave. The satin weave floats one warp yarn over four or more weft yarns and then is tied down with one thread (4/1, 5/1, 6/1, 7/1, or 8/1). The order of interlacing is staggered, so

Warp sateen is used for many printed cotton fabrics

the result is a smooth face with no wales. Many satin-weave fabrics are woven in very fine threads that increase the luster of the cloth. Satin weaves are also used intensively in cotton decorator fabrics. Satin weaves that float weft or filler yarns on the face of the goods are termed horizontal satins, satines, or warp sateens. In addition, satin weaves often form the background for damask and brocade.

The satin weave produces a lustrous smooth face

Jacquard weave. Frenchman Joseph Marie Jacquard invented a loom attachment in the eighteenth century that became known as the Jacquard loom. Hole-punched cards are strung in sequence high above the loom. As the

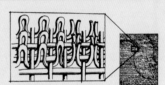
Jacquard weave

wires carry each card into position above the loom, the holes allow some of the threads to raise and keep others in position, producing large, complex patterns. This loom today takes a long time to thread and set up, but then large runs of fabric can be produced at relatively little expense. Jacquard fabrics include matelassé, damask, brocade, brocatelle, and figured velvets.

Pile weave. The pile weave inserts supplementary warp or weft threads into the fabric as it is woven. The extra threads may be looped or cut pile. Examples are velvets, corduroys, and **terry cloths.**

Cut and uncut pile weave

Nonwoven Textiles

Needle-Constructed Fabrics

These are fiber mats, webs, or extruded (flowed then solidified) textiles used for fabric backings or for upholstery, wall, and carpet padding. An increasing number of fabrics today are

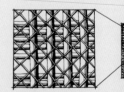
Lace construction

needle-constructed by knitting, **tufting,** and interlocking. Knitted fabrics comprise the majority in constructions such as single and double knits and rachel or warp knits for casement draperies. Arnache and malimo needle machines use multiple needles to chain stitch or interlock threads onto a cloth as it is formed. Lace is a needle-constructed fabric.

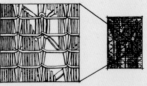
Malimo and arnache

Rachel knits

Layered or Compounded Fabrics

As the name *layered* implies, this group of fabric construction takes more than one production step to complete. Examples of layered or compounded fabrics include **embroidery:** hand, crewel, and schiffli (machine embroidery). Appliqué, the layering of additional fabrics by gluing and/or stitching, is also a compound cloth. **Tufting** is the method by which the majority of carpets are constructed today. Tufting punches yarns into a base fabric. In carpet, the tufted yarn is held in place with a layer of latex adhesive and then adhered to a secondary backing of polypropylene (see Chapter 12). Chenille bedspreads are also tufted fabrics.

Table 13.5 | Fabric Dyeing and Printing

Dyestuff. A water-soluble coloring matter that is mixed with water and chemicals to make a liquid solution or dye bath.

Pigment. A nonsoluble coloring agent that is held onto the surface of fabrics with resin binders. It looks more like paint; white, gold, silver, and other metallic special finishes are pigments.

Stock dyeing. Dyeing natural fibers before they are spun into yarn.

Solution or **dope dyeing.** Adding dyestuff to the man-made-fiber solution before extrusion.

Yarn dyeing. Dyeing the yarn by the skein, by the package, on a beam, or through space dyeing (different colors of the skein, package, or beam).

Piece dyeing. Dyeing a full length of woven fabric (45 to 150 yards long). Types of dyeing include beck, jig, padding, pressure jet, union dyeing, and cross dyeing.

Dye lot. When a new dye bath is constituted, several pieces are dyed at once. The new solution may vary slightly from previous batches of the same color, so may not perfectly **match** other dye lots.

Affinity. The attraction of certain chemical compositions to certain fibers. Chemical affinities must be carefully matched.

Cross dyeing. Two fibers of different affinities dyed in the same bath, accepting the dye in different ways.

Hand printing. Techniques that print fabric through hand-only labor.

Silk-screen printing. A stencil technique using a thin fabric with a film painted or transferred. Ink is **squeegeed** across, penetrating where the film is absent. A new screen is needed for each color.

Rotary screen printing. A fully automatic silk-screen process wherein the screens are wrapped around circular drums that rotate the ink onto fabric that moves beneath the rotary screens.

Roller printing. A mechanical printing method employing a large engraved metal cylinder, which is continuously inked as fabric moves around it.

Resist or **reserve printing.** A mechanized process in which a pattern is printed with a chemical paste that resists the dye. The background is colored and the design is light and neutralized.

Heat-transfer printing. Decals are dispersed-transferred from waxed paper to the cloth under heat and pressure.

Air-brush printing. Use of hand-operated mechanical pressure inkjet guns that spray dye over a stencil.

Etch or **burn-out printing.** Prints a design with a chemical that dissolves one of the two or more fibers in a fabric to leave some areas more sheer and the nonprinted areas more opaque. Typical is burning out cotton in a cotton/polyester semisheer fabric.

Colorfast. Resistant to fading.

Weaving is the interlacing of lengthwise continuous **warp yarns** that are strung on the loom with crosswise **filling** or **weft yarns** to form a fabric. The order of interlacing determines the type of weave. There are five basic types of weaves: **plain, twill, satin, Jacquard,** and **pile.** A fabric may be composed of a single weave, variations of a single weave, or a combination of weaves.

Finishes

Finishing is the process of converting textiles from their raw or gray goods (greige) state (dingy gray without pattern, color, or textural interest) into an identifiable fabric for interior design. **Finishes** can be broken into two main categories: **finishing** and **coloring.** Both of these processes take place at a variety of times. For example, the fabric may receive prefinishing steps, then be dyed, and be further finished for aesthetics and/or durability. Or the cloth may be dyed first and then treated with finishes later. Most fabric goes through an average of six different finishing steps or processes before it is ready to market.

Many fabrics are **prefinished,** such as **preshrinking** or **heat setting.** A common prefinish is **mercerizing,** which subjects cotton or linen to caustic soda. This increases the fiber's ability to absorb dye and increases luster, causing the yarn to become rounder and more consistent.

Finishes may be **durable**—those able to withstand repeated cleaning—or **nondurable** or **soluble**—those that will be removed with cleaning and will need to be reapplied.

Figure 13.7 These yellow and blue fabrics provide visual stimulus in this otherwise simple traditional interior. *Angela Adams/Olivia Cabot Interior Design/photo © Brian Vanden Brink*

Coloring

Coloring of fabric takes place in two general ways: by **dyeing** and by **printing.** Table 13.5 lists terms that are used to help us understand the materials and processes used in the coloring of fabric.

Standard Finishes

Standard finishes are also called **chemical, wet,** or **functional finishes.** Their purpose is to improve the performance of the fabric or its resistance to environmental factors. Standard finishes may be durable or nondurable.

Examples of standard finishes are **antistatic, wrinkle-resistant, flame-retardant, mothproofing, soil-release,** and **soil-** and **water-repellent** finishes.

Decorative Finishes

Decorative finishes may be durable or nondurable. These are also termed **mechanical** or **surface treatment finishes.** They may determine the decorative identity of the fabric, such as chintz (done by **durable press calendering**—flattening and shining with hot heavy rollers). Other decorative finishes may brighten, deluster, soften, add texture, or press or engrave designs to the surface of the fabric.

Obtaining Fabric

Fabrics for interior design travel an interesting road from their natural or compounded raw goods state (greige or gray goods) to our homes and the places where we work or visit. The fibers discussed in this chapter are woven, knitted, or extruded into goods that need an average of six finishes to become marketable.

While some fabrics stay on the market for several years, there is an amazing turnover in current fabrics. Every six months, new fabric lines are introduced to the interior design marketplace (the spring line and the fall line), reflecting current styles, trends, favored fibers, colors, and finishes. Design inspiration is sought the world over for design trends in color, pattern, and texture.

Fabrics obtained from interior designers are purchased through a jobber who sells cut orders "to the trade." In metropolitan locations, the designer may take a client to an **open showroom,** where samples of the "lines" carried by a fabric company (or fabric house) are displayed. Selections are made from individual samples or swatches or from bound sample books. **Showrooms** that do not allow the client to accompany the de-

signer are termed **closed showrooms.** Designers order fabrics for their clients as cut yardage, or occasionally by the half bolt (about 30 yards) or full bolt (about 60 yards). Clients may also purchase decorator fabrics directly from retail stores. Although retail selection usually consists of overruns and discontinued or flawed goods, the fabrics are useful, appealing, and less costly.

Fabric—The Champion of Versatility

Fabric is a malleable element that can be used in more ways than any other material. Fabric softens the straight lines of the interior while complementing and establishing an interesting counterpoint to them. Fabric is used at the window as draperies and curtains, shades, top treatments, and trimmings. On furniture, fabric serves as upholstery, slipcovers, pillows, trimmings, and throws (blankets or afghans). In the kitchen and bath, fabric "linens" dry and caress our bodies as well as our precious and everyday objects. Fabrics also function as floor cloths and wall and ceiling treatments.

Because of its affordability and availability, fabric can be utilized in every room in the house. This is in itself a remarkable achievement of our civilized and modern society, for in past centuries, even nobility did not enjoy the quantity and easy care of luxurious fabrics that we take

Figure 13.8 Subtle, neutral fabrics fill this restful bedroom as bedspread, draperies, Roman shade, upholstered chair and headboard, throw and pillows. *Sara Bengur Interior Design/photo © Brian Vanden Brink*

Figure 13.9 A striking contemporary motif of large flowing gold swirls on a sea of jewelled aqua is complemented with a smaller pattern of abstract leaf shapes reminiscent of Moorish tiles. These fabrics have a three-dimensional quality achieved by incorporating rayon and polyester with metallic yarns.
Courtesy of Duralee® Fabrics

for granted today. Today we also have the ability to keep our fabrics clean, fresh, and appealing. We know how to maintain fabrics and extend their life span.

If we so desire, we can change the interior design by rotating fabrics seasonally or by keeping up with current color and style trends that last only one to three years. We can replace fabrics as they wear out, as our lifestyles change, or as our needs evolve. Or we can choose durable and timeless fabrics that will be just as appealing ten or twenty years after we bring them home.

Fabric may be used lavishly or sparingly. However it is to be applied, the work-order form must be completed accurately for correct fabrication and installation. Since some fabrics and labor are so costly, it is crucial that interior designers be well trained to shoulder the responsibility of overseeing correct specification, fabrication, and installation.

The Human Touch

Fabric humanizes interiors. It can establish quietude and seclusion as it absorbs sound. Fabric can give a sense of personal space; it is selected with personal preference as a prime criterion. Fabric surroundings can be psychologically appealing and uplifting. Seeing a familiar fabric, whether a handmade heirloom or store-bought textile, gives us a sense of belonging and comfort. As we select our fabrics and their use, we reveal to others our values and lifestyles.

In past centuries, smooth, elegant fabrics were the exclusive right of the wealthy. As fabrics became more readily available and as man-made fibers imitated fabrics of luxury inexpensively, the wealthy saw, to their dismay, that anyone could achieve a pseudo-elegance. Those with money and taste have often turned to a new sensual pleasure of handwoven, unique fabrics, rustic or refined. These fabrics are costly because of the complexity of the construction and finishing processes or the relative obscurity of their source. Textiles are brought back from exotic travels or obtained through exclusive interior design firms to establish a look that cannot be easily copied. In this way, fabric establishes identity and status.

Fabric appeals to the visual, tactile, and emotional senses; it can stimulate or excite, be dramatic or theatrical, even produce a sense of intrigue and fascination. Fabric can enliven and cheer through light, bright, or pastel colors and patterns; it can draw us to the earth with coarse, rugged textures, patterns, and colors; and fabric can lift us above earthly cares with soothing texture, neutralized color, and subtle pattern.

Fabric can establish seclusion and privacy by shutting out the world and can satisfy the deep human craving for indulgence in that which gives pleasure.

Fabric Aesthetics

Often a fabric is preferred because of its beauty and emotional appeal, and this is as it should be, providing the fabric is also a durable and an appropriate selection. Three attributes—color, pattern, and texture—form the basis for personal choice. These three form criteria for judging the appropriate use of the fabric, whether the fabric is in itself good design, and whether combinations of fabrics are tastefully and discriminately used.

Color

It is often finding just the right color in a fabric that clinches the selection. Color preferences are often deep rooted and should always be respected. Color affects the mental and physiological health and well-being of those who live with it.

There are guidelines in selecting color for fabric coordination that will give security to both the professional and the layperson when making fabric color decisions. These guidelines are listed in Table 13.6.

Figure 13.10 A high-key, light value color scheme coordinates the Victorian-inspired floral fabrics, ticking stripe wall covering, and circular braided rug in this storybook cottage interior. *Weston & Hewitson Architects/photo © Brian Vanden Brink*

Pattern

Pattern establishes the character and personality of a fabric. Pattern can firmly tie a fabric to a period whose patterns look good together because they evolved around a cohesive "spirit of the times" predominated by one social, political, or artistic/architectural movement. This spirit or character must remain consistent in order for the patterns to coordinate and look right. Some guidelines for coordinating fabric patterns are included in Table 13.7.

Texture

To the touch and to the eye, fabrics are textural. From smooth and refined (satin, velvet, damask, brocade) to sturdy and coarse (tweed, matelassé, frieze, bouclé), fabric is aesthetically appealing because of textural relief. Relief is the way the surface reads—the peaks and val-

leys, highlights and shadows. This added third dimension gives depth and interest to fabric and accounts for much of its appeal. Guidelines to careful texture coordination of fabric are suggested in Table 13.8.

Livability, Flexibility, and Durability

Other important criteria for selecting fabrics include:

- **Livability** Interior design fabrics should be not only aesthetic but also comfortable for the people who live with them. For residential design, consider the lifestyle—how formally or casually do you want to live and entertain? Match the lifestyle to textures, patterns, and colors that will be livable and thematic.
- **Flexibility** Fabrics that are neutral in theme can be flexible as the decor changes, even seasonally. Pillows, trim colors, slipcovers, table covers and linens, and

Table 13.6 | Fabric Color Coordination Guidelines

- Colors are typically either pure and clear or neutralized and dulled. Colors should be used together with other colors from these same families.
- Warm and cool colors can have either warm or cool undertones, produced by mixing other colors into the dye. In complementary schemes, either the warm or the cool hue should dominate.
- Consider the color of the light and how it will affect the fabric colors. Always try out fabric combinations on site to be certain they will coordinate under lighting conditions in that room. It may become necessary to change the quality, type, and direction of the light to coordinate and enhance the fabric color scheme.
- Look carefully at the orientation and needs of the room and its inhabitants. Is it a cold, north room that needs cheerful colors, or is it a hot, south or west exposure that cries for cooling hues?
- Vary intensity or brightness within the fabric color scheme. If all the fabrics are intense, the scheme may prove unlivable, and if all colors are dull, the scheme may prove uninteresting. The law of chromatic distribution has proved its validity: Large areas are dull and neutralized (light, medium, or dark), and small areas are really bright. Midsized objects are middle intensities.
- Be sensitive to value distribution. Light values above, medium around, and dark colors below have consistently proved pleasing. However, some schemes can be very successful as all light (high-key), all medium, or all dark (low-key) values. Some schemes even reverse the standard distribution to light below, dark above. High-value contrast (light next to dark) is stimulating and dramatic; low-value contrast (blended values) is soothing and pleasant.
- Consider what colored fabrics do to each other. Colors should enhance, support, and beautify one another, never compete or cause visual irritation.
- Avoid too many coordinated fabrics with exactly the same dyes in varying colors and patterns. Although these coordinated "designer fabrics" can be lovely, there is also pleasure derived from searching many sources and finding fabrics that do not perfectly match as much as they blend and complement. This approach takes effort and time but is ultimately worth the hunt.

Figure 13.11 A coordinated mix of lively patterns in rich, bold colors brings the flavor of French Provence to this casual sitting area. © Mary McCulley/Imagestate

- Fabric color schemes that are sensitively coordinated will feel natural and interesting, with an almost destinylike rightness. It is the skill in the coordination that produces this effect.

Table 13.7 | Guidelines for Coordinating Patterned Fabric

- Look to the source of the fabric, its period or inspiration. If it is an adaptation, does it still possess the integrity and color of its origination?
- The pattern itself should be handsome, well proportioned, and livable, whether or not it is authentic.
- When bringing together more than one pattern, vary the scale of the fabrics—for example, a large pattern with a small one.
- Add appropriate support patterns and textures, such as correctly scaled stripes and geometrics with a floral or abstract pattern and plain-textured fabrics.

- Consider the thematic goals of the overall look of the interior. If, for example, the fabrics are to replicate the look of English Country, then seemingly conflicting patterns of printed textiles will work because they are authentic. The seemingly haphazard appearance looks lived-in, hence its strong appeal. If the look is American Country, then small-scale calico-chintz or sateen fabrics will pull off the look well. If a formal look is desired—say, a Georgian or French room—then the patterns should be elegant brocades and damasks.

window treatments can alter a room's appearance while furniture style remains. Storing off-season fabrics requires only modest space. Of all the elements in an interior, fabric makes the quickest and most effortless design statement.

- **Durability** Fabrics intended for much use and even abuse, such as often-used upholstery, will stand the test of time better if they are patterned or textured and have medium tones or values. Fabrics that are very light or very dark will show spots and stains readily. Very low end (economical) or very high end (costly) fabrics may require more frequent cleaning. Fabrics should look great after repeated cleaning. Fabric strength and longevity is due to fiber, yarn, and construction factors. Weaknesses in fabrics include:

  - Fuzzing—tiny fibers working to the surface.
  - Pilling—fibers working into balls or pills.

Table 13.8 | Guidelines for Coordinating Fabric Textures

- Textures used together must be compatible. For example, leather is not usually compatible with refined damask or brocade but is with matelassé or tweed. Lace is not in character with dramatic modern textures, but it complements moiré or velvet.
- Harmony is a key to good texture coordination. There must be a unified theme or ambience, a period or style, that holds together all fabrics in a scheme. There must also be variety in order to achieve harmony. For example, in a formal setting there may be velvet, damask, satin, sheer, moiré, and other different textures of the same character. A Country French provincial setting uses tapestry, ticking, toile de Jouy, tweed, and woven herringbone or plaid.
- The textures should be appropriate to their intended use. Fabrics as upholstery should feel comfortable. Wall fabrics should coordinate with the level of formality, and all appointments should be selected to be pleasing for their use. Refer to Table 13.9 for a comparison of fabric weights and applications or uses. Also refer to the "Decorative Fabric Glossary" at the end of the chapter for definitions, weights, constructions, and finishes of fabrics by name.

Figure 13.12 These fabric textures are not only appealing to sight and touch, but also are in harmony with the other textures in the interior. © *Peter Aaron/Esto*

- Fading—color loss from excessive light exposure or repeated cleaning.
- Lack of serviceability—difficult to clean.

Aesthetic durability is another consideration; faddish colors and patterns will date quickly, whereas more neutral or classic fabrics will stand the test of time.

Fabric Weight and Applications

Fabric may be categorized by weight and by specific use or application. Table 13.9 lists four basic categories of weight and the common uses for fabrics that fall in each category. In the "Decorative Fabric Glossary" at the end of the chapter, each fabric is given a weight designation that can be cross-referenced to the information in this chart.

Nonresidential Considerations

Fabrics installed in nonresidential buildings must meet minimum requirements for durability, colorfastness, and fire safety. These minimum acceptable standards are written as specifications by an architect or interior designer. The interior designer then selects fabrics that meet the specifications or requirements listed in Table 13.10.

Table 13.9 | Fabric Weight and Applications

Weight	Application and Use
Sheer, thin, very lightweight fabrics	Bed hangings, canopies, bed curtains, window curtains, sheer curtains/draperies, window semi-sheer casement and contract draperies, soft top treatments, thin table coverings, wall curtains
Lightweight fabrics	Accessory items and trimmings, casements, curtains, draperies, shades, top treatments, kitchen linens, lamp shades, supported bedspreads, table cloths
Medium-weight fabrics	Bedspreads, pillows and accessories, bath linens, slipcovers, supported upholstery, wall and partition upholstery, window treatments—draperies, heavier curtains, shades, stiff top treatments
Heavyweight fabrics	Bedspreads (tapestrylike), floor cloths, wall upholstery, wall hangings and tapestries, upholstery

Decorative Fabric Glossary

Antique Satin
A lightweight drapery fabric in a sateen or horizontal satin weave with slubs that imitate spun shantung silk. Most antique satins are one color, though the warp and weft yarns may be dyed different colors to produce iridescence; may also be printed. Suitable for bedspread fabric if quilted.

Armure
Medium-weight fabric in one color with small woven repetitive dobby figures. Plain-weave ribbed background cloth.

Arnaché
Needle-constructed lightweight casement cloth. Weft

Figure 13.13 Today's luxurious bedroom fabrics are often understated elegance, seen as semisheer and opaque fabrics in unpatterned textures. © *Scott Frances/Esto*

Table 13.10 | Criteria for Nonresidential Fabric Specifications

- **Cost.** Nonresidential installations typically have a strict budget.
- **Durability.** The ability of a fabric to exist for a long time without significant deterioration. Durability includes:
  1. Abrasion resistance—the fabric's ability to withstand friction, rubbing, or grinding. Tests are conducted to rate abrasion resistance.
  2. Colorfastness—resistance to both sun fading and fading from cleaning. Fabrics can be tested and rated for colorfastness.
  3. Resistance to crocking—crocking is the rubbing off of color onto another fabric or onto the skin.
  4. Strength or tenacity—the actual or physical strength of the fiber. The strength of a fabric is based also on the way the yarns are spun and plied, the closeness of the weave, and the thickness of the fabric.
- **Dimensional stability.** The ability of a fabric to maintain its original size and shape dimensions. This includes:
  1. Resistance to sagging—elongation or sagging may occur in fabrics that absorb moisture (hydrophilic fibers) when humidity is high or the fabric is wet-cleaned.
  2. Resistance to hiking—hiking up or shrinkage can occur when humidity drops or fabrics dry out.

  The lack of dimensional stability in hung fabrics through sagging and hiking is called the yo-yo effect—the bottom hem becomes quite uneven.
- **Resilience.** The fabric's ability to return to its original shape after stretching or elongation. In upholstered fabrics, dimensional stability also includes resilience, or the ability to bounce back to its original shape. Resilience is the result of two qualities:
  1. Flexibility—stretching and rebounding.
  2. Strength or tenacity—a fabric lacking strength, which tears easily, is termed *tender*.
- **Resistance to static electricity.** An important consideration where static electricity buildup may affect delicate instruments, such as computers, or where they may be a source of fire ignition.
- **Resistance to insects and microorganisms.** Necessary to prevent fabric disintegration and the spread of disease, particularly in hospitals and institutions.
- **Flammability resistance.** Fibers in nonresidential settings must meet the rigid fire code. Fabrics are tested for flammability, smoke density, and toxicity.
  1. Flammable or inflammable—fabrics that catch fire easily or are highly combustible, such as cotton, linen, rayon, and acetate.
  2. Flame resistant—natural fibers (wool, silk) that do not ignite easily, are slow-burning, and will often self-extinguish.
  3. Fire retardant—man-made fibers that are flame resistant (not easily combustible, slow burning, may self-extinguish). These are modacrylic, saran, polyvinyl chloride, nomex, and novoloid. Fire-retardant fabrics may be flammable natural fibers (cotton, linen, rayon, and acetate) that have been given chemical finishes to inhibit their flammability. These treatments are termed flame-retardant finishes.
  4. Nonflammable or flameproof—fibers that will melt but will not burn are asbestos, metal, and fiberglass.
- **Flame-retardant finishes.** These are chemical applications that enhance a fabric's ability to withstand or resist combustion. Most flame retardants provide one of the following degrees of durability:
  1. Nondurable—a water-soluble compound that is removed with wet cleaning, requiring reapplication.
  2. Semidurable—a compound that will resist wet-cleaning but not dry-cleaning solutions.
  3. Durable—treatments that will withstand repeated dry cleaning and are permanent, lasting the lifetime of the fabric.

threads are inserted just ahead of the multiple-needle lockstitch knitting.

Batik

A lightweight to medium-weight hand-printed textile. Certain areas are waxed; then the fabric is dyed. For two or more colors, each preceding wax layer is removed, and wax is reapplied in a different pattern. A crinkled pattern is achieved by crumpling the fabric and cracking the wax. Primitive or ethnic batik patterns from Indonesia and Africa are reproduced by mechanical silkscreen or roller printing.

Batiste

A thin, semisheer curtain/drapery fabric.

Bengaline

A medium-weight horizontal or weft-ribbed fabric produced with fine warp and plied or grouped filling yarns. Strong and refined cloth.

Bird's-Eye

A lightweight to medium-weight fabric with small dobby woven all-over diamond patterns in one color. Originally a toweling/linen fabric, cotton is used most often.

Bouclé

Medium-weight to heavyweight knitted or woven cloth. Looped bouclé novelty yarns give a tightly curled, bumpy surface texture to the fabric.

Bouclé Marquisette

Fine leno-weave sheer marquisette with bouclé weft or filler yarns. Originally glass curtains of nylon; today of polyester and used as lightweight casement fabric.

Broadcloth

Lightweight cotton plain taffeta weave with fine horizontal ribs. Yarn twist or tightness is slightly irregular. Also a finely napped twill weave wool in various weights.

Brocade

Medium-weight formal Jacquard weave with supplemental warp or weft woven into the fabric to give an embroidered, often colorful, design. Background weave is often satin. Threads not tied down are carried as "floats" on the back of the fabric. Cut floats make broché brocade.

Brocatelle

Medium-weight Jacquard fabric with slightly heavier and puffier surface than damask. Fine cloth with two sets of warp and weft.

Buchram, Buckram, or Crinoline

Lightweight fabric, in width 3, 4, or 5 inches, stiffened and used as drapery heading interfacing. Plain weave or nonwoven web of cotton, linen, jute, or synthetic fiber.

Burlap

Medium-weight jute fabric in plain, loose weave; also called gunnysack cloth. Coarse texture, solid colors. Natural and synthetic fibers imitate jute burlap.

Burn-out

A method of printing designs into semisheer or lightweight casement cloths. Usually a cotton polyester base fabric printed with an acid design that eats or dissolves the cotton. Edges around the burn-out area are often printed with pigment ink to seal edges. Also used to produce eyelet holes. Also called etch printing.

Calico

Lightweight cotton or cotton/polyester fabric similar to broadcloth. Usually printed in small country-style multicolored floral patterns.

Cambric

Semisheer to lightweight plain-weave cotton or linen fabric, often printed. May be finished dull and soft or stiff with a sheen. Also called handkerchief linen.

Canvas

Versatile medium-weight to heavyweight cotton fabric in plain or twill weave. May be dyed any color and has many uses such as upholstery, shades, and awnings.

Casement

Lightweight to medium-weight casual drapery fabric. Plain or combination weave or needle-constructed fabric. Interesting texture, color, and pattern through dyed novelty yarns and weave variations. May be semisheer, translucent, or opaque.

Chambray

Lightweight cotton or blend fabric in plain, balanced weave. Yarns are slightly slubbed in both directions. Usually white warp and colored weft or filling.

Chenille

Medium-weight to heavyweight fabric with chenille yarns that are fuzzy and resemble soft pipe cleaners. Velour textures are common.

Chevron

Regular and repeated zigzag pattern, also called herringbone, formed by reversing the twill weave. Fabric is of natural and/or synthetic fibers. Medium weight to heavyweight.

Chiffon

Sheer, very lightweight ninon or voile drapery fabric. Also a soft finish given to a fabric, such as chiffon velvet.

Chintz

Lightweight fine cotton or cotton/polyester plain-weave fabric. Solid colors or floral or exotic prints. Most often sized or glazed—hence, glazed chintz. It is a multipurpose fabric.

Corduroy

Medium-weight to heavyweight pile-weave cotton or cotton-blend fabric. Lengthwise cords or wales are named according to width:

> pinwale corduroy—narrow wales
> wide-wale corduroy—large wales

Crepe

A fine yarn that is twisted so tightly that it gives a pebbly or crinkled surface in woven fabrics. Crepe may be plain or satin weave and includes the following types:

> canton crepe—heavy fabric with ribs
> chiffon crepe—soft finish thin crepe
> crepe-de-chine—sheer, very thin, limp crepe
> crepon crepe—heavy crosswise ribs
> faille crepe—fine horizontal ribs
> flat crepe—smooth, fine surface
> plissé crepe—puckered or crinkled surface

Cretonne

Medium-weight unglazed printed cotton fabric slightly heavier than chintz. Versatile decorative fabric similar to toile.

Crewel Embroidery

Medium-weight compound fabric. Base cloth is basket weave of cotton, linen, or wool, with hand or machine embroidery of worsted wool. Patterns are meandering vine and floral motifs based on English interpretations of the Eastern Indian tree-of-life motifs.

Crinoline
Same as buchram.

Damask
Medium-weight Jacquard fabric with reversible pattern, historically a large floral or Renaissance design. Contemporary damasks are medium-weight in a variety of designs; multiple-use fabric.

Denim
Medium-weight sturdy twill cotton or cotton/polyester cloth. Navy-colored denim is jeans fabric; cream or white denim is drill.

Dimity
Thin, very lightweight semisheer fabric in plain weave with a crisp finish. Vertical warp spaced ribs or cords are formed with heavier or piled threads. Checks may also be woven in. One color or contrasting thread may form the ribs, cords, or checks.

Dotted Swiss
Plain- or leno-weave swiss is sheer curtain fabric, within tiny embroidered or flocked dots or squares in spaced sequence.

Double cloth
Same as matelassé.

Duck
Durable medium-weight cotton fabric in oxford weave similar to canvas. Different-sized weft threads and the addition of colored stripes may vary the appearance.

Embroidery
A thread or set of threads sewn onto a fabric for surface ornamentation. Types include:

piecework—embroidery done by hand
crewel embroidery—tree-of-life motifs originating in India done by hand-guided machine using a looped crewel stitch
schiffli embroidery—decorative machine embroidery for mass production

Eyelet
Lightweight cotton, cotton/polyester, or other blend plain-weave fabric with schiffli-embroidered designs and small burn-out or etched dots that are part of the design. The fabric is usually a solid white, cream, or pastel color with matching or accenting embroidery. Also comes in

smaller widths—usually 5, 7, 11, and 14 inches—with scalloped borders.

Faille
A lightweight, finely woven fabric generally of cotton, silk, acetate, rayon, or blends, with horizontal or weft ribs that are slightly heavier and flatter than taffeta. When these ribs are pressed or calendered in a watermark design, faille becomes moiré.

Felt
A nonwoven fabric made of wool and perhaps hair and cotton fibers compressed with moisture, heat, and agitation. Felt comes in many weights, from craft felts to upholstery and interlining felts.

Flamestitch
A pattern originally from the Early English Renaissance that represents the flames of a fire and is loosely a chevron design. Flamestitch patterns are multicolored and may be embroidered, woven, or printed on various weight cloths.

Flannel
Any fabric that is woven and then brushed to achieve a soft nap. Types include:

cotton flannel, flannelette—lightweight, thin fabric used for flannel sheets
outing flannel—medium weight, suitable for upholstery; pilling may be a problem
french flannel—fine plain-weave flannel
melton flannel—heavyweight cotton and/or wool dense plain weave; used for interlining and stiffening as a support fabric
suede flannel—two-sided nap, trimmed and pressed

Foam back
Loose adjective for a latex or other synthetic coating laminated, flowed, or sprayed onto the back of drapery and upholstery fabrics to increase energy efficiency and/or dimensional stability.

Frieze or Frisé
Heavyweight, sturdy nylon upholstery fabric with a looped pile. May be a Jacquard weave to achieve a sculptural or ribbed effect. Types include:

Grospoint—frieze in even or staggered rows with large loops; may also be Jacquard woven
petit point—very small loops; resembles fine hand needlepoint

Gabardine
Steep-pitched twill fabric woven of natural or synthetic yarns; lightweight to medium weight. Surface has obvi-

ous diagonal ribs that are tightly woven of fine, lustrous yarns.

Gauze
Very thin (sheer or semisheer) loosely woven fabric used for curtains and draperies.

Gimp
Narrow braid trimming in many designs for drapery and upholstery. Also term for metallic cording.

Grenadine
Thin, sheer leno-weave curtain fabric. May be flocked or swivel lappet embroidered with small dots or designs.

Grosgrain
Narrow trimming ribbon or textile with round, even, heavy ribs in the weft or crosswise direction.

Herringbone
Originally a medium-weight wool fabric. Pattern is a novelty or complex twill that is a regular zigzag pattern. Named after the spinal structure of the herring fish. May also be woven or printed on lightweight, medium-weight, and heavyweight fabrics and in a variety of natural or synthetic fibers.

Homespun
Coarse, lightweight wool, linen, or cotton fabric from Early American hand-spun and handwoven plain-weave textiles. Today in nearly any fiber, a textile that imitates this look. May be natural colors with flecks of vegetable matter. May also be simple stripes or checks.

Hopsacking
Similar to plain homespun yet less sturdy. Usually woven in a loose, semiopen basket weave and given a soft finish. Lightweight casement fabric.

Houndstooth
Medium-weight to heavyweight fabric with woven twill pattern in contrasting color that resembles squares with projecting toothlike corners called four-pointed twill stars. Originally a coarse provincial wool fabric, now in a variety of fibers and may be woven in finer yarns.

Interfacing
A lightweight, stiffened woven or nonwoven fabric that is usually placed between decorative and lining fabric to give body and firmness. White or solid colors.

Interlining
A thick, lofty woven or nonwoven textile of natural or synthetic fibers used to insulate against noise or heat and/or cold. May be a polyester batt or lambs' wool batt, for example.

Jacquard
Any textile woven on the Jacquard loom, which permits large designs to be machine woven. Used for both cloth and carpeting, Jacquard fabrics are brocade, brocatelle, matelassé, lampas, tapestry, and moquette velvet.

Jersey
Single vertical knit fabric that includes tricot and some stretch knits. Fabric is usually lightweight, though some upholstery stretch jersey fabrics are medium-weight.

Khaki
Multipurpose twill or plain-weave fabric of a greenish, dusty, earthy beige. Lightweight to medium-weight cotton or blend fibers.

Knit
Knit fabrics are produced on multiple-needle knitting machines and include:

> rachel, raschel knit—warp knit casement fabrics
> single or jersey—lightweight knit with weft ribs used for fabrics such as tricot
> double knit—heavier knit textiles
> stretch knits—elastomeric threads for stretch upholstery
> Knit terry cloth—knit toweling

Lace
A lightweight machine-made or handmade, needle-constructed fabric of natural or synthetic yarns. Open, floral, or geometric patterns sometimes on a net background, lace is typically used for curtains, draperies, and table settings. Geometric lace for contrast settings is sometimes termed architectural lace.

Lampas
Medium-weight Jacquard fabric with a plain or satin background and figures of contrasting colors in both the warp and weft in ribbed, plain, or twill weave.

Lappet
Swivel or discontinuous (no floats carried on back) embroidery accomplished with an attachment to the plain or dobby loom.

Lawn
Fine, thin fabric that is the base cloth for batiste, organdy, and printed sheer fabrics. Usually cotton, linen, rayon, or blends.

Leno

A variation of the plain weave in which pairs of warp threads are twisted in hourglass fashion as they interlock weft threads to give strength and texture. Used in thin, very lightweight, marquisette sheers as well as lightweight casement fabrics.

Lining

A lightweight support fabric (cotton, synthetic fibers, or blends) in plain or sateen weave sewn onto or used as a separate backing for the decorative fabrics.

Malimo

Casement, contemporary fabric where groups of weft yarns are chain stitched together in clear monofilament thread with multiple needles. Groups of warp threads may also be laid and stitched into the top of the weft groups.

Marquisette

A thin, sheer curtain or drapery cloth of natural or synthetic fibers in a leno weave. Slightly heavier than ninon or grenadine.

Matelassé

A heavyweight textile in Jacquard weave of two sets of warps and wefts. Background surface appears puffy or cushioned since the sets of threads are woven together only where the pattern is. Also called double cloth or pocket weave.

Moiré

Lightweight to medium-weight faille fabric embossed with a watermark moiré pattern. A versatile fabric.

Muslin

Thin cotton cloth of a plain balanced weave similar to lawn but stiffer. Muslin forms the base for several cotton fabrics. May be natural (bleached or unbleached), dyed, or printed. Also lower-thread-count bed sheets.

Mylar

Trade name of the DuPont Corporation for a clear or metallized extruded material. Use in flat sheets such as reflective wallpaper backgrounds or cut into ribbons, texturized, and woven to achieve a novelty-textured fabric.

Needlepoint

Heavy upholstery-weight textile of tight hand-stitched wool yarn on art canvas net. Types include:

petit point—finer needlepoint using very tiny stitches
grospoint—coarser, larger embroidered stitches

Net

Historically made by hand as a base for lace, now a machine-, needle-, and open-construction thin textile with a background of square, diamond, hexagonal, or irregularly shaped mesh.

Ninon

Very fine sheer drapery and curtain fabric in pair warp thread plain-weave variation. Usually of polyester in varying widths up to 118 inches seamless. It has excellent drapability, crisp body, and a lustrous appearance. Sometimes called French voile, triple voile, or tergal voile.

Organdy

Plain-weave sheer curtain and drapery cloth of natural or synthetic fibers (originally cotton), which is given a stiff, very crisp finish. A semisheer organdy is called semiorgandy.

Ottoman

Natural or man-made fibers woven in a medium-weight to heavyweight fabric with broad, round weft threads that produce a horizontal rib. Fine warp threads completely cover the large-, even-, or alternate-sized filling yarns.

Oxford Cloth

A lightweight cotton or cotton/polyester fabric in an oxford variation of the plain weave: Pairs of warp threads are grouped together and carried over and under a heavier filling yarn. Often used as a base cloth for decorative prints and may be woven with slightly heavier yarns to produce a medium-weight fabric. Oxford cloth is traditionally a finely woven shirting cloth.

Paisley

A printed or woven pattern in lightweight or medium-weight fabrics. The curved pear, leaf, or water drop shape originated in India but is named for a city in Scotland where woolen paisley shawls have been produced for centuries.

Pellon

Stiffened interfacing fabric that is a trademark of the Pellon Corporation.

Percale

Lightweight plain-weave cotton or cotton/polyester fabric in a fine yarn and high thread count. Finely woven bed sheets are generally percale. Percale is finished to a variety of lusters from soft to stiff or given a textured plissé finish.

Pile Fabric

Medium-weight to heavyweight fabric with an extra set of warp or weft threads that are woven or knitted into the fabric to produce a deep surface texture. Examples include velvets, terry cloths, friezes, and corduroys.

Piqué

Lightweight to medium-weight versatile cloth in a plain-weave variation, which inserts raised cords, stripes, or geometric patterns. The rib or cord usually runs lengthwise in the face of the goods. Types include:

bird's-eye—lightweight diaper cloth, small geometric three-dimensional weave

goose-eye—larger bird's-eye with diamond-shape pattern in relief, lightweight

dimity—thin, semisheer fabric with lengthwise ribs of heavier threads

ribcord or pinwale—medium-weight fabric with lengthwise ribs, often used for bedspreads and draperies

embossed piqué—design pressed or calendered into face of fabric

waffle piqué—three-dimensional square patterns

Plaid

Lightweight, medium-weight, or heavyweight yarn dyed, woven, or printed with a design consisting of stripes in both warp and weft directions that cross at intervals to form different colors in square or rectangular patterns. Plaids may be plain or twill weave. Variations include:

tartans—Scottish clan plaids
plaidback—reversible plaid

Plissé

A sheer, thin, or lightweight fabric given a blistered or puckered surface through chemical treatments.

Polished Cotton

Lightweight to medium-weight plain or sateen weave cotton fabric with smooth, lustrous yarns. Sateen weave is also called glosheen. Unglazed chintz may be classified as polished cotton.

Poplin

Lightweight to medium-weight fabric with pronounced horizontal ribs. Weft threads are heavier than warp. Often a base cloth for decorative print fabrics.

Quilted Fabric

Any fabric that is lined and usually interlined with a lofty batt and then hand or machine stitched through so that stitches show both front and back. Pinsonic quilting is often used for mass-produced bedspreads, where layers are fused together with ultrasound heat in a predetermined pattern.

Rachel, Raschel Knit

Also called warp-knit casement, a lightweight drapery fabric where knitted warps form the body of the fabric.

Rep, Repp

A horizontally or vertically ribbed fabric in plain weave with heavier threads in one direction. Durable medium to heavy fabric with many applications. High-quality reps are often of wool.

Sailcloth

Same as duck, sometimes heavier.

Sateen

A horizontal satin lightweight to medium-weight fabric. Used for linings and printed decorator fabrics in natural or man-made fibers.

Satin

A basic type of weave where warp threads float over four to eight weft threads and then are interlaced or tied down with one weft thread. Fine thread yields a smooth, lustrous surface. Lightweight to medium weight. Types include:

antique satin—horizontal slubs to imitate silk shantung

lining satin—lightweight drapery lining fabric

ribbed satin—resembles faille or calendered into satin moiré

satin damask—background satin with Jacquard pattern; lighter weight known as ticking satin

upholstery satin—heavier-weight satins, may be the base cloth for Jacquard weaves

Schiffli

Any fabric with machine-embroidered designs, other than dotted swiss, eyelet, and swivel or lappet embroidery. Threads may be one color or variegated. Embroidered on fabric from very sheer to very heavyweight and in simple to complex patterns.

Scrim

Very thin plain-weave cloth with loose construction. Types include:

theater scrim—sheer, curtain-weight, softer, more drapable

upholstery scrim—woven or nonwoven web dust cover fabric for the bottom of upholstered pieces.

Seersucker

Lightweight to medium-weight cotton or cotton blend plain-weave fabric. Crinkled or puckered surface usually in spaced stripes or plaids, permanently woven. Or permanent puckers are formed in polyester by heat-setting.

Serge

Lightweight to medium-weight fabric in natural or synthetic fibers (originally silk) in durable, crisply finished twill weave.

Shade Cloth

Plain or plain-weave variation, such as canvas, poplin, or oxford. Medium weight to lightweight, it is stiffened to become roller shade fabric. Also called Holland cloth.

Shantung

Originally a spun silk fabric with slubs that formed interesting and exotic textures. Shantung today is a lightweight fabric of natural or synthetic fibers. Fabrics that imitate shantung are antique satin (sateen-weave rayon/acetate) and antique taffeta (plain weave).

Sheer

A translucent or transparent thin, very lightweight curtain or drapery fabric. Examples include ninon, chiffon, grenadine, marquisette, swiss, and voile.

Slubs

Yarns with slight irregularities in diameter and profile, originated with wild silk yarns where filaments are knotted or joined.

Strié

Also called jaspé, meaning shadow stripes, a sateen or satin weave with colored warp threads that produce a finely blended vertical stripe. Lightweight to medium-weight multipurpose fabric in natural or synthetic fibers or blends.

Suedecloth

A lightweight to medium-weight synthetic knit or woven textile with brushed nap that imitates genuine suede.

Swiss

A very thin, semisheer curtain fabric of plain weave. It is a crisply finished fabric and may be embellished with woven or flocked dots or figures. Originally of cotton, today it is often polyester. Also called swiss muslin.

Taffeta

A plain, balanced weave in lightweight fabric of natural or man-made fibers. Weft threads are slightly larger, creating a fine horizontal rib. Types include:

moiré taffeta—calendered as moiré; pressed ribs make the classic watermark pattern
faille taffeta—heavier ribbed taffeta
antique taffeta—horizontal slubs, a reversible fabric
paper taffeta—very crisp finish, often woven in plaid patterns

Tapestry

A plain-weave technique used to produce heavy, complex, handwoven European pictorial tapestries. These are now most often Jacquard-weave fabrics with multiple warps and wefts and are very heavy fabric. Tapestry techniques are also used for handmade flat, reversible folk rugs and further apply to a large category of fabric and nonfabric wall hangings or textiles. Tufted wall hangings may also be referred to as tapestries.

Terry

Medium-weight pile weave used for absorbent cotton terry cloth toweling. Loops may be cut for a plush or velour surface texture or left uncut as loops.

Textured Polyester

Lightweight to medium-weight multipurpose fabric with heat set, permanent textures.

Ticking

Originally a twill navy blue and cream vertically woven striped fabric used to make ticks (mattress and pillow casings). Today a woven or printed stripe, in one color on cream or white. Multiuse fabric. Mattress ticking may also be a satin damask fabric, called damask ticking or ticking damask.

Toile

A lightweight to medium-weight cotton or linen fabric similar to muslin or percale in plain or sometimes twill weave. It is similar to a heavier unglazed chintz. Toiles are typically roller- or screen-printed in one color: gold, navy, green, red, or black on a cream background. Types include:

toile de Jouy—eighteenth- and nineteenth-century rural scenes and people; originating in Jouy, France
federal toile—American federal buildings and eagles
country toile—contemporary provincial floral patterns

Tricot

Nylon jersey knit that has a weft-only stretch. Lightweight, limp fabric.

Tufted Fabric

A pile fabric that is formed by tufting a yarn into a woven background. Early American tufted bedspreads are one example. Some upholstery fabrics and all tufted carpets utilized this method. The fabric may be tufted with a small handheld tufting gun or on a large machine that utilizes multiple needles, tufting entire sections in rapid sequence.

Tweed

Heavy upholstery-weight textile in plain balanced or variation weave or (originally) twill-weave variation. Plain and twill weaves may also be combined. Made first of wool in Scotland, today's tweeds may be of wool, nylon, or a combination of natural and man-made fibers in solid colors, a heathered effect, or plaid.

Union Cloth

A coarse, medium-weight cloth that is approximately 50 percent cotton, 50 percent linen. Yarns are calendered or flattened somewhat. Union cloth may be dyed one color or printed and often resembles a very coarse chintz. Versatile fabric with many uses.

Velour

A heavy pile fabric with a soft, velvetlike texture that includes some velvets and all plush-pile surface cloths, such as velour terry.

Velvet

Woven pile fabric with a soft yet sturdy face. May be of one or more fibers, including cotton, linen, wool, silk, rayon, acrylic, and nylon. Types include:

> antique velvet—streaks pressed or woven in: slubs on woven back, or slight strié effect

> brocaded—etch-printed or burn-out pattern, often exposing the woven background
> chiffon velvet—thick, soft surface finish velvet
> crushed velvet—varies from light to heavy crushing of pile
> electrostatic velvet—flocked, rather than woven pile, usually bold color and pattern
> embossed velvet—bas-relief roller calendering to produce pressed-in pattern
> moquette velvet—exposed ground with floral historic patterns of cut and uncut looped pile in Jacquard weave
> panne velvet—pile lays flat, pressed in one direction
> plush velvet—deeper pile, sometimes crushed
> upholstery velvet—deep thick pile and sturdy back
> velveteen—short, cotton-faced pile and back
> printed velveteen—roller or screen printed, typically in floral or geometric patterns

Vinyl

Extruded polyvinyl chloride (vinyon) synthetic fabric flowed onto a woven, knitted, or nonwoven base cloth. Medium-weight to heavyweight upholstery fabric, which is also called imitation leather or artificial leather.

Voile

Sheer, transparent fabric in plain weave with tightly twisted yarns. Often has a stiff finish. May have novelty effects such as piqué stripes, printed patterns or stripes, or woven with nubby yarns for novelty voile.

Chapter 14 | Art and Accessories

Fine Art 356

Decorative Art 360

Objects from Nature 366

Other Accessories 367

The Use of Accessories 368

Nonresidential
Considerations 370

© *Kathryn Taylor*

Art has been an integral part of interiors since prehistoric times, when early humans painted the walls and ceilings of caves with images expressing their relationship to the world they knew. Throughout every period of history, people in cultures the world over have created works of art that served to enhance, embellish, and even sanctify the interiors they occupied. In today's society, we have devised categories such as fine art and decorative arts as a way of organizing the myriad of things we see that have artistic qualities. Works of art add great distinction and individuality to interiors because their selection represents personal taste and experience.

Fine Art

The **fine arts** are concerned with the creation of two- and three-dimensional works of art, designed as expressions of beauty and faith or as a statement of the personal meaning or feeling of the artist. The great **masters** are those throughout the ages who have excelled in the creation of art and whose work has passed the test of time to become what we call **classics.** Every era has its masters, and these men and women were often aware of each other and the work produced by each artist. This mutual awareness often produced similarities in philosophy, technique, subject matter, or other areas of influence. Art historians have classified the work of the masters into **schools** according to these similarities and influences. Many of the masters were equally comfortable drawing with a pencil, painting with a brush, or working sculpture with their hands. The fine arts include **sculpture, painting, mosaic, drawing,** and **printmaking.**

Sculpture

Sculpture is a three-dimensional art form created by carving stone; working clay, wood, or other materials; or casting or assembling metal. Sculpture may represent the human form, animal forms, or other forms from nature in a realistic, conventionalized, or abstract fashion.

Bas-relief is French for "low relief." It is a type of sculpture carved or cast in a flat manner where the design is raised from the background to create a three-dimensional effect. Bas-relief is often seen in friezes (sculptural panels or bands) used on exteriors, in interiors, and even on furniture and small decorative objects.

Painting

Painting is a one-of-a-kind, two-dimensional art form created with colored **pigments** and a num-

ber of different **vehicles** (substances that give the pigment form and body). The paint can be thinned with different **media** and manipulated by pouring, dripping, splashing, or applying with brushes, sponges, or **palette knives** to many different surfaces such as plaster, wood, canvas and other textiles, paper, glass, or any material or surface capable of holding the paint.

- **Oil paint** is colored pigment mixed with linseed oil or varnish and thinned with turpentine. Oil painting is very versatile because the color application can be thick or thin, opaque or transparent. Oils tend to be one of the most permanent types of painting, which may account for their popularity with collectors.
- **Watercolor** is colored pigment mixed with **gum arabic** and thinned with water. The pigments are slightly transparent. Because the water used as a medium dries quickly, the artist must work rapidly to complete the painting. This technique typically imparts a fresh, underworked quality to the finished piece.
- **Acrylic** can duplicate the appearance of oils and watercolors. It is made of plastic and can be mixed with several kinds of media or thinned with water. Its appearance can be opaque or transparent. The untrained eye may find it difficult to distinguish acrylics from the older, more traditional oils and watercolors. Many artists enjoy the versatility provided by a single medium capable of so many different effects.

Figure 14.1 Fine art pieces like these oil paintings add great individuality and interest to interiors. © *Kathryn Taylor*

- **Tempera,** one of the oldest types of paint, is pigment mixed with egg and thinned with water. It is somewhat transparent but more opaque than watercolor. Budding artists at kindergarten easels often use a form of tempera to create their bright, fresh, uninhibited paintings, and tempera poster paints are frequently used to create banners and posters. However, the tempera used by fine artists is much more refined than poster paint. Fine tempera is often called **gouache.**
- **Fresco** is the Italian word for "fresh" and denotes a combination of pigment and limewater applied with brushes to fresh, damp plaster. When it dries, the pigment and plaster become unified. The artist must work quickly, and plaster is applied only as far as the artist can work before it dries. Frescoes were often used to decorate the ceiling and walls of Renaissance buildings.

Mosaic

Mosaic is a two-dimensional art form made of **tesserae** (small pieces of marble, tile, or colored glass) fitted together to form a pattern. The design is held in place with plaster or cement. The Romans used mosaics to decorate their floors, and artists in the Byzantine empire took the art of mosaic to a high level of perfection. The interiors of Byzantine churches shimmer with scintillating mosaic designs of great beauty.

Drawing

Drawings are also one-of-a-kind, two-dimensional art forms produced with pencil, pen and ink, charcoal, chalk, crayon, or grease pencil on paper or other surfaces. Drawing is considered a fundamental skill for artists. Drawings are produced as finished works and also as preliminary studies in the development of paintings, sculpture, and other art. The work of the masters often includes a large body of drawings that were used as studies for later work and now stand by themselves as treasured art pieces.

Printmaking

Printmaking is a method of creating mass-produced two-dimensional fine art. Prints are produced in limited editions by the artist, who prepares a screen, plate, block, or stone and then makes a numbered set of prints. The artist signs and numbers the prints that are of acceptable quality. The numbers read as a fraction and indicate how many copies were made and the order in which they were printed. For example, 8/10 would indicate that a particular print was the eighth print out of a total of ten. Generally, the smaller the number of prints produced, the greater the value. Several screens, plates, or blocks representing different parts of the design can be utilized to create multicolored prints. When using more than one run of color, each plate, screen, or block must be carefully registered (aligned) to produce a clear and even print.

- A woodcut or wood **block print** is made by carving a design into the flat surface of a piece of wood. The background is cut away, leaving the pattern standing out in relief. The block is then inked and printed to create a negative or reverse pattern on the paper. A wood engraving is executed in the same way, except that the pattern is carved into the harder end grain of the wood, a technique that usually results in a finer and more precise design.
- A linoleum block print is made by cutting a pattern into a piece of heavy-gauge linoleum. The process is similar to the woodcut process except that the design will have less detail in the form because of the softness of the linoleum. Woodcut, wood engraving, and linoleum block printing are all forms of **relief printing** because the portion of the pattern that receives the ink and does the printing stands out in relief.
- **Engravings** are prints made from a metal plate that has lines hand-engraved (scratched) with a tool called a burin. These lines make small impressions or grooves in the plate. The plate is covered with ink and then wiped clean, leaving ink only in the grooves. The plate and paper are pressed together so that the ink is transferred from the grooves in a negative impression onto the paper.
- **Etchings** are made by covering a metal plate with an acid-resistant substance such as wax. The artist uses a needle to draw through the wax. The plate is immersed in an acid bath that bites or etches the design into the metal wherever the wax has been scratched away. After the plate is etched and the remaining wax removed, the plate is used to print in the same manner as an engraving. Because wax is less difficult to cut than a metal plate, etching designs tend to be less rigid than engravings. Engravings and etchings are forms of **intaglio,** where printing is done with the ink in the plate's recesses.
- **Lithographs** are produced on the principle that water and grease repel each other. The artist creates a design on a smooth limestone block or metal plate with a grease pencil or with a brush and tusche (a waxy liquid). The block or plate is then chemically treated to attract ink to the greasy design and water (which repels the ink) to the untouched portions of the stone or plate. The stone or plate is then charged (wetted) with water and ink and pressed together with the paper to create a negative image.
- **Serigraphy** or **silkscreen** is a printmaking process that utilizes a fine screen of silk or other fiber and stencils cut to create a positive, direct (not reversed) image.

The stencils are applied to the screen and ink is squeegeed across the pattern, forcing a thin layer of ink onto the surface being printed through the open areas of fabric where there is no stencil.

Rubbings, Reproductions, and Graphic Art

- **Rubbings** are not a true form of printmaking, though they are often framed and used in much the same way as prints. Rubbings are made by placing a sheet of paper over a flat metal or stone plaque—such as a grave marker or an architectural detail that has a flat bas-relief or a raised pattern. The paper is then rubbed with a crayon or chalk to create a direct image of the pattern beneath. The quality of the piece is determined by the care and skill of the person doing the rubbing.

- **Reproductions** are copies of the artist's work and are an important educational tool. Without them, people unable to visit the world's museums would find it difficult to study the history of art. When specifying reproductions, it is important to remember that once the original piece of art is complete, the quality control of the reproduction is generally out of the artist's hands; the quality of reproductions ranges from excellent to poor. Reproductions may be the same dimensions as the original or may be scaled from postcard size to full poster size or larger. Color quality of reproductions may also vary. For example, colors that were red in the original may appear violet in the reproduction. Despite these drawbacks, reproductions are an affordable means of bringing great art into the interior.

- **Graphic art** includes posters designed to publicize athletic contests, concerts, plays, shows of artists' works, and other cultural events. Maps, botanical drawings, architectural drawings, fashion illustrations, book illustrations, and even some mechanical or architectural drawings may also have value as graphic art. These are often worthy of display on the merits of their fine design and, in time, may become valuable. Posters and other graphics are an important resource for people who love art but are unable to afford paintings and other art forms.

Obtaining Fine Art

Art can be found at many locations in a vast range of prices. The works of the great masters are generally sold for enormous sums at auction houses like Christie's or Sotheby's in London and New York. Some less well-known but important pieces are sold by art and antique

Figure 14.2 Graphic art in the form of posters is affordable yet attractive. © *Jessie Walker Associates*

dealers who operate retail shops and galleries. Contemporary artists are usually represented by galleries and dealers who act as agents for the artist. Galleries may specialize in a certain type of art such as historic, Oriental, or Western. Art-minded communities and organizations often sponsor art festivals where artists informally display and sell their work. Some businesses and corporations sponsor art shows or display artists' works that may be purchased.

People who have less to spend on art pieces should know that art teachers and artists who need to finance travels and studies will often sell their work at relatively reasonable prices and artists frequently will barter services for art. Schools of art may have shows of student work, much of which is for sale. Because they have not usually established a reputation, students tend to sell their work at lower prices.

Economical graphic art or posters can be purchased—sometimes obtained without charge—directly from museum shops or from organizations sponsoring the event being publicized in the poster. Old posters, prints, and maps can frequently be found at flea markets or bookshops. When collecting art, one should be prepared to pay fair market prices, though the price is less important than the quality and appeal of a piece.

Print shops specialize in graphic designs from museums, galleries, shows, and other cultural events. In addition, this type of shop will often have fine photography in poster format and reproductions of the masters' works in varying sizes of posters. It is important to be discriminating and choose pieces of fine quality and lasting value.

Obtaining art for our homes is certainly a matter of personal taste, but the more we learn about art, the greater our level of enjoyment and appreciation. The design of a home is a reflection of personal style, and the art chosen for such settings should also be a statement of

discrimination and taste. Unfortunately, many people are underexposed to quality art. Designers or consultants could be used to help make wise selections, but the most pleasing and personal collections belong to persons who put forth the effort to become knowledgeable about art and its history. Not everything that is advertised as original art is worthy of collection. Knowledge, training, and exposure are the only means to ensure wise selection. Following are some important guidelines to help develop the confidence to choose fine-quality art:

- Do not be intimidated by a blank wall—it may have more appeal than a piece of poor art. Take the time and steps necessary to develop confidence in your ability to choose.
- Those who are seriously interested in collecting art will study its history. This can be done formally or

Figure 14.3 A clean, structural, large-scale interior is enhanced by just a few well-chosen paintings. © Peter Aaron/Esto

informally with classes or independent study. Study of art history builds a sincere appreciation and understanding of art and those who created it.

- Taking art classes and attempting to actually create works of art add profound depth to the appreciation of art and help build the ability to see quality.
- Visiting museums of fine art to observe firsthand the works of the great masters and contemporary artists sharpens the ability to discriminate. It provides the kind of exposure that enables a buyer to detect the difference between real art and the poor-quality pieces we see advertised as "original oil paintings."
- As with anything of real value, it takes time and effort to build an understanding and appreciation of art. It is a lifelong pursuit and an important part of the process of developing the ability to discriminate. It is a goal worth the effort, however, because of the satisfaction that fine art provides.

Preparing Art for Display

When purchasing a piece of art, it may be necessary to select a **frame, mat** (heavy flat paper frame), or some other means of display that will show the piece to best advantage and add to its quality and character. Frames are available in unassembled kits or are ready-made from art shops, from paint stores, on the Internet, and by mail. In some places there may be hobby shops or specialty shops where customers can cut mats and make and assemble their own frames. However, with truly fine pieces of art, it may be worthwhile to consult a qualified framer who understands art conservation and can advise on the proper method and materials for displaying and preserving art pieces. Following are some suggestions for framing fine art:

- Generally, oil paintings are framed but left unglazed (not covered with glass). They may be framed with heavy, elaborate period frames that often include a fabric liner to separate the painting from the frame. Contemporary oils and acrylics may be left unframed, or they may be treated with a simple, minimal frame.
- Watercolors, drawings, photographs, and prints are frequently framed behind glass with simple, narrow frames and a mat that keeps the painting from touching the glass. Clear glass is preferable to **nonglare glass** or **Plexiglas.** Nonglare glass does not allow clear color and line transmission. Plexiglas is subject to scratching and bowing. Posters can be framed like watercolors or prints but can also be mounted behind glass with no frame, with the glass and backing held together by clips. When mounting paintings, prints, graphic designs, or reproductions, it is important not to cut or **crop** the piece to make it fit a frame. Cropping destroys the value of the work.

- For permanent display, matting and other materials that will come in contact with the art should be acid-free. Look for matboards sold as archival, museum, or conservation quality. Avoid buffered matboard, which is acidic. Be aware that artworks framed before about 1980 are likely to have acidic mats, which are subject to deterioration.

Decorative Art

The **decorative arts** include utilitarian pieces such as mirrors, tableware, baskets, clocks, screens, lamps, books, tapestries, and rugs as well as nonutilitarian pieces like figurines or statuettes. **Objets d'art, bibelots,** and **curios** are French terms used to describe both utilitarian and nonutilitarian objects of artistic value and beauty. Furniture, also considered a decorative art, is discussed in Chapter 9, "Furniture Selection."

Not all pieces created as decorative art have strict artistic value. **Kitsch** is a German term that connotes bad taste and is applied to pretentious or foolish art and design. In our contemporary world we are inundated by objects of mediocre or poor design. As people develop the ability to discriminate, they can sift out the kitsch from their environment and replace it with that which is fine and uplifting. It is worth the effort to find good design in decorative and functional objects because it enriches and deepens our appreciation for true beauty. Both good and bad design can be found at every price level, and many times it costs no more to choose good design.

Mirrors

In the fourteenth century the skilled artisans of Venice discovered that a layer of **quicksilver** sandwiched between a piece of tin and a piece of glass (a process called **silvering**) created a mirror. Today, mirrors are often used to add depth, a feeling of spaciousness, and sparkle to interiors. They can be obtained in many sizes and framed to harmonize with period styles or used in sheets large enough to cover entire walls. However, many people find it uncomfortable to have to look at themselves in a mirror for prolonged periods when sitting or standing. Large areas of mirror on several different walls may visually duplicate the elements of a design in a manner that creates visual confusion and makes the space seem smaller. Mirror finishes or types include clear glass, smoked glass, **Venetian glass** (veined), **beveled glass, leaded glass,** and **etched glass.**

Tableware and Cookware

Tableware is the term that describes plates, cups, drinking vessels, and flatware or eating utensils. Artisans through the ages have lavished their finest creativity and the best developments of technology on the creation of beautiful and useful pieces for the table and kitchen. Materials of all kinds have been used to create tableware and cookware, and today plastics and other innovative space-age products are used alongside more traditional materials such as ceramics, glass, wood, and metal for the design of quality pieces. (The same materials are also used to create a wide variety of functional and decorative objects such as small sculpture, planters, containers, bookends, desk sets, and dressing or grooming accessories.)

Ceramics

Ceramics are made from clay that has been molded in its softened form into useful shapes and then fired or baked at high temperatures in an oven called a **kiln.** The soft clay can be molded by hand, formed in molds, or thrown on a potter's wheel run by motor or foot power. Clay mixed with water to the consistency of thick cream is called slip and is used to fill molds and for other functions in the ceramic process. **Glazes** are thin layers of glass fired onto ceramic pieces to produce a glossy surface, to add colored effects, and to make the pieces nonabsorbent and sanitary. Glazes may be dull or shiny, clear or colored, and can be used by the ceramist to create decorative effects. Following is a list of ceramic types:

- **Porcelain** is the highest-grade ceramic body. It is made of fine, white clay **(kaolin)** and **feldspar** (crystalline materials) and is fired at very high temperatures that **vitrify** the clay (change it to a glasslike substance), harden the glaze, and make the piece breakage-resistant. Porcelain is sometimes used in the manufacture of fine dinnerware, vases, figurines, and other decorative objects. Porcelain may be plain or decorated with colored glazes and patterns.
- **China** was the designation given by Europeans in the sixteenth century to the porcelain imported from the Orient. It contains a large percentage of animal bone ash (hence the term bone china) that produces a hard, translucent porcelain. Today, the terms china and porcelain are generally used synonymously.
- **Stoneware** is a heavy, durable, thick pottery used for less formal dinnerware, serving and cooking pieces, and other art objects. Stoneware finishes may be less formal and show flecks and speckles in the clay or glaze. Stoneware finishes vary from natural browns, grays, and bluish grays to bright, lively colored patterns.
- **Earthenware** is the most coarse and inexpensive of the ceramic bodies. It is derived from red earthen clays and often finished like a common clay flowerpot. It is fired at lower temperatures, making it softer and less durable. Earthenware products are sometimes referred to as terra-cotta, an Italian term that literally means

Figure 14.4 A collection of blue and white porcelain, fresh flowers, and a botanical print makes a pleasant vignette.
© Jessie Walker Associates

"cooked earth." It is commonly used for baking and serving pieces and other decorative pieces for the interior and garden.

Glass

Glass is used to fashion decorative objects, dishes, serving pieces, and drinking vessels of all shapes and sizes. The quality and design of glassware ranges from inexpensive molded glass to fine lead crystal:

- Molded or **pressed glass** is a method for mass-producing glass. Molten glass is poured into forms or molds of metal or wood. The mold often leaves a seam where the molds meet. The molding process can be used to form simple and functional glass shapes or to imitate the look of cut glass.
- **Cut** or **etched glass** is decorated with patterns incised with chemicals or abrasives. The cut patterns are quite clear, and the etched designs have a frosted appearance.
- **Enameled glass** is layered with a porcelainlike finish.
- **Cased glass** is a layer of clear glass encased in a layer of colored glass.

- **Gilded glass** has a layer of silver or gold applied to its surface. Enameled, cased, and gilded glass are often engraved or cut to reveal patterns in the sparkling clear glass layer underneath.
- **Crystal** is a high-grade glass containing lead. Because of legal requirements, American lead crystal contains less lead than European lead crystal. Higher lead content makes the glass softer, allowing the glassmaker to cut more intricate designs. Fine lead crystal sparkles beautifully in the light and rings or sings when tapped lightly with a fingernail. Crystal is used to create art objects, serving pieces, and drinking vessels. **Stemware** is the name given to formal drinking pieces with a slender pedestal and raised bowl.

Wood

Wood, aside from its use in construction and sculpture, was used historically to make crude plates, utensils, and serving pieces. Today it is still used to create beautiful art objects, both carved and plain, as well as serving pieces, handles for metal utensils and cookware, spoons, and other cooking implements.

Metals and Alloys

Metals and **alloys** such as aluminum, brass, chrome, iron, steel, and stainless steel, together with gold, silver, pewter, bronze, and copper, are common materials used to fashion art objects, cookware, serving pieces, dinnerware, flatware (silverware), fixtures, and hardware:

- Gold, a bright, lustrous yellow, is the most precious, costly, and prestigious metal and was used historically to create dishes, flatware, drinking vessels, candle holders, and other objects of art. Because of its great expense, gold is used principally today as a plating for metal pieces or as paper-thin sheets applied to objects in a process known as **gold leaf. Gold electroplate** is a type of flatware created by the electrolytic process of layering pure gold over a silver/nickel alloy (silver plate).
- Silver is a bright, lustrous, gray-white metal used in the manufacture of objects of art and tableware. **Sterling silver** is the finest and most costly, being by law at least 92.5 percent pure silver. Sterling will tarnish and must be polished and protected from the air. It becomes more beautiful with use, developing a soft **patina** of almost invisible scratches. **Sterling II** is a flatware that combines silver handles with stainless steel blades, bowls, and tines, costing about half as much as sterling silver. **Silver plate** is made of a silver/nickel alloy electroplated with pure silver. It is the most affordable type of silverware and is also used as a base for gold electroplate.
- **Stainless steel** is also used to make attractive, affordable flatware and serving pieces. These pieces are pop-

Figure 14.5 Beautiful table linens, china, stemware, silverware, and flowers contribute to a gracious dining experience. *Ivee Fromkin, Interior Designer/photo © Melabee M. Miller*

ular because they do not tarnish or scratch easily, and they are strong, durable, and dishwasher safe. Some designs feature handles of wood or colorful plastic.
- **Pewter** is a soft, dull gray alloy of tin, copper, lead, and **antimony** used to create dishes, drinking vessels, candle holders, and other art objects. Historically pewter was considered poor man's silver. Today, though it is less costly than sterling, pewter is expensive. Once considered dangerous because of its lead content, pewter is now often made without lead and is safer and easier to care for. Pewter adds character and warmth to informal, **provincial** (country) settings. Less expensive imitations of pewter are made of cast aluminum.
- **Copper** is a bright, shiny, pinkish brown metal used principally for cookware, because of its ability to conduct heat. When copper is allowed to tarnish, it first turns reddish brown and then a beautiful blue-green called verdigris. To maintain the original copper color and shine, it must be polished with copper paste and a soft cloth. Some copper pieces are coated with lacquer or other finishes that prevent tarnishing. These finishes must be removed if the piece is to actually be used for cooking or if a tarnished finish is desired.

- **Bronze** is a deep reddish brown alloy of copper and tin used primarily for sculptural pieces or plaques.
- Iron is cast or wrought (shaped and bent with heat) to make lighting fixtures, candle holders, and other decorative accessories. **Cast iron** is molded in its molten form to create substantial cookware and some art objects. **Wrought iron** pieces and heavy cast pieces such as corn pone or muffin molds, skillets, and Dutch ovens are frequently used as decorative accessories in less formal, country settings.

Plastics

Plastics are used extensively to create informal tableware and other accessories for interiors. Plastic is generally less expensive than the other materials discussed in this chapter and can be used to create designs of great appeal and integrity. For example, some contemporary plastic dishes are bright, colorful, and well designed. Because they are relatively inexpensive, one can indulge in a splash of color without undue concern for budget. Plastic is sometimes used in a lighthearted manner to imitate natural materials such as glass or metal. This is particularly true in the manufacture of disposable objects that are not meant to be taken seriously. When plastic is used to imitate natural materials in a serious manner, the design becomes questionable. For example, plastic molded to resemble carved wood or fine cut crystal might only be considered kitsch.

Baskets

Baskets are woven for function, each type or shape reflecting its specific use. Produced by almost every culture in the world, baskets incorporate beautiful patterns using materials such as wicker and willow. Because of their decorative nature, baskets make excellent additions to informal interiors, particularly when they serve a useful purpose such as a container for plants, bread, fruit, or fragrant **potpourri.**

Clocks

Today, timepieces such as **hourglasses, sundials,** and antique clocks are collected as objects of art. Looking at fine clocks with intricately designed cases, we appreciate the cabinetmakers and furniture designers whose creative genius turned scientific instruments into functional and decorative art. The design of clocks has changed over the years. Today's **high-tech** clocks are often the work of industrial or product designers rather than furniture craftspersons, and these frank, sleek designs may be as beautiful in their own way as the handcrafted pieces of the past. Clocks may be displayed on shelves, mantels, brackets, or walls, or they may be floor clocks. Large-scale floor clocks are often referred to as grandfather clocks, and those of a slightly smaller scale are called grandmother clocks. Clocks are frequently included as a feature in appliances such as radios, microwave ovens, stoves, and video equipment. These often utilize a digital display system that indicates the hour and minutes as digits instead of using the traditional clock face.

Screens

Screens are hinged or sliding panels designed to divide and separate spaces or create areas of privacy. In today's interiors, screens are used as dividers, wall art, window treatments, and as backgrounds for furniture. Screens can be made of wood with solid panels or **louvers, lattice,** pierced wood, or wrought iron. Screens are also custom-made items that might be upholstered, covered with mirrors, painted, lacquered, papered, or treated in other interesting ways.

- Antique screens from Europe and America, with details appropriate to period styles, are attractive additions to interiors as functional dividers or simply as objects of art. Such screens were often traditionally used to create dressing spaces in bedrooms and bathrooms.

Figure 14.6 Coromandel screen.

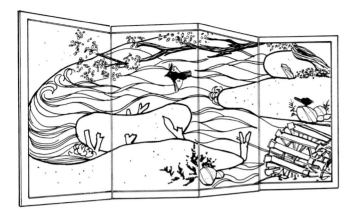

Figure 14.7 Byobu screen.

- **Coromandel** are large Chinese black-lacquered folding screens, decorated with low relief, all-over patterns. They were introduced into Europe in the seventeenth century by the East India Company.
- **Byobu** are small-scaled folding Japanese screens. They are decorated with scenes painted on silk or paper and are generally used as wall hangings, on tables, or as freestanding pieces in today's interiors.
- **Shoji** or fusuma are traditional Japanese screens made of mulberry or rice papers mounted onto a wooden frame. The frames are set into tracks or grooves as sliding panels or hinged and freestanding and used as partitions. Shoji are exterior sliding panels or window screens, and fusuma are decorative interior sliding room partitions or doors. Translucent **transoms** set above the screens add light through a grid or intricate design patterns.
- Near Eastern screens are intricately patterned pierced wooden screens from Islamic cultures. The piercings create a "blind" from which it is possible to see out without being seen. Islamic design was taken to Spain in the eighth century by invading **Moors**. The Near Eastern influence can also be seen today in the screens of Mexico and other countries with **Hispanic** ties. Today, many pierced wooden screens are made in India and imported to Western countries.

Decorative Lighting Fixtures

Lighting fixtures have evolved over the centuries from torches, oil- and gas-burning vessels, and candle holders into the electric fixtures we use today. (Architectural lighting and principles of lighting are discussed in Chapter 5, "Lighting and Technology.") Some of today's most common lighting fixtures are electric versions of historical lighting pieces. It is also common to see decorative objects such as metal **tea caddies** (antique tea containers), **ginger jars, cloisonné** (enameled metal) and porcelain vases, as well as figurines and other sculptural pieces,

made into table lamps. Luminaire is the technical term used by lighting designers and engineers to describe table lamps, floor lamps, and ceiling- or wall-mounted lighting fixtures such as chandeliers and sconces. (The term luminaire distinguishes these lighting fixtures from the technical usage of the term lamp, which refers to a lightbulb or fluorescent tube.) Following is a list of the most common **art-lighting** luminaires:

- **Table lamps** are designed to sit on the table for general lighting of a space or for reading, writing, and other specific tasks. Traditional designs usually incorporate a shade to diffuse the light.
- **Floor lamps** serve the same basic purposes as table lamps but are designed to stand on the floor.
- **Torchère** is a historical term that was used to describe a candle table or candle stand. Today it describes a type of floor lamp that casts its light upward onto the ceiling.

Figure 14.8 Table lamps.

Figure 14.9 Sconces.

Figure 14.10 Chandeliers.

Figure 14.11 Fine bed linens add to the luxurious feeling of this setting. *Courtesy of DuPont "Teflon" soil and stain repellent*

Second-hand hardcover books are sometimes purchased and displayed like stage props. These look attractive in settings such as restaurants and shops where the design is intended to create a homey atmosphere. In a residential setting, books purchased as props may be visually pleasing but will lack the emotional appeal of books that have been read and loved. Books stashed in attics or garages might be an untapped resource that could add a warm finishing touch to interiors.

Walls of books make a suitable background for furniture groupings; they are a welcome addition to almost any interior. They can be interspersed with objets d'art or plants to create pleasing compositions. Interesting books and magazines placed on tables for browsing make stimulating accessories. A home office or children's homework room is an excellent place to display books, allowing them to serve as an active reference library as well as an attractive display. Entries, living rooms, family rooms, dining rooms, kitchens, bedrooms, and even bathrooms are all appropriate locations for books. A formal dining room used only occasionally for meals might double as a library or study; the table would be useful for reading or writing, and the books would make a pleasant background for occasional dining.

- **Sconce** is a wall-mounted luminaire of any style that has descended from wall-mounted torches or candle holders.
- **Chandelier** is a decorative, ceiling-mounted, hanging, or pendant-type luminaire. This type of fixture functions best in high-ceiling rooms and in areas where a strong focal point is the intent of the design.

Many antique and contemporary lighting pieces are used simply as objets d'art. Candle holders made of metal, wood, and ceramic—and various styles of oil and gas lamps—are often collected and displayed because of their aesthetic appeal and not because of a need for light. Candlelight is used to create a special mood because, like firelight, it has a moving and scintillating quality that is not commonly duplicated with electric luminaires. **Neon lamp** designs created for advertising or as pieces of art are sometimes seen in today's interiors. Such pieces are far more important as decorative art than as light.

Books

Books are not only decorative but also appealing because of their unity of form and variety of color and texture. They may also lend a certain amount of emotional warmth to a space because, when read, they become like old friends, associated with all kinds of memories.

Textiles

Textiles serve important functional and decorative purposes as accessories. Linen, the name of the natural fiber derived from the flax plant, today is used to describe the fabric products of natural, artificial, or blended fibers used on the dining table, the bed, and the towel rack. These items are an important part of the appearance of a completed interior and should be chosen in harmony with the other elements of the design. Fine, traditional white linens are still considered classic, but today linens also provide an opportunity to add color and pattern to appropriate settings. Because they are relatively inexpensive, linens reflect the constantly changing color and design trends. Textiles are also used in the form of rugs and carpets, **tapestries,** and other types of hangings to add warm finishing touches to interiors. The following represent some of the uses of textiles as accessories:

- Table linens include tablecloths, napkins, place mats, and runners. These are made in every possible shape and of many fibers. The artificial fibers are generally easier to care for, but the natural fibers have a fine look and feel that are difficult to duplicate. A table beautifully set with linens, tableware, and flowers chosen to create a harmonious and stimulating mood can be an important part of the pleasure of a good meal.

- Bed linens are sheets, pillowcases, **pillow shams** (removable, decorative pillow covers), **dust ruffles**, bedspreads, blankets, comforters, quilts, and **duvets** (nondecorative comforters) and their covers. These are available in a wide array of colors and styles. Today, bed linens are the domain of the designer and are manufactured in classic whites as well as designs compatible with every type of interior.
- Bath and kitchen linens consist mainly of towels. These are generally made of linen, cotton, or cotton terry cloth, all of which are absorbent and easy to launder. Linen (flax) cloths are particularly good for drying glassware, because they are lint-free and shine glass nicely.
- Rugs and carpets are discussed with floor coverings in Chapter 12, "Floor Materials and Coverings." The types of rugs generally considered to be accessories are art rugs, designer rugs, and Oriental rugs, particularly when they hang on the wall.
- Tapestries and hangings were used for hundreds of years to provide actual physical warmth to the interior environment. They were used to cover the windows and walls of cold and damp castles; as bed hangings to protect from drafts, to keep in the warmth, and to provide privacy; and as table covers. Their use today is far more decorative, although they may provide a certain amount of psychological warmth because of their texture, pattern, and color. Traditional European tapestry designs are still being manufactured today, and contemporary artists are creating textile hangings with innovative methods of construction and design.
- Handwoven or constructed fabric or textile pieces that hang on the wall are called **fabric art** or soft sculpture. Handmade antique or new coverlets or quilts are also used as wall hangings and table covers.

Objects from Nature

Plants

Plants add life and interest to interiors because they are continually growing and changing and because of their free-flowing and sculptural forms. Each type of plant has a distinctive quality of design that makes it better suited to one style of interior than another. For example, the cactus has a strong, bristling, hard-edged quality and a dramatic sculptural form well suited to clean, structural interiors. The Boston fern is soft and feathery—character-

istics that make it suitable in both traditional and contemporary environments where it adds textural variety. When selecting plants, pay close attention to the shape, texture, and suitability to the area where they are to be placed.

Plants need adequate light, proper temperatures, and careful feeding, watering, and cleaning. These needs vary according to the type of plant. Some are sturdy, whereas others are quite sensitive to environmental changes. Any room with abundant natural light, whether direct or indirect, can house plants. The humidity produced by running water makes bathrooms and kitchens especially good places for plants that dry out easily. In some interiors such as greenhouses and solariums, plant care may be the very reason for the room's existence.

Plants look healthy and well formed in floral shops or nurseries because they have been raised in greenhouses under controlled conditions. Yet when they are moved into typically overheated, overcooled, or dry human environments, they often become sickly. Living with plants from day to day, it is easy to be unaware of how bad a sickly plant might appear.

People who have the ability to raise and maintain healthy plants are said to have a green thumb. Those who

Figure 14.12 Fresh flowers breathe life into any interior.
© *Kathryn Taylor*

do not have green thumbs or whose interior environments are not conducive to healthy plants may need to consider alternatives. One alternative is commercial plant services, available in many places. These plant services care for greenery on a contract basis and will advise as to the type of plant that does best in a given setting. These firms may sell or lease the plants and in some cases will offer a warranty for their products and service. Another alternative is to seek professional advice on selection and care so that a plant will thrive in its new environment.

Some plants will survive very well with artificial light, but in dark environments with dramatic lighting like certain restaurants and lounges, artificial plants may be a suitable alternative. Fortunately the quality of artificial plants is improving. Today silk leaves and blooms are combined with actual trunks and plastic stems to create fairly convincing artificial plants, trees, and flowers. Both real and artificial plants need regular cleaning in order to continue to look their best.

Flowers and Greenery

Any time of the year, one can find growing or natural things that can be brought indoors to brighten the environment and lift the spirits. Cut flowers from the garden or florist add color and life to interiors. Arrangements can be very formal and precise, like the Japanese **ikebana,** in which flowers are arranged according to strict, ancient rules of placement. Geometric bouquets purchased through florists remain popular, but bouquets of spring or summer blooms that appear to have been brought straight in from the garden and loosely arranged in an artistic way are often more pleasing because they have soft flowing lines that imitate the way flowers actually grow.

Flowers can be used as single blooms or massed in myriads of color and texture combinations. But when flowers are not available, or simply as a change of pace, other natural and growing things can be used seasonally to bring life to interiors. For example, wreaths or baskets full of pine boughs and cones can be used all through the winter, not just at Christmas, to add a touch of greenery. In the early fall, branches of bright autumn leaves are cheerful, and in late fall and early winter, bowls, baskets, or sprays of hardy berries like pyracantha bring visual warmth to a cool season. Bowls or baskets full of apples, horse chestnuts, or other late-fall delights are attractive and long-lasting. Pumpkins, gourds, and winter squash or piles of lemons, limes, or oranges make fine winter displays. In the spring, blossoms from fruit trees or pussy willows and corkscrew willows are interesting alternatives to flower arrangements.

In the summer there is a wonderful array of flowers available, but other growing things can be equally exciting. Fresh summer fruits and vegetables in interesting arrangements can be beautiful. Freshly cut herbs from the garden make unusual greenery for flower arrangements and are also very appealing by themselves in monochromatic arrangements. Dried herbs, grasses, and weeds make long-lived compositions if arranged with restraint and care. Ivy pulled from the garden is also long-lasting when placed in water. With so many possibilities, there is no need to despair the lack of a green thumb. Creating arrangements of flowers and other types of plant life is a pleasing and creative activity.

Selecting the container is a delightful part of the creative process. A beautifully designed vase is a fine way to display flowers, but anything that will hold water is fair game for arrangements. Watertight containers can often be hidden inside baskets and other porous or leaky objects to make them flower-worthy. Some of the most interesting arrangements may be created in very unusual containers. For example, an old rusty disk from a tiller on a farm could hold a fall arrangement, a wicker picnic basket could be filled with summer garden flowers, and a small copper teakettle could complement a sweet country bouquet.

Other Natural Objects

Consider this list of other objects from nature that often find their way into interior environments:

- Sea shells and rocks can be displayed as decorative accessories. Large shells can be mounted on specially designed pedestals or displayed on a table or shelf as any other art object. Small shells can be massed together in baskets, glass bowls, or any appropriate container where their beauty can be fully appreciated. Rocks can be displayed in much the same way as shells, massed together or mounted on stands. The beauty of some rocks becomes evident only after cutting and polishing, which often reveals natural designs of amazing beauty.
- Animal skins and hunting **trophies** may add an exotic or rustic quality to certain interiors. However, they may provoke objections on grounds of sensitivity, concern for conservation, or cruelty to animals. This should be a matter of careful discrimination.
- Fish tanks or aquariums can also bring life to interior environments. However, like plants, they require meticulous upkeep in order to be attractive—a dirty aquarium or sick fish are anything but appealing. As with plants, there are also services available in some areas for maintaining aquariums and fish.

Other Accessories

There are a number of other things in our environments that are products of rapidly developing and constantly

Figure 14.13 Here, a collection of antique boxes provides a distinctive counterpoint to the other furnishings. © *Jessie Walker Associates*

changing technology. Appliances, computers, video systems, audio systems, and telephones are important elements of an interior. These are chosen primarily for their function, although they may be good design as well. They should be considered an important part of the design and be accommodated with sensitivity to their function and aesthetic appeal.

The Use of Accessories

Collections

Many of us enjoy collecting objects, and the collections usually say something about the background, travels, or experiences of the collector. Some collections are worthy of display and impart a personal quality to the environment. These collections might be pieces of fine art, porcelain or other ceramics, antique toys, shells, books, bottles, or other glass pieces, stamps, coins, guns and swords, photographs, or any pieces of personal interest. When there is inadequate space for an entire collection, the finest pieces should be selected for display, grouped and arranged in harmony with the principles and elements of design.

The Japanese Approach to Displaying Collections

The Japanese are widely esteemed for their aesthetic sensitivity. There is much to be learned from the way they collect and display objets d'art in their traditional environments. The traditional Japanese home had a specially designated area called the **tokonoma,** which was a type of shrine for the display of one or two art objects and an arrangement of flowers (ikebana). These displays were changed regularly, and pieces were often chosen to honor a special guest. Objects not on display were safely stored for later use. This approach to the display of art objects is characterized by the excitement of bringing out old and treasured pieces that have been packed away for a time and then rediscovered. These possessions become new again and are used with refreshed appreciation.

This clean or minimal philosophy is in harmony with the idea that "less is more"—a concept that has been a hallmark of the modern design movement and is still the favored approach to many designs. Such designs, stripped of all unnecessary embellishment, can be appealing because they create a sense of space and freedom. Neat, well-ordered spaces devoid of mess and clutter can be peaceful and calming as well. Any object placed in this kind of environment is important because it does not compete visually with other elements of the design. Therefore, a carefully selected art piece or accessory can become a focal point in the room.

The Victorian Approach to Displaying Collections

During the Victorian era of the nineteenth century, there was a tendency to fill every available inch of space with **knickknacks.** Shelves and tables were crowded with objets d'art. When new pieces were introduced, the others were pushed a little more tightly together to make room for the new piece. Everything was on display.

This approach, still common today, is sometimes called organized clutter. Some environments may appear this way due to a lack of organization and planning, an inability to part with anything, or a desire to create a feeling of nostalgia. To others, however, each object in the

Figure 14.14 A tokonoma from the traditional Japanese house.

space may have special significance and may add to the warmth of the environment.

Some interiors are appealing because of their clean, streamlined approach to art and accessories, while others are interesting and charming because they are filled with personal treasures. Somewhere between the extremes of Japanese and Victorian philosophies of accessory display lies comfortable and pleasing middle ground that suits an environment and provides the right balance of emotional support for the users.

Overall Considerations

When selecting any kind of art for an interior, it is important to keep the principles and elements of design in mind. Artworks and objects that fit with the proportions, line, texture, color, and other characteristics of a room's design will complement that room. Conversely, art that may be exquisite on its own will look out of place and detract from its surroundings if placed in an interior whose design characteristics are at odds with it.

Function is another factor to consider in selecting and arranging art. A fragile sculpture, for example, should not be placed near a high-traffic doorway, even if the visual effect of the placement is stunning. It would be poor design to place watercolors that are vulnerable to shifts in humidity above a sink or to place a woven hanging that cannot be cleaned near a window that is usually kept open, admitting dust and pollutants. The subject matter of art, too, can be chosen in relation to the function of the interior. For example, while botanical prints of fruit and vegetables may be appropriate in a number of different places, they are particularly well suited to a kitchen or dining room. These functional factors need not stand in the way of creativity or good taste, but they are worth considering as part of the decision-making process.

Emotionally Supportive Design

Art, accessories, and furnishings have the power to provide emotional support because they are often links to esteemed people or events. This is why a piece of furniture or cherished piece of porcelain often serves as a **memento** of a person, time, or place. Those who emigrated from one country to another or who, in years past, moved from civilized surroundings to settle the wilderness often carried and protected treasured objects from their past into their uncertain futures. Preserving a fragile remembrance from the past and keeping it undamaged through the years is a remarkable accomplishment and source of pride. Today, these same objects are passed from one generation to another with great respect and love.

A photograph, a certificate, and **memorabilia** such as pressed flowers, a tiny christening gown, a watch or medal, and even a map can also preserve a memory and help recall an important time in one's life. Objects collected while traveling serve as reminders of exciting places and experiences. Well-designed pieces received as gifts from cherished friends may be decorative and also serve as remembrances of those people.

Drawings and crafts created by children are part of the emotional support system of a family and should be displayed with pride to encourage creativity. Such pieces often have artistic merit, and a child seeing the work on display is encouraged to continue the creative endeavors. These pieces could be matted and displayed in a place of honor or simply taped to the refrigerator door. It is the recognition that counts.

Human beings generally want to be surrounded by the things they love, whether it be in large doses or one object at a time. The clutter approach is not more correct than the minimal philosophy, merely better suited to certain interiors and individual needs. It is important to determine what kind of a balance is most pleasing to us and appropriate to our interiors; we should be careful not to discard well-loved pieces simply because we might not be completely confident of their aesthetic quality. For example, to some, a porcelain figurine might seem to be valueless kitsch. To another it might represent a cherished childhood memory, or it may have belonged to a dear friend or relative. We alone can make those determinations of value, and it is the inclusion of valued art and accessories that makes an environment emotionally supportive as well as a statement of personal experience.

Figure 14.15 Organized clutter.

Figure 14.16 Industrial design educator Doug Stout's office provides the setting for an unusual link with his native Britain and his lifelong fascination with trains. His bookshelf displays part of his collection of British locomotives and rail cars purchased during visits to England and Scotland. They are not only visually appealing but serve as an important cultural tie with his past. *John Wang and Doug McIntosh, photographers*

Figure 14.17 The interior of the Salt Lake City International Airport features large-scale paintings of the ruggedly beautiful southern Utah landscape. *Andrew Arnone and Darlene Langford, photographers*

Nonresidential Considerations

Art and accessories in nonresidential interiors create a feeling of finish and add the important element of human interest to spaces that could otherwise be quite impersonal. For this reason, many nonresidential design projects have specific budgets for artwork. The decision on how to spend those budgets usually belongs to the architect, the designer, a committee, or an art consultant. Sadly, sometimes the art budget is extremely limited or consumed by cost overrides in other areas. At the other end of the spectrum are the large corporations that collect art not only for its aesthetic value but for investment as well. Some of these have staff members whose sole responsibility is the acquisition of art and its dispersement to permanent collections throughout the corporation. Other nonresidential venues function as unofficial art galleries, displaying work from sources such as schools and community artist guilds on a rotating basis.

Many large nonresidential projects such as offices, hotels, and hospitals benefit from the use of art, though not always in permanent collections. These interiors are usually redesigned every few years, and a change in the art is often part of the new design program. Selecting pieces for this kind of design project requires extreme sensitivity, because not only must the art be purchased in large quantities but it must also be chosen for its relationship to the elements of the design, its price, and its aesthetic merit. Success in this kind of art selection is not as common as it should be, but the errors made in these situations can provide one key to understanding how to select quality art.

Fine art, regardless of price, cannot be exclusively tied to a decorative scheme by color or some other element—it must have its own aesthetic merit. If a new design program truly demands a change in the art, then the pieces being removed, if they have aesthetic merit, should still be of value in some other setting. If they have no value ten years after their initial installation, then they probably had no

be wise to ask ourselves, What will be the value of this piece ten years from now? If it can weather the test of time, it will be well chosen.

Some designs such as restaurants and boutiques often require the selection of art and accessories keyed to a theme such as English Tudor or Country French. This kind of project may be like creating a stage setting, and each piece of art and every accessory will be selected because it reinforces the concept for the design. This often requires some research into the history of the decorative arts to ensure that selections are supportive and appropriate to the stated theme.

One of the most crucial aspects of a design is its relationship to the users. Designers may find it discouraging to return to a design for a postoccupancy evaluation and find that things have changed; for example, the pristine reception area has been invaded by the receptionist's personal items, and the manager's wall is covered with postcards and pictures of the family. It is human nature to surround ourselves with things we love, and design must accommodate that tendency so that the work environment can be pleasant

Figure 14.18 Accessories are the key ingredient of the interior design at the Hard Rock Café in Dallas, Texas. © *Norman McGrath*

aesthetic merit to begin with. Such pieces of decorator art or motel art will only find their way to incinerators or dusty thrift-store tables. Finding good-quality prints, reproductions, or originals at the price points required by large projects may demand some effort. However, the search is worth the impact that good-quality art creates in an interior design. When judging a piece of art, it might and supportive in every way. If a design is so clean that it forces management to create policies prohibiting personal belongings, then it has failed to meet the emotional needs of its users. It should not be difficult to provide a surface for photographs or cards and a space for personal mementos. Such considerate planning, rather than detracting from, will add vitality to the design.

Chapter 15 | Historic Design

Early Influences 374

The English Influence in America 386

American Styles 396

Modern Design (1857–Present) 420

Putting Things in Perspective 437

© Peter Paige

Early Influences

The design we see today is the result of centuries of influence, development, and change. It is difficult to separate innovations from the factors that shaped them. Even those trends that claim to be free from previous influence have some basis in the experience and technology of preceding generations. Some of the most significant and influential architectural designs originated in classical Greece, Imperial Rome, the Middle Ages, and the Italian Renaissance.

Greece (Fifth Century B.C.)

The Parthenon, considered one of the most beautiful buildings in the world, is the classical embodiment of ancient Greek architecture. This magnificent combination of sculpture and architecture, designed to honor the goddess Athena, rests on an outcropping of rock called the Acropolis in the capital city of Athens. The Parthenon, built during the fifth century B.C. (golden age), was partially destroyed in 1687 by a bombardment during the Turko-Venetian war. But even in its ruined state it is an inspiring sight.

The construction of the Parthenon is solid marble, generally without mortar. The triangular roof trusses were wooden and covered with terra-cotta tiles. The building, designed by Ictinus and Callicrates, is beautifully proportioned. Through minute adjustments to the curvature of the horizontal lines and by manipulation of the shape, placement, and inclination of the columns, optical illusions were created that make the Parthenon appear visually perfect.

One of the Parthenon's finest features was its sculpture, which was executed principally by the sculptor Phidias. Much of the original sculpture was taken to England during the nineteenth century by British collector Lord Elgin. These extraordinary pieces are now housed as a collection called the Elgin Marbles in the British Museum in London.

The Parthenon shows clearly the characteristics of Greek architecture. The entire building rests on a base called the **stylobate,** which can be approached from any angle (the actual entrance was in the rear). The **columns** (supporting posts that carry the weight of the roof) form a **colonnade** (row of columns) around the exterior of the building. A **lintel,** or crosspiece, called the **architrave** rests on the **capitals** at the top of the columns. The capital is a decorative detail that helps distinguish one

style or **order** of Greek architecture from another. A second set of beams rests on top of the architrave and runs the length and width of the building. On the exterior, these beams are covered with a decorative panel called the **frieze.** The architrave and frieze form the support for the triangular trusses of the roof. The trusses extend beyond the architrave and frieze and create an overhang called the **cornice.** The architrave, frieze, and cornice together form a combination of the three details known as the **entablature.** The row of roof trusses extends forward and backward to the front and rear of the building. The triangular shape of the roof forms a **pediment** (like a **gable**) at the front and rear. The pediment holds a triangular panel of sculpture called the **pediment frieze.**

The Greek Orders

As stylistic details evolved, certain types of entablatures were more compatible with certain columns and capitals, and distinct styles or orders were born. The three Greek orders are **Doric, Ionic,** and **Corinthian.**

The simplest and apparently the oldest order is the Doric. The shafts of Doric columns are **fluted** in shallow curved sections and have no base, resting directly on the stylobate. The Doric capital consists of a square **abacus** (plate) at the top and a simple curved **echinus** (dish) below. The Doric entablature has a plain architrave and a frieze divided into **triglyphs** and **metopes.** Triglyphs are blocks divided by vertical channels, and metopes are panels placed between the triglyphs, often decorated with sculpture in low relief.

The Ionic order is a more recent development, though it appears to be related to earlier Egyptian and Near Eastern prototypes. It consists of a capital with two front-facing scroll **volutes,** whose design may have been derived from animal horns or shells. Below is a molding of **egg and dart** with a second lower molding of **bead and reel** or **anthemion** relief designs. The column itself is thinner than the Doric and is fluted with separated

Figure 15.1 Even in its ruined state, the Parthenon of Athens is a timeless example of classical Greek design. *Su Davies/Life File/Getty Images*

Figure 15.2 The classical Greek and Roman orders: (A) Doric, (B) Ionic, (C) Corinthian, and (D) Tuscan. *(A) © Scala/Art Resource, NY; (B) © Bob Firth/ Imagestate; (C) © Gregory Edwards/Imagestate; (D) © Peter Aaron/Esto*

Figure 15.3 The Pantheon in Rome with its coffered dome is a remarkable Roman temple originally dedicated to all the gods. *Giovani Paolo Panini, The Interior of the Pantheon, ca. 1740. Oil on canvas, 4 ft. 2½ in. × 3 ft. 3 in. National Gallery of Art, Washington, DC. Bridgeman Art Library.*

semicircular grooves and finished at the bottom with a molded base that rests on the stylobate. The Ionic entablature is narrower than the Doric and features an architrave that rises in three distinct planes. It has an undecorated frieze or one decorated in a continuous band of sculpture and a cornice that projects less than the Doric.

The Corinthian order was not widely used by the Greeks but was adopted by the Romans. The Corinthian capital is shaped like an inverted bell and embellished with two rows of **acanthus leaves.** The bell shape is topped with four small volutes that support each corner of a square abacus. The Corinthian cornice may also be enriched with square **dentil** ornament. Table 15.1 is an overview of Greek design.

Greek Furniture Classics

The Klismos is one of a group of beautiful reproductions of Greek furniture pieces taken from depictions on archaeological artifacts. The pieces, designed by **T. H. Robsjohn-Gibbings** (1905–76), are made in Greece by Saridis S. A. and are distributed in America by Gretchen Bellinger, Inc.

Rome (200 B.C.–A.D. 400)

During the Imperial Age of Rome (beginning in the first century B.C.), Greece was annexed and absorbed into the Roman Empire. At that point, Rome began to overshadow the Greek civilization it had conquered, though the Romans never reached the level of artistic achievement attained by the Greeks. **Classical Roman** designs were magnificent and showy but never executed with the care and craftsmanship that characterized Greek design. That is probably to be expected because the far-flung Roman Empire had a massive program of building, and such meticulous care would have been impractical. The construction spread to every corner of the Empire—from Spain in the west to Asia Minor in the east and from Africa in the south to England and Germany in the north.

The Romans adapted Greek design to suit their needs, but they also brought to the style their own materials and unique engineering techniques. The Romans incorporated the **roundheaded arch** and **barrel vault** with the post and lintel, often in the same building. The perfection of the arch and vault led to the development of the dome. Bricks and concrete made from volcanic ash and lime facilitated rapid and sturdy construction. The brick and concrete were faced with a veneer of marble or plastered with stucco.

The Roman orders include the Doric, Ionic, and Corinthian styles as well as two orders developed by the

Table 15.1 | Greek Design

Classical Details

- Pediment
- Cornice
- Frieze
- Entablature
- Architrave
- Capital
- Column
- Stylobate

The Greek Orders

Doric   *Ionic*   *Corinthian*

Ionic Capital with Decorative Details

- Egg and dart
- Volute
- Anthemion
- Bead and reel
- Fluting

Greek Klismos with Saber Legs

The Parthenon
Athens, Greece

Romans: the **Tuscan** and **Composite.** The Roman Doric order varies most from the Greek original. The Roman version, which incorporates a base on the column, is less massive, and the column is often left unfluted. The Roman Ionic and Corinthian orders are almost identical to the Greek, varying mostly in small details of decoration. The Tuscan order is a simplified version of the Roman Doric, without flutes or ornamental moldings. The Composite order, as the name implies, is a combination of the Corinthian and Ionic orders. Large volutes, together with a band of egg-and-dart and bead-and-reel moldings, are borrowed from the Ionic capital, and two rows of acanthus leaves are taken from the Corinthian order. The resulting design is even more decorative than the Corinthian capital.

The Roman temple was based on the design of Greek temples but differed from them in at least two important ways. First, the Roman temple was built on a raised **podium** instead of a stylobate and was approached only from the front by means of a single set of steps. Second, the interior space (**cella**) was expanded to the edge of the podium and filled the area that would otherwise form a porch at the sides and rear of the building. The exterior walls were lined with half columns that formed a continuous line with the columns of the covered porch or **portico** at the front of the building. The Maison Carrée (c. 16 B.C.), Nimes, France, is an excellent example of a small Roman temple. The Pantheon (A.D. 120) in Rome is an important example of a circular Roman temple. The building, which was dedicated to all the gods and later consecrated as a Christian church, features a large dome (over 142 feet in diameter) that rests on a round drum-shaped cella. The round domed space is called a rotunda. The interior is lighted by an open **oculus** (circular opening at the top of the dome), 142 feet above the floor. The exterior incorporates a portico attached to the circular body of the building.

Much of what remains of Roman domestic design was rediscovered in 1754 with the first excavations of **Pompeii** and **Herculaneum**—cities buried and preserved by the eruption of Mount Vesuvius in A.D. 79. The House of the Vettii, an example of a Pompeiian house, opened into an **atrium** (a space open to the sky). The atrium contained a pool, which held rainwater collected from the roof. The rear section of the house opened into a colonnaded garden area called the **peristyle.** These houses also typically had libraries, picture galleries, kitchens, and rooms for sculpture, dining, sleeping, and conversation and reading.

The terms classical and classicism are often mentioned in conjunction with architectural design and detailing. These terms refer to the use or adaptation of Greek and Roman forms, motifs, and proportions in the designs of subsequent periods. The Roman orders and their proportions were documented and preserved in drawings by **Vitruvius,** a first-century Roman architect. Correct classi-cal proportions are often referred to as **Vitruvian proportions.** Table 15.2 illustrates aspects of Roman design.

Color in Antiquity

Color has played an important role throughout history. Colors have reflected climate, political and social atmosphere, and trade with or exposure to other cultures. Today as we view the ruins of antiquity, we have only a glimpse into the real colors enjoyed by peoples of every era in history. These colors are useful to interior designers today as historic interiors are re-created, restored, or adaptively reused.

Colors of ancient Greece included stellar, slate, and mist blues; scarlet; pale violet; pale and medium malachite and olive greens; sun yellow; ivory white; marble pink; clay beige; copper brown; and charcoal. Fragments of color on the Parthenon in Athens show us that blue was dominant, with figures in realistic tints of yellow, pink, and pale blue.

Classical Roman interiors were decorated with painted stucco and colorful mosaics, accented with rich fabrics. The brilliance and relative clarity of colors such as magenta (the imperial purple), rich gold, Pompeii red, and Roman greens, accented with black, surprised the Western world upon their discovery at Pompeii and Herculaneum.

The Middle Ages (800–1500)

With official acceptance of Christianity in Rome, the faithful in Italy began the construction of churches. These were built in a style known today as **Early Christian** and were an important influence on the styles that followed. By the year 1000, all of Europe was Christian. The barbarians who repeatedly streamed out of the north to sack Rome and the rest of southern Europe had intermarried, converted to Christianity, and in fact become Europeans. The lives of these people were inextricably tied to the church in a manner that is difficult for us to comprehend today. The church took care of every need, whether spiritual, physical, or intellectual, and in return everyone was expected to contribute money and labor to the building of churches.

Many of the Early Christian buildings were destroyed by fire, and in the eleventh century a new style of church with a fireproof stone ceiling became popular. These buildings used the roundheaded Roman arch and vault as forms for windows, doors, and ceilings. The French term **Romanesque,** meaning "Roman-like," is the designation given to the architecture of this period. In England the same style is generally called **Norman** after William I (the Conqueror) of Normandy, who conquered England in 1066.

The **Gothic** style grew out of Romanesque around 1135; it first appeared at the church of Saint-Denis near

Table 15.2 | Roman Design

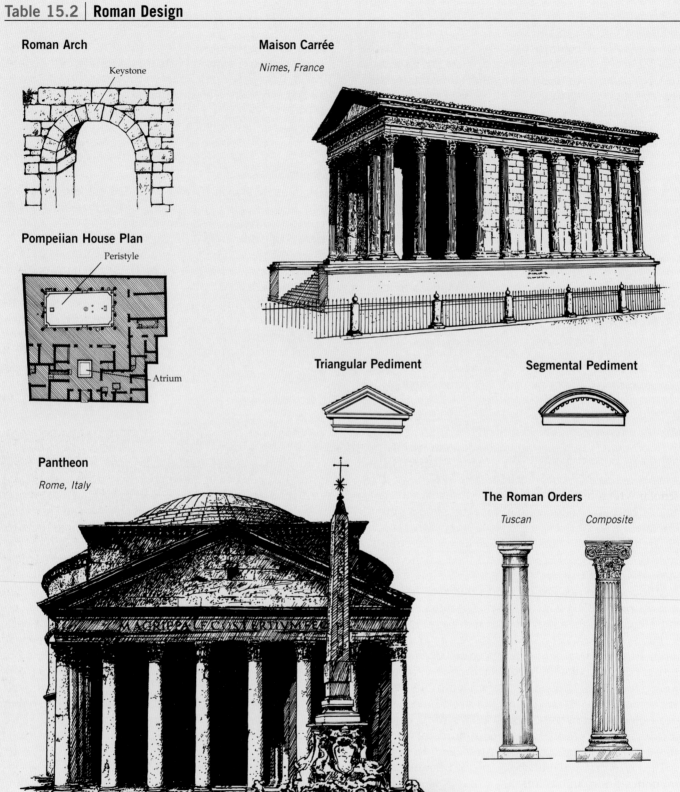

Roman Arch

Keystone

Pompeiian House Plan

Peristyle

Atrium

Maison Carrée

Nimes, France

Triangular Pediment

Segmental Pediment

Pantheon

Rome, Italy

The Roman Orders

Tuscan   *Composite*

Figure 15.4 Canterbury Cathedral has an impressively scaled tower over its crossing, a typical feature of English Gothic churches. © *David A. Taylor*

choir stalls and organ were located there. The end of the main body that frequently houses an altar is called the **apse.** The nave is divided on each side from the **aisles** by an **arcade** (row of arches). The aisles run along the sides of the nave and continue behind the choir and apse. The aisles are not as tall as the nave and extend only as high as the aisle arcade. Some churches have windows that open from the aisles to the exterior of the building, while others have small chapels that are entered from the aisles and run parallel to the nave and choir. The chapels radiate off of the apse aisle or **ambulatory.**

The area between each opposing set of aisle arches is called a **bay.** Each bay is divided by tall **piers** (columns) that carry the weight of the

Paris, France. The name Gothic, which has become synonymous with design from the **Medieval era,** or **Middle Ages,** was first applied by Vasari, a post-Renaissance scholar who must have decided that the style was no further advanced than that of the barbaric Goths in the sixth century. He and his contemporaries probably felt that the designers of the Renaissance had corrected the architectural drift away from the classicism of ancient Greece and Rome. Today, with added perspective, Gothic design and architecture are considered one of the finest achievements of all time.

Gothic architecture incorporates the **Gothic arch** (pointed arch), which led to the development of a very complex and ingenious system of vaulting that allowed the buildings to rise to great heights. These tall spaces draw the eye upward and inspire feelings of reverence and awe. The churches, often built over the **crypt** (basement) of earlier Romanesque churches, were laid out in the shape of a **Latin cross** or **cruciform.** The main body of the church, filled by worshippers, is called the **nave.** The nave is broken by the **transepts,** which extend outward on both sides from the **crossing** (the area where the nave and transepts cross). Beyond the crossing, the main body of the church is called the **choir** (or **quire**) because the

Figure 15.5 At Notre Dame de Chartres Cathedral in France, the arcade, triforium, and clerestory are easily seen within the interior. © *Paul M.R. Maeyaert*

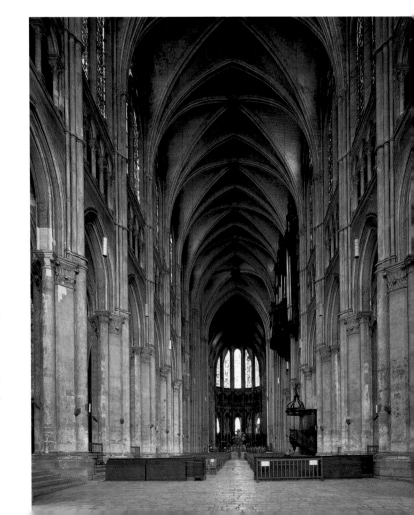

ceiling, the trusses, and the roof. The **ribs** that form the framework of the ceiling spring from **brackets** carved as part of the pier and reach across the ceiling to the opposite side, creating **vaults.** As the style developed, the vaulting became increasingly more complex and ornate. In some churches, large, decorative, carved medallions, called **bosses,** are attached to the ceiling where the ribs cross.

The wall between each of the piers is open at the floor level along the aisle arcade. Above the arcade is another set of openings called the **triforium.** In some cases the triforium serves as a gallery for looking into the nave and choir. In other churches the triforium is shallow and has no room for passage. The large openings above the triforium are the **clerestory windows.** These windows, as well as the windows on the aisle, are divided into smaller sections by vertical stone dividers called **mullions.** The lower part of the windows is divided into smaller pointed windows called **lancets.** The lacelike pattern of stone above the lancets is called **tracery.** The windows are often filled with **stained glass.** Stained glass consists of pieces of plain, colored, and painted glass, fitted together with lead strips called **came** to make patterned panels of glass that are fixed to the metal framework between the mullions of the window. Light entering the windows and filling the building was symbolic of the presence of God. The quality of colored light added further to the feeling of mysticism.

The relatively slender piers support the tremendous weight of the roof and stone ceiling and have a tendency to bow outward unless they are braced. Consequently, the weight of the roof of the nave is carried outward from the wall, above the roof of the aisles, by curved horizontal braces called **flying buttresses.** These connect with tall vertical structures, called **buttresses,** built on the exterior walls of the aisle. These grow increasingly thick in steps as they reach toward the ground and carry the weight from the flying buttresses.

Each country developed characteristics that distinguished the church designs of that area. For example, elegant flying buttresses were a striking feature of many French Gothic churches. English churches often had two sets of transepts, wide fronts, and tall towers over the crossing. Italian Gothic churches were covered with elaborate patterns in contrasting colors of marble. Every area of Europe produced beautiful Gothic churches, and when one stops to consider the sacrifice, hardship, devotion, and ingenuity required to build them, they become monuments to an age of faith. Table 15.3 shows elements of Medieval design.

Late Medieval domestic design continued well beyond the end of the Gothic era into the seventeenth century, particularly in the homes of the common people. The common houses from the end of the Middle Ages were constructed of stone, brick, or timber. These houses had steeply pitched roofs and small **casement windows** (that swing in or out) made with **leaded glass** panes (small panes held together with lead strips, like stained glass). The **timber-framed houses** utilized two types of **infill** to form the walls between the timbers. Panels of woven sticks called **wattle** were fixed, like lath (groundwork for plastering), to the timber frame and then covered with coarse plaster known as **daub.** The second type of infill was brickwork called **nogging.** The houses often featured an overhang or jetty at each story. These may have provided additional space in cramped city settings, but their use in less crowded areas suggests that overhangs were mostly a detail of style. Another theory is that the jetty helped to keep rainwater away from the foundation. Roofs were frequently **thatched** with bundles of reeds attached to the roof timbers and shaped and cut into smooth rounded curves. **Slate roofs** were made of thin, flat pieces of stone fashioned into shingles. Wooden shingles were also used in some areas. These Late Medieval common houses were the prototype for the seventeenth-century American houses. The English versions of this style are often referred to as Tudor, because this type of building was common during the reign of the Tudor kings and queens. Table 15.4 contains examples of Late Medieval design.

Medieval Color

Although color in castles and homes during the Medieval era was somewhat somber, the impact of color seen in the magnificent stained-glass windows throughout Europe

Figure 15.6 The Anne Hathaway Cottage in England, with its thatched roof, is a fine example of Late Medieval design. © *Kathryn Taylor*

Table 15.3 | Medieval Design—Romanesque and Gothic

Romanesque Arches

Gothic Church Interior Elevation

Gothic Church Cross Section

Gothic Church Plan

Notre Dame Cathedral: Gothic

Tracery

Mullion

Lancet

Pointed Gothic arch

Clerestory

Triforium

Arcade

Ribbed vault

Flying buttresses

Bracket

Buttress

Nave

Aisle

Apse

Ambulatory

Choir

Transept

Crossing

Aisle

Nave

Bay

Table 15.4 | Late Medieval Design

Late English Medieval Interior

Interior Details

Floors. Stone, wood plank
Walls. Timber frame with daub-and-wattle infill
Windows. Casement with leaded panes
Doors. Wooden plank
Chimneypiece. Large brick or stone with wooden-beam mantle
Ceiling. Beamed
Stairs. Simple, tucked away

Hall's Croft

Stratford-Upon-Avon, England

still impresses us today. Techniques used to create these colorful masterpieces were temporarily lost until research revived the production of colored stained glass during the Victorian era (1842–1910). Colors of the Middle Ages and previous periods were governed by symbolism and were not freely and creatively used.

The Influence of Asia

The cultures of the East have been influential in European and Western design since the time of the Crusades, when Europeans were introduced to the wonderful textiles, rugs, and other goods produced by the peoples of the Near East. Asian commodities continued to be imported to the West by land until 1492, when the fall of Constantinople closed those trade routes to the East. The thirst for Asian products remained strong, however, and Columbus set sail looking for a new sea route to Asia. With the establishment of the East India Company by the English

and the United East India Company by the Dutch at the beginning of the seventeenth century, Asian goods became readily available in Europe and even made their way to America.

Fine Chinese porcelain, lacquer work (Coromandel) screens, chests, and other pieces of furniture, as well as Chinese rugs, have been important features of Western interior design for centuries. Features of Chinese design including motifs such as fretwork, and details from Chinese furniture have been regularly incorporated into Western design. In the eighteenth century, the French created fanciful designs based on their notion of Chinese design, which they called **Chinoiserie.**

American architects were interested in traditional Japanese architecture. Early twentieth-century designers like the Greene brothers and Frank Lloyd Wright were influenced by the detail and fine craftsmanship of the traditional Japanese house. Shoji screens have inspired contemporary interior-architectural detail, and Japanese art pieces such as lanterns and byobu screens are prized accessories in Western interiors.

From Near Eastern Islamic cultures, Westerners have chosen architectural elements such as the horseshoe arch and the onion dome—a feature Islam borrowed from Byzantium—to embellish their buildings. During the nineteenth-century Victorian era, a picturesque architectural style known as Exotic or Oriental Revival was based on Islamic design. The beautiful rugs made by Islamic weavers have been prized in Western interiors since the time of the Crusades of the Middle Ages. Table 15.5 shows examples of Asian influence.

The Renaissance (1420–1650)

The **Renaissance** began in Florence, Italy, in the fourteenth century and marked the rebirth of classical influences in architecture, art, and many other areas of human endeavor. The architectural Renaissance moved through Europe by means of **pattern books** containing drawings and descriptions published by leading architects and designers from Italy, France, and Holland. These books, along with the writings of Vitruvius, discovered in 1414, influenced architecture until the nineteenth century.

The Renaissance palace was a boxlike city fortress with massive gates opening onto a roofless courtyard or atrium around which the house was built. The exterior of the palace was divided into three distinct stories by means of different textured stone, ranging from **rusticated** on the ground level to smooth on the third story, or by means of protruding rows **(courses)** of stone carved to form entablatures. The entablatures were visually supported by flat, false columns called **pilasters,** which progressed from the Doric order on the ground level to Ionic and Corinthian on the second and third levels. The top of the palace was finished with a very large overhanging cornice. The windows on the ground level were small and covered with iron bars. The second floor, or **piano nobile** (the noble level), and third floor had larger, well-proportioned windows. The **facade** (front face) of the building was arranged in a symmetrical fashion.

The Renaissance architect whose work had the greatest impact on English and, subsequently, American architecture was a sixteenth-century stonecutter-turned-architect named Andrea Palladio. Palladio's work, centered at Vicenza near Venice, included some public buildings but focused mainly on the design of villas for wealthy farmers. The most famous of these is the Villa Rotonda (1567). This house sits at the crest of a hill with a fine view in every direction. The basic form of the building is a plain box on a raised Roman podium. A portion of the podium extends outward on all four sides to create staircases. The four sets of steps lead up to four Roman Ionic porticoes. The house has a narrow attic story topped with a **hipped roof** of terra-cotta tiles that rises gently to support a low **drum** and shallow dome. The windows of the main floor are topped with triangular pediments supported by curved brackets called **modillions.** The Renaissance architects did not always try to duplicate the designs of Greece and Rome but adapted their proportions, forms, motifs, and orders to create a new and important style. See Table 15.6 for examples.

Renaissance Furniture Classics

The Renaissance witnessed the development of furniture that was adapted in every country where its influence

Figure 15.7 The Medici Palace in Florence, Italy, is a fortress-like city house from the Renaissance. *Alinari/Art Resource*

Table 15.5 | The Influence of Asia

Coromandel Screen

Byobu Screen

Chinese Tables

Chinese Chippendale Chair

Chinese Chairs

Persian Oriental Rug

Chinese Porcelain Vase

Chinese Textile

Chinese Rug

Chinese Cupboard

Table 15.6 | Renaissance Design

Palazzo Rucellai

Florence, Italy

Textile Description

Colors. Rich and vibrant reds, blues, golds, and greens predominate

Patterns. Large-scale florals, the artichoke, the pomegranate

Textures. Plain and figured velvet, tapestry, silk brocade, and damask

Savonarola Chair

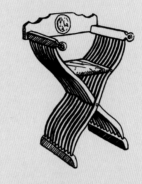

Dante Chair

Renaissance Textiles

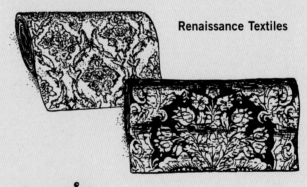

Villa Rotonda, Andrea Palladio

Vicenza, Italy

was felt—from Spain to England, and from Scotland to Germany. Some of those important pieces remain classics even today. For example, the Dante and Savonarola chairs, designed during the Renaissance, are still seen in today's interiors. These are X-frame chairs patterned after Roman folding chairs. The Savonarola chair is made of a series of X-shaped slats, while the Dante chair has a double X frame and usually an upholstered seat.

Renaissance Color

The Renaissance was a time of rebirth of artistic and architectural pursuits. No longer tied strictly to symbolic color, artists discovered the freedom to creatively use color. Color became a pleasing, decorative, and satisfying element for artists and patrons alike. Oil paintings reveal rich, sensuous hues such as garnet and persimmon reds, bright copper, deep cobalt blue, blue-green, medium blue, pale and deep greens, medium and deep malachite greens, rich and dull brown, marble and ivory cream and white, and metallic gold. Renaissance color elements migrated from Italy northward to Europe, notably France, Germany, the Lowlands, and England, and then finally to America.

The Baroque Period (1580–1750)

The Baroque period is often considered the final phase of the Renaissance, and it represents the full flowering of the classical tradition reintroduced by Renaissance designers. Baroque design incorporates all of the classical elements such as columns, pediments, pilasters, entablatures, rounded arches,

Figure 15.8 Baroque scroll pediment.

and domes. However, it takes on an exaggerated form in terms of scale and ornamentation. Baroque design is large scaled, bold, and even theatrical, with dramatic effects of light and shadow. Ceilings are painted with incredible realistic scenes floating in the clouds and with angels hovering overhead. The architectural forms are taken to extremes and made to undulate and twist. The facades of the churches curve in and out, the interior spaces are rounded without corners, and columns are twisted. Hence the origin of the term *baroque,* which comes from the Portuguese *barroco,* or imperfect pearl with its undulating, irregular surface.

The materials of Baroque design are rich marbles, gilded metals, and ornately painted plaster. The overall effect is impressive. The style was called "Jesuit" in France, which reflects an important function of Baroque design. Many Catholics converted to Protestantism during the Reformation, and the Jesuit order was given the

mission to bring back the faithful—which it did through the coercion of the Inquisition and the enticement of the lavish Baroque style.

The Baroque style began in Italy, spread to France, and eventually made its way to Great Britain and northern Europe. As it moved north it became less exuberant, however. For example, the French found Bernini's design for the Louvre far too outlandish for their taste. However, the scale and showy quality of the style was perfectly suited to the Palace of Versailles, built for Louis XIV; it was built not so much as a home but as a symbol of Louis's and France's power. Sir Christopher Wren, the great English designer, studied French Baroque designs and simplified them even more. The influence of the Baroque style, by the time it made its way to the American Colonies, had lost its showiness and appeared in simplified form in the beautifully refined details of the Early Georgian style.

The English Influence in America

The Seventeenth-Century English Medieval Style (1608–95)

Settlers arriving in America from England in the early part of the seventeenth century quickly built crude, temporary

Figure 15.9 Melk Abbey in Austria demonstrates the exuberance, richness, and emotionally rendered classical forms typical of Baroque design. © Paul M.R. Maeyaert

Table 15.7 | Seventeenth-Century English Medieval Design

Exterior Characteristics

- English Medieval construction—brick, stone, timber with daub and wattle or nogging, and clapboard siding
- Steeply pitched gabled roof
- Small casement windows with leaded panes
- Overhang or jetty with pendants (optional)
- Buttressed chimneys (optional)
- Columned chimneys (optional)
- Stone-ender chimneys (optional)
- Projecting entry (optional)
- Saltbox (optional)
- Gambrel roof (optional)

Influences

- Late English Medieval domestic architecture
- Early English Renaissance architecture

Residential Examples

- Adam Thoroughgood House (1640), Princess Anne County, Virginia
- Corwin House (c. 1675), Salem, Massachusetts
- Eleazer Arnold House (before 1676), Johnston, Rhode Island
- Henry Whitfield House (1639), Guilford, Connecticut
- Whipple House (1638), Ipswich, Massachusetts
- Bacon's Castle (c. 1665), Surrey County, Virginia
- Thomas Clemence House (1680), Johnston, Rhode Island
- Parson Capen House (1683), Topsfield, Massachusetts

Nonresidential Examples

- St. Luke's Church (1632), Isle of Wight County, Virginia

Thoroughgood House

Brick Construction

Arnold House

Stone-Ender

Whitfield House

Stone Construction

Corwin House

Clapboard Construction

(continued)

Seventeenth-Century English Medieval Design (continued)

Brewster Chair

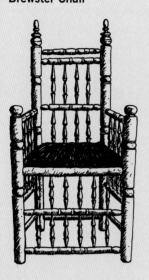

Carver Chair

Gateleg Table

Interior Details

Floors. Wide wooden plank
Walls. Stucco
Windows. Small casement with leaded panes
Doors. Planks (later paneled)
Chimneypiece. Large, open, brick fireplace for warmth and cooking; large wooden mantel beam; board-and-batten palisade wall
Ceiling. Beamed
Stairs. Simple, modified, wooden, double-turn, with wooden balustrade

Sunflower Chest

Seventeenth-Century English Medieval Interior

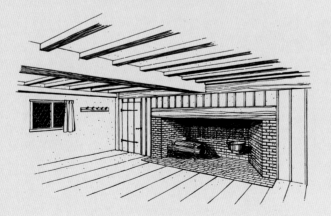

Typical Three-Part Casement Window with Leaded Panes

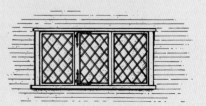

shelters. However, as soon as conditions permitted, they constructed permanent buildings of the style they had left in England. Because these settlers were generally not from the wealthy class, they were probably unacquainted with the Renaissance style; instead, they were accustomed to Medieval construction methods and design. The result is the **Seventeenth-Century English Medieval style** (see Table 15.7).

Seventeenth-century American houses featured varied use of materials and distinctive characteristics in each area of the country. Brick was prevalent in the South where lime to make mortar was more available than it was elsewhere. In New England, timber houses were often covered with **clapboard,** a sheathing of hand-split oak. Houses sided with clapboard were also common in East Anglia, the English region that had been home to many of the early American settlers. In Rhode Island several houses—called **stone-enders**—were built with stone chimneys that covered the end of the building.

The Medieval characteristics of the seventeenth-century American houses were the use of stone, brick, and timber construction, daub and wattle, nogging, jetties with decorative **pendants,** small casement windows with leaded panes, chimneys built in the shape of Gothic buttresses **(buttressed chimneys),** and steeply pitched, gabled roofs. **Saltbox roofs,** though not necessarily Medieval, were English. The saltbox slopes to the rear from the ridge of the roof to a level below the line of the front eaves and usually covers a lean-to addition at the back of the house. These additions were probably made in response to the need for more space. The saltbox was generally an addition made to an existing house, but by the eighteenth century some houses were built with saltbox roofs. The **gambrel roof,** with two different pitches on each side, was also used somewhat during the seventeenth century, but it was more popular on the vernacular houses of the eighteenth century. This type of roof, which was also English, was practical because it allowed more space in the garret (attic).

Seventeenth-Century Furniture Classics

Seventeenth-century furniture was brought from England by settlers or made in America with rather primitive methods. The pieces are solid, sturdy, and unpretentious. Chests were important storage pieces and were frequently carved or decorated with split spindles, a method of **embellishment** also common in England. Chairs were straight and rigid with **turnings,** probably because turning was a relatively simple yet decorative way to make legs and **stretchers.** Two important examples are the Carver and Brewster chairs. These chairs are almost identical except that the Brewster chair has many more spindles than the Carver chair. The gateleg table with turned legs is another important piece from the period that has never really gone out of fashion.

Color in Seventeenth-Century America

Seventeenth-century colors tended to be earth colors seen in pewter, wood, and unbleached muslin, as well as in the simple homespun checks in indigo blues, yellows, and madder reds. Colors, limited as they were, tended to be dull, natural, and faded.

The Early Georgian Style (1695–1750)

The classical style of the Renaissance began to be widely accepted in England primarily due to the work of Sir Christopher Wren, Surveyor of the King's Works (royal architect). In 1666, when the **City of London** was destroyed by fire, Wren was commissioned to rebuild St. Paul's Cathedral as well as fifty-two smaller churches. His designs for churches and royal buildings were classical with some rich Baroque ornamentation. The influence of Wren extended to the building of houses as well. These medium-sized, Wren-Baroque-style houses were the prototype for American houses during the first half of the eighteenth century. Compared to the seventeenth-century Medieval houses, the **Early American** Georgian houses seemed splendid. They were, however, versions of middle-class English residences. The very large homes and palaces of the English aristocracy and royalty were not used as models for homes in the colonies.

At the beginning of the eighteenth century, Colonial America was prospering, and certain segments of society were ready for more elaborate houses. The new Wren-Baroque style of architecture was introduced in Williamsburg, Virginia, at the end of the seventeenth century. The Wren Building (1695) at William and Mary College in Williamsburg—the first example of the new style in America—though much less elaborate than most of Wren's English designs, is very much like his Chelsea Royal Hospital (1682) in London.

Residences in the new style began to appear in America after the beginning of the eighteenth century. The first few years of the 1700s saw the death of Queen Anne and the accession to the British throne of George I. He was succeeded by George II, George III, and George IV, who gave their name to the **Georgian** era. The new architectural style popularized by Wren in England a quarter of a century earlier is called **Early Georgian** in America.

The basic form of the Early Georgian house was a rectangular two-story box, broken by five symmetrically placed bays (sections of wall that include window and door openings). Brick was the preferred building material in the South, painted clapboard or brick were used in New England, and stone was common in the mid-Atlantic colonies. Where brick or stone were used, the first and second stories were frequently divided by a **stringcourse** or **beltcourse.** One or two Early Georgian–style houses built after 1750 include the use of **quoins** (decorative corner block details), which were more common in the Late

Figure 15.10 The MacPhaedris-Warner House, a fine Early-Georgian dwelling in Portsmouth, New Hampshire, features a cupola and balustrade on its roof. *© David A. Taylor*

Georgian style. Because these houses were larger, they required more than one chimney, and the chimneys were frequently placed at opposite ends of the house. Like the English prototypes, the houses had **hipped roofs,** which slope from the ridge in all four directions to the eaves. The roof was often broken by dormer windows that projected to provide light for the attic story. Some builders of independent spirit ignored the English prototype and incorporated gambrel or gabled roofs into their designs. Such variations give these houses a distinctly American feeling.

Medieval details from the seventeenth century, such as casement windows with leaded panes, were replaced by **sash windows;** a door flanked with pilasters and crowned with a classical pediment took the place of the simple Medieval doorway. Pediments were the simple **triangular** type, rounded **segmental pediments** (the arch is a segment of a circle), or the more ornate, Baroque-style **scroll pediments.** On some of these buildings, pediments were also used above the windows. The rafters were extended far enough to create an overhang that was treated like a classical cornice, often with **modillions** or **dentil trim.** A few of these houses had railings or **balustrades** around the ridge of the roof and a windowed tower called a **cupola.** Kitchens, servants' quarters, dairies, and other types of service areas were frequently located in **outbuildings** away from the main body of the house.

Some of these outbuildings were attached to the houses during the twentieth century, altering their original appearance.

Early Georgian Furniture Classics

Both the William and Mary and Queen Anne furniture styles were popular during the Early Georgian era. However, it is the **Queen Anne** style that has remained popular and is still loved and used today.

The Queen Anne tea table was a popular piece in eighteenth-century England and America as tea drinking became increasingly fashionable and the serving of tea a highly refined art. The tea table is characterized by its **cabriole legs** with **club feet.** Below the **apron,** the knee of the leg may be carved with a shell or other motif.

The Queen Anne **wing chair** evolved from a seventeenth-century sleeping chair; the wings provided support for a nodding head. The wing chair is upholstered and has typical Queen Anne cabriole legs, some versions with **stretchers,** others without.

Queen Anne chairs feature upholstered seats, round-shouldered hoop backs with a vase- or fiddle-shaped splat, cabriole legs generally without stretchers, and club feet. The **side chair** is armless, and the **armchair** has open arms in various forms, the most common of which is the gooseneck or shepherd's crook arm with its beautifully shaped curve.

The Queen Anne lowboy and highboy are important case pieces from the eighteenth century. The **lowboy** is a raised chest on cabriole legs, generally with two drawers or a single wide drawer and two smaller square drawers in the curved **apron** (the face of the chest just below the drawers). The **highboy** is created when a chest of four or five drawers is placed on top of the lowboy. The top of the highboy may be crowned with some type of **pediment,** but most often it will be flat with a slight cornice. Table 15.8 shows Early Georgian design.

Early Georgian Color

Early Georgian colors were the Renaissance colors imported from England and France, with a preference for greens and dark dull blues; deep olive greens (examples of Colonial Williamsburg colors); and some golds, oranges, and browns reminiscent of English Medieval interiors.

The Late Georgian Style (1750–90)

The style called **Late Georgian** came to America in English pattern books. These contained drawings of houses, floor plans, and details that could be built with little or no

Table 15.8 | Early Georgian Design and Queen Anne Furniture

Exterior Characteristics

- Two-story rectangular block
- Built of brick, clapboard, or stone
- Symmetrical facade with five or more bays
- Hipped roof, often with dormer windows
- Tall end chimneys
- Sash windows
- Cornice with dentils or modillions
- Stringcourse (optional)
- Pediment and pilasters at doorway or windows (optional)
- Balustrade (optional)
- Cupola (optional)
- Gabled or gambrel roof (optional)
- Quoins (optional)

Influences

- Christopher Wren
- English-Baroque middle-class houses (late seventeenth century)

Residential Examples

- Westover (c. 1730), Charles City County, Virginia
- Governor's Palace (1706–20), Williamsburg, Virginia
- MacPhaedris-Warner House (1718–23), Portsmouth, New Hampshire
- Brafferton Indian School (1723), Williamsburg, Virginia
- The President's House (1723), Williamsburg, Virginia
- Hunter House (1746), Newport, Rhode Island
- Carter's Grove (1750), James City County, Virginia
- Wentworth-Gardner House (1760), Portsmouth, New Hampshire

Nonresidential Examples

- Christ Church—"Old North" (1723), Boston, Massachusetts
- Trinity Church (1725–26), Newport, Rhode Island
- Independence Hall (1731), Philadelphia, Pennsylvania

Westover

(Before Wings Were Added)

Governor's Palace

Williamsburg, Balustrade and Cupola

Early Georgian Interior

(continued)

Early Georgian Design and Queen Anne Furniture (continued)

Queen Anne Highboy

Early Georgian Textiles

Queen Anne Armchair

Queen Anne Wing Chair

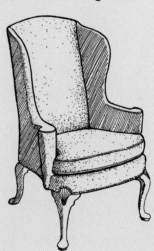

Queen Anne Tea Table

Interior Details

Floors. Wooden plank

Walls. Large raised wooden panels, unpainted; also, plain plaster with chair rail

Windows. Sash

Doors. Paneled

Chimneypiece. Flush, framed with simple, projecting bolection molding

Ceiling. Flat, plain

Stairs. Wooden U-stair with turned balusters

Textile Description

Colors. Williamsburg (dull medium value) blue, green, or rose were predominant, influenced by the Renaissance; recent tests at places such as Colonial Williamsburg and Mt. Vernon, Virginia, have revealed that these colors may have originally been more vibrant than what we see today

Patterns. Authentic or adapted Renaissance floral sprays

Textures. Woven damasks and brocades, velvets, and some plain or satin textures

architectural training. One of the most significant of these books was James Gibbs's *A Book of Architecture* (1728), which had reached America by 1751 at the latest. His designs had great appeal for Americans because they were conservative in scale and within their means. Also, unlike his contemporaries, Gibbs showed a strong tendency to maintain much of the richness of the Wren-Baroque design, which was suited to American taste. Gibbs's book contained illustrations of homes designed with a central house or block, connected to symmetrical dependencies (outbuildings) by straight or curved passages or wings. Such dependencies created a forecourt in the Palladian manner. Gibbs also designed houses in the Wren-Baroque style—as simple self-contained rectangular houses without wings or dependencies. His designs include the use of rusticated stone, balustrades, quoins, and pilasters, details too ornate for use by other Palladian architects of his time. Gibbs often designed houses with a two-story projecting pavilion or **breakfront.**

The breakfront topped with a triangular pediment above the roofline is the most distinctive feature of the Late Georgian–style house. In most other respects, it is similar to the Early Georgian style—a rectangular box with five or more bays, hipped roof, and tall end chimneys. The hipped roof is often lower-pitched than the Early Georgian roof and may, in rare cases, feature a balustrade or **parapet wall** (solid railing-height wall) at the eaves that hides the roof. The Late Georgian house may have a portico or a bracketed cornice, as well as pilasters and pediments at the doorway. The door may be crowned with a roundheaded **fanlight** (a rounded, over-the-door window), and the windows in the dormers may also be roundheaded. These houses may also feature a roundheaded arched window with lower rectangular windows on each side called a **Palladian window.** (They bear that name because they resemble an architectural detail used by Palladio on several of his designs.) When placed above a front door or at the end of an important room, they create an impressive focal point. The standard windows on the Late Georgian house are frequently capped with **crown** or **jack arch lintels,** which are trapezoid-shaped stone pieces with a wedge-shaped keystone. Corner trim is plain or quoined, and sometimes this style features two-story pilasters.

Late Georgian Furniture Classics

In the late Georgian period the Chippendale furniture style was popular. This style, like the Queen Anne style, remains a favorite today.

Chippendale furniture was designed during the mid-eighteenth century by Englishman **Thomas Chippendale** (1718–99). His book of designs, *The Gentlemen and Cabinet-Maker's Director* (1754), featured 160 plates with drawings of furniture pieces. Because the designs were published in book form, any skilled woodworker could build or adapt

them, and as a result, their popularity soon spread throughout the British Isles and America. Chippendale's drawings showed the influence of French (Louis XV), Chinese, Gothic, and Neoclassic designs. The Chippendale chair is characterized by its upholstered seat, cabriole legs with claw and ball feet, and a yoke-shaped back with an ornately carved splat. The backs might be carved in the form of ribbons, in Gothic tracery, in Chinese **fretwork,** or into pierced slats forming a **ladder-back.** The Chippendale cabriole legs joined the **apron** in the same manner as the Queen Anne cabriole legs. On some pieces a straight square leg known as the **Marlborough leg** was common.

The Chippendale wing chair is similar to the Queen Anne wing chair, but generally has either Marlborough legs or cabriole legs with claw and ball feet and is larger scaled.

The Chippendale **camel-back sofa** is an upholstered piece with a **serpentine**-shaped back that dips and rises from rolled arms to a hump in the center. The sofa has either cabriole legs with claw and ball feet or Marlborough legs with or without stretchers.

The **block front** is a furniture detail associated with John Goddard (1724–85) of Newport, Rhode Island. The block front, which was applied to Chippendale-style case pieces, consists of a front panel divided into three alternating vertical convex and concave sections. The inside section is concave, the two outside sections are convex, and the top of each section is finished with a carved convex or concave shell.

The Chippendale breakfront is a case piece designed in such a way that the front plane of the piece is broken (i.e., part advancing and part receding). The breakfront was commonly built as a **secretary** or a china cupboard and had an enclosed cabinet below and open shelves with glass doors above. The breakfront was also popular in succeeding periods and appears in several styles.

The Chippendale highboy, like the Queen Anne highboy, consists of a low, two-drawer chest on legs (lowboy) with an additional chest of drawers above. The chest is topped by a scroll pediment with a **finial.** In the eighteenth century, Philadelphia was an important center for furniture manufacture. The Philadelphia highboy, with its magnificent carving, is a particularly beautiful example of the American version of the Chippendale style. Table 15.9 contains examples of Late Georgian design.

Late Georgian Color

Late Georgian colors were peach, ivory, Wedgewood blue, opal pink, and green with clean and creamy white backgrounds of English garden-printed fabrics. More intense colors such as reds, golds, and deep greens and blues were still often seen in rich imported textiles such as silks, fine cottons, linens, and in the increasingly popular Oriental rugs.

Table 15.9 | Late Georgian Design and Chippendale Furniture

Exterior Characteristics

- Same basic form as the Early Georgian house
- Two-story projecting pavilion or breakfront with pediment
- Small portico over doorway (optional)
- Two-story double portico (optional)
- Building massed into symmetrical blocks and connections; Palladian massing (optional)
- Doorways with roundheaded fanlights, bracketed cornices, or pilasters and pediments (optional)
- Corners untrimmed or trimmed with quoins or pilasters (optional)
- Crown lintels (optional)

Influences

- James Gibbs and other English Palladian architects
- English pattern books

Residential Examples

- Tyron Palace (1770), New Bern, North Carolina
- Mount Pleasant (1761), Philadelphia, Pennsylvania
- Longfellow House (1750), Cambridge, Massachusetts
- Mount Airy (1758–62), Richmond County, Virginia
- Lady Pepperell House (1760), Kittery Point, Maine
- Miles-Brewton House (1765–69), Charleston, South Carolina
- Brandon (1765–70), Prince George County, Virginia
- Hammond-Harwood House (1773–74), Annapolis, Maryland

Nonresidential Examples

- St. Michael's Church (1752–61), Charleston, South Carolina
- First Baptist Meetinghouse (1774–75), Providence, Rhode Island
- Redwood Library (1758–50), Newport, Rhode Island
- Brick Market (1761–62), Newport, Rhode Island

Mount Pleasant

Tyron Palace

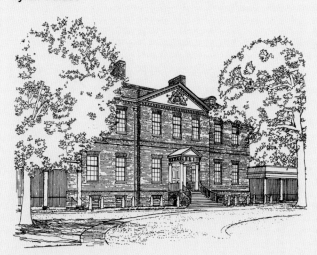

Palladian Window

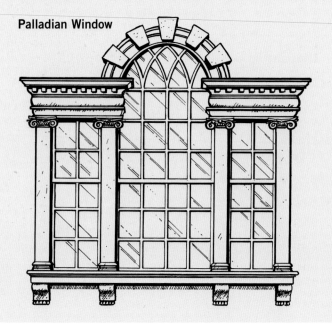

Late Georgian Interior

Late Georgian Design and Chippendale Furniture (continued)

Chippendale Philadelphia Highboy

Interior Details

Floors. Wooden plank

Walls. Large raised wooden panels, painted; also, dado with wallpaper above

Windows. Sash

Doors. Paneled, moldings with ears (molding breaks to form squares at corners)

Chimneypiece. Flush, with molding forming ears, and often with cornice and frieze; cornice forms mantel, over mantel with ears

Ceiling. Flat, plain or decorated with anaglypta (raised patterns)

Stairs. Wooden U-turn, turned balusters

Textile Description

Colors. Baroque and Rococo influence; more vivid colors—red, gold, blue, turquoise or teal, and rich coral sometimes lightened to soft peach

Patterns. Renaissance patterns still in use and strong influence of Chinese and Rococo motifs; English garden block-printed patterns

Textures. Smooth silklike textures in damask and brocade, printed cotton fabrics from slightly coarse to very refined; some velvets

Chippendale Block-Front Chest

Newport, Rhode Island

Chippendale Breakfront

Chippendale Camel-Back Sofa

Chippendale Wing Chair

(continued)

Late Georgian Design and Chippendale Furniture (continued)

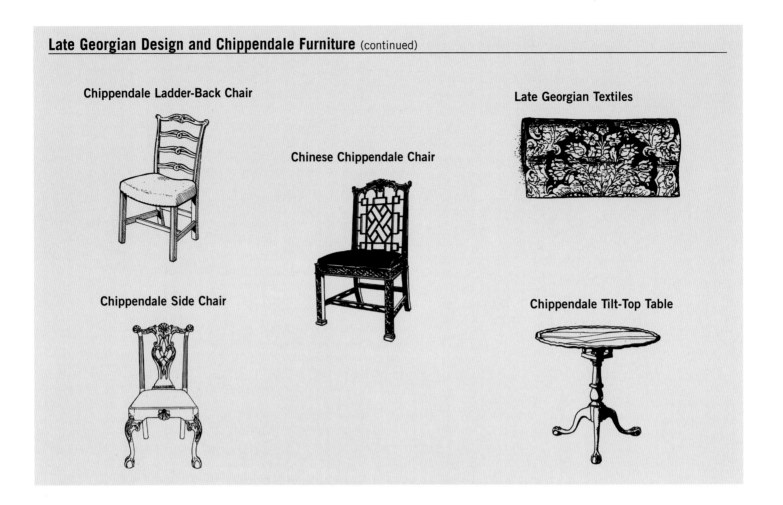

Chippendale Ladder-Back Chair

Chinese Chippendale Chair

Late Georgian Textiles

Chippendale Side Chair

Chippendale Tilt-Top Table

American Styles

The Federal Style (1790–1830)

In the decades after the Revolutionary War, Americans sought to define a style of design that would depart from European models and express the ideals of the new nation. To a large extent they expanded on trends that had already developed on the American continent before independence. However, the resulting style, which came to be called Federal, was in reality still heavily influenced by European design—particularly that of the British architect **Robert Adam** (1728–1792).

After Adam visited the Italian excavation sites at Pompeii and Herculaneum, he used his drawings of ancient Roman and Renaissance design to create a **Neoclassic** style. **Federal**-style houses generally are beautiful American adaptations of the Adam style from Georgian England. The typical Federal house has a symmetrical facade of five bays and, like the English prototype, usually has three stories. A few Federal houses have longer second-story windows that extend to the floor. These second-story rooms were the public spaces of the house and were given more importance with the larger windows—a concept related to the Renaissance idea of the piano nobile.

The windows on the third level were usually smaller than the other two, a characteristic also typical of the English prototype. The Federal doorway was sometimes sheltered by a small portico similar to those designed for English **terrace houses** (row houses). The door itself was commonly topped with a roundheaded or delicate elliptical fanlight and flanked with a narrow set of windows called **sidelights.** The elliptical fan shape, discovered on the walls of Herculaneum, was possibly the most versatile and significant motif of the period. The fan was doubled to form ellipses known as **paterae.** These were used in every possible decorative fashion: furniture hardware, inlaid wood patterns on furniture, plaster patterns for ceilings, and elliptical room plans. The roof on the Federal house was low pitched and hipped and often featured a balustrade at the eaves.

The Federal period includes the work of Boston architect Charles Bullfinch, Samuel McIntire of Salem, and English transplant Benjamin Latrobe. Bullfinch's work was widely copied in the pattern books of the day and was likely the basis for much late eighteenth-century and early nineteenth-century architecture in New England. McIntire was a skilled carver as well as an architect, and his interiors and exteriors reflect the master's touch.

Federal Furniture Classics

The Hepplewhite and Sheraton style from England was fashionable during the Federal period. The Hepplewhite/Sheraton chairs are typical of the delicate Neoclassic style of the late eighteenth century. **George Hepplewhite** (d. 1786) produced a book called *The Cabinet-Maker and Upholsterer's Guide* (published posthumously in 1788), which contained furniture designs inspired by the work of Robert Adam. **Thomas Sheraton's** (1751–1806) *The Cabinet-Maker and Upholsterer's Drawing Book,* published in 1791, was filled with variations of Hepplewhite's designs. Because both men worked in the same style, it is often difficult to distinguish their designs. The distinctions are usually based on very slight differences in detail such as the direction of the curve on a drawer front or the shape of a chair back. Their chair designs featured straight square or **reeded** round, tapered legs without stretchers. The chair with the rectangular back is considered typical of the Sheraton style, and the shield- or heart-shaped back chairs are typical of Hepplewhite designs.

The Hepplewhite/Sheraton **sideboard** or **buffet** is a serving piece with drawers, raised on straight tapered legs. If the side drawers are concave, the piece is considered a Hepplewhite piece; if they are convex, it is considered a Sheraton piece.

The Hepplewhite/Sheraton **pembroke table** is a **drop-leaf occasional table** with a drawer in the apron. The top, when open, is oval in shape, and the legs are straight and tapered, without stretchers. Table 15.10 contains examples of Federal design.

Federal Color

Colors during the Federal period were light and pastel. Americans were influenced by the French Neoclassical colors such as cream; powder green and pink; French lilac and turquoise; Sevres blue (a clear medium blue); Pompadour blue and DuBarry red (soft colors named after Louis XV's mistresses); and accentuated gold and silver tones. English and Americans added Robert Adam colors to the spectrum: a clear spring green called Adam green, dove gray, pale lavender, faded red, deep olive green, grayed green and blue, warm pink, and the Wedgewood jasperware colors, which were tones of blue, warm coral pink, creamy sage, or stark white—sometimes accentuated with gold leaf.

Jeffersonian Federal

Thomas Jefferson was not only an important statesman but also a fine architect, and his designs represent an important divergent style during the Federal period. Unlike the mainstream of Federal design, which was based on English prototypes, Jefferson based his work on the designs of classical Rome. In his role as statesman, Jefferson traveled to Europe where he saw remnants of Roman cul-

ture. He considered the ancient style appropriate for the new American republic and patterned his most famous nonresidential buildings after two well-known Roman temples. The Rotunda at the University of Virginia (1822–26) at Charlottesville is the American incarnation of the Pantheon in Rome, and the State House (1785–92) at Richmond, Virginia, is a larger version of the Maison Carreé in Nimes, France. His home, Monticello (1768–82), at Charlottesville, Virginia, features a prominent temple-like portico that foreshadowed the ensuing Greek Revival style. The time Jefferson spent in France had a strong effect on the layout of Monticello as well as its dome—both were inspired by eighteenth-century Parisian hôtels (town houses). Jefferson's work constitutes a significant and influential departure from the typical Federal style.

The Vernacular Tradition (Seventeenth Century–Present)

In spite of over a century of exposure to classical influences, grassroots American architecture held tenaciously to the English Medieval tradition. Generally it was only the wealthy upper class who built the classically inspired houses discussed thus far. The vast majority of people living in America built adaptations of the new styles using the sturdy Medieval house form with its gabled roof, while others remodeled existing seventeenth-century houses, adding new details to make the Medieval house more stylish and up-to-date. For example, during the Early Georgian period symmetrically placed sash windows and pilastered and pedimented doorways gave the gabled house a feeling of the new style.

During the Federal period, the addition of fanlights and sidelights at the doorway imparted a sense of belonging to the era. These hybrid houses are referred to as **vernacular,** which literally means "common," and implies the houses were adapted by local builders and developed regional characteristics. It also implies a naive, unschooled approach to design quite different from that which attempted to copy faithfully the fine English houses. Vernacular design may result from lack of exposure or resources, or it may represent a strong-willed independence or personal preference. Vernacular is not a negative term; most vernacular houses are charming and, in fact, are the most enduring type of house in America. The majority of colonial-style homes built today are vernacular versions of the Georgian- or Federal-style houses. Though vernacular is generally considered a quality rather than a style, one type of vernacular house is so distinctive and well known that it has become a style: Cape Cod.

The Cape Cod Cottage (Seventeenth Century–Present)

The dwellings characteristic of rural Cape Cod, Massachusetts, have come to typify the American small house.

Table 15.10 | Federal Design and Hepplewhite/Sheraton Furniture

Exterior Characteristics

- Five-bay, three-story, box-shaped facade of brick, stucco, or clapboard
- Smaller windows on upper story
- Second-story windows to floor (optional)
- Doorway with fanlights and sidelights
- Flattened hipped roof with optional balustrade at eaves
- Classical detail from earlier periods such as the crown lintel, portico, Palladian window, stringcourse, and quoins (optional)

Influences

- Robert Adam
- English Georgian design

Residential Examples

- Pingree House (1804), Salem, Massachusetts; Samuel McIntire, architect
- Pierce-Nichols House (1782), Salem, Massachusetts; Samuel McIntire, architect
- Harrison Gray Otis House (1796), Boston, Massachusetts; Charles Bullfinch, architect
- Nathaniel Russell House (before 1809), Charleston, South Carolina
- Amory Ticknor House (1804), Boston, Massachusetts

Nonresidential Examples

- State House (1795–98), Boston, Massachusetts; Charles Bullfinch, architect
- Baltimore Cathedral (1804–18), Baltimore, Maryland; Benjamin Latrobe, architect
- Lancaster Meeting House (1816–17), Lancaster, Massachusetts; Charles Bullfinch, architect
- United States Custom House (1819), Salem, Massachusetts

Federal Interior

Fanlight and Sidelights

Pingree House

Federal Design and Hepplewhite/Sheraton Furniture (continued)

Hepplewhite/Sheraton Style Pembroke Table

Hepplewhite Sideboard (Buffet)

Hepplewhite Shield-Back Chair

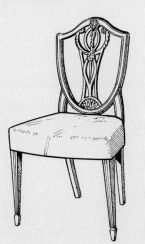

Sheraton Square-Back Chair

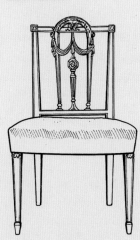

Hepplewhite Bow-Back Sofa

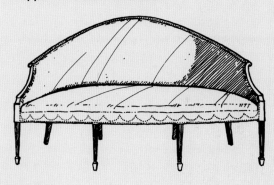

Federal Textiles

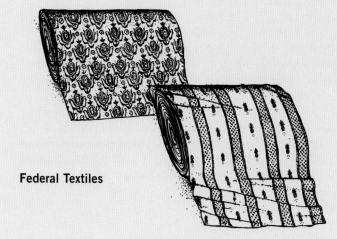

Interior Details

Floors. Wooden plank
Walls. Plain plaster
Windows. Sash
Doors. Paneled, with fanlights used as transoms, sidelights
Chimneypiece. Projecting, classical, in the Adam style, with a raised panel in the center of the frieze
Ceiling. Plain, plaster with cornice molding
Stairs. Various configurations; wooden with turned balusters

Textile Description

Colors. Pastel, light, creamy dull colors accented with white or a little rich color
Patterns. Fine stripes, garlands, bows, ribbons, oval shapes, classic Greek and Roman urns and motifs, tiny florals; in America also the pineapple (symbol of hospitality)
Textures. Plain satin, refined damask and brocade, plain and antique taffeta, batiste, moiré, voile, chintz (crisp cotton textures)

The Cape Cod cottage is a one-story gabled house, usually finished in shingle siding that was allowed to weather to a soft gray in the salty coastal air. In the eighteenth century, the steep Medieval-style roof was lowered and sash windows and classical doorway details were added to make the houses more in step with the times. A few houses had slightly bowed roofs, called **rainbow roofs,** attributed to shipbuilders. (This type of house with a gambrel roof is called a Cape Ann house.) The eaves of the houses are very shallow, which gives them a crisp, boxy character. The size of the houses varied: a one-room half house of three bays, a four-bay, three-quarter house with one large and one small room, or a full-sized, five-bay double house containing two full-sized rooms with the doorway in the center. The Cape Cod house has maintained its popularity since it was introduced in the seventeenth century.

Figure 15.11 Stanton Hall in Natchez, Mississippi, exemplifies the stately quality of the Greek Revival style. © *David A. Taylor*

Vernacular Furniture Classics

Several pieces of vernacular furniture used by the common people throughout the eighteenth and nineteenth centuries still have great appeal for today's interiors. The American **ladder-back chair** is an important piece based on an English prototype. It has a frame made of straight members turned in a fashion that resembles a string of sausages (called sausage turnings) and joined with stretchers. The ladder-back chair would often appear in more humble homes or in the kitchens and servants' quarters of grander homes. Like some other provincial chairs, the ladder-back chair has a seat of woven rush.

The Welsh dresser or **hutch** is a side piece with cupboards, drawers, and a set of open shelves above. The hutch is descended from a sixteenth-century French kitchen cupboard and was popular in England in the seventeenth century as well as in Early America.

The American **Windsor chair,** as the name implies, is based on an English prototype. The Windsor chair is characterized by its saddle-shaped seat, turned legs with stretchers, and spindle back. The early versions were invariably painted. The most common backs are the curved bow or loop back and the comb back. Some later Windsor chairs featured legs turned to resemble bamboo. The English Windsor chair has a pierced splat and may have cabriole legs (see Table 9.1, p. 241). Vernacular design is shown in Table 15.11.

The Greek Revival/American Empire Style (1820–60)

The **Greek Revival** grew out of the spirit of the times and was a natural expression of the growing independence of American culture. Greek mythology, culture, and often even the classical Greek language were part of educational training during the early nineteenth century. Literature and art often alluded to the ancient Greeks, and the Greek war of independence from Turkey had focused the world's attention on modern Greece. The Greek style was not tied directly to English influences. In fact, the Greek Revival was the first style that was truly harmonious with the American vernacular taste for the gabled house. The gabled end of the house, when turned toward the street, became a Greek temple facade. It was adaptable enough to make it suitable for fine city dwellings as well as regional vernacular houses.

The style found acceptance everywhere in the country, but it varied so much in its interpretation that it is difficult to identify a single set of characteristics. The one characteristic that seems to be universal is the use of all or part of the Greek temple form on a one- or two-story dwelling. The most extravagant examples feature a full Doric, Ionic, Corinthian, and even Roman Tuscan colonnade with a complete entablature, and the most unassuming interpretations are those where the gabled end forms an extremely simple pedimented facade that is turned toward the street. The Greek Revival door opening was generally flanked by sidelights and headed by an oblong transom (over-the-door window). The doorway

Table 15.11 | Vernacular Design

Cape Cod Exterior Characteristics

- Small half house, three-quarter house, or full-sized house
- One story (some two-story versions built in Nantucket, Massachusetts)
- Gabled or rainbow roof, less steeply pitched than the Medieval houses (gambrel roofs make a Cape Ann house)
- Sash windows directly under the eaves
- Shallow eaves
- Doorway with simplified pilasters and entablature
- Shingle siding (some clapboard)

Influences

- Seventeenth-century Medieval houses
- Early Georgian houses
- New England ship carpenters

Residential Examples

- Kendrick House (c. 1790), Orleans, Massachusetts
- Shadrach Standish House (1730), Halifax, Massachusetts
- Hezekia Swain-Maria Mitchell House (1790), Nantucket, Massachusetts

Vernacular Georgian

Deacon's Bench

Cape Cod Cottage

(continued)

might be framed by a full portico or simply trimmed with pilasters and an entablature; pilasters were sometimes used to give definition to the facade. The basic two-story temple form might be given additional space with one-story flanking wings.

American Empire Furniture Classics

The interior and furniture styles of the Greek Revival are referred to as **American Empire** style. Much of the furniture from the American Empire era was based on French and British prototypes. The French Empire and English

Vernacular Design (continued)

Gateleg Table

Ladder-Back Chair

Textile Description

Colors. Natural colors or neutrals (off-white, brown gray) and colors that came from natural sources—madder or cranberry red, indigo blue, dull gold from birch leaves or other plants

Patterns. When they were found, simple stripes and checks, stenciled or embroidered floral or folk patterns

Textures. Homespun, muslin, flannel, broadcloth, burlap, ticking, handspun coarse textures

Bow-Back Windsor Chair

Comb-Back Windsor Chair

Welsh Dresser/Hutch

Butterfly Table

Vernacular Textiles

Regency styles date from the early nineteenth century, during the reign of Napoleon in France and George IV in England. Much of the furniture from this period was heavy, based on designs from Rome, yet some of the chairs were amazingly light and delicate—inspired by a new appreciation for the designs of classical Greece, and maintaining much of the delicacy of the previous Louis XVI and Sheraton styles. The Empire and Regency designs made their way to northern Europe and America, where the styles are known respectively as **Biedermeier** and American Empire or **Regency. Duncan Phyfe**

(1768–1854), a Scottish cabinetmaker who worked in New York, is famous for his delicate Regency-style furniture. His designs often incorporated the lyre or harp as a prominent motif. Until recently, only the Phyfe designs from this period had widespread popularity. However, today the heavier **French Empire** and Biedermeier styles find wide acceptance as antiques, and their reproductions are being manufactured in larger numbers.

The **Hitchcock chair** is a vernacular design by **Lambert Hitchcock** (1795–1852), a Connecticut designer. The chair shows the influence of Duncan Phyfe and English

Table 15.12 | Greek Revival Design and American Empire Interiors and Furniture

Exterior Characteristics

- Bold forms with an emphasis on strength rather than delicacy
- Greek temple form with pediment (gabled end) oriented toward the front
- Porticoes and colonnades with two-story Greek columns
- Some use of Roman Tuscan columns
- Exterior finish of stone, brick, wooden siding, or stucco
- Sash windows
- Door openings flanked with sidelights and headed with oblong transoms, or flanked with pilasters and crowned with an entablature

Influences

- Previous classical styles
- The architecture of classical Greece and Rome
- Some French influence

Residential Examples

- Andalusia (1836), Bucks County, Pennsylvania
- Joseph Bowers House (1825), Northampton, Massachusetts
- Russell House (1828–30), Middletown, Connecticut (now Honors College, Wesleyan University)
- Shadows-on-the-Teche (1830), New Iberia, Louisiana
- James Lanier House (1844), Madison, Indiana
- Dunlieth (1847), Natchez, Mississippi
- Alonzo Olds House (1848), Rushton, Michigan

Nonresidential Examples

- Philadelphia Water Works (1819), Philadelphia, Pennsylvania
- Girard College (1833), Philadelphia, Pennsylvania
- Second Bank of the United States (1924), Philadelphia, Pennsylvania
- Quincy Market (1825), Boston, Massachusetts
- Hibernian Hall (1835), Charleston, South Carolina
- Congregational Church (1838), Madison, Connecticut

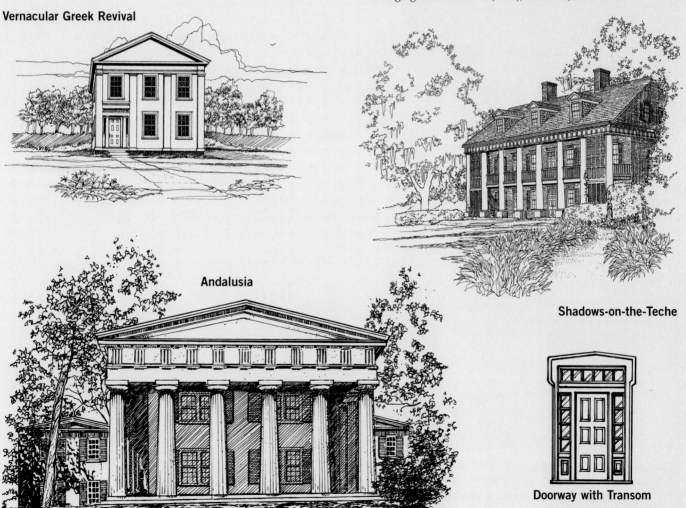

Vernacular Greek Revival

Andalusia

Shadows-on-the-Teche

Doorway with Transom

(continued)

Greek Revival Design and American Empire Interiors and Furniture (continued)

American Empire Console Table

American Empire Interior

American Empire Fainting Sofa/Grecian Sofa

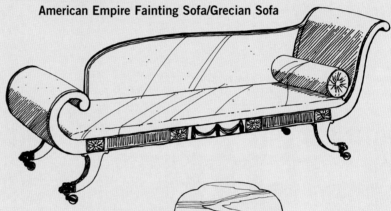

American Empire Textiles

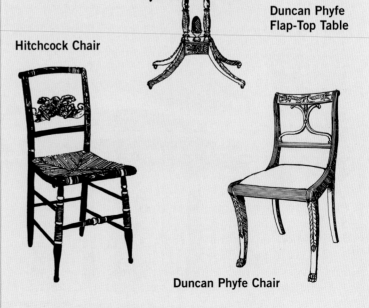

Hitchcock Chair

Duncan Phyfe Flap-Top Table

Duncan Phyfe Chair

Interior Details

Floors. Wooden plank, patterned broadloom carpet
Walls. Plain plaster or chair rail
Windows. Sash or French doors
Doors. Paneled, heavy molding; wooden transom with cornice
Chimneypiece. Projecting, classical, black marble, or faux painted
Ceiling. Plain with crown or cornice molding, anaglypta
Stairs. Several configurations; curved was popular; wooden with turned balusters

Textile Description

Colors. French-inspired color schemes included rich vivid red, gold, deep green, brown, and royal purple; these were also used in America and were sometimes softened to pale mauve, spun honey, dull greens and browns, and dull gray-violet
Patterns. Plain satin background with isolated small motifs such as the laurel wreath, the star or snowflake, honeybee, or classical urns; also the griffin, festooning, both broad and blended satin stripes
Textures. Plain satin, antique taffeta and silk textures, various sheer and semisheer fabrics

Regency designs and is characterized by its black painted finish, turned legs, rush or cane seat, and gold stenciled fruit and flower decoration. Greek Revival and American Empire design are shown in Table 15.12.

Empire Color

The Empire style, which was strongly influenced by French taste, was a reflection of Napoleon's campaigns and personal admiration for the classical interiors. The colors that predominated are bright royal red and gold; emerald to olive green; majestic purple and brown; and accents of pale mauve, cream, white, or black. The bold color statements were seen particularly in upholstery, draperies, and broadloom woven (Wilton and Axminster) carpeting.

The Victorian Age in America (1837–1901)

The **Victorian era** in America corresponds to the reign of Queen Victoria of England from 1837 to 1901, though the architectural styles attached to her name extended beyond the turn of the century and coexisted with the radical new architectural developments of the Modern era. This coexistence was less than peaceful and may account for the scorn that was heaped upon Victorian design during the middle of the twentieth century.

Victorian architecture is not a single style but a succession and **eclectic** mixing of styles. Some of the styles have their roots in the philosophies of the nineteenth century. For example, the Gothic Revival was fired by the notion that pagan buildings (Greek and Roman) were not fit for Christian living—the only suitable style for Christians was Gothic. However, those who adopted the styles were likely less concerned with philosophy than with aesthetics.

The nineteenth century saw the full bloom of the Industrial Revolution and a rapid succession of advancements that radically changed the way people lived. The fireplace and stove were replaced by central heating. Gas lighting and, eventually, electric lighting took the place of oil lamps and candles. Indoor plumbing made the outhouse and water pump things of the past. The modern lifestyle with its many conveniences, often taken for granted today, was developed by the Victorians.

The advancement of technology also paved the way for migration from the farm to the city, where industry was creating a growing middle class and a new wealthy class. This rapid change in society seemed to trigger a proliferation of decorative styles and treatments that have become the hallmark of Victorian design. As each new Victorian style developed, elements of former styles were retained and adapted to create an eclectic design patchwork that signaled the end of classical dominance. Each new variation in style was historical in nature but lacked the authenticity of the original styles upon which they were based. They were re-creations of a distant and romantic past by craftspersons in possession of the new technology of the Industrial Revolution. The most important of these styles were the Gothic Revival, Italianate, Egyptian Revival, Oriental, Mansard, Stick, Shingle, and Queen Anne styles.

Victorian Furniture Classics

Because the Industrial Revolution spawned a large furniture industry, many new pieces and styles emerged during the nineteenth century. Foremost among the styles were the Gothic Revival advocated by Englishman **Charles Eastlake** (1793–1865), the Rococo Revival, and the Renaissance Revival.

Eastlake wrote a book called *Hints on Household Taste* that discussed furniture of good taste based on Medieval and Japanese influences. He was opposed to the rapid changes in style and the machine construction so common during the Victorian era. The calls of Eastlake and others for a return to the simple handcraftsmanship of

Figure 15.12 Longwood in Natchez, Mississippi, is an octagonal house in the Oriental Revival Style characterized by its onion dome. © *David A. Taylor*

Table 15.13 | Victorian Design

Gothic Revival Exterior Characteristics

- Steeply pitched gables (sometimes combined with low-hipped roof)
- Parapets or battlements (low walls on the roof) that are crenellated (notched)
- Towers, spires, and finials on the roof
- Stone construction (finer houses only)
- Vertical wooden siding of board and batten (these wooden houses are called Carpenter's Gothic)
- Lacy wooden version of Gothic tracery called gingerbread used to decorate eaves and porches
- Pointed Gothic and flattened Tudor arches used for window, door, and veranda framing
- Leaded pane windows

Residential Examples

- Lyndhurst (1838), Tarrytown, New York; Alexander Jackson Davis, architect
- Greystone (c. 1859), Pevely, Missouri
- Town Office Building (1847), Cazenovia, New York; Andrew Jackson Downing, architect

Nonresidential Examples

- St. Patrick's Cathedral (1858–79), New York, New York; James Renwick, architect
- Brooklyn Bridge (1869–83), New York, New York
- Baptist Church (1878), North Salem, New York
- Calvary Presbyterian Church (1883), Portland, Oregon

Italianate Exterior Characteristics

- Also called Italian and Tuscan, inspired by Italian country houses and Prince Albert's design of Osborne House in England
- Low-pitched hipped or gabled roof
- Wide overhanging cornices with large brackets
- Square tower with a low pitched roof (optional)
- Belvedere (lookout with windows in tower)
- Roundheaded windows (optional)
- Ornate versions of classical details such as modillions and pediments
- Often used for New York brownstone and other city row houses

Residential Examples

- David Mayer Farmhouse (1867), Lancaster, Pennsylvania
- Edward King House (1845), Newport, Rhode Island
- Mills-Stebbins House (1849–51), Springfield, Massachusetts
- Morse-Libby House (1859), Portland, Maine

Nonresidential Examples

- Haughwout Building (1857), New York, New York (cast-iron facade)
- Sanger-Peper Building (1874), St. Louis, Missouri (cast-iron facade)

Gothic Revival

Italianate Style

Gothic Revival, Calvary Presbyterian Church

Victorian Design (continued)

Egyptian Revival Exterior Characteristics

- Not philosophically suited for residential design but was considered appropriate for cemetery gates, tombs, and mausoleums (perhaps because of the Egyptian preoccupation with the afterlife and preparation for death)
- Also used for prisons and churches
- Featured sloping walls with wide cornices

Nonresidential Examples

- Whaler's Church (1844), Sag Harbor, New York
- Gates, Grove St. Cemetery (1848), New Haven, Connecticut

Oriental Exterior Characteristics

- Also called Moorish or Persian, inspired by Islamic design
- Pointed and horseshoe Moorish arches used for doorways, windows, and porches
- Bulbous onion domes used to crown towers or belvederes

Oriental Revival, Longwood

Egyptian Revival, Whaler's Church

Residential Examples

- Longwood (1860), Natchez, Mississippi
- Olana (1870–72), near Hudson, New York

Nonresidential Examples

- Wise Temple (1866), Cincinnati, Ohio

Mansard Exterior Characteristics

- Also called Second Empire and influenced by nineteenth-century French design
- Also called General Grant Style because it was popular during the presidency of Ulysses S. Grant
- Mansard roof crested with a low, wrought-iron railing
- Dormer windows that rest on or break through the line of the eaves
- Quoins (optional)

Residential Examples

- Governor's Mansion (1871), Jefferson City, Missouri
- John DeKoven House (1874), Chicago, Illinois
- Governor's Mansion (1878), Sacramento, California
- Iolani Palace (1882), Honolulu, Hawaii

Nonresidential Examples

- City Hall (1872–1901), Philadelphia, Pennsylvania
- Grand Union Hotel (1872), Saratoga Springs, New York
- McKinley High School (1872), Lincoln, Nebraska
- Hill County Courthouse (1890), Hillsboro, Texas

Mansard Style

(continued)

Victorian Design (continued)

Stick Exterior Characteristics

- Victorian version of Late English Medieval house
- Steep gables
- Stickwork patterning applied to represent vertical, diagonal, and horizontal timber construction
- Jetties or overhangs

Residential Examples

- Griswold House (1862–63), Newport, Rhode Island
- Emlen Physick House (1879), Cape May, New Jersey

Stick Style, Griswold House

Shingle Exterior Characteristics

- Inspired by colonial seaside dwellings like the Cape Cod, Cape Ann, and Nantucket houses; appeared first as resort houses on the eastern seaboard
- Covered with shingles
- Small paned windows

Residential Examples

- Kragsyde (1884), Manchester-by-the-Sea, Massachusetts
- Dr. John Bryant House (1880), Cohasset, Massachusetts; Henry Hobson Richardson, architect
- William Low House (1887), Bristol, Rhode Island; McKim, Mead, and White, architects
- Frank Lloyd Wright House (1889), Oak Park, Illinois; Frank Lloyd Wright, architect

Shingle-Style, Kragsyde

Victorian Design (continued)

Queen Anne Exterior Characteristics

- Features a variety of decoration and surface embellishments such as stone, rounded fish-scale shingles, clapboard, stickwork, lathwork, turned balusters, and fretwork
- Strong horizontal lines or bands
- Combination of gabled and steep-hipped rooflines
- Turret (towers) often rounded with round pointed roofs
- Rounded gazebos—part of the veranda
- Moon gate arch—part of the veranda (optional)
- Some use of stained glass

Residential Examples

- Miss Parks House (1876), Cape May, New Jersey
- Glenmont (1880), West Orange, New Jersey
- Haas-Lilienthal House (1886), San Francisco, California

Nonresidential Examples

- Hotel del Coronado (1888), Coronado, California

Queen Anne Style

Victorian Interior

Interior Details

Floors. Wood plank
Walls. Plain plaster with wallpaper
Windows. Sash—large panes of glass
Doors. Paneled; some sliding pocket doors
Chimneypiece. Projecting carved marble, with a round-headed arched opening
Ceiling. Mass-produced crown moldings, anaglypta patterns, and chandelier medallions of plaster
Stairs. Various configurations, straight run favored; wooden with turned balusters and elaborate newel posts

Textile Description

Colors. Called the mauve decades—due to the many varieties of dull, somber reds; also deeper values of green, blue, violet, and gold; backgrounds were often off-white or black
Patterns. Copied and adapted, stylized and combined from many sources including Gothic, Egyptian, Byzantine, Oriental, Neoclassic, Rococo, Renaissance, with plenty of large- and small-scale floral and lacy patterns
Textures. Velvets of every description, woven Jacquard fabrics from very smooth to very heavy, cotton prints, lace, and heavy trimming

---

Victorian Belter/Rococo Revival Armchair

Victorian Gothic Revival Side Chair

(continued)

Victorian Design (continued)

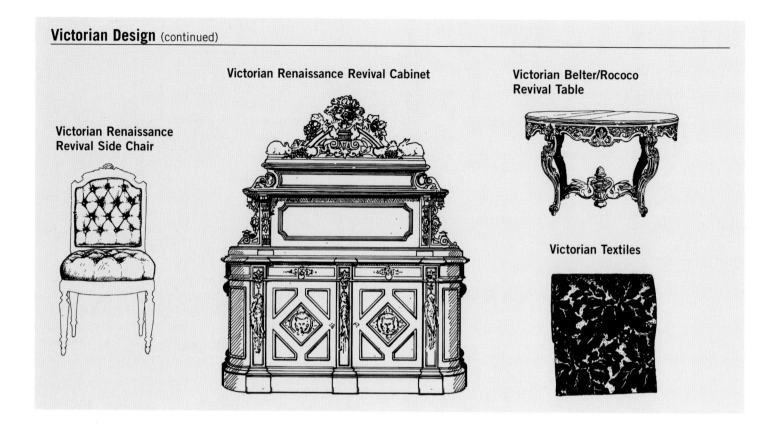

Victorian Renaissance Revival Side Chair

Victorian Renaissance Revival Cabinet

Victorian Belter/Rococo Revival Table

Victorian Textiles

the Middle Ages did little to stem the tide of mass production, but it did heighten the taste for Gothic design.

The Rococo Revival was based on eighteenth-century French Rococo designs and featured a fantastic array of curved lines in both wooden and upholstered pieces. **John Henry Belter** (d. 1865) created heavily carved pieces of furniture from laminated rosewood, and his name is often associated with the Rococo Revival style.

The Renaissance Revival was influenced in part by the writings of Eastlake. A return to clean, straight lines was seen as an Eastlake principle, and many of the rectilinear designs actually came to be known as the Eastlake style. Renaissance Revival pieces also bear a strong resemblance to Louis XVI furniture. This style is also characterized by the use of a segmental pediment form in many pieces. Victorian design is seen in Table 15.13.

Victorian Color

The Victorian period was an age of richly furnished eclecticism. This era is often referred to as the mauve decades, supporting colors such as deep, old-looking red and faded rose red or mauve, wine and dark violet, taupe, and black. Also seen were sage, dark olive, clear green, dark and creamy gold, tobacco brown, rust, and accents of royal blue, bright red and magenta in traditionally designed textile patterns. From the turn of the century

through the 1930s, many pure revivals were seen, and colors were often documented to the era of the revival.

Other Influences in America

The Shaker Influence

In contrast to contemporary Victorian designs, Shaker furniture was particularly simple. The **Shakers** were a nineteenth-century religious group whose beliefs included the design of furniture free from excessive decoration. The Shaker chair has straight legs with straight stretchers and straight uprights with simply formed slats or a woven back. Like the woven backs, the seats are generally webbed with cotton tapes. The uprights and arms might be finished with simple finials, and the top rail was sometimes designed to accommodate a folded blanket.

The Shaker candlestand is a small **tripod pedestal table** of beautiful proportions and delicate lines. Like other Shaker pieces, it is remarkable because of the purity of its design and its suitability in contemporary environments. Table 15.14 shows Shaker design.

The Swedish Influence

Seventeenth-century Scandinavian settlers introduced the house type for which America is most famous—the log cabin. The log house was a typical Scandinavian rural

Table 15.14 | Shaker Design

Shaker Rocker

Shaker Candlestand

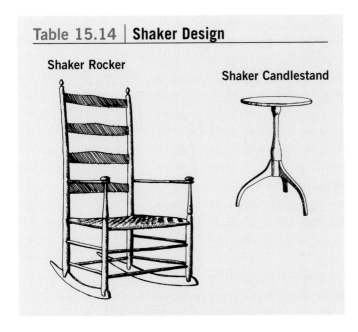

Figure 15.13 The log cabin is a Swedish contribution to American culture.

architectural form adapted by eighteenth- and nineteenth-century settlers of many origins. As Americans pushed the country's borders westward, the log cabin made a strong and quick shelter.

Closer to our own time, the simple dwelling has been adapted for the construction of rustic cabins and resort hotels, such as Old Faithful Inn (1904) at Yellowstone National Park.

The German Influence

The German settlers in Pennsylvania used the plentiful local gray and brown fieldstone to build houses that varied only slightly from the mainstream of American English architecture. The Germans, or Deutsch, were mistakenly called Pennsylvania Dutch, a designation that has endured.

The Pennsylvania Dutch have long been noted for their arts and crafts. The marriage chest, used to hold a young woman's dowry, was often painted in an artistic and decorative manner and is a good example of the Pennsylvania Dutch style. Table 15.15 shows German design.

The Dutch Influence

Nothing remains of the seventeenth-century Dutch buildings in New York City (originally New Amsterdam), and of all the Dutch houses in America, the most distinctive type may not even be Dutch. Historians differ as to whether the so-called Dutch house, with the bell-shaped gambrel roof and flaring eaves, was an American or Flemish development. Regardless of its origins, the house type has come to be known as Dutch Colonial. Unlike the Dutch, who were merchants, the Flemish settlers were generally farmers and built fine farmhouses. Table 15.16 shows an example of a Dutch house.

The French Influence

The architectural characteristics of the houses of French settlers along the southern part of the Mississippi River were distinctive but not all were strongly tied to the architecture of France. Instead they represented an adaptability to the warm and wet climate and waterlogged terrain of that region.

The stucco-covered houses with steeply pitched hipped roofs built by Norman French settlers were soon fitted with an encircling porch called a **galerie.** The roof was extended at a lower pitch to cover the galerie, forming a **bonnet roof** ideally suited to protect from rain and heat. French doors and casement windows opened onto the galerie and allowed the air to move freely through the house. The galerie with French windows and doors was also an important feature that persisted in the design of Greek Revival and Victorian houses of the area. These French details imparted a quality of elegance that is still associated with southern culture. Low piers raised some French houses above the dampness. Some houses were built above a raised basement—it was used as a service area and also offered protection from flooding or dampness in areas with high water tables.

The French town houses of New Orleans were built around galeried garden courtyards. During the Victorian era, with the advent of cast iron, galeries were also added to the front of the houses. These galeries of lacelike cast iron, though found elsewhere, are a symbol of New Orleans and add a touch of character that makes that city particularly charming. Table 15.17 shows an example of a French house.

Table 15.15 | German/Pennsylvania Dutch Design

Exterior Characteristics

- Large, simple, rectangular construction
- Built of roughly finished fieldstone or brick
- Transom over front door
- Sash windows
- Gabled or gambrel roof
- A narrow, overhanging rooflike projection between the first and second stories, called a **pent roof** (optional)
- **Cantilevered** (unsupported) triangular portico (optional)

Residential Examples

- Troxell-Steckel House (1756), Egypt, Pennsylvania
- Thompson-Neely House (1710), Washington Crossing, Pennsylvania
- Georg Mueller House (1752), Milbach, Pennsylvania
- Peter Wentz House (1758), Worcester, Pennsylvania

Nonresidential Examples

- Washington's Headquarters (1758), Valley Forge State Park, Pennsylvania
- Trout Hall (1770), Allentown, Pennsylvania

Pennsylvania Dutch Marriage Chest

Pennsylvania Dutch, Wentz House

Table 15.16 | Dutch Design

Exterior Characteristics

- Houses of stone, brick, or clapboard
- Gambrel roof with a line that breaks near the ridge
- Flaring eaves that give the roof a bell shape
- Sash windows and doors typical of mainstream English/American design

Residential Examples

- Dyckman House (1783), New York, New York
- Zabriskie–Von Steuben House (1752), Hackensack, New Jersey
- Richard Vreeland House (1786), Leonia, New Jersey
- Jacobus Demarest House (1719), Bergen County, New Jersey

Dutch Design, Dyckman House

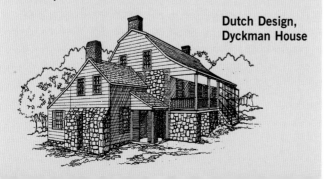

The influence of France is not limited to the Mississippi basin. Many Americans of all ancestries have admired French style. French design has always been considered sophisticated and the court styles of Louis XV, Louis XVI, and today the Empire style have been widely accepted. Design from the provinces of France is a less formal but nonetheless sophisticated version of French taste loved by Americans to this day.

French Furniture Classics. The French pieces so widely used and accepted today come principally from the Rococo period of Louis XV (as well as the transitional Régence period that preceded it), the Neoclassical Louis XVI period, and the provincial countryside of France. The French Régence **fauteuil** is an open armchair from the period of **French Régence** (1715–23), between the reigns of Louis XIV and Louis XV. The piece is characterized by the use of cane for the back and seat, cabriole legs, and stretchers between the legs.

The Louis XV fauteuil is an open armchair from the **Rococo** (1723–74) or **Louis XV period.** The lines of the chair are curvilinear, it has no stretchers, and it has an upholstered seat and back. The line of the cabriole leg continues without a break into the line of the apron.

Table 15.17 | French Design

Exterior Characteristics

- Galerie
- French doors
- French windows
- Bonnet roof, sometimes with dormer windows
- Frequently built over a raised basement

Residential Examples

- Madame John's Legacy (c. 1727), New Orleans, Louisiana
- La Veuve-Dodier House (1766), St. Louis, Missouri
- The Fortier-Keller House (1801), St. Charles Parish, Louisiana
- Le Pretre Mansion (1836), New Orleans, Louisiana

French Design, Madame John's Legacy

Figure 15.14 Country French charm is seen in the ladder-back chair and the neoclassically inspired bed. *Photo from Laura Ashley's archive of past product lines*

(A)

(B)

Figure 15.15 (A) San Carlos de Borromeo in Carmel, California, is considered one of the jewels of the California Spanish missions. (B) These adobe-style buildings in Santa Fe have strong ties to local culture and are well suited to the New Mexican climate. *(B) Photo by Markus Fant*

between the armrest and the seat, but on the bergère that space is filled with cushioning and fabric.

The chaise à capucine or fauteuil à la bonne femme is a ladder-back chair with a rush seat from the provinces of France. Provincial designs were influenced by court styles, so the chair may feature straight or curved lines, depending on the influence. Most of the fine reproductions feature curved back slats and legs.

The Country French **armoire** is a large carved wardrobe used for storage. Like the fauteuil à la bonne femme, the design of the armoire was influenced by the designs at court and may show asymmetrical elements common to the Rococo style or the rectilinear qualities of Louis XVI designs. See Tables 15.18, 15.19, and 15.20 for examples of French design.

The Spanish Influence

The earliest Spanish settlement in America was at St. Augustine, Florida, predating English settlement in Virginia by nearly fifty years. However, due to lack of colonization, frequent destruction and rebuilding, and repeated English inhabitation, no significant influences of these original Spanish settlements remain.

Spanish Missions. The Spanish also controlled the area along the southwestern border of the United States, from present-day Texas to California. Traces of Spanish influence can be seen throughout that region, particularly in the design of missions and churches. These were vernacular designs incorporating Spanish detailing contributed by the missionary-priests, together with the local materials and construction methods employed by the indigenous Indians.

Some examples of remaining Spanish-style missions include:

- San José y Miguel de Aguayo (1768–78), San Antonio, Texas
- San Xavier del Bac (1783–97), near Tucson, Arizona
- San Carlos de Borromeo (1797), Carmel, California

Southwest Adobe Style. In New Mexico, the Southwest Adobe style has endured. Colonists of European extraction arrived in New Mexico early in the seventeenth century and began building houses using the same methods

The Louis XVI fauteuil is an open armchair from the French Neoclassic (1774–93) or **Louis XVI period.** The piece is characterized by the rectilinear lines of classical design. The chair back is generally either oval or rectangular, and the straight tapered legs have no stretchers.

The French **bergère** is an upholstered armchair with fully upholstered sides. The fauteuil has an open space

Table 15.18 | French Rococo/Louis XV Design

French Rococo Interior

Interior Details

Floors. Parquet

Walls. Large, rectangular, painted wooden panels, often with carved or painted asymmetrical, curvilinear designs; French paneling is called boiserie

Windows. Long French casement or French doors

Doors. Paneled, double doors

Chimneypiece. Projecting, ornate carved marble, curvilinear opening

Ceiling. Flat, plain, cove molding

Stairs. Stone U-stair, with ornate wrought-iron balustrade

Textile Description

Colors. Colors were soft and feminine—turquoise, rose, warm creamy yellow, pale sage green

Patterns. Shells were quite popular, along with ribbons, scrolls, loveknots, country folk in country scenes, and Chinese chinoiserie motifs—pagodas, architecture, nature scenes, fretwork, and Chinese people in native dress

Textures. Fabrics were very refined and smooth—taffeta, chiffon, damask, brocade, velvet, lampas, batiste

Régence (Pre-Rococo) Fauteuil

Open Armchair

Rococo Console Table

Rococo Bergère

Upholstered Armchair

Rococo Commode

Low Chest of Drawers

Rococo Bureau-à-Cylindre

Rolltop Desk

Rococo Fauteuil

Open Armchair

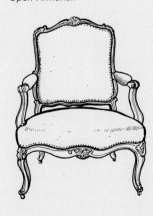

Rococo Textiles

Table 15.19 | French Neoclassical/Louis XVI Design

French Neoclassical Interior

Interior Details

Floors. Parquet wood
Walls. Large, rectilinear, painted wooden panels
Windows. Tall French casement or French windows
Doors. Paneled, double doors
Chimneypiece. Projecting, carved marble, rectilinear with corner-block designs
Ceiling. Flat, plain, with decorative cornice
Stairs. Stone U-stair, with wrought-iron balustrade

Textile Description

Colors. Pastel, light, creamy dull colors accented with white or a little rich color
Patterns. Fine stripes, garlands, bows, ribbons, oval shapes, classic Greek and Roman urns and motifs, tiny florals
Textures. Plain satin, refined damask and brocade, plain and antique taffeta, batiste, moiré, voile

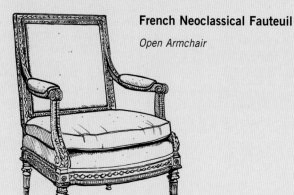

French Neoclassical Fauteuil

Open Armchair

French Neoclassical Bergère

Upholstered Armchair

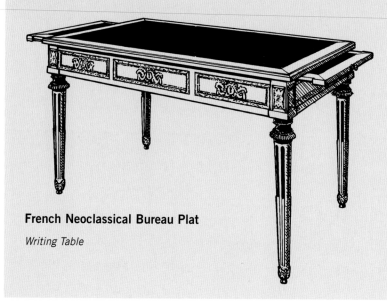

French Neoclassical Bureau Plat

Writing Table

French Neoclassical Textiles

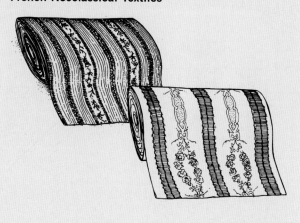

Table 15.20 | Country French Design

Country French Interior

Interior Details

Floors. Wooden plank, terra-cotta tile
Walls. Stucco or papered
Windows. French casement
Doors. French doors
Chimneypiece. Simple version of Renaissance hooded fireplace, also, carved natural wood version of Rococo chimneypiece with curved opening
Ceiling. Plain or beamed
Stairs. Various configurations of wooden stairway with plain balusters

Textile Description

Colors. In the Provinces, the colors were deep and somber—royal blue, cranberry red, goldenrod yellow, rich avocado green, accents of black; printed textiles sport light, lively florals
Patterns. Shells were quite popular, along with ribbons, scroll, love knots, country folk in country scenes, and Chinese chinoiserie motifs—pagodas, architecture, nature scenes, fretwork, and Chinese people in native dress
Textures. Fabrics included tapestry, printed toile de Jouy, floral fabrics, sturdy twill ticking, and woven tweeds such as houndstooth and herringbone

Country French Armoire

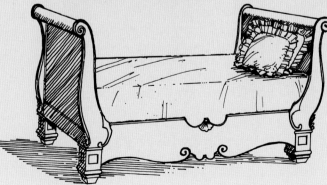

Country French Panetière

Bread Keeper

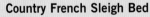

Country French Textile

Country French Sleigh Bed

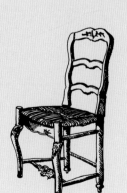

Country French Ladder-Back Chair

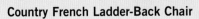

Table 15.21 | Southwest Adobe Design

Exterior Characteristics

- Thick, irregular, adobe walls with rounded corners
- Mud-colored stucco finish on exterior walls
- Deep-set windows and doors
- Vigas (log beams) protrude through the walls
- Flat roofs
- Portal (porch) with wooden post and lintels decorated with carved double corbels called zapatas

Residential Examples

- Palace of the Governors (c. 1610—restored to its nineteenth-century appearance), Santa Fe, New Mexico
- Casa San Ysidro (eighteenth century), Corrales, New Mexico
- Filipe Delgado House (c. 1872), Santa Fe, New Mexico

Nonresidential Examples

- San Francisco de Asis (c. 1772), Rancho de Taos, New Mexico
- Mission Church (c. 1710), Santa Ana Pueblo, New Mexico

Southwest Adobe Interior

Southwest Adobe Design, Palace of the Governors

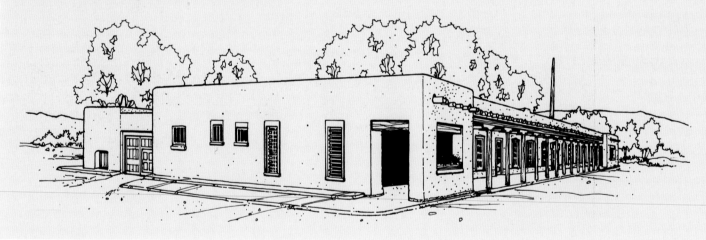

employed by the local Pueblo Indians. The Indian dwellings, or **pueblos,** were communal structures of **adobe** (clay bricks) several stories high. The Indians reached the upper stories by means of ladders. The thick adobe bricks are natural insulators in a climate that is hot in the summer and cold in the winter. Adobes are made by forming clay (bonded with straw) in wooden frames about 1½ feet long and drying the bricks in the sun. Adobe "melts" in the rain and is stuccoed with clay and straw to slow deterioration. The mud imparts a grayish-brown to pink color that varies according to the clay used.

The irregular walls support the large log roof beams, known as **vigas,** which are not cut to size but protrude through the walls. These make a convenient place to dry chilies and hang other objects. The beams are covered with thin sticks called **latillas** that are laid across the vigas in parallel fashion or herringbone patterns and form the ceiling of the structure as well as the base for roofing material. Originally the roof was made of sod or packed earth and required constant repairs (today they are made of more durable materials). The early pueblos had no windows, but during the eighteenth century the settlers began to incorporate paned windows deeply set into the thick adobe walls.

The first settlers' houses were built, Spanish style, around an open courtyard. The house served as a for-

Southwest Adobe Design (continued)

Territorial Style

} Pretil

Zapatas

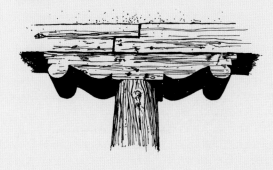

Interior Details

Floors. Wood plank or tile
Walls. Stucco
Windows. Casement
Doors. Plank or paneled
Chimneypiece. Irregular, rounded, stuccoed adobe, corner fireplace with a round, arched opening
Ceiling. Vigas and latillas
Stairs. Early versions generally one story; contemporary versions incorporate various configurations and styles

Textile Description

Colors. Authentic Spanish colors are either dramatic and bold red, gold, and black (all used sparingly as accents) or dull, sun-drenched, very livable colors. The dull pastel colors have influenced Western trends of recent years. The influence from Latin America gives accent colors of brilliant blue-green, chartreuse, vivid violet, and sunshine yellow
Patterns. Geometric patterns based on American Indian motifs, stripes
Textures. Heavy, coarse matelassé, tweed, homespun textures, leather

Southwest Textiles

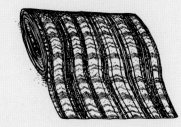

Corbel Brackets

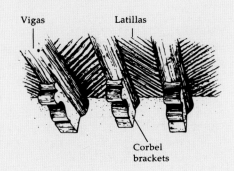

Vigas   Latillas

Corbel brackets

---

tress, opened to the interior with no exterior windows, and was entered through a sturdy wooden gate. As the threat of attack lessened with the years, the house took on a friendlier aspect, opening to the front, which often includes a covered porch or **portal.** The porch is supported by sturdy posts capped with a carved double **corbel** or bracket called a **zapata,** and topped with lintels.

When brick became available, it was used to form a row of trim along the top of the adobe walls. The trim, called **pretil,** is a protection for the weaker adobe and is characteristic of the **Territorial style** frequently seen in Santa Fe. It is a vernacular version of classical design and may feature dentil trim, simple pediments above the windows, and square painted columns in imitation of the Greek Revival. Special ordinances in Santa Fe and Taos permit building only in the Adobe (or Territorial) style, giving both those cities a unique architectural continuity found in few other places. Table 15.21 contains examples of the Southwest Adobe style.

The California Ranch House. Early California ranch houses (c. 1820), like the Southwest Adobe houses, were flat-roofed structures built of adobe. However, the flat roof soon gave way to the low-pitched, gabled, red tile roof, which was more practical in a rainier climate. Because there was less need for protection, the house was

Figure 15.16 This building in Santa Fe, New Mexico, is an example of the Territorial style. Note the boxed columns and the brick pretil as well as the lack of vigas. © *David A. Taylor*

The Beaux Arts Influence (1881–1945)

Beaux Arts is not a style. Rather, it is the influence on the training of architects, either direct or indirect, of **L'École des Beaux Arts** in Paris, France. At the beginning of the 1880s, in the midst of Victorian eclecticism and informality, Richard Morris Hunt, the first American architect trained at L'École des Beaux Arts, designed a home for the Vanderbilt family in New York that was elegant, refined, and historically correct. Thus, America was launched on a new sea of historical influence in architecture. The training at L'École des Beaux Arts focused on historical design in its most minute details. This type of training, which became the standard for American architectural schools, produced designers who were capable of creating the magnificent palaces and châteaus demanded by the new rich, as well as accurately styled smaller homes for those of less means.

By the early years of the 1900s, most American architects were being trained in the historical Beaux Arts tradition, and its influence was felt in most areas of the country. Much of the traditional, historical architecture of the Tudor, French, Dutch, Georgian, Federal, Greek Revival, Spanish, and Colonial styles, in the pre–World War II neighborhoods of the country, shows the Beaux Arts influence. Row houses or town houses also came from the drawing boards of Beaux Arts architects. Without understanding this significant influence, it is difficult to account for much of the period-style architecture that surrounds us. Table 15.23 shows examples of Beaux Arts buildings.

Modern Design (1857–Present)

It was the Victorians and their technological developments that laid the groundwork for modern architecture. Use of reinforced concrete, structural steel, plate glass, plumbing, and central heating were nineteenth-century developments. The Victorians had also experimented with novel floor plans, as well as new types of architectural massing. Some tend to think of the changes that

generally not enclosed with a walled court but open and rambling with a covered porch running the length of the house. The original houses do not exist in numbers sufficient to warrant listing their characteristics. Their significance lies in the fact that they are thought to be the precursor of the twentieth-century rambler or ranch-style house found in many parts of the country. These builder/developer houses, so well suited to the informal California lifestyle, soon found acceptance in other parts of the country. Many of the newer versions have been adapted to the point where any similarity to the originals is purely coincidental.

Monterey Design. The Monterey house is a California vernacular style that blends mainstream American English influence, local influence, and the ingenuity of its first builder. Thomas Larkin, a merchant from Boston, was the United States Consul to California when Monterey was the colonial capital. The two-story house he built in Monterey was made of adobe but built with a Georgian central hall floor plan, paned windows, and a low, hipped, shingled roof. Larkin designed the roof to cover a second-story balcony and a porch that surrounded the house like the French galerie (Larkin likely arrived at the design independent of French influence). The Larkin house was the prototype for several other houses and nonresidential buildings in the vicinity, and today the style, built throughout California and the West, is called Monterey (see Table 15.22).

Table 15.22 | Monterey Design

Exterior Characteristics

- Two stories
- Hipped or gabled roof of tile or shingles
- Second-story balcony, cantilevered or supported with posts
- Sash windows
- Generally stucco covered

Residential Examples

- Thomas Larkin House (1835–37), Monterey, California
- Los Cerritos Ranch House (1884), Long Beach, California

Nonresidential Examples

- Thomas Larkin House (1835–37), Monterey, California (also used as a store)
- Old Customs House (1827), Monterey, California

Monterey Design, Larkin House

gave birth to modern architecture as radical. In reality, it is sometimes difficult to know exactly where modern architecture begins. It begins with new technology.

The Skyscraper (1857–Present)

The skyscraper is a New York and Chicago phenomenon. It was in Chicago that the metal skeleton, which is the basis for skyscrapers, was developed. However, previous innovations also contributed. The installation of the first practical passenger elevator in New York's Haughwout Building in 1857 paved the way for the tall buildings that steel would make possible. The Brooklyn Bridge (1883) had shown that steel could carry far heavier loads than iron. In that same year, William Le Baron Jenney planned the eleven-story Home Insurance Building using a skeleton framework of steel. This building demonstrated that skyscrapers could reach incredible heights without the support of thick walls. The walls could be as thin as glass; the weight of the building was carried on the steel skeleton.

Figure 15.17 Architect Julia Morgan's Hearst Castle is an extravagant example of Beaux Arts architecture on a mountaintop overlooking the central California coast. © David A. Taylor

Table 15.23 | Beaux Arts Influence

Exterior Characteristics

- Vary according to the intended style of the building

Residential Examples

- Biltmore (1890–95), Asheville, North Carolina; Richard Morris Hunt, architect—French Renaissance
- The Breakers (1892–95), Newport, Rhode Island; Richard Morris Hunt, architect—Italian Renaissance
- Marble House (1892), Newport, Rhode Island; Richard Morris Hunt, architect—French Neoclassical
- Hearst Castle (1919–47), San Simeon, California; Julia Morgan, architect—Spanish Renaissance
- Benjamin Winchell House (1922), Fieldston, New York; Dwight James Baum, architect—Dutch Colonial
- Conkey House (1934), Santa Fe, New Mexico—Southwest Adobe

Nonresidential Examples

- Boston Public Library (1895), Boston, Massachusetts; McKim, Mead, and White, architects—Italian Renaissance
- Union Station (1907), Washington, D.C.; Daniel H. Burnham, architect—Classical
- County Courthouse (1920), Santa Barbara, California; William Mooser, architect—Spanish

- Woolworth Building (1913), New York, New York; Cass Gilbert, architect—Gothic Skyscraper
- Palace of Fine Arts (1915), San Francisco, California; Bernard Maybeck, architect—Classical
- Grauman's Chinese Theater (1927), Los Angeles, California; Meyer and Holler, architects—Chinese
- Savoy Plaza Hotel (1928), New York, New York; McKim, Mead, and White, architects—Classical French Château Skyscraper

Beaux Arts Influence, Late Medieval (Tudor) Style

French Renaissance Style, Beaux Arts Influence, Biltmore

The master of the skyscraper was Chicago architect Louis Sullivan. To Sullivan is attributed the famous philosophy that "form follows function." He designed a number of important skyscrapers (some with partner Dankmar Adler) and started a building trend that has not yet ceased and has left its mark on almost every corner of the globe.

Examples of early skyscrapers include:

- The Auditorium Building (1889), Chicago, Illinois; Adler and Sullivan, architects
- The Wainwright Building (1891), St. Louis, Missouri; Louis Sullivan, architect
- Monadnock Building (1892), Chicago, Illinois; Burnham and Root, architects
- Reliance Building (1895), Chicago, Illinois; Daniel H. Burnham, architect
- The Guaranty Building (1895), Buffalo, New York; Adler and Sullivan, architects
- Carson Pirie Scott & Co. (1904), Chicago, Illinois; Louis Sullivan, architect

Art Nouveau/Jugendstil (1890–1910)

Art Nouveau was a new style that emerged at the turn of the century in France, Belgium, Scotland, and Austria (where it was called Jugendstil). Its exponents attempted to create designs unrelated to any previous style. Art Nouveau drew inspiration from nature and incorporated vines and flowers, often in extremely sinuous and twisted form, as well as animal forms such as lizards and peacocks.

Art Nouveau/Jugendstil Furniture Classics

The Vienna café chair, corbu chair, and **bentwood** rocker are pieces designed by the German craftsman Michael Thonet (1796–1871) and manufactured in Austria during the last half of the nineteenth century. Thonet invented a process for bending wood that gives these pieces their beautiful curvilinear design and eliminates the need for complex joinery. Today these chairs are manufactured by Thonet.

The Prague chair, a bentwood and cane piece arranged in a square composition, was designed at the turn of the century by **Josef Hoffmann** (1870–1956), a member of the **Vienna Secession** and founding member of its offshoot, the **Wiener Werkstätte** (Vienna Workshops).

The Fledermaus chair, with its distinctively shaped back and ball pendants, is Hoffmann's 1905 design. The Fledermaus and Prague chairs are also available from Thonet.

The Hill chair and Argyle chair are striking perpendicular Art Nouveau pieces created by scotsman **Charles Rennie Mackintosh** (1868–1928). They are constructed of black ebony with padded seats and are distinguished by a high back treatment. The Hill chair, considered an extraordinary design for the period, was particularly influential with the Secessionists in Vienna. See Table 15.24 for examples.

The Craftsman Style (1905–1929)

In the second half of the nineteenth century, the English Arts and Crafts movement advocated simple handcraftsmanship in reaction to the shoddiness and poor design of machine-made, mass-produced products of the Industrial Revolution. At the beginning of the twentieth century, this craftsman philosophy had a significant impact on American designers like the Greene brothers and Gustav Stickley.

The Craftsman-style house was developed primarily by California architects Charles Greene (1868–1957) and Henry Greene (1870–1954), known as Greene and Greene or as the Greene brothers. Around 1903 they created designs for simple Craftsman-style bungalows that were given much attention by magazines such as *House Beautiful, Good Housekeeping,* and *Ladies' Home Journal.* Designs for small model homes in the style were published in *Ladies' Home Journal* and in the *Craftsman* magazine published by Gustav Stickley (1848–1942). Stickley was one of the greatest proponents of the style; the associated Craftsman-style furniture from this period is often called by his name. The publications provided working drawings for Craftsman houses that could be built for under

Figure 15.18 This home at the foot of the Utah Wasatch Mountains is a faithful and attractive contemporary re-creation of the Craftsman style. © *David A. Taylor*

Table 15.24 | Art Nouveau/Jugendstil Furniture Classics

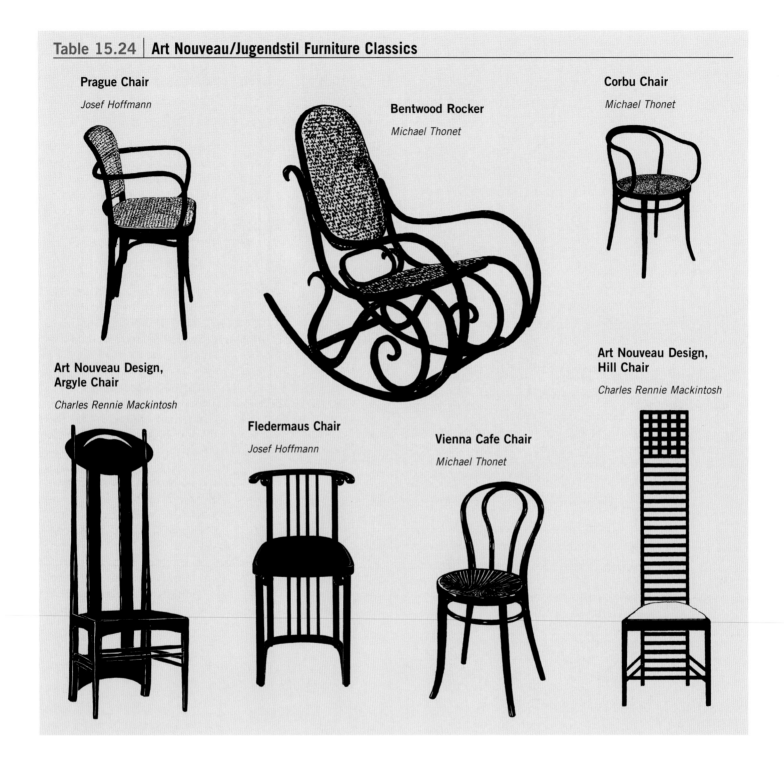

Prague Chair

Josef Hoffmann

Bentwood Rocker

Michael Thonet

Corbu Chair

Michael Thonet

Art Nouveau Design, Argyle Chair

Charles Rennie Mackintosh

Fledermaus Chair

Josef Hoffmann

Vienna Cafe Chair

Michael Thonet

Art Nouveau Design, Hill Chair

Charles Rennie Mackintosh

$1000. Prefabricated versions of the style could also be purchased from Sears and Roebuck; the components were shipped to the nearest railway station complete with instructions for assembly. The Craftsman-style house enjoyed wide acceptance during the first thirty years of the twentieth century and is highly regarded again today for its cozy, cottagelike qualities.

These homes, crafted of wood, featured low-pitched gabled roofs; wide, bracketed overhangs with exposed rafter tails; full and partial porches supported by well-scaled piers or columns; and shingle, brick, stone, or clapboard siding. The gardens, porches, and loggias were extensions of the houses, creating harmony with their setting, a concept referred to as organic.

Figure 15.19 The Craftsman style enjoys great contemporary acceptance. *Jack Silverio, Architect/ photo © Brian Vanden Brink*

Figure 15.20 The Robie House exemplifies Frank Lloyd Wright's Prairie style.

Craftsman Furniture Classics

The English Arts and Crafts movement included designers/philosophers William Morris (1834–96) and John Ruskin (1818–1900). They rejected machine construction and advocated simple handcraftsmanship. Gustav Stickley agreed with their ideas about the beauty and honesty of traditional handcrafted design and natural materials. He disseminated these ideas in his *Craftsman* magazine. In addition to being a magazine publisher, Stickley was, first and foremost, a furniture designer and manufacturer. The chairs and sofas he designed were rectilinear with vertical back slats, straight flat arms, exposed mortise and tenon joints, and leather seats. He also designed a number of case pieces and tables with comparable lines and details. Craftsman or Stickley-style furniture has recently experienced the same kind of high regard enjoyed by Craftsman-style homes.

Craftsman Color

The dominant color in the Craftsman home was the reddish-brown of fumed oak and chestnut loved and recommended by Stickley and used extensively in wall paneling and floors. The use of natural wood finishes imparted a dark and cozy feeling. The color palette for walls and textiles advocated by Stickley included colors from nature such as muted pumpkin, sage, soft golds, and tans. Also used were deep leaf greens and cobalt blues. Hammered metals such as copper and iron added color to the Craftsman interior. See Table 15.25 for illustrations of the Craftsman style.

Frank Lloyd Wright's Organic Architecture (1908–Present)

Often considered America's most important architect, Frank Lloyd Wright (1867–1959) successfully broke the cycle of historically styled design typical of the Victorian age and the prevailing Beaux Arts architectural training. Like the Greene brothers, Wright felt that a home should relate to its setting. The long, low, horizontal lines of the Robie House (1908), Chicago, Illinois, were in harmony with the prairies of the great Midwest. He called his designs the Prairie style and referred to them as organic. He designed over thirty-five houses for his neighbors in Oak Park, a Chicago suburb.

One of the Wright's most famous designs is the Edgar J. Kaufmann residence (1939), Fallingwater, in Bear Run,

Table 15.25 | Craftsman Design

Exterior Characteristics

- Low-pitched roof (front-gabled, side-gabled, and hipped)
- Triangular dormers with three or four grouped windows; or low, flat, horizontal shed dormers with clustered windows
- Widely projecting, unenclosed eaves with exposed rafter tails and triangular, cutout brackets
- Sided with shingles, brick, clinker brick (appears to be melted), clapboard, stone, or a combination of these
- Squared, pop-out bays
- Eight- (or six-) over-one, sash or fixed windows
- Front porch (full or partial width)
- Massive, short, square columns, or clustered columns resting on substantial piers

Influences

- William Morris and the English Arts and Crafts movement
- John Ruskin's aesthetic philosophies

Residential Examples

- David B. Gamble House (1908), Pasadena, California; Greene and Greene, architects
- Craftsman Farms (1911), Parsippany, New Jersey; Gustav Stickley, architect

Craftsman Bungalow

Gamble House

Greene Brothers

Nonresidential Examples

- First Church of Christ, Scientist (1901), Berkeley, California; Bernard Maybeck, architect

Craftsman Interior

Inglenook

Craftsman Shed Dormer

Craftsman Design (continued)

Stickley Armchair

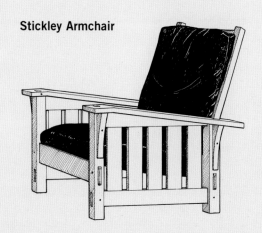

William Morris Textiles

Craftsman Eight-Light Door

Stickley Cabinet

Stickley Settee

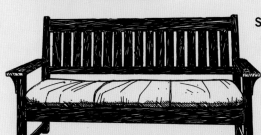

Interior Details

Floors. Oak or chestnut hardwood

Walls. Wooden wainscot, often with a plate rail; plain, painted plaster; stenciled friezes; wallpaper

Windows. Fixed or sash, eight- or six-over-one; pop-out bays; small square windows flanking chimneypiece; some picture windows

Doors. Flush with a single light (pane); plank with hammered-metal straps; two-paneled with a projecting, bracketed shelf under three or four lights; hammered-metal hardware on doors

Chimneypiece. Tile surrounded by bracketed mantlepiece, some hammered-copper hoods, some stone or brick chimneypieces; inglenooks: the fireplace is recessed in an alcove, often with flanking benches

Ceiling. Beamed or plain, painted plaster

Stairs. Straight-run, single- or double-turn wooden stair with large square newel posts and square balusters; stairways tucked between rooms in some small versions

Textile Description

Colors. The natural brown colors of leather were common. Textile and wallpaper designs by William Morris were compatible with Craftsman interiors. Morris, like Stickley, favored colors from nature: pumpkin; sage, sea foam, and leaf greens; light, true, and cobalt blues. Accents of red were also seen among the blues and greens

Patterns. Complex leaf and flower and/or fruit patterns with occasional use of animals such as birds or rabbits

Textures. Smooth cotton prints, leather, rich tapestries, and simple homespuns

(A)

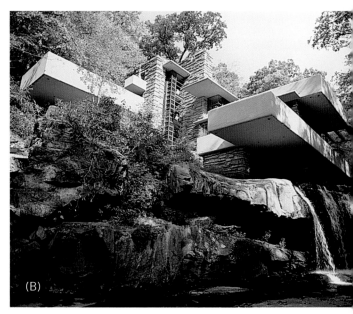

(B)

Figure 15.21 Frank Lloyd Wright's Fallingwater. (A) The extensive use of stone reinforces the organic concept of the design. (B) The house appears to grow out of its setting. *(A) © Norman McGrath (B) © Sergio Penchansky/Photo Researchers, Inc.*

Pennsylvania. The house is dramatically situated over a waterfall where it appears to grow out of the stones that support it. Fallingwater is, however, also an example of how Wright incorporated the concepts and principles of the International style—which had become popular in the 1930s—into his masterful organic design. The broad, light-colored, horizontal bands of the cantilevered terraces and balconies show the marriage of the International and Organic styles—two significant directions in modern architecture.

Characteristics of Organic Design
- Materials that harmonize with nature
- Architectural forms in harmony with the setting
- Well-established relationship from the inside of the house to the outdoors
- Flexible floor plan: open planning

Art Deco (1918–45)

The **Art Deco** style, though modern in spirit, incorporated the kind of rich ornamentation typical of the Beaux-Arts era. Architects, trained in that decorative historical tradition, left the past behind, creating sleek, modern

Figure 15.22 This house in San Antonio, Texas, is a pleasing combination of Art Deco and International style elements. *© David A. Taylor*

designs devoid of specific historical reference. The designs were symbols of the optimism, confidence, and forward thinking of the "Roaring Twenties." Art Deco is a slick and flashy style that epitomized all that was new and modern. Its rich vocabulary of motifs was inspired by the machine, modes of speeding transportation (locomotives and ocean liners), plants and other natural forms, and even some elements of historical design.

The Art Deco style is characterized by rigid geometric forms, zigzags, chevron patterns, stepped pyramid forms, stylized billows of clouds, and stylized human and animal forms. Preferred materials were shiny metals, polished stone or marble, and etched mirrors and glass.

As an architectural style it was used for the design of skyscrapers, movie palaces, and even some post offices and other government buildings. The style has hundreds of vernacular applications in every corner of the country, and its influence can even be seen in unlikely places such as churches, gas stations, and grocery stores.

Its residential application was principally as an interior style and was simply called modern. Examples of Art Deco nonresidential buildings include:

- Richfield Oil Building (1929), Los Angeles, California
- Chrysler Building (1930), New York, New York
- Empire State Building (1931), New York, New York
- Rockefeller Center (1931–40), New York, New York

Art Deco Color
Art Deco colors were appropriate to typically sleek forms and geometric shapes. Favorite colors were rose, mauve, silver and black, and warm yellow-greens trimmed with gold and mustard yellow.

The International Style (1932–Present)

The **International style,** as the name implies, crossed international borders and drew inspiration from several European schools of thought. From the thinking of the **De Stijl** movement in Holland, the **Bauhaus** in Germany, and **Le Corbusier** in France came the principles that dominated and gave form to the International style.

Though isolated examples existed before, the new style was introduced into the mainstream of American design in 1932 by Philip Johnson and Henry-Russell Hitchcock when they organized the first exhibit of modern architecture at the Museum of Modern Art in New York City and published a book called *The International Style.* The definition of the new style advanced by these men rapidly gained acceptance and established a formula or framework in which less-imaginative architects could design. The style gained further momentum when many leaders of the International Movement immigrated to America during World War II. **Walter Gropius, Ludwig Mies van der Rohe** (1886–1969), and **Marcel Breuer** (1902–81), all associated at one time with the Bauhaus,

Figure 15.23 The Chrysler Building in New York is an Art Deco monument.

Figure 15.24 Philip Johnson's home in Connecticut, known as the "glass house," is a jewel of International style design. © Norman McGrath

became teachers of the new style in the United States.

In some ways, the International style is the antithesis of Wright's Organic style. The Organic style harmonizes with its setting, while the International style stands out in clear contrast. The materials of the International style are bold and hard edged: concrete, structural steel, glass, and stark, white stucco. The architectural approach is minimalist, not adding any unnecessary embellishment, and the plan is open and unencumbered. This architecture is not as "forgiving" as the organic or historical designs; there is little place for the wear and tear of human use and the gentle softening that comes with time. In order to appear pleasing, these clean pure designs must be impeccably maintained. Because of its stark cleanliness, the style has not lent itself to the charming vernacular versions of previous styles.

After the years of historical eclecticism, the International movement was like a breath of fresh air. There is a purity and cool elegance to this approach that is beautiful and refreshing, but trends never continue unaltered. It is noteworthy that one of the International style's first American proponents, architect Philip Johnson, moved away from strict adherence to its principles to embrace allusions to classical pediments and Gothic spires.

International Furniture Classics

The Wassily lounge chair (1925), the world's first bent tubular steel chair, was designed by Marcel Breuer, one of the foremost designers of the Bauhaus in Germany. The Bauhaus school of art, architecture, and design attracted some of the world's finest designers from 1919 to 1933. The chair was named for **Wassily Kandinsky** (1886–1944), an important artist and Bauhaus faculty member. Breuer was one of the first of many designers to take advantage of the possibilities of this versatile combination of materials.

The Cesca chair is another bent tubular steel design by Breuer. The Cesca chair has a wood-framed seat and back of cane mounted on a cantilevered frame. The cantilever design has no back legs and was a remarkable breakthrough made possible by the strength of the metal. Both the Wassily lounge and Cesca chair are manufactured by Knoll International and Thonet.

The MR chair, made of tubular steel and wicker or leather, was designed in 1926 by Ludwig Mies van der Rohe, the last director of the Bauhaus. The MR chair, like the Cesca chair, is designed on the cantilever principle.

The Barcelona collection was designed by Mies van der Rohe for his German pavilion at the Barcelona International Exhibition of 1929. The Barcelona chair and Barcelona stool are constructed on a double X frame of polished stainless steel and are meticulously upholstered in tufted leather. The Barcelona table has an X-shaped frame of polished stainless steel with a glass top.

The Brno chair is Mies van der Rohe's 1930 design for the Tugendhat House in Brno, Czech Republic. The cantilevered design has great strength and visual appeal. The Brno chair, the Barcelona collection, and the MR chair are all manufactured by Knoll International, Inc.

The Grand and Petit Confort chairs were designed in 1929 by Swiss-born French designer **Charles-Edouard Jeanneret-Gris** (1887–1965), better known as Le Corbusier.

The Grand Confort has a basketlike frame of bent tubular steel with a series of leather cushions forming the seating unit. The Petit Confort is the same design in smaller scale.

The Basculant chair was designed by Le Corbusier in 1928. The chair has a frame of tubular steel with seat and back of calf skin and arm straps of leather.

The Pony Chaise, designed by Le Corbusier in 1928, is an adjustable **chaise longue** with a frame of chromium-plated tubular steel, a base of matte-textured steel, and pony skin or leather upholstery. These three Le Corbusier designs are manufactured by Atelier International. Table 15.26 shows examples of the International style.

Scandinavian and Mid-Century Design

Scandinavian and Mid-Century Furniture Classics

Scandinavian and mid-century American designers made important contributions to modern furniture manufacture, exploiting new materials as well as earlier methods such as bending wood.

Armchair 406 is a 1935 cantilever design by **Alvar Aalto** (1899–1976) of Finland. The flexible bent laminated plywood frame has a seat and back of woven fabric. Armchair 406 is manufactured by ICF.

The Pedestal group was created by **Eero Saarinen** (1910–1961) in 1956 and was a significant design of a furniture collection without the traditional four legs. The single base of the table and chairs is made of aluminum,

Figure 15.25 Mies van der Rohe's Farnsworth House in Plano, Illinois, is a striking example of the International style. *Courtesy of the Landmarks Preservation Council of Illinois*

Table 15.26 | International Style

Exterior Characteristics

- Open plan
- Simple, logical, rectilinear structured forms
- Generally flat roofed
- Asymmetrical
- Large areas of glass (often arranged horizontally)
- Use of concrete, stucco, and metal
- Long, uninterrupted white wall planes
- Contrasts with setting

Residential Examples

- Waler Gropius House (1937), Lincoln, Massachusetts; Walter Gropius and Marcel Breuer, architects
- Glass House (1949), New Caanan, Connecticut; Philip Johnson, architect
- Edgar J. Kaufmann House, Fallingwater (1936), Bear Run, Pennsylvania; Frank Lloyd Wright, architect
- Lovell Beach House (1926), Newport Beach, California; Rudolph Schindler, architect

- Lovell-Health House (1927), Los Angeles, California; Richard Neutra, architect
- Farnsworth House (designed 1946, built 1950), Plano, Illinois; Ludwig Mies van der Rohe, architect

Nonresidential Examples

- 860-80 Lake Shore Drive (1952), Chicago, Illinois; Ludwig Mies van der Rohe, architect
- Lever House (1952), New York, New York; Skidmore, Owings, and Merrill, architects
- Crown Hall (1956), I.I.T., Chicago, Illinois; Ludwig Mies van der Rohe, architect
- General Motors Technical Center (1956), Warren, Michigan; Eero Saarinen and Associates, architects
- Seagram Building (1958), New York, New York; Ludwig Mies van der Rohe and Philip Johnson, architects

International Style

Philip Johnson

International Style

Walter Gropius

International Style Interior

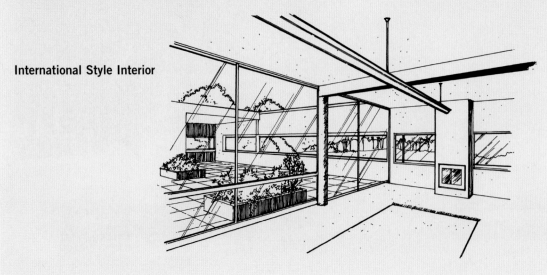

International Style (continued)

Modern Textiles

Barcelona Chair

Ludwig Mies van der Rohe

Cesca Chair

Marcel Breuer

MR Chair

Ludwig Mies van der Rohe

Grand Confort

Le Corbusier

Pony Chaise

Le Corbusier

Wassily Lounge

Marcel Breuer

Brno Chair

Ludwig Mies van der Rohe

Basculant Chair

Le Corbusier

Interior Details

Floors. Hard, smooth—marble or tile
Walls. Plain plaster, glass
Windows. Large areas of glass with minimal framing
Doors. Flush, plain
Chimneypiece. Simple rectangular opening with no trim
Ceiling. Plain plaster
Stairs. Open riser, no embellishment

Textile Description

Colors. Several color palettes have been evident during the twentieth century. Bright primary colors are one; natural neutrals are another. Dulled, neutralized colors and even psychedelic or vivid chroma colors have all been used, according to decades; now, modern trends are established every one to two years

Patterns. Where pattern did exist, it has been abstract and stylized, often reflecting modern art and architectural grid systems. Some patterns were adapted from nature forms

Textures. Textures include leather, handwoven textures (authentic or machine produced), nubby semisheer and casement fabrics, cane, animal hides, woven textures for upholstery

and the shell of the seating pieces is made of fiberglass. The tabletop may be marble, glass, wood, or laminate. The Pedestal group is manufactured by Knoll International.

THE chair is a classic Scandinavian design by Denmark's **Hans Wegner** (b. 1914). The 1949 piece is the epitome of fine craftsmanship featuring a beautifully joined wooden frame with a seat of cane or upholstery. THE chair is manufactured by D.S.I.

The Number Seven Chair was designed by Danish architect **Arne Jacobsen** (1902–71) in 1955. It features a single molded/bent piece of plywood for the seat and bent chrome tubular steel legs. The chair was originally manufactured in natural beech wood as well as with black and white finishes but today is available in a variety of colors. The Number Seven Chair is one of the most successful designs in Danish furniture history, with over 5 million having been sold. It is manufactured by Fritz Hansen.

The Egg Chair, designed by Arne Jacobsen in 1957, is a fabric-covered, foam-molded fiberglass shell with a loose cushion and a base of cast aluminum. The Egg Chair was created for the Royal SAS Hotel in Copenhagen. Jacobsen designed the hotel and all its fixtures and furniture. Like much mid-twentieth-century design, the Egg Chair has enjoyed increased favor at the start of the new millennium. Fritz Hansen of Denmark has manufactured the Egg Chair since 1958.

The Eames lounge chair was designed in 1956 by **Charles** (1907–78) and **Ray Eames.** The lounge was designed for comfort featuring a chair and ottoman with metal bases, bent laminated wood frames, and carefully padded leather upholstery. The lounge was a great success and, like many of the classics, has been widely copied. The original design is manufactured by Herman Miller.

The Bertoia Wire Group by Italian-born **Harry Bertoia** (1915–78) is a sculptural approach to seating design. The chairs are formed of lattice and are made of a steel rod frame with or without cushions and upholstery. The Bertoia chairs, originally designed in 1956 for Hans and Florence Knoll, are still produced by Knoll International.

The Platner Chair was created in 1966 by architect/designer, **Warren Platner,** as a "graceful, decorative design . . . that enhances the person in it." The nickel-plated steel construction chair is part of a larger group of chairs, tables, and stools called the Platner Collection. Knoll

Figure 15.26 These three Eames lounge chairs are examples of mid-century design. *Courtesy of Herman Miller, Inc.*

International, Inc., New York, has manufactured the Platner Collection since it was introduced in the middle of the last century. Table 15.27 contains several examples of mid-century design.

Mid-Century Color

The outbreak of World War II effectively cut off America from European color influence. Many interior colors were neutral and comparatively drab during the 1940s. Designers, however, turned their attention to the optimistic and bright colors south of the border—Latin American hues that were best represented in the interiors of Hollywood movies.

During the 1950s, research that was initiated before and during World War II was utilized for interiors. Dyestuffs chemically invented and applied to synthetic fibers gave rise to bright, clear, and often gaudy colors: bright yellow, carnation and flamingo pink, Oriental blue, flower red, chartreuse, avocado and pine green, and gold. These colors were usually assigned to artwork or textiles, while backgrounds and even furniture remained monochromatic colors such as rose-beige, pale turquoise, black or white, or neutrals. Colors and design from Scandinavia were introduced during the 1950s, and for the first time in America, blues and greens were stylistically used together.

Contemporary Trends

Design is constantly on the move, keeping pace with changes in technology and taste. Only the passage of time will determine the true classics of today. However, it is worthwhile to study the developments taking place around us so that we can put them into context. The following represent three important contemporary trends in design.

High-Tech

High-Tech design is a celebration of technology in which all the inner mechanical workings, as well as the structural members of the building, are left frankly exposed on both the exterior and interior. High-Tech designers use elements that were obviously designed for industrial use, such as warehouse lighting and industrial shelving, as furnishings within the interior. The greatest exponents

and examples of this style are British: Richard Rogers's Lloyd's of London (1986) and Norman Foster's Hong Kong and Shanghai Bank (1986) in Hong Kong.

Postmodern

Postmodern design grew out of a dissatisfaction with the International modern style. Some people were feeling alienated by the severity of the uniform lines and the regularity of the boxy forms associated with the International style. Postmodernism imbued modern design with a sense of individuality and even frivolity or playfulness. The characteristic forms of Postmodernism are updated classical elements with a decidedly modern twist. Columns, pediments, domes, and arches, often in simplified or stylized form, are the elements that give individuality to Postmodernism. Designers have also borrowed many elements of the Art Deco style such as the step-pyramid and the inverted column. The name most associated with Postmodernism is Michael Graves, whose work for Disney is typical of the whimsical quality of the style.

Deconstructivism

The themes that define Deconstructive design are instability, conflict, and disharmony. The materials of the style are corrugated steel, other raw metals, chain-link fencing material, and raw plywood and chipboard. The frank use of materials is similar to High-Tech, but the application is more chaotic. The best description of Deconstructive design is that it appears as if someone took the design apart and didn't know how to put it back together. Some designs resemble a pile of girders and lumber with the unifying factor being the chaos and disunity. While

Figure 15.27 Machine-like High-Tech Lloyd's of London is unusually juxtaposed with Leadenhall Market, its ornate nineteenth-century Victorian neighbor. © *Kathryn Taylor*

Table 15.27 | Scandinavian and Mid-Century Furniture Classics

Armchair 406

Alvar Aalto

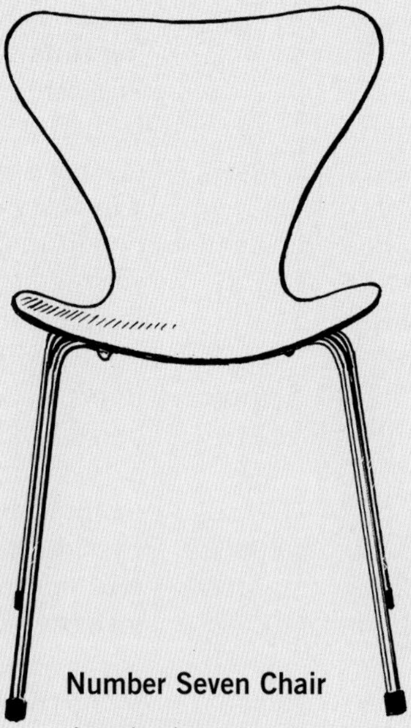

Bertoia Wire Group

Harry Bertoia

THE Chair

Hans Wegner

Number Seven Chair

Arne Jacobsen

Egg Chair

Arne Jacobsen

Pedestal Chair

Eero Saarinen

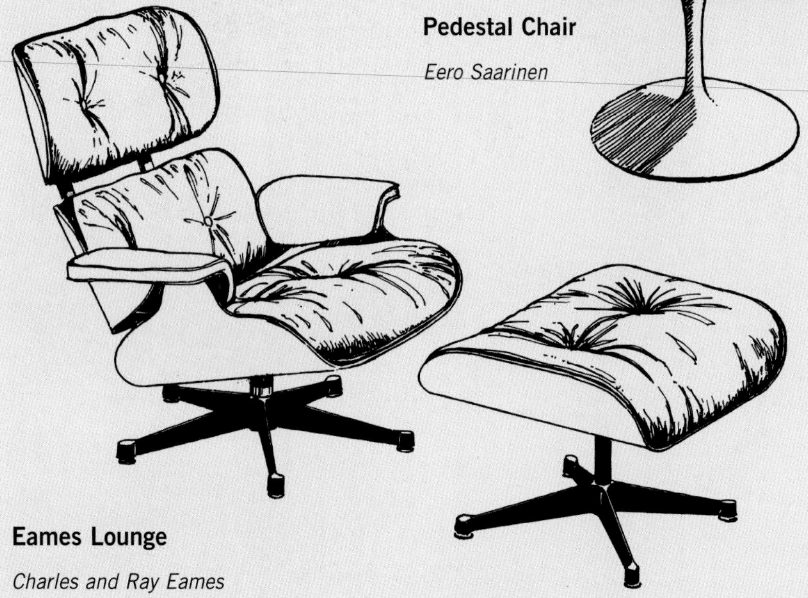

Eames Lounge

Charles and Ray Eames

Platner Chair

Warren Platner

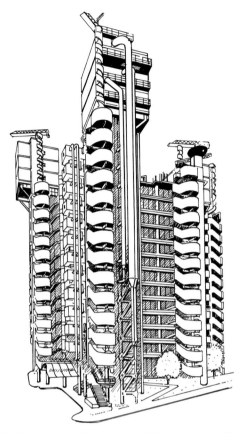

Figure 15.28 The Lloyd's of London building is a beautifully detailed and exciting example of High-Tech design by Richard Rogers.

the descriptions may sound quite grim, the actual product is often exciting. It is a style that has found appropriate application in exclusive but funky clothing stores, bistros, and night clubs. The work of Los Angeles architect Frank O. Gehry, an important proponent of the style, has received international praise and recognition.

Putting Things in Perspective

The styles and influences discussed in this chapter are only a part of the story. There is no style to end all styles. The development of style is an ongoing process, as one style influences another and further variations are born. New technology prompts changes in design, and often some influence of either traditional or modern design reappears.

It takes time to determine the value of a design and to put it into the context of a style. In the past, the classification of styles was done in retrospect by historians with a clear overview. But from our perspective, the design family tree has grown very bushy since the beginning of the twentieth century. We live in an information age filled with self-awareness and are often conscious of every new "ism" that appears on the scene. For the amateur, this can be confusing and discouraging. It may be comforting to realize, then, that many new developments in design, which have mushroomed along with technology, are still being sifted and judged by time.

Figure 15.29 The Keystone House by architect Michael Graves is an excellent residential example of Postmodern design.

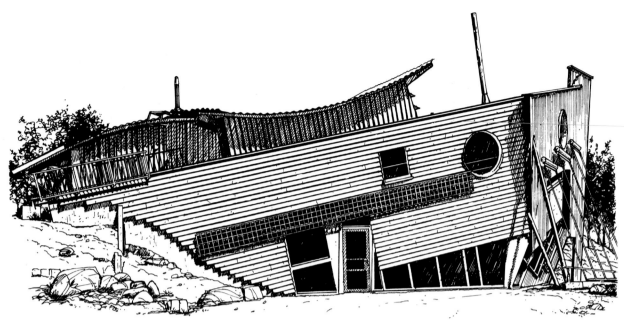

Figure 15.30 This German kindergarten demonstrates the chaotic nature of Deconstructive design.

Figure 15.31 Frank Gehry's Guggenheim Museum in Bilbao, Spain, with its distinctive sculptural shapes and its brilliant titanium skin, is an internationally recognized example of Deconstructive design. *The Soloman R. Guggenheim Foundation, NY/photo: David Heald*

A knowledge of the basic styles and influences listed here is a key to understanding the myriad modes that have grown out of the modern movement and the thousands of vernacular adaptations of each modern and traditional style. Understanding leads to appreciation and enrichment. Our architectural heritage should be cherished and preserved for future generations to enjoy.

Preservation

Preservation is often an emotion-charged subject. Preservationists and developers often disagree over whether a building should be preserved for its historic value or whether it should be removed to make way for new buildings. One problem is that it takes time to determine

Figure 15.32 Adaptive restoration turned this obsolete warehouse into an upscale office building. *Courtesy of Mackey Mitchell Associates, Barbara Elliott Martin photographer*

the historic or aesthetic value of a building. At the point where sufficient time has passed to make that determination, the building may already have disappeared. To address this problem, preservation societies have been established on both local and national levels. The National Trust for Historic Preservation is the largest of such organizations. This Trust was established in 1949 and today helps determine which buildings, neighborhoods, and historic areas should be preserved. From its headquarters in Washington, D.C., the National Trust maintains museums, assists with restoration and preservation projects, and dispenses information to any who need assistance.

Restoration is a research, partial-demolition, and reconstruction process that returns a building to its original state or to some specific state during its history. **Preser-** vation is taking whatever steps are necessary to maintain a building in its present state or the state to which it has been restored. **Adaptive restoration** or reuse is giving new life to buildings of aesthetic or historic worth by remodeling and restoring them for new uses. One of the earliest adaptive restorations was at Ghirardelli Square in San Francisco. In the mid-1960s, the old and unused Ghirardelli Chocolate factory (1915) was turned into a pleasant multilevel shopping center with restaurants and landscaped pedestrian areas. Adaptive reuse has spread across the country reinvigorating many old spaces that no longer serve their original purposes. This concept has been used to turn old buildings into housing, office complexes, theaters, museums, oceanariums, and many other uses.

Glossary

A

A 588 steel The designation given to steel that rusts only to a certain point and in doing so creates its own rustproof finish.

A lamp Designation for an arbitrary-shaped, standard light globe or lamp bulb.

AAHE The American Association of Housing Educators.

Aalto, Alvar (1899–1976) Important Finnish designer of several modern classic furniture pieces.

abacus The slab or pillow above the capital at the top of a column.

abrasion resistance The ability of a material to resist wear from friction, rubbing, or other abrasive action.

abstract design A type of decorative design that may be based on natural or even geometric design, stylized to the point that the source is not recognizable, and the design is therefore open to interpretation.

acanthus leaves A representation of the lobed leaves of the acanthus plant used as a decorative motif.

accent lighting Focusing or highlighting; sometimes called artistic lighting.

accent rug A small rug, also called a scatter or throw rug. Accent rugs may be used for visual accents or to protect the underlying floor material from moisture, dirt, or wear.

accessible design Design that allows users to enter, exit, and use its features without obstruction.

accessories The items in an interior used to give a quality of finish or completion such as paintings, sculpture, books, lamps, vases, flowers, and plants.

accordion door Folding door, with small vertical panels, that stacks against itself.

acetate A man-made fiber of reconstituted cellulose and acetic acid.

achromatic Colors without hue, namely black, white, and gray.

acoustical plaster An irregular plaster surface, usually used for ceilings, designed to absorb rather than reflect sound.

acoustical tile Tile, usually used for ceilings, designed to absorb rather than reflect sound. Acoustical tile is made from fiberboard, fabric- or plastic-coated fiber, or fiberglass.

acrylic A synthetic fiber of over 85 percent acrylonitrile units; used for the manufacture of textiles and furniture.

acrylic paint A synthetic resin, water-based paint.

acrylic sheet A flat plate or sheet of acrylic (a hard plastic) that can be etched to allow special effects. The most common is the exit sign.

active balance Another term for asymmetrical balance where objects that are not alike balance each other, or like objects are placed at unequal distances from a central point. It is termed active because it requires some effort or activity of the eye to analyze or discern the balance.

active solar system A mechanical system of solar heat collection for space and water heating.

actual density The three-dimensional, literal mass or density of a piece of furniture.

Adam, Robert (1728–92) The most influential of four Scottish architect/designer brothers. His English Neoclassic work was influenced by the uncovering of Pompeii and Herculaneum near Naples, Italy.

adaptive restoration Restoring older buildings for purposes other than those for which they were constructed.

adjustable luminaire A light fixture, such as track lighting, that is affixed to a ceiling or wall but can easily be repositioned by the user.

adobe Large building brick made of clay, baked in the sun.

aesthetics The philosophy of art and beauty. The part of art and design that is beautiful and appealing to the senses.

affinity The chemical compatibility of fibers to dyestuffs.

afterimages When the human eye focuses on a strong color for several seconds or minutes, then focuses on a neutral area, the complement of that color will appear in shadow form.

AID The American Institute of Interior Designers combined in 1975 with NSID to form ASID, the American Society of Interior Designers.

air-brush printing Dye sprayed through stencils by pressure ink jet guns.

air compression painting Spray painting powered by an air compression machine that allows paint to be diluted for application.

air-conditioning Cool air piped into an interior through an air-conditioning unit or through a furnace unit.

air-exchange unit Draws fresh outside air into buildings and expels stale, used air. Necessary in a superinsulated and tight structure with few or no windows.

airless paint spraying Mechanical spraying of nondiluted paint.

aisle A passageway separated by an arcade, running parallel to the nave of a church.

Albers, Josef (1888–1976) Color expert in simultaneous and successive contrast. Albers taught at the Bauhaus in Germany and at Yale University.

alkyds, alkyd enamel Oil-modified resin paints. Alkyd enamels produce glossy surfaces.

all-wood Wooden furniture construction where all visible parts are made of wood.

allocate space To assign space; to determine the location and layout of rooms or areas.

alloy A substance formed by fusing one or more metals, or a metal and a nonmetal.

alternate complement A four-color scheme that combines a triad with the direct complement of one of the hues.

alternation A type of rhythm wherein two shapes alternate. A classic example is egg-and-dart molding.

aluminum A lightweight silvery metal.

ambient bank A large, well-lit area which may encompass the entire area or can designate smaller areas, such as walls in a larger space.

ambient general lighting Overall lighting that covers a large area, often in the form of overhead luminaires.

ambulatory A place for walking; the aisle in a cathedral.

amenities Facilities shared by condominium owners or available to renters in luxury apartments. These include swimming pools, tennis courts, and entertainment or athletic facilities.

American Empire (1820–60) The interior design title of the period concurrent with the antebellum Greek Revival homes. Colors are influenced by Napoleonic choices of bold, deep hues.

ampere or amp The measurement of electrical current in a circuit.

anaglypta Embossed wall or ceiling coverings that resemble plaster, hammered copper, or hand-tooled leather.

analogous Colors that are next to each other on the standard color wheel or as they occur in a rainbow or prism. An analogous color scheme usually contains three to six adjacent colors.

analysis A part of a programming process in which information is assessed and priorities established.

ancient Greece, the golden age (fifth century B.C.) Era of the Parthenon and height of philosophical development and architectural excellence.

angular lines Any straight line used in interior design that is neither horizontal nor vertical. Angular lines may be diagonal lines in one direction or even or uneven zigzag lines. Angular lines suggest movement and action.

animal hair felt pad Moderately resilient carpet underlay of 100 percent animal hair felted into padding.

animal skin rugs Rugs of zebra, bear, sheep, and other animal skins.

anodize To put a protective oxide film on metal through an electrolytic process with chemicals and an electric charge.

anthemion A symmetrical stylized Greek flower motif that radiates from a central point at the bottom of the flower.

anthropometrics The study and comparison of human body measurements (i.e., anthropometry).

antimony A silver-white, crystalline, metallic element used in alloys.

antique finish A finish made to appear older by the application of a darker color over the top of a lighter finish.

antique A piece of furniture, fine art, decorative art, or other item of artistic value that is at least 100 years old (U.S. Customs definition).

antiquing Making a painted surface look old with a mellow patina by color washing, glazing, spattering, and dragging techniques. *See also* distressed.

antistatic finishes Reduce conduction or static electricity.

apartment A home unit housed with other units that are rented for living spaces.

apron The face or front piece of a table just below the top, the face of a chair just below the seat, the face of a chest just below the drawers, and the front piece below the windowsill.

apse A semicircular or polygonal projection of a church.

arcade A row of arches and supporting columns.

arch system construction A building type in existence since antiquity; the arch is held together with a splayed keystone under compression.

architect A professional who plans three-dimensional space and creates floor plans and blueprints.

architectural elements The walls, floors, ceilings, windows, doors, fireplaces, cabinetry, and other fixtures or details that are built in to an interior.

architectural glazing *See* glass.

architectural or structural lighting Permanently installed fixtures or luminaires. The wiring must be in place in advance.

architectural rods Nonresidential drapery and curtain rods that are usually drawn with wands or batons rather than a traverse cord and pulley.

architrave The lintel or crosspiece in a classical entablature.

area rugs Rugs that define a specific area, such as a conversation area.

armchair A chair with armrests as distinguished from a side chair without arms.

armoire The French term for a wardrobe or large movable closet.

Art Deco (1918–45) A brief period of design between World Wars I and II that has been repeatedly revived in interior design style and color.

art glass A general term for stained, beveled, leaded, and etched glass used as primary glazing or as hard window treatments.

art lighting A term for luminaires or fixtures that are in themselves works of art where light is the medium of artistic expression.

Art Nouveau (1890–1910) A style of design based on natural floral motifs and colors.

art rug A rug with a decorative texture or pattern of such interest and quality that it can be considered a piece of art.

artificial light Incandescent and fluorescent light. Amount and direction of artificial lighting affect color hue, value, and intensity.

artificial stone A fabricated product that imitates natural stone and is generally used for wall facing.

artistic lighting Another term for accent lighting.

artist's paint Oil or acrylic paint in small bottles or tubes.

Arts and Crafts movement A school of thought at the close of the Victorian era that espoused a return to handmade, quality furnishings rather than machine-made items.

asbestos shingles A fireproof roofing material in several color choices laid in overlapping manner and nailed tight.

ashlar Stone cut into rectangular shapes fitted together with grout.

ASID The American Society of Interior Designers.

asymmetrical balance The placement of different objects on either side of a center point where they balance each other. Also called informal balance, asymmetry requires a discerning eye and sensitivity to achieve the balance.

atrium Latin for "entrance," an entry hall, foyer, or lobby that has a high ceiling or, in ancient Roman houses, is open to the sky.

atrium door A French-door pair with one fixed side. Also called a patio door.

attached dwelling A residential building divided into apartments or sharing walls with adjoining buildings; designed for occupancy by more than one family.

attic window Pivoting window installed in the pitched roof of an attic.

Aubusson rugs Flat tapestry French rugs woven in both historic and contemporary colors and patterns.

Austrian shades Scalloped and gathered shades that fold up. They are full and formal looking.

Austrian valance Valance in the same style as the Austrian shade.

automatic sensor dimmer A device that automatically turns on and controls the level of artificial light to supplement natural light in order to keep the light at an even level of brightness.

auxiliary heating A backup heating method needed for solar energy systems when the sun cannot supply all the heating needs of the interior.

awning window A top- or bottom-hinged window that swings out.

Axminster carpet A Jacquard-woven carpet where colored yarns are inserted as needed. Used extensively in nonresidential carpeting.

B

B lamp A designation for a candelabra lamp or bulb that is a smooth, torpedo-shaped oval.

baccalaureate degree The degree granted by colleges and universities and some design schools following four to five years of general education and specific topic study.

back panel A panel used to cover the back of a case piece; often made of hardboard.

backfilling Plowing excavated dirt into a dug-out area. For example, after a building's foundation is constructed, dirt is backfilled against the foundation's edges.

baffle A device such as a board or grid that deflects light, either to direct it or to prevent glare.

baffled ceiling Ceiling hung with panels of wood, metal, or fabric that serve as a screen.

balance The placement of objects (such as furniture or art), or architectural detail (such as windows or columns), so that it creates visual equilibrium.

balanced light Light from more than one direction meant to eliminate glare and high contrast of light and dark, or unflattering or fatiguing shadows.

ballast The connecting mechanism within a fluorescent lamp.

balloon, pouf, or cloud shades Loosely gathered, full, soft, and billowy shades that pull up from the bottom.

balloon valance Valance in the same style as the balloon shade.

baluster The member that supports the handrail on a stair.

balustrade The railing formed by the newel post, balusters, and handrail.

bamboo shades Shades woven of split bamboo and a cotton warp. Also called matchstick shades.

bank of light A large, well-lit area of light.

Baroque A seventeenth- and eighteenth-century design style characterized by bold, showy, and highly decorative use of classical design elements. The feeling is often luxurious, exuberant, and unrestrained.

barrel vault An arched roof with a roundheaded arch shape.

barrier-free design Design for special populations that presents no physical obstacles or barriers to access and allows free movement in the environment.

bartile Quarry or clay tile (gray or red) roofing material. It is costly but never needs replacing.

base Finish trim used to cover the joint where the wall meets the floor.

base lighting A light placed next to the floor behind a deflector board that directs light upward.

baseboard Base trim made of wood.

baseboard units Plugged-in or prewired units near the floor for room or area heating.

basket weave A variation of the plain weave where groups of warp and weft threads are carried as one. A balanced weave carries the same number in each direction—two over and two under; 3/3; 4/4. An unbalanced basket weave carries uneven groups of threads over and under, such as 2/3 or 3/4.

bas-relief (low relief) The type of sculpture wherein the figures protrude only slightly from the background.

bast fibers Natural cellulosic fibers obtained from the stems and leaves of plant. The best known are linen and jute.

batik A hand process of resist dyeing. A pattern is drawn with wax onto a cloth, then the cloth is dyed. The wax-covered portion will not be colored. The wax is removed and new wax applied to allow other areas of the pattern to be colored.

batting Polyester, cotton, wool, or other suitable fibers formed into sheets for upholstery padding.

battlement A parapet indented or crenellated along the upper line of a building.

Bauhaus A German school of art, design, and architecture that functioned from 1919–33 and espoused the integration of art and technology for the creation of good design. The Bauhaus attracted many important artists and designers and had a significant influence on the development of modern design.

bay The area between columns, piers, or buttresses.

bay or bow rods Traverse or curtain rods that are prebent to a bay or bow window shape.

bay window Projecting window in a square or canted configuration.

bead and reel A molding of alternating round bead shapes and oval or disk shapes.

beadboard Wood paneling with vertical grooves milled into it so that it resembles board-and-batten walls.

beam system construction Solid beams of steel, wood, or concrete supported with a series of posts.

beamed ceiling A ceiling with exposed beams or trusses.

Beau-Grip A registered trademark of Beaunit for viscose rayon.

bed molding *See* crown molding.

beltcourse A projecting row of bricks or stone on the facade that separates one story from another; also called stringcourse.

Belter, John Henry (d. 1865) A New York furniture craftsman best known for his Rococo Revival pieces of carved laminated rosewood.

belvedere A cupola or lantern. The small square towers that rise from the roof of the Italianate buildings of the nineteenth century.

Bemberg A registered trademark of Beaunit for cuprammonium rayon.

bentwood A method of softening wood with steam and then bending it into curved forms.

berber rugs Woven or tufted wood rugs left in their natural color state—white, beige, brown, or charcoal, with flecks of light or dark neutrals.

bergère French term for an upholstered armchair with upholstered side panels between the armrest and seat.

berm A pile of earth used to create a visual or physical diversion or to add variety to a landscape.

Bertoia, Harry (1915–78) Italian-born designer best known for his wire seating group (1956) created for Knoll.

beveled glass Thick, decorative glass with a finished edge that is mitered or beveled at less than ninety degrees.

beveled paneling Paneling with edges cut at an angle other than forty-five degrees.

bibelot French term for a small decorative and often rare object.

Biedermeier The term used to describe the Empire style as interpreted and built by the craftsmen of northern Europe.

bifold door A door with vertical double panels that folds back against itself; frequently used for closet doors.

biotechnology The aspect of technology concerned with the application of biological and engineering data to synthetic products and environments. *See also* ergonomics.

bishop sleeve curtains Drapery lengths pulled into a bloused, poufed effect.

bisymmetrical balance Also called formal or passive balance, the arrangement of like parts or objects in mirror image on each side of a central point.

bleaching A prefinishing process for natural fibers that whitens gray goods. Also the chemical lightening of the natural wood color as part of the wood finishing process.

blinds Slats or louvers held together with cords or on a pulley system. Blinds may be horizontal or vertical. Sometimes pull or pouf shades are called blinds.

block front A furniture detail used on the front section of case pieces. The block front consists of a series of three panels—the two outside panels come forward and the center panel is recessed.

block print A two-dimensional art form printed from a flat wooden or linoleum block on which the background has been carved away, leaving a raised design pattern.

block printing A hand-printing technique in which blocks (usually wood) are carved, inked with fabric dye, and pressed onto the fabric.

blueprints Floor plans printed in blue ink and used for construction plans.

board and batten Vertical wooden siding made of parallel boards with narrow strips of wood (battens) to cover the cracks.

boiserie French term for wood paneling; typically Rococo.

bolection A rounded, projecting molding.

bonded (rebonded) foam Carpet underlay (padding) of chopped foam and filler materials bonded together by heat, pressure, and some adhesives.

bonnet roof A hipped roof with two pitches. The top is steeply pitched and the bottom, which covers a porch, is low pitched; used on houses of French influence.

bonus room An unfinished room, often in a basement or attic, that is suitable for finishing as a guest room, home office or studio, family or media room.

border A strip of companion wall covering used to trim and accent. Packaged in five-yard spools.

boss A projecting ornament at the intersection of ribs in the Medieval church.

bow window A curved projecting window (in the shape of a bow).

bracket An angle-shaped support.

bracket lighting A light placed on the wall behind a bracket board that directs light upward and downward.

braided rugs Strips of fabric braided, then sewn together in ovals or circles. Originated in Colonial New England.

brainstorming Generating ideas without stopping to judge their quality.

brass A yellowish alloy of copper and zinc.

breakfront A case piece whose front plane is broken with receding or advancing sections. Also, the projecting section of the facade on Late Georgian houses that is topped with a pediment.

breast The front of the fireplace and chimneypiece.

Breuer, Marcel (1902–81) Important designer/architect associated with the Bauhaus and known for the design of several classic chairs.

brick Clay and other additives formed into rectangles and dried in the sun or fired in a kiln oven; used for walls and floors.

brilliants Several pinpoints of light that produce a glittering effect.

broadloom carpet Woven or tufted carpet typically twelve feet wide.

bronze A deeply colored, reddish brown alloy of copper and tin used to make sculptural pieces.

brush painting Application of paint with a handheld brush. Ideal for small areas and detail work.

brushed finish A lustrous (but not shiny) finish achieved by brushing a series of uniform scratches into metal.

bubble planning The first step of diagramming where bubbles represent zones and are placed in proximity relationships.

budgeting The facet of a design project that dictates the amount of money to be spent on various aspects of the job.

buffet *See* sideboard.

buffet-style dining Where guests serve themselves a meal from a table or sideboard (balancing the plate on the lap may be implied).

building inspector An official whose job is to inspect new or remodeling construction for structural soundness and safety features.

building systems Components of a building that are permanent. These include HVAC, electrical and lighting systems, and plumbing.

bulb More accurately the lamp bulb or lamp, it is the glass container that houses the filament of incandescent lighting and in fluorescent lighting contains phosphorus and gas.

bullnose A 180-degree rounded wooden edge on the starting step (also on a table or cabinet top).

burl veneer Made from scarlike wood growth or from root wood that imparts a complex, swirling grain pattern to the veneer.

burn-out printing *See* etch printing.

business accounting software Enables computers to keep accounting records.

buttress A structure built against a wall to strengthen it.

buttressed chimney In Medieval construction, a stepped chimney built in the shape of two buttresses placed back to back.

buyer One who selects lines or companies whose furnishings are sold in furniture and department stores.

byobu Small-scaled decorative folding Japanese screens.

Byzantium The ancient Roman name for today's Istanbul, also called Constantinople (330–1453 A.D.). The city was the capital of the Byzantine Empire, which encompassed much of what is today Greece and western Turkey. Known for its colorful tile mosaics, installed in architecture in many parts of the empire.

C

C lamp A cone-shaped lamp or light bulb.

C.O.M. Customer's own material—purchased by the customer from someone other than the furniture manufacturer for upholstery on a selected piece.

cabinetry Fine finish woodwork, as opposed to rough carpentry.

cabinetwork *See* cabinetry.

cable system construction A method of nonresidential building where a canopy is held in place with steel cables hung from a central column.

cabriole leg An S-curved leg typical of the Régence and Louis XV periods in France and the Queen Anne and Chippendale eras in England and America.

CAD *See* computer-aided design.

café curtains Curtains that cover the bottom half of a window.

calendering A finishing process of ironing under heat with a large cylinder roller. The roller may have raised patterns to imprint designs, and the fabric may also be glazed with a resin, then calendered to produce a high sheen or other special finishes.

came The lead strips used to secure the pieces of glass in leaded or stained glass windows.

camel-back sofa A sofa with a serpentine back that rises to a hump in the center.

candela, candlepower, or candle The unit of luminous intensity from which other measurements of light are calculated.

candlestand A small pedestal table, originally used to accommodate a candlestick or lamp.

cane Thin strips of rattan or bamboo used to weave mesh for chair seats and chair backs.

canister A luminaire shaped like a can that contains a lamp at the top or the bottom.

canted Beveled or tilted at an angle.

cantilever A projecting or overhanging structure anchored at one end so that no outside support is required.

Cantrese A registered trademark of DuPont for nylon.

capital The decorative head of a column or pillar.

Caprolan A registered trademark of Allied Chemical for nylon and polyester.

Carpenter's Gothic The wooden, board-and-batten version of the Gothic Revival style.

cascades Zigzag-shaped panels of fabric that usually frame swags or festoons.

case goods Furniture without upholstery such as desks, chests, and dressers.

cased glass Clear glass encased in a layer of colored glass.

casement draperies A strongly textural-looking fabric in a woven or knitted construction. Screens light, cuts down on glare, and provides daytime privacy.

casement window A side-hinged window that swings in or out.

casing A layer of fabric between the padding and the actual cover in upholstery.

cast iron Iron cast in a mold.

cathedra The bishop's chair from which the term cathedral is derived.

cathedral ceiling A high, open, gabled ceiling.

cathedral window A pointed window set in the gable of a room with an open ceiling.

Caucasian or Turkish rugs Oriental rugs of a coarser weave than Persians, in geometric patterns and often vivid colors.

cella Literally a cell. The interior space of a Roman temple.

cellulosic fibers A classification of natural fibers that come from plants and are made up of cellulose, cotton and linen being the most commonly used. Also a classification of man-made fibers that begin with cellulose, such as rayon and acetate.

cement A powder of silica, alumina, lime, and other materials. Mixed with water and aggregate, cement becomes concrete.

central air-conditioning Cool or temperate air controlled from a central unit and distributed through ducts and vents.

Central and South American rugs Folk rugs from natives of Central and South American countries.

central vacuum system A vacuum located in one unit with plumbed pipe and outlets where the hose is attached. The wall plate covering the outlet activates the system when it is lifted.

ceramic tile White clays fired to a point of vitrification. It comes in many sizes, shapes, colors, and patterns; a strong, hard material for walls, floors, and ceilings.

ceramics The art of modeling and baking in clay.

chair rail A molding placed on the wall at chair-back height.

chaise longue A French term that literally means long chair. It has an elongated seat designed for reclining.

chandelier A decorative, ceiling-mounted, or pendant-type luminaire consisting of several branches for candles or electric lamps.

chemical finishes *See* standard finishes.

Chevreul, M. E. (1786–1889) French chemist who was head of dyestuffs at Gobelin Tapestry Works near Paris. Chevreul researched and published theories that were forerunners to the Standard Color Wheel theory.

chimneypiece The decorative detail that covers the firebox and flue.

china Designation given by Europeans to porcelain from the Orient.

Chinese rugs Oriental rugs woven in Chinese traditional or contemporary patterns in a deep, sculptured pattern.

Chinoiserie A French term for Chinese-inspired design, first popular in the seventeenth and eighteenth centuries.

chipboard *See* particleboard.

Chippendale, Thomas II (1718–99) An important English cabinetmaker known for the designs published in his book, *The Gentleman and Cabinet-Maker's Director.*

choir The section of the church where the choir sings.

chopped urethane A foam product made from particles of urethane bonded with other materials, often used as a carpet underlay.

chroma The relative brightness or intensity of a particular hue or color. Low chroma is dull; high chroma is bright. Chroma, also called intensity, is a designation of the Munsell color system.

chromium (chrome) A shiny silver metal resistant to rust.

circuit A wiring hookup that forms a path through which electrical current may flow.

circulation Movement from place to place within an environment.

cissing Dropping mineral spirits onto wet spattered paint to make shadows of the spatters.

City of London The one-square-mile area that encompasses what was once Roman and Medieval London.

clapboard Thin, horizontal, overlapping, exterior wooden siding.

classic A work of the highest excellence able to stand the test of time.

classical Rome (200 B.C.–A.D. 100) The Roman era of political conquest and architectural achievement. Roman design was discovered by the Western world when the excavation of Pompeii began in 1754.

clearance Space required by code or law around a combustible heating unit (stove, fireplace, or furnace) so that nearby materials will not ignite. Also, the clear space between users and the objects they are passing.

clerestory window Window placed at the top of the wall or in the highest story of the nave or choir of a church.

cloisonné Decorative objects made by soldering metal strips into a pattern on a metal piece and filling the space between the strips with enamel.

closed floor plans Floor plans with many rooms that are totally private from other rooms, having solid walls and accessed only through a door that may also close.

closed showrooms A design-oriented store for placing orders of merchandise. They deal only with professional interior designers; clients are not allowed to enter.

closed stair A stairway with walls on both sides. Also called a housed stair.

club foot A round, pad-shaped foot on a cabriole leg.

coated fabric wall coverings Fabric layered with vinyl to become wall coverings.

cobblestone Large rounded stones such as river cobbles set into concrete and used mainly as nonresilient hard wall materials.

code A federal, state, or local ruling, law, or regulation that stipulates building safety and health requirements. Examples include nonflammable materials or firestops.

coffered ceiling A ceiling formed with recessed boxes or coffers.

coil spring A cylindrically shaped spring used for upholstery cushioning.

cold-air returns Ducts used in forced-air heating systems to return cooled air to the heat source for warming.

cold-cathode lighting The term for all colors of neon lighting.

collectors Units to capture the sun's energy or heat for active and passive solar heating.

Colonial American (1640–1770) The period prior to the Revolutionary War that included Medieval and Early and Late Georgian interiors.

colonnade A row of columns, often forming a corridor.

color An element of design, color is pigment in paint or part of the visible spectrum of light that enables us to see hues. It incorporates the study of hue, value, and intensity as well as color schemes, color application, and color psychology.

color consultants Professionals who are trained and skilled in selecting colors for products, architecture, or interiors. May be on-staff or work freelance on a per-job basis.

color deficiency An impaired ability to perceive and distinguish colors, and/or light versus dark values.

color-group moods Groups of color that produce emotional response, such as light and bright colors producing feelings of spontaneity and happiness.

color harmony The selection and arrangement of colors to be pleasing to the eye and to the senses.

color washing Applying a coat of thinned, sometimes translucent, paint over a white or colored ground.

colored incandescent lighting Accomplished with colored glass lamps or by colored screens or filters placed over a white light.

colorfast The ability of a dyed or printed fabric to resist color loss from cleaning, light fading, or atmospheric impurities.

coloring A general term for dyeing and printing textiles.

column A tall upright supporting shaft.

columned chimney A chimney formed in the shape of one or more columns.

combination Wooden furniture construction with more than one type of wood in the exposed parts of the piece.

combination felt padding Carpet underlay felt pad of some animal hair and some synthetic fiber.

combination floor plans A floor plan with areas that are open and other rooms that are closed.

combination weave A fabric employing more than one type of weave; for example, plain and twill weaves seen side by side in a fabric.

combing A paint application technique in which a comb or similar toothed object is dragged across the surface of newly applied, wet paint.

combustion lighting Candlelight and firelight.

communication systems Intercom, computer network, and telephone systems that connect people within the building or beyond the building.

compact fluorescent lamps (CFL) Small fluorescent lamps that consume one-fifth of the power and can last up to thirteen times longer than incandescent. May connect to an incandescent fixture.

compartmental bathroom A bathroom in which the separate functions are housed in small rooms that open to each other.

complementary colors Colors that are in opposite position on the color wheel. Complementary colors have the greatest contrast of all the color combinations, each making the other more vivid. Types of complementary combinations include direct, split, triadic, double, tetrad, and alternate complements.

Composite A Roman architectural capital style composed of volutes from the Ionic order and acanthus leaves from the Corinthian order.

compounded fabrics *See* layered fabrics.

computer hardware The components of a computer system: the keyboard, monitor, computer power drive, printer, and plotter. It can also include large mainframe computers.

computer network Connective cables that allow computer terminals within an office or design firm to access the same information.

computer programs The software that operates the computer hardware. Programs are instructions, information, and databases that allow the machine to operate specific functions. These include graphics, CAD, word processing, and so on.

computer terminal A keyboard and monitor that are connected to a mainframe. Also, a personal computer that can be connected to other computer terminals via a computer network system.

computer-aided design (and/or drafting) CAD (CADD) Computer software that enables the designer to draw, draft, arrange furnishing components, and compose simulated perspectives of a proposed interior space.

concept An idea for the solution to a problem.

conceptual drawings Drawings that show the concept or idea for a design.

concrete A mixture of sand, water, and portland cement that dries to a hard material; used for floors and walls, footings, foundations, and exterior flatwork.

condominium An individually owned home in a complex. The owner pays a monthly or yearly charge to maintain common landscaping and recreation and/or fitness facilities.

construction drawings *See* working drawings.

continuing education Skills, training, and knowledge gleaned by the professional interior designer through seminars and networks sponsored by professional organizations, institutions, and corporations.

contract design Design based on a contractual arrangement with the client. Usually synonymous with nonresidential design.

contrast The difference that exists between two colors, values, or shapes. A large difference is termed sharp contrast, high contrast, or vivid contrast; small differences are termed low contrast. Contrast makes individual objects more meaningful.

control The monitoring unit or thermostat needed for a furnace or an active solar heating system.

conventional design A type of decorative design taken from nature and adapted, stylized, or conventionalized. The pattern is still recognizable as the nature object (flowers, for example) but is not reproduced in its naturalistic state.

conventional traverse rods Drapery rods with a cord-and-pulley system for operating pleated draperies.

conversation pit Seating areas designed and built in as an integral part of the environment. The name pit implies a sunken area, but this type of seating could be designed on a platform or on floor level.

cool colors Green, blue-green, blue, blue-violet, and violet.

cool white deluxe fluorescent lamps A quality, balanced spectrum lamp whose light does not appear cold and unflattering.

coordinating fabric Decorative fabric printed in the same pattern as, or one that harmonizes with, wallpaper. Also called companion fabric.

cope To cut a section of paneling to fit an adjoining piece.

copper A bright, shiny, reddish brown metal used for cookware, tableware, decorative objects, and building components.

corbel *See* bracket.

Corinthian A Greek and Roman architectural style that features a capital decorated with acanthus leaves.

cork, cork wall coverings Lightweight, resilient bark of the cork oak, a broadleaf evergreen tree that grows in the Mediterranean region. Cork is coated with vinyl for floors and is an ingredient in linoleum. It is used in sheets or tiles or laminated to paper for wall coverings.

corner blocks Triangular blocks of wood attached at an angle across the corner of a joint for added strength.

corner fireplace A fireplace situated in the corner of a room.

cornice A wooden top treatment for draperies, frequently shaped on the bottom. Also, the projecting top section of a classical entablature. Found on the exterior under the eaves and on the ceiling where it meets the wall on the interior.

cornice lighting A lamp or line of light placed next to the ceiling with a board in front to direct the light downward.

cornice molding A more ornate form of crown molding.

coromandel Large Chinese black-lacquered folding screens.

corridor A passageway or hallway; usually indicates a nonresidential application.

cost analysis The proposed budget, including the design fee for a project or the economic feasibility of the design work. The result of programming research.

cost per square foot The total cost of the home or building, or the total cost of building one floor divided by the number of square feet.

cottage curtains Curtains often used in tiers or layers with ruffles around the edges.

cotton A natural cellulosic fiber obtained from the boll (fruit of the cotton plant). Cotton comes in short, medium, and long staple fibers and is an absorbent, soft, comfortable fiber. It dyes easily and is used in many printed decorative fabrics and in toweling.

cotton rugs Accent, scatter, or area rugs woven of cotton. Many are handwoven in India.

course A horizontal row of brick or masonry.

cove molding A concave, rounded molding placed where wall and ceiling meet.

coved ceiling A ceiling with a concave, rounded radius where the ceiling meets the wall.

covered-frame wall fabric method Fabric wrapped and stapled around a lath frame, then hung or affixed to a wall.

Craftsman style A style of architecture and interior design developed in the late 19th century, featuring exposed beams, right-angled furniture, and rustic decoration. Its early proponents were the Greene brothers and Gustav Stickley. Also called Mission style.

crenellation The notches or indentations in a parapet.

critical path The time frame and overlapping order of every step in the building and finishing process.

crocking The rubbing off of excess dyestuffs onto another fabric or onto the skin.

crop To trim or cut an art piece to fit a frame.

cross dyeing Two fibers of different affinities dyed in the same bath; the colors will be accepted differently.

cross section A vertical drawing of a slice through the interior of a building, showing the relationships among walls, beams, rooms, stairs, and other architectural elements.

crossing The area of a cross-shaped church where the nave and transept cross.

crowding Where people are grouped together in tightly restricted areas.

crown lintel *See* jack arch lintel.

crown molding Trim placed where the wall and ceiling meet. Also called bed molding.

cruciform Floor plan in the form or shape of a cross.

crypt An underground vault, especially in a church, often used for burial.

crystal A high grade of glass containing lead.

cubic feet or footage The width multiplied by the length of a room and then by its height. The volume of space we walk through. Rooms with very high ceilings have greater cubic footage than those with lower ceilings.

cultured stone A hard synthetic material, lighter in weight than actual stone. Cultured stone is made to imitate a smooth-finished onyx or marble, suitable for interior applications, and to resemble fieldstone, suitable for exterior use.

cupola A small-domed structure rising above a roof.

curio A rare or curious art object—a curiosity.

curtain rods Plain or nontraverse rods of metal or wood.

curtain wall construction *See* metal or space frame system.

curtains A general term for fabric window treatments that are shirred or sometimes pleated but usually stationary or hand operated.

curved lines Flowing lines, part of the elements of design. Large curves are smooth and gracious; small curves can give a feeling of activity in the interior.

curved staircase A staircase with a curved radius.

custom design Any design that is planned and executed according to individual specifications—not mass produced.

custom floor plan One that is executed by an architect or designer to meet the needs of the space—custom tailored to the design program.

cut glass Glass incised with an abrasive to create decorative patterns.

cut length The length of unhemmed fabric window treatments.

cut pile A carpet texture formed by shearing the carpeting to one or more heights.

D

dado A section of paneling that extends from the floor only as high as the chair rail.

dado cap A molding used to finish the top of a dado.

damper The movable piece in a fireplace that controls the airflow and escape of smoke.

database catalog Information and graphic symbols programmed into a database software program. Useful in CAD and in business applications.

database programs Software programs that manage, organize, and retrieve files used for working on documents, graphics, and CAD.

daub A coarse plaster used as infill wall finish in Medieval timber-framed buildings.

David Brewster Color theory Another designation for the Standard Color Wheel theory.

De Stijl An early twentieth-century Dutch aesthetic philosophical movement best represented by the work of painter Piet Mondrian.

debt-to-income ratio This ratio used by mortgage lenders compares the total monthly debt, including housing costs, to the total income. This figure should not exceed 36%. It is written as follows: Housing Costs+Debts divided by Gross Income=36% or less.

decorative arts Arts such as ceramics, metal work, textiles, and furniture that are suitable as decoration.

decorative design A classification of design wherein the building, furniture piece, or object is decorated with ornamentation. Decorative design is broken into four categories: naturalistic, conventional, abstract, and geometric.

decorative finishes A term for a group of finishes that add decorative appeal to fabrics. Examples of mechanical decorative finishes include various calendering, flocking, and napping finishes. Chemical decorative finishes include etch or burn-out printing and finishes that add brightness, softness, texture, stiffening, and delustering.

decorative luminaire Another term for portable luminaire, consisting of plug-in, movable luminaires such as table and floor lamps. Also refers to an architectural or built-in luminaire that is decorative.

decorator rods Metal drapery rods that are decorative with traverse cord-and-pulley workings.

deep pile A carpet texture in which the loops are cut to a relatively long length. Also called shag carpet, especially if cut long enough that the yarns flop over.

dehumidifier A unit connected to an air-conditioning unit that draws off excess humidity as a part of the cooling system.

demographics The statistical data of a particular population.

dentil A decorative trim of projecting rectangular blocks.

design A term that describes a process of designing a building, furnishings, or composite interiors. Design also refers to the plan or scheme that made the end product possible in its executed form, material(s), and size.

design drawings A general term for plans, elevations, working drawings, renderings, schematics, and other two-dimensional representations of a design project.

design process The sequence of steps in creating and executing a design project.

designer rugs Custom-design tufted or woven area rugs.

desk manager software Programs with specific options for managing a business.

detached dwelling A single home on a lot of its own.

detail A drawing showing an enlargement of a construction component, usually provided when clarification or additional information is needed.

deWolfe, Elsie (1865–1950) The greatest and best known of the society interior designers who paved the way for the modern interior design profession.

dhurrie rugs Originally cotton, now wool flat tapestry weave reversible rugs. Most are imported from India to meet Western demands.

diagonal lines Lines running at a slanting or oblique angle that may go one (or more) direction in an interior. Diagonal lines suggest movement and action.

diagramming The graphic process of planning space on paper or on a computer using CAD software.

diffusers The glass or plastic cover over a luminaire that serves to soften the light and spread it evenly over the area.

digital subscriber lines (DSL) A structured wiring system that enables telephone wires to carry signals at increased speed and with increased capacity. DSL can be retrofitted in existing homes.

dimensional stability The ability of a fabric to maintain or return to its original shape.

dimmable fluorescent system A lighting apparatus utilizing an electronic dimming ballast and special wiring to operate a dimmable fluorescent lamp with a wall-box dimmer switch. It is a fire hazard to use a nondimmable fluorescent lamp in a dimmer circuit.

dimmer switch A manual or automated mechanism that controls the variable brightness of a lamp.

direct complement Two colors that are directly across from each other on the color wheel.

direct glare Glare from an insufficiently shielded light source directly into the line of vision.

direct glue-down A method of laying carpeting where a layer of adhesive is applied to the floor and the carpet is laid directly on top of it, with no pad.

direct lighting Lighting that shines directly on the desired area.

direct pasteup Gluing fabric or wall coverings up with paste or adhesive.

direct solar gain Heating an area through direct exposure of sunshine to the occupied space.

discharge printing A process that removes the dyed color in patterned areas and replaces it with another color.

distressed A finish made to appear old or antique by the intentional addition of dents, scratches, and flecks of paint during the finishing process. *See also* antiquing.

distribution Carrying air heated by active or passive solar systems to the various areas or rooms within a building.

doctor of philosophy Ph.D., or doctorate degree; a possible requirement for full-time, tenure-track teaching positions in colleges and universities.

dome An inverted round-dish or cup-shaped ceiling.

dome system construction An arch rotated in a circle to become a dome.

domestic Oriental rugs Jacquard machine-woven rugs in Oriental rug designs.

doorjamb The vertical piece forming the side of a door frame.

dope dyeing *See* stock dyeing.

Doric Greek and Roman architectural style with fluted columns and plain capital.

dormer window A window that projects from the attic.

double complement Two sets of direct complementary colors next to each other on the color wheel.

double glazing Filling a window opening with two layers of glass that provide insulation and increase energy efficiency at the window. Also known as twin glazing.

double roll A roll of wall covering with approximately seventy-two square feet or double the area of a single roll.

double-hung Two layers of draperies, an overdrapery and an underlayer. Also, two sets of shutters, one installed directly above the other.

double-hung sash Sash window where both sections are operable.

double-shirred valance A valance shirred, or gathered, at the top and bottom.

double-turn stair A stair that makes two ninety-degree turns on two separate landings.

double-wide mobile home A mobile home that is fabricated into sections the size of a single-wide trailer, then fitted together to become twenty-four to thirty feet wide and twenty to forty feet long.

dovetail A series of fan-shaped joints used to connect drawer fronts and sides.

dowel A type of joint in which a third piece (the dowel) is glued into holes drilled in the two pieces being joined.

down Soft, fine feathers used as filling in some upholstered cushions.

draft dodgers A sand-filled tube of fabric or a heavy rug placed against a door to prevent cold air infiltration.

drafting The drawing by hand, machine, or computer of floor plans.

draftsman A person who drafts, draws, or produces floor plans and blueprints.

dragging A paint application technique in which a dry paint-brush is pulled across the wet paint, producing a surface texture of uneven lines. Dragging may be used to produce many curved, angular, and wood-grain effects. *See also* combing.

drapability The characteristic of a fabric to fall nicely into folds when draped.

draperies Pleated fabric hung with hooks on a traverse rod. Also refers to stationary side panels, tied-back fabric, and occasionally long shirred panels.

draw draperies Operable panels hung on a cord or wand-operated traverse rod.

drawings One-of-a-kind, two-dimensional art forms produced with pencil, pen and ink, charcoal, chalk, crayon, or grease pencil on paper or other surfaces.

drop-leaf table A table with a fixed center section and side flaps that can be lowered or raised and held up with various types of supports. Also called occasional table.

dropped-pendant luminaires Simple, suspended luminaires dropped from the ceiling with a cord or chain.

drum A cylindrical portion of a building used as the base for a dome.

drywall Another term for wallboard, sheetrock, or plasterboard; wall material made of pulverized gypsum rock.

duct work or ducts Metal or plastic pipes that funnel heated or air-conditioned air throughout an interior.

duplex A twin home dwelling—two units sharing one roof and foundation.

durable finishes Chemical or decorative finishes that remain on the fabric through repeated cleaning.

durable press calendering A decorative mechanical finish that resin presses for durability and pattern impressions.

durry rugs *See* dhurrie rugs.

dust panel A panel, usually of hardboard, placed between drawers to keep dust and other objects from passing between levels.

dust ruffle A gathered, pleated, or tailored fabric covering that extends from the mattress of a bed to the floor.

dutch door A double door, split in half horizontally, with independent top and bottom sections.

duvet A nondecorative comforter that is covered with a removable cover.

dye lot A single run of color printing of wallpaper or fabric, using a particular batch of dye. Background and decorative design colors may vary somewhat with each new dye lot.

dyeing The process of coloring done in one of several stages: in the viscose solution (man-made fibers), as stock (natural fibers), the yarn state, or the fabric piece goods state.

dyestuff A water-soluble coloring matter used to make a dye bath solution.

Dynel A registered trademark of Union Carbide for modacrylic.

E

ER lamps *See* R, ER lamps.

Eames, Charles (1907–78) and Ray (1912–88) An important husband-wife design team responsible for several modern classic furniture pieces.

Early American (1650–1750) A general term for American Provincial or country New England interiors.

Early Christian (A.D. 330–800) The architectural period following the official recognition of the Christian church by the Roman government.

Early Georgian (1695–1750) Architectural period that first brought the design and elegance of the English Renaissance to America.

ears Moldings on panels, door frames, or chimneypieces that break to form small molded squares at the corners.

earthenware Coarse and inexpensive ceramic body used for dinnerware and accessory pieces.

easements Short bends in the handrail that allow it to change direction.

Eastlake, Charles (1793–1865) Nineteenth-century English designer and scholar who advocated the Gothic Revival style. Wrote *Hints on Household Taste*.

echinus An oval-shaped molding between the shaft and the abacus on a column.

eclectic A mixture of stylistic influences or a mixture of styles.

economy The relative cost of items as related to an allotted budget.

effects of crowding The effects of crowding are inordinate exposure to sounds, smells, and touch.

efficacy Lumens per watt is a measure of the efficacy or efficiency of the light source.

egg and dart A molding of alternating egg shapes and dart or arrowhead shapes.

eggshell enamel A hard finish semigloss paint.

egress The way out; exit.

eight plex An apartment building containing eight units.

electrical raceways Encased wiring covers, usually installed along baseboards, that carry electrical and telephone cables.

Raceways allow ready access so that wiring can be modified without tearing into walls.

elements of design The tactile portion of interiors that can be manipulated by the designer. These are space, shape or form, mass, line, texture, pattern, light, and color.

elevation A flat, two-dimensional drawing of a straight-on (orthographic) view of an object, an exterior facade, or an interior wall.

embellishment Decoration or ornamentation added to an object or an interior.

embossed loop pile A looped pile surface carpet with high and low, or multilevel, loops; creates a random pattern.

embossed wall coverings Wallpapers with an imprinted, three-dimensional design.

embroidery The hand or machine stitching of threads or yarns to create a pattern on the surface of an otherwise completed fabric.

emphasis A principle of design that indicates attention is given to a certain area within an interior. Emphasis is also called focal point.

enamel paints Oil-based or sometimes water-based paints that are hard and glossy.

enameled glass Glass that has been encased with an opaque vitreous layer.

energy consciousness A term often associated with window treatments—covering windows to keep in winter heat and exclude summer solar gain or heat.

energyguide A label that allows consumer to compare the average yearly energy costs of similar major appliances.

Energy Star label Affixed to thirty categories of products, including appliances, electronics, lighting, office equipment, and heating and cooling equipment to verify a minimum of 10 percent less energy consumption. Also verifies the most efficient products in terms of clean air, using construction materials wisely, and conservation of water.

engravings Prints made from a hand-engraved metal plate.

entablature A decorative architectural section made up of cornice, frieze, and architrave.

envelope A passive solar building system wherein air circulates in a double-wall construction around the house and includes a south-facing solarium.

epoxy paint Used to paint over metal or water-filled surfaces. Contains hardeners.

equilibrium A state of physical or visual balance or equality.

ergonomics The study of the relationships between, on the one hand, human form and movements and, on the other, furniture and other products people use. *See also* biotechnology.

etch printing A decorative chemical finish printed with acid to burn out one fiber—usually cotton in a cotton/polyester blend—to leave a sheer pattern.

etched glass Glass that has been engraved with a pattern by hand or by use of an abrasive cutting tool, a corrosive substance, or sandblasting.

etchings Prints made from metal plates that have patterns and designs chemically etched into their surface.

European handmade rugs French Savonnerie and Aubusson, Portuguese needlepoint, and Spanish rugs.

evaporative cooling system Also called swamp cooling, the system is based on air flowing through a wet pad. Useful and economical in arid climates.

execution The final phase of the design process where the design plans are implemented.

exotic style *See* Oriental Revival.

exposed aggregate Pebbles set into and protruding above a concrete base. Hard flooring and wall material.

exterior elevation A flat, two-dimensional drawing of a straight-on (orthographic) view of a given side of a building's exterior.

exterior veneer The finish building material on the exterior, such as masonry (brick, stone) or siding (metal, wood, stucco).

extrude/extrusion To force out through a small opening; a method used to form tubular steel. Also, man-made fibers formed by forcing a viscose solution through a spinnerette.

eyeball A recessed spotlight that shines at an angle on a wall or object.

F

F lamp A flame-shaped, often fluted lamp for decorative fixtures such as a candelabra.

FIDER The Foundation for Interior Design Education and Research, which establishes standards for design education. Also a design school accrediting body.

fabric art Handwoven or constructed fabric or textile pieces that hang on the wall.

fabric finish Any of a variety of treatments that render a fabric more resistant to bacteria, static, wrinkling, flammability, insects, soil, or humidity damage or that increase insulative qualities. A fabric finish may also prepare a fabric for coloring, apply dye or prints, or add aesthetic or decorative effects.

fabric shades Vertically or horizontally operated shades of fabric, including roller, Roman, balloon, and Austrian shades.

fabric wall coverings Heavy wall coverings made sturdy and substantial with a fabric, rather than paper, backing. Used for vinyl and nonresidential wall coverings.

fabric-backed wall covering A heavy-face wallpaper or other heavyweight wall covering, such as vinyl, that is laminated to a supportive layer of fabric. Often used in nonresidential interiors.

facade The front or principal face of a building.

face weight Yarn weight of carpeting per square measure. Heavier weights indicate more face or pile yarn, or greater density.

fanlight A half-circle or half-ellipse-shaped window placed above a door or in a pediment.

fascia or fascia board A flat horizontal band or board, especially below a ceiling or roof, or at the end of rafters or eaves.

fauteuil French term for an open armchair.

Federal (1790–1830) The post-revolutionary period in America.

feldspar Crystalline materials mixed with kaolin to make porcelain.

felt padding Animal and/or synthetic fibers compressed and needlepunched; used for carpet underlay to protect carpet without great resilience.

festoon Another term for swag, a half circle of fabric pleated or folded on the ends.

fiber felt padding *See* felt padding.

fiberglass or glass fiber A mineral material made of spun glass fibers, used in applications such as textiles, insulation, roof shingles, windows, and tub enclosures. Trademarked by Owens Corning as Fiberglas®.

fieldstone Any type of large, rugged rocks used for flooring or walls.

filament The continuous man-made fiber strand extruded through the spinnerette. Filaments are combined and spun into threads or yarns. Natural filaments are silk and horsehair.

fillers Preparatory materials for surfaces to be painted. Used to fill in nail holes, cracks, or other imperfections.

filling yarns The set of yarns woven crosswise into the set of long warp yarns that are threaded onto a loom. Also called weft.

fine arts The arts of architecture, painting, drawing, sculpture, and printmaking, as well as music, literature, drama, and dance.

finial An upward-pointing finishing ornament for pediment, post, or spire.

finish carpenter One who creates custom woodwork and cabinetry.

finish package The woodwork in an interior, including items such as built-in shelving, cabinets, case piece units, baseboard/door/window trim, and railings.

finish plumbing The installation of sinks, toilets, and faucet hardware.

finished length The length of a finished, hemmed fabric window treatment.

finished pile weight Weight in ounces per square measure of finished carpeting.

finishes Paint and stain used for cabinetry, walls, trim, and other hard surfaces. *See also* fabric finish.

finishing Processes or chemicals that render fabrics more durable or decorative.

fire alert system A network or single unit that senses heat or smoke, then alerts the occupants through a shrill noise.

fire retardant Certain man-made fibers such as modacrylic, saran, and PVC that resist burning but are not flame-proof.

firebox The part of the fireplace that contains the fire.

fireplace insert An enclosed stove unit that can be placed in an existing fireplace to make it more efficient.

fish-scale shingles Small shingles with round or pointed sawtooth ends used to create decorative surface effects on the nineteenth-century Queen Anne–style houses.

fixed window A window that cannot be opened.

fixture Something that is fixed in place or an element or feature of a setting. Pieces other than typical furniture that are placed in the environment by the designer, such as pieces of specialized equipment, custom-designed work spaces, or counters. Plumbing fixtures are the sinks, toilets, and various bathtubs and hot tubs. Lighting fixtures are also called luminaires.

fixture or luminaire The structured or decorative unit that holds the lamp or bulb and the electric connectors. In fluorescent and HID lighting, it also contains the ballast.

flagstone Hard, nonresilient stone that splits into sheets, used for paving and flooring.

flame resistant A term referring to fabrics such as wool, silk, nylon, olefin, and polyester that do not ignite easily, are slow-burning, and will often self-extinguish.

flame-retardant finishes Chemical finishes that make a fabric that is constructed of a flammable fiber become resistant to fire ignition and spread. Chemical applications that render a fabric less flammable.

flame-retardant paints Paints with additives that inhibit combustibility.

flammability resistance Ability of background textiles to resist catching on fire and/or sustaining a flame. Nonresidential code requirement.

flammability tests Tests that measure the rate of ignition, the rate of flame spread when the source of the fire is removed, how long the fabric continues to burn, how long it remains in a red-glow state, and the density and toxicity of the fumes. These tests are conducted to meet stringent nonresidential state and local fire codes.

flammable or inflammable A term that refers to fabrics, such as cellulosic cotton, linen, rayon, and acetate, that easily catch on fire or are highly combustible.

flat British term for an apartment.

flat paint Any type of paint that dries to a matte or nonshiny finish.

flatbed screen printing The traditional method of stencil silkscreen printing where screens are manually or mechanically moved and paint squeegeed across by hand.

flatwork Concrete laid flat for foundation and garage floors, sidewalks, and driveways.

Flemish gable A gable incorporating steps, curves, or both.

flexibility The ability of a fabric to stretch and rebound to its original shape; a necessary characteristic in upholstery fabrics.

flexible wall coverings A general term for wall coverings that may be bent or manipulated to fit a shape or surface.

flickering light An uneven source of light such as candlelight, firelight, or electric lamps that imitate this effect.

flitch The half or quarter log that is cut to make lumber for furniture construction.

floccati, or flokati, rugs Area rugs woven or knitted with tufts of sheared goat's hair left in its natural cream or brown color.

flocked carpet A method of producing a carpet pile similar to velvet. Fibers are electrostatically charged, then embedded in a glue-coated fabric backing.

flocked wallpapers Wallpapers with chopped fibers affixed to the surface in a decorative pattern.

flocking A decorative process of adhering patterns of tiny fibers to the surface of a fabric; often seen in sheers and flocked dotted swiss fabrics.

floodlight A reflective lamp spotlight with a wide-beam spread.

floor lamp Luminaires designed to sit on the floor for task or general lighting.

floor plans The two-dimensional layout of rooms. Part of the working drawings and blueprints used to construct a space.

flowing lines A type of curved lines that suggest graceful continuous or growing movement.

flue The chimney pipe above the firebox in a fireplace.

fluoresce To glow or become fluorescent.

fluorescent light Produced by an arc, or discharge, between two electrodes inside a glass tube filled with very low-pressure mercury vapor that produces ultraviolet (invisible) radiation in wavelengths. These activate the white phosphorus lining of the lamp, causing it to glow and converting the ultraviolet energy into visible light.

fluorescent lighting Artificial lighting produced by charging mercury argon gas. Light is clear and relatively shadowless. Cool fluorescent lighting may produce a bluish cast.

flush door A flat door whose surfaces are flat, with no raised or sunken panels.

flush-face fireplace A fireplace whose planes are flush with the wall in which it is built.

flute A groove in the shaft of a column.

flying buttress An inclined brace that spans from the wall to a supporting abutment and receives the outward thrust of the wall.

foam rubber pads Carpet underlay of foam rubber.

focal point Also known as emphasis or center of interest, a focal point draws the eye to an area or object and holds the interest of the viewer. Architectural focal points include picture windows and fireplaces.

foil/mylar wall coverings A mirrorlike shiny or reflective background.

folded plate system construction A building system of thin reinforced concrete in a folded, zigzag roof pattern.

folk rugs Flat tapestry rugs handmade by an ethnic group in native design and color.

footcandle A measurement of the amount of direct light hitting a surface.

footlambert A measurement of the amount of light reflected off a surface.

forced-air heating A conventional furnace-powered heating system in which the hot air is blown through ducts and enters rooms through registers.

form The three-dimensional shape of an object.

formal areas The spaces in residential design where structured visiting, dining, and entertaining take place away from kitchen and other work spaces.

formal balance Another term for symmetrical, bisymmetrical, or passive balance.

foundation The footings and basement walls that support the building, usually made of concrete.

foundation drawings Plans showing the structural details of a building's interface with the ground, including footings, anchor bolts, breaks in walls, and drains.

four plex A four-unit apartment building.

frame A case or border made to enclose a picture.

framing or framework The wooden or metal skeleton structure used for the majority of buildings today.

framing plans Projections of a building from the lowest level to the roof, showing columns, beams, and joists.

freestanding fireplace A self-contained fireplace unit that is away from the wall.

freestone A general term for building stones that are easily cut or carved, usually limestone or sandstone.

French door Double casement-type door that opens in or out.

French Empire (1804–20) The period during the time of Napoleon in France.

French Régence (1715–23) The period between the reigns of Louis XIV and Louis XV in France.

fresco A painting made on fresh wet plaster with pigment and lime water.

fretwork Patterns of flat interlocking bands or trelliswork.

frieze A horizontal band of two- or three-dimensional ornamentation. In classical architecture, the section of the entablature above the architrave and below the cornice. In textiles, a carpet whose yarns are tightly twisted, producing improved resilience and a somewhat rough texture.

full-spectrum lighting Light that contains all color wavelengths.

full-aniline leather Leather processed with a transparent dye that lets the grain show through.

full-grain leather Leather that retains the natural texture and imperfections of the animal hide.

function A normal or characteristic action or some duty required in work. Used here to refer to anything that takes place within a given environment.

functional finishes *See* standard finishes.

furnace The mechanism that heats air or water by electricity, natural gas, coal, or oil and either blows the heated air through ducts or pumps hot water to radiators.

furnishings Furniture and accessories, and fixtures such as lighting and appliances.

fuse-bonded carpet Carpet yarns directly tufted into a liquid rubber or latex backing that solidifies to hold in the tufts.

fuzzing The working loose of fibers to the surface of the textile.

G

G lamp A spherical or globe-shaped bulb.

gable The triangular end of a house formed by the pitched roof.

galerie A covered porch on the houses of French influence.

gambrel roof A roof line with a double pitch, flatter at the top and steeper at the bottom like a red barn.

garret Same as attic.

gazebo A small, open garden house.

general contractor A builder who is licensed to construct or oversee construction of all building phases.

general lighting *See* ambient general lighting.

generic A general type of man-made fiber that is significantly different from other fibers and thereby has been granted a name, such as nylon, by the Federal Trade Commission. Within each generic group are up to dozens of trademarks or trade names produced by various chemical companies.

genuine Wooden furniture construction with veneers of a particular wood, over hardwood plywood, on all the exposed parts of a piece.

geodesic dome system construction A building system enclosing spaces with curved, triangular steel truss work. The interior structure must be independent of the dome.

geometric design A classification of decorative design based on geometric shapes: circles, squares, rectangles, and triangles.

Georgian A term used to describe design during the period when George I through George IV ruled England.

gilded glass Glass that has been encased in a layer of gold.

ginger jar A bulbous oriental ceramic pot and lid, designed to hold ginger.

gingerbread The decorative trim used on Victorian buildings.

glare Strong, steady, daylight or artificial light that can cause irritation, fatigue, and heat buildup.

glare-free Lamps that have silvered lining.

glass A hard, brittle material of molten silica sand and soda or potash, lime, and possibly metal oxides. Clear, transparent, or colored; used for window glazing, mirrors, walls.

glass, architectural glazing Glass used to fill window openings; term usually refers to nonresidential installations.

glass block Semihollow blocks of translucent glass primarily for non-load-bearing walls.

glass curtains A historic term for sheers shirred onto a curtain rod and placed next to the glass.

glass tile Vitrified tiles of dense glass composition. Imported from France.

glaze A colored or transparent liquid applied to clay objects that hardens and becomes glasslike when baked at high temperatures.

glazing The process of filling an opening with glass. Also, transparent paint colors overlayed in sequence, producing various gradations of color in a painting.

glide The mechanism on the bottom or sides of a drawer upon which it slides.

gloss enamel Hard, oil-based paint that dries to a shine or gloss.

gold electroplate A process for creating gold-plated silverware.

gold leaf Extremely thin sheets of gold used in gilding.

golden age *See* ancient Greece.

golden mean A pleasing line of division that is placed between one-half and one-third of the height or length of an object, such as tieback draperies or a chair rail.

golden section A theory of pleasing proportions based on the sequence 2:3:5:8:13:21, ad inf., where a portion or section of a line relates best to its neighbors in measurements of these or equivalent increments.

Gothic (A.D. 1150–1550) A period and style in western Europe characterized by pointed arches and steep roofs.

Gothic arch A pointed arch that is the principal form in Gothic architecture.

gouache Any water-soluble, opaque watercolor. Often used as a synonym for tempera.

gradation A type of rhythm wherein sizes of shapes graduate from large to small or small to large. Also seen in varying color values from dark to light or light to dark.

grain The markings and textures in a piece of wood created by the arrangement of the fibers.

granite A very hard crystalline rock used for floors and walls.

graphic art Artwork such as posters, fashion illustrations, and book illustrations created primarily for commercial purposes but having aesthetic merit.

graphic artist A designer who specializes in two-dimensional signage, graphics, type, and design motifs or logos.

graphics The visual signs in a retail space that direct customers to departments or to certain goods. Also, the term used for putting on paper the stages of space planning from bubble diagrams to the finished floor plans.

grass cloth Woven grasses laminated to a paper backing and used as wall covering.

gray goods or greige Woven fabrics in their natural fiber state before bleaching and prefinishes. Pieces of bolt length may not be gray but a dingy off-white.

grazing or graze Light shining at a very steep angle that emphasizes the texture of the surface.

great hall The large, multipurpose area in the English Medieval house.

great room An open area in contemporary homes that combines the living room, family room, dining room, and perhaps the kitchen, office, and/or library.

Greek Revival (1820–60) Architectural style that contained American Empire interiors.

green design An approach to design in which preservation of the natural environment is a primary consideration. Green design specifies renewable and biodegradable materials. It utilizes solar, climate, and site factors to minimize the energy consumed by the completed building.

Greene brothers Charles (1868–1957) and Henry (1870–1954) Greene, also known as Greene and Greene. Southern California architects who developed and popularized the Craftsman-style bungalow.

greenhouse effect Phenomenon in which captured solar heat from long sun rays penetrates glass, bounces off materials and furnishings, and becomes shorter, weaker, and unable to repenetrate the glass.

greenhouse window Projecting glass box for growing plants.

Gropius, Walter (1883–1969) German-born architect known for his modernist style. Gropius was director of the Bauhaus design school (1919–28) and later chaired the architecture department at Harvard University (1938–52).

grounding receiver The third hole in an electric outlet required for fixtures and appliances that consume a lot of power to be connected into the circuit and to prevent electric shock.

gum arabic A sticky substance from gum trees that is soluble in water and hardens when exposed to air, used as a vehicle for watercolor.

gypsum board *See* wallboard.

H

HID (high-intensity discharge) lighting HID lamps establish an arc between two very close electrodes set in opposite ends of small, sealed, translucent or transparent glass tubes. The electric arc generates heat and pressure high enough to vaporize the atoms of various metallic elements inside the lamp, causing the atoms to emit large amounts of visible-range electromagnetic energy.

HVAC The acronym for heating, ventilation, and air-conditioning. A central HVAC system maintains an even temperature and circulates fresh air through the interior.

hand The relative softness or coarseness of a fabric; the way it feels to the touch.

hand printing Textile processes such as batik, tie-dye, block printing, and hand silkscreen and stencil printing.

handrail The rail for grasping while ascending a stair.

hard window coverings Art glass, blinds, screens, shades, and shutters.

hardboard Compressed wood fibers formed into panels with embossed designs or a wood/plastic laminated surface.

hardware The metal fittings on furniture such as drawer pulls and keyhole covers. Also, the components that make up a computer: the keyboard, the computer power drive unit, the monitor or screen, the printer, and the plotter.

hardwood Tough, heavy timber of compact texture taken from trees with broad, flat leaves such as oak and walnut.

harmony A congruous combination of parts into a pleasing whole; the result of unity and variety balanced together in an orderly, agreeable arrangement.

hearth The slab that forms the base of a fireplace and extends into the room.

heat gain Solar heat that penetrates the interior through glass; desirable in winter and undesirable in summer.

heat loss The interior heat lost in winter back through glass to the outside. To prevent heat loss, movable insulation or insulative window treatments are employed.

heat pump A geothermal heat exchange system, usually composed of a sealed length of liquid-filled underground tubing connected to a heat exchanger that feeds into the building's ventilation ductwork. It utilizes the relatively constant, moderate temperatures found several feet beneath the earth's surface to provide heat and/or cooling.

heat setting The setting in of permanent creases or folds in polymer fabrics by heating the fold to the point of polymer flow (beginning to melt), then rapidly cooling the fabric.

heat-transfer printing Decals that are dispersed-transferred from waxed paper to a cloth under heat and pressure.

Hepplewhite, George (d. 1786) An important English furniture designer who produced a series of drawings published as *The Cabinet-Maker and Upholsterer's Guide.*

Herculaneum *See* Pompeii and Herculaneum.

high contrast The difference between small areas of light and the dark area surrounding it. *See also* high-contrast values.

high key All colors in an interior that are light or high in value.

high rise A building containing several levels or floors of apartments, condominiums, or offices.

high tech A product of high technology.

high values Light variations of a hue; a hue with various amounts of white added.

highboy A tall four- or five-drawer chest mounted on a dressing table (lowboy). Also known as a tallboy.

high-contrast values A wide division of color value in an interior—very light colors contrasted with very dark colors.

high-efficiency furnace A furnace that uses less energy and delivers a higher output. The unit costs more initially.

high-gloss paint Any paint that dries to a very shiny finish.

hiking up The shrinking of a draped fabric that has absorbed moisture, then dried.

hipped roof A roof without a gabled end that slopes in four directions.

Hispanic Having to do with Spain or Portugal.

Hitchcock, Lambert (1795–1852) An American furniture designer known best for his Hitchcock chair with its black painted finish, stenciling, rush or cane seat, and delicate lines.

Hitchcock chair *See* Hitchcock, Lambert.

Hoffmann, Josef (1870–1956) Member of the Vienna Secession and founding member of the Wiener Werkstätte. He is best known for his design of the Prague chair and Fledermaus chair.

hollow-core door A veneered door with a hollow core filled with cardboard honeycomb.

hologram A three-dimensional image projected by splitting a laser beam.

home automation Central control of all energy-using fixtures and devices.

home designer A design professional who specializes in creating residential floor plans, typically CAD plans.

hooded fireplace A fireplace with a projecting hood to catch the smoke.

hook-and-loop fasteners A two-part fastening system of nylon loops on one tape and a fuzzy nylon surface on another that stick together and can be pulled apart. The best-known brand is Velcro.

hooked rugs A traditional method of making decorative rugs of strips of fabric, punched through a jutelike backing with a special hook.

horizontal lines Horizontal lines serve to visually widen or lengthen an interior and, when dominant, produce feelings of relaxation and repose.

horizontal satin See sateen.

horseshoe arch An arch whose apex is wider than its base, resembling a horseshoe in profile. Horseshoe arches are a typical feature of Near Eastern and Central Asian architecture.

hourglass A piece for telling time with two globes of glass connected by a narrow neck that allows a quantity of sand to pass during a specified time.

housed stair A stair attached to walls on both sides. Also called a closed stair.

housing-to-income ratio Home financing or lending institutions require that monthly housing costs generally not total more than 28 percent of the gross monthly income. This housing-to-income ratio is expressed as: Housing Costs divided by Gross Income = 28% or less.

hue Another word for color, such as the hue red. Often used to mean pure spectral colors as opposed to shades, pastels, etc. An important designation in the Munsell color system.

humidifier An attachment to a furnace that adds moisture or humidity to the air. (Heating interior air strips it of moisture.)

hutch A side piece with cupboards and drawers and a set of open shelves above; also called a Welsh dresser.

hybrid solar energy system A passive solar system augmented with fans, ducts, blowers, or other mechanical devices.

hydrophilic A fiber that readily absorbs moisture, such as natural and man-made cellulosics and natural protein fibers.

IBC The Institute of Business Designers.

IDC The Interior Designers of Canada.

IDEC The Interior Design Educators Council.

IDS The Interior Design Society.

IFDA The International Furnishings and Design Association (formerly the National Home Fashions League).

IFI The International Federation of Interior Architects/Designers.

IIDA The International Interior Design Association.

ikebana Traditional Japanese method of arranging flowers according to strict rules of placement.

illusion lighting The artistic science of creating illusion through specialty lighting.

incandescent lighting Light produced by heating fine metal filament until it glows. Warm incandescent lighting produces a yellowish cast to colors.

incident solar radiation The energy collected from the sun to power active solar panels/systems. Also called insolation.

independent living The ability of elderly or handicapped persons to live at home and care for themselves because the space is planned to accommodate their needs.

indirect passive solar gain Heat from sunshine that is gathered in a location apart from the primary living space of a building, such a Trombe walls, a thermosiphoning system, roof monitors, or a solar greenhouse. Also called isolated passive solar gain.

indirect lighting Produced by throwing light against a wall, floor, or ceiling to light a general area.

indoor air quality The condition of the breathable atmosphere in a building.

infill Materials used to fill the space between the timber frame of a building.

informal areas Areas for relaxed, spontaneous living, and entertaining.

informal balance Also known as asymmetrical, optical, or occult balance, it is the state of equilibrium reached through the arrangement of unlike objects or parts on each side of a central point.

infrared (IR) transmission A wireless system that uses infrared waves to operate electronic devices or enable one electronic device to communicate with another.

ingress The entrance to a building.

in-house designer An interior designer who is a salaried staff member of a large organization; responsible for the interior design or facilities management of new and existing buildings owned by that organization.

inlaid vinyl Flooring in which successive layers of vinyl granules are built up to suggest texture.

insolation *See* incident solar radiation.

Insulating Concrete Forms (ICF) Large, hollow blocks, forms, or molds that have built-in insulation. They are stacked in place and filled with reinforcing bar and concrete to create structurally sound walls ready to accept final exterior and interior finishes. Replacing wood-framed structural building systems, they produce interiors that are comfortable (no drafts or cold spots), quiet, energy efficient, flexible, safe, and healthy (no rotting or molding), are termite and pest resistant, and have a two-hour burn rating.

insulation A material such as fiberglass that prevents heat transfer. Commonly used in batts (fiber blanket rolls), rigid panels, shredded recycled paper, or other materials.

insulative window treatments Any window covering that deters heat loss and solar gain.

intaglio Printing from plates where the design is recessed below the surface of the plate. Those recesses hold the ink.

intensity The relative pureness or brightness of a color, as opposed to the dullness or neutralization of that hue. Also called chroma.

intercom An electrical system that allows people to communicate within a building; also carries taped or radio music heard through speakers.

interface Interdependency of design phases that must be accomplished simultaneously or consecutively. Also, a computer term in which different terminals can access the same information through a central mainframe computer or a networking system.

interior architecture The nonresidential aspect of interior design that may entail remodeling and work with building systems.

interior building systems The systems that are a part of the interior: plumbing, HVAC, electrical.

interior design package Materials and furnishings installed when a building's construction is complete, such as carpeting and rugs, window treatments, wall coverings, and furniture.

interior elevation A flat, two-dimensional drawing of a straight-on (orthographic) view of a given wall of a building's interior, showing any cabinetry, trim, millwork to be installed.

interior environmental control system The systems that produce a livable environment in a building, such as plumbing, heating, air-conditioning, and electrical wiring.

interior finish components The structural items and fixtures that are installed in the final phase of construction; including wall, ceiling, and floor materials; cabinetry and woodwork, and optional wall and window coverings.

intermediate hues Six hues on the standard color wheel that are produced by mixing a primary and secondary color. They are yellow-orange, red-orange, red-violet, blue-violet, blue-green, and yellow-green. Also known as tertiary hues.

International style An early twentieth-century design style based on concepts developed simultaneously in several international locations, including the Bauhaus in Germany. The style is simple, clean, functional, and modern in spirit.

interrelationship of functions The way areas work together or depend on one another to function effectively.

Ionic Greek and Roman architectural style with scroll-shaped capital.

iron A heavy black metal.

Islamic design Styles of architecture and furniture prevalent in the Near East.

isolated passive solar gain Heat from sunshine that is gathered in a location apart from the primary living space of a building, such as a Trombe wall, thermosiphoning system, roof monitor, or solar greenhouse. Also called indirect passive solar gain.

Itten, Johannes (1888–1967) A colorist who taught at the Bauhaus in Germany and at Yale University. He authored several books, including *The Art of Color* and *The Elements of Color*.

J

jack arch lintel A trapezoidal lintel with a wedge-shaped keystone used as decoration above windows. Also called a crown lintel.

Jacobsen, Arne (1902–71) Danish architect/designer known for his Number Seven chair (1955), and Swan and Egg chairs (1957).

Jacquard A loom attachment named after its French inventor that allows complex patterns to be woven in rapid succession. Jacquard fabrics include brocade and brocatelle, damask, lampas, matelassé, and patterned velvets.

jalousie window A louvered glass window.

Jeanneret-Gris, Charles-Edouard (1887–1965) Important architect/designer better known as Le Corbusier. Designer of several modern classic furniture pieces.

joint A closure, such as the mortise and tenon, where two pieces of wood are fastened together in furniture construction.

joists The heavy beams that support the floor and rafters.

Journal of Interior Design The scholarly, refereed journal of the Interior Design Educators Council.

jute A cellulosic bast fiber obtained from the inner stalks of the jute plant and grown in India.

juxtaposition Placement of colors next to each other.

K

Kandinsky, Wassily (1886–1944) A Russian artist associated with the Bauhaus.

kaolin A claylike substance used in making porcelain. The name comes from Kaoling, a mountain in China where kaolin was first mined.

keystone The stone at the top of an arch that is angled on the sides, stabilizing compression and friction.

kilim rugs Flat tapestry folk rugs that originated in Romania.

kiln An oven capable of controlled high temperatures used for baking or firing clay objects.

kilowatt hour The work done by 1,000 watts in one hour. Consumers of electricity pay for their use by the kilowatt hour.

kitsch A German term that describes bad taste and is applied to pretentious or foolish art.

knickknack A small ornament article.

knitted carpet A sturdy pile carpet that is constructed by knitting with multiple needles.

knitted fabrics Needle-constructed interlocking fabrics such as single and double knits, laces, rachel warp knits, arnache and malimo fabrics. Knitted fabrics offer speed of construction, variety in patterns, and lacy effects, and either stretch or dimensional stability characteristics.

L

LED *See* light-emitting diode.

L'École des Beaux Arts A school of art, design, and architecture in Paris, France, noted for its emphasis on historical studies.

lacquer A type of varnish made from shellac or gum resins dissolved in ethyl alcohol or other quick-drying solvents.

ladder-back chair A chair back with a number of horizontal slats like a ladder.

laminate Wood particleboard with a hard, durable composite vinyl layer bonded over it, used for flooring and countertops.

laminated foam One or more densities of polyurethane foam laminated together to form a single pad.

lamination The process of building up in layers or attaching a single ply as with plywood, foam, or plastic laminates.

lamp The technical term for light bulb.

lancet A narrow, pointed arch window.

landings The platforms of a stair where it begins, ends, or turns.

laser A device containing a crystal, gas, or other suitable substance in which atoms, when stimulated by focused light waves, amplify and concentrate these waves, then emit them in a very intense, narrow beam.

Late Georgian (1750–90) The American period that utilized English Georgian design and Chippendale furniture.

latex A rubber-based synthetic polymer extruded or sprayed on as a coating or backing to hold woven fabrics or tufted carpets stable.

latex paint A water-based paint that is easy to apply and cleans up with soap and water when still wet.

lath Thin strips of wood laid parallel and nailed onto building studs. Historic method of plastering walls is to apply it over lath.

lathwork Grids or panels made with strips of lath, used as screens, trellises, or decorative trim on verandas.

latillas Sticks laid cross the vigas to form the ceiling of the southwest Adobe houses.

Latin cross The Western Christian cross with a tail longer than the top and arms.

lattice A panel consisting of metal or wooden strips that are interlaced or crossed to form a grid with regular spaces.

law of chromatic distribution A rule governing the distribution of color intensity or brightness. The most neutralized colors are used in the largest areas, and the smaller the size or area, the brighter or more intense the chroma proportionately becomes.

layered or compounded fabrics A group of fabric constructions that require more than one step to complete. Examples include embroidery, appliqué, and tufting.

Le Corbusier *See* Jeanneret-Gris, Charles-Edouard.

leaded glass Glass windows made of small pieces held together with lead caming to form a pattern.

leather The tanned hide of cattle or swine, largely used for upholstery. Leather is strong, comfortable, and has a long life span.

leather tiles Actual pieces of leather cut into shapes and applied as wall or floor tiles. Resilient semipermanent materials.

leno weave A variation of the plain weave that has warp thread in hourglass twists where the weft or filling threads are woven in.

letter of agreement The legal contractual arrangement between the design firm and the client that spells out responsibilities and services of both parties.

level-loop carpet Woven or tufted carpet with an uncut pile of even loops; used in both residential and nonresidential interiors.

level-tip carpet Woven or tufted carpet with some loops higher than others. Surface has a smooth, velvetlike texture.

life-cycle costing Calculating the overall cost of an item by dividing its purchase price by the number of years of expected use.

lifestyle The way an individual or group lives.

light An element of design that is broken into two types: natural (sunlight) and artificial.

light pipe An acrylic pipe that conducts light along its corridor. The light source can be sunlight or artificial light.

light-emitting diode (LED) A solid-state, filamentless lamp with an extremely long life expectancy.

lighting as art Use of light as a medium to create artistic effects.

lighting designer A design professional who specializes in maximizing both the practical and the aesthetic effectiveness of lighting in interiors.

lighting plan The portion of the working drawings or blueprints that shows where the lights, switches, and outlets are to be placed in a building and how they are connected to one another and to the circuit-breaker box. Also called the wiring plan.

limestone A calcite stone with a uniform, matte texture. It is versatile for building because it can be cut or carved without splitting.

line The deliberate connection of two points as seen in planes and outlines of shapes. An element of design.

line of credit The total cost of merchandise that may be purchased by a designer on credit on behalf of the designer's clients.

line or outline lighting Lighting the perimeter of an object to give emphasis or even lighting.

linen The best known of the cellulosic bast fibers, obtained from the inner stalks of the flax plant. Linen is strong and absorbent and varies from a coarse jutelike texture to fine table damask linen textures.

linenfold A medieval panel motif resembling folded linen.

linoleum A soft resilient flooring of ground wood and cork, gum, color pigments, and oxidized linseed oil. Production is limited.

lintel A horizontal crosspiece over a door or a window or between two columns.

lithographs Prints made from a stone or metal plate to which the pattern or design has been applied with a special grease pencil or wax.

long, formal curtains Having a shirred or tabbed heading, these long curtains can be hand operable or stationary.

long-life bulb An incandescent bulb that lasts from 2,500 to 3,500 hours.

loose cushions Pillows that are part of an upholstered piece but left unattached in the upholstery process.

Louis XV period (1723–74) The period during the reign of King Louis XV of France. Also known as the Rococo period and characterized by ornate, curvilinear, asymmetrical design.

Louis XVI period (1774–93) The period during the reign of King Louis XVI of France. Also known as the French Neoclassic period and characterized by rectilinear, classically inspired design.

louvered door Door with louvered panels.

louvers Horizontal slats in a shutter, screen, or window, slopped downward (or movable) to control light and air passage.

low contrast The difference between colors whose values (lightness vs. darkness) are very close—such as all light colors or all dark colors.

low key A color scheme in a variety of dark values.

low value Hues that have been darkened.

lowboy A low chest of drawers raised on legs, used as a dressing or serving table. With the addition of a tall chest, it becomes a highboy.

low-contrast values Values near each other, such as dark and medium values or medium and light values, for example.

low-voltage lamps Bulbs that consume little energy.

lumber-core door Same as solid-core door.

lumens A measurement of the amount of light flow.

luminaire A lighting fixture.

luminance The intensity of light in a given surface or area.

luminous ceiling Incandescent or fluorescent lights around which a box is framed and finished, with the cover over the lights made of translucent glass or plastic.

luminous panels Fluorescent or incandescent lights set into a wall or floor and covered with translucent glass or plastic.

lux The unit of illumination, equal to one lumen per square meter.

luxury homes Spacious or luxurious homes with high-quality detail, cabinet work, and furnishings.

M

Mackintosh, Charles Rennie (1868–1928) Scottish designer/architect, influential with the Vienna Secessionists and designer of the Hill chair.

mainframe computer A large computer into which smaller computer terminals or personal computers can be accessed. Mainframes can handle complex data, problems, and CAD with speed and accuracy.

maintenance The labor required to maintain a material—tasks such as sweeping, vacuuming, dusting, mopping, scrubbing, or waxing.

man-made fibers Chemically derived and extruded from a viscose or liquid solution.

mansard roof A hipped roof with two pitches. The bottom pitch is very steep and the top pitch flatter, so it is usually not seen from the ground.

mantel The projecting shelf of a chimneypiece.

marble A very hard stone cut into slabs and polished for floor and wall materials. Smooth and formal, white or colored with streaks of color.

marbling Imitating polished marble stone with paint.

markets, marketing centers Convenient clusters of trade sources that market goods and services wholesale to interior designers.

Marlborough leg A straight, square furniture leg with a square foot.

marquetry Patterns created by laminating contrasting pieces of thin wood (and other materials) into a veneered surface.

masonry block construction Walls or foundations of cinder block or concrete block without any wooden framework.

mass An element of design that denotes density or visual weight within an object. Heavier mass or density will often make an object appear larger than one that has little mass or empty space within its shape.

massing Gathering or forming into a mass. The pulling of objects into a group so that together they have more visual weight or importance than they do separately.

master of arts degree (M.A.) A degree that may be considered a terminal degree in interior design education.

master of fine arts degree (M.F.A.) A degree that may be considered a terminal degree in interior design education. M.F.A. degrees require a fine arts skill and showing of work. It is considered the design education equivalent of a doctor of philosophy (Ph.D.) degree.

master of science degree (M.S.) A degree that may be considered a terminal degree in interior design education.

masters Those whose art has passed the test of time to become classic.

mat A border of mat board or other material, used as a frame or part of the frame of a picture.

match The same color from one dye lot to another.

materials Textiles and other substances used for floor and wall coverings, window treatments and upholstery, cabinetry, trim, and other physical components of an interior.

materials and finishes boards Boards used to show pieces of the materials and finishes that have been selected for a design.

matte paint Any paint that dries to a flat, nonshiny finish.

McIntire, Samuel (1757–1811) American architect and designer of houses and public buildings in Salem, Massachusetts. McIntire is best known for the beautifully carved woodwork in his interiors.

mechanical finishes A classification of decorative fabric finishes that include calendering, napping, and flocking. Also called surface treatment finishes.

media The substances used to dilute paint—water for watercolor and turpentine for oil paint. Also the means or methods an artist uses to produce a work.

Medieval era (A.D. 800–1500) The Middle Ages or Medieval era in Europe was a time of poverty for the masses but in architecture was a period of great cathedral building and colorful stained glass windows.

melamine A synthetic compound used to make plastic laminates.

mementos Remembrances or souvenirs of a person, a place, or an event.

memorabilia Things and events worthy of remembrance.

mercerization A process of treating natural cellulosic fibers (cotton and linen) with caustic soda to enlarge and make the fibers more uniform, increase the luster, and better accept and hold dyes.

metal Aluminum, tin, brass, stainless steel, and other chemical compounds that are formed into strips, tiles, or sheets for use as wall, ceiling, and furniture materials.

metal blinds Originally known as venetian blinds, metal blinds provide the look of two-inch wood blinds at less cost and with less stacking space required.

metal or space frame system Strong, lightweight steel skeleton framework based on the forms of geometry.

metameric effect A phenomenon in which colors appear different under different lighting due to the spectral energy distribution in the materials.

metamerism The effect of light on color that causes a color to appear differently in different types of light.

metope The space between the triglyphs on the frieze of the Doric entablature.

Mexican tile Clay tile fired at low temperatures. Natural terra-cotta color or hand-painted in bright colors, glazed and unfired.

Middle Ages *See* Medieval era.

midtones Colors at their normal value or saturation point.

Mies van der Rohe, Ludwig (1886–1969) An important architect/designer associated with the Bauhaus. Designer of several modern classic furniture pieces.

millwork Stock- and custom-milled woodwork in the form of cabinetry, shelving, panels, and molding.

miniblinds One-inch wide, concave metal slats held together with nylon cord. Slats or louvers are adjustable and are excellent for light and glare control.

mini-mainframe computer A computer about the size of a personal computer but with greater capacity and power somewhat similar to a mainframe computer.

mirror Glass with the back coated with silver or a silver amalgam (compound) to give the surface a reflecting quality; used on walls, ceilings.

Mission style *See* Craftsman style.

miter To cut at a forty-five-degree angle. A joint where two diagonally cut pieces meet at right angles and are nailed or screwed together.

mobile home A house trailer for temporary or permanent housing.

mobile home park An area where only mobile homes are placed.

modacrylic A synthetic long-chain polymer fiber consisting of 35 to 85 percent acrylonitrile units. It is a soft, buoyant fabric that is inherently flame resistant and used extensively for nonresidential draperies where fire codes must be met.

modillion A projecting decorated bracket; also called a console.

monitor The computer hardware screen component.

monochromatic A color scheme using one color in any of its varieties, plus some white and black.

mood lighting Low-level lighting that creates an ambience or mood that is cozy or inviting.

Moor A Moslem of mixed Berber (North-African) and Arab ancestry.

Moroccan rugs Handmade pile rugs from North Africa that have geometric patterns and are coarsely woven.

Morris, William (1834–96) A British designer of the Arts and Crafts movement who produced wallpaper, furniture, tapestries, carpets, stained glass windows, and accessories.

mortise and tenon A joint that utilizes a square hole carved in one of the pieces being joined and a projection that fits the hole in the other.

mosaic Small pieces of glass tile or stone fitted together and held in place with cement to create a pattern or design. Used for floor, ceiling, or wall decorations or accessories.

mosaic tile Small tiles fitted together with grout to form a pattern in floors, walls, and countertops.

mothproofing A finish that renders a fabric, especially wool, unpalatable to moths and other destructive insects.

motivational lighting A lighting specialty that utilizes brightness, dullness, and darkness to motivate people to behave in a certain manner. It utilizes principles of psychology as well.

motorized rods Drapery rods that are electronically operable. Used for large or hard-to-reach installations.

movable insulation Interior or exterior insulation that protects against excessive heat loss or solar gain.

movable louver shutters Wooden shutters with slats or blades that can be adjusted.

mullion A vertical dividing piece in an opening, especially a window.

multilevel living Housing that contains one or more changes of planes in addition to the main floor: an upstairs, downstairs, or step-down or step-up areas.

multilevel-loop pile carpet A looped pile carpet with various levels woven or tufted to create texture or a pattern.

multiple-outlet strips Casings with spaced outlets that are prewired or portable, useful in home workbenches, home offices, and other work spaces.

multiuse areas Rooms or areas with more than one purpose or function.

Munsell, Albert H. (1858–1918) American colorist whose system, based on hue, value, and chroma notation, is widely used in design.

Munsell theory Based on three attributes—hue, value, and chroma—where exact color matching is possible through a notation system.

mural A series of wallpapers hung in sequence to depict a scene. Also, a large-scale scenic wall painting.

N

NASAD The National Association of Schools of Art and Design.

NCIDQ The National Council for Interior Design Qualification.

NCIDQ examination An examination administered to interior designers after a minimum of two years of professional work experience. Must be passed for full acceptance into several of the professional design organizations.

nap The fuzzy surface of a fabric formed by short hairs or fibers.

natural A wood finish without any added color or stain.

natural fiber rugs Animal skins, berber rugs, cotton rugs, floccati rugs, sisal/maize mats, and wool rugs.

natural light Sunlight.

natural saturation point The amount of naturally occurring white or black value in a pure hue according to the Munsell system for color notation.

natural textiles Come from either cellulosic fibers (cotton, linen, jute), or protein sources (silk, wool, leather) which are derived from natural sources.

natural thermal flow The convection or movement of heated air up and/or toward cold air and the consequent dropping of cool air.

natural traffic pattern The pattern of movement users will follow in an environment if their circulation is not hampered or obstructed.

naturalistic design A classification of decorative design that is a copy or representation of something in nature. It is realistic decoration or ornamentation.

Navajo rugs Handwoven flat tapestry rugs in earth-tone neutral colors and geometric patterns. Woven in the southwestern United States by members of the Navajo tribe.

nave The main section of the church where the worshipers stand or sit.

needle-constructed fabrics Fabrics made or decorated with automated sets of needles, including knits, laces, some casements, and schiffli embroidery.

needlepoint rugs Hand or machine-made rugs, most often from China or Portugal, with small stitches of wool yarn on an art canvas background.

needlepunched carpet Carpeting constructed of fibers held together by needlepunching or interlocking the fibers by meshing together with barbed needles. Used primarily in indoor-outdoor and nonresidential applications.

negative space The area between the forms in a two- or three-dimensional design. Empty or void space not filled in with furnishings, accessories, or mass.

Neoclassic (1790–1830) The period in America influenced by the excavations of Pompeii.

neon lamp A thin glass tube containing a gaseous element (neon) that glows when charged with electricity. The tubes can be bent into any shape for artistic or advertising purposes.

neon lighting The red spectrum of cold cathode lighting formed with neon gas.

network of lighting Interconnected wiring of lights indicated on the lighting or wiring plan in nonresidential buildings.

neutralized colors Any hue that is dulled or grayed or lessened in brightness or intensity.

neutrals Black, white, and gray. Brown is a hue, derived from orange, but it is often referred to as a neutral, as are beige, tan, and the colored spectrum of off-whites.

newel post An upright that receives and supports the handrail at critical points on a stair.

niche The rounded, half-domed end of a room, or a similar recess in a wall.

nogging Brickwork used as infill between timber framing.

nonarchitectural lighting Portable luminaires.

noncellulosic fibers The range of synthetically composed man-made fibers that begin as chemicals and organic substances other than cellulose. Also known as synthetic fibers.

nondurable or soluble finishes These are fabric finishes that are removed with repeated washing or dry cleaning.

nonglare glass Clear glass with a faintly textured surface that does not reflect light.

nonrenewable resources Materials that cannot be reproduced in a sustainable manner. They include materials such as plastics that are made from fossil substances, and materials such as stone and metals that are mined.

nonresidential design Interior design work for which the client is not a residential occupant.

nonresidential wall coverings Wall coverings that meet standards or codes for durability, fire safety, and low maintenance. Wider and in longer rolls than residential wall coverings.

nonresilient flooring materials A category of materials that are hard and have no give or resilience.

nonwoven textiles A group of fabrics such as felt, webbing, and films that are processed into fabrics without going through the yarn stage.

Norman The name given to the Romanesque architectural style in England.

nosing The rounded edge of a tread.

novelty twill A twill weave that changes direction to create a pattern such as herringbone.

nubuck Top-grain leather that has been buffed on the upper side to a soft, velvety nap.

nylon A long-chair synthetic polymer fiber that consists of amides linked to aramide ring molecules. Nylon is a versatile, durable fiber used extensively for carpeting and upholstery.

objets d'art French term for any object of artistic worth.

occasional chair A chair kept away from the main seating area that can be pulled up and used occasionally, as needed.

occasional table A small table that can be moved and used for any purpose as needed.

occult balance Another word for asymmetrical, informal, active, or optical balance. The balance is not the same on each side but is achieved through arranging until the composition "feels right" and is therefore somewhat mysterious.

oculus Literally "an eye." The circular opening at the top of a dome.

off-gassing The process of allowing volatile fumes and gases to dissipate. Newly installed wall and floor coverings, and new upholstered furniture, often require an off-gassing period.

oil paint Colored pigment mixed with linseed oil or varnish and thinned with turpentine.

oil-based paints Paints that must be thinned and cleaned up with solvents or paint thinners. Durable, scrubbable finish. Requires a long drying time and has a strong odor.

olefin A synthetic, long-chain polymer fiber consisting largely of ethylene or propylene. Olefin is durable and economical. Used for carpet face and backing and for upholstery.

one-turn stair A stair that turns ninety degrees at a landing.

onion dome A pointed dome whose apex is greater in diameter than its base, resembling the shape of an onion. It may be squatly or elongated. Onion domes are found on churches, mosques, and other large buildings in a broad geographical area extending from Germany and the Balkans to Russia and India.

open floor plan A concept in interior and architectural planning where areas are left open, without wall divisions. The open areas can be used in a flexible manner to accommodate varying functions.

open office planning A large office space in which workstations are divided only by systems furniture and other furnishings.

open plan *See* open floor plan.

open showroom A wholesale trade source that allows clients to accompany the designer into the showroom.

open stair A stair not attached to the wall.

open-riser stair A stairway that is open because it has no risers.

operable window A window that can be opened.

opposition A form of rhythm wherein right angles meet or light and dark areas contrast in a rhythmic sequence.

optical balance Same as asymmetrical, informal, active, or occult balance. Judged by the eye, or optical sense.

optical color mixing *See* subtractive color mixing.

optical density The appearance of a pattern or item as heavy or dense or filled in, and therefore judged as heavy mass.

orders The styles of Greek and Roman architecture.

ordinary incandescent lamps Incandescent bulbs that last from 750 to 2,500 hours.

organizational tool programs Software that analyzes, organizes, and synthesizes information. Used for writing specifications, critical paths, and word processing.

Oriental Revival A style inspired by Islamic design, first popular in the mid- to late nineteenth century.

Oriental rugs Hand-knotted (handwoven) pile rugs from the Near and Far East woven in complex floral or geometric patterns. Used for area, art, and accent rugs and wall hangings. May be very valuable.

orientation The direction (N, S, E, W) windows face in a room. The natural daylighting of the different orientations each has a unique effect on colors.

Ostwald theory A system for analyzing color based on the color and the amount of white or black added to the hue.

Ostwald, Wilhelm (1853–1932) A physicist who won the 1909 Nobel Prize for chemistry and who turned his research to color, producing the well-known book *The Color Primer*.

ottoman An oversized upholstered footstool. Sometimes called a hassock.

outbuildings Buildings situated away from a house used historically for kitchens, dairies, carriages, or servants' quarters.

outlet strips Prewired or plugged-in casings that contain several outlets in a row.

outlining Painting contrasting colors or white values on architectural molding.

overcrowding An excessive number of people working or living within a given space.

overlay A sheet of velum or tracing paper placed over a rough design to improve and refine it.

oxford weave Variation of plain weave in which two fine warp threads are interlaced with one heavier weft thread.

P

PAR lamp Reflective parabolic aluminized reflector lamp with heavy, protective glass and a focused beam. Silvering is used to establish the beam spread and the reflective quality.

PL lamp Compact twin fluorescent bulb.

PS lamp A pear-shaped incandescent lamp, often with a long neck.

pad painting The application of paint with a flat fibrous pad.

padding A general term for carpet underlay or the cushioning layer covering the springs in upholstery.

paint A liquid oil-, water-, resin-, alkyd-, acrylic-, or epoxy-based material that is applied by spraying, brushing, rolling, or pad painting. Dries to a flat, semigloss, gloss, or high-gloss finish.

painting A one-of-a-kind, two-dimensional art form created with color pigments and a number of different substances (vehicles) that give the paint form and body.

palette knife A small, usually flexible knife used to mix paint on the artist's paint tray (palette) or to apply paint to the surface being painted.

Palette theory Another name for the Standard Color Wheel theory.

palisade wall A paneled fireplace wall formed of boards and battens.

Palladian window An arched window flanked on each side by lower sidelights.

paneled door A traditional door formed with stiles, rails, and panels.

paneling Sheets of wood used for wall and ceiling finish materials. May be solid wood or veneered (sandwiched).

panel-track wall fabric installation Metal tracks available for installing fabric on the wall. Used most often in nonresidential settings.

paper wall covering Paper front and back; no vinyl coating.

papier-mâché A material used for the construction of furniture and accessories made from paper pulp and glue. During the nineteenth century these pieces were often painted black and inlaid with mother-of-pearl.

parapet A low wall on the edge of a roof, bridge, or terrace.

parquet The decorative, geometric arrangement of short lengths of wood plank for floors and sometimes walls.

particleboard A solid panel formed by compressing flakes of wood with resin under heat and pressure.

passive balance Another term for symmetrical or formal balance where items are identical on each side of a central point, and therefore no judgment of the composition is needed.

passive solar gain Heat from sunshine that collects through the natural transfer of radiation, conduction, and/or convection.

pastel A neutralized color achieved by mixing one or more complementary or contrasting colors with the basic hue to produce a tone, and then adding white.

paterae Oval (or round) shapes used as ornament, often decorated with rosettes.

patina A finish that comes with use and time to wood and metal.

patio door *See* atrium door.

patio home A small home set on a narrow, shallow building lot.

pattern An element of design; the arrangement of shapes and perhaps value (light and dark contrast) or relief (high and low areas) brought together to make a random or predictable design.

pattern book Books of patterns for houses, furniture, and architectural detail published for general use.

pattern repeat Wall covering or fabric pattern measurement from the top of one pattern to the top of the next, or from one pattern to another horizontally.

payback period The number of years that a purchase (such as a solar energy installation) takes to pay for itself.

pediment A decorative design detail that originated with the triangular section of the Greek trussed roof. The pediment was adapted from a triangle into a rounded segmental pediment, a broken pediment, which is open at the top, and an ornate scroll pediment. Pediments are used for furniture and architectural embellishment.

pediment frieze The sculptural design within the pediment.

peelable wall covering Wall covering that can be peeled away from a substrate (backing or lining), which is suitable to be repapered.

pembroke table An occasional table with drop leaves and a drawer in the apron.

pendants Decorative downward projections used to embellish architectural and furniture designs.

pent roof A narrow, overhanging rooflike structure above the first story on Pennsylvania German houses.

perfatape A wide paper tape applied to sheetrock seams with plasterboard compound or mud.

perimeter lighting Lighting around the outside of a room or an area. Perimeter lighting visually expands space.

peristyle A continuous row of columns around a building. Also used to designate the colonnaded garden area at the rear of a Roman house.

permanent installations Structural or finish materials that are not likely to be replaced due to their cost or difficulty to install or remove.

Persian rugs The finest of the Oriental rugs, traditionally from Persia (today Iran). High knot count, complex, usually floral patterns.

personal computer A small computer for home or small-business use.

personal space The invisible "bubble" of space that surrounds us and that we consider to be our own.

perspective sketch A three-dimensional sketch or rendering of an interior space drawn in perspective with vanishing points.

pewter A soft, dull-gray alloy of tin, copper, lead, and antimony used to make tableware.

Phyfe, Duncan (1768–1854) A New York furniture builder, originally from Scotland, known for his Regency-style pieces.

piano nobile The principal floor of a building; usually a raised first floor.

picking out Highlighting features on molding, such as dentil trim or carved bas-relief, with paint.

piece dyeing Coloring a bolt or length of fabric after it is woven into cloth.

pier Same as a column but without its details and proportions.

pigment A compound that is the coloring agent for paint, ink, crayons, and chalk. A nonsoluble coloring matter that is held onto the surface of the fabric with a resin binder.

pigmenting Coloring or dyeing. Also, the process of treating leather with chemical dye.

pilaster A flat, false, decorative column.

pile The surface of a carpeting that has depth. Rounded loops are called uncut pile, while cut loops are called cut pile.

pile density Closeness of stitches (woven) or tufts of a carpet. Greater or tighter density yields a more durable product.

pile weave A weave that utilizes a third set of threads that form a depth or a pile in the surface. Types of pile weave include velvet, terry cloth, and corduroy.

pilling Tendency of fibers to work into small balls or pills.

pillow sham A removable decorative pillowcase.

plain slicing method used to cut a log parallel to a line through its center—produces a vaulted or cathedral-like grain.

plain weave The interlacing of threads or yarns in a one-over, one-under sequence.

plan drawing A flat, two-dimensional, scaled drawing of an environment as seen from above.

plane of light A bank of light; a well-lit area.

planned development A tract of land that is developed into housing of a specific style, size, price range, and type (attached dwellings, single detached dwellings, luxury dwellings).

plantation shutters Louvered shutters with wide blades. Used in the South during colonial days as screens to encourage ventilation during the hot months.

plaster A thick, pasty mixture of sand, water, and lime used for smooth or rough wall and ceiling textures.

plasterboard Another name for drywall, Sheetrock, or gypsum board, plasterboard is a wall material made of pulverized gypsum rock and commonly used as a wall finish material.

plastics Synthetically produced, nonmetallic compounds that can be molded, hardened, and used for manufacture of various products.

plate rail A narrow shelf for displaying plates.

Platner, Warren (1919–) American architect/designer who created the Platner Chair (1966) and other furniture pieces in the Platner Collection. Platner worked in the offices of Eero Saarinen.

pleated shades Factory-manufactured polyester fabric shades permanently heat set into one- to three-inch pleats. May be metallized on the reverse for energy efficiency.

pleated valances A fabric top treatment that is given fullness through pleating.

plenum The space between the suspended ceiling grid and the ceiling. This space often contains mechanical systems.

Plexiglas A highly transparent, lightweight, thermoplastic acrylic resin made into sheets like glass. Unlike glass, it is not easily broken.

plies Thin layers of wood laminated together to make plywood.

plotter A computer mechanical drawing printer that can produce drafting, two- and three-dimensional illustrations, and perspectives.

plumbing The systems that carry water, sewage, or central vacuums.

plumbing chase A thick wall containing plumbing.

plush carpet A tufted carpet with a dense, short, even pile in solid colors. Originally intended to imitate the pile of an Oriental rug.

plywood A product made of thin sheets of wood glued together in layers.

pneumatic system construction Air-inflated or air-supported structures.

pocket door A door that slides into a pocket recessed in the wall.

podium The base on which Roman buildings are built.

point or pinpoint lighting Spotlighting a tiny area for emphasis or a glitter effect.

polyester A synthetic long-chain polymer fiber of polymer ester. A durable, dimensionally stable fiber that is highly versatile. Most sheer and semisheer fabrics are of polyester. Used for residential carpeting and scatter rugs and for wall covering fabrics that are often used in nonresidential interiors.

Polypropylene A modified olefin fiber used for artificial turf, tufted indoor-outdoor carpeting, and nonwoven (needle-punched) carpets and tiles. Also used for a primary and secondary backing for some carpeting. A registered trademark of Thiokol for olefin.

polyurethane A synthetic resin used to make foam for cushions and as a base for varnish.

Pompeii and Herculaneum (destroyed A.D. 79, excavation began 1754) Sister cities on the Bay of Naples (southern Italy) that contained prosperous classical Roman architecture, preserved by the ashes and lava mud flow of Mount Vesuvius. Archaeological excavations resulted in the introduction of the Neoclassic or Classic Revival style in Europe and America.

pool of light A circle of light thrown by a downlighter or spotlight.

porcelain The highest grade of ceramic. Made of fine white clay.

porphyry A granitelike texture achieved by crisscross brushing, then stippling, spattering, and finally cissing paint. Also a type of stone.

portable computer A keyboard, monitor, and drive unit that folds into the size of a briefcase, also called Notebook.

portable luminaires Nonarchitectural lighting such as table and floor lamps or plug-in wall lights.

portable space heaters Small units that produce heat for a small area or a room. Types include electric and propane heaters; they vary in their size, output, electricity consumption, and safety.

portal The porch on a Southwest Adobe house.

porthole window A round window, named for its resemblance to a ship's porthole.

portico A classical porch formed by a roof with supporting columns.

positive space Space filled in with a two- or three-dimensional form or shape.

post-occupancy evaluation (POE) The formal process of looking at a design once it is in use to see how well it is functioning.

potpourri French term for the mixture of dried flower petals used to perfume a room.

power-line carrier (PLC) system A structured wiring system that enables AC power wires to carry coded communications signals, forming an interface between household appliances and a computer. PLC systems can be retrofitted in existing homes.

Prang theory Another name for the Standard Color Wheel theory.

prefinishes Processes that prepare a fabric for coloring, decorative, or functional finishes. Prefinishes include scouring, preshrinking, bleaching, mercerizing, and sizing.

prepasted wall coverings Wall coverings with a dry paste or adhesive preapplied to the back which is moistened, then pasted to the wall or ceiling.

preservation Maintaining a building in its present state or the state to which it has been restored.

preshrinking A prefinish process of subjecting a fabric to wet or dry heat to cause it to shrink and stabilize before further finishing or coloring.

pressed glass Decorative glass formed in molds.

pretil A row of brick trim used to cap the adobe walls of the Territorial-style Southwest Adobe houses.

pretrimmed wall coverings Wall coverings with selvages trimmed off at the factory.

primary focal point The main point of emphasis in an environment. The object, area, or grouping that first catches the eye.

primary hues Red, yellow, and blue, as based on the Standard Color Wheel theory.

primers Liquid preparations that seal the surface and prepare it for paint application.

principles of design Scale, proportion, balance, rhythm, emphasis, and harmony (unity and variety).

printing Applying color to a finished cloth by hand (batik, tie-dye, stencil) or mechanical processes (automated silk screen, roller, transfer).

printmaking A method of mass-producing two-dimensional art pieces by various means. *See also* block prints, engravings, etchings, lithographs, and serigraphs.

priscilla curtains Sheer, semisheer, or muslin curtains with ruffles on all edges, on the ties, and as a valance; they meet at the center or crisscross; a colonial and Victorian style.

privacy draperies A white, an off-white, or perhaps a colored fabric installed on a traverse rod next to the window to be drawn closed at night for privacy.

private zones Areas within a home that dictate privacy—the bedroom and the bathroom, for example.

problem statement A short declaration that identifies a design project according to purpose, location, and those for whom the design is being created.

product design The design of furniture, accessories, or other components that are marketed in the design field.

profile An outline of user characteristics, habits, background, and design preferences that helps determine the direction a design should take.

program Everything that happens or must be accomplished in an interior. It also is the written document that describes what will take place in an interior.

programming The research phase of the design.

progression A type of rhythm wherein shapes repeat in diminishing or escalating sizes or where colors graduate from light to dark. Also called rhythm by gradation.

project management Overseeing calendars, critical paths, and deadlines so that a design is completed in a timely manner.

project managing tools Documents and administrative systems used to accomplish a design project, particularly the critical path and punch list.

projecting fireplace A fireplace that projects beyond the wall plane to which it is mounted.

proportion The relationship of parts to a whole in terms of size, detail, or ornamentation. Good proportion is pleasing and functional.

protected aniline leather *See* semi-aniline leather.

protein fibers Natural fibers or fabrics whose source is animal based: wool, silk, and includes the textile leather.

provincial Rustic; local; from the provinces or countryside.

proxemics The way people use space and the way that use is related to culture.

pueblo Communal dwelling of the Pueblo Indians.

punch list A checklist of items to be completed before final building inspection and occupation.

Q

quarry tile Rust-colored tiles that are fired at lower temperatures than ceramic tiles and valued for their natural terracotta coloration. Typically square or hexagonal shapes.

quarter slicing A method used to cut logs where the blade meets the grain at right angles to the growth rings, resulting in a straight, striped grain.

Queen Anne (1665–1714) Queen of England (1702–14) whose name is given to the period design style during her reign, and also to an elaborate style of Victorian architecture popular in the late 19th century.

quicksilver An alloy of mercury and tin used for mirror backing.

quire Alternate British spelling for choir. *See* choir.

quoin Projecting or contrasting brick or stone laid at the corner angle of a building.

R

R, ER lamps Lamps with a built-in, reflective surface.

R-20, R-30, R-40 Indicate the degree of beam spread in reflector lamps.

Rabat rugs Moroccan rugs in a deep, hand-knotted pile with simplified Oriental designs.

radial balance A type of balance that is seen in the same way as radiation from a central point.

radiant heat Electrical conduit or water (steam) heat plumbing in ceilings, floors, or walls that radiates heat.

radiation A type of rhythm (a principle of design) illustrated by elements radiating out in nearly every direction from a central point, such as spokes of a wheel or concentric circles.

radiators Wall or baseboard units that contain steam heat or another heated fluid medium, permanent or portable.

radio frequency (RF) transmission A wireless system that uses radio frequency waves to operate electronic devices or enable one electronic device to communicate with another.

rag rug A plain weave rug woven with strips of fabric, historically rags or recycled clothing.

ragging and rag rolling Wet paint or glaze is partially removed by dabbing with a rag or rolling the paint off with a rolled rag or plain newsprint paper.

rail The horizontal section of a frame for a panel or door.

rain gutter The metal gutter and downspouts that channel rain and snow runoff from the eaves down the side of the building to the ground.

rainbow roof A curved, gabled roof, attributed to ships' carpenters, used on some Cape Cod houses.

raised hearth A hearth built on a platform or cantilevered in front of a raised fireplace.

rambler A one-story detached home with or without a basement. The social, work, and private zones are located on the main floor.

random carpet texture *See* level-tip carpet.

rapid-start fluorescent lamps Eliminate flickering as the gases quickly activate the phosphorus in the light. May also be controlled with a dimmer switch.

rattan A climbing palm with slender, tough stems used to make wicker.

rayon A regenerated cellulosic man-made fiber that imitates the luster of silk at a lower cost. Primarily used for drapery and upholstery.

rebar Bendable steel bars set into concrete for reinforcement and to deter cracking.

rebonded foam *See* bonded (rebonded) foam.

recessed adjustable lighting Architectural luminaires that are fixed into the ceiling. The lamps can be adjusted to the desired angle.

recessed downlight A canister that fits into the ceiling and casts pools of light downward.

recessed luminaires A general term for luminaires that fit into the ceilings where the light is noticeable but the fixture is not.

reeding Rows of parallel convex beads or moldings used to embellish a column or leg. If the piece is grooved with concave moldings, it is fluted.

refinement or refining The process of placing overlays of tracing paper to improve a space plan design.

reflecting glare Excessive light reflecting from a shiny object, for example sunlight reflecting off a glass tabletop.

refraction The bending of a ray of heat, light, or sound.

Regency The period or style of English architecture that paralleled American Greek Revival. *See* American Empire.

registers (heat registers) The metal grill that covers the duct opening of the HVAC system.

reinforced concrete Concrete (a mixture of cement and a mineral aggregate) that is strengthened by setting steel bars or wire mesh into the mixture while it is wet.

relief printing Printing from a pattern that stands out in relief, as is done with a block print.

Renaissance The great rebirth of classical art and learning during the fourteenth, fifteenth, and sixteenth centuries.

rendering An artist's conception or perspective of a finished building exterior or interior, usually done in full color.

renewable resources Materials that can be reproduced in a sustainable and timely manner, such as natural-fiber textiles, wood, leather, and organic pigments.

repetition A type of rhythm wherein shapes, forms, lines, or colors are repeated in a congruous manner.

reproductions Printed copies of an artist's work.

research Examining all factors that influence a design.

resilience The ability of a fabric or flooring to return to its original shape.

resilient A material with some give or ability to bounce back.

resist or reserve printing Coating the fabric with a chemical paste that resists the dye, then dyeing the fabric. The area not printed receives the color.

restoration A research, demolition, and reconstruction process to bring a building back to a specific state of its history.

retainer fee A deposit given to the designer upon the client's signature on the letter of agreement that retains or hires the services of the designer.

retrofitting Adding an electrical, telecommunications, home automation, solar, or other system to an existing building.

reverberation Echoing of sound waves.

reversible cushions Loose cushions that can be turned to avoid excessive soiling and wear.

rhythm A principle of design seen in an interior as a visual flowing pattern or regular recurrence. The path the eye follows. Types of rhythm include repetition, alternation, progression or gradation, transition, opposition or contrast, and radiation.

rib A projecting band on a ceiling or vault.

riser The vertical member of a stair between two treads.

Robsjohn-Gibbings, T.H. (1905–76) Designer of a group of Greek furniture reproductions, including the Klismos chair.

Rococo *See* Louis XV period.

roller painting Paint application with a roller—a sleeve of soft fibrous pile fabric that can hold and release the paint evenly. Faster than brush painting. It tends to spatter but is very useful for large areas such as walls and ceilings.

roller printing A fabric printing method whereby dye is applied to raised figures on a cylinder, then stamped or transferred to fabric as it rolls over the cylinder.

roller shade Flat fabric or plastic material on a roller rod, which is operated with a spring or pulley mechanism.

rollikan rug A flat tapestry folk rug from Scandinavia that often incorporates simplified floral patterns and stripes.

Roman shade A fabric shade that folds up from the bottom accordion style. May be interlined for energy efficiency.

Romanesque (A.D. 800–1150) The Medieval architectural period based on Roman design.

roof monitors Clerestory windows, skylights, and cupola windows that catch heat from the sun and allow ventilation for excess summer heat.

roof trusses A joist and rafter system that forms the triangular construction of a roof.

rotary screen printing A mechanized silkscreen process where the screens are wrapped around a circular drum that rotates the ink onto the fabric moving beneath the rotary screens. It is a fast and efficient process.

rotary slicing A method of shaving a continuous layer of wood from a log that has been mounted on a lathe, producing a broad, open grain.

rotogravure or roto A printed pattern overlaid with layers of vinyl for sheet flooring.

rotunda A round, domed room.

rough electrical The wiring installed when the building is framed.

rough heating The installation of furnace and duct work systems when the building is framed.

rough plumbing The installation of pipes to carry water and sewage and central vacuum.

round wire tufting/weaving Carpet construction technique that yields even, round loops.

roundheaded arch An arch formed in a perfect half circle, not flattened. A Roman or keystone arch.

row house Another term for town house.

rubber A natural or synthetic composition that yields a resilient, solid or marble-patterned flooring.

rubber-backed tufted carpet Carpeting tufted into a foam rubber backing that serves as a pad or underlay. Direct glue-down installation.

rubbings Designs made by placing a sheet of paper over any object with a flat, raised pattern and rubbing it with a special crayon.

rubble Stone or rocks set or installed to produce an uneven, random surface.

rush A grasslike marsh plant used to weave chair seats and floor mats.

rusticated Rough-surfaced masonry or stone.

rya rugs Deep pile shaglike rugs handknotted with abstract, contemporary patterns from Scandinavia.

S

Saarinen, Eero (1910–61) Architect/designer, creator of the pedestal furniture group.

safety lighting Lighting required by code or building ordinances to protect the health and safety of the public. Examples include exit signs, aisle lighting, and lighting for stairs and landings.

sagging Irregular elongation or stretching of a drapery fabric due to increased humidity or moisture in the air.

saltbox roof A gabled roof with one slope longer and lower than the other.

sandstone A granular stone that may be used as floor or wall materials, laid at random or in a rectangular, ashlar pattern.

saran A synthetic long-chain polymer of vinylidene chloride. Saran is fire retardant and used alone or in fabric blends.

sash curtains Sheer or semisheer fabric shirred (gathered) onto a rod at the top and bottom of the window frame.

sash window A double window (one panel above, one below) that is opened by raising or lowering one of the panels that slides up and down in its frame.

sateen, satine, or horizontal satin A satin weave where the weft or filler threads float over five to eight warp threads, then are tied down under one in an irregular manner that produces a smooth surface.

satin or eggshell paint A paint that dries to a finish slightly less shiny than semigloss but more lustrous than flat.

satin weave A smooth, often lustrous fabric weave where warp threads float over five to eight weft or filling threads, then are tied down under one. There are no ridges or wales.

Savonnerie rug A hand-knotted pile rug from France, originally woven at the Savonnerie Tapestry Works and patronized by King Louis XIV. Historic and contemporary patterns.

scale A principle of design that evaluates the relative size and visual weight of objects. Classifications of scale include small or light, medium, large or heavy, and grand (extra large).

scatter rugs Small rugs (sometimes called throw or accent rugs), often with a tufted cut pile, used in residential areas where water is likely to spill or where dirt is tracked in. Usually of polyester or nylon.

schedule The chart that indicates the finish material used on floors, walls, and ceiling and lists types of doors and windows.

scheduling Arranging for subcontractors and craftspeople who build or finish portions of a building and its interior to complete their work within a time frame.

schematics Quick drawings used to generate or show ideas.

schools Groups of artists with like philosophies whose work has similar characteristics.

sconce A wall-mounted luminaire.

screens A general term for a sliding or freestanding frame filled with wood, paper, fabric, or other materials, which may be placed in front of a window or used as a divider.

scroll pediment A pediment with a flat bottom and two curved volutes at the top, often with a finial between the volutes.

scrubbable Wall coverings that can be repeatedly washed with detergent solutions.

sculpture The art of fashioning figures and forms of wood, clay, plastics, metal, or stone.

sculptured carpet A carpet with more than one height to the pile, which gives a pattern to the whole.

sculptured-loop carpet A multilevel-loop carpet, the same as embossed-loop carpet.

sealed environment A building with nonoperable or fixed windows; HVAC provides warm, cool, and clean air.

sealers A liquid used to prepare a surface for painting.

seasonal affective disorder (SAD) A condition with symptoms of fatigue and depression affecting some people who are deprived of natural light during the long winter season.

secondary focal point The point (or points) of emphasis in an environment that is (are) subordinate to the primary focal point because of size, location, color, or other design factors.

secondary hues Green, orange, and violet, as based on the Standard Color Wheel theory.

secretary A desk with drawers below and bookcase above.

security system A wiring system that detects unlawful entry.

segmental pediment A pediment with a flat bottom and a curved radius at the top.

semi-aniline leather Leather colored with a transparent dye and treated with additional substances to increase color saturation and resistance to stains. Also called protected aniline leather.

semidetached houses A term for housing in which portions of walls and roofs are common to two or more units.

semi-durable A fabric finish that will withstand dry, but not wet cleaning.

semigloss paint A paint that dries to a luster between flat and shiny; it contrasts nicely with both and hides fingerprints.

semihoused stair A stair attached to the wall on one side.

semitrimmed wall covering Wall coverings with only one selvage trimmed off. The selvage edge is overlapped with the next strip or trimmed off at the site.

sericulture Cultivated silk production.

serigraph An art print made by passing ink through a fine screen that has been covered with a cut stencil to form the pattern. Also called silk screen.

serpentine Literally, like a snake; a line that curves in and out as on a chest front or camel-back sofa.

Seventeenth-Century English Medieval style The design style of seventeenth-century America, inspired by the late Medieval designs of England. Architecture, interiors, and furniture were all strongly influenced by English prototypes.

shade A neutralized color achieved by mixing black with a hue.

shade (window) *See* roller shade.

shading Blending painted color values from light to dark across a wall or ceiling. Also a slatted polyester shade.

shading devices Interior or exterior window coverings that deter solar gain from penetrating the interior.

shag A carpet texture in which the loops are cut to a relatively long length, usually long enough that the yarns flop over. Also called deep pile carpet.

shake shingles Wooden roof shingles, somewhat irregular in width, that weather to a gray color.

Shakers A late eighteenth-century, early nineteenth-century religious sect whose beliefs included the design of furnishings devoid of excessive decoration.

shape An element of design that is the contour or outline of an external surface of a form.

shaped valance A flat fabric top treatment with a shaped or curved bottom hem. Interlined with stiffening fabric and/or batting and sometimes quilted.

shed ceiling A ceiling with a single slope.

sheer draperies and curtains Transparent or translucent fabric hung next to the glass. Called draperies if pleated and hung on a traverse rod, curtains if shirred or gathered onto a curtain rod.

sheet vinyl Rolls of vinyl in widths up to twelve feet, glued down directly to a prepared surface. May have a cushioned backing, and the thickness of the vinyl surface may vary with the quality.

Sheetrock Also known as drywall, gypsum board, or plasterboard; a rigid wall material made of pulverized gypsum rock. *See* wallboard.

shellac A finish film for wood made by dissolving a secretion of the lac bug in denatured alcohol.

Sheraton, Thomas (1751–1806) An important English furniture craftsman best known for the designs published in his book *The Cabinet-Maker and Upholsterer's Drawing Book.*

Shibusa A Japanese approach to color harmony based on ratios and proportions found in nature. The goal of a Shibui color scheme is to create a mood of tranquility.

shingles Wood, asbestos, or tile components commonly used as a finish material on angled (gable or hipped) roofs.

shirred curtains Fabric gathered onto a rod with or without a ruffle at the top.

shirred valance A fabric top treatment gathered onto a curtain rod.

shoji screens Wooden frames and divider grids filled with translucent mulberry or rice paper. Used in traditional Japanese homes and contemporary Western residential and nonresidential interiors as well.

showrooms Wholesale businesses usually located in marketing centers where the designer may see lines of merchandise, place orders, or buy furnishings.

sick building syndrome A term for unacceptably poor air quality in a building, often attributed to dirty HVAC ductwork, low air-volume exchange, and/or a pollution source near the building's air intake vents.

side chair An armless chair without full upholstery.

side draperies Stationary panels hung on each side of a window.

sideboard A dining room serving piece with space for storing tableware. The French term buffet and the Italian terms credenza or credence are also used to describe this type of piece.

sidelights Vertical, narrow windows used on each side of a door.

silhouette lighting Accomplished by shining a light directly on an object to produce a shadow echoing the shape of the object.

silk A natural protein fiber obtained from the filament of the silk moth cocoon. Silk is lustrous, is smooth to slubby, and has a dry hand. It has long been woven into fabrics of luxury and prestige.

silk screen *See* serigraph.

silk-screen printing A traditional method of stencil printing, done by squeegeeing ink through stencils on sheer silk stretched on wooden screens. Originally it was a hand technique. Now flatbed printing automates the moving of fabric under the screens and the raising and lowering of the screens, and rotary screen printing further speeds the process by rotating the pattern onto the fabric with no hand labor. Silk screening accounts for a large portion of printed textile designs today.

silver plate Flatware made from an alloy of silver and nickel, electroplated with pure silver.

silvering The process of coating glass with quicksilver to make a mirror. Also, any process of applying silver or silverlike substances.

simultaneous contrast The juxtaposition or near placement of opposing, often intense colors that contrast with each other, possibly causing a vibrating afterimage where they border.

single family residence (SFR) A detached dwelling, or house, designed for occupancy by one family.

single glazing Filling a window opening with one layer of glass.

single roll One bolt of wall covering containing approximately thirty-six square feet.

single-hung sash Sash windows in which only the bottom section is operable.

single-wide mobile home A mobile home that is approximately twelve to fifteen feet wide and twenty to forty feet long.

sinuous wire spring An essentially flat spring bent in a zigzag fashion used in upholstered furniture, typically in the back rest.

sisal and maize mats Natural cellulosic fiber mats that are coarse and rough to the touch.

site plans Drawings showing a building's situation on the land, including legal boundaries, key reference points, and hookups for water, sewer, and electricity.

sizing A thin liquid painted on a surface before hanging wall coverings. It seals against alkali, lessens the paste quantity needed, and provides some grip for the wallpaper.

sketch A rough, quick illustration of a proposed space or a detail of the space.

skylight An opening for light set into the roof and ceiling.

slate A finely grained metamorphic rock used for roofing and flooring. Colors vary from grays to greenish or reddish grays to browns and blacks.

slate roof A roof covered with thin sheets of stone, used like shingles.

sliding windows Windows that slide horizontally.

slipcovers Fitted covers that can be placed over the original upholstery and secured with snaps or other fasteners.

Smart House Registered trademark of the National Home Builders' Association for home automation.

smoke detector A fire-alarm device that sounds when triggered by excessive smoke in the air.

smooshing A paint application technique in which a plastic sheet is placed on wet paint and then peeled off, leaving a slightly marbled texture.

social zones Areas for formal or informal social interaction.

soffit The trim applied to the eave, or the boxed projection above cabinets or over a sink.

soffit lighting Architectural lighting built into a soffit.

soft window treatments Fabric treatments: curtains, draperies, shades, and top treatments.

software Computer program that accomplishes specific tasks.

softwood Light, easily cut wood taken from cone-bearing trees such as pine and redwood.

soil-release finish Allows a fabric to more readily absorb water and free soil to be lifted out with mild detergent.

soil-repellent or soil-resistant finishes These are sprayed onto the surface of a fabric, forming a temporary barrier that prevents soil from penetrating the fabric. If the soil or stain is not removed quickly, it can be forced into the fabric through tiny cracks in the finish. The soil may then be locked under the finish, making it very difficult to remove.

solar energy Energy from sunlight which can be harnessed for heat and electricity.

solar greenhouses A greenhouse living space that is also a passive solar collector; a solarium.

solar heat gain Heat from sunshine collected through glass walls or windows. May be absorbed, stored, and released through many of the hard background materials such as stone, tile, brick, and concrete.

sole proprietorship An interior design business owned by one person.

solid Wooden furniture construction with solid pieces of wood in all the external or visible parts of the piece.

solid-core door A veneered door with a core of solid wood pieces. Also called lumber-core door.

soluble finish *See* nondurable finish.

solution or dope dyeing The addition of dyes or coloring matter to the viscose solution in man-made fibers before they are extruded. The dyes then become colorfast and will not fade. The process is more costly than other methods of dyeing and must be done well in advance of the finished product, making solution-dyed color somewhat risky in today's market of rapidly changing color trends.

solvent A liquid for thinning and cleaning up oil-based paints.

sound board An insulative material in rigid form that prevents audible sounds from being heard; usually used beneath drywall.

Southwest Adobe style An architectural style prevalent in Spanish-settled areas of North America, which survives today particularly in New Mexico. It features adobe brick construction with heavy wood beams.

space An element of design consisting of a continuous expanse of distance without forms, which is divided with walls, partitions, and furnishings. Filled space is termed positive space and empty space is called negative space.

space heating Heating the area or space where people live and work by passive or active solar means or by mechanical devices such as furnaces or space heaters.

space planning The allotment of spaces to create a workable floor plan. The organization and division of spaces into rooms or areas to meet specific needs.

space-saving device Any means of maximizing the existing space, thereby making a space seem larger.

Spanish rugs Hand-knotted pile rugs with a coarse, sparse weave. Classified with folk rugs.

spattering A method of adding texture to painted surfaces by flipping extra paint onto a surface with a filled brush.

special rodding Drapery rods that can be bent and suited to custom or special installations.

specifications The written list of materials and furnishings, itemized according to company, stock number, color, and other pertinent ordering information, and the location where the goods will be installed. Also, in nonresidential architecture, the criteria of minimum durability, cost, and safety requirements of finish materials written or specified by an architect.

specifier A type of designer whose role is limited to selecting or specifying which products or specifications will be used.

spectral colors The wave bands of solar energy that correspond to visible frequencies. From longest to shortest wave length, spectral colors are red, orange, yellow, green, blue, and violet, as seen in a rainbow.

spectral energy distribution The inherent color characteristics of an object or material due to the type and amount of dyes or pigments. This can cause the object or material to appear as different colors under different kinds of light; also describes the color of the light source. *See* metamerism.

spectral light The visible frequencies of energy that humans perceive as light and colors, as in a rainbow.

spinnerette The shower head–like device through which man-made fiber viscose solutions are forced to create monofilament. The size and shape of the holes in the spinnerette can be changed to give various characteristics to the fibers.

spiral staircase A corkscrew-shaped staircase.

splat The vertical wood panel in the center of a chair back.

split complement Consists of a hue and the two colors on each side of its direct complement.

split-entry home A two-level home in which the entry is located in the center, and the person entering walks upstairs to the kitchen/living/dining areas and the bedroom/bath areas, and downstairs to the family room, extra bedrooms, and storage areas. Has a raised basement.

split-level home A three- or four-level home with half flights leading from one area to the next.

sponge rubber pad Carpet underlay. The most common example of sponge rubber is waffle padding.

sponging Applying paint with sponges for texture and color overlay.

spotlight A luminaire that focuses light in one direction, casting a pool of light.

spray painting Paint application through a spray nozzle. Fast and economical for large applications. Should be followed with a roller to smooth out the paint.

square feet or footage The width multiplied by the length of a room or building. The two-dimensional floor space.

squeegee An implement with a strong, straight crosspiece edged with rubber used to spread a thin layer of ink across and through a silk screen.

stain Color mixed with water, oils, or other agents and applied to wood as part of the finishing process.

stained glass Colored and clear glass set into patterns and hung in front of windows or used as the window glazing itself sandwiched between plain glass.

stainless steel An alloy of steel and chromium.

stains Liquids that penetrate wood with color.

stairwell The open space filled by a stair.

Standard Color Wheel theory Based on three primary colors—red, yellow, and blue—and the variations derived by mixing these, plus black and white. Colors are arranged in a circle, with secondary and tertiary or intermediate colors placed between the primary colors.

standard finishes Applied to fabrics to enhance durability. Also known as wet, chemical, or functional finishes.

staple Short fibers that vary from approximately one-half to two inches. Staple yarns offer greater bulk, insulation, and area coverage.

stapled wall fabric Fabric attached to a wall by staples.

starting step The first step of the stair.

state of the art The current or latest technology; the newest developments.

steel A hard alloy of iron and carbon.

stemware Designation given to fine drinking glasses with raised bowls, stems, and bases.

sterling II Flatware with sterling silver handles and stainless steel blades, tines, and bowls.

sterling silver Finest type of silverware; 92.5 percent pure.

Stickley, Gustav (1848–1942) Furniture designer and exponent of the Craftsman, or Mission style. Published the magazine *The Craftsman*.

stickwork Flat battens used on Victorian buildings to create patterns in imitation of Medieval timber framing.

stile The upright section of a frame for a panel or door.

stippling A paint application technique similar to sponging that uses a stippling brush to dab on a colored glaze or paint, revealing some of the base color.

stock dyeing The coloring of natural fibers (particularly wool) in the raw-goods state (stock) before they are spun into yarns.

stock plans Floor plans that are mass produced and purchased, usually by mail order, by anyone wishing to build that home.

stone Any hard rock used for flooring or wall materials.

stone-ender A seventeenth-century house with stone-covered chimney ends, common to Rhode Island.

stoneware A heavy, durable, thick pottery used for less-formal dinnerware.

storage Space planned for keeping foodstuffs, linens, tools, clothing, and other items owned by people. It also refers to needs of a nonresidential interior to keep extra stock merchandise, office supplies, or other goods. Also, the reservoir for storing thermal energy in a solar system.

storm windows Glass or plastic removable windows that add insulation. Summer storm windows are tinted as a shading device.

stove A freestanding wood- or coal-burning heating unit.

straight lines Lines that directly connect two points; horizontal and vertical lines.

straight run A stair that makes no turns.

strapping tape method A temporary method of attaching fabric to a wall. Rolls or circles of strapping tape are affixed to the wall and to the fabric.

strength or tenacity The inherent ability of a fiber or material to withstand stress without breaking.

stretchers Crosspieces used to brace and strengthen table and chair legs.

stringcourse See beltcourse.

stringer The supporting member in a staircase.

strip lighting A lighting fixture in which several lamps or bulbs are aligned in a strip. Used in grooming areas around mirrors.

strippable A wall covering that can be stripped or completely removed from a wall. Applies to most vinyl wall coverings.

structural design A basic or general category of design wherein the design is intrinsic to the structure—one cannot be separated without destroying the other.

structural systems The components of new or remodeling construction that make up the structure: footings and foundation, as well as the framework (or other systems) that supports the building and to which the finish materials are applied.

structured wiring Specialized wiring for home automation and multimedia appliances.

stucco Rough textured plaster or cement for covering walls.

stylobate The base upon which the Greek temple rests. Contains steps on all sides.

subcontract An agreement for specialized work performed by a subcontractor, a person or firm hired to install or build a particular feature of a building's construction or finish work.

subcontractor A person who performs a single task in construction such as foundation work, framing, electrical, plumbing, HVAC, finish work (millwork or woodwork), or tile or floor laying.

subfloors The material (usually wood) nailed to the framework on which the finish floor materials are laid.

subtractive color mixing The phenomenon in which the frequencies of colors placed very near one another are blended. Subtractive color mixing is what enables us to perceive an almost infinite range of colors beyond the spectral colors.

subtractive color theory The phenomenon in which the frequencies of light striking an object are absorbed, or "subtracted," except for the frequencies corresponding to the colors with which the object is pigmented. The frequencies not absorbed are reflected, and we perceive them as colors.

suede Leather that has been buffed to a soft, velvety nap.

Sullivan, Louis (1856–1924) Called the father of American architecture, he felt that the form of a building should follow its function.

sundial A timepiece that shows the time by a shadow cast by a pointer.

superinsulation Extra-heavy insulation of walls, foundations, ceilings, and attic areas to conserve energy; requires thicker than conventional walls.

surface treatment finishes See mechanical finishes.

surface-mounted fixture A structural or decorative luminaire that is mounted onto the ceiling.

surround The noncombustible material that separates the opening of a fireplace from the wall or mantel.

surrounds (tub or shower) The tile, marble, or imitative plastic finish material used to protect the wall against water in showers and bathtub areas.

suspended ceiling A ceiling formed of metal grids and acoustic panels, hung from the superstructure of a building.

suspended fixtures Structural (pendant) or decorative (chandelier) luminaires hung on a cord or chain from the ceiling.

sustainability The ability of a design to be sustained over a long period of time without becoming obsolete; also the ability of a design to impact the environment as little as possible and consequently sustain it.

swag holders Metal or resin hardware that supports swagged fabric.

swags Also called festoons. Semicircles of fabric folded at the top to form a soft or precise curved fabric top treatment. Often finished with a cascade on each side of the swag or arrangement of swags.

swamp cooler *See* evaporative cooling system.

swinging door (one way) The typical side-hinged door.

switched outlet An electrical outlet controlled by the flip of a switch.

symbolism The use of historic color where each color held significance or symbolized a value.

symmetrical balance Also called bisymmetrical, formal, or passive balance, it is mirror-image arrangement of parts or elements.

synthesis Bringing together the research data in the programming process.

synthetic fibers The group of fibers that do not begin as cellulose but as chemicals or other natural elements chemically altered or composed into a viscose solution and extruded through a spinnerette. This group includes nylon, acrylic, modacrylic, polyester, olefin, saran, spandex, vinyon, latex, fiberglass, and metallic fibers. Also known as noncellulosic man-made fibers.

systems furniture Component pieces that can be chosen and assembled to create work spaces according to the needs of the user. As needs change, new components can be added and unneeded elements can be eliminated.

T

T lamp Tubular shaped lamp or bulb.

tab curtains Flat panel curtains with tabs or strips sewn into loops at the top, then threaded onto a dowel rod.

table lamp Luminaires designed to sit on a table for task or general lighting.

tackless strip The thin board with recessed-head tacks or staples protruding toward the wall. The strip is nailed down and the carpet is attached over the top to hold it in place for wall-to-wall installations over padding.

tapestry A plain or Jacquard weave of heavy decorative textiles.

tar paper A heavy, black, waterproof paper applied to the roof before the shingles and sometimes on the outside of foundation walls.

task lighting Bright, concentrated light for accomplishing specific tasks.

tatami mats Woven sea grass mats in various thicknesses. A traditional Japanese floor material, they will not hold up to heavy traffic.

tea caddy Metal container used to import tea during the eighteenth century, often decorated with oriental motifs and designs.

tea table A small table, tall enough to accommodate serving tea from a seated position.

technical drawings Floor plans, elevations, and detailed drawings of architectural detail, cabinetry, storage, and built-in units.

technology tools Computer software and documents used to accomplish a design project, including such applications as CAD, scheduling and critical path systems, budget and purchasing systems.

telephone system A network of connected telephones within a building or office.

tempera Paint made with pigment mixed with egg and thinned with water.

tempered glass Glass toughened by heating and rapid cooling.

tenant improvement The designer works with the client who will occupy a nonresidential space. The design work within an established budget is paid for by the developer.

tender A state of weakness in a fabric wherein it easily can tear.

tensile system construction A tentlike building system.

tenure-track position A full-time college or university appointment that offers tenure, or the status of holding one's position on a permanent basis.

terrace houses Matching row houses that became popular in England during the eighteenth century.

terra-cotta An Italian term for cooked earth used to describe hard, durable reddish brown clay products, such as that used to make roof tiles.

terrazzo Chips of marble set into concrete and polished. A hard nonresilient flooring for residential and nonresidential interiors.

Territorial style The later, more classical version of the Southwest Adobe–style houses of New Mexico, showing the influence of Greek Revival architecture.

territoriality Personal attachment to a certain territory or space.

terry cloth A pile fabric with uncut loops, used for towels.

tertiary hues *See* intermediate hues.

tesserae Pieces of colored glass and stone used to make mosaics.

tetrad complement A variation of a direct complementary scheme consisting of four colors equidistant (equally spaced) on the color wheel.

textile wall coverings Fabrics laminated to a paper backing and sold in rolls or bolts.

texture The relative smoothness or roughness of a surface read by the eye (visual texture) or with the hand (tactile texture). Texture is produced in several ways: by material, color, line, relief, and finish.

texturizing Adding crimp, kink, or waviness to a man-made monofilament thread or yarn to increase bulk and loftiness and to add textural interest. An uneven surface applied to drywall or sheetrock by blowing on a thin plaster mixture, then sanding it semismooth.

texturizing paint Thick paint that can be applied to imitate stucco.

thatched roof A roof covered with reeds or straw intended to shed water.

thematic design Interior design based on a theme, such as traditional, country, or ethnic.

thermal pane A type of double glazing in which two layers of glass are produced with a pocket of air for insulation.

thermoplastics Plastics that change their form by heating.

thermoset plastics Plastic compounds that are hardened by heat.

thermosiphoning A passive solar system of collecting heat through spaces in the walls or roof, then drawing the heat into ducts and forcing it into the interior through fans and registers.

thermostat A device that controls the furnace or air-conditioning by maintaining a preset temperature.

thin shell membrane construction A self-supporting membrane of reinforced (mesh) concrete or sprayed foam.

Thonet, Michael (1796–1871) A German craftsman best known for his bentwood furniture designs.

Tibetan rugs Rugs woven in the Himalayan region for export. Characterized by very coarse yarns, abstract, indistinct patterns and earthy colors.

tieback draperies Panels of pleated or shirred fabric tied back at a soft curve and held with ties (strips of fabric), or cords, or metal holdbacks.

tieback holders Concealed hardware to hold the ties or decorative metal rosettes that hold the draperies in the tieback position.

tie-dye A hand process for coloring fabric where a fabric is folded into various shapes, then tied with string and immersed in a dye bath. Where the folds and tied portions are thick, the dye will not penetrate, creating interesting abstract patterns.

tiered curtains Short curtains layered to overlap vertically.

tight An interior that is sealed or that has few or no windows for natural ventilation; requires HVAC system or air-exchange units for fresh air.

tile A flat, geometrically shaped wall, floor, and countertop finish material of kiln-baked clay.

timber frame A frame of heavy timbers used as the structure system for a building.

tint A neutralized color achieved by mixing white with a hue.

toe-kick or riser lighting Lighting in the toe-kick area beneath a corner, or on the stair riser just beneath the tread.

toe-mold lighting Lighting under the toe-kick area of stairs or cabinets.

tokonoma A small alcove with a low, raised platform reserved for display of aesthetic and sacred objects in the traditional Japanese home.

tone A neutralized color achieved by mixing one or more complementary or contrasting colors with the basic hue.

tongue and groove Strips of wood milled to fit together and interlock with a filet and a groove.

top treatments Any fabric used as a short covering at the top or above a window or window treatment.

top-grain leather The outer, most durable layer of the hide.

torchère In history a tall candlestand. Today a floor lamp that casts light upward onto the ceiling.

town house Another term for a dwelling that is narrow, one or two room(s) wide, and two or three stories high. It shares walls with one or two similar town houses, and one roof spans all the units.

tracery A term used to describe the lacelike ornamentation in stone or woodwork of Gothic design, often seen in windows.

track lighting A track that holds and connects several adjustable spotlights.

trade sources Wholesale companies that market goods and services to the trade or the interior design profession.

trademarks or trade names Names given by chemical companies to a generic fiber that identifies it as their product. Trademarks are registered with the Federal Trade Commission and may be accompanied by a small TM following the name.

traffic Movement of users through an area or along a route.

traffic pattern The pattern created by tracing the movement of a user through an area or along a route.

transepts The part of a cross-shaped church that extends at right angles to the nave. (The arms of the cross.)

transgenerational Design that functions for users in various stages of life (from different generations), implying that the design can be used continually without change over a long period.

transition A type of rhythm that leads the eye without interruption from one point or area to another.

transom A window over a door.

transport Moving the sun's heat through a liquid medium to the storage area in an active solar system unit.

transportation design A facet of nonresidential design: airlines, buses, trains, and automobiles.

traverse rods Rods equipped with cords and pulleys to draw draperies opened and closed.

travertine A light-colored limestone used for nonresilient floors and hard wall materials.

tread The portion of the stair that is stepped on.

triadic complement Three colors equidistant (equally spaced) on the color wheel, such as red, yellow, and blue.

triangular pediment A pediment in the shape of a triangle.

triforium A gallery above the arches of the arcade in the nave of a church.

triglyphs The three decorative vertical grooves on the frieze of the Doric entablature.

triple glazing Three layers of window glass for insulation.

triple roll A roll or bolt of wall covering containing approximately 108 square feet or three times the area of a single roll.

tripod pedestal table A three-legged table; the legs converge to form a single pedestal.

Trombe wall A passive solar system of glass (that collects and amplifies heat) placed in front of a dark masonry wall (that absorbs and slowly releases the heat into the interior).

trompe l'oeil "Trick the eye." Painted surfaces or wall covering in realistic three-dimensional scenes.

trophies Mounted fish, animals, animal heads, and skins.

true divider Windows glazed with individual panes, rather than snap-in grids.

trusses Triangular reinforcing in wood or metal that distributes the load effectively. A framework for supporting a roof.

Tudor arch A flattened Gothic arch popular in the Tudor era.

tuft bind A measurement indicating the strength of the latex layer that holds tufts of carpet yarns in place.

tufted carpets The method by which most carpeting is produced for both residential and nonresidential interiors. Multiple needles threaded with yarn are simultaneously punched into a loosely woven primary backing. The tufts are held in place with a layer of latex, then adhered to a secondary backing of jute or polypropylene.

tufting A needle construction technique of inserting yarns into a woven or knitted fabric to create a pile. Examples include many cut pile carpets and traditional patterned chenille bedspreads. Also, tying back fabric and padding in such a way as to create patterned, pillowed surface in upholstery. Also the most common type of carpet construction.

tufts or stitches per square inch A measurement indicating the density of the tufts or woven stitches in carpeting.

tungsten filament Another name for incandescent lighting.

tungsten halogen lamp Lamp in which the filament is surrounded with halogen gas that reacts with the tungsten, producing a bright light.

turnings Decorative spindles formed by turning a piece of wood on a lathe and cutting designs into the wood with a sharp knife or chisel as the piece spins.

Tuscan A simplified version of the Roman Doric style without fluting on the column.

twill weave The interlacing of yarns in a sequence such as three over, one under, which creates a distinct diagonal rib or wale. A novelty twill may reverse, creating fabrics such as herringbone or houndstooth.

twin glazing *See* double glazing.

twin home A dwelling that adjoins via a common wall only one other dwelling. A semidetached house.

U

U-stair A stair that makes a 180-degree turn at a single landing.

undertones The addition of a small amount of one hue to another, rendering the latter slightly warm or cool.

unity A component of harmony that provides a change or relief from sameness in an interior through differences in the design and furnishing elements.

universal design Design that meets the needs of all users, without drawing attention to those with disabilities.

upgrade Of a quality surpassing that of the standard allotment in new construction. Upgrades may be specified for paint or wall coverings, carpeting, or other materials.

upholstered cornice A wooden top treatment that is padded, then covered with a decorative top treatment.

upholstered walls Padded, then fabric-covered walls.

uplighters or uplighting Canisters, spotlights, or floodlights that cast light upward to the wall or ceiling.

urethane foam Synthetic foam used for carpet and upholstery padding.

user Anyone who will use a completed design.

user friendly Often refers to computer hardware and software that are relatively uncomplicated and easy to operate.

utility plans Drawings showing a building's mechanical systems, such as heating, ventilation, air-conditioning, plumbing, and electrical.

V

vacuforming A process of forming plastic in a mold in which all the air is drawn out to form a vacuum that forces the plastic around the mold.

valance lighting A light over the top of a window placed behind a board that directs light both upward and downward.

value The relative lightness or darkness of a hue according to the amount of white or black inherent in or added to the hue.

value contrast Hues or neutrals that differ in value. High-value contrast is seen when light and dark values are used together; low-value contrast refers to similar hues or neutral values.

value distribution The placement of differing values in an interior to create a balanced and pleasing effect.

vapor barrier A heavy-gauge plastic applied to walls or insulative window treatments to prevent moisture and air penetration.

variety A component of harmony made possible through repetition or similarity of objects or elements in an interior.

varnish A finish film for wood made by dissolving resinous substances in oil or alcohol.

vault A ceiling constructed on the principle of an arch. An arched roof.

vaulted system construction A tunnel-like arch system of building.

Vedic architecture A system of architecture inspired by ancient Hindu texts. Vedic buildings typically have doors and windows oriented to the sun's path, are centered around an open courtyard or solarium, and use Vedic proportions in both their overall structure and their details.

Vedic proportions Proportions for design and building based on principles in the ancient Hindu texts known as the Veda (Sanskrit for "knowledge"). These proportions often use a ratio of 1:1, resulting in squares and cubes as basic design forms.

vehicle In painting, the binding agent that holds the particles of pigment together and creates the film that adheres to the surface being painted.

veiling glare A reflected image of a light source, such as a lamp, that obscures all or part of a task area, such as a glossy book page or a television screen.

velvet weave carpet A cut-pile woven carpet with no design. Colors are solid or utilize variegated yarns.

veneer A thin ply of beautifully grained wood laminated to plywood or solid woods.

Venetian glass Delicate and fine glassware made at or near Venice, Italy. A term used to describe glass mirrors with an antique or veined appearance.

ventilation Natural fresh air through windows or through a central HVAC unit that circulates clean air through a building.

veranda A long covered porch along the front and/or side of a building.

vernacular Design executed by local craftspeople, reflecting a regional, naive, or unschooled quality.

vertical lines Up-and-down lines that lift the eye and give dignity and formality to interiors.

vertical louvers Movable louvered blinds with vertical, rather than horizontal, slats.

vestibule An air-lock entry consisting of two doors and a compartmentlike room that prevents excessive heat or cold from entering the building.

Victorian Era (1837–1901) The English and American era that coincided with the reign of Queen Victoria. It paralleled the Industrial Revolution, during which time many styles were seen. Victorian design is characterized by revivals of nearly every previous historical style, together with rapid technological development.

Vienna Secession A group of young Viennese artists and craftsmen including Otto Wagner, Josef Hoffmann, and Joseph Maria Olbrich who broke away from the mainstream of traditional art and design around 1897. The group eventually evolved into a more formal workshop—the Wiener Werkstätte headed by Josef Hoffmann.

viga A large pole beam used to support the roof of Southwest Adobe houses.

vinyl Polymerized vinyl (ethylene), essentially a plastic compound, extruded into sheets for floor and as wall coverings. Also a coating for wall coverings and fabrics.

vinyl composition A resilient hard flooring of vinyl and other compounds.

vinyl latex wall coverings Wall coverings that are vinyl through to the backing, which is usually a fabric. They are usually very durable, heavy, and scrubbable.

vinyl tile Extruded vinyl sheets cut into square tiles.

vinyl wall coverings Any wall covering with a vinyl surface, including vinyl-protected, vinyl latex, and coated fabric wall coverings.

vinyl-protected wall coverings Wall coverings, usually paper, with a coating of vinyl, which makes the covering washable.

vinyon A synthetic vinyl chloride long-chain polymer generally extruded in sheet form, and often imitating leather, suede, or nearly any surface texture. Often called vinyl or PVC (polyvinyl chloride).

virtual reality Computer simulation of a three-dimensional physical environment and its visual, auditory, and other sensory aspects.

visual acuity An enhanced ability to see, and especially to distinguish colors.

visual proportion The way a proportion might appear regardless of actual dimensions or proportions.

visual weight The weight or scale an object appears to have, regardless of actual weight.

vitrify To change into a glasslike ceramic by high heat.

Vitruvian proportions Correct classical proportions as recorded by Vitruvius.

Vitruvius A first-century Roman architect and writer responsible for standardizing classical architectural forms.

volts or voltage The measurement of power that comes through the power line.

volute A spiral or scroll.

W

wainscot Medieval wooden paneling that may or may not reach to the ceiling.

wale A pronounced rib or raised cord that may run vertically with the warp, horizontally with the filling threads or weft, or diagonally as in a twill weave.

wall composition The arrangement of furniture, architectural openings, and accessories against a wall.

wall coverings A general term for paper, cloth, vinyl, and other products designed to be pasted onto walls.

wall washer A general term for a series of lights that wash a wall. These may be recessed adjustable lights or eyeball spotlights, for example.

wallboard A term for rigid wall materials installed in sheets or boards: Sheetrock (gypsum board), Masonite, paneling. Also called drywall.

warm colors The hues on the color wheel generally considered to produce feelings of warmth. They are red-violet, red, red-orange, orange, yellow-orange, yellow, and yellow-green.

warm white deluxe fluorescent lamp Contains a warm light spectrum similar to incandescent lighting.

warp threads or yarns The lengthwise or vertical fabric yarns that are threaded onto the loom and form the basis for woven fabric and rugs.

wash A soft plane of light from spotlights or track lighting.

washable A wallpaper term meaning that the paper can be gently cleaned with a little soap and water.

water closet A toilet.

watercolor Paint made solid with gum arabic and thinned with water. Also a painting created with this type of paint.

waterproofing Coating the building's foundation with a sealant such as a tar mixture, tar paper, or plastic.

water-repellent finish A functional, wet, or standard finish that allows the fabric to shed or repel moisture and stain due to condensation or excessive humidity.

watt or wattage A unit of electric power equal to the power of one ampere (amp) as compared to one volt.

wattle A panel of woven sticks used as infill for timber framing or as fencing materials.

weatherstripping Thin strips of insulation, usually with a sticky side, that insulate around windows and doors to prevent cold air infiltration.

weft threads or yarns Inserted over and under the warp threads to create a woven fabric. Also called filling yarns.

Wegner, Hans (b. 1914) Important Danish furniture craftsman, designer of several modern classic pieces.

welt A fabric-covered piping cord sewn between two pieces of the covering in upholstery.

wet finishes See standard finishes.

wicker A general term for furniture, baskets, or other objects woven from twigs.

Wiener Werkstätte See Vienna Secession.

Wilton Broadloom loop-pile carpeting woven on a Jacquard loom. All colors used in the carpeting are carried beneath the carpet face, creating a thick, heavy carpet.

windbreak Trees, hedges, or fences that provide protection from wind.

window wells The corrugated metal or concrete form that keeps dirt away from basement windows.

windowsill The horizontal ridge or shelf beneath the glass, usually with the frame.

Windsor chair Originally an English chair with cabriole legs and a shaped splat. The Windsor chair became common during the eighteenth century in America and featured a carved seat, spindle back, and turned legs.

wing chair An upholstered easy chair with a high back and wings on each side for resting the head.

wire construction See round wire tufting/weaving.

wiring plan The portion of the blueprints or working drawings that indicate placement of all electric wiring, fixtures, switched outlets, and connections. Also called the lighting plan.

wood blinds Thin flat slats of wood made into miniblinds. They take more stacking space and are more costly than metal miniblinds.

wood filler A paste or liquid used in the wood-finishing process to fill the natural pores of the wood and create a smooth surface.

wood frame or wood truss system The conventional system of framing a building with wood studs, joists, rafters, and beams, reinforced with the herringbone (zigzag) truss system between joists.

wood graining Brushing on a glaze and drawing wood grains and lines with an artist's brush.

wood molding Narrow strips of concave and/or convex wood molding. May also be plastic.

wood plank Flooring of strips of wood. Planks may be laid in even width strips or random plank (three different widths).

wood rods Curtain and drapery rods of solid wood, often fluted.

wood- or coal-burning stove A self-contained stove, usually of cast iron, that burns wood or coal for space heating.

wool Natural protein staple fibers taken from the fleece of sheep and the hairs of goats. Wool—absorbent, resilient, and flame resistant—is used in high-quality upholstery, wall, and window textiles for both residential and nonresidential use. Also used for carpeting. Oriental and folk rugs.

wool rugs A term for natural fiber rugs or carpeting left in its undyed state. The most common is the berber rug.

word-processing programs Software programs that offer options in text writing.

work zones Areas for tasks such as food preparation and office work.

working drawings The final mechanical drawings that are used to obtain bids and construct a design.

Wren, Sir Christopher (1632–1723) One of England's most important and influential architects, responsible for building London's city churches after the great fire of 1666.

Wright, Frank Lloyd (1869–1959) A great American architect who believed that a building should relate to its setting. He designed the complete building, including interiors and furniture.

wrinkle-resistant finish Treating a fabric with a functional finish process so it does not easily wrinkle.

wrought iron Iron that is welded and forged into different shapes.

Y

yarn dyeing Coloring yarn before it is woven or knitted into a fabric.

yo-yo effect Uneven high and low areas along the bottom hemline of a draped fabric due to alternating humidity absorption and drying.

Z

zapata Carved decorative corbel on the porch of the Southwest Adobe house.

zero-clearance fireplace unit A fireplace unit that can be set into combustible walls with no clearance.

zigzag lines Lines that reverse upon themselves in a regular order, such as a herringbone pattern, or in an irregular order, such as a flame pattern.

zones Areas that have similar functions or purposes, such as work zones, social zones, private zones, and storage zones.

Index

A

Aalto, Alvar, 431
Abacus, 374
Abstract design, 76
Acanthus leaves, 375, 377
Accent lighting, 108f, 109, 109f
Accessible design, 47–48
Accessories
    scale of, 220
    use of, 368–69
Accessory apartments, 181
Accordion doors, 256, 256f
Accounts management, 29
Acetate, 332, 332t, 334t
Achromatic (no-color) grays, 90
Acoustical tile, 191, 277t
Acoustic design, 32
Acoustic designers, 34f
Acoustics, 194–95
Acropolis, 374
Acrylic, 332, 335t
Acrylic carpet fibers, 318t
Acrylic paint, 356
Acrylics, 234
Acrylic sheets, 110
"Active" balance, 61–62
Active solar systems, 195–98
Actual density, 68
Adam, Robert, 25, 267, 396, 397
Adaptable compact fluorescent (CF) lighting, 119
Adaptive restoration, 439f, 440
Adaptive reuse, 32, 38f, 41
Adjustable luminaires, 115
Adjustable track lighting, 117
Adobe-style buildings, 414t, 418
Afterimages, 94–95, 99
Air-conditioning. See Heating, ventilation, and air-conditioning (HVAC)
Air exchange, 204
Air-exchange units, 190
Air pollution, in the interior environment, 44–45
Air purifiers, 204
Aisle or egress lighting, 119
Aisles, 379
Albers, Josef, 88
Alloys, 362
All-wood construction, 231
Alternate complement colors, 87
Alternation, 63
Alternative building system methods, 172
Aluminum, 232–33
Ambient bank, 110
Ambient lighting, 108, 112f
Ambulatory, 379
America
    Beaux Arts influence in, 420, 422t
    Dutch influence in, 411
    English influence in, 386
    French influence in, 411
    German influence in, 411
    Seventeenth-century, 389
    Shaker influence, 410
    Spanish influence in, 414

Swedish influence in, 410–11
    See also American styles
American Empire
    color, 405
    console table, 404t
    fainting sofa/Grecian sofa, 404t
    furniture classics, 401
    interior, 404t
    interiors and furniture, 404t
    textiles, 404t
American National Standards Institute, 24
American styles, 396–440
    Federal style (1790-1830), 396–97
    Greek Revival/American empire style (1820-60), 400–405
    Jeffersonian federal, 397
    Modern design (1857-present), 420–40
    Vernacular tradition (seventeenth century-present), 397–400
    Victorian age (1837-1901), 405–10
Americans with Disabilities Act of 1990, 46–47
Ampere or amperage, 114
Amusement park design, 32
Anaglypta, 267, 268f
Analogous color schemes, 84, 85f, 86, 86f
Analysis, 16
Andalusia, 403t
Angled ceilings, 267
Angular (diagonal or zigzag) lines, 69, 70, 71
Animal-hair felt padding, 320
Animal skins, 326, 367
Anne Hathaway Cottage, England, 380f
Anodized, 233
Antehmion, 374
Anthropometrics, 212, 238
Antimony, 362
Antique boxes, 368f
Antique oriental rugs, 322
Antiques, 232
Antiquity, color in, 377
Antistatic, 340
Anything Goes! ® Carpet, 317f
Apartment buildings, 180
Apartments, 180
Appliances, 144, 147–50
    energy usage, 148
    planning considerations, 149
    price point vs. energy costs, 149
    upscale, 139f
Applied design, 76
Apron, 390, 393
Apse, 379
Aquariums, 32, 367
Arcade, 379, 379f
Architects, 29, 69, 184, 187, 188
Architectural details
    cabinetwork, 268
    ceilings, 266–68
    doors, 254–57
    fireplaces and chimneypieces, 264–66
    nonresidential considerations, 268–69
    stairs, 260–63
    walls, 252–54
    windows, 257–60
Architectural elements, balance with furniture, 217
Architectural glazing, 278t
Architectural lighting, 115
Architectural openings, 220
Architectural rodding, 301t

Architectural space planning, 32
    See also Space planning
Architectural techniques, evolution of, 201f
Architecture, 25
    new, 4
    scale of, 59
Architrave, 374
Arch systems, 202t
Area rugs, 321, 321f
Argyle chair, 423, 424t
Armchairs
    Armchair 406, 431, 436t
    Queen Anne, 390, 392t
Armless chair, 242t
Armoire, 246t, 414
Armure, 345
Arnaché, 345–46
Arnold House, 387t
Art and accessories
    decorative art, 360–66
    emotionally supportive design, 369
    fine art, 356–60
    nonresidential considerations, 370–71
    objects from nature, 366–67
    other accessories, 367–68
    overall considerations, 369
Art and accessory dealerships, 32
Art Deco style, 428f–429f, 435
Art glass, 303t
Artificial lighting, 73, 83, 104–10
    fluorescent lighting, 106, 107
    incandescent lighting, 104–5
    low-voltage lighting, 105–6
    strategies, 102f
    tungsten halogen lighting, 105
Artistic lighting, 109
Artist's loft, 159f
Art lighting, 109f, 364
Art nouveau/Jugendstil furniture classics, 423, 424t
Art of Color, The (Itten), 88
Art pieces, hanging, 220, 221f
Arts and Crafts movement, 423, 425
Asbestos, 44, 191, 204
Ashlar, 274t
Asia, influence of, 382–83, 384t
Asymmetrical furniture groupings, 216f, 217
Asymmetrical (informal) balance, 60, 61–62, 61f
Athena, 374
Atria, 45, 46, 377, 378t
Attached dwellings, 175, 180–82
Attic windows, 260
Aubusson rugs, 325
Aubusson tapestry, 327f
Automatic doors, 47f, 49f
Automatic sensor dimmers, 123
Auxiliary heating, 198
Average or mediocre design, 76
Awnings, 46
Awning windows, 258, 258f
Axminster carpets, 319

B

Backfilling, 189
Backlighting, 73
Back panels, 232
Back-to-back plumbing, 193f
Bacteria, 44

Bad design, 76
Baffled ceiling, 34f, 114, 269, 269f
Balance, 58, 60–62
    "active," 61–62
    of architectural elements with furniture, 217
    asymmetrical (informal), 60, 61f–62
    bisymmetrical, 61
    of form, 68
    of furniture, 216–17
    of horizontal, vertical, and curved lines, 69f
    occult, 61–62
    optical, 62
    passive, 61
    radial, 60, 62
    symmetrical (formal), 60f, 61
Balance lighting, 110
Ballasts, 107
Balloon (pouf or cloud) shades, 297t
Baluster, 262
Balustrades, 262, 390, 390f
Bamboo, 236
Bamboo flooring, 42f, 313t
Bamboo shades, 303t
Banisters, 262
Barcelona chair, 433t
Barcelona collection, 431
Barcelona stool, 431
Barcelona table, 431
Baroque period (1580-1750), 386
Barrel vault, 375
Barrier-free design, 48
Barrier-free entrance, 49f
Bartile, 191
Basculant chair, 431, 433t
Baseboard, 254
Baseboard units, 193
Base lighting, toe-mold lighting, 116
Base molding, 254, 254f
Basic human needs, 128
Baskets, 363
Bas-relief, 356
Bast fibers, 332
Bath linens, 366
Bathrooms
    design, 31f
    designed for an assisted living facility, 51f
    family, 154–57
    floor plan, 156f
    master, 153–54, 154f–155t
    mirrors visually expand the space of, 161f
    for motion-impaired individuals, 50
Batik, 346
Batiste, 346
Batting, 236
Batts, 190
Bauhaus school, 25, 429, 430
Bay rods, 301t
Bays, 379, 389
Bay windows, 258, 259f
Bead-and-reel moldings, 374, 377
Beadboard, 253f, 281t
Beamed ceilings, 267–68
Beam systems, 203t
Beauty, in floor materials, 309
Beaux Arts influence (1881-1945), in America, 420, 421f, 422t
Bed linens, 366
Bedrooms, for motion-impaired individuals, 50–51
Beltcourse, 389
Belter, John Henry, 410
Bengaline, 346
Bentwood rocker, 423, 424t
Berber rugs, 326–27
Bergère, 242t
Berms, 13, 201
Bernini, 386
Bertoia, Harry, 434
Bertoia Wire Group, 434, 436t
Beveled, 252, 255
Beveled glass, 360

Beyond™ Home Hub2, 121f
Beyond™ iCEBOX FlipScreen, 120
Bibelots, 360
Bids, 23
Biedermeier, 402
Bifold doors, 256, 256f
Biltmore, 422t
Bird's-eye, 346
Bisymmetrical balance, 61
Blacks, 90
Blanket wrapping, 42
Bleaching, 232
Blinds, 292
Block front furniture, 393
Block print, 357
Blown (loose) insulation, 190
Blueprints. See Working drawings
Board and batten paneling, 253, 254f, 281t
Bold colors, 89
Bonnet roof, 411
Books, 365
Bosses, 380
Bouclé, 346
Bouclé marquisette, 346
Bow-back windsor chair, 402t
Bow rods, 301t
Bow windows, 258, 259f
Box-shaped grouping, 224f
Bracketed cornice, 393
Bracket lighting, 116
Brackets, 380
Braided rugs, 325, 325f
Braille, 53f
Brainstorming, 16, 21
Brass, 233
Breakfronts, 246t, 393
Breast, 264
Breuer, Marcel, 25, 429, 430, 431
Brewster chair, 388t, 389
Brick, 276t–277t, 389
Brick flooring, 312t
Brigham Young University library underground
    addition, 206f–207f
Bright light, 113
Bright-light therapy, 111
Brilliants, 109
British Museum, 374
Brno chair, 431, 433t
Broadcloth, 346
Broadloom carpets, 316, 317–19
Brocade, 191, 347
Brocatelle, 347
Bronze, 363
Brooklyn Bridge, 421
Brown, 90–91
Brownstones, 181
Brushed metal, 233
Bubble planning, 173
Buchram (buckram or crinoline), 347
Buffet, 246t
Buffet-style dining, 210
Builders, 29
Building blocks, 204
Building materials
    indigenous, 15
    representations of, 177f
Built-in indirect lighting, 115
Bullfinch, Charles, 396
Bullnosed, 262
Burlap, 347
Burl veneer, 231
Burn-out, 347
Business skills, 26
Busy lines, 70
Butler, Lee Porter, 201
Butler's pantry, 144
Butler's tray table, 247t
Butterfly table, 247t, 402t
Buttoned upholstery, 237f
Buttressed chimneys, 389

Buttresses, 380
Buying, 32
Byobu screen, 364, 364f, 383, 384t
Byzantium, 383

C

Cabinet, closet, and storage design, 32
Cabinetmakers, 30, 30f
Cabinetwork (cabinetry), 268
    details, 185f
    standard sizes of, 151t
Cable systems, 203t
Cabriole legs, 390
Café curtains, 295t
Calendered (rolled) plastics, 235
Calico, 347
California Ranch House, 419–20
California Spanish missions, 414t
Callicrates, 374
Cambric, 347
Came, 380
Camisole panel, 296t
Candela, candle, or candlepower, 103f, 114
Candelabrum, 63
Cane furniture, 236
Canopy bed, 248t
Canted, 258
Canterbury Cathedral, 379t
Cantilever design, 431
Canvas, 347
Cape Cod Cottage, 397, 400, 401t
Capitals, 374
Carbon dioxide, 44
Carbon monoxide, 44
Careers
    nonresidential interior design, 31–32
    residential interior design, 31
    specialized design, 32
    teaching interior design, 35–36
Carpeting, 316–28, 366
    Broadloom, 316, 317–18
    cost per square yard, 308
    deep-pile, 320t
    durability, 329
    fibers, 317, 318t
    fuse-bonded, 319
    installation and padding, 192, 320
    knitted, 319
    maintenance and cleaning, 321
    needlepunch, 319
    for nonresidential installation, 328–29
    patterned, 42, 328f
    plush, 319f
    rubber-backed tufted, 319
    shag, 320t
    texture, 319–20
    tufted broadloom carpets, 319
    Velvet weave, 319
    wall-to-wall, 321f
    Wilton, 317f, 319
    woven broadloom carpet, 317
Carver chair, 388t, 389
Cased glass, 361
Case goods, 230–31, 232
Casement, 347
Casement draperies, 294t
Casement windows, 258, 380
Casing, 237
Cast iron, 363
Cast-iron pipe, 192
Category 5 unshielded twisted-pair cable, 121
Cathedral ceilings, 267
Cathedral windows, 259, 260f
Caucasian or Turkish rugs, 323, 323f
Caulking, 46
Ceiling boxes, fluorescent, 119
Ceiling fan, 43f

Ceiling lighting, luminous, 108
Ceilings, 266–68
    angled, 267
    architectural details, 266–68
    baffled, 34f, 269, 269f
    beamed, 267–68
    cathedral, 267
    coffered, 63, 268f, 269, 269f
    coved, 268
    flat, 267
    materials, 191
    nonresidential, 305
    plaster, 267
    shed, 267
    structural beamed, 267f
    suspended, 269f
    treatments, 290
    vaulted, 266f
    See also Wall and ceiling materials
Cella, 377
Cellular (honeycomb) shades, 297t
Cellulosic fibers, 332
Cement, 189
Center for Universal Design, 41
Central air-conditioning system, 194
Central air-conditioning unit, 194f
Central heating, 193
Central plumbing, 192–93
Central vacuum systems, 192
Ceramics, 361
Ceramic tile, 276, 277t, 311t
Ceramic tile floor, 328f
Certified Kitchen Designer, 34
Cesca chair, 431, 433t
Chair rails, 60, 254, 254f
Chairs
    Argyle chair, 423, 424t
    Barcelona, 433t
    Basculant, 431, 433t
    bow-back windsor, 402t
    Brewster, 388t, 389
    Brno, 431, 433t
    Carver, 388t, 389
    Cesca, 431, 433t
    THE Chair, 434, 436t
    Chinese, 384t
    Chinese Chippendale, 384f, 396t
    Chippendale, 393, 395t, 396t
    club, 244t
    Comb-back windsor, 402t
    Corbu, 424t
    Country French ladder-back, 417t
    Dante, 286, 385t
    Duncan Phyfe, 404t
    Eames lounge chair, 434, 434f
    Egg Chair, 434, 436t
    ergonomic, 240, 240f
    Fledermaus, 423, 424t
    Grand Confort, 431
    Hepplewhite shield-back, 399t
    Hill chair, 423, 424t
    Hitchcock, 402, 404t
    ladder-back, 244t, 245t, 400, 402t, 413t, 414
    Lawson lounge chair, 242t
    MR chair, 431, 433t
    Number Seven Chair, 434, 436t
    occasional, 217
    open armchairs, 241t
    Pedestal Chair, 436t
    Petit Confort chair, 431
    Platner Chair, 434, 436t
    Prague, 423, 424t
    Queen Anne, 390, 392t
    Shaker, 410
    Sheraton Square-back, 399t
    Stickley armchair, 427t
    tub, 244t
    Victorian Belter/Rococo Revival armchair, 409t
    Victorian Gothic Revival, 409t
    Victorian Renaissance Revival side chair, 410t

    Vienna cafe chair, 424t
    Wassily lounge chair, 430
    Windsor, 242t, 400
    wing, 244t
    x-frame, 386
Chaise longues, 243t–244t, 431
Chambray, 347
Chandeliers, 115, 364f, 365
Chelsea Royal Hospital, London, 389
Chenille, 347
Chest of drawers, 245t, 246t
Chest on chest, 245t
Chevreul, 84, 87
Chevron, 70, 347
Chiffon, 347
Children's spaces, 9f, 157f–158
Chimneypiece, 264
China (tableware), 361
Chinese chairs, 384t
Chinese Chippendale chairs, 384t, 396t
Chinese cupboard, 384t
Chinese design, 382
Chinese fretwork, 393
Chinese porcelain, 382
Chinese porcelain vase, 384t
Chinese rugs, 324, 324f, 382, 384t
Chinese tables, 384t
Chinese textiles, 384t
Chinoiserie, 382
Chintz, 347
Chipboard, 230
Chippendale, Thomas: *The Gentlemen and Cabinet-Maker's Director*, 393
Chippendale block-front chest, 395t
Chippendale breakfront, 393, 395t
Chippendale camel-back sofa, 393, 395t
Chippendale chairs, 393
    ladder-back chair, 396t
    side chair, 396t
    wing chair, 395t
Chippendale furniture, 393, 394t–396t
    highboy, 393
    Philadelphia highboy, 395t
    secretary, 231f
    tilt-top table, 396t
Choic (quire), 379
Chopped urethane, 320
Chroma, 88, 99
Chromatic distribution, law of, 90
Chromium (chrome), 233
Chrysler Building, 429, 429f
Churchill, Winston, 4, 238
Circular grouping, 224f
Circular lines, 70
Circulation, 210
City of London, 389
Clapboard, 389
Classical details, 376t
Classical Roman designs, 375
Classicism, 252
Classics, 356
Cleanup, 147
Clearance, 193, 212, 212f–213f
Clerestory windows, 45, 46, 258–59, 259f, 379f, 380
Climate, 10, 12
    affect on color, 83
    mild, 11f
    and shape of space, 175
Cloisonné, 364
Closed floor plan, 175
Closed showrooms, 340
Closed stair (enclosed by walls), 262f
Closets, for motion-impaired individuals, 51
Club chairs, 244t
Club feet, 390
Coal-burning stoves, 193
Codes, 16, 24
Coffered ceilings, 63, 268f, 269, 269f
Coffers, 268
Coil springs, 236

Coir, 332
Cold-air returns, 193, 210
Cold-cathode lighting, 104, 107, 118
Cold-cathode light sculpture, nonresidential interior, 112f
Collections, 368–69
    of British locomotives and rail cars, 370f
    Japanese approach to displaying, 368
    Victorian approach to displaying, 368–69
Collectors, 197
Colonnade, 374
Color, 59, 66f, 74
    alternate complement, 87
    in antiquity, 377
    Art Deco, 429
    bold, 89
    complementary, 86, 86f
    cool, 84, 94, 96f
    deep value, 162f
    deficiency, 82
    direct complement, 85f, 86
    distinctive, 83f
    double complement, 86
    high-contrast, 89
    in hospitality facilities, 98–99
    how we see, 82–83
    intensity, 74
    in medical facilities, 98
    medieval, 380, 382
    in mid-century design, 435
    in nonresidential interiors, 98–100
    in office interiors, 99
    placement, 92
    in production plants, 99–100
    progression, 63
    Renaissance, 386
    in residential interiors, 97–98
    in restaurant settings, 100f
    Seventeenth-century America, 389
    spectral, 82
    subtractive, 82
    tetrad complement, 86
    and texture, 92
    trends, 95, 97
    triadic complement, 86
    values, 74
    Victorian era, 410
    visually determines scale, 59
    warm, 84, 94, 95f
    washing, 286f
    Wedgewood jasperware, 397
Color Association of the United States (CAUS), 97
Color associations, common, 95t
Color consultants, 97
Colored lighting, 113
    fluorescent, 107
    incandescent, 104
Color-group models, 94
Color harmony
    considerations in, 88–90
    neutralized colors, 89–90
    neutrals, 90–92
Color-influencing factors
    climate, 83
    color placement, 92
    light, 92f
    seasons, 83
    texture and material, 92
    value distribution and contrast, 92–93
Coloring, 339, 340
Color Marketing Group (CMG), 97
Color mixing
    optical, 82
    subtractive, 82
Color Notation, 87
Color organizations, 97t
Color Primer, The (Ostwald), 88
Color psychology, 74
    afterimage simultaneous contrast, 94–95
    color trend market, 95–97

Color samples, 89
Color schemes, 72
    monochromatic, 84, 85f, 86f
    neutralized, 89–90, 97–98, 98f
    split complementary, 85f
Color theory
    Munsell theory, 87–88
    Standard Color-Wheel Theory, 84–87
    subtractive, 82
Color wheel, 74, 84f–87
Columns, 252, 374
Comb-back windsor chair, 402t
Combination felt padding, 320
Combination (open and closed) plans, 175
Combination wood furniture, 231
Combing, 286f
Combustion lighting, 83, 103–4
"C.O.M." (customer's own material), 237
Communication design, 32
Communication systems, 125
Compact fluorescent lamps (CFL), 45, 106f, 107
Compacting, 189
Complementary color scheme, 86, 86f
Composite order, 377, 378t
Compounded textiles, 336
Compression ring, 203t
Computer-aided design and drafting (CADD), 29, 32, 36, 173, 186
Computer-generated animations, 27, 29
Computer-generated drawings, 25f, 29f
Computer networks, 125
Computers, 27, 29
Computer skills, 26
Computer software, 186
Concept development, 16–21
Concepts, 16
Conceptual drawings, 21
Concrete, 189, 276t–277t
Concrete block, 276
Concrete flooring, 312t
Conduction, 198, 198f
Cones, 82
Conservation, 39, 193, 201
Console table, 247t
Constructing the building, 188–201
Construction details, 186f
Construction documents, 186–87
Construction drawings, 21
Construction/project management, 32
Consulting fees, 36
Contemporary trends
    deconstructivism, 435, 437
    high-tech, 435
    postmodern, 435
Continuing education units (CEUs), 27
Contract design, 23
Contrast, 63
Control, 198
Convection, 198, 198f
Conventional design, 76
Conventional traverse rods, 300t
Conversational distance, 215f
Cooktop arrangements, for motion-impaired individuals, 50f
Cool-beam lamp, 113
Cool colors, 84, 94, 96f
Cool lighting, 83
Cool white deluxe lamps, 107
Coped, 253
Copper, 233, 362
Copper pipe, 192
Corbel brackets, 419, 419t
Corbu chair, 424t
Corduory, 347
Corinthian order, 374, 375, 375f
    Roman, 377
Cork, 281t, 315t
Corner blocks, 231
Corner fireplace, 265, 265f
Cornice lighting, 116

Cornice moldings, 254, 255f
Cornices, 298, 374, 390
Coromandel, 364, 382
Coromandel screen, 363f, 384t
Corwin House, 387t
Cost
    floor coverings, 308–9
    maintenance, 15–16
    not the issue in design, 76–77
    per square foot, 133, 174
    replacement, 15
Cottage curtains, 295t
Cotton rugs, 328, 333t
Counter dimensions, for motion-impaired individuals, 50f
Country French, 413t
    armoire, 417t
    interior, 417t
    ladder-back chair, 417t
    panetière, 417t
    sleigh bed, 417t
    textile, 417t
Courses, 383
Coved ceilings, 268
Cove molding, 254, 255f
Coverings, of upholstered furniture, 237
Crackle finishes, 286f
Craftsman magazine, 425
Craftsman style, 423f–425f, 426t–427t
    color, 425
    Craftsman Bungalow, 287f, 426t
    eight-light door, 427t
    furniture classics, 425
    shed dormer, 426t
Craftspeople, 27, 30, 30f
Creative lighting, 83f
Creativity, 79
Crepe, 347
Cretonne, 347
Crewel embroidery, 347
Crinoline, 347, 348
Critical path, 188, 195, 196t
Cropping, 360
Crossing, 379
Cross sections, 185f, 187, 188f
Crowding, 215
Crown (bed) moldings, 254, 254f
Crown lintels, 393
Cruciform, 379
Crypt, 379
Crystal, 362
Cubic footage, 173
    calculation of, 173f
Culture
    and ideas of comfort and function, 238
    and proxemic patterns, 212, 214
    relationships, 13
Cupola, 390, 390f
Curios, 360
Curtain rods, 300t
Curtains, 294, 295t–296t
Curtain wall construction, 201f, 204
Curved lines, 69, 70, 71
Curved staircase, 263
Curved walls, 174f
Cushioning, for upholstered furniture, 236
Custom cabinets, 268f, 269
Custom designs, 240
Custom floor plans, 183–84
Custom ("to-order") building, 25
Cutaway view, 188f
Cut glass, 361
Cut-pile, 319

D

Dado, 252, 252f, 287f
Dado cap, 254

Dado molding, 60
Damage, inspection for, 21
Damask, 348
Damper, 264
Dante chair, 385t, 386
Dark values, 93, 93f, 99
Data management, 29
Daub, 380
David Brewster Color theory. *See* Standard Color-Wheel Theory
Deacon's Bench, 401t
Debt-to-income, 134
Deconstructive design, 435, 437, 438f
Decorative arts, 25
    baskets, 363
    books, 365
    clocks, 363
    decorative lighting fixtures, 364–65
    mirrors, 360
    screens, 363–64
    tableware and cookware, 360–63
    textiles, 365–66
Decorative design, 75f, 76
Decorative fabric glossary, 345–53
Decorative finishes, 340
Decorative luminaire lamps, 109
Decorator rods, 300t
Deep-pile carpets, 320t
Deep value colors, make a space feel smaller, 162f
Defects, 183
Deforestation, 42
Dehumidifier, 194, 194f
Demographics, household, 7
Denim, 348
Dentil ornament, 375, 390
Dentil trim, 390
Design
    concept statement, 17
    considerations, 39
    discernment and excellence, 76–79
    emotionally supportive, 369
    for the handicapped, 32
    for large gatherings, 32
    preferences, 16
    specialties and related factors, 32t
    for 21st century living, 165f
Design centers, 28f
Design development, 16–23
    design concept development, 16–21
    execution, 21–22
    working drawings and specifications, 21
Design elements. *See* Elements of design
Designer 800, 82f
Designer fees, 36
Designer rugs, 326, 327f
Design longevity, and sustainability, 40–41
Design principles. *See* Principles of Design
Design process, 5t
    letter of agreement, 5
    nonresidential considerations, 23–24
    postoccupancy evaluation, 23
    problem statement, 6
    research and programming, 6–16
Design-review commissions, 41
De Stijl movement, 429
Details, 29f, 187
deWolfe, Elsie, 25
dhurrie rugs, 324
Diagonal lines, 70
Diagramming, and floor plans, 173–75
Diffuser lenses, 119
Diffusers, 115
Digital subscriber lines (DSLs), 122
Dimity, 348
Dimmable fluorescent lighting, 107
Dimming controls, 119, 123
Dining cabinetry, 147
Direct complement colors, 85f, 86
Direct glare, 114
Direct glue-down, 320

Direct lighting, 108
Direct solar gain, 198, 199f, 200f
Disabled persons, accessibility, 24
Discernment, power of, 76
Dishwashers, 149
Distinctive objects, 15f
Distressed, 232
Distribution, 198
Doctor of philosophy (Ph.D.), 35
Do-it-yourself building, 187–88
Domes, 267
Domestic oriental rugs, 326
Dome systems, 203t
Doorjamb, 256
Doors, 254–57
Doric order, 374, 375, 375f
  Roman, 377
Dormers, 260
Dotted Swiss, 348
Double cloth, 348
Double complement colors, 86
Double glazing, 258, 258f
Double-hung sash window, 259
Double-turn stair, 263, 263f
Dovetail joints, 232
Dowels, 231–32
Down cushions, 237
Draft dodgers, 195
Drafting, 26, 32
Draperies, 294t–295t
Drapery hardware, 294, 300t–301t
Draw draperies, 294t
Drawings, 356, 357
Drop-leaf occasional table, 397
Dropped-pendant luminaires, 115
Drum, 383
Drywall, 191
DuBarry red, 397
Duck, 348
Ductwork, 193, 194f, 204
Dulux, 82f
Duncan Phyfe, 402
  chair, 404t
  flap-top table, 404t
Duplex, 180
Durability, 15
  of floor materials, 309
  of furniture for nonresidential use, 249
Durable finishes, 339
Durable press calendering, 340
Dust panels, 232
Dutch Colonial, 411
Dutch design, 412t
Dutch doors, 257, 257f
Dutch influence, in America, 411
Dyckman House, 412t
Dyeing, 340
Dyestuffs, 82

E

Eames, Charles, 434
Eames, Ray, 434
Eames lounge chair, 434, 434f, 436t
Early Christian style, 377
Early Georgian style (1695-1750), 386, 389–90,
  391t–392t, 397
  color, 390
  furniture classics, 390
  interior, 391t
  textiles, 392t
Earthenware, 361
Easements, 262
East India Company, 382
Eastlake, Charles: *Hints on Household Taste*, 405, 410
Eastlake style, 410
Echinus, 374
Echo noise, 13

Eclectic styles, 405
Economic factors, 14–16
Edgar J. Kaufmann residence, 425
Egg-and-dart motif, 63, 374, 377
Egg Chair, 434, 436t
Egyptian Revival, 407t
Electrical raceways, 122–23
Electricians, 26f
Electricity, measuring, 114t
Elements of Color, The (Itten), 88
Elements of design, 58, 59t, 66–67
  color, 74
  light, 73–74
  line, 69–71
  mass, 68–69
  pattern, 71–73
  shape or form, 67–68
  space, 66–67
  texture, 71
Elevation, 29f
Elgin, Lord, 374
Elgin Marbles, 374
E-mail, 29
Embellishment, 389
Embroidery, 338t, 348
Emotionally supportive design, 369
Emphasis, 58, 63–64
  in furniture arrangements, 217–18
  placement of, 71
Empire State Building, 201f, 429
Enameled glass, 361
Energy conservation
  active and passive solar systems, 195–201
  and lighting, 45–46
  and windows, 46
  and window treatments, 305
Energy consumption, minimizing, 43f
Energy Guide labels, 148, 149
Energy Star label, 148, 149
English Gothic, 379t
Engravings, 357
Entablatures, 374, 383, 401
Entertainment center design, 32
Entertainment rooms, 159
Entryway planning, 136, 139
Envelope concept, 201
Environmental considerations, 10–13, 39–46
  air pollution in the interior environment, 44–45
  green design, 32, 42–43
  lighting and energy conservation, 45–46
  sustainability, 39–42
  water conservation, 42
  windows and energy conservation, 46
Environmental hazards, 13
"Environmentally Preferable Products," 43
Environmental Protection Agency (EPA), 43
Environmental safety, 32
Equilibrium, 60
Ergonomics, 75, 238–39
  chairs, 240f
  nonresidential furniture, 240, 249
  placement of the computer screen, 239f
  superchairs, 240
Etamerism, 82–83
Etched glass, 360, 361
Etchings, 357
Ethics, 39
European rugs, 325
Evaporative cooling system, 194
Excellent or fine design, 76
Execution, 21–22
Exhaust, 44
Existing home, buying, 182–83
Exotic woods, 42, 383
Exposed aggregate flooring, 309t
Exterior elevations, 186–87
Exterior finishing, 191
Exterior veneer, 190
Extruded materials, 204, 232
Extruded textiles, 336

Eye, training, 77–79
Eyeball lighting, 117
Eyeball spotlights, 107f, 108
Eyelet, 348

F

Fabric art, 366
Fabricators, 30
Fabric-covered wall, 289–90
Fabric glossary, 345–53
Fabrics
  aesthetics, 341–45
  color coordination guidelines, 343t
  construction, 336–38t
  durability, 344
  dyeing and printing, 339t
  fibers, 332–36
  finishes, 339–40
  flexibility, 342, 344
  humanizing of interiors, 341
  livability, 342
  maintenance guidelines, 336, 336t
  nonresidential considerations, 345
  obtaining, 340
  pattern, 342
  texture, 342, 344f, 344t
  versatility, 340–45
  weight and applications, 345t
Fabric wall coverings, 290t
Fabric window shades, 294, 297t
Facade, 383
Face weight, 329
Facilities management, 33
Facilities managers, 33f
Faille, 348
Fallingwater, 425, 428, 428f
Familiarity, 14
Family bathrooms, 154–57, 156f
Family room, with billiard table, 158f
Fanlights, 257, 258, 258f, 397, 398t
Farnsworth House, 431f
Fascia, 191
Fashion
  changing, 5, 97
  vs. longevity, 41
Fauteuil, 241t, 412
Federal style, 396–97, 398t
  color, 397
  elliptic fanlight, 258f
  furniture classics, 397
  houses, 396
  textiles, 399t
Feldspar, 361
Felt padding, 320, 348
Festoons, 298t
Fiber felt padding, 320
Fiberglass, 278t
Fibers, 332–36
  carpet, 317, 318t
  comparison of, 333t–336t
  fuzzing, 344
  man-made, 332, 332t, 334t–335t, 341
  pilling, 344
Fieldstone, 274t
Filaments, 332, 332t
Filling, 339
Financial considerations, 36
Financing, 134
Fine art, 356–60
  drawing, 357
  mosaic, 357
  obtaining, 358–60
  paintings, 356–57
  preparing for display, 360
  printmaking, 357–58
  rubbings, reproductions, and graphic art, 358
  sculpture, 356

Finial, 393
Finish carpenters, 268
Finished pile weight, 329
Finishes, 21
    antique, 232
    chemical, 340
    crackle, 286f
    decorative, 340
    durable, 339
    functional, 340
    mechanical, 340
    natural, 232
    nondurable, 339
    paint, 284t
    soil-repellent, 340
    soluble, 339
    standard, 340
    surface treatment, 340
    verdigris, 233
    water-repellent, 340
    wet, 340
    wood, 232
Finishing, 339
Finish package, 191
Finish plumbing, 192
Fire alert systems, 124, 125
Firebox, 264
Fire extinguishers, 14
Fireplaces, 104, 139f, 193, 264f–266
    components, 264f
    inserts, 193, 266
    lighting from, 109
Fire prevention, 14
Fireproof shingles, 191
Fish tanks, 367
Fixed windows, 258
Fixtures
    installation, 192
    standard sizes of, 151t
Flagstone, 310t
Flame-retardant, 340
Flamestitch, 70, 348
Flannel, 348
Flap-top table, 247t
Flat inverted box pleat valances, 298t
Flat Roman shades, 297t
Flats, 181
Flatwork, 189
Fledermaus chair, 423, 424t
Flexibility, planning for, 163–64
Flexible wall covering, 289
Flickering lighting, 113
Flitch, 231
Floccati (flokati) rugs, 327
Floor coverings
    calculations and costs, 308–9
    floor requirements and specifications, 308–9
    hard and resilient, 309–16
    nonresidential considerations, 328–29
    rugs, 321–28
    soft floor coverings, 316–18
Floor lamps, 108, 364
Floor plans, 172–73, 186
    defined, 173
    design, 32
    and diagramming, 173–75
    evolution of, 128f
    fourplex, 180f
    and housing, 175–88
    obtaining, 183–86
    one-and-one-half-story, 178f
    split-level home, 180f
    split-level home, remodeled, 183f
    symbols, 175
    two phases of schematics or graphics in the
        evolution of, 163f, 172f
    two-story, 179f
    types, 175
Flounce top panel, 296t
Flowers, 366f, 367

Flowing lines, 69, 70
Flue, 264
Fluorescent lamps, 45, 73
Fluorescent luminaires, 83, 104, 106f–107
    compact, 106f
    retrofitted, 119
    shapes of, 106f
Fluoresces, 106
Flush doors, 255, 255f
Flush-face fireplace, 264, 265f
Fluted, 374
Flying buttresses, 204, 380
Foam back, 348
Foam blocks, 190
Foam rubber pads, 320
Foams, 204, 237, 320
Focal point, 63–64, 65f
    primary and secondary, 217–18
Folded plate systems, 203t
Folk rugs, 324–26
Food preparation countertop-cabinet-top areas, 146
Food storage cabinetry, 146
Footcandle or footlambert, 114
Forced-air heating, 193
Forensic consultation, 33
Forest management, 42
Form, 59, 66f
Formal curtains, 296t
Formaldehyde, 45
Formal space, 139, 141f
Formal symmetrical balance, 60f
"Form follows function," 75
Form (shape), 59, 66f, 67f–68
    balance of, 68
    "Form follows function," 75
    and furniture arrangement, 220
Foster, Norman, 435
Foundation drawings, 187
Foundation for Interior Design Education and
    Research (FIDER), 26
Foundations, 189
Fourplex, 181
Four-poster bed, 248t
Frames, art, 360
Frames, for upholstered furniture, 236
Frame system, 202t
Framing, 189–91
Framing plans, 184f, 187
Freestanding fireplace, 266
Freezers, 149
French Aubusson rugs, 326f
French Baroque designs, 386
French casement window, 259f
French design, 413t
French doors, 5f, 256–57, 257f
    with a round fanlight, 256f
French Empire, 402
French furniture classics, 412–14
French influence, in America, 411
French neoclassical
    bergère, 416t
    bureau plat, 416t
    fauteuil, 416t
    interior, 416t
    textiles, 416t
French Régence, 412
French Renaissance style, 422t
French Rococo/Louis XV design, 415t–416t
French Savonnerie rugs, 326f, 327f
Fresco, 357
Fretwork, 382
Frieze or Frisé, 348, 374
Frieze yarns, 319f
Front doorway, 254–55
Full-aniline leather, 235
Fuller, Buckminster, 203t
Full-grain leather, 235
Full-spectrum light, 82, 102
Function, 136
    and culture, 238

and furniture, 210–12, 238
and lifestyle, 7–8
multi-functional design, 11f
and nonresidential space planning, 164–68
and space planning, 128, 129
Functional finishes, 340
Fungi, 44
Furnace, 193
Furniture
    design, 33
    harmony, 237–39
    identification, 241t, 248t
    restaurant, 248f
    "suites" of, 237–39
    types, 239–40
Furniture arrangement
    balance, scale, and mass, 216–17
    and circulation, 210
    combined functions, 210, 211f
    for conversation, 215
    and electric and phone connections, 210
    elements and principles of design, 216–22
    emphasis, 217–18
    form and space, 219–20
    function, 210–12
    human factors, 212–16
    line and harmony, 218–19
    mechanical functions, 210
    nonresidential considerations, 225–27
    and proportion, 221–22
    rhythm, 217
    in a square room, 221f
    See also Furniture groupings; Furniture selection
Furniture groupings
    box-shaped groupings, 223
    circular groupings, 223–24
    L-shaped groupings, 223
    parallel groupings, 224
    solo groupings, 224–25
    straight-line groupings, 222–23
    U-shaped groupings, 223
Furniture retail sales or rental business, 33
Furniture selection
    anthropometrics and ergonomics, 238–39
    function, 238, 238f
    metal furniture, 232–34
    nonresidential considerations, 240, 249
    other furniture materials, 234–36
    upholstered furniture, 236–37
    wooden furniture, 230–32
Fuse-bonded carpets, 319
Fusuma, 364

G

Gabardine, 348
Gable, 374
Gabled house, 400
Galerie, 411
Gallery style hanging, 221f
Gamble House, 426t
Gambrel roof, 389
Game rooms, 222
Garbage disposals, 150
Gateleg table, 247t, 388t, 402t
Gauze, 349
Gehry, Frank O., 204f, 437
General and ambient lighting, 107, 107f
General contractors, 29, 187, 188
General zones, 128f
Generic fibers, 332
Genuine, 231
Geodesic domes, 203t
Geometric design, 76
George I, 389
George II, 389
George III, 389
George IV, 389, 402
Georgian era, 389

German influence, in America, 411
German/Pennsylvania Dutch design, 412t
Ghirardelli Square, San Francisco, 440
Gibbs, James: *A Book of Architecture*, 393
Gilded glass, 362
Gimp, 349
Ginger jars, 364
Glare, 73, 113–14, 119
    natural, 102
    types of, 114t
Glass, 278t–279t
Glass block, 278t
Glass doors, 255
"Glass house," 430f
Glassware, 361–62
Glazes, 361
Glazing (transparent paints), 257–58, 283
Glides, 232
Goddard, John, 393
Gold electroplate, 362
Golden mean, 60
Golden rectangles, 60
Golden section, 60, 60f
Gold leaf, 362
Good or fair design, 76
Good taste, cultivating, 79
Gothic Revival, 405, 406t
Gothic style, 377, 379, 381t
    arch, 379
    Church, cross section, 381t
    Church, interior elevation, 381t
    Church plan, 381t
    structural block construction with flying
        buttresses, 201f
Gouache, 357
Governor's Palace, 391t
Grab bars, 50, 51f
Graceful aging, 309
Gradation, 63
Grains, 230
Grand Confort chair, 431, 433t
Grandfather clocks, 363
Grandmother clocks, 363
Granite, 274t, 310t
Granite countertops, 277t
Graphic art, 358, 358f
Graphic design and illustration, 33
Graphics, 173
Graves, Michael, 435
Gray, 90
Grazes, 110
Great hall, 161
Great rooms, 13, 161
    features and trends for, 143–44
Greece (fifth century B.C.)
    architecture, 374
    colors of, 377
    design, 376t
    furniture classics, 375
    orders, 374–75f, 376t
    temple form, 400
Greek Revival, 400–405, 400f, 403t
Greenbelts, 41
Green design, 173, 201
    of an award-winning New York skyscraper, 205f
    assistance for designers, 42–43
Greene, Charles, 423
Greene, Henry, 423
Greene brothers, 382, 423
Greenery, 367
Greenhouse, 113
    dining area in, 14f
    rooms, 200f
    and solarium design, 33
Greenhouse effect, 198
Greenhouse window, 259, 260f
Green products, 42
Green spaces, 41
Grenadine, 349
Gretchen Bellinger, Inc., 375

Griswold House, 408t
Grommet panel, 296t
Gropius, Walter, 25, 429
Grosgrain, 349
Grounding receiver, 124
Guggenheim Museum, Bilbao, Spain, 438f
Gum arabic, 356
Gym-spa facility, 166
Gypsum board, 191

H

Hall, Edward T., 212
Halls Croft, 382t
Halogen lamps, 45, 104f
Hammer-beam ceilings, 266
Handrail, 262
Handrail diagram, 49f
Hangings, 366
Hard and resilient floor materials
    guidelines for selecting, 309–16
    for nonresidential settings, 328
Hardboard, 230
Hard Rock Café, Dallas, Texas, 371f
Hard-surface floor-covering design, 33
Hardware
    case goods, 232
    design, 33
Hardwood, 230
Harmony, 58, 63, 64–66
    color, 88–92
    floor materials, 309
    furniture, 237–39
    placement of furniture, 219, 219f
Haughwout Building, 421
Health-care facilities. See Medical facilities
Health club/recreational facility design, 33
Hearst Castle, 421f
Hearth, 264
Heat gain, 291
Heating, ventilation, and air-conditioning (HVAC),
    10, 13, 193–94
    fresh-aid intakes for, 45
    heat pump, 194
    microbial contamination, 44
    in nonresidential interiors, 204
Heat loss, 292
Heat setting, 339
Heavy mass, 68
Hepplewhite
    bow-back sofa, 399t
    shield-back chair, 399t
    sideboard (buffet), 399t
Hepplewhite, George: *The Cabinet-Maker and
    Upholsterer's Guide*, 397
Hepplewhite/Sheraton furniture
    Pembroke table, 397, 399t
    sideboard or buffet, 397
Herculaneum, 377
Heritance® hardwood shutters, 293f
Herringbone, 70, 336f, 349
HID (high-intensity discharge) lighting, 104, 116, 118
High-contrast colors, 74, 89, 93, 94, 109
High-efficiency furnace, 193
High-key interiors, 93f
High-tech clocks, 363
High-Tech design, 435, 435f
High-technology devices, 188
High values, 93
Hill chair, 423, 424t
Hipped roof, 383, 390, 393
Hispanic, 364
Historic buildings
    early influences, 374–86
    homes, 77
    mass density as the measure of strength, 204
Historic furniture pieces, 68

Historic preservation, 33
Hitchcock, Henry-Russell, 429
Hitchcock, Lambert, 402
Hitchcock chair, 402, 404t
Hobby areas, 159
Hoffmann, Josef, 423
Hollow core, 255
Holograms, 110
Home automation system
    controls for programming, 138f
    for existing houses, 121f–122
Home builder, 187
Home designer, 186
Home Insurance Building, 421
Home office
    located within a family room, 141f
    planning, 139, 141
    station with ergonomic chair and natural light,
        144f
    where to locate, 141–43
HomePad refrigerator with computer screen, 148f
Homespun, 349
Home theater, 158
Hong Kong, square feet per person, 175
Hong Kong and Shanghai Bank, 435
Hooded fireplace, 265, 265f
Hooked rugs, 325
Hook-ups, 192
Hopsacking, 349
Horizontal lines, 70, 71
Horseshoe arch, 383
Hospital design, 168f, 169f
Hospitality facilities
    colors and patterns, 98–99
    design, 23f, 33
    space planning, 167
Hospitals, space planning, 167
Hotels, 167
Houndstooth, 349
Hourglasses, 363
Housed stair, 263
Housing
    floor plans and, 175–88
    types of, 175–82
Housing-to-income ratio, 134
Hue, 74, 87–88
Hue identity, 88–89
Human factors
    anthropometrics, 212
    crowding, 215
    proxemics, 212–15
    standard clearances, 212
    territoriality, 215–16
Human scale, 59
Humidifiers, 193
Hunt, Richard Morris, 420
Hutch, 246t, 400
Hybrid solar energy system, 198

I

Ictinus, 374
Ikebana, 367
Illusion lighting, 118
Incandescent (common filament) lamps, 45, 73, 104,
    105t
Incandescent luminaires, 83, 104–5
    retrofitting, 119
Incident solar radiation (insolation), 195
Indian dhurrie rugs, 324f
Indirect and isolated passive solar gain, 198–99
Indirect lighting, 113, 116t
Indo-Aubusson rugs, 324
Indoor air quality, nonresidential spaces, 204
Indoor-outdoor living, 158
Industrial facilities, 33
Industrial Revolution, 405
Infill, 380

Informal balance, 62
Information-age home automation systems, 120–21
Information-age wiring and installation, 121
Infrared (IR), 122
Inglenook, 426t
In-house corporate design, 33
Inquisition, 386
Installers of materials, 30
Insulating Concrete Forms (ICF), 190
Insulation, 10, 13, 172–73, 190, 195
    window frames, 46
    window treatments, 195
Intaglio, 357
Integrated solarium, 200f
Intensity, 88
Interaction, 13
Interaction of Color (Albers), 88
Intercom systems, 124f
    in nonresidential installations, 125
    wiring, 125
Interest rates, 134–35
Interfacing, 349
Interior design
    careers in, 31–36
    future of, 36
    language of, 3
    need for, 4–5
    profession of, 24–36
    residential and nonresidential, 3–4
    resources, 27–36
    skills, 25–26
Interior Design Bookshop, New York City, 28f
Interior design education programs, topics of study, 27t
Interior designers
    must understand the aspects of construction, 188
    oversee the work of fabricators, 26f
    training and professional development, 26–27
    work closely with subcontractors, 26f
    work with fabric samples, catalogs and computers, 29f
Interior elevations, 187
Interior environmental control systems, 172, 190
Interior finish components, 172, 191–92
Interior lighting, manipulating mood with, 113
Interior space, shaping, 175
Interlining, 349
Intermediate hue, 84
International Business Machines (IBM), Purchase, New York, 73f
International Colour Authority (ICA), 97
International Conference of Building Officials, 24
International style, 252, 428f, 429–31, 430f, 431f, 432t–433t
    furniture classics, 430–31
The International Style, 429
Internet, 27, 29
Intimate distance, 212, 214f
Inverted pleat draperies, 295t
Ionic Capital, with decorative details, 376t
Ionic order, 374, 375, 375f
    Roman, 377
Iron, 233
Islamic design, 383
Italianate style, 406t
Itten, Johannes, 88

Jack arch lintels, 393
Jacobsen, Arne, 434
Jacquard loom, 317
Jacquard weave, 336f, 337f, 338t, 339, 349
Jalousie window, 259, 260f
Jeannert-Gris, Charles-Edouard (Le Corbusier), 431
Jefferson, Thomas, 397
Jeffersonian Federal, 397
Jenney, William Le Baron, 421

Jersey, 349
"Jesuit" style, 386
Johnson, Philip, 429
Joining methods, 231–32
Joints, 231
Joists, 190
Journalism, 33
Justice design, 34
Jute, 332, 333t
Juxtaposition of hues, 92

Kandinsky, Wassily, 25, 430
Kaolin, 361
Kelly Wearstler Interior Design, Los Angeles, 24f
Keystone House, 437f
Khaki, 349
Kilim rugs, 324
Kilowatt-hour, 114
Kitchen linens, 366
Kitchen planning
    cabinetry considerations for, 146t–147t
    working triangles, 150f
    zones and the working triangle, 144–50
Kitchens
    contemporary, 148f
    with custom design elements, 145f
    design, 34
    designers, 33f
    features and trends for, 143–44
    and great room planning, 143–50
    heart of many homes, 13
    for motion-impaired individuals, 50
    structurally designed, 74f
    well-planned, 144f
Kitsch, 76, 360
Klismos, 375
Klismos, with Saber legs, 376t
Knee-hole desk, 245t
Knickknacks, 368
Knit, 336, 349
Knitted carpets, 319
Knoll International, 434
Kohler Ingenium flushing system, 42f

Lace, 349
Lacquer, 232, 233
Lacquer work, 382
Ladder-back, 393
Ladder-back chairs, 244t, 245t, 400, 402t, 413t, 414
Laminated (sandwiched) foam, 237
Laminate flooring, 313t–314t, 314t
Lamination, 230
Lamp, 45
Lampas, 349
Lamp shades, 105t
Lancets, 380
Landings, 262
Landscaping, 34
Lanterns, 383
Lappet, 349
Large-scale furnishings, 59
Large space, 67
Larkin, Thomas, 420
Larkin House, 421t
Laser lights, 110
Late Georgian style (1750-90), 390–95, 394t–396t
    color, 393
    furniture classics, 393
    interior, 394t
    textiles, 396t
Late medieval (Tudor) style, 380, 382t, 422t
Latex, 319

Latillas, 268, 418, 419t
Latin cross, 379
Latrobe, Benjamin, 396
Lattice screens, 363
Laundry room planning, 151–52
Law, 34
Lawn, 349
Law of Chromatic Distribution, 90, 90f
Law office design, 34
Lawson lounge chair, 242t
Layered or compounded fabrics, 336, 338t
Leaded glass, 360, 380
Leadenhall Market, 435f
Leadership in Energy and Environmental Design (LEED™) Green Building Rating System, 42–43, 44
Lead paint, 204
Leather, 332, 334t
Leather floor materials, 315t
Leather furniture, 234f, 235
L'École des Beaux Arts, 420
Le Corbusier, 429
LEDs (light-emitting diodes), 119
Leno, 350
Letter of agreement, 5, 36
Level loop, 320t
Level-tip cut and loop texture, 320t
Library design, 34, 142f, 143
    reception area, 166
Licensing, 27
Life-cycle costing, floor materials, 309
Life safety, nonresidential buildings, 208
Lifestyle profiles, 7, 8
Light, 59
    affects all other elements, 73
    affects pattern, 73–74
    affects the perception and appearance of color, 92f
    measuring, 114t
    and the mind and body, 110–14
    plane of, 110
    pool of, 110
    quantity of, 257
    spectral, 82
Lighting, 13
    accent, 108f, 109, 109f
    adaptable compact fluorescent (CF), 119
    adjustable track, 117
    aisle or egress, 119
    ambient, 108, 112f
    architectural, 115
    art, 109f–110
    backlighting, 73
    balance, 110
    and balance of furniture arrangement, 217
    base, 116
    bracket, 116
    bright, 113
    built-in indirect, 115
    candlelight, 103f
    cold-cathode, 104, 107, 118
    cool, 83
    cornice, 116
    creative, 83f
    as design element, 102
    direct, 108
    as element of design, 34, 73–74
    and energy conservation, 45–46
    eyeball, 117
    fireplace, 109
    fixed and adjustable, 117t
    flickering, 113
    full-spectrum, 82
    for the future, 115–16
    general, 107, 107f
    HID (high-intensity discharge), 116, 118
    illusion, 118
    indirect, 113, 116t
    library, 143
    line, 110
    luminous ceiling, 108
    mood, 109, 113

motivational, 118
natural, 45, 46, 73, 73f, 102–4, 111f, 116
nonarchitectural, 115
outline, 110
perimeter, 110, 110f
pinpoint, 110
point, 110
riser, 116
safety, 119
silhouette, 110
soffit, 116, 191
strip, 117
structural, 115
task, 108, 108f
toe-kick, 116
track, 108
valance, 116
  See also Artificial lighting; Luminaires
Lighting economy, 115, 117t, 119
Lighting effects, categories of, 107–10
Lighting fixtures, 115, 124, 364–65
Light pipes, 45, 46, 110
Light switches, 123
Limestone, 274t, 310t
Line, 59, 66f, 69f–71
  combining, 71
  and furniture arrangement, 219, 219f
  psychological effects of, 70t
Line lighting, 110
Linen, 332, 333t
Linenfold, 252
Linenfold panel, 252f
Linens, 365f–366
Lining, 350
Linoleum, 315t
Linoleum block print, 357
Lintel, 374
Lithographs, 357
Lloyd's of London, 435, 435f, 437f
Load-bearing walls, 190
"Location, location, and location," 183
Log cabin, 410–11, 411t
London shades, 297t
Long-life bulbs, 114
Long-term care facility, reception area, 54f
Longwood, Natchez, Mississippi, 405f, 407t
Loose cushions, 237
Louis XV design, 412
Louis XVI design, 386, 410, 414
Louvered doors, 256, 256f
Louvered shutters, 292
Louvers, 363
Lowboy, 390
Low contrast, 74
Low-E glazing, 46
Low-key scheme, 93, 93f
Low values, 93
L-shaped groupings, 223f
Lumber core, 255
Lumens, 114
Luminaires, 104, 115, 364
  decorative, 109
  fixed and adjustable, 115
  fluorescent, 83, 104, 106f–107
  portable, 108, 115
Luminance, 102
Luminous ceiling lighting, 108
Luminous panels, 115
Lux, 114
Luxury apartments, 181
Lyocell, 335t–336t

M

Machine-made rugs, 326
MacIntosh rose design, 337f
Mackintosh, Charles Rennie, 25, 423
MacPhaedris-Warner House, 390f

Madame John's Legacy, 413t
Maintenance costs, 15–16
Maison Carrée, 377, 378t, 397
Maize, 332
Maize mats, 327
Malimo, 350
Management, 34
Man-made fibers, 332, 332t, 341
  cellulosic, 334t
  noncellulosic/synthetic, 334t–335t
Mansard style, 407t
Mantel, 264
Manufacturer's representatives, 34
Marble, 304f, 310t
Marketing, 35
Marketing centers, 27
Marlborough leg, 393
Marquetry, 231
Marquisette, 350
Marriage chest, 411
Marts, 28f
Masonite, 230
Masonry block construction, 202t
Mass, 59, 68–69, 216, 216f, 217
Massing, 68–69, 68f
Master bathroom, 153–54, 154f–155t
Master bedroom, utilizing vertical open attic space, 153f
Master of arts (M.A.), 35
Master of fine arts (M.F.A.), 35
Master of science (M.S.), 35
Masters, 356
Master suite planning, 152–54
Mat, 360
Matelassé, 350
Materials
  and color, 92
  selection of, 16, 21
Materials boards, 21
McIntire, Samuel, 25, 396
Mechanical finishes, 340
Media, 77–78, 356
Media room, 158, 158f
Medical facilities, 33, 35
  philosophy of color, 98
  space planning, 167
Medici Palace, Florence, Italy, 383f
Medium-density fiberboard (MDF), 230
Melamines, 234
Melk Abbey, Austria, 386f
Mememto, 369
Memorabilia, 369
Mercerizing, 339
Metal, 278t–279t, 279t
Metal, types of, 232–34
Metal furniture, 232–34
  types of metal, 232–34
  used in outdoor settings, 233f
Metal or space frame, 202t
Metal shingles, 191
Metals tableware and cookware, 362
Metal tieback holders, 301t
Metamerism, 82f
Metopes, 374
Mexican tile, 277t, 311t
Mid-century design, 434f, 435
Middle Ages (800-1500), 377–82
  color, 380, 382
  design, 381t
  domestic design, 380
Midtones, 93
Mies van der Rohe, Ludwig, 25, 429, 431
Mildew, 44
Miniblinds, 303t
Mirror, 278t–279t, 279t
Mitering, 253
Miter joints, 232
Mobile home, 179
Modacrylic, 335t
Model homes, 77

Modern design (1857-present), 420–40
  art deco (1981-45), 428–29
  art nouveau/Jugendstil (1890-1910), 423, 424t
  contemporary trends, 435–40
  craftsman style (1905-1929), 423–25
  Frank Lloyd Wright's organic architecture (1908-present), 425, 428
  International style (1932-present), 429–31
  Scandinavian and mid-century design, 431, 434–35
Modern textiles, 433t
Modest living
  example of, 40f
  and sustainability, 39–40
Modillions, 383, 390
Moiré, 350
Mold, 44
Molded plastic doors, 255–56
Molding, 192f, 253–54, 255
Monitoring, 29
Monochromatic color scheme, 84, 85f, 86f
Monterey design, 420, 421t
Monticello, 397
Mood lighting, 109, 113
Moors, 364
Morgan, Julia, 421f
MoriMoto Restaurant, Philadelphia, 113f
Morris, William, 25, 425
Mortgage payment, comparison of monthly, 135t
Mortise and tenon, 232
Mosaic, 356, 357
Motels, 167
Mothproofing, 340
Motion impairment, design recommendations for people with, 48–51
Motivational lighting, 118
Motorized rods, 301t
Mount Pleasant, 394t
Movable insulation, 195
MR chair, 431, 433t
Mullions, 380
Multi-functional design, 11f
Multiple-outlet strips, 124
Multiplex units, 180–81
Multiuse areas, 136, 161
Munsell, Albert H., 87
Munsell color notation system, 87f, 88
Munsell color wheel, 87f, 97
Munsell theory, 87–88, 92
Museum design, 35
Muslin, 350
Mylar, 350

N

Napoleon, 402
Naps, 237
National Association of Home Builders (NAHB), 120, 173
National Council for Interior Design Qualification (NCIDQ) examination, 27
National Trust for Historic Preservation, 440
Native American accessories, 15f
Natural cellulosic fibers, 333t
Natural fiber rugs, 326–28
Natural fibers, 332
Natural finishes, 232
Naturalistic design, 76
Natural light, 45, 46, 73, 73f, 102–4
  into the interior, 111f
  in nonresidential settings, 116
Natural Protein fibers, 333t–334t
Natural saturation point, 88
Natural thermal flow, 198
Natural traffic pattern, 211, 212f
Natural wool rugs, 328
Nature, 78
Navajo rugs, 324–25, 325f
Nave, 379

Near Eastern Islamic cultures, 383
Near Eastern screens, 364
Needle-constructed fabrics, 336, 338t
Needlepoint, 350
Needlepoint rugs, 325
Needlepunch carpets, 319
Negative space, 67, 220, 220f
Neoclassic high position, 293f
Neoclassic style, 396
Neon lights, 107, 118
Nesting tables, 63, 246t
Net, 350
Networking
    with clients, 29
    with other designers, 29
Neutralized colors, 89–90, 97–98, 98f
Neutralized yellow, 89f
Neutrals, 90–92, 98f
    examples of interiors furnished in, 91f
New architecture, requires complete designs, 4
New construction, 130
    flexibility in planning and customizing, 131f
    master bedroom with luxury features, 131f
    rules, 132–33
    traditional character, 133f
Newel post, 262
New oriental rugs, 322
New Orleans French town houses, 411
Niche paint, 287f
Niches, 267
Ninon, 350
Nitrogen oxides, 44
Nogging, 380
Noise control, 13, 194
Nonarchitectural lighting, 115
Noncellulosic fibers, 332
Nondurable finishes, 339
Nonglare glass, 360
Nonrenewable resources, 39
Nonresidential spaces, 3f–4, 23–24
    carpets, 320, 329
    communication and safety systems, 125
    details, 268–69
    fabric specifications, 346t
    flat fee for designing interiors, 36
    furniture design, 225–26, 227, 240, 249
    lighting, 116, 119
    materials, 304–5, 306
    noise control, 194
    plumbing, HVAC, and indoor air quality, 204–8
    profile for, 23
    space planning, 164–68
    using advanced technology, 204f
    wall coverings, 304
    wiring, 124
Nonresilient flooring materials, 308
Nonwoven textiles, 336, 338t
Norman style, 377
Northern Light, 111
Nosing, 262
Notre Dame de Chartres Cathedral, 379f, 381t
Nova products, 238f, 239f
Novelty twills, 338t
Nubuck, 235
Number Seven Chair, 434, 436t
Nylon, 334t
Nylon carpet fibers, 318t

O

Objets d'art, 360
Occasional chairs, 217
Occult balance, 61–62
Oculus, 377
Off-black, 90
Off-gassing, 44, 45

Office buildings
    color trends, 99
    design, 35
    space planning, 168
Off-white, 90
Oil paintings, 356, 356f
Olefin, 332, 335t
Olefin/Polypropylene carpet fibers, 318t
One-and-one-half story floor plans, 179
One-inch movable louver shutters, 303t
One-turn stair, 263
One-turn stair (with landing), 263, 263f
Onion dome, 383
Online real estate services, 183
Open armchairs, 241t
Open arrangement, 10f
Open floor plan, 161–62, 175
Open-riser stair, 262
Open showroom, 340
Open stair (no walls), 262f, 263
Operable windows, 258
Opposition, 63
Optical balance, 62
Optical color mixing, 82
Optical density, 68
Orange peel, 191
Orders, of Greek architecture, 374
Ordinary incandescent lamps, 114
Organdy, 350
Organic design, 428, 430
Organization, and modest living, 39–40
Organized clutter, 369f
Oriental grasses, 332
Oriental philosophies, 62
Oriental Revival, 383, 405f, 407t
Oriental rugs, 321–24
    Caucasian or Turkish rugs, 323
    Chinese rugs, 324
    Persian prayer rugs, 323
    Persian rugs, 322
    Tibetan rugs, 323–24
Orientation, 83, 102
    and need for light and glare control, 292
    and shape of the space, 175
    and windows, 257
Ornament, visually determines scale, 59
Ornamentive design, 76
Ostwald, Wilhelm, 88
Ostwald theory, 88
Ottoman fabric, 350
Ottomans, 68, 242t
Outbuildings, 390
Outdoor living space, 157f
Outline lighting, 110
Ovens/ranges/cooktops, 149
Overcrowding, 175
Overhands, 46
Overlays, 173
Oxford cloth, 350
Oxford plaid, 336f
Ozone, 44

P

Pacific Design Center, Los Angeles, California ("the Blue Whale"), 30f
Pad and tackless strip, 320
Padding, 236
Paint, 282–86
    contrasting color on trim, 283f
    finishes, 284t
    painting guidelines, 283–84
    paint-texturizing techniques, 285t
    texturing techniques, 286f
    types of, 284t
Painters, 26f
Paintings, 356–57, 359f, 370f
    hanging, 221f

Paisley, 350
Palace of the Governors, 418t
Palace of Versailles, 386
Palazzo Rucellai, 385t
Palette knives, 356
Palette theory. *See* Standard Color-Wheel Theory
Palisade wall, 253
Palladian manner, 393
Palladian window, 257, 258, 258f, 393, 394t
Palladio, Andrea, 383
Paneled doors, 255, 255f
Paneling, 252
Pantheon, Rome, 375f, 377, 378t
Papier-mâché, 234
Parallel groupings, 225f
Parapet wall, 393
Parisian pleat draperies, 295t
PAR lamp, 105
Parquet, 313t
Parthenon, 374, 376t
Particleboard, 230
Passive balance, 61
Passive solar systems, 198–201, 198f
Pastels, 90
Paterae, 396
Patina, 78, 309, 362
Patio home, 179
Pattern books, 383, 396
Patterned carpet, 42, 328f
Patterned fabric, guidelines for coordinating, 343t
Pattern psychology, 73
Patterns, 59, 71–73
    character of, 72
    combined, 71–73, 72f
    scale of, 72
    visually determine scale, 59
Pedestal Chair, 436t
Pedestal group, 431, 434
Pedestal table, 247t
Pediment frieze, 374
Pediments, 374, 390, 393
Pellon, 350
Pembroke table, 247t
Pendants, 389
Pendelton blanket patterns, 15f
Pennsylvania Dutch, 411
Pennsylvania Dutch marriage chest, 412t
Percale, 350
Perfa-tape, 191
Perimeter lighting, 110, 110f
Peristyle, 377, 378t
Persian Oriental rugs, 322, 322f, 323f, 384t
Persian prayer rugs, 323, 323f
"Personal digital assistant," 188
Personal distance, 214, 214f
Personal pieces, 4f, 6f
Personal space, 79, 214
Personal style, finding, 79
Perspective sketches, 173
Pewter, 362
Phidias, 374
Philadelphia highboy, 393
Phosphorus, 106
Photo Therapeutics, 111
Physical location, 12–13
Physically handicapped, making buildings accessible to, 24
Piano nobile, 63, 383
Pictures, hanging, 220
Pied-è-terre, 181–82
Piers, 379
Pigments, 82, 235, 356
Pilasters, 252, 252f, 383, 390, 393, 401
Pile density, 329
Pile fabric, 351
Pile weave, 338t, 339
Piña, 332
Pingree House, 398t
Pink, 96f
Pinpoint lighting, 110

Piqué, 351
Plaid, 351
Plain basket weave, 338t
Plain leno weave, 338t
Plain oxford weave, 338t
Plain slicing, 231
Plain weave, 336f, 338t, 339
Plan drawing, 218
Plane of light, 110
Plantation shutters, 303t
Plants, 366–67
    toxins, 45
Plasterboard, 191
Plaster ceilings, 267
Plasters, 280t
Plastics, 204
    furniture materials, 234–35
    informal tableware and accessories, 363
Plate rail, 252
Platner, Warren, 434
Platner Chair, 434, 436t
Platner Collection, 434–35
Pleated shades, 297t
Plenum, 269
    egress lighting connected through, 208f
    systems in, 208f
    systems within, 208
Plexiglas, 260, 360
Plies, 230
Plissé, 351
Plumbing chase, 192, 204
Plumbing fixture design, 35
Plumbing systems, 13, 192–93
    for nonresidential interiors, 204
    three stages of, 189
Plush carpets, 319f
Plywood, 230
Pneumatic systems, 203t
Pocket doors, 163, 256, 256f
Podium, 377
Point lighting, 110
Polished cotton, 351
Pollution, 39
Polyester, 332, 335t
    batting, 237
    carpet fibers, 318t
Polylactic acid fiber (PLA), 335t
Polyurethane, 232, 234
Polyurethane foam, 237
Pompadour blue, 397
Pompeii, 377
    house plan, 378t
Pony Chaise, 431, 433t
Poor design, 76
Poplin, 351
Porcelain, 361
Portable appliances, 150
Portable luminaires, 108, 115
Portable space heaters, 193
Portal, 419
Porthole windows, 258, 258f
Portico, 377, 401
Portuguese needlepoint rugs, 326f
Positive space, 67
Posters, 358f
Postmodern design, 435, 437f
Postoccupancy evaluation (POE), 23
Potpourri, 363
Power-line carrier (PLC) systems, 121–22
Prague chair, 423, 424t
Prairie style, 425, 425f
Prang theory. *See* Standard Color-Wheel Theory
Prefinished, 339
Presbyterian Church, 406t
Presentation boards, 22f
Preservation, 438, 440
Preshrinking, 339
Pressed glass, 361
Pretil, 419
Prevailing winds, 12–13

Primary focal point, 218, 218f
Primary hues, 84
Principles of design, 58–66
    balance, 60
    emphasis, 63–64
    harmony, 64–66
    proportion, 59–60
    rhythm, 62–63
    scale, 58–59
Printing, 340
Printmaking, 356, 357–58
Priscilla curtains, 295t
Privacy, 13
    draperies, 294t
    and windows, 257
Private zones, 129, 130f
Problem statement, 6
Product design, 35
Product evaluation, 35
Production plants, 99–100
Product searches, 29
Professional organizations, 30–31
Professionals in related fields, 29–30
Profile, 7
Programming, 6–16
    codes, 16
    design preferences, 16
    economic factors, 14–16
    environmental factors, 10–13
    lifestyle and function, 7–8
    mechanical considerations, 13
    psychological and sociological considerations, 13–14
    relationships, 8
    space requirements, 8, 10
    users, 7
Progression, 63
Projecting fireplace, 265, 265f
Project management, 29, 172
Proportion, 58, 136
    of decoration, 76
    and furniture arrangement, 221–22
    of a long narrow room, 222f
    ratio and, 59–60
Protein fibers, 332
Provincial settings, 362
Proxemics, 212–15
Psychological space, 10
Psychology of color, 74
Public distance, 214, 215f
Publicity and public relations (PR), 35
Public spaces, 77, 168
Public transportation, space planning, 167
Pueblo Indian design, 13
Pueblos, 418
Punch list, 195, 197t
Purchasing agent, 35
PVC polyvinyl chloride pipe, 192

Q

Quadplex, 181
Quarry tile, 277t, 312t
Quarter slicing, 231
Queen Anne style, 389, 390, 391t–392t, 409t
    armchair, 390, 392t
    chairs, 390
    Highboy, 392t
    tea table, 390, 392t
    wing chair, 390, 392t
Quicksilver, 360
Quilted fabric, 351
Quoins, 389

R

Rachel, Raschel knit, 351
Radial balance, 60, 62
Radiant heat, 193
Radiation, 63, 198, 198f
Radiator, 193
Radio frequency (RF) transmission, 122
Radon gases, 44, 45
Rafters, 190
Ragging or rag rolling, 286f
Rag rugs, 325, 325f
Rails, 252
Rainbow roofs, 400
Rain gutters, 191
Raised hearth, 265
Raised numerals, 53f
Raised ranch style, 179
Rambler, 179
Ramie, 332
Rammed earth, 43f
Ramps, 46, 48
Ranch style, 179
Random cut and loop texture, 320t
Rapid-start fluorescent lamps, 107
Ratio and proportion, 59–60
Rattan, 235–36
Raw-fiber stage, 332
Rayon, 332, 332t, 334t
Real estate developer, 35
Rebar, 189
Rebond, 320
Recessed downlights, 111f, 117
Recessed luminaires, 115
Recycling, 39, 42, 201
"Reduce, reuse, recycle, and repair," 39, 41
Reeded legs, 397
Refinement, 173
Reflecting glare, 114
Reflective lamps, 105t
Reformation, 386
Refract, 13
Refrigerators, 149
Refurbishing, 5, 132f
Régence (Pre-Rococo) fauteuil, 415t
Regency design, 402
Registers, 193
Reinforced concrete, 189
Relationships
    of each function, 8
    well-defined, 8f
Relaxed Roman, 297t
Relief designs, 374
Relief printing, 357
Remodeler, 187
Remodeling, 5, 131–33
    advantages of, 132
    disadvantages of, 132
    older homes, 133f
    plans, 182f
    rules of, 132–33
Remote-control devices, 119
Renaissance (1420-1650), 252, 383–86, 385t
    color, 386
    furniture classics, 383, 386
    palace, 383
    textiles, 385t
Renaissance Revival, 410
Rendering, 21, 22f, 35, 173
Renewable resources, 39
Rep, Repp, 351
Repetition, 62f–63
Reproductions, 358
Residential build-in systems, 124–25
Residential program, 17t–20t
Residential space, 2f, 7
    analyzing the design of, 77f
    for 21st century living, 165f

and well-being, 4
wiring plan, 122f
Resilient flooring materials, 308, 314, 315t–316t
Resource efficiency, and sustainability, 39
Resources, 39
Restaurants
colors, 100f
design, 35
space planning, 167
Restoration, 33, 440
Restrictive covenants, 174
Retail design, 35, 99
Retailers, 30, 35
Retainer fee, 36
Retrofitting, 46, 198
Reupholstering, 42
Reverberation, 13
Reversible cushions, 237
RG-6 quad-shielded coaxial cable, 121
Rhythm, 58, 62–63
by gradation, 62f
by opposition, 63f
in placement of furniture, 217
by radiation, 64f
Ribs, 380
Rice to Riches, effective lighting, 104f
Richfield Oil Building, 429
Riser, 262
Riser lighting, 116
River cobbles, 274t
Robie House, 425f
Robsjohn-Gibbings, T. H., 375
Rockefeller Center, 429
Rocks, 367
Rocky Mountain Institute, 45
Rococo Revival, 405, 410
Rococo style, 412, 414
bergère, 415t
Bureau-à-Cylindre, 415t
commode, 415t
console table, 415t
fauteuil, 415t
textiles, 415t
Rods, 82
Rogers, Richard, 435
Roller shades, 303t
Rollikan rugs, 325
Rolltop desk, 245t
Roman arch, 378t
Roman design, 378t
Roman domestic design, 377
Romanesque, 377, 381t
Romanesque arches, 381t
Romanian kilim, 324f
Roman orders, 375, 375f, 377, 378t
Roman shades, 297t
Roman temple, 252, 377
Rome (200 B.C.-A.D. 400), 375–77
Roof, 190–91
Roof monitors, 199, 199f
Roof overhand, 200f
Roof trusses, 190
Room-sized rugs, 321f
Rotary slicing, 231
Rotunda, 267, 377
Rough electrical, 190
Rough heating, 190
Rough materials, 194
Rough plumbing, 190, 192, 192f, 204
Roundheaded arch, 375
Roundheaded fanlight, 393
Round windows, 258
Round-wire construction, 320t
Row houses, 181, 420
Rubber-backed tufted carpets, 319
Rubber floor materials, 315t
Rubbings, 358
Rubble, 274t
Rugs, 321–28, 366
authentic oriental rugs, 321–24

designer rugs, 326
European handmade rugs, 325
folk rugs, 324–26
machine-made rugs, 326
natural fiber rugs, 326–28
for nonresidential installation, 328–29
Rush furniture, 236
Ruskin, John, 425
Rusticated, 383
R-value, 46
Rya rugs, 325

S

Saarinen, Eero, 431
Safety, 14
environmental, 32
floor materials, 309
lighting, 119
nonresidential buildings, 208
Sailcloth, 351
Salon design, 35
Saltbox roofs, 389
Salt Lake City International Airport, 370f
San Carlos de Borromeo, 414, 414t
Sandstone, 274t
San José y Miguel de Aguayo, 414
San Xavier del Bac, 414
Saran, 332
Saridis S. A., 375
Sash curtains, 296t
Sash window (nine over nine), 260f
Sash windows, 259, 261f, 390
Sateen, 351
Satin, 351
Satin weave, 338t, 339
Sausage turnings, 400
Savonarola chair, 385t, 386
Savonnerie rugs, 325
Scale, 58–59
of architecture, 59
of windows and room space, 58f
Scandinavian and mid-century furniture classics, 431,
434–35, 436t
Scandinavian book case, 41f
Scandinavian rya rugs, 325f
Scheduling, 187, 188, 190f
Schematics, 16, 21, 22f
Schiffli, 351
Schools of art, 356
Sconces, 108, 364f, 365
Scottish Lomond Clan Tartan, 336f
Screens, 363–64
Scrim, 351
Scroll pediments, 386f, 390
Sculpture, 356
Sculptured multilevel textures, 319f
Sea shells, 367
Season, affect on color, 83
Seasonal affective disorder (SAD), 111, 113
Secondary focal point, 218
Secondary hues, 84
Secretary, 245t, 393
Security, 14, 257
Security systems, 14, 124, 125
Seersucker, 352
Segmental pediments, 378t, 390
Self-valanced draperies, 291f
Semianiline (protected) aniline, 235
Semiantique oriental rugs, 322
Semi-detached house plan, 181f
Semi-detached houses, 181
Semi-housed stair, 263
curved, 263f
wall on one side, 262f
Serge, 352
Sericulture, 332
Serigraphy, 357

Serpentine-shaped, 393
Service areas, 33f
Service/storage cabinetry, 147
Set design, 35
Settees, 242t, 243t
Seventeenth-century English medieval style (1608-95),
386–89, 387t–388t
Sevres blue, 397
Shade cloth, 352
Shades, 89, 291f, 292f, 294, 297t, 303t
Shade trees, 46
Shading devices, 195, 291
Shadows-on-the-Teche, 403t
Shag carpets, 320t
Shaker candlestand, 411t
Shaker chair, 410
Shaker design, 411t
Shaker rocker, 411t
Shakers, influence in America, 410
Shake shingles, 191
Shantung, 352
Shape. See Form
Shaped valances, 298t
Shed ceilings, 267
Sheer draperies, 294t
Sheer fabric, 352
Sheetrock, 191, 192f, 267, 291f
Sheet vinyl, 308, 316t
Shellac, 232
Sheraton, Thomas: The Cabinet-Maker and Upholsterer's
Drawing Book, 397
Sheraton Square-back chair, 399t
Shibusa, 89
Shingles, 190
Shingle-style, Kragsyde, 408t
Shirred, 296t, 298t
Shoji screens, 257, 257f, 303t, 364, 382
Shopping malls and retail stores, space planning, 167
Showcase homes, 77, 78f
Showroom designer, 35
Showrooms, 28f, 340
"Sick-building syndrome," 44, 204
Side chairs, 241t, 390
Side draperies, 305f
Sidelights, 259, 260f, 396, 397, 398t, 400
Signage graphics, 33
Silhouette lighting, 110
Silhouette shades, 291f
Silk, 334t
Silkscreen, 357
Silver, 362
Silvering, 360
Silver plate, 362
Simultaneous contrast, 94–95
Single family residence (SFR), 175, 179
Single glazing, 258, 258f
Single-hung sash window, 259
Sinks, 150
Sinuous wire (no-sag) springs, 236
Sisal, 332
Sisal mats, 327
Site, 12, 175
Site plans, 187
Skins, 204
Skylights, 45, 46, 111f, 118f, 200f, 260, 260f
Skyscrapers, 204, 421
Slab, 276
Slab stone, 308f
Slab system, 202t
Slash-and-burn farming, 42
Slate, 273f, 311t
Slate roofs, 380
Sleigh bed, 248t
Sliding glass door, 255f
Sliding windows, 260, 261f
Slipcovers, 237
Slubs, 352
Small-scale details, 59f
Small-scale furnishings, 59
Small spaces, 66–67

Smoke detectors, 14, 124, 124f
Smoking, 45
Social distance, 214, 215f
Social zones, 128–29, 130f
Sofas, 243t
Soffit lighting, 116, 191
Soft floor coverings, carpeting, 316–28
Soft sculpture, 366
Soft window coverings, 290, 293–94
Softwood, 230
Soil-release, 340
Soil-repellent finish, 340
Solar design, 35
Solar energy, 172
Solar exposure, 13
Solar gain, 257, 291
Solar greenhouses, 199, 199f
Solarium, 113
Solar systems, 198–201
    active, 195–98
Solid, 231
Solid core, 255
Solo grouping, 225f
Soluble finishes, 339
Sound board, 190
Sound waves, 13
Southwest adobe style, 414, 418t–419t
Southwest textiles, 419t
Spa Café, Cliff Lodge, Snowbird, Utah, 103f
Space frames, 204
Space heating, 193
Space planning, 59
    brainstorming, 129–30
    children's spaces, 157–58f
    economic considerations, 133–34
    entry or foyer, 136, 139
    factors that affect economy, 134
    family bathrooms, 154–57
    features and benefits, 136
    for flexibility, 163–64
    formal living spaces, 139
    functional analysis, 128
    for furniture arrangement, 220–21
    hobby and special-use areas, 159
    home office, 139, 141–43
    indoor-outdoor living, 158
    interrelating functions, 129
    kitchen and great room, 143–50
    laundry room, 151–52
    library, 143
    living with less space, 161
    long-range, 135–36
    making large spaces seem smaller, 162
    master suite, 152–54
    measurements of, 173–75
    media and entertainment rooms, 158–59
    new construction *versus* remodeling, 130–33
    nonresidential considerations, 164–70
    and the principles and elements of design, 160–64
    prioritizing needs and wants, 128
    residential, for the human scale, 136t
    shaping, 175
    space-reducing devices, 162
    space requirements, 8–10
    space-restricting devices, 66
    space-saving devices, 161–62
    storage, 159–60
    stretching space, 161
    traffic patterns, 162–63
    unequal allotment, 66
Spanish influence, in America, 414
Spanish missions, 414
Special design considerations, as fundamental goals, 55
Special needs users, considerations for, 46–48
Special populations, design for, 48–54
    elderly, 53
    hearing impaired, 51–52
    motion impaired, 48–51
    visually impaired, 52

Special-use areas, 159
Specifications, 21, 29, 187
Spectral colors, 82
Spectral energy distribution, 83
Spectral light, 82
Spinnerette, 332, 332t
Spiral staircase, 263, 263f
Split complementary color scheme, 85f, 86
Split entry, 179
Split level, 179
Split spindles, 389
Sponge rubber pads, 320
Sponging, 286f
Spotlights, 108, 110f
Springs, for upholstered furniture, 236
Square footage, 173–75
    calculation of, 173f
    proportional to the cost of the building or home, 133
St. Paul's Cathedral, 389
Stability, 14
Stained glass, 303t, 380
Stainless steel, 233, 362
Stains, 232
Staircases, 260–63, 262f, 263f
    components, 262f
    traditional, 263f
Standard Color-Wheel Theory, 84–87
Standard finishes, 340
Standard ring top panel, 296t
Stanton Hall, Natchez, Mississippi, 400f
Starting step, 262
State House, Richmond, Virginia, 397
Steel
    for nonresidential furniture and fittings, 233
    weathering, 233
Steel-framed houses, 189, 204
Stemware, 362
Steps, 48
Sterling II, 362
Sterling silver, 362
Stewardship, 40
Stickley, Gustav, 423, 425
Stickley armchair, 427t
Stickley cabinet, 427t
Stickley settee, 427t
Stick style, 408t
Stiles, 252
Stock plans, 186
Stone, 274t–275t, 308
Stone-enders, 389
Stone flooring, 309t–311t
Stoneware, 361
Storage, 159–60, 159f, 197–98
Storm windows, 258
Stout, Doug, 370f
Stoves, 266
Straight (horizontal or vertical) lines, 69
Straight-line grouping, at the Grand Hotel on Mackinac Island, Michigan, 222f
Straight lines, 70
Straight run, 263
Straight-run stair, 263f
Stretchers, 389, 390
Strié, 352
Stringcourse, 389
Stringer, 262
Strip lighting, 117
Structural building components and systems, 172
    acoustics, 194–95
    foundation, 189
    framing, 189–91
    HVAC systems, 193–94
    interior finish components, 191–92
    interior systems, 190–91
    nonresidential buildings, 202t–203t
    for nonresidential interiors, 201–8
    plumbing systems, 192–93
Structural design, 74f, 75–76
Structural lighting, 115

Structural soundness, 183
Structured wiring, 121
Stylobate, 374
Subcontractors, 30, 187, 188
    hiring yourself, 187
Subfloors, 190, 309
Subtractive color theory, 82
Suede, 235
Suedecloth, 352
Sunbrella® fiber trims, 337f
Sundials, 363
Sunflower chest, 388t
Sun room, 200f
Superinsulated structure, 190
Surface-mounted downlights, 117
Surface-mounted luminaires, 115
Surface treatment finishes, 340
Surrounds, 191–92, 264
Suspended ceilings, 269, 269f
Suspended luminaires, 115
Sustainability, 39–42, 201
Swag holders, 301t
Swags, 298t, 305f
Swamp cooler, 194, 194f
Swatch board, 28f
Swedish influence, in America, 410–11
Swinging doors, 163
Swiss fabric, 352
Switched outlets, 123–24
Switches, 123
Symbols
    for appliances, walls, stairs, and mechanical support equipment, 176f
    door and window, 176f
    plumbing fixture, 176f
Symmetrical (formal) balance, 60, 61
Symmetrical furniture groupings, 216f, 217
Symmetry, 61f
Synthetic fibers, 332
Systems furniture, 42, 226f, 239–40, 239f
    maintenance of, 33f
    planning for, 226–27

T

Tab curtains, 296t
Table desk, 245t
Table lamps, 108, 118f, 364, 364f
Table linens, 365–66
Tableware, 360–63
Tableware storage cabinetry, 147
Tackless strips, 320f
Taffeta, 352
Tall case clock, 245t
Tapestry, 352, 365, 366
Tar paper, 190
Task lighting, 108, 108f
Tatmi mats, 327–28
Tea caddies, 364
Tea table, 247t
Technical drawing, 26
Technology, 119–20
Technology tools, 172
Telecommunication device for the deaf (TDD), 52
Telephone systems, 13, 125
Tempera, 357
Tempered glass doors, 255
Tensile systems, 203t
Terrace houses (row houses), 396
Terrazzo, 310t
Territoriality, 215–16
Territorial style, 419, 419t, 420f
Terry, 352
Terry cloths, 338t
Tesserae, 357
Tetrad complement colors, 86
Textile art, 327f
Textile design, 35

Textiles, 365–66
Texture, 59, 71
    of carpeting, 319–20
    and color, 92
    fabrics, 342, 344f, 344t
    under foot, 52f
    of log walls, 72f
    and upkeep, 71
    variety of smooth and interesting, 71f
    wall, 280t
Textured door handle, 52f
Textured polyester, 352
Texturizing, 191
Texturizing yarns, 332
Thatched, 380
THE Chair, 434, 436t
Theory of design, 58
Therapeutic light devices, 111
Thermal pane, 258
Thermoplastics, 234
Thermoset plastics, 234
Thermosiphoning, 199, 199f
Thermostat, 193, 198
Thiel, Philip: *Visual Awareness and Design,* 94
Thin shell membranes, 203t
Thonet, Michael, 423
Thoroughgood House, 387t
Three-dimension shapes, 68
Three-part casement window with leaded panes, 388t
Tibetan rugs, 323f
Ticking, 352
Tieback draperies, 60, 295t
Tieback holder, 301t
Tiered curtains, 295t
Tightly curved lines, 70
Tight superinsulation, 190
Tile, 276t–277t, 311t–312t
    flooring, 308f
    installation costs for, 308
Tilt-top table, 246t
Timber-framed houses, 380
Tints, 89–90
Titlement, 27
Title registration acts, 36
Tobacco smoke, 44
Toe-kick lighting, 116
Toe-mold lighting, 116
Toile, 352
Toilet
    diagonal approach, 51f
    side approach, 51f
Tokonoma, 368, 368f
Tones, 90
Tongue-and-groove, 253
    paneling, 254f
Top grain leather, 235
Top treatments, 294
    types of, 298t–299t
Torchère, 364
Town houses, 181, 420
Tracery, 257, 380
Track lighting, 108
Trademarks, 332
Trade names, 332
Trade resources, 27
Traffic patterns, 162–63, 172f
    and furniture arrangement, 210–12f
    nonresidential buildings, 168, 170
    nonresidential furniture arrangement, 227
Training specialists, 35
Transepts, 379
Transgenerational design, 41
Transition, 63
Transoms, 260f, 364, 400, 403t
Transom windows, 259–60
Transporatation design, 35
Transport, 197
Trash compactors, 150
Traverse rods, 293
Travertine, 311t

Treads, 262
Triadic complement colors, 86
Triangular pediment, 378t, 390
Tricot, 352
Triforium, 379f, 380
Triglyphs, 374
Trio® Convertible shade, 292f
Triple glazing, 258
Triplex, 180
Tripod pedestal table, 410
Trombe walls, 198–99, 199f
Trompe l'oeil, 282, 282t
Trophies, 367
Tropical rain forests, 42
True Sun, 111
Truss system, 189, 190
Tub chairs, 244t
Tufted broadloom carpets, 319
Tufted fabric, 352
Tufting, 237, 237f, 329, 338t
Tungsten filament, 104
Tungsten halogen lamp, 105
Turkish oriental rugs, 322f
Turnings, 389
Turnkey design, 35
Turrets, 260
Tuscan order, 375f, 377, 378t
Tweed, 353
Twill weave, 336f, 338t, 339
Twin homes, 181, 181f
Two-dimensional shapes, 67–68
Two Gray Hills rugs, 325
Two-inch metal blinds, 303t
Two-story floor plans, 179
Tyron, 394t

U

Ultralume, 82f
Ultraviolet radiation, 106
Undertones, 89, 90
Uniform Building Code (UBC), 24
Union cloth, 353
United Airlines terminal, O'Hare Airport, Chicago, 109f
United East India Company, 382
Unity, 64, 66f
Universal and transgenerational design, 35, 46, 47, 144
    and sustainability, 41–42
University of Virginia at Charlottesville Rotunda, 397
Upholstered cornices, 298
Upholstered furniture, 236–37
Upholsterers, 30f, 236f
Upholstery process, 236f
Upkeep, floor materials, 309
Upkeep costs, doors, 254
Uplighters, 108
Urea formaldehyde, 230
Urethane foam, 320
U.S. Green Building Council (USGBC), 43
Users, 7
U-shaped groupings, 223f
U-stair (with one landing), 263, 263f
Utility plans, 187

V

Vacuformed plastics, 235
Valance lighting, 116
Valances, 298t
Values, 88, 92
    distribution, 92
    distribution based on nature, 93
    normal, 88t
    scale, 94f

Vapor barrier plastic, 190
Variety, 64
Varnish, 232
Vaulted ceiling, 266f
Vaulted skylights, 174f
Vaulted systems, 202t
Vaults, 267, 380
Vehicles, for painting, 356
Veiling glare, 114
Velour, 353
Velvet, 353
Velvet weave carpets, 319
Veneer, 231
Venetian glass, 360
Ventilation, 194
Verbal communication skills, 26
Verdigris finish, 233
Vernacular Greek Revival, 403t
Vernacular style, 397, 401t–402t
    furniture classics, 400
    Georgian design, 401t
    textiles, 402t
Vertical lines, 70, 71
Vertical louvers, 303t
Vertical space, 220–21
Vestibules, 195
Vibrating simultaneous contrast, 95
Victorial Gothic Revival side chair, 409t
Victorian age (1837-1901), 405–10
    color, 410
    design, 406t–410t
    furniture classics, 405
    Renaissance Revival cabinet, 410t
    Renaissance Revival side chair, 410t
    textiles, 410t
    Victorian Belter/Rococo Revival armchair, 409t
    Victorian Belter/Rococo Revival table, 410t
Videoconferencing, 29
Vienna cafe chair, 424t
Vienna Secession, 423
View, 12, 257
Vigas, 268, 418, 419t
Villa Rotonda, 383, 385t
Vinyl, 234, 315t, 332, 335t
    composition, 315t
    fabric, 353
    resilient sheet flooring, 316t
    tile, 316t
Virtual reality, 36
Viscose-solution stage, 332
Visual acuity, 82
Visual communication skills, 26
Visual impairment, unobstructed walking space for those with, 53f
Visual proportion, 222
Visual weight, 216
Vita-Light, 111
Vitruvian proportions, 377
Vitruvius, 377
Voile, 353
Volatile organic compounds (VOCs), 44
Volt or voltage, 114
Voluntary Simplicity, 40
Volutes, 262, 374, 377

W

Wainscot, 252
Wale, 338t
Wall and ceiling materials, 190, 252–54
    hard or rigid wall materials, 273–81
    moldings, 253–54
    nonresidential considerations, 304–6
    overview of, 272t
    paint, 282–86
    selection guidelines, 272–73
    wall composition, 220
    wood paneling, 252–53

Wallboard, 191, 280t
Wall coverings, 286–90
  coral plaid, 287f
  fabric, 288t, 289–90
  guidelines, 286–87
  terms, 288t
  types of, 289t
Wallpaper, 192
Wall sconces, 118f
Wall textures, rough, 280t
Wall-to-wall carpeting, 321f
Wants, 128
Warm colors, 84, 94, 95f
Warm light, 83
Warm white deluxe lamps, 107
Warps, 319
Warp yarns, 339
Warranties, 183
Wash, 110
Wassily lounge chair, 430, 431, 433t
Waste management, 39
Waste plumbing, 193
Watercolor, 356
Water conservation, 42
Water disposal systems, 192
Waterfall Roman shade, 292f, 297t
Water features, 138f
Water heaters, 192, 193
Water intake system, 192
Waterproofing, the foundation, 189
Water-repellent finish, 340
Wattle, 380
Watt or wattage, 45, 114
Weather, 10, 12
Weatherstripping, 195
Weaves, types of, 339
Wedgewood jasperware colors, 397
Weft, 317
Weft yarns, 339
Wegner, Hans, 434
Welsh Dresser/Hutch, 402t
Welts, 237
Wentz House, 412t
Westover, 391t
Wet finishes, 340
Whaler's Church, 407t
Wheelchairs, space required for passage and turning, 49f–50
White, 90
Whitfield House, 387t
Whiton, Sherrill, 3
Wholesalers, 30
Wicker furniture, 235, 235f
Wiener Werkstätte, 423
William and Mary College, 389
William Morris textiles, 427t
William Morris wall covering, 287f
Williamsburg, Virginia, 389

Wilton carpets, 317, 317f, 319
Windbreaks, 13
Windows, 190
  architectural details, 257–60
  attic, 260, 261f
  awning, 258, 258f
  bay, 258, 259f
  bow, 258, 259f
  casement, 258, 380
  cathedral, 259, 260f
  clerestory, 45, 46, 258–59, 259f, 379f, 380
  and energy conservation, 46
  fixed, 258
  French casement, 259f
  greenhouse, 259, 260f
  jalousie, 259, 260f
  operable, 258
  and orientation, 257
  Palladian, 257, 258, 258f, 393, 394t
  porthole, 258, 258f
  and privacy, 257
  round, 258
  sash, 259, 260f, 261f, 390
  scale of, 58f
  sliding, 260, 261f
  storm, 258
  three-part casement window with leaded panes, 388t
  transom, 259–60
  and view, 12f
Windowsills, 191
Window treatments, 35
  aesthetic coordination, 290–91
  alternative, 294
  calculating yardage for, 302t
  considerations, 290–94
  and energy consciousness, 291–92
  and light control, 292
  nonresidential, 305–6
  operational control, 293
  privacy, 291
  soft window coverings, 293–94
  types of alternative, 303t
Window wells, 189
Windsor chairs, 242t, 400, 402t
Wing chairs, 244t, 390, 392t, 395t
Wiring plans, 123–24
  lighting symbols for, 123f
Wish list, 136, 137t–138t
Wood, 189, 281t
  blinds, 303t, 305f
  exotic, 42
  filler, 232
  flooring, 313t–314t, 314t
  inherent beauty of, 140f
  paneling, 252–53f, 281
  planks, 313t
  rods, 300t

  shutters, 293f
  wood-framing system, 189f
  See also Wooden furniture
Wood-burning stoves, 193, 193f
Wooden furniture
  all-wood construction, 231
  case goods, 230–31
  hardwood and softwood, 230
  joining methods, 231–32
  other forms of wood, 230
  wood finishes, 232
  wood grains, 231
Wooden tableware and cookware, 362
Wool, 333t
Wool carpet fibers, 318t
Working drawings, 21, 186–87
Working triangle, 144–50
Work zones, 128, 129f
World Financial Center, New York City, 64f
Woven broadloom carpet, 317–19
Woven fabric construction, 338t
Wren, Christopher, 386, 389
Wren-Baroque style, 389, 393
Wright, Frank Lloyd, 382, 425, 425f
Wrinkle-resistant, 340
Written program, 16
Wrought iron, 363
Wrought iron rods, 300t

X

X-frame chairs, 386

Y

Yellow acetate lens, 54f

Z

Zapatas, 419, 419t
Zero-clearance fireplace units, 193, 264
Zigzag lines, 70
Zones
  general, 128f
  and kitchen planning, 144–50
  private, 129, 130f
  social, 128–29, 130f
  within zone, 129
Zoning, and nonresidential buildings, 164–68